Lecture Notes in Computer Science 4102

Commenced Publication in 1973
Founding and Former Series Editors:
Gerhard Goos, Juris Hartmanis, and Jan van Leeuwen

Schahram Dustdar José Luiz Fiadeiro
Amit Sheth (Eds.)

Business Process Management

4th International Conference, BPM 2006
Vienna, Austria, September 5-7, 2006
Proceedings

Volume Editors

Schahram Dustdar
Vienna University of Technology
Distributed Systems Group (DSG), Information Systems Institute
Argentinierstrasse 8/184-1, 1040 Wien, Austria
E-mail: dustdar@infosys.tuwien.ac.at

José Luiz Fiadeiro
University of Leceister
Department of Computer Science
Leicester LE1 7RH, UK
E-mail: jose@fiadeiro.org

Amit Sheth
University of Georgia
Department of Computer Science
415 Graduate Studies Research Center, Athens, GA 30602-7404, USA
E-mail: amit@cs.uga.edu

Library of Congress Control Number: 2006931678

CR Subject Classification (1998): H.3.5, H.4.1, H.5.3, K.4.3, K.4.4, K.6, J.1

LNCS Sublibrary: SL 3 – Information Systems and Application, incl. Internet/Web and HCI

ISSN 0302-9743
ISBN-10 3-540-38901-6 Springer Berlin Heidelberg New York
ISBN-13 978-3-540-38901-9 Springer Berlin Heidelberg New York

Springer is a part of Springer Science+Business Media

springer.com

Printed in Germany

Typesetting: Camera-ready by author, data conversion by Scientific Publishing Services, Chennai, India
Printed on acid-free paper SPIN: 11841760 06/3142 5 4 3 2 1 0

Preface

The 4th International Conference on Business Process Management (BPM 2006) was held in Vienna, Austria, on September 5–7, 2006, organized by the VitaLab, Distributed Systems Group, Institute of Information Systems, Vienna University of Technology.

The present volume collects the papers accepted for presentation at the main conference. A series of co-located workshops were held together with BPM, the proceedings of which are published as volume 4103 of Springer's *Lecture Notes in Computer Science* series.

Paper submission was strong and geographically well distributed: 78 papers originated from Europe, 32 from Asia, 14 from the Americas, 11 from Oceania, and 3 from Africa, to a total of 40 different countries.

All papers were reviewed by at least three referees and competition for acceptance was very high: of the 138 submitted papers, only 20 were accepted as full research papers (14% acceptance rate), 5 as industrial papers and 15 as short papers. Further to these, invited lectures were delivered by Donald Ferguson – an IBM fellow, Dave Green – an architect for Microsoft's Windows Workflow Foundation, and Edwin Khodabakchian – Vice President of Product Development at Oracle. We want to thank our keynote speakers and their organizations for their invited presentations.

We take this opportunity to thank the members of the Program Committee and the additional reviewers for their tremendous effort in guaranteeing the scientific quality of BPM. We would also like to thank the Steering Committee for their constant support.

We are also indebted to the local organization staff for their timely and precious support, in particular to Florian Rosenberg and Eva Nedoma for their invaluable help in making BPM 2006 a reality. We thank Marco Aiello for the help in assembling this volume. Last but not least, we would like to express our gratitude to Frank Leymann (Industrial Chair), Johann Eder (Workshop Chair), and Jan Mendling (Demo Chair).

We hope you will find the articles in the present volume a valuable and up-to-date picture of the state of the art in research on business process management and its industrial impact.

June 2006

Schahram Dustdar, Jose Fiadeiro, Amit Sheth
BPM PC Chairs 2006

Organization

BPM 2006 was organized by the VitaLab, Distributed Systems Group, Institute of Information Systems, Vienna University of Technology.

Executive Committee

General Chair:	Schahram Dustdar (Vienna Univ. of Technology, Austria)
Program Co-chairs:	Schahram Dustdar (Vienna Univ. of Technology, Austria) Jose Fiadeiro (Univ. of Leicester, UK) Amit P. Sheth (LSDIS lab, Univ. of Georgia, and Semagix, Inc., USA)
Industrial Chair:	Frank Leymann (Univ. of Stuttgart, Germany)
Workshop Chair:	Johann Eder (Univ. of Vienna, Austria)
Demo Chair:	Jan Mendling (Vienna Univ. of Economics and Business Administration)
Local Organization:	Florian Rosenberg, Chair (Vienna Univ. of Technology, Austria) Martin Vasko (Vienna Univ. of Technology, Austria) Eva Nedoma (Vienna Univ. of Technology, Austria) Gudrun Ott (Vienna Univ. of Technology, Austria) Margret Steinbuch (Vienna Univ. of Technology, Austria)

Program Committee

Wil van der Aalst, The Netherlands
Rama Akkiraju, USA
Gustavo Alonso, Switzerland
Karim Baina, Morocco
Steve Battle, UK
Boualem Benatallah, Australia
Djamal Benslimane, France
M. Brian Blake, USA
Christoph Bussler, USA
Jorge Cardoso, Portugal
Fabio Casati, USA
Malu Castellanos, USA
Sanjay Chaudhary, India
Francisco Curbera, USA
Peter Dadam, Germany
Jörg Desel, Germany
Asuman Dogac, Turkey
Marlon Dumas, Australia
Schahram Dustdar, Austria
Johann Eder, Austria
Jose Fiadeiro, UK
Dimitrios Georgakopoulos, USA
Stefania Gnesi, Italy
Claude Godart, France

Paul Grefen, The Netherlands
Kees van Hee, The Netherlands
Arthur ter Hofstede, Australia
Gerti Kappel, Austria
Dimitris Karagiannis, Austria
Haim Kilov, USA
Kwang-Hoon Kim, Korea
Akhil Kumar, USA
Frank Leymann, Germany
Peri Loucopoulos, UK
Zongwei Luo, Hong Kong
Axel Martens, USA
Mike Papazoglou, The Netherlands
Barbara Pernici, Italy
Olivier Perrin, France
Manfred Reichert, The Netherlands
Hajo Reijers, The Netherlands
Wolfgang Reisig, Germany
Heiko Schuldt, Switzerland
Marek Sergot, UK
Amit Sheth, USA
A Min Tjoa, Austria
Farouk Toumani, France
Vijay Vaishnavi, USA
Kunal Verma, USA
Mathias Weske, Germany
Michal Zaremba, Ireland

Referees

Fuat Akal
Bugrahan Akcay
Taiseera Al Balushi
Lachlan Aldred
A. K. Alves de Medeiros
Samuil Angelov
Danilo Ardagna
Donald Baker
Maurice ter Beek
Ralph Bobrik
Lindsay Bradford
Stephan Breutel
Roberto Bruni
Antonio Bucchiarone
Cinzia Cappiello
Martin Carpenter
Andrzej Cichocki
Marco Comuzzi
Remco Dijkman
Yishu Ding
Boudewijn van Dongen
Rik Eshuis
Alessandro Fantechi
Hans-Georg Fill
Nadine Froehlich
Mario Fusani
Joy Garfield
Andreas Glausch
Jose Gomes
Christian Guenther
Ozgur Gulderen
Farshad Hakimpour
Sandra Hintringer
Peter Hoefferer
Christian Huemer
Anke Hutzschenreuter
Monique Jansen-Vullers
Yildiray Kabak
Shubir Kapoor
Dimka Karastoyanova
Kwang-Hoon Kim
Oliver Kopp
Gerhard Kramler
Marcello La Rosa
Christoph Langguth
Marek Lehmann
Lei Li
Beate List
Rong Liu
Niels Lohmann
Jeroen van Luin
Dominic Müller
Peter Massuthe
Franco Mazzanti
Harald Meyer
Stefano Modafferi
Thorsten Moeller
Nataliya Mulyar
Enrico Mussi
Bela Mutschler
Tuncay Namli
Martin Nemetz
Mariska Netjes
Alex Norta
Olivia Oanea
Alper Okcan
Mehmet Olduz
Justin O'Sullivan
Raju Pavuluri
Maja Pesic
Horst Pichler
Marco Pistore
Frank Puhlmann
Jan Recker
Guy Redding
Anne Rozinat
Nick Russell
Tayfun Sen
Alexander Serebrenik
Natalia Sidorova
Michael Springmann
Christian Stahl
Iain D. Stalker
Veronika Stefanov

Ibrahim Tasyurt
Irene Vanderfeesten
Senthil Velayudham
Eric Verbeek
Laura Voicu
Jochem Vonk
Marc Voorhoeve
Kenneth Wang
Ton Weijters
Daniela Weinberg
Matthias Wieland
Manuel Wimmer
Zixin Wu

Sponsoring Institutions

We acknowledge the support of the following companies and institutions.

Ultimus

Austrian Computer Society

Stadt Wien

TU Wien

Table of Contents

Invited Talks

Monitoring and Mining

Service Composition

Process Models and Languages

Dynamic Process Management

Service Composition

Applied BPM

Industrial Papers

Short Papers

Enterprise Business Process Management – Architecture, Technology and Standards

Donald F. Ferguson[1] and Marcia Stockton[2]

[1] IBM Fellow, SWG Chief Architect, IBM Software Group, USA
dff@us.ibm.com
[2] Senior Technical Staff Member, IBM Software Group, USA
mls@us.ibm.com

Abstract. All enterprises' operations require integrating information, and processing information with applications. This has been true for decades, if not centuries. Information and application integration has evolved from completely person centered verbal communication (blacksmith to apprentice), through paper documents-mail-fax, email and Web page interactions. The information and applications control the flow of goods and operations on them. *These are the business processes of the economy.* Coming from vastly different starting points, the evolutionary paths of business designs and IT architectures are converging, in a striking example of convergent evolution. In some cases, enterprises are almost purely information processing businesses, e.g. insurance. The past few years have seen explosive growth in direct program-program interaction for application integration, removing manual steps to yield tremendous improvements in reliability and efficiency. Controlling the sequence of program interactions and information flow, and knowing the status of the flows, are fundamental to an enterprise's functions. Automating, monitoring and optimizing the flow is the field of business process management. The past two years have seen the emergence of several architectural and standards based innovations. This paper, with a focus on the end-to-end model, provides a technical overview of the standards, architecture, programming and runtime models that make modern BPM possible.

1 Model – Assemble – Deploy – Manage (MADM)

Business professionals collaborating with IT professionals define a model (architecture) of the business. Often the model is simply a set of "business processes," e.g. steps to process a purchase order. Additionally, the model may include business artifacts (purchase order, bill of materials), policies (schedule premier customers ahead of others) and the business components (shipping department, finance and accounting). The business model could include key performance indicators (KPIs). Examples of KPIs include: percentage of purchase orders that complete without manual intervention, or average dollar value of submitted shopping carts. These KPIs directly measure business performance, e.g. profit, customer satisfaction. Figure 1 provides an overview of end-to-end *business process management (BPM).*

The fundamental goal of BPM is to iteratively and coherently describe and implement the business model through the development stage, into running systems and monitoring KPIs. This is what distinguishes BPM from more classic approaches

S. Dustdar, J.L. Fiadeiro, and A. Sheth (Eds.): BPM 2006, LNCS 4102, pp. 1 – 15, 2006.

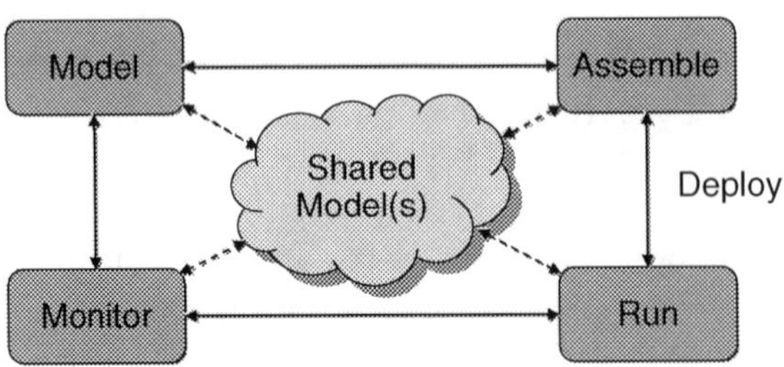

Fig. 1. BPM Loop

to application development and execution. Existing systems are often vertically integrated applications, with only fragmentary views of the business. The systems typically do not report on satisfaction of business goals, or if they have this capability to any extent, it was added after the fact.

Many recent innovations -- service oriented architectures, Web services and standard languages for describing business processes, business artifacts, business events and services -- make BPM goals more achievable.

This paper provides an overview of the recent innovations. The breadth of standards and concepts often make seeing the forest difficult, as there are many, changing trees. There are, however, an emerging set of architecture models that integrate the many concepts. The models also enable consumable, progressive discovery and application of the concepts. Moreover, the emerging architecture naturally represents the *business architectures and business models.* The business architecture and BPM/SOA architectures' evolution are converging.

1.1 Model

The most popular modeling tools are white boards, followed closely by Microsoft Office. However, there is an increasing trend to more formal and rigorous modeling. Some organizations use focused tools, e.g. WebSphere Business Modeler [1] or Intalio [2]. Others use tools that extend spreadsheets, documents or diagrams to incrementally support business process modeling. Formal modeling has two major benefits:

1. Precise notation: The well-defined semantics of formal models can capture information in an unequivocal manner, whereas if you use PowerPoint® or white boards, people who were not in the room do not know what dotted arrows or purple circles mean.
2. Reliable hand-offs: Modeling tools can generate implementation templates and the structure of the supporting applications (SOA services), business processes and artifacts. This is less error-prone than reading documents and guessing the desired application behavior. *Bad things happen when programmers guess.*

Surprisingly the connection between model and assemble (build) is bidirectional. Organizations often use modeling tools to reverse engineer systems to explain the existing applications to business professionals.

1.2 Assemble

Historically, programmers think of "building" an application, or elements of an application. The trend is increasingly moving to a*ssembling* an application, or business process. Packaged and pre-existing applications provide much of the necessary function. Implementing the business model and its changes often simply requires assembling (and configuring) existing applications into a *composite application* that integrates the existing systems. A business process, coordinating the integrated composite application, is often accompanied by development of some new services to complete the business process. Assembly has two sub-models:

1. Structure: Which services, processes and artifacts comprise the composite application? What are the governing policies? …
2. Behavior: What are the sequences/control flows of calling the applications? What is the data flow? What are the state transitions? …

An example of assembly tools is WebSphere Integration Developer [3]. Many other companies have similar capabilities, e.g. SAP [4].

1.3 Deploy

The newly assembled, existing and configured applications run on an IT infrastructure (systems, application servers and middleware, packaged applications, pub/sub systems …). The deploy phase maps the application artifacts and configuration information to the systems and software environments. The incremental nature of deployment creates enormous challenges. The applications, processes and data formats *change while existing applications and transactions are executing*. Imagine changing the flight control system of a trans-Pacific flight.

Unexpectedly, information technology (IT) systems and application management itself is evolving to a BPM model. Rolling out patches, upgrading software, etc. are business processes. Products are evolving in this space, e.g. IBM IT Service Management [5]. Standards evolving in the IT governance space include IT governance processes (IT Infrastructure Library [6]), and the use of SOA and Web services to manage applications and systems (Management Using Web Services [1], Web Services Distributed Management [7], WS-Management [8]). The essential realization is that complex IT management functions like call center/trouble ticket or software upgrade approval are essentially business processes. Moreover, many business processes are a mix of IT activities and application activities. The business process for adding a new employee will update payroll systems, employee profile systems and issue configured PCs, activate LAN ports and VPN user ids.

The IT Service Management solutions and standards:

- Define long-running, complex IT management operations using business process modeling, which implement the processes using SOA centered workflow/BPM engines.
- Provide SOA Web service APIs for management agents.
- Use portals to integrate manual steps within the service management processes. The portals support user interfaces to applications, work lists, etc.

- Use Web service based events to monitor processes and compute KPIs, e.g. average time to resolve a problem ticket.
- Build integrated information models for configuration information. The systems use Web service to perform information integration and federated databases.
- Warehouse/analyze business process events; automate reactions to event patterns.

1.4 Monitor

Monitoring is the observation of the executing composite applications. *IT monitoring* observes throughput, response, resource utilization, problem events, etc. This enables change, for example allocating more servers, to improve satisfaction of business goals (for example, the time to process a purchase order). *Business monitoring* observes the execution of the solution. (For example, did a purchase order fail a credit check or require manual intervention? Emit an event when a credit check fails.)

The stream of business events enables intervention and reaction. Assume a credit check fails. Part of the business process definition may be *event filters*, which look for events or event streams matching a pattern. A filter for the credit check failure event may trigger an email or instant message to the account representative. Aggregating events into summaries interesting to employees, and making the summaries available through email or a Web portal is extremely common.

A common element of business models is *key performance indicators.* How does the business measure the success of their business model? The business may want to achieve a target value for purchase orders; a business not achieving its goal may want to modify personalization and product suggestions on their portal. The business may want to reduce cost by eliminating manual approval of purchase orders; if not meeting the goal, they might modify the approval-automation rules in the rule systemapproval. Business events supply the data for computing KPIs. The solutions can warehouse the events and perform analytics to compute KPIs.

The event and KPI models are *explicit elements of the business process model.* These elements flow through all steps in the MADM loop. Business modeling defines the taxonomy and formats for events, the KPIs and the event filters and actions. The assemble phase realizes the model constructs; the deploy and run phases emit the events. Standards emerge in this space, for example the Web Services Distributed Management Event Format.

1.5 Nirvana

The preceding exposition restates the well-known BPM Nirvana. We have been striving for enlightenment for years, if not decades. What is different now? We provided some insight in the preceding sections. The remainder of the paper articulates technical changes that make the goals more achievable.

2 Business Architecture and IT Architecture

Businesses have components: factories, departments, teams. Unfortunately, businesses are very rarely designed from a top-town perspective. Poor or haphazard business designs, with ill-defined interfaces between components and no clear understanding of components' behavior, are much more common than well-conceived ones. Enterprises evolve from mergers and acquisitions, and local decisions over lines of business and geographical units, often resulting in duplications such as disjoint, multiple shipping departments or administration systems.

Convergent evolution is a powerful, descriptive and prescriptive theory. Kangaroos and Kangaroo Rats are not closely related, but have similar locomotion. Platypuses and otters are not closely related, but are similar. In each case, the pair of similar animals independently acquired similar solutions to certain problems that it faced in its environment. Convergent evolution explains the similarity between the evolution of enterprise *business architectures* and SOA; both evolved in parallel to address the same kinds of problems, and not-so-coincidentally arrived at very similar approaches.

Enterprises are evolving towards well-factored and defined *business components* [9]. Business components offer well-defined services with standard business object formats. The business architecture detects redundant components and sub-components. Once detected, the enterprise can consolidate or divest the redundant components (to the extent their vision for a streamlined business design dictates).

The new business architecture enables selective externalization and flexible placement of components. In fact, many enterprises "own" almost none of the business components; their business model is the composite, aggregate solutions.

There is large body of literature on the benefits of the new business architecture (please see the reference for case studies and references). Our key observation is the close alignment of the *business architecture* and the *SOA technical model.* It is fundamentally this parallelism – in an apparent example of convergent evolution — which enables the IT realization of an enterprise to match the business architecture.

There is a second, subtler observation. Historically, the industry focused on changing IT to make it more responsive to the business needs. Yet modern, SOA based IT solutions have evolved to an effective architecture. Going forward, we foresee a slight change in emphasis: *similar pressures will cause the business to be more like IT.*

There are many definitions of "service" and service-oriented architecture. We will use the following definition [10]:

> *A Service is a set of functionality provided by one entity for the use of others. ... Opacity is a core component [i.e., trait] of services. Each Service has a Service Description. A Service Description is a set of metadata declaring all aspects of a service necessary for a Service Consumer to understand the service's externally inspectable aspects.*

These definitions are correct, but are not sufficient to provide a SOA realization of a business architecture that supports BPM. For example, business components provide services to other business components, but *also use services.* The Service Component Architecture [11] is an evolving set of specifications to define a *SOA component model.* Many of the elements of SCA directly support BPM.

The definition of service description identifies the needs for metadata. SCA brings together several standards and patterns for formalizing this metadata. The standards are: XML Schema Definition (XSD), Web Services Description Languages (WSDL) , WS-Policy, BPEL4WS, and Elements of the Unified Modeling Language.

Finally, SOA relies on loose coupling and flexible binding. If service ***A*** needs to invoke an operation ***O***, the service (component) to use may be selected at runtime. The specific shipping service to use may depend on the purchase order, current business contracts, etc. Loose coupling and flexible binding are accepted concepts in SOA. The technical architecture we describe in Section 3 identifies the architecture models for *mediation* and integrating *event driven processing* with SOA. These concepts offer greater flexibility than dynamic binding. The message transport mechanism, the *enterprise service bus (ESB),* contains active logic within its message-processing components, which can, for example, transform messages into a format compatible with the message recipient or modify routing based on a message's payload.

Integrating a set of standards provides a more complete, coherent model that facilitates the business process modeling and assembly phases. It also provides a more complete, concrete rendering of business concepts in an IT model. Extensions to the architecture, which are patterns for services/components, improve the fidelity for representing business designs. The ESB allows dynamic connections between business processes and the services it choreographs.

An additional element of SCA is an increasingly portable programming model for services components. This model, which extends beyond language-specific approaches like J2EE, offers many benefits to both programmers and CIOs, most notably avoiding vendor lock-in to specific products. SOA flexibility is as valuable to business architectures and business process management as it is to IT implementation. Consider that the evolution of a business component architecture may dictate migration of business functions to partners, service providers, etc. A portable approach to implementing services and components facilitates this flexibility.

3 Architecture Overview

This section refines the concepts previewed in Section 2. Much of the application architecture focus is ensuring that the *application (SOA) architecture* supports the *business architecture.* There is a special emphasis on coherence of the business process models and the SOA models. This coherence helps integrate the modeling phase of a solution with the assembly, run and monitor phases. So, the first element of the application architecture we describe is the *process model.* A process choreographs a dynamic set of services. We follow the process concepts with modeling and assembly of dynamic sets of services.

A second tenet of the application architecture is well-defined services, metadata and flexible binding. These are key requirements for mapping the business architecture to the application architecture. To ensure flexibility and responsiveness to changing business designs, the portfolio of services and the processes must be able to evolve independently. We explain a general set of approaches to service description and metadata, and an evolving standard architecture (the Service Component Architecture).

To be useful, a service must be executable. Runtime products that support the *monitor* phase of the BPM lifecycle play an extremely important role in SOA and SCA. Section 3.3 describes the integration of monitoring/management with SOA and SCA.

Existing systems, such as CICS and IMS, offer robust support for change management. Programmers for these systems find them intuitive and easy to program. Many of these benefits derive from applying a set of well-known best practices or design patterns. Similar patterns are emerging for SOA, and we briefly enumerate the core patterns.

3.1 Application Architecture

3.1.1 Composition – Processes and Structure

3.1.1.1 Business Processes – Motivation. Figure 2 provides an overview of two approaches to building SOA business solutions. The first approach, labeled inflexible, is just that. The solution is inflexible and violates two SOA design principles. Two services access the same data (S1 and S2 access D2). This violates the principle of well-defined interfaces. The two services effectively communicate through private data signals. The services' implementations (e.g. S1) also orchestrate or choreograph other services within their implementations. How do these violations cause inflexibility? Three problems are salient:

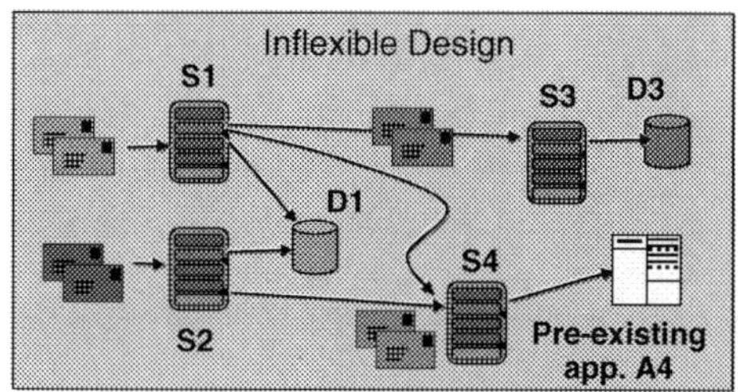

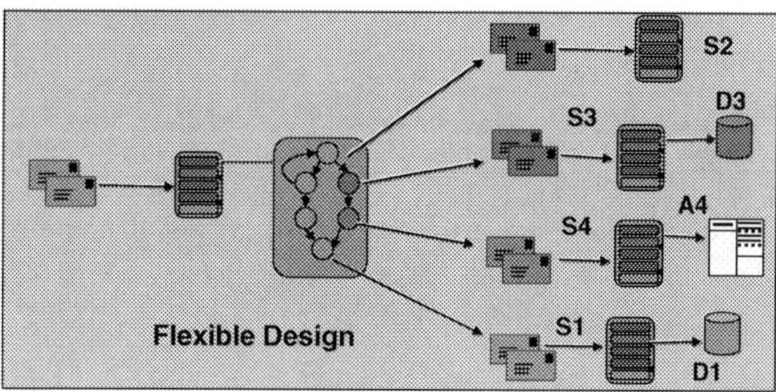

Fig. 2. Well-designed Business Processes

1. The ability to independently evolve and refine services provides flexibility.
2. Embedding sequences and control flows for service invocation within the code of a service makes change difficult
3. Embedded signaling through data and encapsulated (implicit) service choreography make flexible modeling and monitoring more difficult.

Figure 2 also provides an example of a more flexible design. Services are atomic elements; their implementation may access data, call pre-existing applications (e.g. A4), use libraries, etc. A key design principle is the sharing of data between services is prohibited; services may not even call applications that share data. Another principle is that all aggregation and control flow of service operations must be external to the atomic services, and reside in a well-defined business process.

3.1.1.2 Behavioral Composition. Experience with products and solutions reveals three fundamental approaches to composing the behavior of services to form business processes and composite applications. 1) *A control flow and composite activity* model -- The standard approach to control flows and composite activities is BPEL4WS. There are many documents on BPEL4WS, and we will not discuss it here. 2) A state machine model -- State machines are also widely understood, and we will not discuss them. 3) A message flow/event model.

SCA takes an interesting approach to behavioral composition. On first examination, SCA's primary focus seems to be structural composition, which we will discuss below. The evolving SCA specifications and products introduce three sub-types/kinds of SCA components. WebSphere Process Server/WebSphere Integration Developer/WebSphere ESB are examples:

1. There is a component kind for BPEL4WS, which supports control flow and composite activity composition.
2. A *Business State Machine* is component kind that implements a state machine model. A component has a current state and state machine. For any state, only certain operations are enabled. The state machine changes state based on the called operation, and may execute a private operation on the transition. There are also state entry and exit guards.
3. WebSphere Enterprise Service Bus provides support for composition through event and message flows, including composing primitives and sub-flows into a larger composition. We will briefly discuss this model below (Section 3.1.5).

In SCA, BPEL4WS processes, state machines and ESB event/message flows are SCA components. Externally, these component types look like any other. Programmers implement behavioral composition by writing new SCA components that behaviorally compose other components. The programmer may add the new components to an application or solution, or develop a separate module that performs the composition.

This approach may appear to violate some of the principles we articulated in Section 3.1.1.1, e.g. embedding control flow in components.

3.1.1.3 Business Processes – Structural Composition. A service component in SCA documents the interfaces it supports and the interfaces it requires. We explain the details of the approach to documenting the interface in Section 3.1.2. Figure 3 provides an overview of structural composition. The model "wires" required interfaces to implemented interfaces. Interface compatibility can consider all aspects of the metadata describing the interface. Programmers wire service components together to create assemblies called *modules*. The model is recursive: modules may export interfaces and require interfaces. Assemblers can then wire modules together to build subsystems and solutions.

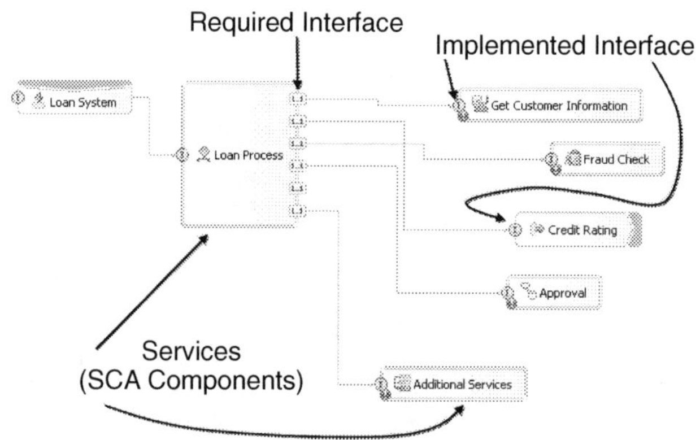

Fig. 3. Structural Assembly

The wiring approach simplifies the process of assembling services into new solutions, and modifying the services that comprise a solution. The key benefit is that all service components have the same external model. Programmers can perform assembly without being aware of the component's implementation.

Finally, assembly can be dynamic. The model is not static. Because of loose coupling and the enterprise service bus functions, modules and solutions can change rapidly.

3.1.2 Service Components, Service Description and Business Artifacts

A component implements one or more interfaces, which it defines in WSDL. (Many SCA implementations will support defining interfaces in native languages, e.g. COBOL, to simplify the developer's task; tools then generate any necessary WSDL.) The component also identifies one or more *required interfaces.*

Another key element, not yet explicitly part of SCA, is a *business artifact.* Services and their operations are the *verbs* that implement an enterprise's business model: *create purchase order*, *approve* purchase order. Business artifacts are what the verbs manipulate, e.g. *account, purchase order.* WS-ResourceFramework [17] is an evolving standard for integrating Web services and business artifacts. WebSphere Process Server and WebSphere Integration Developer support *business state machines (BSMs).*

Most literature on SOA and Web services assert that Web services are stateless. This is true only in a narrow sense. Most Web services manage and manipulate state data, i.e. the business artifacts. The opacity requirement for services implies that the business artifacts are not externally visible, and the service's operations completely describe its behavior. There are three ways in which a business artifact becomes externally visible, however.

1. Its operations send and receive messages, which projections from an underlying data model.
2. *Service description* metadata expresses relationships between service operations and the artifact's state, incidentally providing intuitive monitoring data. One can ask, "What is the state of my purchase order?"

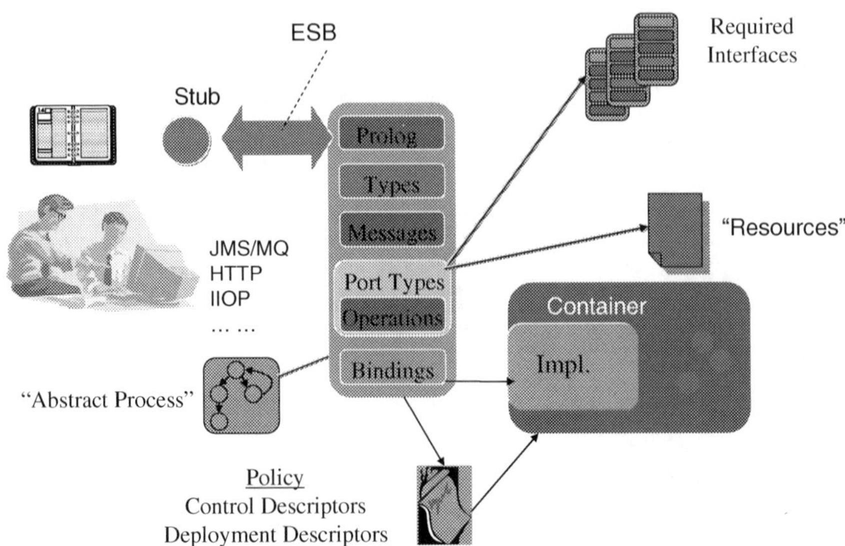

Fig. 4. Components and Interfaces

3. The additional metadata provided by business artifacts, lifecycle states, operations and messages aid in service discovery and binding, ensuring that consumers and providers have a common understanding of business artifacts and their behavior.

Business artifacts and state machines have limited ability to express behavior. For the description of aggregate behavior spanning multiple operations, interfaces and artifacts, BPEL4WS introduces the notion of an *abstract process*. The abstract process projects a service component's "business process" from the perspective of a consumer or provider.

The evolving Service Component Architecture provides a rich set of constructs for describing the interface syntax and behavior of services. The model is *consumable* and *incremental.* Solution developers can start with simple interfaces, as outlined here, and gradually increase sophistication. Despite having a *logical external model,* a component's innards are typically completely opaque.

3.1.3 Policy

The preceding service description concepts focused on documenting *what* a service/component does: e.g. it *creates, approves,* and *cancels* purchase orders. Equally important is *how* the component implements its functions and what it expects of callers or services that it calls. A component may have policy annotations on the interfaces and other elements. The policy annotations typically describe quality-of-service related concepts. For example,

- Does the component require that callers sign or encrypt messages? What certificate authorities does the component trust?
- The component may require reliable messaging, ensuring that there are no duplicate messages or out-of-order messages.

Web service standards such as WS-Transactions [12], WS-ReliableMessaging [13], and WS-SecureConversation [14] define formats and protocols on top of the base SOAP and HTTP protocols. The standards provide additional quality of service for interactions. The standards and protocols may offer parameter choices, e.g. what message digest algorithm may be used in a security protocol. Each Web service interoperability specification typically has a companion extension to WS-Policy [15] that allows services to document the details of protocols that it supports/requires.

The base policy framework supports Boolean composition of policy statements, for example AND/OR/NOT. This allows a service to specify sets of policies that it supports. During binding, the infrastructure performs a *policy intersection* to determine a choice of policy settings that both the caller and called support.

3.1.4 Bindings

Most BPM systems support protocols in addition to SOAP/HTTP. Metadata associated with a component documents support for other protocols. The binding may support for the policies natively, for example reliable messaging on WebSphere-MQ.

3.1.5 Enterprise Service Bus

Wiring is a powerful concept because of its simplicity and intuitive model. The approach appears limiting and in conflict with the flexible, dynamic and loose coupling of SOA. The service component model provides a layered approach to increasing flexibility and function. Logically, all wires flow through an *enterprise service bus.* Wires offer a continuum of function ranging from a direct, design-time connection between components, to a logical connection resolved at runtime based on specified metadata, to a mediation that routes dynamically based on message content, to an actor in a complex publish-subscribe system.

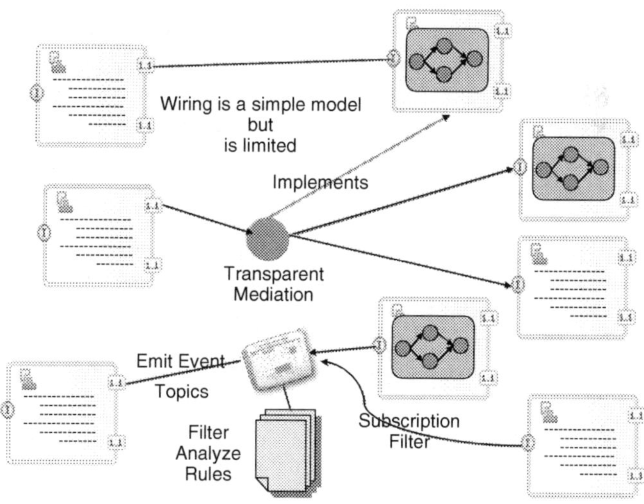

Fig. 5. Enterprise Service Bus

ESB tools support composing basic mediations into composite mediations. The example above is a composite of routing and transformation; other typical mediations include side effects (e.g. logging), and augmentation (adding pertinent data to messages).

The key benefit of the ESB mediation model is flexibility. New services or new versions of services can join the bus. An integration specialist can change service request routing transparently to existing, deployed services and modules.

It is important to note that some ESB function may execute within application endpoints, providing performance levels comparable to a traditional implementation.

3.1.6 Configuration and Customization

Service components are highly configurable. Configuration may occur during assembly or at runtime. Some component kinds are inherently configurable. For example, rule sets, BPEL4WS processes and business state machine are effectively documents that an engine interprets. Configuration is as simple as changing the underlying document and setting an "as of time" for the change to take affect.

SCA defines a property model for binary components. The component may define an accompanying "document" that declares parameters that configure the component's behavior. An example might be the maximum value of a PO. Developers set the properties during assembly. It may also be possible to change the properties for deployed components, for example by inserting mediations.

3.2 Runtime Architecture and Deployment

Figure 6 provides an overview of the two key concepts in the runtime architecture. The first concept is the *container abstraction.* Logically all components, including business processes, execute/reside in a container. The container "wraps" the component, pre- and post-processing all service invocations. The pre-post processing implements the policies associated with the component. For example, if the component specifies that message from a sender must be in order and digitally signed, the container implements these functions before passing it to the business logic.

The container abstraction and policy have many advantages. Implementing quality of service logic should be separate from business logic. The necessary policies may change over time, or from composite application to composite application. Using the declarative model enables this flexibility. Most runtimes support a service provider interface (SPI) for adding new quality-of-service functions and policy types.

The runtimes typically support several *container kinds*, including workflow engines, the ESB, containers for code (J2EE™ application servers), XML enabled databases, etc. The containers may be on separate runtimes and machines, or often within a single runtime. Finally, *distinguished services*—such as transaction/coordination manager, logging, authorization and authentication—may be available on the bus.

A complete application has associated metadata that defines the components, modules and their versions. The metadata also defines the container types for each component. Modern deployment systems like Tivoli Provisioning Manager [16] implement deployment and change-management business processes for solution deployment and update.

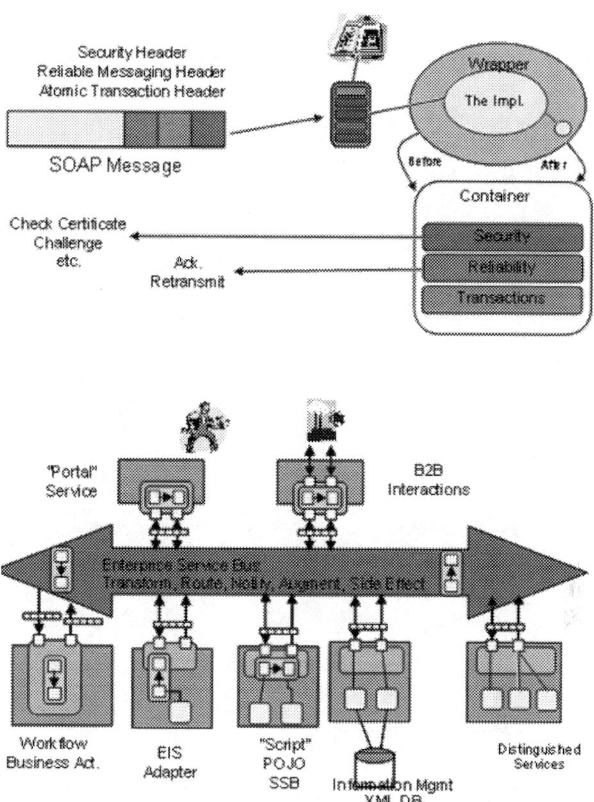

Fig. 6. Runtime Architecture

3.3 Monitoring and Management

Business process monitoring and management occurs through a *business event* model. The modeling and assembly phases define explicit business events. For example, there may be an explicit "emit business event" activity in a state machine or BPEL4WS process. The component may emit this event in the same way that code logs a condition or an exception. Containers also support dynamic, automatic event generation. For example, the container may emit business events when messages arrive for a component. The event includes the input message and response. Most BPEL4WS containers support configurable monitoring of BPEL4WS processes, emitting business events for selected activity transactions.

There may be a mismatch between the emitted event format and the observer's expected format. Business events flow through the ESB, which enables routing, transformation, etc. Many ESB systems also support mediations that use rules or logic to examine event streams looking patterns. When the mediation detects a pattern, it emits an event indicating that the pattern occurred. The mediation may also invoke an operation on a service when recognizing the pattern. This enables automated execution of business processes, rules, and so forth, when specific conditions occur.

Business process management systems also enable the logging of events to a data warehouse for business intelligence, and the connection of end-user dashboards to the event system.

4 The Role of Standards

Standards play a key role in business process management. Standards are the mechanism for integrating applications and infrastructure between companies, lines of business, geographies in a multinational company, etc. Many people are familiar with and understand interoperability standards like SOAP/HTTP and WS-Interop.

Standards play two other roles:

- They enable interoperability between different organizations development tools (and management products), and between products provided by different software vendors. For example, SOAP/HTTP provides runtime interoperability between service **A** and service **B.** The developers use the services' WSDL, XSD, WS-Policy, BPEL4WS abstract processes, etc. to develop the services.
- They also enable *portable* services, components and modules. This area is evolving. J2EE™ is one example. BPEL4WS/BPELJ, XSL and XQuery are other (mostly) portable models. Finally, WS-Policy and policy grammars for infrastructure also enable portability.

5 Summary and Future Directions

Business process management and monitoring is becoming THE way that enterprises implement their business models. SOA and Web services have enabled BPM to grow and expand. As the standards continue to emerge, BPM will become progressively more powerful. This is especially true because the standards enable cross-enterprise collaboration, globalization, etc. Much of the emphasis on BPM derives from two observations:

1. SOA, components and BPM, and the architecture of businesses (componentization, partnership, outsourcing, …) are co-evolving to similar design points. Thus, BPM and SOA are the natural ways to implement flexible business models.
2. The industry is realizing that many problems previously solved with non-BPM concepts are in-fact ideally suited for BPM. Complex systems management and data center governance processes are an example. Application development and governance itself is a *business process management problem.*

BPM and SOA are not complete, however. The BPM platform exposes several open problems and directions for research:

- Modeling is a powerful, useful concept. Model constructs and environments have only rudimentary support for reasoning about and analyzing the model. Simulation and testing are the state of the art.
- Beauty is in the eye of the beholder. One of programmers' most common questions is, "What makes something a good service? Should I surface my database through

one "mondo service," or have a service per table?" Experiential guidance and tool support for service identification, factoring, etc will be increasingly critical.

– Most business processes integrate people and commercial data processing applications. Web service and Grid service models have converged. This make calling just-in-time optimization, simulation, etc in business processes possible. Our industry is only at the beginning of understanding and exploiting these capabilities.
– There has been recent discussion of "situation applications," "ad hoc applications" or "just-in-time" applications. These applications are targeted for a very specific, usually short duration and narrowly scoped problem. In some sense, the applications are the natural evolution of wikis, spreadsheets and Web services. Simple BPM concepts will increase the power and flexibility of these applications.

References

1. http://www-306.ibm.com/software/integration/wbimodeler
2. http://www.intalio.com/
3. http://www-306.ibm.com/software/integration/wid/
4. http://www.sap.com
5. http://www-306.ibm.com/software/tivoli/features/it-serv-mgmt/
6. http://www.itil.co.uk/
7. http://www.oasis-open.org/committees/tc_home.php?wg_abbrev=wsdm
8. http://msdn.microsoft.com/ws/2004/10/ws-management
9. Linda S. Sanford, Dave Taylor. *Let it Grow – Escaping the Commodity Trap.* Pearson Education, 2006. ISBN 0-13-148208-4.
10. http://www.oasis-open.org/committees/tc_home.php?wg_abbrev=soa-rm.
11. http://www-128.ibm.com/developerworks/library/specification/ws-sca/.
12. http://www.ibm.com/developerworks/library/ws-coor/
13. http://www.ibm.com/developerworks/webservices/library/ws-rm/
14. http://www.ibm.com/developerworks/library/ws-secon/
15. http://www.ibm.com/developerworks/library/ws-polfram/
16. http://www.ibm.com/software/tivoli/products/prov-mgr/
17. http://www.oasis-open.org/committees/wsrf/

BizTalk Server, Windows Workflow Foundation, and BPM

Dave Green

Microsoft Corporate Campus
One Microsoft Way
Redmond, WA 98052, USA
davgreen@microsoft.com

Abstract. The release of BizTalk Server 2006 in March, and the upcoming releases of Windows Workflow Foundation and BizTalk Server 2006 R2 are milestones in Microsoft's BPM strategy. This talk is about how BizTalk Server and Windows Workflow Foundation work together, how Microsoft thinks about and supports BPEL, how Microsoft partners can add and are adding value to this picture, and how all these pieces combine to deliver a BPM solution.

S. Dustdar, J.L. Fiadeiro, and A. Sheth (Eds.): BPM 2006, LNCS 4102, p. 16, 2006.

Analyzing Interacting BPEL Processes*

Niels Lohmann, Peter Massuthe, Christian Stahl, and Daniela Weinberg

Humboldt–Universität zu Berlin
Institut für Informatik
Unter den Linden 6
10099 Berlin, Germany
{nlohmann, massuthe, stahl, weinberg}@informatik.hu-berlin.de

Abstract. This paper addresses the problem of analyzing the interaction between BPEL processes. We present a technology chain that starts out with a BPEL process and transforms it into a Petri net model. On the model we decide *controllability* of the process (the existence of a partner process, such that both can interact properly) and compute its *operating guideline* (a characterization of all properly interacting partner processes). A case study demonstrates the value of this technology chain.

Keywords: Business process modeling and analysis, Formal models in business process management, Process verification and validation, Petri nets.

1 Introduction

To an increasing extend interorganizational cooperation is crucial for enterprises to meet the new challenges of ever faster changing business conditions and the growing number of competitors in all kinds of business fields.

In this context, *services* play an important role: they serve as the basic building blocks of such interorganizational cooperations. Recent publications apply the term service in different contexts with varying denotations (see [1] for a survey). A common understanding is that a service basically encapsulates self-contained functions that interact through a well-defined interface via asynchronous message passing.

A service can typically not be executed in isolation – services are designed for being invoked by other services, or for invoking other services themselves. The interaction of services is described by the paradigm of *service-oriented computing* (SOC) [2]. Thereby, two different approaches can be distinguished: *service orchestrations* consider one particular service that directs the logical order of all other services, whereas *service choreographies* consider the case where individual services work together in a loosely coupled network. The participants of such interactions are called *partners*.

The most common implementation of services are *web services*. The *Business Process Execution Language for Web Services* (BPEL, also known as WS-BPEL

* Partially funded by the BMBF project "Tools4BPEL".

S. Dustdar, J.L. Fiadeiro, and A. Sheth (Eds.): BPM 2006, LNCS 4102, pp. 17–32, 2006.

or BPEL4WS) [3] is an accepted language to describe web services. We shall refer to a web service that is described in BPEL as a *BPEL process* or *process* for short.

A choreography of BPEL processes may cause nontrivial interaction between them. Thus it is a challenging task to decide whether the whole choreography of processes interacts properly, i. e. it is free of deadlocks and there are no messages being sent that cannot be received any more. There are two main reasons for non-proper interaction: (1) a process may have an erroneous design. For instance, the process may contain an internal choice relevant for the expected behavior of a partner, but the partner is not informed which decision is actually made; (2) the interactional behaviors of two processes of the choreography exclude each other. For example, the processes run into a situation where one process waits for a message of the other one and vice versa.

Thus a BPEL process needs to be analyzed thoroughly before it is deployed. For this purpose, we can make use of several results in the context of the analysis of services and of backing BPEL processes with a formal semantics. In [4] the notion of *controllability* was developed. A service is *controllable* if there exists a partner such that both interact properly. Thus an erroneous design of a service itself is detected by analyzing its controllability. We further developed the *operating guideline* of a service. The operating guideline characterizes all properly interacting partners in a compact way [5]. With the aid of the operating guideline it can be checked whether the interactional behaviors of two services exclude each other. As a formal model for BPEL processes *open workflow nets* (oWFNs) [6], a special class of Petri nets, are used. Further, we developed a feature-complete Petri net semantics for BPEL [7]. The semantics allows for an automatic transformation of BPEL processes into Petri net models [8]. The resulting Petri net models are well-suited for computer-aided verification. The verification, however, is restricted to the internal behavior of a BPEL process so far and does not consider the interactional behavior.

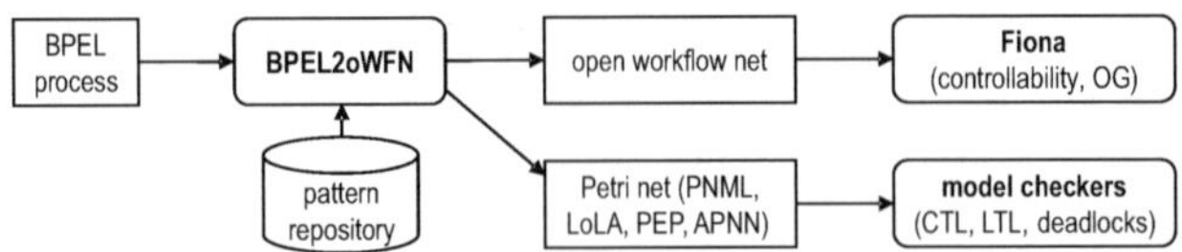

Fig. 1. Proposed tool chain to analyze BPEL processes

In this paper we extend the analysis of BPEL processes presented in [8] by interactional behavior. We introduce two tools – BPEL2oWFN and Fiona. BPEL2oWFN transforms a BPEL process into an oWFN. That way it is possible to analyse the interaction between BPEL processes with Fiona, a tool that decides controllability and computes the operating guideline. Thus, we present a technology chain (Fig. 1) that starts out with a BPEL process, transforms it into an oWFN or a Petri net and that finally analyses the process by either using Fiona or by using a common model checker. Throughout this paper we restrict ourselves to the interaction of two processes only. For the interaction of more than two processes, some theoretical results [9] exist, which are not implemented yet.

The rest of the paper is organized as follows: in Sect. 2, we provide an overview of the general concepts of BPEL and introduce our model, open workflow nets. We also explain controllability of oWFNs and operating guidelines for oWFNs. A BPEL example process, an online shop, is presented in Sect. 3. Section 4 explains the concepts of our advanced transformation and translates the online shop into an oWFN. The resulting oWFN is then analyzed in Sect. 5. We present a slightly modified version of that process in Sect. 6 and analyze it, too. In Sect. 7 we describe related work in detail. Finally, we conclude with directions to future research.

2 Background

2.1 BPEL

The *Business Process Execution Language for Web Services* (BPEL) [3], is a language for describing the behavior of business processes based on web services. For the specification of a business process, BPEL provides *activities* and distinguishes between basic and structured activities. A basic activity can communicate with the partners by messages (`invoke`[1], `receive`, `reply`), manipulate data (`assign`), wait for some time (`wait`) or just do nothing (`empty`), signal faults (`throw`), or end the entire process instance (`terminate`).

A structured activity defines a causal order on the basic activities and can be nested in another structured activity itself. The structured activities include sequential execution (`sequence`), parallel execution (`flow`), data-dependent branching (`switch`), timeout- or message-dependent branching (`pick`), and repeated execution (`while`). The most important structured activity is a `scope`. It links an activity to a transaction management and provides fault, compensation, and event handling. A `process` is the outmost scope of the described business process.

A fault handler is a component of a scope that provides methods to handle faults which may occur during the execution of its enclosing scope. Moreover, a compensation handler can be used to reverse some effects of successfully executed activities. With the help of an event handler, external message events and specified timeouts can be handled.

2.2 Open Workflow Nets

Open workflow nets (oWFNs) [6] are a special class of Petri nets and can be seen as a generalized version of van der Aalst's workflow nets [10]. As a substantial difference, in an oWFN the interface of a service is explicitly represented as sets of input and output places. In our model we concentrate on control flow aspects

[1] We use a typewriter font for BPEL activities.

of services and abstract from data (like, e. g., the content of messages). For data with finite domain, however, important message content can be represented in our approach. For instance, a channel receiving messages with Boolean values can be represented by its separation into two channels: one for messages with content *true* and one for messages with content *false*. Hence, oWFNs provide a simple but formal representation of services, still preserving sufficient information to analyze proper interaction of such services.

We assume the usual definition of Petri nets. An *open workflow net* is a Petri net $N = (P, T, F)$, together with (1) an *interface* $I = in \cup out$ such that $I \subseteq P$, $in \cap out = \emptyset$, and for all transitions $t \in T$ it holds: if $p \in in$ ($p \in out$), then $(t, p) \notin F$ ($(p, t) \notin F$), (2) a distinguished marking m_0, called the *initial marking*, and (3) a set Ω of distinguished markings, called the *final markings*. The places in *in* (*out*) are called *input* (*output*) places. The *inner* of an oWFN N can be obtained from N by removing all interface places, together with their adjacent arcs. As a convention, we label a transition t connected to an input (output) place x with $?x$ ($!x$).

Throughout this paper we only consider *acyclic* open workflow nets, i. e. nets where the transitive closure of F contains no cycles. As an example, consider the oWFN N_1 depicted in Fig. 2.

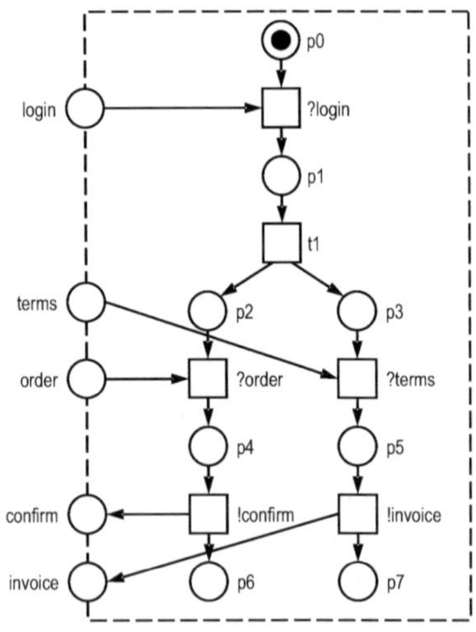

Fig. 2. An example oWFN N_1. The net has three input places, login, terms, and order, and two output places, confirm and invoice. The initial marking m_0 is [p0] which denotes one token on place p0. N_1 has only one final marking, [p6,p7].

In m_0 the net waits for the login message from a partner. If the message arrives, transition ?login can fire and produces a token on place p1.

Then, firing transition t1 yields the marking [p2,p3]. This means that the net is ready to concurrently receive an order message (order) and a terms of payment message (terms). The order is confirmed (!confirm) and the terms of payment are followed by an invoice (!invoice). If both transitions have fired, the final marking [p6,p7] is reached.

The interplay of two oWFNs N and M is represented by their *composition*, denoted by $N \oplus M$. Thereby, we demand that the nets only share input and output places such that an input place of N is an output place of M and vice versa. The oWFN $N \oplus M$ can then be constructed by merging joint places and merging the initial and final markings. Merged places become internal to $N \oplus M$.

A marking (sometimes called a *state*) m of N is called a *deadlock* if m enables no transition. An oWFN in which all deadlocks are final markings is called *weakly terminating*. Obviously, the net N_1 in Fig. 2 itself is *not* weakly terminating. N_1

requires a partner who sends and receives messages. N_1 is not able to reach its final marking [p6,p7] on its own. Given an oWFN N, we call an oWFN S a *strategy* for N iff $N \oplus S$ is weakly terminating.

2.3 Controllability of oWFNs

Intuitively, controllability of an oWFN N means that N can properly interact with some other net. Formally, N is *controllable* iff there exists a strategy for N. Like the soundness property for workflow nets (cf. [10]), controllability is a minimal requirement for the correctness of an oWFN.

In [4] we developed an algorithm to efficiently decide the controllability of an oWFN N. Intuitively, the algorithm tries to construct (synthesize) a strategy, i. e. an oWFN S, which imposes the weak termination property of $S \oplus N$. If the construction fails, N is not controllable. If it succeeds, N is controllable and we have constructed a strategy, S. This construction is, in fact, a problem known in the literature as *controller synthesis* (see [11]). Technically we do not construct a strategy S, i. e. an oWFN, but an *automaton* that reflects the interactional behavior of S instead. To avoid confusion, we call the constructed automaton *controller*, but denote it with S as well.

To construct such a controller S, we first construct the *interaction graph* (IG) of N which has also been introduced in [4]. The IG represents a controller's point of view of N. A node of the graph represents the set of all states that N can reach by consuming (already present) messages or producing messages itself. The actual state of N is hidden for S. S knows the history of sent and received messages only. From that information, in each node, S can deduce a *set* of states of N which *contains* the state that N is really in. Thus a node of the graph represents a *hypothesis* of the controller with respect to the actual state of N.

S can control the net in a limited way by sending or receiving messages. Each edge of the graph represents an *event* of S. A *sending event* (labeled by !) means that S sends a message to N. The new message may enable N to fire previously disabled transitions, i. e. deadlocks may get "resolved". A *receiving event* (labeled by ?) of S represents the receiving of a message by the controller. Thereby, the controller gets some more knowledge about the state that N might be in.

In the constructed IG, we then look for a controller S for N. The controller is a subgraph of the IG containing the root node and fulfilling the following property: for every node v of the subgraph and each deadlock in v which is no final marking, there exists an event at v that resolves that deadlock and leads to a node of the subgraph again. This property can easily be checked while the IG is constructed. The oWFN is controllable iff such a controller can be found. In a final step, the controller could be transformed into an oWFN by using the theory of regions, for instance. This oWFN is then a strategy by construction.

As an example, the IG of the oWFN N_1 (see Fig. 2) is depicted in Fig. 3. As we can see in the IG of N_1 each deadlock in any node (except for the final marking in the last node) is resolved. Hence, the IG itself represents a controller, and we conclude that N_1 is controllable. Please note that two other subgraphs constituting controllers can also be found in the IG of N_1.

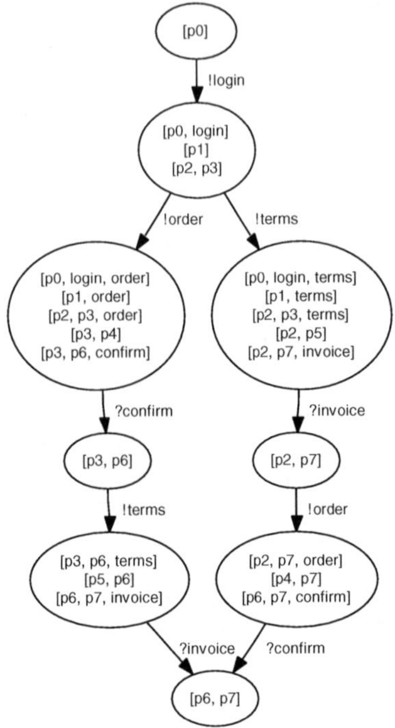

Fig. 3. The IG for the net N_1 of Fig. 2. The first node of the IG represents the hypothesis that the controller of N_1 has about N_1 when neither messages have been sent nor received: the net must be in state [p0], which is a deadlock. Hence, the first node contains the state [p0] only.

However, sending a login message resolves the deadlock. Hence, we add an edge labelled with the sending event !login and a new (yet empty) node to the IG. N_1 is now in state [p0,login] and may fire transition ?login reaching the state [p1]. After successively firing all enabled transitions the next reachable deadlock is [p2,p3]. So the new node contains the states [p0,login], [p1], and [p2,p3].

Now one of two sending events is possible: !order or !terms. So we add two edges and two empty nodes, and so on.

The last node of the controller represents the states where N_1 can be in after all the messages are exchanged. There is only one deadlock, [p6,p7], in that node which is the final marking of N_1.

2.4 Operating Guidelines for oWFNs

The IG of an oWFN N contains only *some* controllers of N. For a representation of *all* controllers (all properly interacting partners) of N, the concept of the *operating guideline* (OG) for N was introduced in [5]. As we did in the section before, we do not directly represent the strategies as oWFNs, but represent their behaviors as automata.

The OG of N is constructed as follows: in a first step, an extended interaction graph for N is computed which considers more events than the original one. This results in a controller performing more events than the one given by the original IG. In [9] it has been proven that *every* (properly interacting) controller must be a subgraph of the constructed one. Unfortunately, the converse is not true – only subgraphs that fulfill some further conditions are controllers for N, too. The second construction step is devoted to these conditions. In [5] we have shown that it is possible to code the conditions as a Boolean formula for each node of the controller. For a node v, the formula at v is in conjunctive normal form (CNF) over the events at v. Adding the corresponding formulae to the controller results in an annotated controller, the *operating guideline* for N.

The OG characterizes the set of all strategies for an oWFN and can be read as follows. We are allowed to remove nodes (except for the root node) and edges from the OG as long as, in each node v, the formula at v is still satisfied. To evaluate such a formula, the (remaining) outgoing edges constitute an assignment of truth values to the literals of the formula: an outgoing edge from node v with label x assigns *true* to the literal x in the formula at v. Each subgraph that can be constructed this way is a controller per construction.

Operating guidelines can be used to efficiently check whether two oWFNs will interact properly even before actually composing them. Given a controller representing an intended partner's behavior, we developed an algorithm to check whether it is characterized by the OG or not [12].

Figure 4 shows the operating guideline of the oWFN N_1 depicted in Fig. 2. In a node of the OG, the corresponding annotation is depicted. The reachable states of N_1 are hidden.

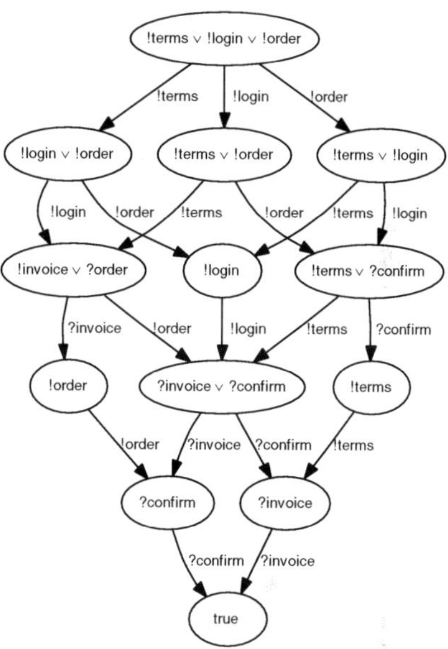

Fig. 4. The OG for the oWFN N_1 of Fig. 2. The annotation of the first node is a disjunction (!terms ∨ !login ∨ !order), i. e. a one-clause CNF formula. It means that every controller must, as its first event, send one of the three corresponding messages. The controller of Fig. 3, for instance, performs the event !login which is obviously correct according to the OG. The OG also allows a controller which first sends its order to N_1. This possibility results from the proposed asynchronous way of interaction. Even if the order was sent first, it would keep pending on the place order until N_1 has consumed the login message sent later.

The annotation true of the last node means that no event has to be performed any more.

In sum, the OG of N_1 characterizes 77 different controllers for N_1.

3 Example Process: Online Shop

In this section we present an online shop as our example process. It is a simple but realistic business process and a modification of an online shop presented in [13]. The online shop's BPEL specification consists of 15 activities and an event handler and is depicted in Fig. 5. We abstract from the BPEL syntax and use a more intuitive graphical notation: a box frames an activity. For structured activities the corresponding BPEL construct is additionally depicted in the top left corner of the box. We use icons for basic activities, optionally with a message name shown below it. A sequence is depicted by arcs whereas concurrent activities are grouped in parallel separated by a dashed line.

When the online shop receives the login information from a customer, its business strategy distinguishes between already known customers and new customers. In case of a known customer the left branch is executed: first the shop expects an order, and then it sends the invoice to the customer. In case of a new customer

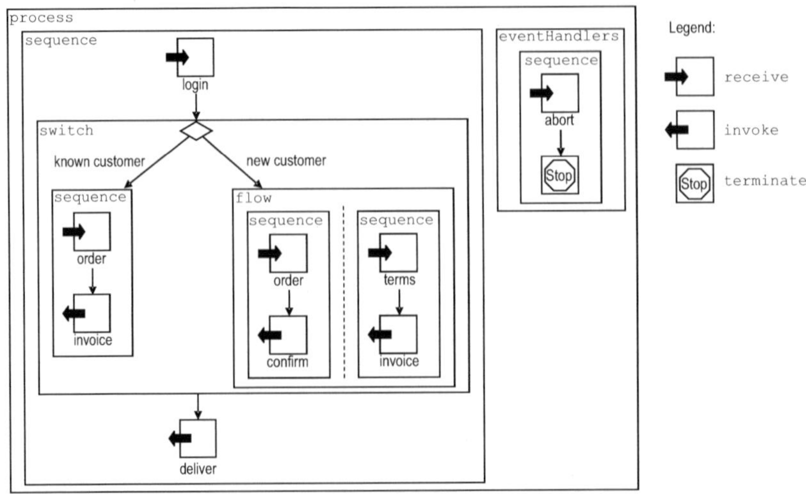

Fig. 5. The online shop process

(right branch) the shop initiates two tasks concurrently: in the first task (left sequence) the shop first receives the order and then confirms it. In the second task (right sequence) the shop receives the terms of payment before it sends an invoice to the customer. In either case the shop finally sends the delivery information to the customer. The customer may send an abort message at any time. We modeled this as an onMessage event handler that receives the abort message and then terminates the whole process. In Fig. 5 we depicted the event handler as a box, too. The expected message is also depicted by a receive icon.

4 Translating BPEL to Open Workflow Nets

4.1 Petri Net Semantics for BPEL

Our goal is to formally analyze BPEL processes. To achieve this goal we translate a BPEL process into an open workflow net using the semantics of [7]. As the semantics itself is not the focus of this paper, we only summarize the main ideas of it. The semantics is guided by the syntax of BPEL. In BPEL, a process is built by plugging instances of BPEL constructs together. Accordingly, we translated each construct of the language separately into a Petri net. Such a net forms a *pattern* of the respective BPEL construct. Each pattern has an interface for joining it with other patterns as it is done with BPEL constructs. The semantics aims at representing all properties of each BPEL construct within its respective pattern.

Please note that a pattern itself is not an open workflow net. Only the composition of all patterns of the activities of the process forms an open workflow net. The collection of patterns forms our Petri net semantics for BPEL. The semantics is complete (i. e. it covers all the standard and exceptional behavior of BPEL) and formal (meaning it is suitable for computer-aided verification). However, to decide controllability or to construct the operating guideline of a BPEL process it is not necessary to model all features of BPEL. As an example, Fig. 6(a) shows the `receive` activity "login" as it is used in the online shop. Figure 6(b) shows its corresponding Petri net pattern that is used to check controllability in the following sections. It is an abstraction of the original pattern of the semantics and does neither model variables nor correlation sets. As a means of simplification, we also do not model the occurrence of BPEL standard faults in the whole process.

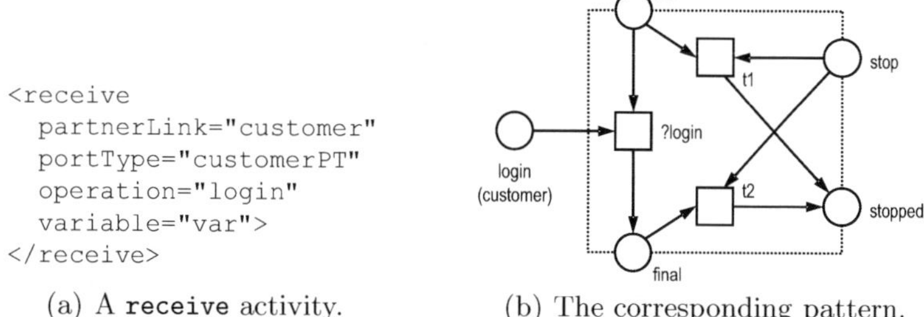

(a) A `receive` activity. (b) The corresponding pattern.

Fig. 6. The input place login is determined by the given `partnerLink`, `portType`, and `operation`. The dotted box frames the pattern. The places on the frame (init, final, stop, and stopped) describe the interface of the pattern used to join it with other patterns. The execution of the activity can be stopped any time by marking place stop and firing either `t1` or `t2`.

4.2 The Tool BPEL2oWFN

The described Petri net semantics for BPEL was prototypically implemented in the tool BPEL2PN [8]. The resulting Petri net does not model the interactional behavior and therefore only allows for verification of the internal behavior. Another drawback of BPEL2PN is its "brute-force" mapping approach which results in huge models for BPEL processes of realistic sizes and therefore does not permit efficient analysis.

To scale down the model size we pursue three objectives. (1) We improve the Petri net patterns of the semantics. (2) We choose specific (smaller) patterns from a repository with the help of information gained by static analysis. (3) We use structural simplification rules to compact the generated Petri net model and thus reduce its state space. These features were implemented in the tool BPEL2oWFN[2], the successor of BPEL2PN. BPEL2oWFN is capable of generating oWFNs and other file formats (PNML, low-level PEP notation, APNN, and LoLA low-level nets) and thus supports a variety of analysis tools.

Novel patterns. The Petri net semantics as described in [7] was designed to formalize BPEL rather than to automatically generate compact Petri net models that are necessary for computer-aided verification. Some patterns were designed

[2] Available at `http://www.informatik.hu-berlin.de/top/tools4bpel/bpel2owfn`

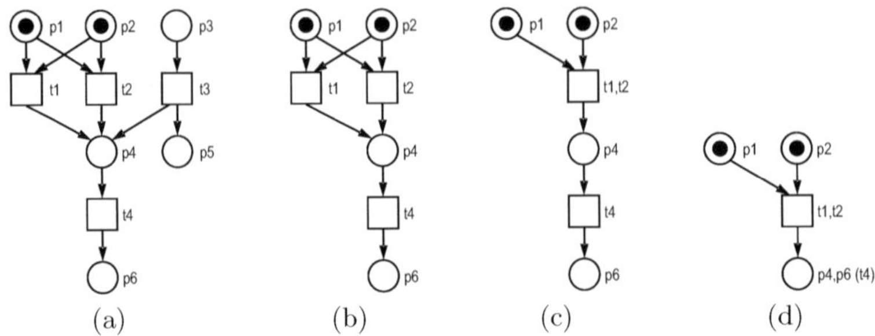

Fig. 7. The implemented structural reduction rules. From the original net (a) all structural dead places and transitions are removed (b). Then duplicate transitions are merged (c), and simple sequences are collapsed (d).

to be easily understood and made use of quite "expensive" constructs such as reset arcs. We improved these patterns and replaced them by less intuitive patterns with simpler structure. As mentioned before, we abstract from data and model data-driven decisions by non-determinism. As a result, the generated oWFN is a 1-safe low-level Petri net which improves the verification performance.

Static analysis. Instead of mapping each BPEL activity to a single pattern modeling its behavior in all possible contexts, BPEL2oWFN employs a repository of several patterns for each activity. Each pattern (e. g. the `receive` pattern in Fig. 6(b)) is designed for a certain context or to preserve specific properties only. To choose the most compact pattern for a certain verification task, we perform static analysis (see [14] for an overview) for the BPEL process.

Structural simplification. Finally, we use structural reduction rules to further scale down the size of the generated Petri net model w. r. t. the requirements of the given analysis task. Currently, three reduction rules are implemented: at first, all structural dead places and transitions are removed. Secondly, duplicate transitions are merged. Thirdly, simple sequences (a transition with exactly one place in its preset and postset) are collapsed. As the nodes of the IG consist of sets of reachable markings, structural reduction may dramatically scale down the size of the IG. The rules are exemplified in Fig. 7.

4.3 Translating the Online Shop

Using BPEL2oWFN, we now translate the online shop example process into an oWFN[3]. The generated net originally has 112 places (including 4 input and 3 output places), 117 transitions, and 371 arcs. Structural reduction simplifies the net to 61 places (including the 4 input and 3 output places), 58 transitions, and 191 arcs. The structural reduction also affects the state space of the inner of the generated oWFN. The number of reachable states is reduced from 510 to 205.

[3] As the process terminates after receiving an abort message, we modeled the event handler to receive at most one abort message. Thus, the generated oWFN is acyclic.

5 Analyzing the Interaction of oWFNs

5.1 The Tool Fiona

Fiona[4] is a tool to automatically analyze the interactional behavior of a given oWFN N. Fiona provides two techniques: it checks for the controllability of N, and it calculates the operating guideline for N. Fiona uses oWFNs as its input which is the output of BPEL2oWFN. Thus we can easily analyze BPEL processes.

Depending on the goal the user wants to achieve (controllability analysis or calculation of the operating guideline) the tool either builds up the interaction graph or the operating guideline. Fiona computes the nodes and the events of the respective graph as described in Sect. 2. To compute the states of the graph nodes we use efficient algorithms that were implemented in the model checking tool LoLA [15].

To find a controller in the computed graph (IG or OG), each of its nodes is analyzed. The analysis is done while the graph is constructed. It is a backward analysis starting at the leaf nodes. The analysis makes use of colors: black nodes are yet to be analyzed, blue nodes denote nodes of the controller and red nodes are not part of the controller. Initially, each node is colored black. If we have calculated a leaf node of the graph which contains only such deadlocks that are final markings, we color this node blue. If a leaf contains further deadlocks, it is colored red (since every such deadlock is not resolved). An internal node becomes blue if there exists for each deadlock (which is no final marking) an activated event leading to a blue node again. If this is not the case, the node becomes red. In case of building the OG, the analysis additionally computes the Boolean annotation of the node. Finally, each node has been colored either blue or red. The graph contains a controller iff the root node is blue. The controller is constituted by the largest connected blue subgraph that contains the root node.

Fiona implements several optimizations: for instance, the red color of a node can sometimes be concluded before all of its successors are known. For such a node, we do not need to compute the remaining successors, since they cannot be part of the controller later on. Furthermore, not all states in a node must be stored to compute the successors – these states are rejected.

5.2 Analyzing the Online Shop Model

We now want to analyze our online shop example from Sect. 3. Firstly, we use Fiona to calculate the IG of the corresponding oWFN which we got from Sect. 4.3. The IG consists of 16 nodes and 19 edges. A blue subgraph can be found that has 8 nodes and 8 edges, containing the root node. Thus this subgraph constitutes a controller and the online shop is controllable.

The controller found reflects the intended behavior of a customer. First he sends a login, followed by an order. Then he must be able to either receive an invoice (in case he is known to the shop) or to receive the confirmation (in case

[4] Available at `http://www.informatik.hu-berlin.de/top/tools4bpel/fiona`

he is a new customer). If he actually has received the confirmation, he must send a terms of payment message. After that he will receive the invoice. In either case he finally receives the delivery information. At any time he may abort. We did not depict the IG due to the lack of space and because it can be found as a subgraph in the corresponding OG. The latter has 12 nodes and 15 edges and is depicted in Fig. 9(a). Compared to the IG, the OG contains more interleavings of sending or receiving messages. For instance, a customer may reverse the order of sending the login and the order message.

6 The Online Shop Revised

Let us take a look at the online shop presented in Sect. 3 once again. The shop now modifies its business strategy: every known customer that orders something can choose a gift. The modified online shop is depicted in Fig. 8.

The changes only affect the left branch of the switch. The shop initiates two tasks concurrently now: in the first task (left sequence) the shop first receives the order and then confirms it. In the second task (right sequence) the shop receives which gift is chosen before it sends the invoice to the customer. The rest of the process is as in Fig. 5.

The analysis with Fiona reflects that this simple change has a crucial effect on the behavior of the process. The IG of the revised online shop has 32 nodes and 40 edges. The corresponding controller inside the IG consists of 6 nodes and 5 edges which is less than the original controller of Sect. 5.2. Our algorithm concludes that the process is controllable, too. However, the reflected strategy is not the intended one. The controller in the IG represents a customer who sends an abort message during the interaction.

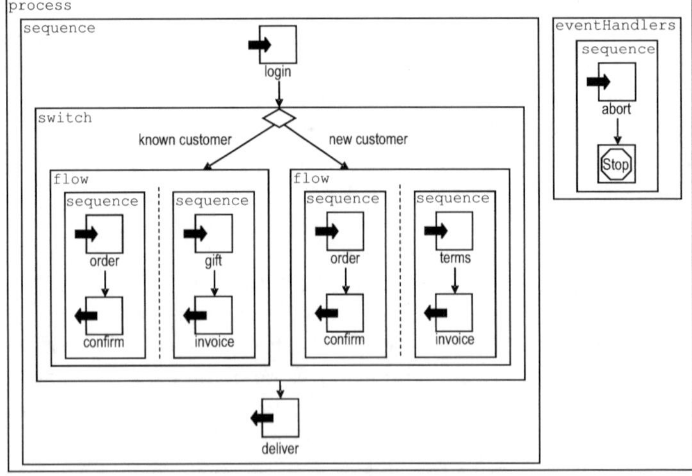

Fig. 8. The modified online shop

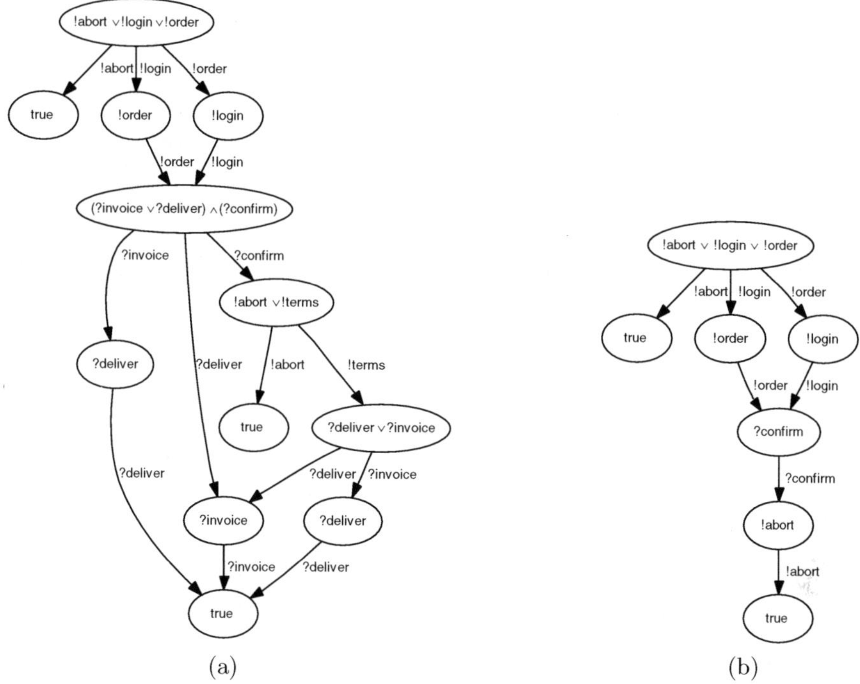

Fig. 9. Operating guidelines (a) of the original online shop of Fig. 5 and (b) of the modified shop of Fig. 8. The OG in (a) characterizes different intended customers of the original shop, whereas the OG in (b) documents that there is only one possible way to interact with the modified shop: to abort.

The IG represents only one customer's behavior. For further information we need Fiona to calculate the OG. It is depicted in Fig. 9(b) and consists of 7 nodes and 7 edges. A closer look at the OG reveals that actually *every* customer of the modified shop must eventually send an abort message. This surely means that the process is controllable. However, the way this is done is obviously a not intended one. There is no way that a customer can get what he has ordered from the process.

Let us take a look at what went wrong when we modified our online shop from Sect. 3. We can see that the shop does not communicate its inner decision about which branch (known customer, new customer) is chosen. In the original online shop (Fig. 5) the controller must send an order, but receives either an invoice or a confirmation w. r. t. which branch the shop has chosen before. That way the controller knows what branch the shop is actually in and hence knows how to continue. In contrast, in the modified shop the controller must send an order and receives undistinguishable confirmation messages in either case. The modified shop expects a choice of a gift in case it decided for the known customer branch. In the other case it expects the terms of payment. The controller, however, does not know about the decision of the shop. That means, it does not know what message to send. This is reflected by the OG of the new shop as well (see Fig. 9(b)): in the situation where a partner receives the confirmation he does not know whether the shop decided for the left or the right branch. Hence, he can choose either to send a gift choice or the terms of payment. In either case it is not guaranteed that the message will always be consumed, and therefore it should not be sent in the first place. However, sending an abort is always correct.

This simple example shows that even a small modification of a process may result in an unintended interactional behavior. The effect on the interactional behavior of a BPEL process is not obvious. Since this is not obvious even for small processes as in our shop example, it is even more challenging for BPEL processes of realistic size. In general, processes may have a complex structure that it is not possible to detect such erroneous structures in the BPEL process manually. With the help of the operating guideline we can see if there exists a controller that interacts with our process as we have expected it during the process design.

7 Related Work

Several groups have proposed formal semantics for BPEL. Among them, there are semantics based on finite state machines [16,17], the process algebra Lotos [18], abstract state machines [19,20], and Petri nets [21,7]. The group of van der Aalst also follows a Petri net-based approach [21]. Their semantics, however, does not cover the communication of BPEL. It enables several analysis methods including the detection of unreachable activities and BPEL standard faults like "conflicting receive" (two concurrent receive activities are waiting for the same input message). Further, it is possible to perform a reachability analysis for the garbage collection of unconsumable messages later on. Those methods are implemented in the tool WofBPEL [22].

In [23] BPEL processes are transformed into an annotated subset of oWFNs, *BPEL annotated Petri nets* (BPNs). The transformation is oriented on a modified version of our semantics [7], which does not include most of the fault and compensation handling. For BPNs a technique for analyzing the controllability has already been introduced in [13] – the *communication graph*. It is similar to our proposed IG. As a main difference, this graph performs communication *steps*, where each step consists of a (possibly empty) sending phase followed by a (possibly empty) receiving phase. Therefore, the communication graph tends to be more complex than our IG (cf. [4]).

8 Conclusion and Further Work

We presented a framework to formally analyze the interactional behavior of BPEL processes. Both the translation from BPEL into compact Petri net models as well as the further analysis of controllability and the computation of the operating guideline are implemented which allows for a fully-automatic analysis. The results show that we can detect non-trivial model flaws of interacting BPEL processes that would have been hard or impossible to find manually.

In the current translation approach we use static analysis to compact the generated model only. However, it is possible to check certain properties statically, i. e. without generating a model at all. In future work we want to use control flow analysis to detect unreachable (thus dead) activities or other design flaws. To further support this analysis, we have to add data aspects to our model and replace non-determinism by data-driven decisions.

To analyze interactions consisting of more than two interacting processes, existing theoretical results have to be integrated into Fiona. In addition, algorithms to decide controllability and to compute the operating guidelines of cyclic oWFNs have to be established to complete the analysis spectrum.

To support the redesign of erroneous (e. g. not controllable) services, the analysis results (e. g. counter-examples) have to be translated back into BPEL source code. This will be extremely helpful to support process designers during the modelling.

Finally, our tool Fiona is not restricted to analyze BPEL processes only. Since Fiona uses oWFNs as its input we have a very general formalism at hand that can be used to model various kinds of interacting processes. Therefore Fiona can, for instance, also be used to analyze interorganizational workflow as well.

References

1. Hull, R., Benedikt, M., Christophides, V., Su, J.: E-Services: A Look Behind the Curtain. In: PODS '03, New York, USA, ACM Press (2003) 1–14
2. Papazoglou, M.P.: Agent-Oriented Technology in Support of E-Business. Communications of the ACM **44**(4) (2001) 71–77
3. Andrews, T., et al.: Business Process Execution Language for Web Services, Version 1.1. Technical report, BEA, IBM, Microsoft (2003)
4. Weinberg, D.: Reduction Rules for Interaction Graphs. Technical Report 198, Humboldt-Universität zu Berlin (2006)
5. Massuthe, P., Schmidt, K.: Operating Guidelines – An Automata-Theoretic Foundation for Service-Oriented Architectures. In: QSIC 2005, Melbourne, Australia, IEEE Computer Society (2005) 452–457
6. Massuthe, P., Reisig, W., Schmidt, K.: An Operating Guideline Approach to the SOA. AMCT **1**(3) (2005) 35–43 To appear.
7. Stahl, C.: A Petri Net Semantics for BPEL. Techn. Report 188, Humboldt-Universität zu Berlin (2005)
8. Hinz, S., Schmidt, K., Stahl, C.: Transforming BPEL to Petri Nets. In: BPM 2005. Volume 3649 of LNCS., Nancy, France, Springer-Verlag (2005) 220–235
9. Schmidt, K.: Controllability of Open Workflow Nets. In: EMISA. LNI, Bonner Köllen Verlag (2005) 236–249
10. Aalst, W.: The Application of Petri Nets to Workflow Management. Journal of Circuits, Systems and Computers **8**(1) (1998) 21–66
11. Ramadge, P., Wonham, W.: Supervisory Control of a Class of Discrete Event Processes. SIAM J. Control and Optimization **25**(1) (1987) 206–230
12. Massuthe, P., Schmidt, K.: Operating Guidelines – An Automata-Theoretic Foundation for Service-Oriented Architectures. to appear (2006)
13. Martens, A.: Verteilte Geschäftsprozesse – Modellierung und Verifikation mit Hilfe von Web Services. PhD thesis, Humboldt-Universität zu Berlin (2004)

14. Nielson, F., Nielson, H.R., Hankin, C.: Principles of Program Analysis. 2nd edn. Springer-Verlag (2005)
15. Schmidt, K.: LoLA: A Low Level Analyser. In: ICATPN 2000. Number 1825 in LNCS, Springer-Verlag (2000) 465–474
16. Arias-Fisteus, J., Fernández, L.S., Kloos, C.D.: Formal Verification of BPEL4WS Business Collaborations. In: EC-Web'04. Volume 3182 of LNCS., Springer (2004) 76–85
17. Fu, X., Bultan, T., Su, J.: Analysis of Interacting BPEL Web Services. In: WWW '04, ACM Press (2004) 621–630
18. Ferrara, A.: Web Services: A Process Algebra Approach. In: ICSOC, ACM (2004) 242–251
19. Fahland, D., Reisig, W.: ASM-based Semantics for BPEL: The Negative Control Flow. In: ASM'05, Paris XII (2005) 131–151
20. Farahbod, R., Glässer, U., Vajihollahi, M.: Specification and Validation of the Business Process Execution Language for Web Services. In: ASM. Volume 3052 of LNCS., Springer (2004) 78–94
21. Ouyang, C., Verbeek, E., van der Aalst, W.M., Breutel, S., Dumas, M., ter Hofstede, A.H.: Formal Semantics and Analysis of Control Flow in WS-BPEL. Technical report (revised version), Queensland University of Technology (2005)
22. Ouyang, C., Verbeek, E., Aalst, W., Breutel, S., Dumas, M., ter Hofstede, A.: WofBPEL: A Tool for Automated Analysis of BPEL Processes. In: ICSOC 2005. Volume 3826 of LNCS., Amsterdam, The Netherlands (2005) 484–489
23. Martens, A., Moser, S., Gerhardt, A., Funk, K.: Analyzing Compatibility of BPEL Processes – Towards a Business Process Analysis Framework in IBM's Business Integration Tools. In: ICIW'06, IEEE Computer Society Press (2006)

Tracking over Collaborative Business Processes

Xiaohui Zhao and Chengfei Liu

Centre for Information Technology Research
Faculty of Information and Communication Technologies
Swinburne University of Technology
Melbourne, Victoria, Australia
{xzhao, cliu}@it.swin.edu.au

Abstract. Workflow monitoring is a routine function of a workflow management system for tracking the progress of running workflow instances. To keep participating organisations as autonomous entities in an inter-organisational business collaboration environment, however, it brings challenges in generating workflow tracking structures and manipulating instance correspondences between different participating organisations. Aiming to tackle these problems, this paper proposed a matrix based framework on the basis of our relative workflow model. This framework enables a participating organisation to derive tracking structures over its relative workflows and the involved relevant workflows of its partner organisations, and to perform workflow tracking with the generated tracking structures.

1 Introduction

With the trend of booming global business collaborations, organisations are required to streamline their business processes into dynamic virtual organisations [1, 2]. A virtual organisation defines the trading community of a set of participating organisations for conducting collaborative business processes. Normally, the building blocks of a collaborative business process are the pre-existing business processes of participating organisations. Therefore, it is fundamental that a collaborative business process knows how the business process belonging to different organisations are linked together for cooperation [3, 4]. While this kind of cooperation is a prerequisite, organisations must act as autonomous entities during business collaboration. Besides, certain levels of privacy of participating organisations have to be guaranteed. Many existing inter-organisational workflow approaches streamline the related business processes of different organisations, into a *public view* workflow process [5-9]. This public view neutralises the diversity of the perception on collaborative business processes from different organisations, and fails to support business privacy sufficiently. We reckon that different organisations may see different pictures of a collaborative business process, and may need to know and be only allowed to know certain details of the collaboration with their partner organisations. To support this, we have proposed a new approach for collaborative business process modelling called *relative workflow model* [10]. In this model, different *visibility constraints*, *perceptions*, and *relative workflow processes* can be defined for different participating organisations.

Most traditional workflow monitoring approaches, such as WfMC Monitor and Audit specification [11, 12], BEA Weblogic Integration [13], IBM WebSphere MQ Workflow

S. Dustdar, J.L. Fiadeiro, and A. Sheth (Eds.): BPM 2006, LNCS 4102, pp. 33–48, 2006.

[14], the agent based workflow monitoring [15] and the customisable workflow monitoring [16], are mainly applicable either in an intra-organisational setting or in an environment where a public view of a collaborative business process is assumed without privacy concern. To our best knowledge, there is little discussion on workflow monitoring in an inter-organisational environment concerning privacy. This paper aims to fill this gap. Based on the relative workflow model, the tracking structure for a relative workflow process is defined and a matrix based framework is proposed to enable a participating organisation to derive tracking structures over its relative workflow processes and the involved relevant workflow processes of its partner organisations, and to perform tracking based on the generated tracking structures.

The remainder of this paper is organised as follows. Section 2 analyses requirements of workflow tracking in a privacy sensitive environment with a motivating example. In Section 3, we first review our relative workflow approach, then introduce some representation matrices, after that we define the tracking structure of a relative workflow process and discuss the fundamental rules for workflow tracking. Based on these rules, several matrix operations are presented in Section 4 for tracking structure generation, together with the algorithms for generating tracking structures and performing tracking. Conclusion remarks are given in Section 5.

2 Requirement Analysis with Motivating Example

Basically speaking, current *public view* approaches all rely on a single workflow model to support inter-organisational business collaboration. This means that once the workflow model for a collaborative business process is defined, it will be open to all participating organisations. If we follow a public view approach, a participating organisation may not be able to offer different visibilities to different organisations. As such, different partnerships between different collaborating organisations cannot be achieved. In our opinion, the visibility between participating organisations is inherently relative rather than absolute. Our relative workflow approach [10] was proposed based on this "relative perspective" philosophy. This approach discards the public view on the inter-organisational workflow process, and allows different organisations to create different views or relative workflow processes upon the same collaborative business process. These multiple relative workflow processes enable participating organisations behave as autonomous entities and enhance the flexibility and privacy control of business collaboration. In the same time, they bring challenges to inter-organisational workflow tracking.

Figure 1 illustrates a business collaboration scenario where a retailer collects orders from customers, and then purchases products from a manufacturer. The manufacturer may contact a shipper for booking product delivery while making goods with supplies from a supplier. In this scenario, a retailer may track the collaborative business process as follows: After placing an order with a manufacturer, the retailer may contact the manufacturer and enquire about the execution status of the production process by referring, say the order number. Furthermore, the retailer may also contact the shipper via the manufacturer and enquire about shipping information after the manufacturer organises product shipping for the retailer by a shipper.

However, the retailer may not be allowed to enquire about the goods supply information, because that could be confidential information of the manufacturer and is hidden from the retailer. For a manufacturer, it may track same collaborative business process differently. Besides the retailer and shipper, the manufacturer can also track the supplier for goods supply information.

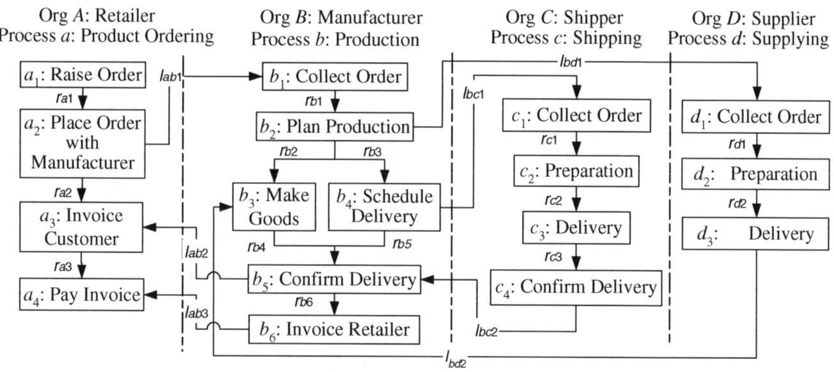

Fig. 1. Inter-organisational collaboration example

From this scenario, we can see that (1) a participating organisation may require tracking other organisations for its involved part of a collaborative business process; (2) each participating organisation may track same collaborative business process differently.

The first point requires collaboration between participating organisations, which is fundamental to inter-organisational workflow tracking. The second point, however, requires that a participating organisation is treated as a fully autonomous entity and can provide different visibilities to different organisations. Obviously, the public view approaches cannot meet the second requirement. Our relative workflow approach can meet both requirements, as we can see from the following sections.

3 Relative Workflows and Tracking Structures

3.1 Relative Workflow Model

In this section, we briefly review the relative workflow model. Figure 2 shows the relative workflow meta model, which has been proposed in [10]. In this model, an *organisation*, say g_1, is considered as an entity holding its own workflow processes called *local workflow processes*. A local workflow process, lp^1, of organisation g_1 can be denoted as $g_1.lp^1$.

As the owner, an organisation naturally has an absolute view of its local workflow processes. On the contrary, the host organisation (the owner organisation) may only allow a restricted view of its local workflow processes to its partner organisations due

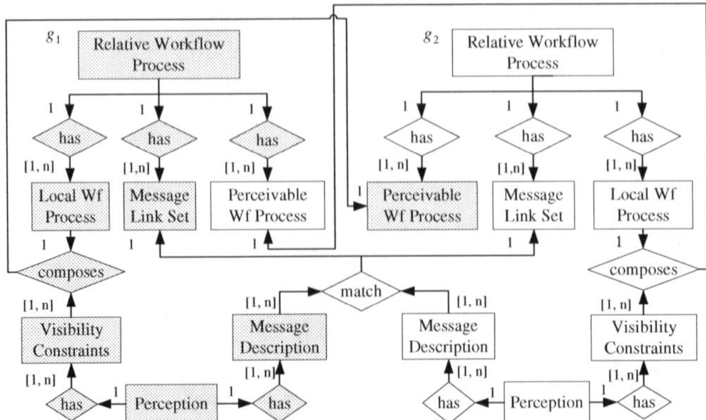

Fig. 2. Relative workflow meta model

to the privacy concern. This restriction mechanism may hide some confidential workflow tasks and related links or set some tasks only observable rather than interactable to some partner organisations according to the partnership. The degree of task visibility are defined by *visibility constraints*, which currently contains three values, viz., "invisible", "trackable" and "contactable", as shown in Table 1.

Table 1. Visibility values

Visibility value	**Explanation**
Invisible	A task is said invisible to an organisation, if it is hidden from the organisation.
Trackable	A task is said trackable to an organisation, if this organisation is allowed to trace the execution status of the task.
Contactable	A task is said contactable to an organisation, if the task is trackable to the organisation and the task is also allowed to send/receive messages to/from this organisation for the purpose of business interaction.

Visibility constraints are used as a component in defining *perceptions*. A perception $p_{g_1}^{g_2.lp}$ defines how organisation g_1 sees g_2's local workflow process lp. In the motivating example, the manufacturer may set up the following content in the set of visibility constraints, $\mathcal{VC}$, of its perception $p_{Retailer}^{Manufacturer.Production}$.

$p_{Retailer}^{Manufacturer.Production}.\mathcal{VC}$ = {("collect order", `Contactable`), ("plan production", `Invisible`), ("make goods", `Trackable`), ("schedule delivery", `Trackable`), ("confirm delivery", `Contactable`), ("invoice retailer", `Contactable`)}

These visibility constraints allow a partial view of the manufacturer's production process for the retailer. This partial view is called *perceivable workflow process*. The perceivable workflow process of g_2's local workflow process $g_2.lp^1$ defined for organisation g_1 is denoted as $g_2.lp_{g_1}^1$.

To represent the diverse partnerships, an organisation may generate a series of perceivable workflow processes of same local workflow process for different partner organisations. And the inter-organisational business interactions are characterised as directed inter process links, such as l_{ab1} and l_{bc2} in Figure 1. In our relative workflow meta model, these inter process links are defined as *message descriptions* before being linked, and *messaging links* after being linked, as shown in Figure 2.

Finally, a *relative workflow process* can be created by combining the messaging links which connect "contactable" tasks of neighbouring organisations. As shown in Figure 2, a relative workflow process consists of three parts, viz. local workflow processes, perceivable workflow processes and relevant messaging links. Such a relative workflow process represents the collaborative business process perceivable from an organisation.

For example, we suppose that the involved organisations in the motivating example set up the following visibility constraints in proper perceptions, together with perception $p_{Retailer}^{Manufacturer.Production}$, which has been given before.

> $p_{Manufacturer}^{Retailer.ProductOdering}.\mathcal{VC}$ = {("raise order", Invisible), ("place order with manufacturer", Contactable), ("invoice customer", Contactable), ("pay invoice", Contactable)};
>
> $p_{Manufacturer}^{Shipper.Shipping}.\mathcal{VC}$ = {("collect order", Contactable), ("preparation", Invisible), ("delivery", Trackable), ("confirm delivery", Contactable)};
>
> $p_{Retailer}^{Shipper.Shipping}.\mathcal{VC}$ = {("collect order", Invisible), ("preparation", Trackable), ("delivery", Trackable), ("confirm delivery", Trackable)};
>
> $p_{Manufacturer}^{Supplier.Supplying}.\mathcal{VC}$ = {("collect order", Contactable), ("preparation", Invisible), ("delivery", Contactable)}.

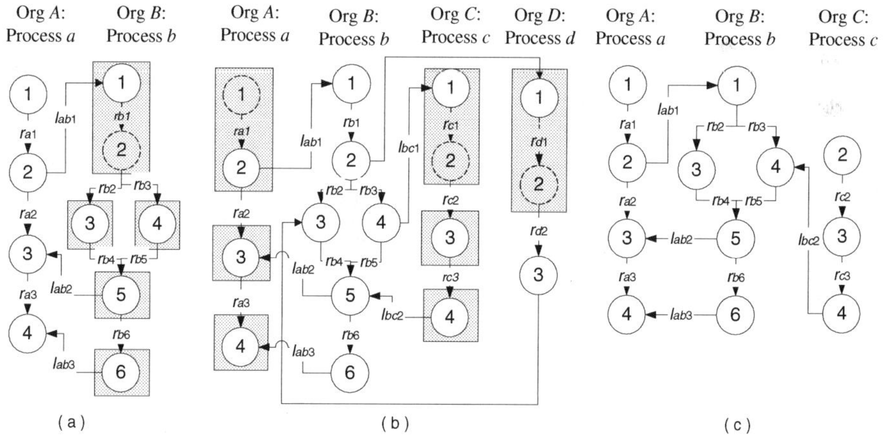

Fig. 3. Relative workflow and tracking structure examples

Since the retailer and the supplier have no partner relationship in the collaborative business process, they do not define perceptions for each other.

According to these visibility constraints, the retailer and the manufacturer may generate corresponding relative workflow processes, as shown in Figure 3 (a) and (b), respectively.

The tasks with dashed circles denote the invisible tasks. These two diagrams clearly illustrate that the relative workflow processes for same collaborative business process may be different from different organisations' perspectives. This reflects the relativity characteristics of our relative workflow approach.

3.2 Representation Matrices

To accurately depict the proposed relative workflow model, we establish several matrices to formally represent key concepts of the relative workflow model.

Self Adjacency Matrix

An n-task workflow process p of organisation g is represented by a special matrix, called *Self Adjacency Matrix* (SAM), which is defined as,

$$D_g^p{}_{n\times n} = [d_{ij}], \text{ where } d_{ij} = \begin{cases} r, \text{ if exists link } r \text{ linking task } t_i \text{ and task } t_j, \text{ where } i < j; \\ 0, \text{ otherwise.} \end{cases}$$

Each element of an SAM denotes an intra process link between tasks, such as r_{a1} and r_{b2} in Figure 1. As a link connecting tasks t_i and t_j is put in d_{ij}, not d_{ji}, where $i<j$, D_g^p is always an upper triangular matrix. For example, process a in Figure 1 can be represented by SAM $D_A^a = \begin{pmatrix} 0 & r_{a1} & 0 & 0 \\ 0 & 0 & r_{a2} & 0 \\ 0 & 0 & 0 & r_{a3} \\ 0 & 0 & 0 & 0 \end{pmatrix}$. Similarly, $D_B^b = \begin{pmatrix} 0 & r_{b1} & 0 & 0 & 0 & 0 \\ 0 & 0 & r_{b2} & r_{b3} & 0 & 0 \\ 0 & 0 & 0 & 0 & r_{b4} & 0 \\ 0 & 0 & 0 & 0 & r_{b5} & 0 \\ 0 & 0 & 0 & 0 & 0 & r_{b6} \\ 0 & 0 & 0 & 0 & 0 & 0 \end{pmatrix}$ and

$D_C^c = \begin{pmatrix} 0 & r_{c1} & 0 & 0 \\ 0 & 0 & r_{c2} & 0 \\ 0 & 0 & 0 & r_{c3} \\ 0 & 0 & 0 & 0 \end{pmatrix}$.

A self adjacency matrix can be used to represent not only a local workflow process but also a perceivable workflow process, a relative workflow process, or a tracking structure, which will be introduced later.

Transformation Matrix

When composing a local workflow process p into a perceivable workflow process for organisation g, the composition is subject to the visibility constraints defined in proper perceptions. The details of this composition can be found in [10]. In this paper, we formalise the composition process as an $n\times n$ triangular 0-1 matrix, called *Transformation Matrix* (TM), which is defined as

$$T_g^p{}_{n\times n} = [t_{ij}], \text{ where } t_{ij} = \begin{cases} 1, \text{ if task } t_j \text{ is composed into task } t_i\ (j \neq i), \text{ or not composed } (j = i); \\ 0, \text{ otherwise.} \end{cases}$$

This matrix can be directly derived from the visibility constraints defined in the corresponding perception, following the task composition algorithm discussed in [10]. Notice, each column has only one element with value "1", because each task can be composed only once or may not be composed at all. For example, the procedure of composing local workflow process b into a perceivable workflow process for organisation A can be described by TM $T_A^b = \begin{pmatrix} 1 & 1 & 0 & 0 & 0 & 0 \\ 0 & 0 & 0 & 0 & 0 & 0 \\ 0 & 0 & 1 & 0 & 0 & 0 \\ 0 & 0 & 0 & 1 & 0 & 0 \\ 0 & 0 & 0 & 0 & 1 & 0 \\ 0 & 0 & 0 & 0 & 0 & 1 \end{pmatrix}$. This composing procedure is conducted by the visibility constraints defined in perception $p_A^{B.b}$.

Likewise, we can calculate that $T_A^c = \begin{pmatrix} 0 & 0 & 0 & 0 \\ 1 & 1 & 0 & 0 \\ 0 & 0 & 1 & 0 \\ 0 & 0 & 0 & 1 \end{pmatrix}$.

Boundary Adjacency Matrix

Finally, we also represent the relevant messaging links in a matrix. The messaging links between two workflow processes, p_1 and p_2, from the perspective of organisation g, can be represented by an $m \times n$ matrix called *boundary adjacency matrix* (BAM), where m is the number of tasks belonging to p_1, and n is the number of tasks belonging to p_2. A BAM is defined as follows,

$$B_g^{p_1|p_2}{}_{m \times n} = [b_{ij}], \text{ where } b_{ij} = \begin{cases} l, \text{ if exists messaging link } l \text{ connecting } p_1.t_i \text{ and } p_2.t_j \\ 0, \text{ otherwise.} \end{cases}$$

For example, the interaction relationship between local workflow process b and perceivable workflow process c at the site of organisation B, can be represented by BAM $B_B^{b|c} = \begin{pmatrix} 0 & 0 & 0 & 0 \\ 0 & 0 & 0 & 0 \\ 0 & 0 & 0 & 0 \\ l_{bc1} & 0 & 0 & 0 \\ 0 & 0 & 0 & l_{bc2} \\ 0 & 0 & 0 & 0 \end{pmatrix}$. Similarly, $B_A^{a|b} = \begin{pmatrix} 0 & 0 & 0 & 0 & 0 & 0 \\ l_{ab1} & 0 & 0 & 0 & 0 & 0 \\ 0 & 0 & 0 & 0 & l_{ab2} & 0 \\ 0 & 0 & 0 & 0 & 0 & l_{ab3} \end{pmatrix}$.

3.3 Tracking Structure

From the discussion in the motivating example section, we see that an organisation's tracking structure is its observable view upon the execution progress of one collaborative business process. Technically, a tracking structure is different from a relative workflow process, because the latter is created by messaging links connecting to *contactable* tasks of neighbouring organisations while the former may go beyond neighbouring organisations through *trackable* tasks.

Unlike the "contactable" visibility value defined in Table 1, the "trackable" value is designed for tracking purpose and can be set on the tasks of the workflow processes belonging to non-neighbouring organisations. We define a tracking structure for each relative workflow process and this tracking structure can be defined by including trackable tasks from its non-neighbouring organisations.

Tracking Structure: A tracking structure *ts* for organisation g's relative workflow process *rp* consists of the following tasks and links.

- The tasks include: (*i*) the tasks of relative workflow process *rp*; (*ii*) the union of task sets of perceivable workflow processes that are *reachable* from g. These perceivable workflow processes may belong to g's neighbouring and non-neighbouring organisations. The reachability of a perceivable workflow process from an organisation is to be discussed in next sub section.

- The links include: (*i*) the links of relative workflow process *rp*; (*ii*) the union of link sets of perceivable workflow processes that are reachable from *g*; (*iii*) the set of messaging links between perceivable workflow processes that are *visible* from *g*. The visibility of a messaging link from an organisation is to be discussed in next sub section.

3.4 Rules

From the definition of a tracking structure, we need to first define the visibility of a messaging link and the reachability of a perceivable workflow process from an organisation. They all depend on the visibility of tasks. For this purpose, we establish the following rules that are used to generate a perceivable workflow process and to determine whether a perceivable workflow process is reachable via visible messaging links and therefore can be included in the tracking structure.

Intra Process Visibility Rule: If a task t in organisation g_1's local workflow process $g_1.lp$ is set invisible to organisation g_2, then t is hidden by composing it into a visible (contactable or trackable) task of $g_1.lp$. The links connecting t will be changed accordingly. The composition procedure will be discussed in the *composition operation* in next section. After composition, $g_1.lp$ becomes a perceivable workflow process $g_1.lp_{g2}$.

Inter Process Visibility Rule: A messaging link l connecting two perceivable workflow processes is said *visible* to organisation g, if and only if both tasks connected by l are visible to g.

Expansion Rule: Let *ts* be the tracking structure for a relative workflow process of organisation g. A perceivable workflow process outside *ts* is said *reachable* and therefore can be included into *ts*, if and only if it has at least one *visible* messaging link connecting a task inside *ts*.

Following the Intra Process Visibility Rule, the original link r_{b1} connecting tasks b_1 and b_2 of process b in Figure 1 becomes invisible in its perceivable form for organisation A in Figure 3 (c) because b_2 is invisible to organisation A. Correspondingly, links r_{b2} and r_{b3}, which connect b_2 and b_3, b_2 and b_4 in Figure 1 respectively, are now changed to connect b_1 and b_3, b_1 and b_4, in Figure 3 (c). Following the Inter Process Visibility Rule, messaging link l_{bc1} connecting task b_4 and task c_1 is not visible while messaging link l_{bc2} connecting task b_5 and task c_5 is visible in Figure 1. Following the Expansion Rule, the perceivable workflow processes of process c is reachable because of the existence of the visible messaging link l_{bc2}. By applying all these rules, we can finally generate a tracking structure shown in Figure 3 (c) for A's relative workflow process shown in Figure 3 (a).

4 Generating Tracking Structures

4.1 Operations

According to the rules discussed in last section, we define three matrix operations for tracking structure derivation.

Operation 1. Composition Operation

As defined in the TM for a local workflow process, each element with value "1" in a non-diagonal position (i, j) stands for a procedure of composing the composed task t_j to the composing task t_i. Under the restriction of the Intra Process Visibility Rule, the following sub rules may apply to this composition:

(1) a link connecting t_j and t_k ($k \neq i$) is changed to a link connecting t_i and t_k;
(2) a link connecting t_i and t_k ($k \neq j$) is unchanged;
(3) a link connecting t_i and t_j is discarded.

The first sub rule requires an operation that can be applied to the SAM defined for the local workflow process. This operation first adds the elements in row j to their corresponding elements in row i, and then sets all elements in row j to zero. This can be achieved by applying a matrix multiplication to this TM and the SAM defined for the local workflow process. A function $f_{reshape}$ is assigned to reshape the result matrix into an upper-triangular form.

For input matrix $M_{n \times n}$, function $f_{reshape}$ is defined as

$$f_{reshape}(M_{n \times n}) = M^{\circ}_{n \times n} = [\, m^{\circ}_{ij} \,], \text{ where } m^{\circ}_{ij} = \begin{cases} m_{ij} + m_{ji}, \; i < j; \\ 0, \text{ otherwise.} \end{cases}$$

The second sub rule identifies the case that needs no action. From the definition of a TM, we can see that the composing tasks of this case all have value "1" on the diagonal line, which takes no effect in the matrix multiplication.

Regarding the third sub rule, we need to check whether there exists a link connecting t_i and t_j in the corresponding TM. This can be easily achieved by checking whether there exists a row that has value "1" at both column i and column j. We can represent the existence of such a link by a boolean expression, i.e. $|f_{row}(i) = f_{row}(j)|$, where $f_{row}(x)$ defines a function that returns the row where column x has the value "1".

Finally, these three sub rules can be merged together as an operation $\otimes$, which is defined on $T_{n \times n} \otimes D_{n \times n} = [\, |f_{row}(i) \neq f_{row}(j)| \cdot \sum_{x=1}^{n} t_{ix} \cdot d_{xj} \,]_{n \times n}$. Hence, organisation g_1 may apply a *Composition Operation* on a local workflow process p to generate a perceivable workflow process for g_2. This can be defined as

$$D^{g_1 \cdot p}_{g_2} = f_{reshape}(T^{g_1 \cdot p}_{g_2} \otimes D^{g_1 \cdot p}_{g_1})$$

Here $D^{g_1 \cdot p}_{g_1}$ and $T^{g_1 \cdot p}_{g_2}$ are the SAMs of g_1's local workflow process p and the corresponding TM for perception $p^{g1 \cdot p}_{g2}$, respectively.

By applying this composition operation, organisations B and C can generate perceivable workflow processes b and c for organisation A in the form of $D^b_A = f_{reshape}(T^b_A \otimes D^b_B) = \begin{pmatrix} 0 & 0 & r_{b2} & r_{b3} & 0 & 0 \\ 0 & 0 & 0 & 0 & 0 & 0 \\ 0 & 0 & 0 & 0 & r_{b4} & 0 \\ 0 & 0 & 0 & 0 & r_{b5} & 0 \\ 0 & 0 & 0 & 0 & 0 & r_{b6} \\ 0 & 0 & 0 & 0 & 0 & 0 \end{pmatrix}$ and $D^c_A = f_{reshape}(T^C_A \otimes D^c_C) = \begin{pmatrix} 0 & 0 & 0 & 0 \\ 0 & 0 & r_{c2} & 0 \\ 0 & 0 & 0 & r_{c3} \\ 0 & 0 & 0 & 0 \end{pmatrix}$.

Operation 2. Connection Operation

According to the Inter Process Visibility Rule, we need to identify the visible messaging links between perceivable workflow processes in order to include perceivable workflow processes of non-neighbouring organisations in the tracking structure for an organisation. For this purpose, we need to identify the visible tasks by simply checking elements valued "1" in diagonal positions of the corresponding TM. We use function f_{diag} to diagonalise TM T into a diagonal matrix T°. Function f_{diag} is defined as follows,

$$f_{diag}(T_{n\times n}) = T^{\circ}_{n\times n},\text{ where } t^{\circ}_{ij} = \begin{cases} 1, \text{ if } t_{ij} = 1 \text{ and } i = j; \\ 0, \text{ otherwise.} \end{cases}$$

The visible messaging link between two workflow processes, for example, g_1's p_1 and g_2's p_2, from the perspective of another organisation, say g_3, can be represented as BAM $B_{g_3}^{g_1.p_1|g_2.p_2}$. The *Connection Operation* connecting $g_1.p_1$ and $g_2.p_2$ for g_3 can be defined as

$$B_{g_3}^{g_1.p_1|g_2.p_2} = (f_{diag}(T_{g_3}^{g_2.p_2}) \cdot (f_{diag}(T_{g_3}^{g_1.p_1}) \cdot B_{g_1}^{g_1.p_1|g_2.p_2})^T)^T$$

This connection operation first requires g_1 to diagonalise TM $T_{g_3}^{g_1.p_1}$, and then perform a matrix multiplication on the diagonalised $T_{g_3}^{g_1.p_1}$ and BAM $B_{g_1}^{g_1.p_1|g_2.p_2}$. g_2 will subsequently use the diagonalised matrix $T_{g_3}^{g_2.p_2}$ to multiply the result matrix from g_1. In the connection operation, proper transposition operations are needed to align the columns of the left hand matrix with the rows of the right hand matrix for matrix multiplication.

Regarding the motivation example given in Section 2, organisations B and C can generate matrix $B_A^{b|c}$ for organisation A to provide the visible messaging links between B's process b and C's process c in A's view.

$$B_A^{b|c} = (f_{diag}(T_A^c) \cdot (f_{diag}(T_A^b) \cdot B_B^{b|c})^T)^T = \begin{pmatrix} 0 & 0 & 0 & 0 & 0 & 0 \\ 0 & 0 & 0 & 0 & 0 & 0 \\ 0 & 0 & 0 & 0 & 0 & 0 \\ 0 & 0 & 0 & 0 & 0 & 0 \\ 0 & 0 & 0 & 0 & 0 & l_{bc2} \\ 0 & 0 & 0 & 0 & 0 & 0 \end{pmatrix};$$

Operation 3. Extension Operation

The Expansion Rule is used for extending the tracking structure to include perceivable workflow processes of both neighbouring and non-neighbouring organisations. Technically, an extension step can be represented as an *Extension Operation*. With a local workflow process p_1 in the tracking structure, organisation g_1 may apply the extension operation to include a local workflow process p_2 of organisation g_2 in the tracking structure. This can be defined as.

$$D_{g_1}^{g_1.p_1|g_2.p_2} = \begin{pmatrix} D_{g_1}^{g_1.p_1} & B_{g_1}^{g_1.p_1|g_2.p_2} \\ 0 & D_{g_1}^{g_2.p_2} \end{pmatrix}.$$

For example, the tracking structure containing process a and b from the view of organisation A, can be described by a composite SAM $D_A^{a|b}=\begin{pmatrix} D_A^a & B_A^{a|b} \\ 0 & D_A^b \end{pmatrix}$, which is obtainable through this extension operation.

4.2 Generation Algorithm

The tracking structure generation can be technically considered as a process of appending a new generated column each time a reachable workflow process is detected. This new generated column consists of a new SAM and a series of BAMs. The new SAM describes the inner structure of this detected workflow process, while the BAMs describe the interaction relationships between the detected workflow process and the processes already included in the structure.

As shown in Figure 4, at the starting point, the tracking structure contains only $D_{g_1}^{g_1.p_1}$, which means that only $g_1.p_1$ is included. Afterwards, g_1 detects that perceivable workflow process $g_2.p_2$ is reachable from $g_1.p_1$, and then appends a column containing $B_{g_1}^{g_1.p_1|g_2.p_2}$ and $D_{g_1}^{g_2.p_2}$ to the tracking structure. Likewise, organisation g_2 may append a column containing $B_{g_1}^{g_1.p_1|g_3.p_3}$, $B_{g_1}^{g_2.p_2|g_3.p_3}$ and $D_{g_1}^{g_3.p_3}$, when g_2 detects that process $g_3.p_3$ is reachable from $g_1.p_1$ via $g_2.p_2$. This appending process continues until all reachable perceivable workflow processes are detected. Because the inter process interaction relationships can only be identified by the organisation (*context organisation*) that owns the "bridging" workflow processes, by which the expansion proceeds, a propagation mechanism is adopted to spread this detection process over all involved organisations. The context organisation for an appending step may change from time to time. Organisation g_1 is called the *original context organisation* of this tracking structure.

$$\left(D_{g_1}^{g_1.p_1}\right)\Rightarrow\begin{pmatrix} D_{g_1}^{g_1.p_1} & B_{g_1}^{g_1.p_1|g_2.p_2} \\ 0 & D_{g_1}^{g_2.p_2} \end{pmatrix}\Rightarrow\begin{pmatrix} D_{g_1}^{g_1.p_1} & B_{g_1}^{g_1.p_1|g_2.p_2} & B_{g_1}^{g_1.p_1|g_3.p_3} \\ 0 & D_{g_1}^{g_2.p_2} & B_{g_1}^{g_2.p_2|g_3.p_3} \\ 0 & 0 & D_{g_1}^{g_3.p_3} \end{pmatrix}$$

$$\Rightarrow\begin{pmatrix} D_{g_1}^{g_1.p_1} & B_{g_1}^{g_1.p_1|g_2.p_2} & B_{g_1}^{g_1.p_1|g_3.p_3} & \cdots & B_{g_1}^{g_1.p_1|g_n.p_n} \\ 0 & D_{g_1}^{g_2.p_2} & B_{g_1}^{g_2.p_2|g_3.p_3} & \cdots & B_{g_1}^{g_2.p_2|g_n.p_n} \\ 0 & 0 & D_{g_1}^{g_3.p_3} & \cdots & B_{g_1}^{g_3.p_3|g_n.p_n} \\ \cdots & \cdots & \cdots & \cdots & \cdots \\ 0 & 0 & 0 & 0 & D_{g_1}^{g_n.p_n} \end{pmatrix}$$

Fig. 4. Tracking structure evolving process

We note that the process shown in Figure 4 starts from g_1's local workflow process $g_1.p_1$ instead of g_1's relative workflow process $g_1.rp$. Actually, $g_1.rp$ can be generated by the first step of the process when g_1 is the context organisation.

Algorithm 1 details the generation procedure. In algorithm 1, function *relatedProc*(p) returns a set of local workflow processes and perceivable workflow processes that have direct interactions with process p. Function *includedProc(trackStruc)* returns all included workflow processes at that moment in tracking structure *trackStruc*, which initially contains an SAM defined on a local workflow process of the original context organisation. Function *BAM*(p_1, p_2, g) returns the BAM between processes p_1 and p_2 from the view of organisation g, using the connection operation. Function *SAM*(p, g) returns the SAM of process p from the view of organisation g, using the composition operation. Function *genOrg*(p) returns the organisation of process p.

Algorithm 1. *genTrackStruc* - Tracking Structure Generation

```
Input:
trackStruc    -  A tracking structure matrix
cxtProc       -  A local workflow process of the context organisation
origCxtOrg    -  The original context organisation that starts the generation
Output:
trackStruc    -  The expanded tracking structure matrix

Step 1        Detect workflow processes
detectedProcSet = relatedProc(cxtProc);
includedProcSet = includedProc( trackStruc );
detectedProcSet = detectedProcSet – includedProcSet;
Step 2        Expand the tracking structure
appendedProcSet = ∅;
for each process p_i ∈ detectedProcSet
    tempB = BAM( cxtProc, p_i, origCxtOrg );
    if tempB is a non-zero matrix then
      newColumn = NULL;
      for each process p_j ∈ includedProcSet
        B = BAM(p_j, p_i, origCxtOrg );
        Append B to newColumn.
/* generate related boundary adjacency matrices of the new column*/
      end for
      D = SAM( p_i, origCxtOrg );
/* generate the self adjacency matrix of the new column */
      Append newColumn and D to trackStruc, using extension operation.
      includedProcSet = includedProcSet ∪{ p_i };
      appendedProcSet = appendedProcSet ∪{ p_i };
   end if
 end for
Step 3        Propagate the detection process
for each process p_i ∈ appendedProcSet
   targetOrg = genOrg( p_i );
   /* Ask targetOrg to call genTrackStruc */
   trackStruc = targetOrg.genTrackStruc( trackStruc, p_i, origCxtOrg );
end for
Step 4        Return the expanded tracking structure
return trackStruc;
```

The tracking structure generation process starts from a local workflow process of the original context organisation, and then spreads to all reachable workflow processes of the involved organisations. When this generation process comes to an organisation, this organisation becomes the context organisation of the above algorithm.

For example, if we starts from the retailer's product ordering process, i.e., process a in the motivating example, this algorithm first detects the workflow processes having direct interactions with process a. Then it checks for each detected workflow process whether it is reachable from organisation A, and if so, the detected process will be included to the tracking structure. In this step, organisation B's process b is included, and the tracking structure is expanded to $D_A^{a|b} = \begin{pmatrix} D_A^a & B_A^{a|b} \\ 0 & D_A^b \end{pmatrix}$. After that, this generation process will be propagated to B, and B repeats the above steps to extend the tracking structure. At this stage, B may find process c and process d, while only process c is included. This is because that the retailer and the supplier do not set up perceptions for each other in this example, and hence no transformation matrix is defined for process d from A. Therefore, the tracking structure is finally expanded to $D_A^{(a|b)|c} = \begin{pmatrix} D_A^a & B_A^{a|b} & B_A^{a|c} \\ 0 & D_A^b & B_A^{b|c} \\ 0 & 0 & D_A^c \end{pmatrix}$, which equals to the diagram shown in Figure 3 (c).

Here, $B_A^{a|c}$ is a zero matrix because there is no direct interactions between processes a and c, and the other sub matrices can be found from the former part of this paper.

4.3 Performing Workflow Tracking

In an inter-organisational workflow environment, there is another issue, i.e., how to keep the correct correspondence between collaborating local workflow instances. From the semantics of a collaborative business process, we can find the cardinality relationship between collaborating local processes, e.g., more than one instance of process a may associate with a single instance of process b for the purpose of batch production. While this kind of cardinality relationship can be determined at build time, the correlation between the particular instances of these processes has to be determined at run time, when they "shake hands".

To perform workflow tracking, we design a data structure, as shown in Figure 5, to keep the necessary information for tracking. This data structure consists of a series of lists, each of which represents the set of instances belonging to a specific local workflow process. Each element of a list has several units to record the workflow execution status. The links connecting elements represent the correspondence between instances of different workflow processes.

The tracking process is similar to a graph traversal process, where the nodes represent the related workflow instances and the arcs represent their messaging links

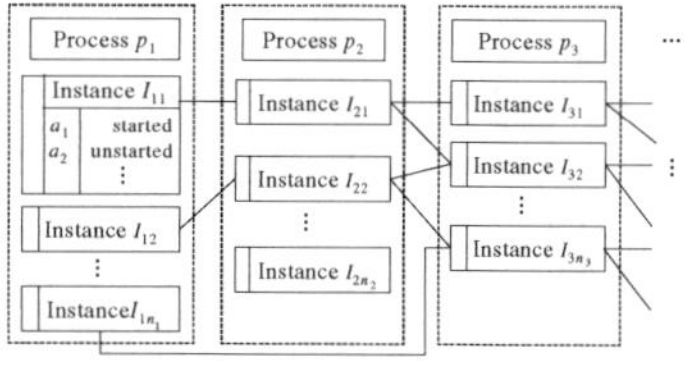

Fig. 5. Tracking data structure

Algorithm 2. ***trackProc*** **- Tracking Process**

Input:
trackStruc - The tracking structure to conduct the tracking
origInstance - An instance of the original context organisation's initial local workflow process defined in *trackStruc*
DS - The tracking data structure
Output:
DS - The updated tracking data structure

```
Step 1      Initialisation
trackInstanceSet = ∅;
stack s=new stack( );
s.push( origInstance );
Step 2      Discover the participating workflow instances
while s is not empty do
  cxtInstance = s.pop( );
  foundInstanceSet = linkedInstances( cxtInstance, trackStruc) – trackInstanceSet;
  for each i ∈ foundInstanceSet
     s.push( i );
     cxtProc = genProc( cxtInstance );
     BAMset = relatedBAMs( cxtProc, trackStruc );
     for each link l of each boundary adjacency matrix B∈ BAMset
/* now, start discovering workflow instances by following each visible messaging link */
        partnProc = partnerProc( B, cxtProc );
        partnOrg = genOrg( partnProc );
        if cxtInstance.l is newly fired then
           newInstanceSet=∅;
           Ask partnOrg to check any new participating instances of partnProc, and set the
instances to newInstanceSet.
           newInstanceSet = newInstanceSet – trackInstanceSet;
/* filter the previous discovered instances */
           for each i ∈ newInstanceSet
              addInstance( partnProc, i );
              addLink( cxtInstance, i );
/* update the tracking data structure */
              s.push( i );
/* and add the newly discovered instance to the stack */
           end for
        end if
     end for
  trackInstanceSet = trackInstanceSet ∪ { cxtInstance };
  /* the set of instances to track */
end while
Step 3      Update the execution status of participating workflow instances
for each instance i ∈ trackInstanceSet
  p = genProc( i );
  targetOrg = genOrg( p );
  Enquire targetOrg for the execution status of i, and then update the status of i in DS.
end for
```

to be tracked. In addition, new participating workflow instances will be identified at the time when visible messaging links are fired.

Details can be found in Algorithm 2. In this algorithm, function *addInstance*(p, i) inserts instance i to the list of process p in the tracking data structure. Function *addLink*(i_1, i_2) creates a link between instances i_1 and i_2 in the tracking data structure. Function *linkedInstances*(i, *trackStruc*) returns the instances linked to instance i in the tracking data structure, according to the tracking structure *trackStruc*. Function *relatedBAMs*(p, *trackStruc*) returns the set of BAMs related to process p, defined in *trackStruc*. Function *partnerProc*(B, p) returns the partner process of p defined in BAM B. Function *genOrg*(p) returns the organisation of process p. Function *genProc*(i) returns the process of instance i.

This algorithm starts from a local workflow instance of the original context organisation. Following the corresponding tracking structure, this algorithm searches along visible messaging links and propagates the execution status queries to all reachable workflow instances with the cooperation of participating organisations. The corresponding tracking structure records the interaction relationship between the processes of these reachable workflow instances. When an inter-organisational interaction is fired, the algorithm will check whether any new workflow instances join the business collaboration. If so, the algorithm will add these workflow instances to the tracking data structure.

5 Conclusion

This paper contributed to the study of workflow tracking across organisational boundaries. Compared with other workflow tracking solutions, the approach proposed in the paper not only enables an organisation to track other organisations for its involved parts of collaborative business processes, but allows different organisations track same collaborative business process differently as well.

In the paper, we deployed a matrix based framework which includes three representation matrices and three matrix operations. Algorithms using these matrices and operations for generating tracking structures and performing workflow tracking are developed. The framework allows an organisation to generate its own tracking structure based on its visibility to other organisations, thus privacy can be protected. The framework also allows a tracking structure to be generated on the fly, thus enables flexibility in workflow tracking. Based on its own tracking structure, an organisation can proactively trace the execution progress of its involved part of a collaborative business process.

Acknowledgements

The work reported in this paper is partly supported by the Australian Research Council discovery project DP0557572.

References

1. van der Aalst, W.M.P., ter Hofstede, A.H.M., and Weske, M.: Business Process Management: A Survey. In Proceedings of International Conference on Business Process Management (2003) 1-12.
2. Osterle, H., Fleisch, E., and Alt, R.: Business Networking - Shaping Collaboration between Enterprises. Springer Verlag (2001).
3. Gans, G., Jarke, M., Lakemeyer, G., and Schmitz, D.: Deliberation in a Modeling and Simulation Environment for Inter-organizational Networks. In Proceedings of Advanced Information Systems Engineering (2003) 242-257.
4. Zdravkovic, J. and Johannesson, P.: Cooperation of Processes through Message Level Agreement. In Proceedings of Advanced Information Systems Engineering (2004) 564-579.
5. Grefen, P., Aberer, K., Ludwig, H., and Hoffner, Y.: CrossFlow: Cross-Organizational Workflow Management for Service Outsourcing in Dynamic Virtual Enterprises. Data Engineering, 24(1) (2001) 52-57.
6. van der Aalst, W. and Mathias, W.: The P2P Approach to Inter-organizational Workflows. In Proceedings of International Conference on Advanced Information Systems Engineering (2001) 140-156.
7. Wetzel, I. and Klischewski, R.: Serviceflow beyond Workflow? IT Support for Managing Inter-Organizational Service Processes. Information Systems, 29(2) (2004) 127-145.
8. Lazcano, A., Schuldt, H., Alonso, G., and Schek, H.-J.: WISE: Process based E-Commerce. IEEE Data Engineering Bulletin, 24(1) (2001) 46-51.
9. Colombo, E., Francalanci, C., and Pernici, B.: Modeling Coordination and Control in Cross-Organizational Workflows. In Proceedings of DOA/CoopIS/ODBASE (2002) 91-106.
10. Zhao, X., Liu, C., and Yang, Y.: An Organisational Perspective on Collaborative Business Processes. In Proceedings of International Conference on Business Process Management. Nancy, France. Lecture Notes in Computer Science (2005) 17-31.
11. WfMC: Workflow Management Coalition Audit Data Specification [WfMC 1015] (1998)
12. WfMC: The Workflow Reference Model, [WfMC 1003] (1995)
13. BEA. Using BEA WebLogic Components http://edocs.beasys.com/wlac/pdf/compguide.pdf (2000)
14. IBM: BPEL4WS Business Processes with WebSphere Business Integration http://ibm.com/redbooks (2004)
15. Wang, M. and Wang, H.: Intelligent Agent Supported Flexible Workflow Monitoring System. In Proceedings of 14th International Conference on Advanced Information Systems Engineering (2002) 787-791.
16. Hur, W., Bae, H., and Kang, S.H.: Customizable Workflow Monitoring. Concurrent Engineering-Research and Applications, 11(4) (2003) 313-325.

Beyond Workflow Mining

Clarence A. Ellis[1], Aubrey J. Rembert[1], Kwang-Hoon Kim[2], and Jacques Wainer[3]

[1] Collaboration Technology Research Group
Department of Computer Science
University of Colorado at Boulder
Boulder, CO 80306, USA
{skip, rembert}@cs.colorado.edu
[2] Collaboration Technology Research Lab
Department of Computer Science, Kyonggi University
Suwonsi Kyonggido 442-760, South Korea
kwang@kyonggi.ac.kr
[3] Institute of Computing, State University of Campinas
Campinas 13084-971, SP, Brazil
wainer@ic.unicamp.br

Abstract. In the domain of Business Process Management and Workflow Management Systems, the log of work transactions executed has been found to be a useful artifact. The ideas, work, and literature on workflow mining have been primarily concerned with examining the workflow event log to rediscover control flow. Workflow mining has generally been defined as "the process of extracting a workflow model from a log of executions of activities". In fact, most of the literature specifically and narrowly is concerned with rediscovering the precedence relations amongst activities. It is generally a hidden assumption that all activities are known a priori because they are listed by label in the workflow event log. In this position paper, we explore the possibility of removing this assumption, and thus performing *workflow discovery* rather than precedence rediscovery. Workflow discovery does not assume that process structure or even activities are known a priori and is concerned with discovering a wholistic perspective of workflow.

Workflow management systems are *people systems* that must be designed, deployed, and understood within their social and organizational contexts. Thus, we argue in this document that there is a need to expand the concept of workflow mining beyond the behavioral perspective to encompass the social, organizational, and activity assignment perspectives; as well as other perspectives. To this end, we introduce a general framework and meta-model for workflow discovery, and show one approach to workflow discovery in a multidimensional perspective.

1 Introduction

A Workflow Management System (WFMS) can be a tremendous aid to an organization in effectively enacting their business processes. But how does the

S. Dustdar, J.L. Fiadeiro, and A. Sheth (Eds.): BPM 2006, LNCS 4102, pp. 49–64, 2006.

WFMS know the particular processes of the particular organization? The answer is BPA (business process analysis) and workflow modeling. These steps result in a model of work within an organization in a language that is logical and rigorous enough to be interpreted by computer software. Realistically, for large organizations, BPA and workflow modeling are complex nontrivial tasks which are known to be time consuming, expensive, and error prone [20]. Furthermore, workflow management systems are "people systems" that must be understood and designed with an eye towards social and organizational contexts. However, this is difficult and elusive to capture within a logical and rigorous description. The result is that workflow management systems tend to be inhibitive to humans, and potentially stifle creativity [15]. Additionally, large organizations are complex dynamic systems; this carries the implication that their workflow processes constantly change. Thus, the formal workflow process models created as a result of BPA and workflow modeling are not only partial and inhibitive, they are typically obsolete! Fortunately, people are frequently quite clever at performing "workarounds" to somehow subvert the WFMS.

Workflow mining has been offered as a solution to the problems described above. Workflow mining has been described as the automatic construction of workflow models from *workflow event logs* produced by process-aware information systems. A workflow event log is typically an interleaved list of events from numerous process instances. Currently, most workflow mining algorithms operate on workflow event logs that, in general, conform to the following schema:

1. work case number
2. activity identifier
3. participant (i.e. person or subsystem performing the activity)
4. date/time

By examining the workflow event log, a workflow mining algorithm can detect the ordering of activity executions for each process instance, and then infer the general process structure. As a simple example of how a typical workflow mining algorithm operates, suppose a we examine the workflow event log of a process that has four activities, a1, a2, a3, and a4. Suppose that all four activities are always executed in some order by each work case. If we observe over a large number of process instances that a1 is always executed first and a4 is always executed last, then we can begin to piece together a workflow process model that requires a1 to complete before all other activities, and a4 to execute after all others. If we find process instances in the log where a2 begins before a3, and other cases where a2 begins after a3, then we can infer that the process begins with a1; after it completes, a2 and a3 execute concurrently; and after they both complete, then a4 executes.

This extremely simple example typifies what current workflow mining algorithms do. It also highlights some areas of further research for workflow mining. For instance, most workflow mining algorithms do not consider the social or organizational contexts of the processes they discover. To our knowledge, there exists only one concrete workflow mining algorithm for discovering the social context of a workflow process [18]. Furthermore, current workflow mining algorithms operate based on the hidden assumption that activities are known a priori. Therefore, the environments in which workflow mining is most suitable are organizations with well defined activities. However, if an organization does not have labels that group the fine-grained actions it performs, the utility of workflow mining is greatly reduced.

What can we do about all this? Well, consider the following workflow dream. You have determined that your company could potentially gain great benefit from a WFMS in efficiency and effectiveness, but your company does not have well-defined notions of activities. One option is to hire an expensive consulting firm; do a nine month study and tediously create a detailed set of workflow descriptions. Alternatively, you could continue doing work as normal, with the exception that your work will be recorded in some type of event log. At some point in the future, this event log will be examined by computer software that will automatically construct a logical and rigorous workflow model for your organization. This scenario is the essence of workflow discovery. The concept of workflow discovery is an extension to workflow mining. It removes the assumption about knowing activities a priori.

In this exploratory position paper, we will present one simple approach to performing workflow discovery. In section 2, we describe the ICN meta-model and the ICN models used as targets of workflow discovery. In section 3, we provide some very simple general techniques for performing workflow discovery. In section 4, we describe some related work. Finally, in section 5 we describe our conclusions and future research directions.

2 ICN Meta-model and Framework

We consider workflow discovery to be a sub-area of Knowledge Discovery in Data (KDD) [16] and we use models formed from the Information Control Net (ICN) meta-model as discovery targets. The Information Control Net (ICN) meta-model is used to create multidimensional workflow models[6,7]. In the ICN meta-model, a multidimensional workflow model consists of a family of models. A model represents either an organizational dimension or an organizational perspective. An organizational dimension is a set of homogeneous organizational objects and a set of zero or more automorphisms over those organizational objects. An organizational perspective is a set of organizational objects and a set of mappings over those organizational objects.

The distinction between an organizational dimension and an organizational perspective is quite subtle. At this point, we need to make a clear distinction between the two. Organizational dimensions represent aspects or properties of an organization while organizational perspectives represent the examination or observation of an organization from one or more dimensions.

Organizational perspectives and organizational dimensions are modeled in the ICN meta-model using an organizational framework, organizational schema, and organizational net. The organizational framework is used to specify classes of organizational objects. The organizational schema is used to specify the set of mappings over the classes of organizational objects. The organizational net is used to specify the dynamic behavior of an organization.

Definition 1 (Organizational Framework). *An organizational framework is a 3-tuple, $F = (G, R, A)$, where G is a class of abstract organizational objects (i.e. goals, constraints, ideals, and policies), R is a class of concrete organizational objects, resources (i.e people, data repositories, and chairs), and A is a class of functional organizational objects, activities.*

Definition 2 (Organizational Schema). *An organizational schema is a tuple, $S = (F, f_s)$ where F is an organizational framework and f_s is a set of early binding mappings over F .*

Definition 3 (Organizational Net). *An organizational net is a 3-tuple, $N = (S, T, f_n)$, where S is an organizational schema, T is a class of tokens, and f_n is a set of late binding mappings over S and T .*

2.1 Some Useful Perspectives

We stress that there are a plethora of perspectives [10], many are important and still unexplored (e.g. the "security" perspective and the "reputations" perspective). Below we provide a brief description of two perspectives, namely the behavioral perspective and the activity assignment perspective. Before we describe these two perspectives, we first describe the dimensions used to realize them.

The activities dimension of an organization depicts what an organization does. The organizational objects of this perspective are a finite set of activities. The precedence automorphism is a typical mapping in this dimension. However, not all organizations have well structured processes. Therefore, not all organizations specify precedence between their activities. The roles dimension emphasizes how an organization is structured. The organizational objects of this dimension are the roles of an organization. The automorphisms over organizational objects in this dimension are highly domain dependent. The participants dimension focuses on the active agents (e.g. people or computers) of an organization. The organizational objects of this dimension are a finite set of participants.

2.2 Behavioral Perspective

The behavioral perspective is formed when we observe an organization through the activities dimension. This perspective describes the control flow of a workflow process. The behavioral perspective is modeled with an ICN Control Flow Model.

Definition 4. *An ICN Control Flow Model is the tuple $CFM = (A, \delta)$ where:*

1. *A is a finite set of activities*
2. *$\delta = \delta_i \cup \delta_o$*
   (a) *δ_i: $A \rightarrow 2^A$ is a multivalued mapping from an activity to a vector of vectors of activities that precede it (2^A is the power-set of A).*

(b) δ_o: $A \rightarrow 2^A$ *is a multivalued mapping from an activity to a vector of vectors of activities that it precedes.*

In the ICN Control Flow Model, there are three types of activities, two that are control activities and one that is a work activity. A control activity alters the control flow of a process. A work activity does not affect control flow, but it usually changes the state of a case. The control activities are the AND-Control and the OR-Control. Informally, an AND-Control can be either an AND-Split, an AND-Join, or both. Symmetrically, an OR-Control can be either an OR-Split, an OR-Join, or both.

In the graphical depiction of an ICN Control Flow Model, precedence is modeled as a directed edge. A work activity is represented by a labeled circle with at most one directed edge leading into it and at most one directed edge leading out of it. An AND-Control is represented by a small dark circle with one or more directed edges leading out of it and/or one or more directed edges leading into it. An OR-Control is represented by a small hollow circle with one or more directed edges leading out of it and/or one or more directed edges leading into it. Figure 1 depicts the graphical representations of the different types of activities in an ICN Control Flow Model.

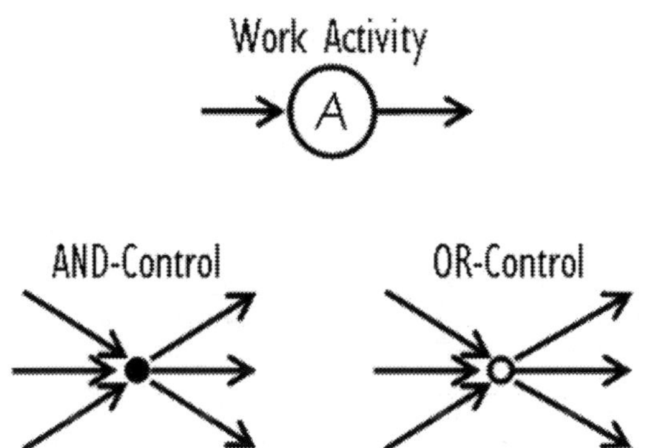

Fig. 1. Activity Types in the ICN Control Flow Model

2.3 Activity Assignment Perspective

The activity assignment perspective is formed by defining a set of relationships between three dimensions: participants, roles, and activities. Depending on the size and nature of an organization, the dimensions involved in this perspective can vary. For a small organization, with say 2 people and a relatively simple organizational process, it is quite adequate and convenient to relate participants directly to the activities they perform. However, in organizations with Very Large Scale Workflow (VLSW)[11], this type of relationship is very impractical; it is more appropriate to relate activities to roles, then relate roles to participants. In this paper, we will assume that the organizations are sufficiently large and have a need for the inclusion of roles in this perspective. The activity assignment perspective is modeled with an ICN Activity Assignment Model.

Definition 5. *The ICN Activity Assignment Model is the tuple* $AAM = (R, A, P, \phi, \zeta)$ *where:*

1. *R is a finite set of roles*
2. *A is a finite set of activities*
3. *P is a finite set of participants*
4. ϕ*:* $A \rightarrow 2^R$ *is a single-valued mapping from an activity to a vector of roles.*
5. ζ*:* $R \rightarrow 2^P$ *is a single-valued mapping from a role to a vector of participants*

Graphically, roles are represented as labeled ovals. Participants are represented as labeled stick figures. The ϕ mapping is represented as directed edges from roles to activities. The ζ mapping is represented as directed edges from participants to roles. Figure 2 depicts an ICN activity assignment model, as it relates to one activity instance.

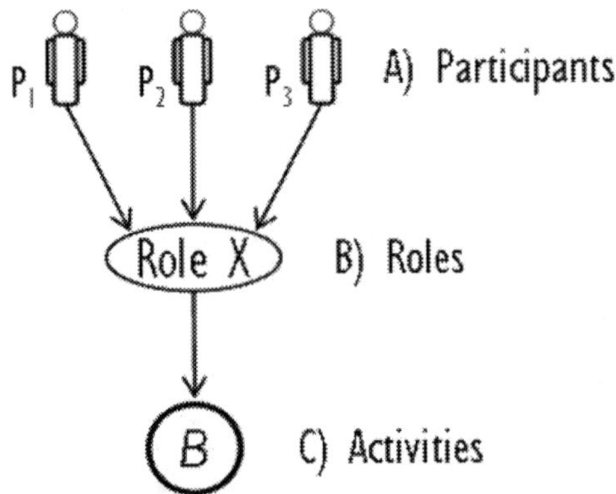

Fig. 2. An ICN Activity Assignment Model

3 Workflow Discovery

In order to describe the concept of workflow discovery in more depth, we consider a hypothetical piece of collaborative software similar to [12] and [4] that allows an organization to computerize its cases and gives participants the autonomy to route those electronic cases. In this software system, the actions of a participant, as they relate to a case, are recorded in a *work transaction log*. A work transaction log consists of a set of work transactions, which are composed of a transaction number, a case number, the state of a case after it has been changed or viewed, the participant that changed or viewed the case, and the time the participant changed or viewed the case.

In the remainder of this section, we describe a simple workflow discovery technique via a simplified order processing workflow example enacted with our hypothetical software system.

3.1 Order Processing Example

Consider the following order processing workflow in Example 1 and assume that it is enacted with our hypothetical collaborative software system. It should be noted that typically this workflow is not known a priori; we only provide this example to give some context to, and simplify the description of, one approach to workflow discovery.

Example 1 (Order Processing Workflow).

1. Receive Order from Customer
2. Check Customer's Credit
3. If Customer Approved for Order
   (a) Send Order to Shipping/Billing Department
   (b) Bill Order to Customer
   (c) Ship Order to Customer
4. If Customer Not Approved for Order, Simply Notify the Customer

Let the electronic order form depicted in Figure 3 represent a process instance of the order processing workflow. Given the electronic order form and our hypothetical collaborative software system, there is a rich set of information that can be discovered about the order processing workflow. For instance, if we observe that a single participant is not responsible for filling out the entire order form, the participants that perform similar actions can be clustered together into roles. Similarly, the actions performed in each work transaction can be clustered into activities. By examining these clusters of activities and roles, we can discover an ICN multidimensional workflow model that is composed of an ICN Control Flow Model and an ICN Activity Assignment Model. In our discussion, we make the simplifying assumption that an activity can occur only once within a workflow process (i.e. no loops and no multiple occurrences of activities). It should be noted that once activities are discovered either the ICN Activity Assignment Model or the ICN Control Flow Model can be discovered.

3.2 Workflow Discovery Techniques

We now describe some techniques to cluster work transactions into activities and cluster participants into roles. We then give general directions about how these clusters can be formed into an ICN Control Flow Model and an ICN Activity Assignment Model. First, we begin with a discussion of a technique for workflow discovery in the behavioral perspective. Then, we move to a discussion about a technique for workflow discovery in the activity assignment perspective.

We will now provide an abstraction to the order form in Figure 3 by associating each label of the order form to a case attribute. If there are n case attributes, we assign a unique integer i, where $1 \leq i \leq n$, to each case attribute from the top to bottom and left to right of the order form. In our order processing workflow example, $n = 22$. The Customer Name attribute of an order, where an order is a process instance or case of the order processing workflow, maps the to the

Order Form

Date : ____________

Customer Information :

1) Name : ____________

2) Number : ____________

3) Address : ____________

4) e-Mail : ____________

5) Phone : ____________ Mobile : ____________ Fax : ____________

6) Item Ordered : ____________

7) Item Quantity Ordered : ____________

Order Processing Status :

1) Order Approved : Yes ☐ No ☐

○ High Interest Rate
○ Medium Interest Rate
○ Low Interest Rate

2) Item Shipped ☐ Ship to Customer Address ☐

Shipping Address : ____________

3) Customer Billed ☐ Bill to Customer Address ☐

Billing Address : ____________

Order Notification Status :

Notified Customer ☐

Notes Comments : ____________

Fig. 3. Order Form for Order Processing Workflow Example

integer 2, and the Ship to Customer Address case attribute maps to the integer 16. It should be noted that the labels YES and NO on the order form do not correspond to case attributes; they are simply labels of the values that can be assigned to the Order Approval case attribute, which maps to the integer 11.

Let the work transaction log of Table 1 be the history of state changes of the order form in Figure 3 for three different orders. The *change set* of a work transaction w_j, denoted by $CS(w_j)$, is the set of case attributes that have changed in the jth work transaction. We employ the *Simple Matching Coefficient* to measure the similarity between change sets of work transactions in order to induce activities. To do this, we represent each change set of a work transaction as a binary string such that the ith position in the binary string corresponds to the ith case attribute. If the ith case attribute was changed during work transaction w_j, then the ith bit in $CS(w_j)$ will be a 1. Alternatively, if the ith case attribute was not changed during w_j, the ith bit in $CS(w_j)$ will be a 0. For instance, in Table 1, the change set $CS(w_1) = \{1, 2, 4, 5, 6, 8, 9, 10, 22\}$ of the first work transaction w_1, maps to the binary string 1101110111000000000001.

Table 1. Work Transaction Log based on the Order Processing Workflow and the Order Form

TRANS NUM	CASE NUM	CHANGE SET	PARTICIPANT	TIME
1	1	$\{1, 2, 4, 5, 6, 8, 9, 10, 22\}$	JOE	12
2	2	$\{1, 2, 3, 7, 9, 10\}$	JACK	23
3	3	$\{1, 2, 3, 4, 5, 6, 7, 8, 9, 10\}$	LISA	36
4	1	$\{11, 12, 22\}$	SHAWN	45
5	3	$\{11, 22\}$	SHAWN	76
6	2	$\{11, 14\}$	SHAWN	80
7	1		MATHEW	120
8	2		MATTHEW	126
9	1	$\{15, 16\}$	JACK	160
10	1	$\{18, 19\}$	JOE	175
11	3	$\{21, 22\}$	LISA	192
12	2	$\{18, 20, 22\}$	LISA	214
13	2	$\{15, 17, 22\}$	JACK	280

Definition 6 (Simple Matching Coefficient). *The Simple Matching Coefficient of binary vectors* $\boldsymbol{x}$ *and* $\boldsymbol{y}$ *is* $SMC = \frac{f_{11}+f_{00}}{f_{01}+f_{10}+f_{11}+f_{00}}$ *where*

- f_{00}=*the number of attributes where* $\boldsymbol{x}$ *is 0 and* $\boldsymbol{y}$ *is 0*
- f_{01}=*the number of attributes where* $\boldsymbol{x}$ *is 0 and* $\boldsymbol{y}$ *is 1*
- f_{10}=*the number of attributes where* $\boldsymbol{x}$ *is 1 and* $\boldsymbol{y}$ *is 0*
- f_{11}=*the number of attributes where* $\boldsymbol{x}$ *is 1 and* $\boldsymbol{y}$ *is 1*

Given two change sets $CS(w_i)$ and $CS(w_j)$, their Simple Matching Coefficient, $SMC(CS(w_i), CS(w_j))$, is a number in the interval [0, 1]. If it is the case that $SMC(CS(w_i), CS(w_j))$ is greater than some user-defined threshold, then $CS(w_i)$ and $CS(w_j)$ are considered similar.

However, using the Simple Matching Coefficient in its current form to compare work transactions with empty change sets (i.e. work transactions 7 and 8 in Table 1) to work transactions with non-empty change sets is problematic. This is because these two situations have different semantics. If a work transaction has an empty change set, then the case was only viewed and not changed. This is, however, a valid action, but we don't want a clustering algorithm to conclude that viewing a case and making very small changes to a case constitute the same activity. To remedy this situation, we modify the Simple Matching Coefficient such that it considers two strings to be dissimilar (i.e $SMC = 0$) if one of the strings contain all 0s and the other string contains a 1 at some position. This is denoted by $mSMC$.

We will now give a high-level clustering technique based on our modified version of the Simple Matching Coefficient. The technique begins by creating for each change set $CS(w_j)$ a change set cluster $C(j)$. Let $\mathcal{C}$ be the set of all change set clusters. For each cluster $C(i)$, $C(j) \in \mathcal{C}$, where $i \neq j$, if the *proximity* of their centers is less than some user defined threshold, the technique merges cluster $C(j)$ into cluster $C(i)$. For simplicity, we consider the *center* of a cluster

$C(i)$, denoted by $center(C(i))$, to be the conjunction of the change sets inside of the cluster. The proximity of two clusters $C(i)$ and $C(j)$ is denoted by the equation

$$proximity(C(i), C(j)) = 1 - mSMC(center(C(i)), center(C(j))) \quad (1)$$

Cluster merging halts when the proximity of the centers of the remaining clusters is greater than some user defined threshold. The remaining clusters in $\mathcal{C}$ become the activities in our organization. We can then use those activities to form *process traces*. A process trace is a sequence of activities ordered on the basis of process execution. A set of process traces can be used as input into traditional workflow mining algorithms to discover the precedence relations between activities. The pseudo-code in Algorithm 1 describes succinctly the technique that we have discussed above.

Algorithm 1. Activity Discovery Technique

Create a cluster for the change set of each work transaction
Add each cluster to $\mathcal{C}$
Let MAX_PROX be the user defined maximum allowable proximity for cluster merging
while $\exists(C(i), C(j) \in \mathcal{C}) : proximity(center(C(i)), center(C(j))) \leq MAX\_PROX$ **do**
    Merge cluster $C(j)$ into $C(i)$.
    Update $\mathcal{C}$ to reflect the merger
end while
Create an activity for each cluster in $\mathcal{C}$

We will now execute the algorithm on the work transaction log in Table 1. First, we transform the change sets of each work transaction into a binary string:

```
(1,  1101110111000000000001)
(2,  1110001011000000000000)
(3,  1111111111000000000000)
(4,  0000000000110000000001)
(5,  0000000000100000000001)
(6,  0000000000100100000000)
(7,  0000000000000000000000)
(8,  0000000000000000000000)
(9,  0000000000000110000000)
(10, 0000000000000000011000)
(11, 0000000000000000000011)
(12, 0000000000000000010101)
(13, 0000000000000010100001)
```

Then we create a cluster $C(i)$, where $1 \leq i \leq 13$, for the change set of each work transaction. Since we are working with a small number of work transactions each with a small number of case attributes, we will assume that clusters should be merged if their proximity is less than or equal to .40 (i.e $MAX\_PROX = .40$). Based on this threshold of proximity, we can combine clusters $C(1)$, $C(2)$,and $C(3)$ into cluster $C(1)$. Next, we can combine clusters $C(4)$, $C(5)$, and $C(6)$ into cluster $C(4)$. Then, we can combine clusters $C(7)$ and $C(8)$ into cluster $C(7)$. Next, we can combine clusters $C(9)$ and $C(13)$ into cluster $C(9)$. Then we can combine clusters $C(10)$ and $C(12)$ to form cluster $C(10)$.

After the execution of this portion of the algorithm,

$$\mathcal{C} = \{C(1), C(4), C(7), C(9), C(10), C(11)\}$$

such that the clusters in $\mathcal{C}$ represent the activities of the order processing workflow. We can now use these clusters to form process traces. We use those process traces as input those into a traditional workflow mining technique such as the model rewriting technique of [21]. To make the precedence relation discovery process easier to understand, we relabel the clusters in $\mathcal{C}$ such that: $C(1)$ = A, $C(4)$ = B, $C(7)$ = C, $C(9)$ = D, $C(10)$ = E, and $C(11)$ = F. A process trace is formed by associating the change set of a work transaction with its corresponding activity and then extracting the sub-sequence of activities that belong to the same case. The result of this step on the order processing workflow is the set of process traces $PT = \{ABCFE, ABCEF, ABD\}$. We can use the rewrite rules of [21] on this set of process traces to produce the ICN Control Flow Model depicted in Figure 4.

Using the discovered activities, we can now discover the roles of the participants in the order processing workflow. The *participant set* of an activity A, denoted by $PS(A)$, is the set of participants that performed activity A. To induce roles, we follow a strategy similar to the discovery of activities described above. Each participant in an organization is assigned a number from 1 to n, where n represents the total number of participants in the organization. We use this information to construct an n-length binary string for each participant set. If participant i performed activity A, then the bit at position i in the binary

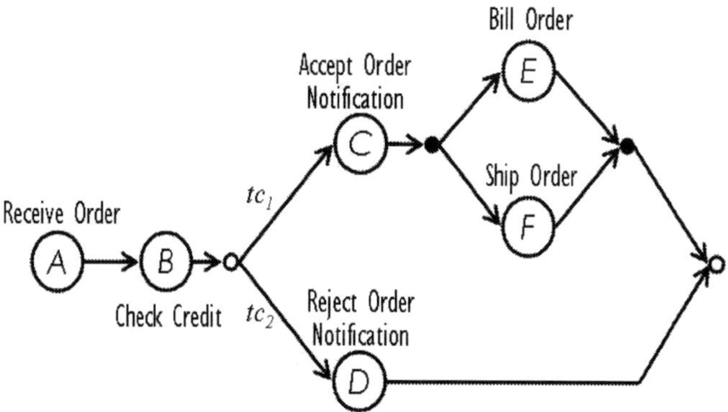

Fig. 4. ICN Control Flow Model of the Order Processing Workflow

string $PS(A)$ will contain a 1. If participant i did not perform activity A, then there will be a 0 at position i in binary string $PS(A)$.

If the participant sets of different activities are similar, we can infer that these participants belong to the same role. We will use Jaccard's Coefficient, a slightly different notion of similarity than the Simple Matching Coefficient, to form roles. We use Jaccard's Coefficient because it takes into account that most participants in an organization don't perform the same activities. For instance, the number of participants that can approve a loan in a bank is small compared to the number of participants that cannot approve a loan. This is contrasted with discovering activities, where it is equally important to know what case attributes have changed as well as what case attributes have not changed, assuming that at least some case attributes have changed (our modified version of SMC).

Definition 7 (Jaccard's Coefficient). *The Jaccard Coefficient of binary vectors* $\boldsymbol{x}$ *and* $\boldsymbol{y}$ *is* $J = \frac{f_{11}}{f_{01}+f_{10}+f_{11}}$ *where*

- f_{00}*=the number of attributes where* $\boldsymbol{x}$ *is 0 and* $\boldsymbol{y}$ *is 0*
- f_{01}*=the number of attributes where* $\boldsymbol{x}$ *is 0 and* $\boldsymbol{y}$ *is 1*
- f_{10}*=the number of attributes where* $\boldsymbol{x}$ *is 1 and* $\boldsymbol{y}$ *is 0*
- f_{11}*=the number of attributes where* $\boldsymbol{x}$ *is 1 and* $\boldsymbol{y}$ *is 1*

Participant sets $PS(A)$ and $PS(B)$ are considered similar if $J(PS(A), PS(B))$ is greater than some user defined threshold of similarity. Only participant sets that have some relatively large intersection are grouped together into roles.

We use the definition of Jaccard's Coefficient to induce clusters and therefore roles from participant sets. The technique begins forming a cluster $C(A)$ for each participant set $PS(A)$. If the proximity of the centers of clusters $C(A)$ and $C(B)$ is less than some user defined threshold, merge $C(B)$ into $R(A)$. Repeat this cluster merging step until no more clusters can be merged. The remaining clusters will become roles. The center of a cluster $C(A)$, denoted by $center(C(A))$ is the disjunction of the participant sets in it. Let $\mathcal{R}$ be the set of participant set clusters. The proximity measure for participant sets is

$$proximity(C(A), C(B)) = 1 - J(center(C(A)), center(C(B))) \tag{2}$$

Algorithm 2 describes compactly the clustering technique discussed above. We will now use this technique on the work transaction data in Table 1. First, we assign integers to the participants. Then, we convert the participant sets into binary strings. Let the following be the participant number assignments: $(1, JOE)$, $(2, JACK)$, $(3, LISA)$, $(4, SHAWN)$, and $(5, MATTHEW)$. The participant sets are $PS(A) = 11100, PS(B) = 00010, PS(C) = 00001, PS(D) = 01100, PS(E) = 10100$, and $PS(F) = 00010$. If we create a cluster for each participant set and let $MAX\_PROX = .40$, after the cluster merging phase, the remaining clusters are: $C(A)$, $C(F)$, and $C(C)$. We then transform these clusters into roles by relabeling the clusters such that $C(A) = R_X$, $C(F) = R_Y$, and $C(C) = R_Z$, relating the participants of a cluster to a corresponding role, and then relate that role to the activities that at least one of the participants in the corresponding cluster performs. We have now formed the ICN Activity Assignment Model of Figure 5.

Algorithm 2. Role Discovery Technique

```
Create a cluster for each participant set.
Add all participant set clusters to R
Let MAX_PROX is the user defined maximum allowable proximity for cluster merging
while ∃(C(A), C(B) ∈ R) : proximity(center(C(A)), center(C(B))) ≤ MAX_PROX do
    Merge cluster C(B) into cluster C(A).
    Update R to reflect the merger
end while
Associate roles to each of the remaining clusters in R
```

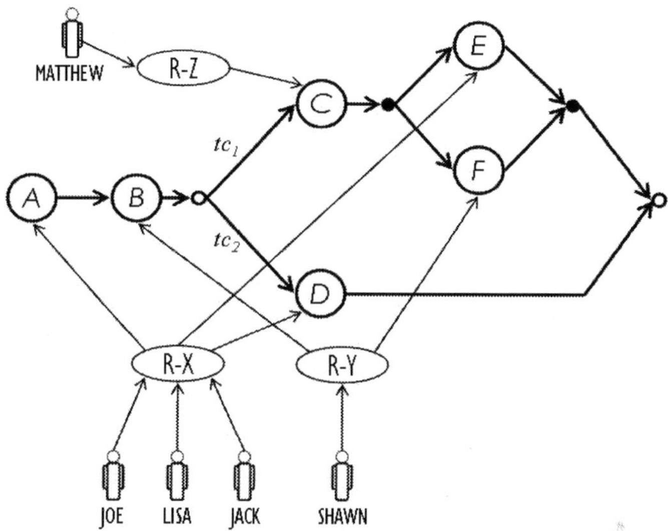

Fig. 5. ICN Activity Assignment Model of the Order Processing Workflow

4 Related Work

To our knowledge, this paper is the first known investigation into multidimensional workflow discovery, which is removing the assumption that activities are known a priori and discovery different perspectives of workflow. As mentioned in the introduction, workflow discovery is an extension to process/workflow mining.

The concept of process control flow discovery is not new; it was first investigated within the context of software processes in [3,2]. However, workflow mining is a new and fledgling field. It was first studied in [1] by Agrawal et al. In that paper, the authors describe workflow mining as a two step process: (1) discover a workflow graph that conforms to the workflow event log and (2) find the edge conditions of the workflow graph. The discovery of edge conditions is a necessary step in this workflow mining algorithm because the target language in this paper can't explicitly represent AND-Control or OR-Control constructs. Agrawal et. al. also describe a method for dealing with iteration and noisy logs.

In [13], Schimm describes a workflow mining algorithm and tool that discovers properly nested block-structured workflow models via a model rewriting approach. Schimm's workflow mining algorithm is based on a workflow algebra. Similarly, Wainer, Kim, and Ellis in [21] describe a technique for inducing properly nested workflow models using model rewriting rules. However, their work did not include a concrete workflow mining algorithm description.

Herbst in [9], describes a machine learning approach to discover sequential and concurrent workflow models in the ADONIS language. Their work introduced problem classes for workflow mining and a heuristic for discovering multiple instances of an activity (the duplicate activities problem). Their algorithm first constructs Stochastic Activity Graphs (SAG)s and transforms these graphs into sequential workflow models in the ADONIS language.

Silva et. al. [14] investigated the idea of discovering probabilistic workflow models from workflow event log data. Their learning algorithm attempts to discover a probabilistic And/Or Graph.

Greco et. al. in [8], take a slightly different approach to workflow mining. They assume that they are given a workflow model and the workflow event log that this workflow model generated. The goal of their algorithm is not to discover a workflow model, but to discover useful knowledge about process instances. They also describe some intractability results.

In [5], Dustdar et. al. explore workflow mining in the context of ad-hoc processes. This is done using the Caramaba [4] process-aware collaboration system. A tool, TeamLog, was built that converted Caramba logs into an XML format that could be used by a workflow mining algorithm.

In [20], van der Aalst et. al. studied workflow mining with Petri Nets as the target language. He and his group have developed the α-algorithm to discover a certain class of Petri Nets. In that paper, they discuss some of the limitations of the α-algorithm, (mining short loops and dealing with noise) and propose extensions. His group has also identified and classified some of the remaining key scientific challenges for workflow mining (e.g the non-free choice construct and hidden activities). In [17], van der Aalst et. al. proposed a genetic algorithm help solve the non-free choice problem. For a good overview of workflow mining, the authors recommend [19].

5 Conclusion and Future Work

In the domain of Business Process Management and Workflow Management Systems, workflow mining has been primarily concerned with examining the workflow event log to rediscover control flow. In this document we have explored the possibility of moving beyond conventional mining, and performing workflow discovery rather than precedence rediscovery. To this end, we introduced a general framework and meta-model for workflow discovery, and showed how discovery can be effectively enacted within a multidimensional perspective.

Future work includes designing concrete discovery algorithms based on live and synthetic data. We are particularly interested in mining in unstructured environments (i.e. no concept of an activity and ad-hoc processes). Work to be done also includes further specification and mining of other perspectives (e.g: the "security" perspective, "data-flow" perspective, the "organizational" perspective, the "social" perspective, the "reputation" perspective, and the "case" perspective). We would like to investigate mining algorithms that address complex iteration constructs (i.e. concurrency within a loop), dynamic change, and that execute in the presence of noisy and incomplete event logs. Conventional workflow mining assumes that many of the elements of the organizational framework are known in advance. As the field matures, we expect to remove more and more of these assumptions, and do more sophisticated workflow discovery.

References

1. Rakesh Agrawal, Dimitrios Gunopulos, and Frank Leymann. Mining process models from workflow logs. In *EDBT '98: Proceedings of the 6th International Conference on Extending Database Technology*, pages 469–483, London, UK, 1998. Springer-Verlag.
2. Jonathan E. Cook and Alexander L. Wolf. Discovering models of software processes from event-based data. *ACM Trans. Softw. Eng. Methodol.*, 7(3):215–249, 1998.
3. Jonathan E. Cook and Alexander L. Wolf. Event-based detection of concurrency. In *SIGSOFT '98/FSE-6: Proceedings of the 6th ACM SIGSOFT international symposium on Foundations of software engineering*, pages 35–45, New York, NY, USA, 1998. ACM Press.
4. Schahram Dustdar. Caramba - a process-aware collaboration system supporting ad hoc and collaborative processes in virtual teams. *Distrib. Parallel Databases*, 15(1):45–66, 2004.
5. Schahram Dustdar, Thomas Hoffmann, and Wil van der Aalst. Mining of ad-hoc business processes with teamlog. *Data Knowl. Eng.*, 55(2):129–158, 2005.
6. Clarence A. Ellis. Information control nets: A mathematical model of information flow. In *SIGMETRICS '79: Proceedings of the 1979 ACM SIGMETRICS conference on Simulation, measurement and modeling of computer systems*, pages 225–240, New York, NY, USA, 1979. ACM Press.
7. Clarence A. Ellis. Formal and informal models of office activity. In *IFIP Congress*, pages 11–22, 1983.
8. Gianluigi Greco, Antonella Guzzo, and Giuseppe Manco. Mining and reasoning on workflows. *IEEE Transactions on Knowledge and Data Engineering*, 17(4):519–534, 2005. Senior Member-Domenico Sacca.
9. Joachim Herbst. A machine learning approach to workflow management. In *ECML '00: Proceedings of the 11th European Conference on Machine Learning*, pages 183–194, London, UK, 2000. Springer-Verlag.
10. Stefan Jablonski and Christoph Bussler. *Workflow Management: Modeling Concepts, Architecture, and Implementation.* International Thomson Computer Press, 1996.
11. Kwang-Hoon Kim and Clarence A. Ellis. Workflow performance and scalability analysis using the layered queuing modeling methodology. In *GROUP '01: Proceedings of the 2001 International ACM SIGGROUP Conference on Supporting Group Work*, pages 135–143, New York, NY, USA, 2001. ACM Press.

12. Thomas W. Malone, Kenneth R. Grant, Kum-Yew Lai, Ramana Rao, and David Rosenblitt. Semistructured messages are surprisingly useful for computer-supported coordination. *ACM Trans. Inf. Syst.*, 5(2):115–131, 1987.
13. Guido Schimm. Mining exact models of concurrent workflows. *Comput. Ind.*, 53(3):265–281, 2004.
14. Ricardo Silva, Jiji Zhang, and James G. Shanahan. Probabilistic workflow mining. In *KDD '05: Proceeding of the eleventh ACM SIGKDD international conference on Knowledge discovery in data mining*, pages 275–284, New York, NY, USA, 2005. ACM Press.
15. Lucy A. Suchman. *Plans and situated actions: the problem of human-machine communication.* Cambridge University Press, New York, NY, USA, 1987.
16. Pang-Ning Tan, Michael Steinbach, and Vipin Kumar. *Introduction to Data Mining.* Addison Wesley, 2005.
17. Wil M. P. van der Aalst, Ana Karla A. de Medeiros, and A. J. M. M. Weijters. Genetic process mining. In *ICATPN*, pages 48–69, 2005.
18. Wil M. P. van der Aalst and Minseok Song. Mining social networks: Uncovering interaction patterns in business processes. In *Business Process Management*, pages 244–260, 2004.
19. Wil. M. P. van der Aalst, B. F. van Dongen, J. Herbst, L. Maruster, G. Schimm, and A. J. M. M. Weijters. Workflow mining: a survey of issues and approaches. *Data Knowl. Eng.*, 47(2):237–267, 2003.
20. Wil M. P. van der Aalst, Ton Weijters, and Laura Maruster. Workflow mining: Discovering process models from event logs. *IEEE Transactions on Knowledge and Data Engineering*, 16(9):1128–1142, 2004.
21. Jacques Wainer, Kwanghoon Kim, and Clarence A. Ellis. A workflow mining method through model rewriting. In *CRIWG*, pages 184–191, 2005.

Adapt or Perish: Algebra and Visual Notation for Service Interface Adaptation

Marlon Dumas[1], Murray Spork[2], and Kenneth Wang[1]

[1] Queensland University of Technology, Australia
{m.dumas, kw.wang}@qut.edu.au
[2] SAP Research Center Palo Alto, USA
murray.spork@sap.com

Abstract. The proliferation of services on the web is leading to the formation of service ecosystems wherein services interact with one another in ways not necessarily foreseen during their development or deployment. A key challenge in this setting is service mediation: the act of retrofitting existing services by intercepting, storing, transforming, and (re-)routing messages going into and out of these services so they can interact in unforeseen manners. This paper addresses a sub-problem of service mediation, namely service interface adaptation, that arises when the interface that a service provides does not match the interface that it is expected to provide in a given interaction. The paper focuses on reconciling mismatches between behavioural interfaces, i.e. interfaces that capture ordering constraints between interactions. It presents a declarative approach to service interface adaptation based on: (i) an algebra over behavioural interfaces; and (ii) a visual language that allows pairs of provided-required interfaces to be linked through algebraic expressions. These expressions are fed into an execution engine that intercepts, buffers, transforms and forwards messages to enact the adaptation logic.

1 Introduction

There is an increasing acceptance of Service-Oriented Architectures (SOAs) as a paradigm for integrating software applications within and across organisational boundaries. In SOAs, independently developed and operated applications are made available as *services* that may be interconnected with one another using standardised protocols and languages. One of the cornerstones of SOAs is the principle that each service operates according to an interface. In a broad sense, a service's interface captures the types of messages that the service can produce and consume, the message encodings and transfer protocols that the service supports or requires, and the dependencies between message exchanges. Armed with such information, developers can build systems that draw upon functionality from multiple services and make them collaborate in complex manners.

Services may be reused across development projects, development teams, or even across organisational boundaries. It is thus normal to expect that services will be reused in context for which they were not originally designed. Consider

S. Dustdar, J.L. Fiadeiro, and A. Sheth (Eds.): BPM 2006, LNCS 4102, pp. 65–80, 2006.

a procurement service which, after sending an order to an order management service, expects to receive one and only one response. Now, consider the case where this procurement service is required to engage in a new collaboration wherein the order management service may send a first response acknowledging the order and accepting or rejecting a subset of its line items, and later on send zero, one or more additional updates to accept or reject the remaining line items as their availability is determined. This interface mismatch is illustrated in Figure 1. The figure shows an interface provided by an existing service (the *provided interface*) and the interface that this service is expected to provide in a new context (the *required interface*). The interfaces shown in this example are taken from industry standards: the provided interface corresponds to a fragment of an xCBL/UBL *order management process*[1] while the required interface corresponds to a RosettaNet *partner interface process.*[2]

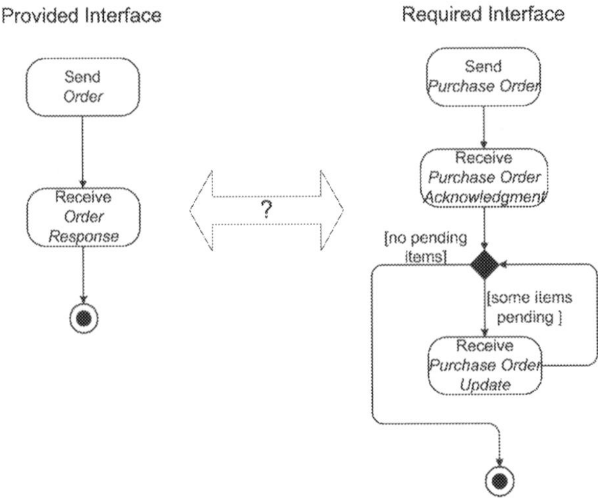

Fig. 1. Interface mismatch scenario

Cast more generally, service reuse leads to situations where a service is required to participate in multiple collaborations where different interfaces are required from it. These "required interfaces" may correspond to different message granularities, message types, and dependencies between message exchanges. Thus, service reuse calls for mechanisms to mediate between the interface natively provided by a service and the various interfaces that are required from it. We call this problem *service interface adaptation.*

Service interfaces can be described from a structural perspective, where the focus is on message types, and from a behavioural perspective, where the focus is on control dependencies between message exchanges. The problem of interface adaptation from the structural perspective has received considerable

[1] `http://www.xcbl.org` and `http://docs.oasis-open.org/ubl/prd-UBL-2.0`

[2] `http://www.rosettanet.org`

attention, leading to a number of transformation definition (e.g. XSLT) and schema mapping tools such as Microsoft BizTalk Mapper, Stylus Studio XML Mapping Tools, and SAP XI Mapping Editor.[3] In comparison, the problem of interface adaptation from a behavioural perspective is still open.

In this setting, the research question that we address can be formulated as follows: how to enable a service implementing a given behaviour (e.g. the behaviour on the left-hand side of Figure 1) to participate in interactions where a different behaviour, yet the same functionality, is required from it (e.g. the behaviour on the right-hand side of Figure 1). Traditionally, this problem is addressed by developing adaptors using programming languages. However, these adaptors are costly to develop and to maintain. Furthermore, the use of programming languages makes it difficult to check that these adaptors correctly implement the intended adaptation logic or that they do not create deadlocks.

Accordingly, we propose a declarative approach to service interface adaptation that emphasises on the behavioural perspective and can coexist with existing approaches to structural interface adaptation. The proposal comprises a visual notation underpinned by an algebra of interface transformation operators. The visual notation provides a declarative means for developers to map between required and provided interfaces. The algebra provides a semantics for the notation and provides a basis for executing these mappings. The proposal has been validated by a prototype tool that mediates between pairs of provided-required interfaces by intercepting, buffering, transforming and forwarding messages according to interface transformation expressions.

The rest of the paper is structured as follows. Section 2 introduces background concepts. Next, Section 3 presents the algebra of interface transformation operators while Section 4 presents the visual notation and its relationship to the algebra. Section 5 then discusses a prototype implementation. Finally, Section 6 compares our proposal with related work and Section 7 concludes.

2 Background

The operators put forward in this paper are defined over *behavioural interfaces*. We view a behavioural interface as a collection of control dependencies defined over a set of message exchanges. Behavioural interfaces complement structural interfaces such as those that can be described in WSDL. Structural interfaces describe the individual message exchanges in which a service can engage (e.g. in terms of message types and transport protocols) while behavioural interfaces are concerned with dependencies between message exchanges. Behavioural interfaces are known under different names, including *abstract process* in BPEL [7] and *collaboration protocol profile/agreement* in ebXML [10].

Various languages can be used to specify behavioural interfaces, e.g. UML Activity Diagrams, BPMN [12] or BPEL. We abstract from the language employed to describe behavioural interfaces by adopting a general definition based

[3] See `http://www.biztalk.org`, `http://www.stylusstudio.com`, and `http://www.sap.com/platform/netweaver/components/xi` resp.

notions from the field of concurrency theory. For illustration purposes however, we depict behavioural interfaces using UML activity diagrams in which actions are named according to the type of message being sent or received.

Behavioural interfaces are defined in terms of *communication action schemas*. A communication action schema[4] is a statement that a service may send or receive a message of a given type. We represent a communication action as a tuple (AN, D, MT) where AN is the name of the action, D indicates whether the action is inbound (receive) or outbound (send) with respect to the service being described, and MT denotes the type of messages that are sent or received by the action. Since the focus is on behavioural aspects, we abstract from the way message types are represented and instead we refer to message types through identifiers. For example, a communication action whereby a procurement service sends a purchase order to an order management service is represented as a tuple *("place order", "purchase order", out)*.

Formally, we define a behavioural interface as a possibly infinite set of traces (or strings) over an alphabet made up of communication actions. A trace t over an alphabet of communication actions defines a linear order and we call this order relation $<_t$. Each token in a trace represents an *instance of a communication action*. Thus, we distinguish between a communication action schema as defined above and instances (i.e. occurrences) thereof that appear in a trace. A trace may contain several instances of the same communication action schema. This is the case of behavioural interfaces that define repetitive behaviour (e.g. the interface on the right-hand side of Figure 1) such that the same action may be executed more than once as part of a single execution of the behavioural interface (e.g. action "Receive PO Update" in Figure 1). Below, we represent traces as lists of communication action instances $[a_1, \ldots, a_n]$.

Different traces of an interface may include instances of different actions. This happens when there is conditional branch in the interface. For example, it may be that for purchase orders with quotes > 500 something is done, while for purchase orders with lower quotes, something else is done. However, we can group the traces of an interface into disjoint groups gt_1, gt_2, ...such that all the traces in a given group gt_i contain the same set of action instances, albeit ordered differently in each trace. Given a group of traces gt of an interface I, we define a run r over interface I as a partial order $<_r$ such that:

$$\forall a_1, a_2 \in Actions(gt)\; a_1 <_r a_2 \leftrightarrow (\forall t \in gt\; a_1 <_t a_2)$$

...where $Actions(gt)$ denotes the set of action instances common to all traces in group gt. If $a_1 <_r a_2$ we say that a_1 *necessarily precedes* a_2.

Consider for example the interface represented in Figure 2. It consists of four traces: $t_1 = [a_1, a_2, a_4]$, $t_2 = [a_1, a_3, a_5, a_6, a_7]$, $t_3 = [a_1, a_3, a_6, a_5, a_7]$ and $t_4 = [a_1, a_3, a_6, a_7, a_5]$.[5] We can cluster these traces into two groups $gt_1 = \{\{t_1\}\}$ and $gt_2 = \{\{t_2, t_3, t_4\}\}$ such that each group corresponds to a run. The run r_1

---

[4] We write *communication action* or simply *action* where there is no ambiguity.

[5] Throughout the paper, we use lowercase to denote action instances and uppercase to denote action schemas. For example, a_1 denotes an instance of action A_1.

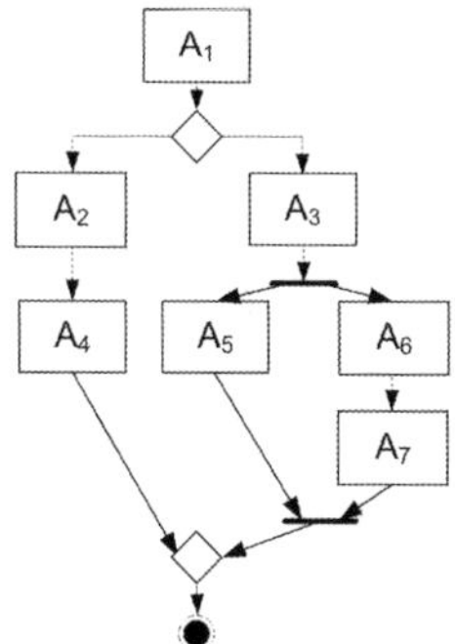

Fig. 2. Sample behavioural interface used to illustrate the notions of trace and run

corresponding to gt_1 is such that $a_1 <_{r_1} a_2$ and $a_2 <_{r_1} a_4$, while the run r_2 corresponding to gt_2 is such that $a_1 <_{r_2} a_3$, $a_3 <_{r_2} a_5$, $a_3 <_{r_2} a_6$, and $a_6 <_{r_2} a_7$.

3 Interface Transformation Algebra

The proposed model for interface transformation is based on a collection of operators for expressing how to go from one behavioural interface to another. We propose six operators namely *flow*, *scatter*, *gather*, *collapse*, *burst*, and *hide*. We do not claim that this set of operators is complete in any sense. However, we have designed each operator based on common mismatch pattern identified in prior work. Specifically, the flow, scatter gather, and hide operators correspond to the mismatch patterns identified in [9,1,3][6], the collapse operator corresponds to the "bundling patterns" supported in SAP XI (see Section 6) while the burst performs the opposite of the collapse.

All six operators are algebraic in the sense that they take as input a behavioural interface (and other parameters) to produce another behavioural interface. In the sequel, an interface taken as input by a transformation operation is called the *source interface* while the interface that is produced is called the *target interface*. The notion of source and target interface are not to be confused with those of provided and required interfaces. The source interface may correspond to the required interface, the provided interface, or to an intermediate interface generated by another operation as illustrated later.

To define the transformation operators, we use the following notations:

- *Interface* denotes the type of all possible behavioural interfaces.
- *Action*<*T*> denotes the type of all possible actions that produce or consume a message of type T. This is a parameterised type.
- *AID* denotes the type of all *action identifiers.*
- *direction*(a) denotes the directionality of action a (inbound or outbound).

[6] The hide operator also corresponds to notions of behaviour abstraction studied in the area of behaviour inheritance [11].

3.1 The Flow Operator

The Flow operator describes a transformation where an action defined in the source interface becomes another action in the target interface. The type of this operator is:

$$Flow : Interface, Action{<}ST{>}, (ST \rightarrow TT), AID \rightarrow Interface$$

The Flow operator takes as input: (i) a source interface SI, (ii) an action SA within this source interface that produces or consumes a message of a type ST, (iii) a function F that converts a message of type ST to a message of another type TT, and (iv) an action identifier ID_{TA}. From there, it produces an interface TI which has the same set of runs as SI except that in each of the resulting runs, every instance of action SA is replaced by an instance of an action TA, such that $direction(SA) = direction(TA)$. The message produced by an instance of TA that replaces an instance of SA (say sa) is obtained by applying function F to the message produced or consumed by sa). Thus, $TA = (ID_{TA}, TT, direction(SA))$. The use of the Flow operator is illustrated in Figure 3.

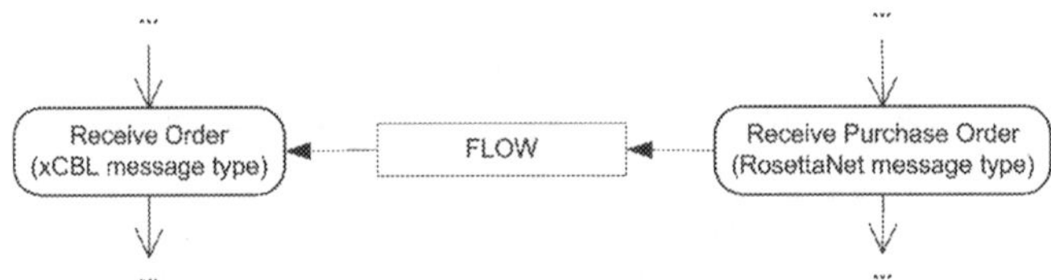

Fig. 3. The Flow operator

3.2 The Gather Operator

The Gather operator is applied when multiple actions from the source interface map to a single action in the target interface. The messages produced by the designated actions in the source interface are combined together using an aggregation function. The use of this operator is illustrated in Figure 4.

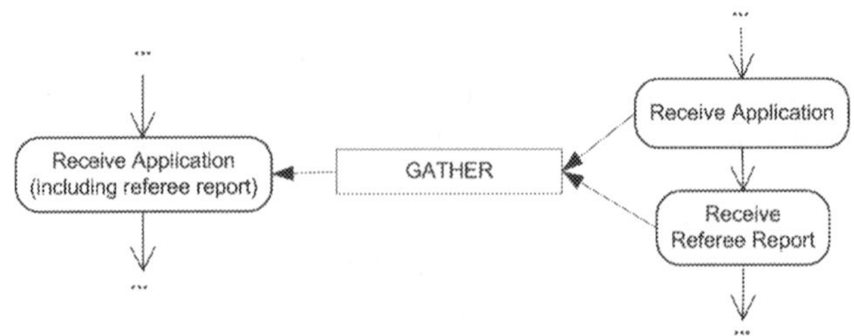

Fig. 4. The Gather operator

The Gather operator is in fact an infinite family of operators $(Gather)_n$ ($n \geq 2$) with the following type:

$$Gather_n : Interface, Action{<}ST_1{>} \ldots Action{<}ST_n{>}, \\ (ST_1 \ldots ST_n \rightarrow TT), AID \rightarrow Interface$$

$Gather_n$ takes as input: (i) an interface SI, (ii) n actions $SA_1, \ldots, SA_n$, (iii) an aggregation function AF, (iv) an action identifier ID_{TA}. The resulting interface TI defines the same set of runs as SI except that in each of these runs, every *consecutive combination* of instances of actions $SA_1 \ldots SA_n$ (say $sa_1 \ldots sa_n$) is replaced by an instance of an action TA (say ta such that $(TA = ID_{TA}, TT, direction(SA))$. Instance ta is placed in the resulting run such that:

$$\forall a \in Actions(r) \setminus \{sa_1, \ldots, sa_n\}(\exists i \in [1..n]\ a <_r sa_i) \Rightarrow a <_{r'} ta \\ \wedge (\forall i \in [1..n]\ a >_r sa_i) \Rightarrow a >_{r'} ta$$

... where r is the original run and r' is the run obtained after replacement of $sa_1 \ldots sa_n$ with ta. Runs r and r' are identical except for this replacement.

The message produced by an action instance ta that replaces a combination of action instances $sa_1 \ldots sa_n$ is obtained by applying aggregation function AF to the list of messages produced or consumed by $sa_1 \ldots sa_n$.

By *consecutive combination* of instances of actions $SA_1 \ldots SA_n$ in a run r, we mean that in between an occurrence of SA_i and an occurrence of SA_{i+1} (where $i \in [1..n-1]$), there is no occurrence of another action SA_j ($j \in [1..n]$) such that $sa_i <_r sa_j <_r sa_{i+1}$. For this definition to make sense, the following precondition must be associated to operator $Gather_n$: the set of actions $SA_1, \ldots SA_n$ should be ordered in a way compatible with their control dependencies in the source interface SI. Specifically, for any given consecutive combination of actions as defined above, the following must hold:

$$\forall i, k \in [1..n], i < k \rightarrow \forall r \in Runs(SI)\ \neg(sa_k <_r sa_i)$$

Another precondition of the $Gather_n$ operator is that all the actions being gathered should have the same directionality, and there should not be an action of the opposite directionality that lies in-between the actions being gathered. Formally:

$$\forall i, j \in [1..n], i \neq j \rightarrow (\forall r \in Runs(SI)\ sa_i \in Actions(r) \rightarrow sa_j \in Actions(r)) \\ \forall i, j \in [1..n], i < j \rightarrow Direction(sa_i) = Direction(sa_j) \wedge \\ \neg\exists sa_m \in Actions(SI)\ Direction(sa_m) \neq Direction(sa_i) \wedge \\ sa_i <_r sa_m <_r sa_j$$

The rationale for this precondition is the following. $Gather_n$ replaces a combination of actions $sa_1 \ldots sa_n$ with a single action ta. If $sa_1 \ldots sa_n$ were "receives" and there was a "send"(say *sendA*) between them ($sa_1 <_r sendA <_r sa_n$), we would have that $sendA <_{r'} ta$ due to $sendA <_r sa_n$ and the definition of $Gather_n$. However, the service implementing SI can not execute *sendA* prior to the execution of ta, since the execution of *sendA* requires information coming from sa_1 ($sa_1 <_r sendA$) and this information is only known once ta has been executed. So on the one hand *sendA* needs to occur before ta and on the other hand it needs to occur after ta. The above precondition prevents this deadlock.

3.3 The Scatter Operator

The Scatter operator is applied when a single action in the source interface is transformed into multiple actions in the target interface.

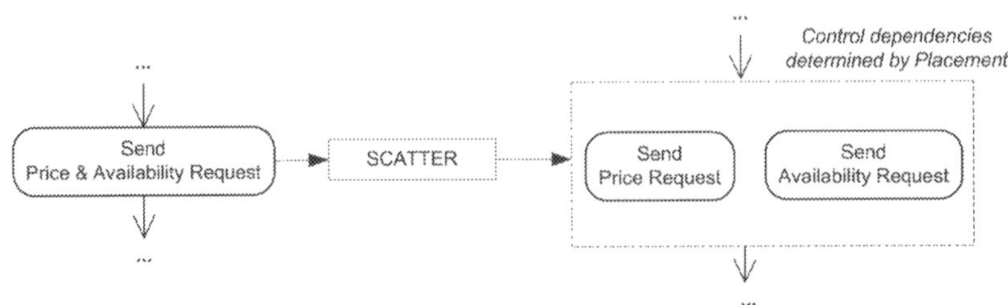

Fig. 5. The Scatter operator

Like with the Gather, $(Scatter)_n$ $(n \geq 2)$ is an infinite family of operators: $Scatter_2, Scatter_3, \ldots$. For a given n, the type of this operator is:

$$Scatter_n : Interface, Action{<}ST{>}, (ST \rightarrow TT_1 \ldots TT_n), \\ Placement{<}Action{<}TT_1{>} \ldots Action{<}TT_n{>}{>} \rightarrow Interface$$

Operator $Scatter_n$ takes as parameter an interface SI, an action SA, a function DS that splits a message into multiple ones, and a partially ordered set of actions $TA_1 \ldots TA_n$ (called a *placement*) all with the same directionality, and returns an interface. The resulting interface TI has the same set of runs as SI except that in every run of SI, every instance of SA is replaced by a subrun containing instances of actions $TA_1 \ldots TA_n$. The actions in the subrun are arranged as described by the placement P. The placement may be represented in many ways. One possible representation (though not necessarily the most expressive one) is as an expression composed using operators SEQ and PAR that represent *sequential* and *parallel* placement respectively. For example given a placement SEQ(TA_2, PAR(TA_1, TA_3)), each occurrence of SA is replaced by a subrun in which TA_2 is executed first followed by both TA_1 and TA_3 in any order.

The messages produced or consumed by the instances of actions $TA_1 \ldots TA_n$ that replace an instance of SA (say sa), are obtained by applying the data splitting function DS to the message produced or consumed by sa.

3.4 The Collapse Operator

The Collapse operator is used when a stream of messages resulting from multiple instances of the same communication action is aggregated into a single message, as illustrated in Figure 6. In this figure, the source interface (left) is such that the shipment notifications are sent incrementally as the products are dispatched. Meanwhile, the target interface (right) requires a single shipment notification.

The type of the Collapse operator is:

$$Collapse : Interface, Action{<}ST{>}, (List{<}ST{>} \rightarrow TT), AID \rightarrow Interface$$

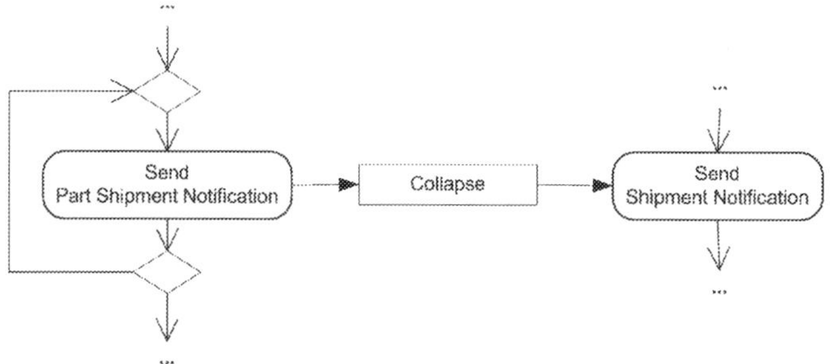

Fig. 6. The Collapse operator

The Collapse operator takes as parameter an interface SI, an action SA, an aggregation function AF, and an action identifier ID_{TA}, and produces a target interface TI. The resulting interface TI has the same set of runs as SI except that in each run, the set of instances of SA (if any) is replaced by a single instance of action TA such that $TA = (ID_{TA}, TT, \mathit{direction}(SA))$. The message produced or consumed by an instance of TA that replaces a sequence of instances of SA (say $sa_1 \ldots sa_n$) is obtained by applying the aggregation function AF to the set of messages produced or consumed by $sa_1 \ldots sa_n$.

The collapse operator requires the execution environment to: (i) track the progress of the source and target interfaces; (ii) perform a reachability analysis each time the source interface changes state;[7] (iii) once the action to be collapsed is no longer reachable from the current state, apply the aggregation function to the set of accumulated messages; (iv) dispatch the aggregated message when the target interface reaches a state where it can consume it.

The collapse operator as defined above is such that all instances of a "source" action are replaced by a single action instance. In some scenarios however, one may wish not to aggregate all instances of the source action, but only a subset thereof up to the point where a milestone is reached. For example, one may need to aggregate all part shipment notifications until an invoice is received, then aggregate the next set of shipment notifications until another invoice is received and so on. In future, we plan to investigate extensions to the Collapse operator that capture more general scenarios.

3.5 The Burst Operator

The Burst operator works in the reverse of the Collapse operator and is used when a single message needs to be split into a stream of messages. This operator is used where the transformed stream of message consists of repeated instances of the same communication action as illustrated in Figure 7.

The type of the Burst operator is:

$$\mathit{Burst} : \mathit{Interface}, \mathit{Action}{<}ST{>}, (ST \rightarrow \mathit{List}{<}TT{>}), AID \rightarrow \mathit{Interface}$$

[7] We can optimise this step so that the analysis is only performed once per state.

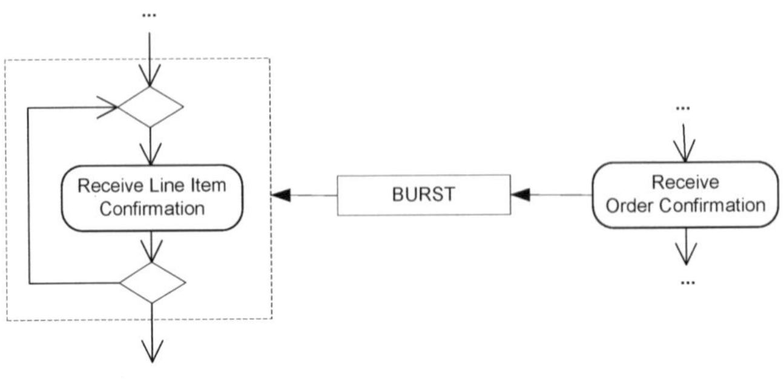

Fig. 7. The Burst operator

The operator Burst takes as parameter an interface SI, an action SA from SI, a function SF, and an action identifier ID_{TA}, to produce a target interface TI. The resulting interface TI has the same set of runs as SI except that in each run, every instance of action SA is replaced by a sequence of instances of an action TA such that $TA = (ID_{TA}, TT, direction(SA))$. The message produced by a sequence of instances of TA ($ta_1 <_r ta_2 <_r \ldots ta_n$) that replaces a single instance of action SA (say sa) is obtained by applying the "splitting" function SF given as third parameter of the Burst operator, to the message produced or consumed by sa.

3.6 The Hide Operator

The Hide operator is used when an action from the source interface is not required in the target interface. Specifically, the action produced by the source interface is to be ignored (i.e. discarded) as illustrated in Figure 8.

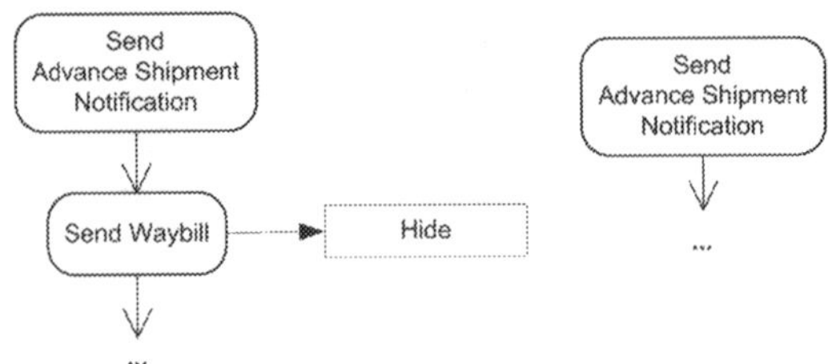

Fig. 8. The Hide operator

The type of the Hide operator is:

$$Hide : Interface, Action{<}ST{>} \rightarrow Interface$$

The Hide operator takes as input an interface SI and an action SA within this interface, and produces as output an interface TI identical to SI, except that in each run of SI, any instance of action SA is removed. Before applying this operator, the developer needs to ensure that the message produced or consumed by the action being hidden is not crucial to the operation of the adapted service.

We have intentionally avoided introducing any operators that handle the scenario where an action from the target interface is needed but is not provided by the source interface. This scenario requires the introduction of business logic in the adaptor, which is undesirable from a software maintenance perspective. Indeed, this would result in the business logic being spread across the service and the adaptors. Subsequently, any change in the business logic would require developers to trace back which adaptors need to be changed.

4 Visual Notation

4.1 Visual Representation of Mapping Expressions

An interface mapping between a provided interface and a required interface is a collection of interface transformation expressions ($E_1, \ldots E_n$). A transformation expression can be either outbound (dealing with "send" actions) or inbound (dealing with "receive" actions).

An interface transformation expression is represented as follows. Each operation in the expression a node linked through edges to other operations or to actions in the required interface or in the provided interface. Edges are directed according to the message flow. Visually, we distinguish two groups of operators: Hide, Flow, Gather, Scatter on the one hand, and Burst and Collapse on the other. Nodes corresponding to the first group can be represented by the same symbol (say a rectangle). They can be distinguished because a Flow node has one incoming and one outgoing edge, a Gather node has multiple incoming and one outgoing edge, a Scatter node has one incoming and multiple outgoing edges, and a Hide node has multiple incoming edges and no outgoing ones. The Collapse and Burst nodes have one incoming and one outgoing edge, so to distinguish them from the Flow, we need to use different symbols. We represent them as concentric rectangles containing two convergent or divergent arrows indicating whether it is a collapse or a burst respectively.

Figure 9 illustrates how interface transformation expressions are visually represented using the example introduced in Section 1. The mapping expressions (namely E_1 and E_2) captured in this figure can be textually expressed as follows:

$$E_1 = \mathit{Flow}(PI, PA_1, F_1, RA_1)$$
$$E_2 = \mathit{Gather}(\mathit{Collapse}(RI, RA_3, F_2, IA), RA_2, IA, F_3, PA_2)$$

The outbound interface mapping expression E_1 is a single-operator transformation expression that converts action PA_1 into RA_1. The inbound interface mapping expression E_2 is a composition of a Gather and a Collapse operator. The Collapse operator is applied first and transforms RA_2 into an intermediate interface containing an action IA that replaces action RA_3. The interface obtained from the Collapse operation is then given as input to the Gather function which merges RA_2 and IA and replaces them with action PA_2.

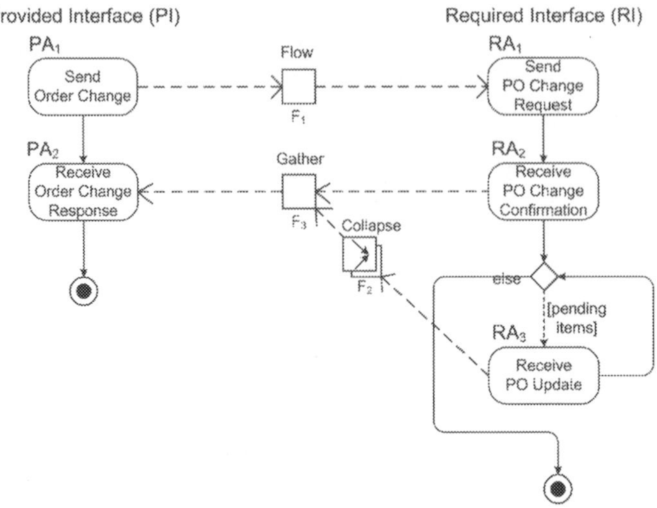

Fig. 9. Example of a visual mapping

Formally, an interface transformation expression is a directed acyclic graph whose sources are actions in one interface (e.g. the required) and whose sinks are actions in the other interface (e.g. the provided interface). For an interface mapping to cover all possibilities, it should be such that every action in the provided interface is the source or the sink of at least one transformation expression.

4.2 Mapping Constraints

Interface mappings may create deadlocks. To detect such deadlocks, we define below a condition that an interface mapping needs to fulfil. We do not claim that this condition covers all possible deadlock scenarios. In future work, we plan to investigate more general conditions.

Given any two expressions $E_i, E_o \in IM$ such that E_i is inbound and E_o is outbound, if there are four actions $A_1 \in TargetActions(E_i)$, $A_2 \in SourceActions(E_o)$, $A'_1 \in SourceActions(E_i)$ and $A'_2 \in TargetActions(E_i)$, then the precedence relation between A_1 and A_2, if any, should be compatible with that between A'_1 and A'_2. Specifically, for every run r of the target interface of E_i such that r contains an instance of action A_1 (say a_1), let a'_1 be an instance of action A'_1 that maps to a_1 through expression E_i. Now assuming that in r there is an instance of A_2 (say a_2) that maps to an instance of A'_2 (say a'_2) through expression E_o, then:

$$a_1 < a_2 \Rightarrow \neg(a'_2 < a'_1)$$

Figure 10 shows a violation of this constraint. The provided interface expects to receive the payment (A_1) before sending the shipment A_2, while in the required interface the opposite holds, thus creating a deadlock. More generally, the rationale for this constraint is that it is not possible to send information that is dependent on other information we have not yet received, nor to receive information that is dependent on other information we have not yet sent.

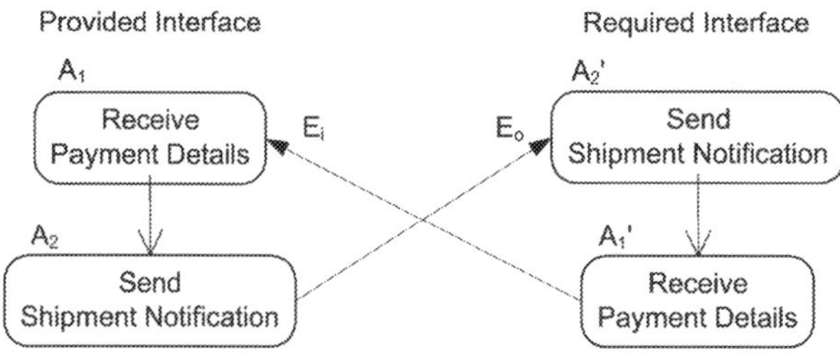

Fig. 10. Example violating the first mapping constraint

5 Tool Support

We are currently developing a prototype implementation of an *interface mapping tool* and a *service mediation engine* that support the visual notation and the algebra respectively. The implementation of the mediation engine has been completed while that of the mapping tool is underway.

The mapping tool is a graphical editor allowing developers to load pairs of provided-required behavioural interfaces and to link them through interface transformation expressions. Behavioural interfaces are represented as BPEL abstract processes supplemented by their corresponding WSDL definitions. Data manipulation functions are coded in XSLT. This provides a hook for connecting the editor with schema mapping tools that produce XSLT as output.

The output of the interface mapping tool consists of the original pair of required-provided interfaces, the transformation expressions specified by the developer, as well as configuration information related the service endpoints that implement the provided and the required interfaces. In line with our aim to abstract away from the language used to describe behavioural interfaces, the engine relies on an abstract representation of behavioural interfaces in the form of Finite State Machines (FSMs) whose transitions are labelled by communication actions. Such FSMs capture the information needed to execute the transformation expressions while abstracting away from evolving technology such as BPEL. This design choice entails however that, when deploying an interface mapping, the mapping tool must convert the BPEL abstract processes that it takes as input into the FSMs used by the execution engine. Translations from BPEL process definitions to FSMs have been studied in the literature, see e.g. [6].

The deployment of an interface mapping into the mediation engine results in the engine exposing a new service endpoint that behaves according to the required interface. An external application or service (say S1) can then send messages to this endpoint managed by the mediation engine which, based on the logic of the corresponding transformation expressions, stores, transforms and eventually forwards messages to the service endpoint that implements the required interface (say S2). Subsequently, the engine intercepts all messages between S1 and S2 and manipulates them according to the transformation expressions.

Messages intercepted by the engine need to be correctly associated to their corresponding service instance. To this end, we impose that every SOAP message intercepted by the mediation engine should contain a WS-Addressing *messageID* and (optionally) a *relatesTo* header. The engine uses these headers to correlate new messages with previously intercepted messages in order to determine the correct service instance to which the new message belongs. Messages with a *relatesTo* header are assigned to an existing service instance, while messages without this header lead to the creation of new instances, unless there is no service registered with the mediation engine that matches the action identifier of the message (SOAP-Action header), in which case the message is put into a pool of unallocated messages. The mediation engine includes an administration console to monitor the current status of service instances managed by the engine and to view histories of intercepted, transformed and forwarded messages.

6 Related Work

Traditionally, the concept of "interface" has been associated to a collection of operations or message type definitions. This view has transpired into WSDL. Accordingly, the problem of interface adaptation has been approached as a schema reconciliation problem. In the case of Web services, this comes down to mapping between different XML schemas which is a well-understood problem [8].

In this paper, we adopt a broader view on interfaces, encompassing behaviour in addition to structure. This view has been advocated in the field of component-based software engineering where the issue of interface adaptation over behavioural interfaces has received some attention. Yellin & Strom [13] define a notion of compatibility of components whose behavioural interfaces (called *protocols*) are described as FSMs. Their work addresses the question of verifying that a given adaptor (specified as a FSM) is able to to reconcile two incompatible behavioural interfaces. The authors assume that the adaptors can not store an unbounded number of messages. Our Collapse operator breaks this assumption. For example, the adaptor specified in Figure 9 needs to store an unbounded number of "updates". The "bounded buffer" assumption is motivated by undecidability issues that arise when verifying properties of adaptors. But as shown in Figure 9, the assumption is unrealistic in the application domain of Web services. Yellin & Strom also discuss how to generate an adaptor from a set of links between *parameters* (i.e. message parts) in the provided interface and corresponding parameters in the required interface. But there is an assumption that the adaptors do not use the equivalent of a Collapse, Burst, or Hide operator.

Another technique for generation of adaptors for behavioural interfaces is defined in [9]. As in Yellin & Strom , the authors deal with mismatches corresponding to the "Flow", "Gather" and "Scatter" operators, not with "Burst", "Collapse" and "Hide". This work also differs from ours in that it does not consider the use of composable transformation operators with a graphical syntax.

More recent research has addressed the problem of interface adaptation in the context of Web services. Benatallah et al. [3] identify a set of "mismatch patterns" between behavioural interfaces and provide templates of BPEL code that developers may reuse to build adaptors that resolve these mismatches. However, the compositionality of these BPEL templates is not considered and thus the approach is not systematic. Similar mismatch patterns are identified in [4] and [1] where high-level architectures for addressing such mismatches are proposed. The ADAPT framework [1] goes further by proposing a notation for N-to-M mappings, i.e. mappings where data coming from N services are collected and repartitioned among M services. This is similar to the Gather and Scatter operators but it does not take into account any information contained in the behavioural interfaces, e.g. the data is forwarded to the target services as soon as it has been collected and in no particular order, whereas our Gather operator forwards messages in a specific order to fulfill the constraints of the target interface. Altenhofen et al. [2] propose a formal model for process mediation based on Abstract State Machine (ASM) specifications. They show how these ASMs can be refined to deal with mismatch patterns such as those identified in [4]. Fuchs [5] proposes another approach to interface adaptation. However, this contribution focuses on reconciling operational differences such as security policies, service level agreement, etc.

SAP eXchange Infrastructure (XI) supports behavioural interface adaptation through so-called "bundling patterns"[8]. These patterns come with process templates that can be used in scenarios where certain types of messages need to be buffered until they are all available and then aggregated into a single message. However, these patterns only address a restricted set of behavioural interface adaptation scenarios and do not provide a systematic approach to the problem.

7 Conclusion and Future Work

In this paper, we introduced a declarative approach to service interface adaptation based on an algebra of six operators over behavioural interfaces; and a visual language that allows pairs of provided and required interfaces to be linked through algebraic expressions. The paper also introduced an architectural view of our execution engine that consumes these algebraic expressions and facilitates message interception, buffering and transformation to enact the adaptation logic.

In future work, we plan to investigate notions of completeness in the context of service interface adaptation that would enable us to characterise the expressiveness of the algebra and to define more powerful extensions or alternatives thereof. One fundamental question that should be addressed is: When can a service implementing a given provided interface be adapted to fit a given required interface without adding new business logic into the adaptor. As discussed in Section 3.6, adding business logic into the adaptors can lead to maintainability issues, since business logic would then be spread across the service and its adaptors, rather than being concentrated in the service. In other words, we envisage that adaptors should be restricted to data transformations and coordination aspects, leaving the business logic entirely within the service.

[8] See `http://tinyurl.com/h427a` and `http://tinyurl.com/kpe3a`.

In addition, we plan to develop techniques to semi-automatically infer possible links between provided and required interfaces. For example, when a send action in a provided interface has an associated message type similar (according to a similarity metrics) to that of a send action in the required interface, we can infer that these two actions should be linked through a Flow operation. By combining these heuristics with similar heuristics developed in the context of schema mapping [8], we seek to design techniques for semi-automatic generation of adaptors for conversational services.

Acknowledgment. This research is funded by a Queensland "Smart State" Fellowship and ARC Linkage Project LP0455394, both co-sponsored by SAP.

References

1. G. Alonso, C. Pautasso, and B. Biörnstad. CS Adaptability Container. Deliverable #11, EU FP5 Project "ADAPT", August 2004.
2. M. Altenhofen, E. Börger, and J. Lemcke. An abstract model for process mediation. In *In Proceedings of the 7th International Conference on Formal Engineering Methods (ICFEM)*, pages 81–95, Manchester, UK, November 2005. Springer.
3. B. Benatallah, F. Casati, D. Grigori, H. R. Motahari Nezhad, and F. Toumani. Developing Adapters for Web Services Integration. In *Proceedings of the 17th International Conference on Advanced Information System Engineering, CAiSE 2005, Porto, Portugal*, pages 415–429. Springer, 2005.
4. E. Cimpian and A. Mocan. WSMX Process Mediation Based on Choreographies. In *Proceedings of the Business Process Management Workshops*, pages 130–143, Nancy, France, September 2005. Springer.
5. M. Fuchs. Adapting web services in a heterogeneous environment. In *Proceedings of the Second IEEE International Conference on Web Services, ICWS 2004, San Diego, California, USA*, pages 656–664, 2004.
6. H.Foster, S.Uchitel, J.Magee, and J.Kramer. Tool support for model-based engineering of web service compositions. In *IEEE International Conference on Web Services (ICWS)*, Orlando FL, USA, July 2005. IEEE Computer Society.
7. R. Khalaf, N. Mukhi, F. Curbera, and S. Weerawarana. The Business Process Execution Language for Web Services. In *Process-Aware Information Systems*. John Wiley & Sons, 2005.
8. L. Popa, Y. Velegrakis, R. Miller, M. Hernández, and R. Fagin. Translating web data. In *Proceedings of the 28th International Conference on Very Large Databases (VLDB)*, pages 598–609, Hong Kong, China, August 2002.
9. H. Schmidt and R. Reussner. Generating adapters for concurrent component protocol synchronisation. In *Proceedings of the 5th IFIP International Conference on Formal Methods for Open Object-Based Distributed Systems (FMOODS)*, Enschede, The Netherlands, March 2002. Kluwer Academic Publishers.
10. UN/CEFACT and OASIS. ebXML Business Process Specification Schema (Version 1.01). http://www.ebxml.org/specs/ebBPSS.pdf, 2001.
11. W. van der Aalst and T. Basten. Inheritance of workflows: An approach to tackling problems related to change. *Theoretical Computer Science*, 270(1-2):125–203, 2002.
12. S. White. Business Process Modeling Notation (BPMN). Version 1.0 - May 3, 2004, BPMI.org, 2004. `www.bpmi.org`.
13. D. Yellin and R. E. Strom. Protocol specifications and component adaptors. *ACM Transactions on Programming Languages and Systems*, 19(2):292–333, 1997.

Automated Service Composition Using Heuristic Search*

Harald Meyer and Mathias Weske

Hasso-Plattner-Institute for IT-Systems-Engineering at the University of Potsdam
Prof.-Dr.-Helmert-Strasse 2-3, 14482 Potsdam, Germany
{harald.meyer, mathias.weske}@hpi.uni-potsdam.de

Abstract. Automated service composition is an important approach to automatically aggregate existing functionality. While different planning algorithms are applied in this area, heuristic search is currently not used. Lacking features like the creation of compositions with parallel or alternative control flow are preventing its application. The prospect of using heuristic search for composition with quality of service properties motivated the extension of existing heuristic search algorithms.

In this paper we present a heuristic search algorithm for automated service composition. Based on the requirements for automated service composition, shortcomings of existing algorithms are identified, and solutions for them presented.

Keywords: Processes and service composition, Process planning and flexible workflow.

1 Introduction

Service Composition is an important approach to aggregate existing functionality into new functionality. Functionality, available as services, is composed and enacted as a process. Creating service compositions is a time-consuming, error-prone manual task. Hence, different approaches for its automation exist [1,2,3,4]. In this paper we present an approach for automated service composition based on a heuristic search algorithm.

Heuristic search is a promising approach for automated planning. Contrary to other planning approaches, it is currently not used for automated service composition. Lacking features prevent the wide-spread usage. But its clear-cut and easy to understand principle makes heuristic search a promising starting point for more elaborated automated service composition approaches. Metric-FF [5] allows planning with numerical properties and the optimization for them. This can be used to implement quality of service properties. Using heuristic search as the basis for semi-automated composition might also be a viable approach.

* This paper presents results of the Adaptive Services Grid (ASG) project (contract number 004617, call identifier FP6-2003-IST-2) funded by the Sixth Framework Program of the European Commission.

S. Dustdar, J.L. Fiadeiro, and A. Sheth (Eds.): BPM 2006, LNCS 4102, pp. 81–96, 2006.

But heuristic search algorithms have some severe shortcomings: Generated plans are totally-ordered. This is critical as it prevents taking advantage of possible parallelism and invoke services in parallel. Heuristic search also does not support alternative control flows. These are required if the exact services to invoke are only known at run-time, based on results of previously invoked services. For example, to process a payment if several different payment options are available the correct service must be invoked according to the payment option. If the payment option is selected only at run-time, the service composition must contain alternative control flows for each possible payment option. Constructing such plans is not supported by classical heuristic search planners.

In the following section a usage scenario is introduced. In section 3 the critical requirements that hinder the usage of heuristic search are presented. Section 4 then proposes extensions to overcome the shortcomings by extending an existing algorithm. The paper closes with a view on related work in section 5 and a conclusion.

2 Usage Scenario

To illustrate the automated service composition approach of this paper a small usage scenario is introduced. It is a payment process that can be part of some larger business process. Figure 1 shows an example for a composition. It starts by determining the credit card company for a given credit card number. Afterwards

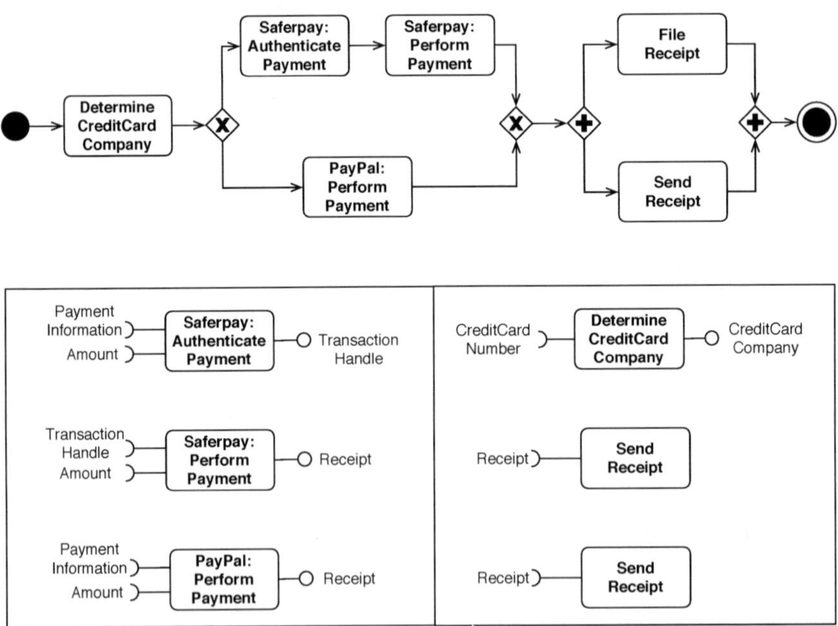

Fig. 1. Payment Composition

the payment is performed with the correct payment service. The payment service of Saferpay[1] actually consists of two services. A payment has to be authenticated before it is performed. This is not necessary for the PayPal[2] payment service. Based on the issuing credit card company, payment through Saferpay, PayPal, or both is possible. Of course, always only one of them is actually used. Finally, the receipt is send to the customer and filed in the database. Based on the actual request, different compositions are possible. If for example the request already states that the credit card is from a specific credit card company supported by SaferPay, the composition only consists of four services: authenticate payment, perform payment, file receipt, and send receipt.

The presented composition algorithm is implemented and used as a part of the Adaptive Services Grid (ASG) project[3]. The scenario is derived from a larger scenario by one of the project partners. The Dynamic Supply Chain Management scenario is about the integration of suppliers in the domain of Internet Service Providers (ISP).

3 Shortcomings of Existing Heuristic Search Algorithms

In [6] we presented elaborated requirements analysis for automated service composition algorithms. Most of these requirements are fulfilled by existing heuristic search algorithms. Hence, we are limiting ourselves to the following critical ones:

1. Parallel control flow
2. Uncertainty in initial state and service effects
3. Alternative control flow
4. Creation of new variables

The first requirement is *parallel control flow*. Compositions consist of service invocations and their ordering. This ordering is the control flow. The straight forward approach is to assume a total ordering between service invocations and perform them sequentially. But in reality service invocations are often only partially ordered. If services do not depend on each other's results and do not conflict with each other, they can be invoked in parallel. This saves execution time. Therefore a composition algorithm must be able to create compositions with control flows that only contain the necessary orderings.

The second requirement is to support *uncertainty in the initial state and service effects*. Executing a service with uncertain effects leads to several new states. This is necessary to represent a service that determines the issuing credit card company based on a credit card number. The exact outcome can only be determined after actually invoking the service for a given credit card number. After invoking a service with uncertain effects we are in more than one possible state. Hence, we might as well start with multiple possible states. Uncertainty in

[1] Saferpay is a registered trademark of Telekurs Group.

[2] PayPal is a registered trademark of eBay Inc.

[3] http://asg-platform.org

the initial state is necessary to express that for a certain fact only the possible values but not the exact value are known. For compositions containing service invocations with uncertain effects starting in an uncertain initial state it must be ensured that they work correctly in all possible situations.

The third requirement – *alternative control flow* – yields from the support of uncertainty in the initial state and in service effects. Invoking the service to determine the issuing credit card company based on the credit card number leads to several possible states. Based on the actual state, different service must be invoked to perform the payment. But determining the actual state can only be done when enacting the composition and invoking the services. To create compositions that work in all possible states it is necessary to support or-splits that lead to alternative control flows.

The fourth requirement – *creation of new variables* – results from the fact that in the data flow of a composition new data is created on the fly. This is not limited to writing the data into an existing variable but also includes the creation of new variables. This is complicated and often not possible in automated planning. This limitation of the planning model, already criticized in [7], simplifies planning. As all the variables are known, all possible service invocations can be calculated in advance. Services that are not invokable because the necessary variables for input or output parameters are missing, can be pruned.

Hence, in this planning model all variables used during composition must be defined in advance. This includes also intermediate variables that are neither used in the input nor in the output. For the payment scenario this means that a variable for the transaction handle of Saferpay must be be defined. It is not obvious why such a variable could be necessary. By adding this variable we are encoding assumptions about possible composition results into the service request. For PayPal the transaction handle is not necessary and other companies might require other intermediate variables. Defining all necessary variables requires a lot of information about the service landscape and at least a rough idea of how the composition could look like (e.g. which services might be used). For a realistic composition approach it is therefore required that activities can create new variables and that the service composer takes these into account.

4 A Heuristic Search Algorithm for Service Composition

In this section a composition algorithm that overcomes all these limitations will be presented. Before starting with the description of the algorithm, the notions of service, service specification, service composition, and service request are introduced. A service is a discrete business functionality. It is described by a service specification:

Definition 1. *A* ***service specification*** $s = (\mathcal{I}, \mathcal{O}, p, e)$ *is a tuple with*

- $\mathcal{I}$*: List of input parameters*
- $\mathcal{O}$*: List of output parameters*

- *p: The precondition of the service is a disjunction-free logical expression and must be satisfied in order to invoke the service.*
- *e: The effect of the service is a disjunction-free logical expression. It describes the changes to the current state resulting from the invocation of the service.*

The afore-mentioned definition states that services have exactly one method to invoke. This differs from the service definition used for example in the WSDL standard [8]. But as WSDL does not specify choreographies, each method can be seen as an individual service and specified separately.

Definition 2. *A* ***service request*** $R = (a_0, g, D)$ *is a triple consisting of the initial state* a_0*, the goal state* g *and a service domain* D*. A state is a logical expression. This concept is refined later. A* ***service domain*** $D = (\mathcal{S}, o)$ *consists of a set of service specifications and and ontology describing the concepts used to specify services.*

A ***service composition*** c *is a list of service invocations* $c = \langle s_1, ..., s_k \rangle$*. A service request is* ***fulfilled by*** *a service composition that starting from the initial state reaches a state that satisfies the goal state by subsequently invoking the services from the composition.*

4.1 Enforced Hill-Climbing

Our algorithm is based on enforced hill-climbing [9]. It is a forward heuristic search in state space. A state is defined as follows:

Definition 3. *A* ***logical expression*** *is defined as:*

- *A logical literal is a logical expression*
- *Two literals composed using the junctors* $\vee$ *(disjunction) and* $\wedge$ *(conjunction) is a logical expression*

A logical expression is disjunction-free if it does not contain disjunctions. A disjunction-free logical expression a *can be divided into the two logical expression* a^+ *and* a^- *where* a^+ *contains all positive literals and* a^- *contains all negated literals. A* ***state*** *is a disjunction-free and negation-free logical expression.*

A logical expression a ***satisfies*** *another logical expression* a' *(written as:* $a \models a'$*) if every positive literal of* a' *is in* a *and no negative literal of* a' *is in* a*.*

State space is the search space that is spanned by the states and the transitions in between them:

Definition 4. *Service* $s = (\mathcal{I}, \mathcal{O}, p, e)$ *is* ***invokable*** *in state* a *if* $a \models p$*.* ***Invoking service*** s *in state* a *leads to a state transition. This can be defined by the state transition function* $\gamma(a, s) = a'$*. If* $a \models p$ *then* $a' = a \bigcup e^+ \setminus \{x | \neg x \in e^-\}$*.*

A state a *has a direct successor* a'*, written as* $a \rightarrow a'$*, if a service* s *exists and* $\gamma(a, s) = a'$*. The successor relation can be inductively extended to indirect successors* $\rightarrow^+ = \rightarrow \bigcup \{(a, a'') | (a, a') \in \rightarrow \wedge (a', a'') \in \rightarrow^+\}$*.*

Enforced Hill-Climbing is an extension of Hill-Climbing. Hill-Climbing uses a heuristic function $h(a, g)$ to select states until the goal is reached. The heuristic $h(a, g)$ delivers an approximation of the distance of the state a to the goal g. Starting with the initial state, a new state is selected from the direct successors. The first successor that is, according to the heuristic, better than the current state is selected and assigned as the new current state. This process is continued until the current state satisfies the goal state. Given an admissible heuristic and a mechanism to prevent visiting states multiple times, the algorithm always terminates. It terminates successfully if it reaches a state that satisfies the goal state. It fails if a state a is reached so that no direct successor a' with $h(a', g) < h(a, g)$ exists.

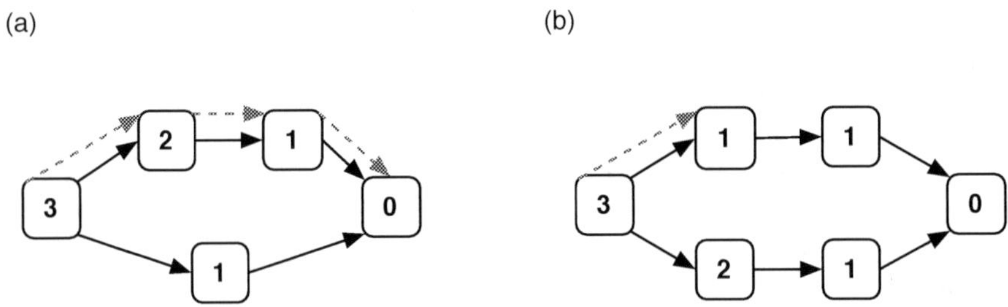

Fig. 2. Hill Climbing is not optimal (a) and incomplete (b)

Hill-Climbing does not create optimal compositions and it is incomplete. Figure 2(a) illustrates the reason for the in-optimality. Displayed are states, their heuristic values, and possible state transitions. If the state with heuristic 2 is evaluated first, it is selected even though a shorter path exists. Another problem is the greediness of Hill-Climbing. Greediness means that optimization is done locally without taking the path to the current state into account. This is only of importance if a cost function is associated with state transitions. Otherwise the admissible heuristic guarantees that greediness does not affect the composition result. Figure 2(b) demonstrates why Hill-Climbing is incomplete: If the upper path is taken, composition fails after the first state with heuristic 1 as no direct successor with a better heuristic can be found. Such a state is called a local maximum.

Enforced Hill-Climbing solves the problem of local maxima by switching to breadth-first search if it gets trapped in a local maximum. This works as depicted in Fig. 3. If the evaluation of a state shows that it is not better than the current states all its direct successor are added to the end of A'. Hence when all direct successors are evaluated and none was better than the current state, Enforced Hill-Climbing starts evaluating the successors of the successors. This is continued until either a better state is found or no reachable states are unevaluated and composition fails. In the situation from Fig. 2(c) Enforced Hill-Climbing switches to breadth-first search in the state with no better direct successors. Through breadth-first search the state with heuristic 0 (the goal) is found and it can finish successfully. Regardless of this extension is Enforced Hill-Climbing

```
a = i
c := empty composition
while ¬(a ⊨ g)
        A' = new Queue
        enqueue(A', {a'|a → a'})
        for a' ∈ A'
                if h(a',g) < h(a,g)
                        add(c,s) with γ(a,s) = a'
                        s = s'
                        goto 3
                else
                        enqueue(A', {a''|a' → a''})
                end
        end
        composition failed
end
composition successful
```

Fig. 3. Enforced Hill-CLimbing

still incomplete but termination is still guaranteed as breadth-first search always terminates. Fig. 4 shows that composition fails if the upper path is taken. The upper path is a dead end and the algorithm is not able to turn around and leave it. As termination is always guaranteed, one approach to deal with incompleteness, as proposed by [9], is to switch to another complete but slower search algorithm (e.g. A*) if Enforced Hill-Climbing fails. The enforcement extension of Hill-Climbing does not affect the in-optimality of the algorithm.

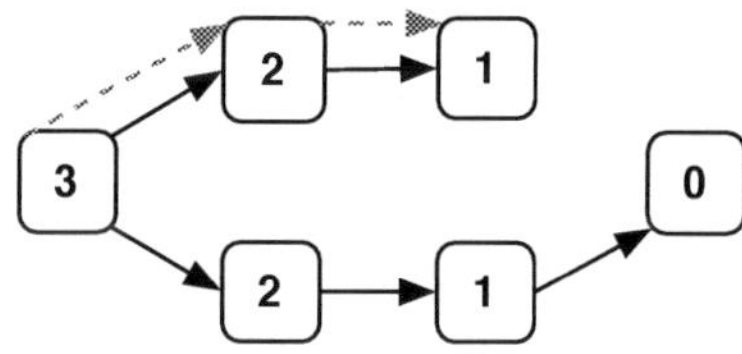

Fig. 4. Enforced Hill-Climbing is incomplete

4.2 Extending Enforced Hill-Climbing

Enforced Hill-Climbing does not support any of the aforementioned requirements. Uncertain effects or initial states cannot be handled by creating alternative control flows. Compositions are strictly sequential and no variables can be created during the composition. In the following we present how each requirement can be addressed.

Implementing requirement 1: Parallel control flow. The first step towards parallel control flow is to support the parallel selection of multiple services. Figure 5 illustrates that this leads to a denser search space as more state transitions are possible. But at the same time paths become shorter.

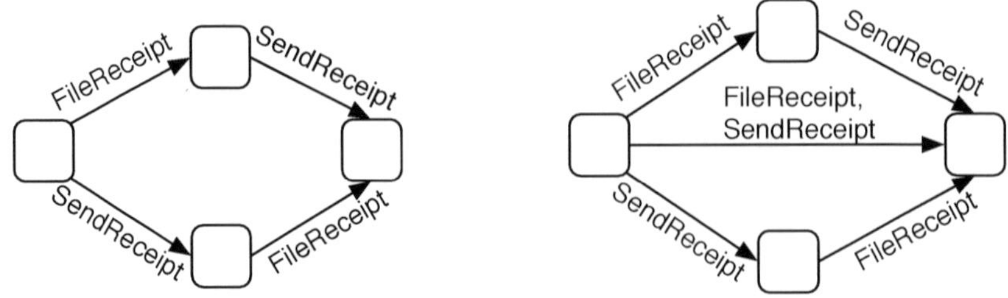

Fig. 5. State Space without and with parallel selection

To invoke services in parallel it must be ensured that they can actually work in parallel. First this means that services where one service creates the precondition of the other service cannot be invoked in parallel. For example, the payment processing must be finished before the receipt can be send. This can be ensured by extending the invocability definition to sets of services: a set of services is invokable in a given state if every service is invokable in the state. But this definition is not sufficient as two invokable services may be in conflict. Before we can define invocability for sets of services we need to define what it means if two services are in conflict:

Definition 5. *Two services* $s_1 = (\mathcal{I}_1, \mathcal{O}_1, p_1, e_1)$ *and* $s_2 = (\mathcal{I}_2, \mathcal{O}_2, p_2, e_2)$ *are in* ***conflict*** *if:*

- s_1 *deletes the precondition of* s_2*:* $\neg x \in e_1 \wedge x \in p_2$
- s_1 *creates a fact whose negation is the precondition of* s_2*:* $x \in e_1 \wedge \neg x \in p_2$
- s_1 *and* s_2 *have inconsistent effects:* $x \in e_1 \wedge \neg x \in e_2$

A set of services $\mathcal{S} = \{s_1, ..., s_n\}$ *is in conflict if two services* $s_i (1 \leq i \leq n)$ *and* $s_j (1 \leq j \leq n)$ *exists which are in conflict.*

Based on this notion we can define invocability and invocation for service sets:

Definition 6. *A set of services is* ***invokable*** *if each service is invokable and it is conflict-free. Given a set of conflict-free services* $\mathcal{S} = \{s_1, ..., s_n\}$ ***invocation*** *of* $\mathcal{S}$ *is equal to the sequential invocation of all* $s_i (1 \leq i \leq n)$ *in arbitrary order. The state transition function can be extended accordingly:* $\gamma(a, \mathcal{S}) = a'$*.*

To support the parallel selection of multiple services one modification of Enforced Hill-Climbing is necessary: Line 8 where the new service is added to the composition must deal with the extended state transition function $\gamma(a, \mathcal{S})$. More than one service can be added to a composition at the same time. As the parallel selection should be reflected in the resulting composition, we need to modify our composition definition. The easiest way to do that would be to extend the previous list of services to a list of service sets. But with respect to further additions we choose another definition:

Definition 7. *A composition $C = (\mathcal{S}, \overset{cond}{\prec})$ consists of a set of service invocations $\mathcal{S}$ and a partial order $\overset{cond}{\prec}$ between them. For two services $s_i, s_j \in \mathcal{S}$ an ordering $s_i \overset{cond}{\prec} s_j$ is defined if s_i was added to the composition before s_j. Here cond is that part of the effect of s_i that is necessary to invoke s_j. Likewise, $s_i \overset{cond}{\not\prec} s_j$ if both were added in the same step.*

Implementing requirement 2: Uncertainty in initial state and service effects. States, preconditions, and effects must include disjunction to support uncertainty. Disjunction in states is not only used to express uncertainty about the initial state. It also used to express several distinct goal states. Disjunction in the precondition of a service allows to express that the service is invokable in different situations. This does not increase the expressiveness as this can be simulated by multiple services. Disjunction in service effects can be used to express uncertainty about the service's outcome. To work with these richer expressions, we introduce a set-based representation of logical expressions with disjunctions:

Definition 8. *Given a logical expression a its disjunctive normal form can be expressed as a set $a_{set} = \{a_1, ..., a_n\}$ of disjunction-free logical expressions. Here each a_i represents one conjunction of the disjunctive normal form.*

A logical expression and its set-based representation can be used interchangeably. When a distinction is necessary we will name the set-based notation a_{set}. When speaking about a state and its set-based representation it is helpful to think of the set-based representation as a set of possible states. The definition for state satisfaction needs to be extended accordingly:

Definition 9. *A state a* ***satisfies*** *another state g if $\forall a_i \in a_{set}\ \exists g_j \in g_{set} a_i \models g_j$.*

Hence, a set of possible current states satisfies a set of allowed goal state if every possible current state satisfies at least one allowed goal states. Now we have developed the foundation to represent uncertainty. Yet it is unclear how we can actually deal with uncertainty during planning. In automated planning two approaches have been developed: conformant planning and contingent planning. Using conformant planning, additional service invocations are added that ensure the correct working of the composition, without actually determining the current state or the actual effects of service invocations. While this is a simple model, it is often not practicable. For example instead of first determining the correct credit card company and then charging the credit card only with the correct payment service, it is tried to charge the credit card using each payment service. While, hopefully, the credit card is only charged once, the other services may charge a fee making the payment process very expensive. Conformant planning makes most sense when controlling robots that lack sensors. In business scenarios another approach is more practicable. Contingent planning introduces the ability to sense the actual value of fact during run-time and then continue accordingly. This means after determining the credit card company for a credit card, the actual value is sensed during run-time and then the correct service is invoked. For the control flow of the composition or-splits must be support that lead to alternative control flows.

Implementing requirement 3: Alternative control flow. In the previous section we extended the notion of states to include uncertainty. Service effects can now include disjunction as well. This means that we can actually reach several alternative states by invoking a service. To support contingent planning it must also be possible to invoke a service if it is only invokable in some of the current states. Figure 6 illustrates this situation. Invoking the service to determine the credit card company leads here to two possible states[4]. In the first state the SaferPay authentication service is invokable and in the second state the PayPal payment service is invokable. Invoking them only changes the state in which they were invokable. As multiple services may be selected (see section 4.2) both services can be selected in parallel changing both states at once. To support this notion, invocation and invokability need to be extended:

Definition 10. *A service* $s = (\mathcal{I}, \mathcal{O}, p, e)$ *is* ***invokable*** *in a state* a *if* $\exists a_i \in a_{set} \exists p_j \in p_{set} a_i \models p_j$. ***Invoking a service*** *in a state* a *leads to a state transition. This can be defined by a state transition function* $\gamma(a, s) = a'$. *If* $a \models p$ *then* $a' = \{a_i | a_i \in a_{set}, \forall p_j \in p_{set}, a_i \not\models p_j\} \cup \{a_i \circ e | a_i \in a_{set}, \exists p_j \in p_{set}, a_i \models p_j\}$. *The operation* $a_i \circ e = \{a_i \bigcup e_j^+ \setminus \{x | \neg x \in e_j^-\} | e_j \in e_{set}\}$ *applies the effect to one logical expression.*

Invoking a service with uncertain effects results in several possible states. If subsequent services cannot be invoked in all states, an or-split is added to the composition. In our example this is the case after determining the credit card company.

For our composition algorithm it is irrelevant which path from Fig. 6 is actually taken, because only necessary orderings between service invocations are added. This is done by linking two service invocations only if one produces the precondition of the other or if they are in conflict. Formally:

Definition 11. *For two services* $s_1 = (\mathcal{I}_1, \mathcal{O}_1, p_1, e_1)$ *and* $s_2 = (\mathcal{I}_1, \mathcal{O}_1, p_1, e_1)$ *a link* $s_1 \overset{cond}{\prec} s_2$ *exists if:*

- $cond \in p_2 \wedge producer(s_1, a, x) \wedge x \in cond$ *where* $producer(s, a, x)$ *is the relation of fact* x *from state* a *produced by service* s
- *or* s_1 *and* s_2 *are in conflict.*

Often it is not only necessary to create alternative branches but to also merge them later. In our example this is necessary after payment has been performed. A first approach to merging might be to detect equivalent states and unify them to one state. In Fig. 6 states E and F seem to be mergable be merged because they represent the same fact: payment has been performed. In reality things are

[4] In reality this might be more, but two is sufficient for presentation.

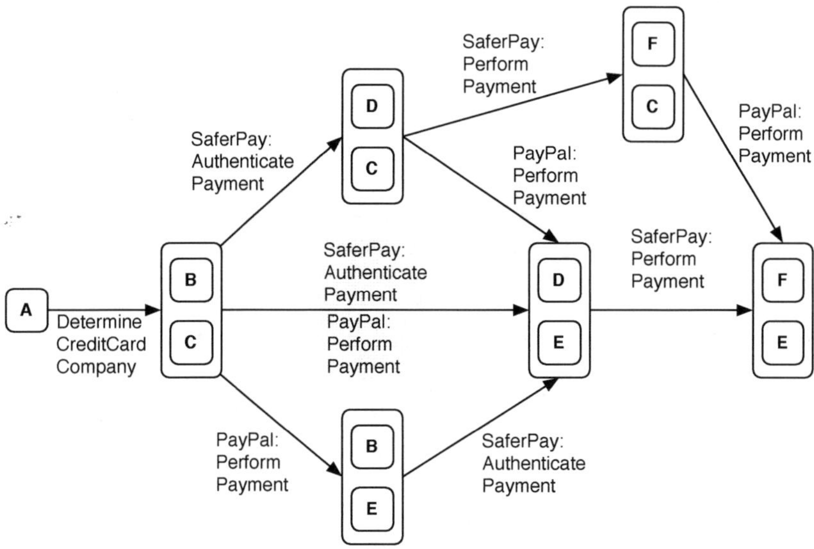

Fig. 6. Extended State Transition

not that easy and calculating state equivalence is hard and may be impossible. As a matter of fact E and F are not really equivalent as F also includes the transaction handle. Although both states mean the same for us, detecting this is not possible. We can only merge states which are exactly identical. This is unproblematic as in the end we are not interested in merging states but merging control flows. This is a lot easier: Control flows can be merged if the current set of services is invokable in some or all possible states. Both succeeding services in our example – filing the receipt and sending the receipt to the customer – can be invoked in both possible states. Hence we can merge the alternative control flows. The inability to merge the states costs us performance, as we have to evaluate more states, but it does not prevent us from doing a merge.

The interesting point about introducing only necessary links is that it renders the parallel selection of service unnecessary. As only necessary links are added, two service that can be invoked in parallel will be composed as running in parallel even if they are selected subsequently. We are still using the parallel selection as it is currently unclear whether its denser search space is a disadvantage or its shorter search paths are an advantage.

Implementing requirement 4: Creation of new variables. Creating new variables is currently not supported by most planners. This results not only from limitations of the language used to describe requests [7] but it also greatly simplifies creating the composition. If all variables are known in advance it is easy to determine which services can be invoked. If we do not specify that a transaction handle variable exists, the SaferPay services are never invokable and hence can be pruned. But as we do not want to specify the transaction handle in our request, this behavior is undesirable.

To solve this problem we need to allow the creation of new variables if a matching variable for the output of a service does not exist. But the unrestricted addition is problematic as this yields a possibly infinite set of states and makes planning semi-decidable [10,11]. Thus we are introducing a very restricted form of variable creation. A variable may only be created if no variable of the same type already exists. While this keeps the problem decidable it may be too restrictive as it fails if two variables of the same type need to be created. We are currently not allowing the deletion of variables, as we have not encountered any practical use for it.

4.3 A Heuristic for Extended Enforced Hill-Climbing

As the heuristic guides the search it is crucial for the performance of the composer. An approach to find a heuristic for a given problem is to relax it (make it simpler). Enforced Hill-Climbing was originally developed together with the *Relaxed Graphplan* heuristic [9]. Essentially it solves a simplified version of the composition request using the Graphplan planning algorithm [12]. We take the length of the generated composition as the heuristic. Graphplan works by first creating a planning graph and then extracting the solution from it. The relaxation or simplification of the problem results from ignoring the negative effects of service invocations. In the presence of negative effects back tracking is necessary during solution extraction. As negative effects are ignored, the heuristic can be calculated in polynomial time [9].

For our algorithm the calculation of the heuristic function can be even more simplified. We skip the solution extraction phase. Why the solution extraction phase was necessary for FF and can be skipped here, will be become evident after we have build up such a planning graph. A planning graph consists of two kinds of

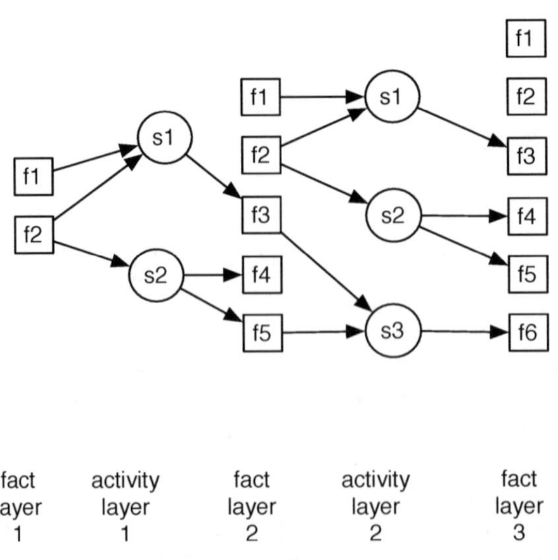

Fig. 7. A Planning Graph

nodes: fact nodes and activity nodes. Fact nodes represent literals (or facts) from states and activities represent service invocations. Starting from the facts of the initial state alternating layers of facts and activities are added until a fact layer is reached that satisfies the goal. Figure 7 illustrates such a graph. Starting from the initial state all invokable services (in this case $s1$ and $s2$) are added to the first activity layer. This activity layer *produces* a new fact layer including all the positive effects of $s1$ and $s2$. Now a new service $s3$ is invokable. The resulting fact layer now includes our goal (e.g. $f6$) and we are finished with building the graph. The original planning graph from Graphplan additionally contains mutual exclusion relations between two activities or two facts if the activities are in conflict or if the facts only result from conflicting activities. If negative effects are ignored no mutual exclusion relations will be added as all conflicts emerge from negative effects. Now the original Relaxed Graphplan heuristic would continue by extracting a sequential solution from the graph. But as we are not interested in the length of a sequential solution we can directly count the number of activity layers and take it as our heuristic. As the resulting composition contains as much parallel invocation of services as possible this is quite a good. The upper-limit for the heuristic is the actual distance from the goal. The value can actually be lower as we are ignoring conflicts. Hence it is admissible.

Like the original Relaxed Graphplan heuristic, this heuristic can be calculated in polynomial time. To reduce space consumption we can use an optimization. As we are only interested in the number of activity layers and we do not want to extract a solution, it is sufficient to just keep the current fact layer and count the number of activity layers used to reach this fact layer. This greatly reduces space consumption.

5 Related Work

As mentioned in the introduction, a lot of different approaches towards service composition exist. Most are adapting existing automated planning algorithms. In [1] a slightly different approach is followed. They designed their own algorithm that finds the necessary services to invoke through backward-chaining and and then identifies additional necessary services in a second forward-chaining phase. In [3] Hierarchical Task Network (HTN) planning is used for service composition. HTN planning is based on the notion of composite tasks that can be refined to atomic tasks using predefined methods. In domains where these methods that are essentially sub-processes exist, HTN planning provides a very fast approach. In [2] the model checking planner MBP is presented. Model checking is based on nondeterministic state-transition systems. States are not represented explicitly. It has the ability to generate conformant and contingent plans. It can also generate cyclic plans and has the notion of extended goals. Through extended goals it is possible to impose requirements not only on the goal state but also on intermediate states. But it is not able to create compositions with parallel control flows as the definition of state transition systems is restricted to invoking just one service per state transition.

We are using heuristic search instead of any of the above-mentioned approaches as heuristic search promises to be easily extensible to support optimization for QoS properties and the adaption towards semi-automated composition. Heuristic search algorithms are currently not used for automated service composition. Our work is based upon previous research by Hoffmann and Nebel who developed the planners FF [9] and Metric-FF [5]. They introduced Enforced Hill-Climbing and Relaxed Graphplan as a heuristic. Metric-FF also supports numerical properties and the optimization for them. This functionality can be used to optimize for QoS properties. As demonstrated earlier their algorithm does not support uncertainty about the initial state or service invocation effects, is not able to compose parallel or alternative control flows, and does not create intermediate variables.

Recently, several extensions to heuristic search algorithms were proposed to support some of the required features [13,14,15,16]. But all of them are based on the restricted planning model imposed by the Planning Domain Description Language (PDDL) and thus are not able to created intermediate variables [7]. LPG [13] performs heuristic search in plan space instead of state space. The nodes of the search space are (partial) plans and transitions between them are plan refinement operations (e.g.: adding an additional service invocation). LPG is a temporal planner and hence supports parallel control flow. Compositions are partially ordered and durations are assigned to service invocations. LPG supports optimization for duration and other numerical properties. It can not deal with uncertainty and it cannot create alternative control flows. Sapa [14] is also a temporal planner and supports optimization for duration and numerical properties. But unlike LPG it does perform search in state space. In that regard it is very similar to FF and Metric-FF. Sapa uses A* as the search strategy. In contrast to Enforced Hill-Climbing is A* complete and optimal if an admissible heuristic is used. We did not use A* because you have to trade in performance for completeness and optimality. Sapa does not support uncertainty and the creation of alternative control flows. Conformant-FF [15] and Contingent-FF [16] are both extension of the original FF planner. They extend it by functionality for conformant planning and contingent planning. Both work with uncertainty through the notion of *belief states*. A belief state is equivalent to our extended state definition and incorporates a set disjunction-free states. It represents the possible states. For Conformant-FF the main difference to FF is the handling of the belief states: Planning starts in a set of possible states and is finished if all the possible current states satisfy the goal. It creates conformant plans without alternative control flows and is therefore not usable for automated service composition. Contingent-FF on the other hand creates contingent plans that include alternative control flows. It is quite similar to out approach. Through its more efficient representation of possible states and further optimizations it has some advantages over our approach. But it does currently not support parallel control flow and alternative control flows are not merged resulting in tree-shaped compositions.

6 Conclusion

In this paper we presented a heuristic search algorithm for automated service composition. It supports the creation of composition with parallel and alternative control flows allowing uncertainty about the initial state and service effects. The ability to create variables during composition ensures its applicability in real world business scenarios. Our implementation currently significantly is slower than FF and its descendants. There are two main reasons for this: a larger search space and missing optimizations. The search space is larger than the one of FF as we search for possible parallel invocations and create intermediate variables on the fly. Several different optimization strategies for heuristic search algorithms have been proposed. With *helpful actions* [9] or *favored actions*[17] a subset of the invokable services representing the most promising ones is defined. Evaluating them first often considerably increases performance. In Conformant-FF and Contingent-FF belief states are represented by the initial state and the invoked service sequence reducing efforts to calculating the actual state. Adapting these optimizations to our approach will increase performance significantly.

Future directions of our research will be directed at extending the composer by numerical state properties. This extension allows for the representation of Quality of Service properties (e.g. price, execution time). Using these properties during composition makes it possible to optimize for desired values. We are also adapting the search algorithm to work in a semi-automated modeling environment. Here a human modeler creates the composition, but the composition component assists him by finding matching services / sub-compositions or verifying that a composition fulfills a given goal.

References

1. Zeng, L., Benatallah, B., Lei, H., Ngu, A., Flaxer, D., Chang, H.: Flexible Composition of Enterprise Web Services. Electronic Markets – Web Services **13** (2003) 141–152
2. Pistore, M., Barbon, F., Bertoli, P., Shaparau, D., Traverso, P.: Planning and monitoring web service composition. In: Workshop on Planning and Scheduling for Web and Grid Services (held in conjunction with The 14th International Conference on Automated Planning and Scheduling. (2004) 70 – 71
3. Sirin, E., Parsia, B., Wu, D., Hendler, J., Nau, D.: HTN planning for web service composition using shop2. Journal of Web Semantics **1** (2004) 377–396
4. Berardi, D., Calvanese, D., Giacomo, G.D., Mecella, M.: Composition of services with nondeterministic observable behaviour. In: Proceedings of the Third International Conference on Service-Oriented Computing. Volume 3826 of Lecture Notes In Computer Science., Heidelberg (2005) 520–526
5. Hoffmann, J.: Metric-FF planning system: Translating "ignoring delete lists" to numeric state variables. Journal Of Artificial Intelligence Research **20** (2003) 291 – 341
6. Meyer, H., Kuropka, D.: Requirements for automated service composition. In Eder, J., Dustdar, S., eds.: Business Process Management Workshops. Volume 4103 of Lecture Notes In Computer Science., Heidelberg, Springer (2006) (to appear).

7. Boddy, M.: Imperfect match: PDDL 2.1 and real applications. Journal Of Artificial Intelligence Research **20** (2003) 133 – 137
8. W3C: Web Services Description Language (WSDL) 1.1. (2001)
9. Hoffmann, J., Nebel, B.: The FF planning system: Fast plan generation through heuristic search. Journal of Artificial Intelligence Research **14** (2001) 253 – 302
10. Chapman, D.: Planning for conjunctive goals. Artificial Intelligence **32** (1987) 333–377
11. Erol, K., Nau, D.S., Subrahamnian, V.: Complexity, decidability and undecidability results for domain-independent planning. Artificial Intelligence **76** (1995) 75–88
12. Blum, A., Furst, M.: Fast planning through planning graph analysis. Artificial Intelligence **90** (1997) 281–300
13. Gerevini, A., Saetti, A., Serina, I.: Planning through stochastic local search and temporal action graphs. Journal of Artificial Intelligence Research **20** (2003) 239 – 290
14. Do, M., Kambhampati, S.: Sapa: A multi-objective metric temporal planner. Journal Of Artificial Intelligence Research **20** (2003) 155 – 194
15. Brafman, R., Hoffmann, J.: Conformant planning via heuristic forward search: A new approach. In Sven Koenig, Shlomo Zilbe Koenig, S.Z., ed.: Proceedings of the 14th International Conference on Automated Planning and Scheduling (ICAPS-04), Morgan-Kaufmann (2004) 355 – 364
16. Hoffmann, J., Brafman, R.: Contingent planning via heuristic forward search with implicit belief states. In: Proceedings of the 15th International Conference on Automated Planning and Scheduling (ICAPS-05), Morgan-Kaufmann (2005)
17. McDermott, D.: A heuristic estimator for means-ends analysis in planning. In: Proceedings of the International Conference on Artificial Intelligence Planning Systems. (1996) 142–149

Structured Service Composition*

Rik Eshuis, Paul Grefen, and Sven Till

Eindhoven University of Technology, Department of Technology Management
P.O. Box 513, 5600 MB Eindhoven, The Netherlands
{h.eshuis, p.w.p.j.grefen, s.till}@tm.tue.nl

Abstract. Composition languages like BPEL and many enactment tools only support structured process models, while most composition approaches only consider unstructured models. In this paper, we outline a semi-automatic approach for composing a set of services with data flow dependencies into a structured process model. These data flow dependencies can be automatically derived from the input and output messages of each service, but some additional user input is needed to annotate dependencies with specific branching types. Heart of the approach is a fully automatic composition algorithm that given an annotated dependency graph constructs a structured composition. We illustrate the approach by applying it to an example case study from the CrossWork project, which studies the dynamic formation of cross-organisational workflows.

Keywords: Process and service composition, cross-organisational process support, formal models in business process management.

1 Introduction

Today, companies more and more focus on their core competences, relying on competences of other companies to deliver requested products or services. The resulting cross-company collaborations give rise to networked organisations, in which one company acts as main contractor and the network partners deliver products and services to the main contractor. The market dictates that these networks are highly agile and efficient. This typically means that networks are formed on an ad hoc basis, depending upon a specific service requested by a customer.

The most promising technology to support this way of working is service-oriented computing. Web services are self-contained functions that are defined in an implementation-independent way, usually in WSDL [8]. Their descriptions are published in a publicly accessible repository. Service consumers can search for specific web services offered by providers and invoke the found web services. Upon request of a customer, a main contractor can search the repository for basic services offered by service providers and orchestrate these into a composite

* This work is supported by the IST project CrossWork (No. 507590) and the IST Network of Excellence INTEROP (No. 508011).

S. Dustdar, J.L. Fiadeiro, and A. Sheth (Eds.): BPM 2006, LNCS 4102, pp. 97–112, 2006.

service that meets the customer's request. When the composite service is enacted, the main contractor (service composer) invokes the basic services in the order specified in the service orchestration.

While BPEL [2] has emerged as standard language for describing service compositions, the actual problem of how to orchestrate a set of given services, still remains open. Formal approaches [10,17,18,22] focus on automated service composition. There, the effect of each service is modelled with a pre- and post-condition. This allows the application of techniques from AI planning and program synthesis to orchestrate the services into a composite service. However, it puts the burden on the service provider to formally specify its services and to annotate the WSDL specifications with this additional information.

Other approaches are more pragmatic and derive graph-based compositions by analysing input/output dependencies between services [5,15]. In graph-based compositions, services are coordinated through control elements like AND-splits, AND-joins, XOR-splits, and XOR-joins. Though such approaches do not require any annotation of the web services, they suffer from another disadvantage: Graph-based process models can contain flaws, for example deadlocks. Executing such a flawed composition could result in failures at run-time, which involves considerable expense to repair.

This problem with graph-based models disappears if the models are structured[1], i.e., if each split has a corresponding join and if the split-join pairs are properly nested [13,16]. Models violating this constraint are similar to programs containing goto's. The most important orchestration language, BPEL, is mainly structured (BPEL only allows cross links between parallel services and parallel blocks). Moreover, the research on workflow patterns has shown that each of the evaluated workflow enactment tools supports structured process models [1]. Thus, considering structured compositions only is a reasonable choice.

The goal of this paper is to outline a semi-automatic approach for composing a given set of services into a structured composition, i.e. a structured process model. The approach consists of several steps. First, dependencies between services are derived based on the input and output messages of each service. Next, these abstract dependencies are typed with concrete branching types like AND and XOR. Finally, the concrete dependencies are used to compose the services into a structured process model. While the first and last step can be fully automated, the second step needs user input, as we argue in Sect. 3.

The remainder of this paper is organised as follows. Section 2 gives an overview of the composition approach. Section 3 defines dependency graphs. We distinguish between abstract and concrete dependency graphs, concrete ones specifying types for branching points. Section 4 defines an algorithm which given an abstract dependency graph, fully automatically constructs a structured

[1] Structured process models should not be confused with structured processes. These latter allow their structure to be specified in any model, including graph-based ones. In that terminology, processes supported by for example groupware are unstructured.

composition without branching types. Next, it defines how concrete dependency graph can be used to type the structured composition. Section 5 discusses how the approach is applied in the CrossWork project [9] to achieve a peer-to-peer integration of black-box workflows. Section 6 gives an overview of related work. Finally, Sect. 7 winds up with conclusions and further work.

2 Overview

To motivate the composition approach, we consider a simple purchasing process which consists of a number of services. Some services output data that is required by other services. The composition has to respect these data flow dependencies. The services and their dependencies are shown in graph form in Fig. 1. Section 3 defines these graph forms formally.

By means of an arrow, we show that some service depends on another service. For example, Make production plan depends on input from Receive order. This dependency information can be easily derived from the signatures of the services (see Sect. 3). If a service has more than one incoming (outgoing dependency), then either all the previous (next) services can be done (AND) or only one (XOR).

Figure 2 shows a structured composition that complies with the dependencies shown in Fig. 1. The circles indicate splits (more than one outgoing edge) and joins (more than one incoming edge). Circles with an A denote AND splits/joins whereas ones with an O denote XOR splits/joins. Note that in structured process models circles come in pairs and that each pair has the same type (either A or O).

Furthermore, note that some dependencies are translated only indirectly into control flow. For example, in Fig. 2 there is no edge connecting Check credit and Create invoice. For graph-structured compositions, such an edge would have been created in the composition. However, there is a path from Check credit to Create invoice, thus the desired dependency is respected by the composition.

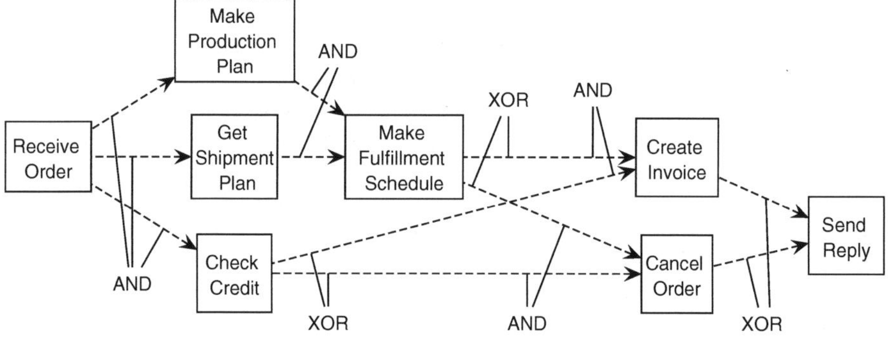

Fig. 1. Services for purchasing process and their dependencies

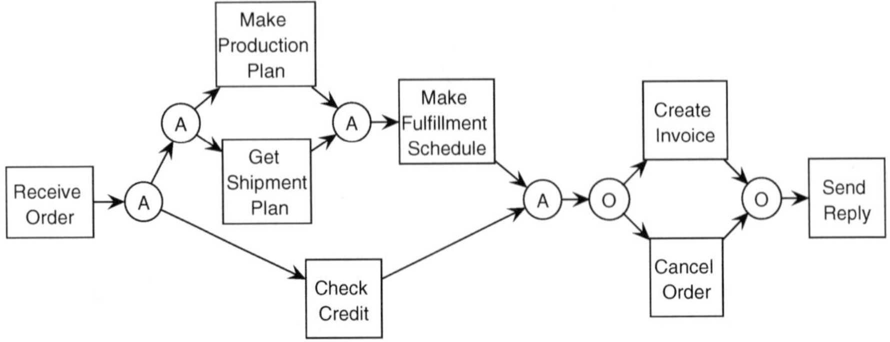

Fig. 2. Structured composition for Fig. 1

In general, however, the composition can be even more different from the data flow, since dependencies might not be structured. For example, a dependency might require a synchronisation between two parallel blocks (blocks are explained in Sect. 4). Such a synchronisation is not allowed in structured process models. This implies that a structured process implementing such a synchronisation looks quite different from the data flow dependency graph.

For example the dependencies in Fig. 3 cannot be implemented straightforwardly in a structured model. Figure 5 shows a flawed composition in which the data flow dependencies are directly translated into control flow dependencies. The composition is flawed because it is not structured: there is a synchronisation between two blocks.

Figure 4 shows a structured composition that does satisfy the dependencies. The dependency graph in Fig. 3 is abstract: it does not contain explicit information about AND and XOR dependencies. Therefore, we use the generic notion of a composite block, indicated with the symbol C inside the circles.

3 Dependency Graphs

First we define and explain abstract dependency graphs. Next, concrete dependency graphs, which extend abstract dependency graphs with specific branching types, are introduced. Finally, we discuss how dependency graphs can be constructed.

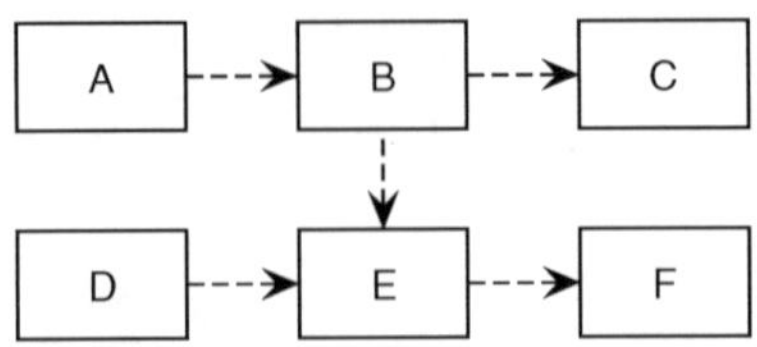

Fig. 3. Services with cross synchronisation dependencies

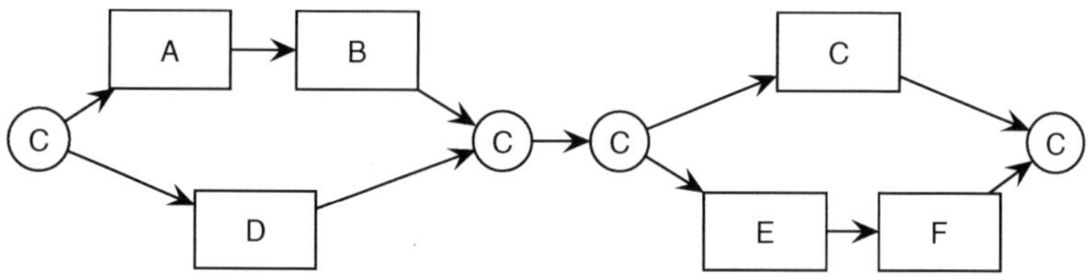

Fig. 4. Structured composition for Fig. 3

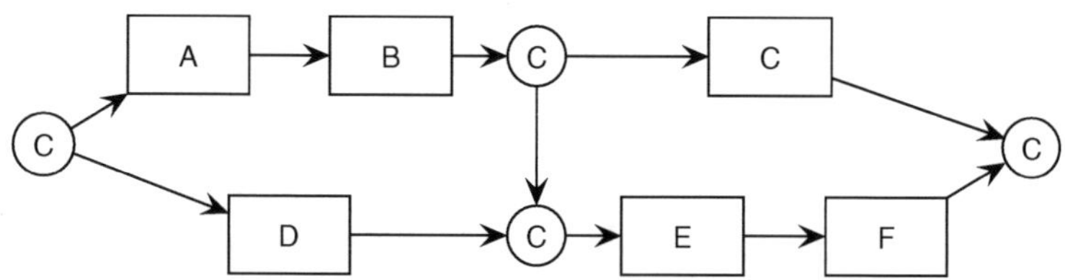

Fig. 5. Non-structured composition for Fig. 3

3.1 Abstract Dependency Graphs

Services communicate with each other through messages. Each message consists of a set of typed data items. Inline with existing work on ontological-based matching of data types in the context of services [6,20], we consider business types here, not low-level data types. For example, a message could comprise a data item of type order and a data item of type customer. Given a message m, we denote by $types(m)$ the set of types of the data items in m. For each service s, $input(s)$ denotes its input message and $output(s)$ its output message. One of these messages is required, otherwise the service does not need to be composed with the other services.

Based on the input/output data types of each service, we can define dependencies between services. If a service a outputs a data item with a certain type and service b needs as input a data item with the same type, then b depends on a. More advanced notions of matching outputs to inputs, for example those based on ontological concepts [6,20], can be easily used instead. If multiple messages refer to the same stateful data item, some additional dependencies based on the states need to be defined, but we do not consider that here.

We capture dependencies between a set S of services in a graph. An *abstract dependency graph* is a tuple (S, E) with

- $S \stackrel{\text{df}}{=} \{s_1, s_2, .., s_n\}$ a set of services
- $E \stackrel{\text{df}}{=} \{(s, s') \in S \times S | type(data(output(s)) \cap type(data(input(s'))) \neq \emptyset\}$

Note that the notion of dependency graph is quite generic and is also used in areas like program analysis and database systems. Other works in service composition like [15] also use dependency graphs.

When defining the algorithm in Sect. 4, we use some auxiliary functions on dependency graphs. Given a service s, its set of pre-condition services, written $pre(s)$ are those services on which s depends. Symmetrically, the set of post condition services of s, written $post(s)$, are those services that depend on s:

$$pre(s) \stackrel{\text{df}}{=} \{x|(x,y) \in E \wedge y = s\}.$$
$$post(s) \stackrel{\text{df}}{=} \{y|(x,y) \in E \wedge x = s\}.$$

For the algorithm, we require that each dependency graph with services $s_1, s_2 \in S$ satisfies the following constraints:

C1 The dependency graph is acyclic.
C2 If there is an edge from s_1 to s_2, then there is no path with length greater than 1 from s_1 to s_2.

The first constraint rules out the construction of loops. The relaxation of this constraint to deal with the construction of structured loops is planned as future work.

The second constraint is needed for the algorithm, but is not very restrictive. Dependency graphs violating the constraint can be easily repaired, by either removing the violating dependency since it is redundant, or by putting an empty service between services s_1 and s_2 for each pair s_1, s_2 of violating services. The latter solution is needed to construct if-then-else compositions with an empty else-branch.

To illustrate the differences, consider the two examples in Fig. 6, which both violate C2. For example (a), the most obvious solution would be to remove the dependency Receive Order→Process Order, since archiving is always done and therefore the dependency is redundant. But for (b), the most logical solution is to include an empty service between Receive Credit Application and Send Notification, since Assess Risk is only required for credit applications over a certain limit (if-then-else construct). Note that we resolved both violations by applying domain knowledge. This obviously implies that we need user input.

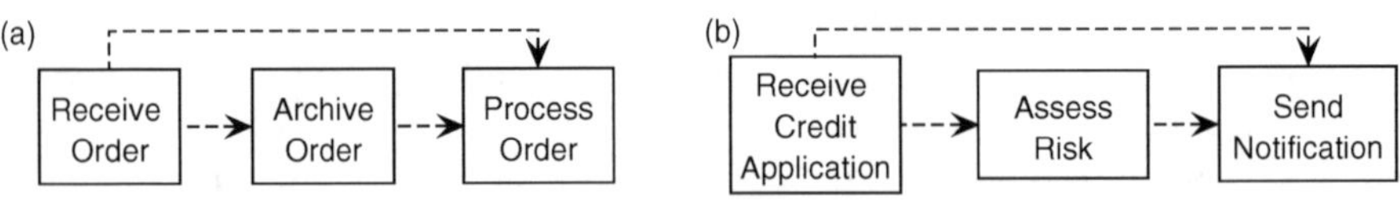

Fig. 6. Two dependency graphs violating C2

3.2 Concrete Dependency Graphs

A *concrete dependency graph* is a tuple $(S, E, join, fork)$ where (S, E) is an abstract dependency graph and functions *join* and *fork* label respectively the incoming and outgoing dependencies of a service with the branching type:

$$join, fork : S \to \{AND, XOR\}.$$

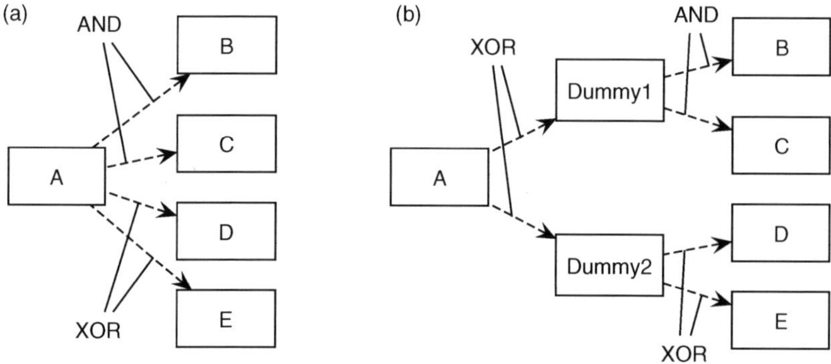

Fig. 7. Invalid dependency graph (a) and valid dependency graph with same dependencies as (b)

We require that $join(s)$ only exists if s has more than one service on which it depends. Similarly, $fork(s)$ only exists if s has more than one service that depends on s.

These functions are only used in the second stage (see Sect. 4.3). Note that inconsistencies can arise in that latter stage, so not every labelling yields a valid composition. We elaborate on this in Sect. 4.3.

The labelling assigns one type only to incoming resp. outgoing dependencies. This might seem restrictive. For example, languages like XPDL [25] allow that some incoming or outgoing links have type AND while other have type XOR. Thus, the dependency graph in Fig. 7(a) would be valid in XPDL. However, we rule it out since it is ambiguous: it is not specified whether for example B and D can be done both or are exclusive.

This restriction can be overcome by using empty services, which have no implementation but whose sole purpose is to describe dependencies. For example, Fig. 7(b) shows a dependency graph with the same services and dependencies as in Fig. 7(a), but now two empty services are included. Now, the dependency between for example B and D is made precise: either B is done or D but not both.

3.3 Constructing Dependency Graphs

Abstract dependency graphs can be derived completely automatically from the signature of the web services, as explained in Sect. 3.1. However, to resolve violations of C2, some user input is needed, as argued in Sect. 3.1.

Concrete dependency graphs are then constructed by the user (a domain expert), by specifying in the abstract dependency graph for each service the type of its incoming and outgoing dependencies. The reason for doing this manually is that message dependencies themselves are usually not sufficient to decide on the type of a dependency. For example, consider two services that both have as input an order for some goods. If both services deal with shipping, they would be exclusive and type XOR would be used. If one service deals with picking up the requested goods from the warehouse and another with calculating the total fee to be paid, both services are required and type AND would be useful.

4 The Algorithm

First, we explain the structured composition language. Next we explain the construction algorithm which takes as input an abstract dependency graph and outputs a structured composition. Finally, we explain how such a structured composition can be typed by analysing the concrete dependency graph.

4.1 Structured Composition Language

Various formalisations of structured workflow models exist [13,23]. We choose here a hierarchical view, where leaf nodes are services and non-leaf nodes are blocks. In the graphical syntax, the beginning and end of a block is demarcated by a split and join node respective.

We consider two kinds of blocks here: composite blocks of type $COMP$ and sequential blocks of type SEQ. In the next section, $COMP$ blocks are annotated with types AND or XOR.

The children of blocks are specified as parameters, a set in case of $COMP$ and a list in case of SEQ blocks. For example $COMP\{SEQ[X, Y], SEQ[Z]\}$ is a process in which X is done before Y and both are done in parallel with or exclusive to Z. The following definition formalises this.

Given a set of S of services, the following inductive definition formalises the set of structured compositions on S:

- Each service $s \in S$ is a structured composition.
- If $X_1, X_2, .., X_n$ are structured compositions, then so are $SEQ[X_1, X_2, .., X_n]$ and $COMP\{X_1, X_2, .., X_n\}$.

In the algorithm, we use some additional functions on blocks. Given a block b, we denote by $children(b)$ the children of b and by $parent(b)$ the unique parent block of b. Since we consider a hierarchical structure, each block has one parent, except the root of the hierarchy which has no parent. Finally, $services(b)$ indicates the set of services that are a direct or indirect child of b. For example, $services(COMP\{SEQ[X, Y], SEQ[Z]\}) = \{X, Y, Z\}$.

4.2 Construction Algorithm

The construction algorithm is listed in Fig. 8. It takes as input a dependency graph and returns a structured composition satisfying the input dependencies. Due to space limitations, we do not provide a formal proof of correctness, but it can be observed that each operation changing the constructed structured composition results in another structured composition. The definition is strongly inspired by an existing algorithm to translate Petri nets into statecharts [11].

```
1: procedure StructuredComposition((S, E))
2:     C := SEQ[constructBlock(Initial(S, E))]
3:     processed := Initial(S, E)
4:     while processed ≠ S do do
5:         toprocess := next(processed)
6:         for each maximal influencing subset I of toprocess do
7:             BlockI := constructBlock(I)
8:             InputI := {s ∈ processed|post(s) ∈ I}
9:             N := the most nested block in C containing all services in InputI.
10:            if N is composite then
11:                NotPreI := {c ∈ children(N)|InputI ∩ services(c) = ∅}
12:                if NotPreI ≠ ∅ then
13:                    PreI := COMP{c ∈ children(N)|InputI ∩ services(c) ≠ ∅}
14:                    N' := COMP({SEQ[PreI, BlockI]} ∪ NotPreI)
15:                    replace N by N' in C
16:                else
17:                    parent(N).append(BlockI)
18:                end if
19:            else
20:                parent(N).append(BlockI)
21:            end if
22:            processed := processed ∪ I.
23:        end for
24:    end while
25:    return C
26: end procedure
```

Fig. 8. Algorithm for constructing structured compositions

In the initial phase, a composition is created (l. 2) from the set of $Initial(S, E)$ of initial services, i.e. the services not depending on any other service:

$$Initial(S, E) = \{s_1 \in S | \nexists s_2 \in S : (s_1, s_2) \in E\}$$

Function $constructBlock(X)$ composes a given set X of services into either a single service (if X is singleton), or otherwise into a composite block consisting of a set of sequential blocks, each containing one service from X.

$$constructBlock(X) = \begin{cases} x & \text{, if } X = \{x\} \\ COMP\{SEQ[x] | x \in X\} & \text{, otherwise} \end{cases}$$

Next, the set *processed* of services in S that are already processed is updated with the initial services (l. 3).

In the main phase, the structured composition is iteratively constructed by processing services in S. In each iteration, first the set of services to be processed in this iteration is determined and put in *toprocess* (l. 5).

A service can be processed next if all services on which it depends have been processed, in other words, all its input data can be delivered by previously processed services. Function *next* returns the services to be processed next,

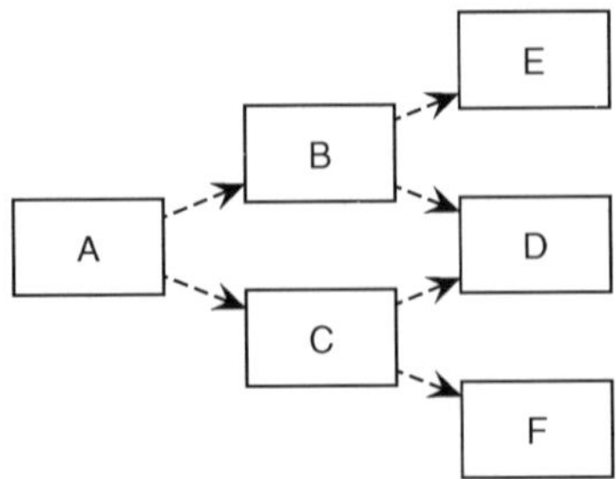

Fig. 9. Example dependency graph

which are those unprocessed services whose pre-condition services have been processed:

$$next(processed, S) \stackrel{\text{df}}{=} \{ \ s \in S \mid pre(s) \subseteq processed \ \} \setminus processed.$$

To explain lines 6-23, we first observe that services in the set *toprocess* cannot be processed one by one. To see why, consider the example in Fig. 9. Suppose services A, B and C have been processed, then *next* returns D, E, and F. Now, D depends on both B and C. To translate this into control flow, the block encompassing both B and C has to end before D. But this implies that the block also ends before E and F. To achieve this, D, E, and F need to be processed as a group.

To define precisely which services need to be processed in a group, we introduce the notion of influence. Two services are *directly influenced* by each other if they depend on the same service, i.e., their pre-conditions overlap. For example, in Fig. 9, services B and C both depend on A, and therefore directly influence each other. Note that each service directly influences itself.

Two services s_1, s_2 *influence* each other if they either directly influence each other or if there is another service s that directly influences s_1 and influences s_2. (Thus, mathematically speaking, the influence relation is the transitive closure of the direct influence relation.) For example, in Fig. 9 services E and F influence each other even though their pre-conditions are disjoint, since D directly influences both E and F.

A set of services is influencing if each of the services influences all other services in the set. An influencing set I of services is maximal compared to set of services X if adding any service $s \in X \setminus I$ would result in a non-influencing set. For example, if in Fig. 9 $X = \{\mathsf{D}, \mathsf{E}, \mathsf{F}\}$, then $I = \{\mathsf{D}\}$ is not a maximal influencing set, since E and F are lacking. Hence, the only possible set I is X itself.

Maximal influencing subsets of services are processed in lines 6-23. To explain these lines, consider the dependency graph in Fig. 1, and suppose the algorithm starts the second iteration. After the first iteration, the constructed composition is $C{=}SEQ$[Receive order, $COMP\{SEQ$[Make Production Plan],SEQ[Get Shipment Plan],SEQ[Check Credit]$\}$]. For the second iteration, the only service to be processed is Make Fulfillment Schedule, so $I = \{$Make Fulfillment Schedule$\}$.

In line 7, first the block comprising the services in I is constructed.

Next, line 8 defines the set $InputI$ of services in *processed* on which services in I depend. For the example, $InputI$ = {Make Production Plan, Get Shipment Plan}.

Set $InputI$ is used next (l. 9) to search the constructed composition for the most nested block N containing all pre-condition services for I. For the example, N=$COMP${SEQ[Make Production Plan],SEQ[Get Shipment Plan],SEQ[Check Credit]}.

If N is a basic service (l. 19), then $BlockI$ can be appended to the SEQ block parent of N (l. 20). Note that by construction, each basic service has a SEQ parent.

If N is a $COMP$ block (l. 10), there are two cases.

- N is a $COMP$ block having some child blocks that do not contain any service pre-condition to I (l. 12). Then the new block $BlockI$ only needs to be appended to those child blocks of N on which services in I depend. Hence, $BlockI$ needs to be inserted into N, rather than appended to the parent of N.
  In the example, child block SEQ[Check Credit] of N does not contain any service input to Make Fulfillment Schedule. Thus, Make Fulfillment Schedule does not need to be appended to Check Credit, but only to the block encompassing Make Production Plan and Get Shipment Plan.
  In line 13 a new composite block $PreI$ is constructed which has only those children of N that contain services on which some service in I depends. For the example, $PreI$ becomes $COMP${SEQ[Make Production Plan],SEQ[Get Shipment Plan]}.
  Next, the new block N' is a composite block, consisting of one sequential child block consisting of $PreI$ followed by $BlockI$, plus the child blocks in $NotPreI$, which do not contain any service that is pre-condition to I (l. 14). For the example, N' =$COMP${SEQ[Check Credit],SEQ[$COMP${SEQ[Make Production Plan],SEQ[Get Shipment Plan]},Make Fulfillment Schedule]}.
  Finally, N' can replace N (l. 15).
- If every child block of N contains a service that is pre-condition to a service in I (l. 16), then $BlockI$ can be simply appended to the SEQ block parent of N (l. 17).

Finally, the constructed composition is returned (l. 25).

4.3 Concrete Dependencies

As explained in Sect. 3, if a service has multiple incoming or outgoing dependencies, these dependencies can be annotated with types. The resulting dependency graph is a concrete dependency graph.

Concrete dependency graphs can be used in a straightforward manner to type composite $COMP$ nodes in the structured composition returned by the algorithm in Fig. 8. If a service s has more than one outgoing dependency, then each $COMP$ block b for which each child has services that depend on s, gets the type $fork(s)$. Symmetrically, if a service s has more than one incoming dependency, then each $COMP$ block b for which each child has services on which s depends, gets type $join(s)$. The following definition defines this formally:

$$type : COMP \rightarrow \{AND, XOR\}$$

$$type(b) \stackrel{\text{df}}{=} \begin{cases} fork(s) & \text{, if for every child } c \text{ of } b,\ services(c) \cap post(s) \neq \emptyset \\ join(s) & \text{, if for every child } c \text{ of } b,\ services(c) \cap pre(s) \neq \emptyset \end{cases}$$

Note that an inconsistent labelling of the concrete dependency graph might lead to conflicting types being assigned to the same block. For example, if in Fig. 1 $join$(Make Fulfillment Schedule) would be XOR rather than AND, this would mean that Make Production Plan and Get Shipment Plan are exclusive, while $fork$(Receive Order) stipulates they are done both. In that case, the structured composition cannot be typed in a consistent way, and the concrete dependency graph should be changed.

5 CrossWork Case Study

In this section, the complete approach is explained by means of a case study from the IST project CrossWork [9]. The goal of CrossWork is to support the dynamic formation of Networks of Automotive Excellence (NoAE). These networks are virtual enterprises, consisting of automotive suppliers that collaborate with each other to deliver a product requested by an OEM. Examples of such a product are the interior of a car or a watertank for a truck. Suppliers need to collaborate since an individual supplier is typically not large enough to handle a product request of an OEM all by itself. An NoAE is formed dynamically, depending upon the specific product request received by one specific supplier (the main contractor). The two main steps in dynamic NoAE formation is finding the partner suppliers that can deliver parts of the requested product (team formation) and constructing a global NoAE workflow that coordinates and integrates the local workflows of the individual suppliers (workflow formation). This paper focuses on the last part.

In the case study, an OEM requests a watertank from one member of a cluster of automotive suppliers. We assume the member has selected the partners. The

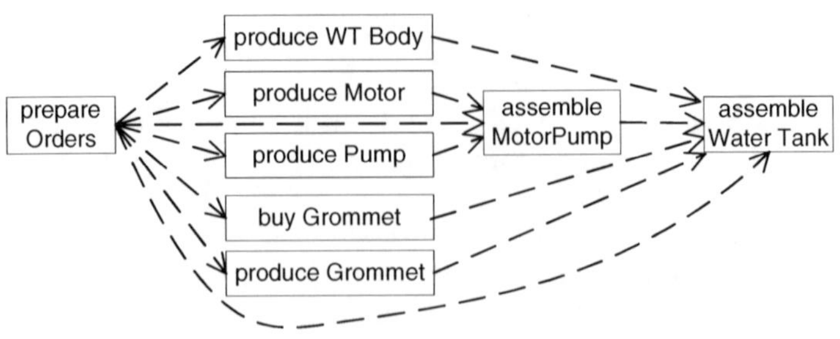

Fig. 10. Abstract dependency graph

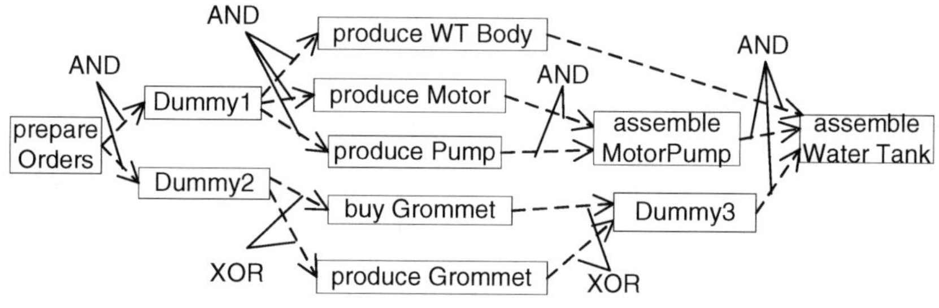

Fig. 11. Concrete dependency graph for Fig. 10

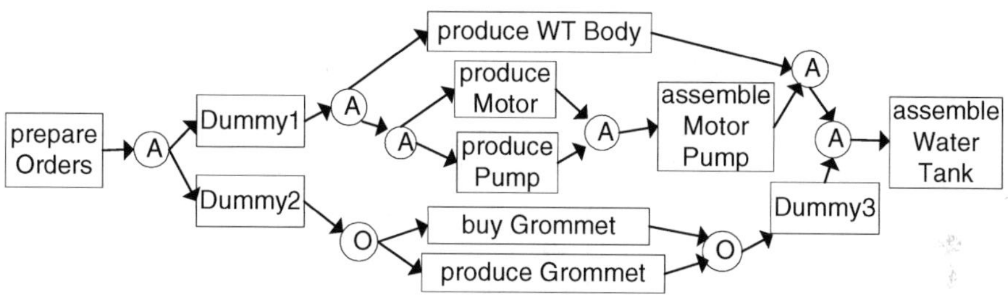

Fig. 12. Structured composition for Fig. 11

workflow of each partner is shown as a black box service in Fig. 10. Thus, the internal structure of the local workflows is hidden, but partner suppliers can offer an external view to the entire network through some additional interfaces [12]. Note that the dependency graph in Fig. 10 violates the second constraint on dependency graphs, since there is an edge connecting Prepare Orders and Assemble Motorpump. Therefore, the user (a domain expert) has to provide a corrected version, and also needs to annotate the dependencies with types. Figure 11 shows a corrected concrete dependency graph. For example, the user has decided that only one of the services produceGrommet and buyGrommet is necessary. Next, three dummy services were needed to obtain a valid typing. Furthermore, some direct dependencies, e.g. between prepareOrders and assembleMotorPump have been removed, because the user decided they are redundant (e.g. prepareOrders delivers input to assembleMotorPump by means of produceMotor).

Finally, the workflow is composed using the algorithm defined in Sect. 4. The result of the composition is shown in Figure 12. This workflow is now ready to be fed into a workflow engine and to organize a production of a watertank. For the demonstrator prototype, a BPEL engine is used.

6 Related Work

The topic of service composition has attracted already the attention of many researchers. Existing approaches can be classified into three categories: manual, partly automated, or fully automated. Approaches in the manual category assume that a user manually designs a service composition, including the binding to concrete web services. In this category we find languages like BPEL [2] and JOpera [21] and concrete composition prototypes [3,26].

In approaches in the semi-automatic category [7,19], the user must provide a composition skeleton which defines the process logic. This skeleton is then instantiated automatically by searching for atomic services that match each of the services specified in the skeleton. The focus of these approaches lies on automatically finding substitute services for a specified service.

Fully automatic approaches (e.g. [4,10,17,24]) mostly come from the field of AI or formal reasoning. These approaches require that web services are specified formally with pre- and post-conditions. This puts a considerable burden on the shoulders of service designers, since WSDL specifications do not require that level of detail and hence need to be annotated with the additional pre- and post-conditions.

Though our approach is semi-automatic, the actual composition algorithm is fully automated. Compared to the automated composition approaches, our approach is much simpler since we do not require formally specified pre- and post-conditions, and thus user do not have to provide as much input as in the mentioned other approaches. Drawback, however, is that our approach is less precise, since service dependencies are less detailed than pre- and post-conditions.

As explained in the introduction (Sect. 1), the work most resembling ours is [5,15]. However, these approaches focus on composing unstructured process models, while we construct structured ones. As shown in Sect. 2, constructing structured models is more complex since data flow dependencies cannot be translated directly into structured control flow. In fact, we are aware of only one other approach [10] that constructs structured process models, but that one is based on formal pre and post-condition reasoning.

Another way of dealing with the unstructuredness problem would be to transform an unstructured process model into a structured one. Some preliminary research has been done on this topic [13,14,16], based on techniques developed in the 70's and 80's to structure sequential programs containing goto's. Unfortunately, converting an unstructured process model into a structured one has revealed to be quite intricate, because process models can contain parallelism while programs are sequential. Consequently, only for sequential process models automated transformations exist. We therefore have adopted an approach in which services are directly composed into a structured process model.

7 Conclusions and Further Work

We have presented an approach for composing services into a structured composition. Though the approach itself requires manual input, a large part of it is fully automated. Key part is an algorithm that given a set of services and their interdependencies, fully automatically constructs a structured composition satisfying the given dependencies. The user must still give input to the algorithm by annotating the dependency graphs. However, this work is a lot less than annotating services with formal pre- and post-conditions, which is required by most other comparable service composition approaches.

Key feature of the approach is that the constructed compositions are structured and make use only of basic workflow patterns that are supported by virtually every workflow tool [1]. This feature enables the constructed compositions to be encoded straightforwardly into any process language including BPEL [2] and other standard languages like XPDL [25]. However, it considerably complicates the composition task, since dependencies cannot be translated directly into control flow links.

For further work, we plan to extend the algorithm to deal with loops. Also, we are currently implementing the algorithm in a prototype in the context of the CrossWork project [9].

References

1. W.M.P. van der Aalst, A.H.M. ter Hofstede, B. Kiepuszewski, and A.P. Barros. Workflow patterns. *Distributed and Parallel Databases*, 14(1):5–51, 2003.
2. T. Anders, F. Curbera, H. Dholakia, Y. Goland, J. Klein, F. Leymann, D. Roller, D. Smith, S. Thatte, I. Trickovic, and S. Weerawarana. Business Process Execution Language for Web Services, Version 1.1. Standards proposal by BEA Systems, International Business Machines Corporation, Microsoft Corporation, SAP AG, Siebel Systems, 2002.
3. B. Benatallah, Q.Z. Sheng, and M. Dumas. The self-serv environment for web services composition. *IEEE Internet Computing*, 7(1):40–48, 2003.
4. D. Berardi, D. Calvanese, G. De Giacomo, M. Lenzerini, and M. Mecella. Automatic service composition based on behavioral descriptions. *International Journal of Cooperative Information Systems*, 14(4), 2005.
5. A. Brogi and R. Popescu. Towards semi-automated workflow-based aggregation of web services. In F. Casati, P. Traverso, and B. Benatallah, editors, *Proceedings of Third International Conference on Service Oriented Computing (ICSOC05)*, Lecture Notes in Computer Science 3826. Springer, 2005.
6. J. Cardoso and A. Sheth. Semantic e-workflow composition. *Journal of Intelligent Information Systems*, 21(3):191–225, 2003.
7. F. Casati and M.-C. Shan. Dynamic and adaptive composition of e-services. *Information Systems*, 26(3):143–162, 2001.
8. E. Christensen, F. Curbera, G. Meredith, and S. Weerawarana. Web Services Description Language (WSDL) 1.1. `http://www.w3.org/TR/wsdl`, 2001.
9. CrossWork consortium. Crosswork project, IST no. 507590. `http://www.crosswork.info`.
10. Z. Duan, A. Bernstein, P. Lewis, and S. Lu. A model for abstract process specification, verification and composition. In *Proceedings of the 2nd international conference on Service oriented computing (ICSOC'04)*, pages 232–241. ACM Press, 2004.
11. R. Eshuis. Statecharting Petri nets. Beta Working Paper Series, WP 153, Eindhoven University of Technology, 2005.
12. P. Grefen. Service-oriented support for dynamic business process management. In D. Georgakopoulos and M. Papazoglou, editors, *Service Oriented Computing*. MIT Press, 2006. To appear.

13. B. Kiepuszewski, A.H.M. ter Hofstede, and C. Bussler. On structured workflow modelling. In B. Wangler and L. Bergman, editors, *Proc. CAiSE '00*, pages 431–445. Springer, 2000.
14. J. Koehler and R. Hauser. Untangling unstructured cyclic flows - a solution based on continuations. In R. Meersman and Z. Tari, editors, *Proc. CoopIS/DOA/ ODBASE 2004*, Lecture Notes in Computer Science 3290, pages 121–138. Springer, 2004.
15. Q. Liang, L. N. Chakarapani, S. Su, R. Chikkamagalur, and H. Lam. A semi-automatic approach to composite web services discovery, description and invocation. *Int. Journal on Web Service Research*, 1(4):64–89, 2004.
16. R. Liu and A. Kumar. An analysis and taxonomy of unstructured workflows. In W.M.P. van der Aalst, B. Benatallah, F. Casati, and F. Curbera, editors, *Proc. 3rd Conference on Business Process Management (BPM 2005)*, Lecture Notes in Computer Science 3649, pages 268–284, 2005.
17. M. Matskin and J. Rao. Value-added web services composition using automatic program synthesis. In C. Bussler, R. Hull, S.A. McIlraith, M.E. Orlowska, B. Pernici, and J. Yang, editors, *CAiSE'02 workshop on Web Services, E-Business, and the Semantic Web, Revised Papers*, Lecture Notes in Computer Science 2512, pages 213–224. Springer, 2002.
18. S.A. McIlraith and T.C. Son. Adapting golog for composition of semantic web services. In D. Fensel, F. Giunchiglia, D.L. McGuinness, and M.-A. Williams, editors, *Proc. of the 8th International Conference on Principles and Knowledge Representation and Reasoning (KR-02)*, pages 482–496. Morgan Kaufmann, 2002.
19. B. Medjahed, A. Bouguettaya, and A. Elmagarmid. Composing Web services on the Semantic Web. *The VLDB Journal*, 12(4):333–351, 2003.
20. M. Paolucci, T. Kawamura, T.R. Payne, and K.P. Sycara. Semantic matching of web services capabilities. In I. Horrocks and J.A. Hendler, editors, *Proc. International Semantic Web Conference (ISWC'02)*, Lecture Notes in Computer Science 2342, pages 333–347. Springer, 2002.
21. C. Pautasso and G. Alonso. The JOpera visual composition language. *Journal of Visual Languages & Computing*, 16(1-2):119–152, 2005.
22. S.R. Ponnekanti and A. Fox. Sword: A developer toolkit for building composite web services. In *Proc. of the 11th International World Wide Web Conference*, 2002.
23. M. Reichert and P. Dadam. ADEPTflex: Supporting Dynamic Changes of Workflow without Loosing Control. *Journal of Intelligent Information Systems*, 10(2):93–129, 1998.
24. P. Traverso and M. Pistore. Automated composition of semantic web services into executable processes. In S.A. McIlraith, D. Plexousakis, and F. van Harmelen, editors, *Proc. Third International Semantic Web Conference ISWC (2004)*, Lecture Notes in Computer Science 3298, pages 380–394. Springer, 2004.
25. Workflow Management Coalition. Workflow process definition interface – XML process definition language. Technical Report WFMC-TC-1025, Workflow Management Coalition, 2002.
26. J. Yang and M. Papazoglou. Service components for managing the life-cycle of service compositions. *Information Systems*, 29(2):97–125, 2004.

Isolating Process-Level Concerns Using Padus

Mathieu Braem[1], Kris Verlaenen[2], Niels Joncheere[1], Wim Vanderperren[1], Ragnhild Van Der Straeten[1], Eddy Truyen[2], Wouter Joosen[2], and Viviane Jonckers[1]

[1] System and Software Engineering Lab (SSEL), Vrije Universiteit Brussel
Pleinlaan 2, 1050 Brussels, Belgium
{mbraem, njonchee, wvdperre, rvdstrae, vejoncke}@vub.ac.be
[2] DistriNet, Katholieke Universiteit Leuven
Celestijnenlaan 200A, 3001 Leuven, Belgium
{kris.verlaenen, eddy.truyen, wouter.joosen}@cs.kuleuven.be

Abstract. Current workflow languages for web services suffer from poor support for separation of concerns. Aspect-oriented software development is a well-known approach to improve this. In this paper, we present an aspect-oriented extension for the WS-BPEL language that improves on current state-of-the-art by introducing an explicit deployment construct, a richer joinpoint model, and a higher-level pointcut language. In addition, the supporting technology is compatible with existing WS-BPEL engines.

Classification. Business process modeling and analysis, processes and service composition.

1 Introduction

Over the last years, *web services* [1] have been gaining a lot of popularity as a means of integrating existing software in new environments. By composing a number of basic web services, new web services can be created that provide more advanced functionality. These compound web services can then be reused in even other web services, which further facilitates software reuse.

Originally, the only way to compose web services was by manually writing the necessary glue-code in programming languages such as C and Java. It quickly became clear, however, that a composition of web services is more naturally captured by dedicated *workflow languages* [2] than by general-purpose programming languages.

Today, the most popular workflow language with regard to the composition of web services is the *Business Process Execution Language* (WS-BPEL) [3]. WS-BPEL builds on the foundations of WSFL [4] and XLANG [5], and can be used to specify both executable business processes and abstract business processes. Executable processes model the behavior of one participant in a composition (i.e. *orchestration*), while abstract business processes specify the externally visible behavior of a composition (i.e. *choreography*). WS-BPEL processes are platform- and transport-independent, and are expressed using XML.

S. Dustdar, J.L. Fiadeiro, and A. Sheth (Eds.): BPM 2006, LNCS 4102, pp. 113–128, 2006.

1.1 Separation of Concerns

In this paper we improve the modularization capability of WS-BPEL in order to provide a better separation of concerns [6] in the workflow specification. In WS-BPEL (and other workflow languages, for that matter) a large number of concerns (such as authorization and billing) cannot be cleanly separated from the main functionality of the workflow specification. WS-BPEL processes suffer from a problem that is named the "tyranny of the dominant decomposition" [7]. A WS-BPEL process can only be decomposed according to the control flow of the process, and concerns that do not align with this decomposition end up scattered across the process specification and tangled with one another. For example, billing requires invoking some billing service each time before and after a certain functionality in the process is provided. This makes it difficult to add, modify, or remove such concerns. Also, because WS-BPEL processes must be specified in a single XML file, complex processes give rise to large XML files which can become difficult to understand, maintain and evolve.

To solve the above problem, we propose to apply *aspect-oriented* decomposition and composition mechanisms to WS-BPEL. Aspect-oriented software development (AOSD) [8] has been gaining a lot of popularity as a means of improving separation of *crosscutting concerns* in software. Examples of such *crosscutting concerns* are security concerns such as access control and confidentiality [9], debugging concerns such as logging [10] and timing contract validation [11], and business rules such as billing [12]. The goal of AOSD is to achieve a better separation of concerns, by allowing crosscutting concerns to be specified in separate modules called *aspects*, so that adding, modifying or removing these concerns does not require changes to the rest of the system.

Traditional aspects consist of two main parts: *pointcut* definitions and *advices*. Points in the program execution where an aspect can be applied (e.g. method invocations in object-oriented programming) are called *joinpoints*. Pointcuts select sets of joinpoints where aspects should be applied; these pointcuts can be expressed using declarative pointcut languages. An advice specifies the concrete behavior that should be executed at certain joinpoints — typically before, after or around the original behavior of the joinpoints. Inserting the behavior defined by aspects at the correct locations in the main program is called *weaving*.

Initial research on AOSD has concentrated on applying its principles to the object-oriented programming paradigm. However, as motivated by Arsanjani *et al.* [13] and others [14,15,16], AOSD has a lot of potential in a web services context, too.

1.2 Web Service Composition in Telecom

The research described in this paper is part of a larger research project, which is named WIT-CASE and is performed in collaboration with Alcatel, and which addresses composition of web services on a telecom service delivery platform. We will therefore illustrate the motivation for our approach by providing examples from within this context. Typical use cases for a telecom service delivery platform include setting up and executing a multi-party conference call. Such use cases mostly have the same general characteristics. For example, the platform needs to check whether the user is allowed to access the functionality he has requested before providing this functionality (authorization), and the user needs to be billed for his usage according to some billing scheme (billing).

Both the authorization and billing concerns are typically crosscutting. Therefore, an aspect-oriented approach can improve the modularization of web service compositions on a telecom service delivery platform. Without support for AOSD, nearly every WS-BPEL process on our platform would start with some authorization code before executing its main functionality, and would perform some billing functionality before and/or after certain resources are used. This means that, when some part of the authorization or billing policies changes, all these processes need to be modified. The presence of more than one authorization or billing policy would even further complicate this situation.

If, on the other hand, support for AOSD is available, crosscutting concerns such as authorization and billing can be expressed separate from the processes' main functionality in dedicated aspects. If authorization or billing policies would change, this would only require changes to the corresponding aspects, and not to the main processes. If one would like to support more than one authorization or billing policy (e.g. fixed fee billing as well as duration billing), it is sufficient to simply implement an additional aspect.

In this paper, we propose an aspect-oriented programming extension for WS-BPEL, named Padus, in order to provide a better separation of concerns. The characteristics of the telecom service delivery platform and the goals of the WIT-CASE project have had a profound impact on the design and implementation of Padus. First of all, the overall workflow specification language should be sufficiently expressive and should support creation of higher-level composition primitives. Moreover, adding AOP support to WS-BPEL should be as less disruptive as possible to the existing tool chain and should introduce as less run-time performance overhead as possible. For these reasons we have chosen to follow an approach in which the design of Padus is based on a logic-based programming language (in order to increase expressive power and ability to construct higher-level composition primitives) and the implementation of Padus is based on a static transformation approach (in order to be compatible with existing tool chain and minimize run-time performance overhead).

The paper is structured as follows. Section 2 describes our AOP language for WS-BPEL, while section 3 describes how this language is implemented. A brief case study is provided in section 4. We present related work in section 5 and state our conclusions in section 6.

2 The Padus Language

We present Padus, an aspect-oriented extension to WS-BPEL, which aims to overcome its lack of support for modularization of crosscutting concerns. It allows introducing crosscutting behavior to an existing WS-BPEL process in a modularized way. Developers can augment WS-BPEL processes with additional behavior at specific points during their execution. These points can be selected using a logic pointcut language, and the Padus weaver can be used to combine the behavior of the core process with the behavior specified in the aspects. Using Padus, the complexity of the core process can be controlled by specifying crosscutting concerns like security and billing in separate aspects.

In this section, we describe the design of the Padus language. We follow the template for describing AOP languages proposed in AOSD-Europe's survey on aspect-oriented programming languages [17]. We describe the language along five dimensions: the joinpoint model (section 2.1), the pointcut and advice languages (sections 2.2 and 2.3), the aspect modules (section 2.4), and the aspect deployment language (section 2.5).

2.1 Joinpoint Model

Joinpoints are well-defined points during the execution of a WS-BPEL process where extra functionality could be inserted. They are related to the activities that are provided in WS-BPEL. Table 1 lists the kinds of joinpoints that are available. Each type is related to a specific WS-BPEL activity, which can be easily deduced from the type's name. The joinpoint model does not only allow behavioral joinpoints but also includes structural joinpoints related to structural WS-BPEL activities (which contain one or more activities themselves).

Table 1. Types of joinpoints available in Padus

Behavioral joinpoints		**Structural joinpoints**	
invoking	replying	sequencing	switching
receiving	assigning	looping ("while")	picking
throwing	terminating	flowing	scoping
compensating	doingNothing ("empty")		

Joinpoints are associated with properties relevant to that particular joinpoint. Some of these properties are related to the attributes and elements of the corresponding WS-BPEL activity. For example, table 2 provides the attributes of "invoking" joinpoints. Additional properties specify, among others, in which WS-BPEL process or structural activity a joinpoint occurs. Dynamic properties, like in which process instance a joinpoint occurs and the value of certain variables, are defined too. Using these properties, one can more precisely select interesting joinpoints.

2.2 Pointcut Language

A pointcut selects a specific set of joinpoints. Pointcuts can be used to specify the joinpoints where additional behavior should be inserted. The pointcut language of Padus is based on logic meta-programming [18,19]. A pointcut can be seen as

Table 2. Attributes of "invoking" joinpoints

Attribute	Type	Description
name	String	An optional name for the WS-BPEL activity
partnerLink	String	The partner link used by the invoke
portType	String	The port type used by the invoke
operation	String	The operation of the port type that is invoked
inputVariable	String	The message that should be sent
outputVariable	String	The variable that should contain the reply message

```
invoking(Joinpoint, 'smsService', 'smsServicePT', Operation),
startsWith(Operation, 'send').
```

Listing 1. Simple pointcut that captures "invoking" joinpoints that invoke an operation of which the name starts with "send"

a collection of constraints on the type and properties of allowed joinpoints. In addition, a pointcut is able to expose certain information (e.g. argument values) so that the advice can exploit this.

The pointcut language defines a predicate for each type of joinpoint. The attributes of the predicate refer to the attributes of that specific type of joinpoint. Table 3 shows the exposed bindings of the invoking predicate. Only the version with the most variables is really required. The others can be written in function of the larger one. The predicates with less variables simply offer extra convenience.

Table 3. Bindings for the "invoking" predicates

Predicate binding	Description
invoking(Joinpoint, Name, PartnerLink, PortType, Operation, InputVariable, OutputVariable)	All allowed attributes
invoking(Joinpoint, Name, PartnerLink, PortType, Operation)	Input and output variable names not bound
invoking(Joinpoint, PartnerLink, PortType, Operation)	Only Partnerlink, PortType and Operation bound

By constraining the attributes of a joinpoint predicate, certain joinpoints can be selected. Pointcuts can combine these predicates with standard predicates that are available in Prolog [20], for comparing basic data types, searching lists, etc. Pointcuts can include negations, and predicates can be combined with conjunctions or disjunctions. The small example in listing 1 denotes a pointcut that covers all "invoking" joinpoints of operations on the `smsServicePT` port type of the `smsService` partner link of which the name of the operation starts with "send".

The pointcut language also offers predicates for constraining or exposing additional (possibly runtime) properties of joinpoints, like for instance the process or process instance a joinpoint occurs in, etc. Table 4 gives an overview of some of these predicates.

Table 4. Predicates for constraining additional properties of joinpoints

Predicate	Description
inProcess(Joinpoint, Process)	Links a joinpoint with the process it is defined in.
inProcessInstance(Joinpoint, ProcessInstance)	Links a joinpoint with the process instance it occurs in.
variableValue(ProcessInstance, Name, Value)	Links the name of a variable to its value in a specific process instance.

Using a logic pointcut language offers significant advantages over more traditional approaches. The pointcuts can use the full power of unification on logic variables (by backtracking). Furthermore, since pointcuts are logic rules that cover joinpoints, new user-defined pointcuts can be reused in the definition of similar pointcuts. The logic engine supporting our pointcut language also allows writing recursive pointcut definitions. The base predicates available in the pointcut language have well chosen names, which can clearly express the intension of the pointcuts and improve readability.

2.3 Advice Language

The advice language is used to specify how the behavior at certain joinpoints defined by a pointcut should be altered. Similar to traditional aspect-oriented systems, advices can either be *added* to the original behavior, or can *replace* the original behavior. New behavior can be introduced by inserting it *before* or *after* certain joinpoints defined by the pointcut. An *around* advice must be used if existing behavior might need to be replaced.

In advices can be used to add behavior inside some activity, like for example add an extra concurrent activity to a flow activity. This cannot be simulated by before or after advices. In some cases, an around advice could be used as a workaround, but this would result in significant code duplication. The *in* advice can not only be used to add new activities in structural WS-BPEL activities, but also to customize the behavior of certain WS-BPEL activities, like for example adding variables to a scope, or adding flow links to any WS-BPEL activity. Table 5 gives an overview of all the situations where an in advice could be used.

Advice code is defined in an XML element that specifies the type of the advice. A pointcut describes the points in the original process to which the advice applies. The extra behavior that should be inserted is specified using standard WS-BPEL elements. For before, after and around advices, this is a WS-BPEL activity. In advices can be used to insert other WS-BPEL elements too, as specified in table 5. For around advices, the `<proceed>` activity could be used to include the original behavior specified by the joinpoint. The pointcut's attributes are exposed to the advice; these can be accessed in the advice by prefixing their name with the '$' character. Listing 2 shows an example of a before advice that logs all invocations of the `smsServicePT` web service. The extra behavior that is inserted is a sequence of two activities: first, the log message

Table 5. Pointcuts where an in advice could be used

Joinpoint	Element	Description
all types	source	Add the activity as source of a flow link.
	target	Add the activity as target of a flow link.
flowing	activity	Add a new parallel activity to a flow.
	links	Add a new link to a flow.
switching	case	Add a new case to a switch.
	otherwise	Add the otherwise element to a switch.
picking	onMessage	Add a new message trigger to a pick.
	onAlarm	Add a new timeout trigger to a pick.
scoping	variable	Add a variable to a scope.
	correlationSet	Add a correlation set to a scope.
	faultHandler	Add a fault handler to a scope.
	compensationHandler	Add a compensation handler to a scope.
	eventHandler	Add an event handler to a scope.
assigning	copy	Add a copy to an assign.
invoking	correlation	Add a correlation element to an invoke.
	catch	Add a specific catcher to an invoke.
	catchAll	Add a generic catcher to an invoke.
	compensationHandler	Add a compensation handler.
receiving	correlation	Add a correlation element to a receive.
replying	correlation	Add a correlation element to a reply.

containing the invoked operation is created; then, this message is sent to the logging service.

2.4 Aspect Modules

An aspect represents one crosscutting concern. As such, aspects can contain several before, after, in and around advices. Listing 3 shows an example aspect that logs the start and end of all invocations of the `smsServicePT` web service. The main sections of an aspect are the using declarations (lines 2–6), the pointcut (lines 8–9) and advice definitions (lines 11–22), and the actual advices (lines 24–30). To allow reuse of pointcuts and advices, aspects can include other aspect files.

```
<before joinpoint="Jp" pointcut="invoking(Jp, 'smsService',  'smsServicePT', Operation)">
  <sequence>
    <assign>
      <copy>
        <from>Logging invocation of operation $Operation</from>
        <to variable="logMsg" part="msg" />
      </copy>
    </assign>
    <invoke partnerLink="logging" portType="log:loggingPT"
            operation="logMessage" inputVariable="logMsg" />
  </sequence>
</before>
```

Listing 2. An advice that logs all invocations of the SMS service

```
1  <aspect name="logSMSInvocations">
2    <using>
3      <namespace name="xmlns:log" uri="logging.example.com" />
4      <partnerLink name="logging" partnerLinkType="log:loggingLT" />
5      <variable name="logMsg" type="log:logMsg" />
6    </using>
7
8    <pointcut name="smsInvocation(Jp, Operation)"
9              pointcut="invoking(Jp, 'smsService', 'smsServicePT', Operation)" />
10
11   <advice name="logMessage(Message)">
12     <sequence>
13       <assign>
14         <copy>
15           <from>$Message</from>
16           <to variable="logMsg" part="msg" />
17         </copy>
18       </assign>
19       <invoke partnerLink="logging" portType="log:loggingPT"
20               operation="logMessage" inputVariable="logMsg" />
21     </sequence>
22   </advice>
23
24   <before joinpoint="Jp" pointcut="smsInvocation(Jp, Operation)">
25     <advice name="logMessage('Invoking $Operation')" />
26   </before>
27
28   <after joinpoint="Jp" pointcut="smsInvocation(Jp, Operation)">
29     <advice name="logMessage('Invoked $Operation')" />
30   </after>
31 </aspect>
```

Listing 3. An example aspect logging the start and end of all SMS service invocations

Adding new behavior usually requires extending the information defined at process-level, too. For example, adding a new invocation to a process usually requires adding a partner link that specifies the interface of the new service, and a new variable that will contain the message that should be sent to that service. The <using> tag (lines 2–6) allows the definition of such information global to the process. It may include variables, partner links, partners, fault handlers, compensation handlers, event handlers and namespaces.

Pointcut expressions can be reused (lines 8–9) by giving them a name and specifying the parameters, which can either be further constrained when reusing the expression, or be referred to from inside an advice reusing the pointcut. Defining a pointcut expression like this generates a higher-level pointcut predicate that can then be used in other pointcut expressions.

The extra behavior that should be inserted in before, after, around and in advices can be reused too (lines 11–22). The advice behavior is given a name and can be parametrized. These parameters can be referred to from inside the advice code with their name (using the '$' prefix). The named advice behavior can be called from within advice code using the <advice> element (line 25 and line 29).

2.5 Aspect Deployment Language

A Padus aspect deployment specifies how aspects should be applied to the base processes and consists of two main parts: aspect instantiation and aspect com-

```
<deployment>
    <!-- the following aspects need to be deployed for the selected processes -->
    <aspect name="..." process="..." id="..." />
    <aspect name="..." process="..." id="..." />
    ...
    <!-- the following precedence declarations are valid for the selected process
         or for all processes if no process is specified -->
    <precedence [process="..."] />
        <aspect id="..." [advice="before|after|around|in"] />
        <aspect id="..." [advice="before|after|around|in"] />
    </precedence>
    ...
</deployment>
```

Listing 4. Aspect deployment specification

position. Aspect instantiation is responsible for instantiating and applying an aspect type to a concrete process. Processes are referenced using their name. It is also possible to select processes in a pattern-based manner using a logic language very similar to our pointcut language. As such, it is for instance possible to select only those processes that invoke a particular service or to select processes whose name starts with a given identifier. Listing 4 illustrates aspect deployment in Padus.

The second part of an aspect deployment, namely the aspect composition, is responsible for specifying the aspect precedence in case multiple aspects apply to the same joinpoint. In case no precedence is specified, the advice is executed in the order in which their corresponding aspects are specified. A precedence declaration overrides this default and is able to specify precedence on a per-advice-type basis. Aspect precedence for a before advice can thus be different than precedence for an after advice. The precedence is also able to vary over several deployments of the same aspect type, as it is bound to the aspect instance's ID and not to its type. Furthermore, the precedence specification can be limited to certain processes only, allowing a custom precedence specification for each process or group of processes if necessary. Similar to aspect instantiation, the process selection can be name-based or pattern-based.

3 The Padus Implementation

3.1 General Architecture

In existing literature on aspect-oriented execution models, two main approaches can be identified:

- **Static Weaving:** In a statically woven approach, the aspect and base-code are woven (i.e. merged) before run-time on either source or byte-code level. At runtime the aspects, like the base code, cannot be redefined, removed nor can new aspects be added.
- **Dynamic Weaving:** A dynamically woven approach uses dedicated techniques to allow weaving at runtime. This allows to dynamically add, remove and redefine aspects.

We opt for a statically woven approach for the execution model of the Padus language. Because the language is used to describe real-time processes in a telecom service delivery platform, performance is extremely important. In contrast to dynamic weaving, static weaving introduces no runtime overhead. Another important advantage is that it does not require a dedicated execution platform (i.e. a modified WS-BPEL engine in our case), which would otherwise seriously limit the applicability of the approach. Figure 1 illustrates the architecture of our weaver. A WS-BPEL process is transformed based on the aspect deployment descriptions. The result is again a regular WS-BPEL process that can be deployed on all WS-BPEL execution engines.

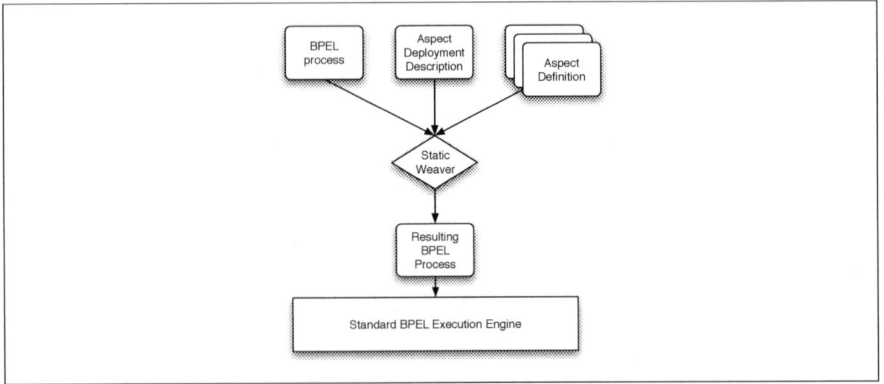

Fig. 1. Padus weaver architecture

3.2 Pointcut Matching and Document Transformation

In order to match the pointcuts and transform the target WS-BPEL specification, the following steps are taken:

- **Translation:** The WS-BPEL process is translated to a set of logic facts in the Prolog language. For every WS-BPEL activity, several facts are generated that define the equivalent activity in Prolog. There is also an explicit backlink to the nodes in the XML tree representation of the WS-BPEL process. This allows for a fast reverse translation process from any given activity to the concrete XML node.
- **Matching:** A logic engine (SWI-Prolog) is used to find all solutions for the pointcut rule. The result is a set of facts representing activities where the aspect is applicable. In case the pointcut defines conditions that are to be dynamically evaluated (such as `variableValue(ProcessInstance, Name, Value)`), partial evaluation is applied to only evaluate the static part of the pointcut. The dynamic part of the pointcut is inserted at the beginning of the advice. If it does not evaluate to true, the advice is not executed.

Separating the dynamic part of a pointcut and inserting the conditional advice is independent from a concrete WS-BPEL process and the result might thus be stored for later deployments of the same aspect.

- **Joinpoint Identification:** All solutions for the rule are translated back to WS-BPEL activities using the explicit back-link generated in the translation process. The result is a set of joinpoints denoted by XPath in the WS-BPEL XML tree where the aspect should be woven.
- **Transformation:** An XML transformation engine (based on XSLT) is used to transform the WS-BPEL document at the joinpoints identified in the previous step. Depending on the concrete advice semantics, a different transformation is applied. For a before advice for instance, the advice process is inserted before the identified joinpoints. Non-WS-BPEL constructs in the advice, such as proceed, have to be translated to valid WS-BPEL activities as well. In case of proceed in an around advice for instance, the replaced behavior of the joinpoint is inserted instead of the proceed activity.

4 Case Study

In this section we show how our aspect language can be used to add billing to a multi-party conference call process. Two types of billing schemes are supported: a *fixed fee billing scheme* where the end user should pay a fixed price at the end of the conference call, and a *duration billing scheme* where the price is determined based on the duration of the conference call. Three aspects are used to represent these two billing schemes:

- A *generic billing aspect* (see listing 5) is used to define concepts common to both billing schemes: the billing service and message definitions (lines 2–6), the pointcuts representing the start and end of a conference call (lines 7–10), and an advice for invoking the billing service (lines 11–14).
- The *fixed fee billing aspect* (see listing 6) introduces one advice that invokes the billing service with a fixed price at the end of the conference call.
- In the *duration billing aspect* (see listing 7), a first advice (lines 6–13) stores the start time of the conference call in a new variable (line 4), while a second advice (lines 14–25) uses this time to calculate the price of the conference call based on its duration and then invokes the billing service.

The logic needed for adding billing to the conference call process is now cleanly modularized and is not scattered across the basic control flow, which is very useful for keeping the complexity of the core functionality under control. Any of the two billing aspects can now be combined with the conference call process, or any other process, greatly improving reusability. The billing scheme can easily be modified afterwards too.

The deployment descriptor in listing 8 specifies how the aspect should be instantiated. Here we apply the `FixedFeeBilling` aspect to the `ConferenceCall` process. Suppose a `SecurityCheck` aspect is used to make sure that only users that are allowed to end the conference call can actually do so. In this case, the

```
<aspect name="Billing">
  <using>
    <namespace name="xmlns:bill" uri="my.billing.uri" />
    <partnerLink name="billing" partnerLinkType="bill:billingLT" />
    <variable name="billingMsg" type="bill:billingMsg" />
  </using>
  <pointcut name="confCallStarts(Jp)"
           pointcut="invoking(Jp, 'ConfCallService', 'confCallPT', 'createConfCall')" />
  <pointcut name="confCallEnds(Jp)"
           pointcut="invoking(Jp, 'ConfCallService', 'confCallPT', 'closeConfCall')" />
  <advice name="billService">
    <invoke partnerLink="billing" portType="bill:billingPT"
           operation="billService" inputVariable="billingMsg" />
  </advice>
</aspect>
```

Listing 5. Aspect defining generic billing concepts

```
<aspect name="FixedFeeBilling">
  <include name="Billing" />
  <after joinpoint="Jp" pointcut="confCallEnds(Jp)">
    <sequence>
      <assign>
        <copy>
          <from>1.5 EUR</from>
          <to variable="billingMsg" part="price" />
        </copy>
      </assign>
      <advice name="billService" />
    </sequence>
  </after>
</aspect>
```

Listing 6. Aspect implementing a billing scheme with a fixed fee

```
<aspect name="DurationBilling">
  <include name="Billing" />
  <using>
    <variable name="startTime" type="xsd:time" />
  </using>
  <before joinpoint="Jp" pointcut="confCallStarts(Jp)">
    <assign>
      <copy>
        <from expression="func:getCurrentTime()" />
        <to variable="startTime" />
      </copy>
    </assign>
  </before>
  <after joinpoint="Jp" pointcut="confCallEnds(Jp)">
    <sequence>
      <assign>
        <copy>
          <from expression="func:calculatePrice(
            bpws:getVariableProperty('startTime'), '0.4 EUR')" />
          <to variable="billingMsg" part="price" />
        </copy>
      </assign>
      <advice name="billService" />
    </sequence>
  </after>
</aspect>
```

Listing 7. Aspect implementing a billing scheme based on duration

```
<deployment>
  <aspect name="FixedFeeBilling" process="ConferenceCall" id="ConferenceCallBilling" />
  <aspect name="SecurityCheck" process="ConferenceCall" id="ConferenceCallSecurity" />
  <precedence process="ConferenceCall" />
    <aspect id="ConferenceCallSecurity" />
    <aspect id="ConferenceCallBilling" />
  </precedence>
</deployment>
```

Listing 8. Aspect deployment specification

`SecurityCheck` aspect should be applied first, to make sure that the billing only occurs if the conference call is actually terminated. Note that in this simple example the default precedence could be used to specify the right order in which the aspects should be applied too, but this might not be the case anymore if more processes and/or aspects were defined.

5 Related Work

AO4BPEL [14] is an aspect-oriented extension to WS-BPEL that allows for more modular and dynamically adaptable web service compositions. Each WS-BPEL activity is a potential join point. In contrast to Padus, AO4BPEL uses the lower-level XPath pointcut language. Pointcuts are too low-level and refer directly to paths in the document tree, which limits their reusability and makes them fragile with respect to evolution of the base process. Furthermore, their approach does not support an explicit aspect deployment construct nor allows for aspect reuse. While AO4BPEL allows for aspect addition and removal while processes are running, supporting this requires a custom-made WS-BPEL engine, which is incompatible with the existing tool chain.

Courbis and Finkelstein [21] present an aspect-oriented language extension very similar to AO4BPEL. They also use XPath as a pointcut language and use a custom WS-BPEL engine for allowing dynamic aspect addition and removal. In contrast to AO4BPEL and Padus, however, the advice language is Java.

The Web Services Management Layer (WSML) [22] uses aspects implemented in JAsCo [23] to capture client-side web service management concerns such as billing, transactions, selection and caching. Compositions of web services are handled by traditional approaches such as WS-BPEL. The WSML is thus complementary to our approach: Padus is able to specify process specific aspects that reflect over the process definition while the WSML specifies service specific aspects independent of process details.

Previous research [18] already showed the advantage of using a logic language for both aspect declaration (defining pointcuts as logical queries) and weaver implementation (representing the program as logical facts) in the context of Smalltalk. The logic meta-programming approach to AOP also allows non-expert programmers to define their own high-level, domain-specific aspect languages.

6 Conclusions and Future Work

The paper presents an extension of WS-BPEL for allowing a better separation of concerns through aspect-oriented programming. The Padus language improves on existing approaches by:

- Providing a rich joinpoint model consisting of all WS-BPEL activities.
- Employing a higher-level logic-based pointcut language that makes the pointcuts less dependent on the concrete document structure. This makes the pointcuts less fragile with respect to evolution of the WS-BPEL process. Because of the higher-level pointcuts, reusing them becomes easier as well.
- Introducing the concept of an *in* advice to add new behavior to existing elements, which extends the expressiveness of the advice language.
- Providing an explicit deployment construct that allows to specify aspect instantiation to specific processes expressively using a logic language. Aspect composition is tackled by an expressive precedence specification that is able to vary depending on the aspect instances, advice types and concrete processes.
- Remaining compatible with the existing infrastructure.

Our aspect-oriented extension for WS-BPEL is an XML-based language and can be defined using an XML Schema [24]. But, similar to specifying a WS-BPEL process using a graphical notation (e.g. BPMN [25]), a more user-friendly graphical notation for aspects can be defined too. We already started on an extension of BPMN that supports the aspect-oriented idea and that can be translated to Padus aspects.

Acknowledgments

This research is partly funded by Alcatel Belgium and the Institute for the Promotion of Innovation Through Science and Technology in Flanders (IWT-Vlaanderen) through the WIT-CASE project.

References

1. Alonso, G., Casati, F., Kuno, H., Machiraju, V., eds.: Web Services: Concepts, Architectures and Applications. Springer-Verlag, Heidelberg, Germany (2004)
2. Du, W., Elmagarmid, A.: Workflow management: State of the art vs. state of the products. Technical Report HPL-97-90, Hewlett-Packard Labs, Palo Alto, CA, USA (1997)
3. Andrews, T., Curbera, F., Dholakia, H., Goland, Y., Klein, J., Leymann, F., Liu, K., Roller, D., Smith, D., Thatte, S., Trickovic, I., Weerawarana, S.: Business Process Execution Language for Web Services version 1.1 (2003) `http://www.ibm.com/developerworks/library/ws-bpel/`.
4. Leymann, F.: Web Services Flow Language (WSFL 1.0). IBM (2001)

5. Thatte, S.: XLANG — web services for business process design. Microsoft (2001) `http://www.gotdotnet.com/team/xml_wsspecs/xlang-c/default.htm`.
6. Parnas, D.L.: On the criteria to be used in decomposing systems into modules. Comm. ACM **15**(12) (1972) 1053–1058
7. Ossher, H., Tarr, P.: Using subject-oriented programming to overcome common problems in object-oriented software development/evolution. In: Proc. 21st Int'l Conf. Software Engineering, IEEE Computer Society Press (1999) 687–688
8. Kiczales, G., Lamping, J., Mendhekar, A., Maeda, C., Lopes, C., Loingtier, J.M., Irwin, J.: Aspect-oriented programming. Technical Report SPL97-008 P9710042, Xerox PARC (1997)
9. De Win, B., Joosen, W., Piessens, F.: Developing secure applications through aspect-oriented programming. In Filman, R.E., Elrad, T., Clarke, S., Akşit, M., eds.: Aspect-Oriented Software Development. Addison-Wesley, Boston (2005) 633–650
10. Kiczales, G., Hilsdale, E., Hugunin, J., Kersten, M., Palm, J., Griswold, W.G.: An overview of AspectJ. In Knudsen, J.L., ed.: Proc. ECOOP 2001, LNCS 2072, Berlin, Springer-Verlag (2001) 327–353
11. Vanderperren, W., Suvée, D., Jonckers, V.: Combining AOSD and CBSD in PacoSuite through invasive composition adapters and JAsCo. In: Proceedings of Net.ObjectDays 2003, Erfurt, Germany (2003) 36–50
12. D'Hondt, M., Jonckers, V.: Hybrid aspects for weaving object-oriented functionality and rule-based knowledge. In Lieberherr, K., ed.: Proc. 3rd Int' Conf. on Aspect-Oriented Software Development (AOSD-2004), ACM Press (2004) 132–140
13. Arsanjani, A., Hailpern, B., Martin, J., Tarr, P.: Web services: Promises and compromises. Queue **1**(1) (2003) 48–58
14. Charfi, A., Mezini, M.: Aspect-oriented web service composition with AO4BPEL. In Zhang, L.J., ed.: Proceedings of the 2nd European Conference on Web Services (ECOWS 2004), Erfurt, Germany, Springer-Verlag (2004) 168–182
15. Cottenier, T., Elrad, T.: Dynamic and decentralized service composition with Contextual Aspect-Sensitive Services. In: Proceedings of the 1st International Conference on Web Information Systems and Technologies (WEBIST 2005), Miami, FL, USA (2005)
16. Verheecke, B., Vanderperren, W., Jonckers, V.: Unraveling crosscutting concerns in web services middleware. IEEE Software **23**(1) (2006) 42–50
17. Brichau, J., Haupt, M.: Survey of aspect-oriented languages and execution models. Technical Report AOSD-Europe-VUB-01, AOSD-Europe (2005)
18. De Volder, K.: Aspect-oriented logic meta programming. In Lopes, C., Kiczales, G., Tekinerdoğan, B., De Meuter, W., Meijers, M., eds.: Workshop on Aspect Oriented Programming (ECOOP 1998). (1998)
19. De Volder, K.: Type-Oriented Logic Meta Programming. PhD thesis, Vrije Universiteit Brussel (1998)
20. Deransart, P., Ed-Dbali, A., Cervoni, L., eds.: Prolog: The Standard Reference Manual. Springer-Verlag (1996)
21. Courbis, C., Finkelstein, A.: Towards aspect weaving applications. In: ICSE '05: Proceedings of the 27th international conference on Software engineering, New York, ACM Press (2005) 69–77
22. Cibrán, M.A., Verheecke, B., Jonckers, V.: Aspect-oriented programming for dynamic web service monitoring and selection. In Zhang, L.J., ed.: Proceedings of the 2nd European Conference on Web Services (ECOWS 2004), Erfurt, Germany, Springer-Verlag (2004)

23. Suvée, D., Vanderperren, W.: JAsCo: An aspect-oriented approach tailored for component based software development. In Akşit, M., ed.: Proc. 2nd Int' Conf. on Aspect-Oriented Software Development (AOSD-2003), ACM Press (2003) 21–29
24. Fallside, D.C., Walmsley, P.: XML Schema part 0: Primer second edition. W3C Recommendation 28 October 2004, World Wide Web Consortium (2004) http://www.w3.org/TR/2004/REC-xmlschema-0-20041028/.
25. White, S.A.: Business Process Modeling Notation (BPMN) version 1.0 (2004) http://www.bpmn.org/.

Process Equivalence: Comparing Two Process Models Based on Observed Behavior

W.M.P. van der Aalst, A.K. Alves de Medeiros, and A.J.M.M. Weijters

Department of Technology Management, Eindhoven University of Technology
P.O. Box 513, NL-5600 MB, Eindhoven, The Netherlands
{w.m.p.v.d.aalst, a.k.medeiros, a.j.m.m.weijters}@tm.tue.nl

Abstract. In various application domains there is a desire to compare process models, e.g., to relate an organization-specific process model to a reference model, to find a web service matching some desired service description, or to compare some normative process model with a process model discovered using process mining techniques. Although many researchers have worked on different notions of equivalence (e.g., trace equivalence, bisimulation, branching bisimulation, etc.), most of the existing notions are not very useful in this context. First of all, most equivalence notions result in a binary answer (i.e., two processes are equivalent or not). This is not very helpful, because, in real-life applications, one needs to differentiate between slightly different models and completely different models. Second, not all parts of a process model are equally important. There may be parts of the process model that are rarely activated while other parts are executed for most process instances. Clearly, these should be considered differently. To address these problems, this paper proposes a completely new way of comparing process models. Rather than directly comparing two models, the process models are compared with respect to some typical behavior. This way we are able to avoid the two problems. Although the results are presented in the context of Petri nets, the approach can be applied to any process modeling language with executable semantics.

Keywords: Process Equivalence, Petri Nets, Process Mining.

1 Introduction

Today one can find a wide variety of process models in any large organization [10]. Typical examples are:

- reference models (e.g., the EPC models in the SAP R/3 reference model)
- workflow models (e.g., models used for enactment in systems like Staffware, FLOWer, FileNet, Oracle BPEL, etc.),
- business process models/simulation models (e.g., using tools such as ARIS, Protos, Arena, etc.),
- interface/service descriptions (e.g., the Partner Interface Processes in RosettaNet, the abstract BPEL processes in the context of web services, choreography descriptions using WSCDL), or
- process models discovered using process mining techniques.

S. Dustdar, J.L. Fiadeiro, and A. Sheth (Eds.): BPM 2006, LNCS 4102, pp. 129–144, 2006.

Given the co-existence of different models and different types of models, it is interesting to be able to compare process models. This applies to different levels ranging from models at the business level to models at the level of software components (e.g., when looking for a software component matching some specification). To compare process models in a meaningful manner, we need to assume that these models have semantics. Moreover, we need to assume some equivalence notion (When are two models the same?) People working on formal methods have proposed a wide variety of equivalence notions [1,11,13], e.g., two models may be identical under trace equivalence but are different when considering stronger notions of equivalence (e.g., bisimulation). Unfortunately, most equivalence notions provide a "true/false" answer. In reality there will seldom be a perfect fit. Hence, we are interested in the *degree of similarity*, e.g., a number between 0 (completely different) and 1 (identical). In other to do so, we need to quantify the differences. Here it seems reasonable to put more emphasis on the frequently used parts of the model.

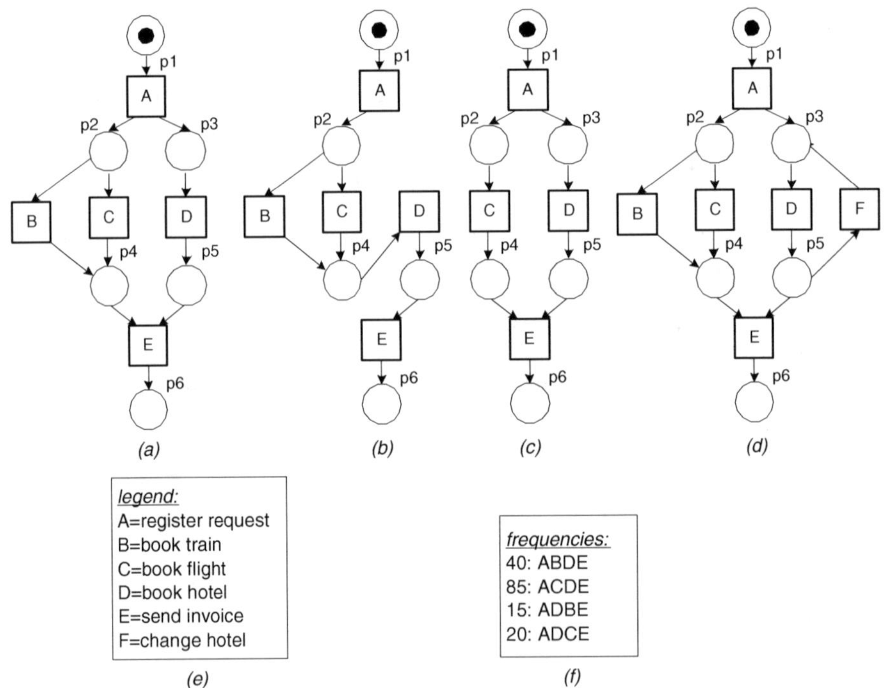

Fig. 1. Running example

To clarify the problem, let us consider Figure 1 where four process models (expressed in terms of Petri nets [16]) are depicted. These models describe the booking of a trip, see the legend for the interpretation of the various transitions in the Petri nets, e.g., C refers to the booking of a flight. Clearly, these models are similar. However, using classical equivalence notions all models are considered different. For example, in process (a) it is possible to have the execution sequence $ADBE$ while this sequence is not possible in (b) and (c). Moreover, the Petri net in Figure 1(d) allows for $ACDFDE$ which is not possible in any of the other models. Note that we focus on the active parts of the net (i.e., the transitions) rather than passive things such as places. Although classical equivalence notions consider the four models to be different, it is clear that some are more similar than other. Therefore, we want to quantify "equality", i.e., the degree of similarity. A naive approach could be to simply compare the sets of transition labels, e.g., nets (a) and (b) have the same transition labels: $\{A, B, C, D, E\}$ while (c) has a smaller set (without B) and (d) has a bigger set (with F). However, models with similar labels can have completely different behaviors (cf. (a) and (b) in Figure 1). Therefore, it is important to consider causal dependencies and the ordering of activities, e.g., to distinguish between parallelism and choice. Another approach could be to consider the state spaces or sets of possible traces of both models. However, in that case the problems are that there may be infinitely many traces/states and that certain paths are more probable.

In this paper, we investigate these problems and propose a completely new approach. *The main idea is to compare two models relative to an event log containing "typical behavior".* This solves several problems when comparing different models. Even models having infinitely many execution sequences can be compared and automatically the relevance of each difference can be taken into account. Moreover, as we will show, we can capture the moment of choice and analyze causalities that may not be explicitly represented in the log.

To give some initial insights in our approach, consider the set of traces listed in Figure 1(f). Each trace represents an execution sequence that may or may not fit in the models at hand. Moreover, frequencies are given, e.g., in the event log trace $ABDE$ occurred 40 times, i.e., there were 40 process instances having this behavior. Figure 1(f) represents some "typical behavior". This may be obtained using simulation of some model or it could be obtained by observing some real-life system/process. All 160 traces fit into the first Petri net (cf. Figure 1(a)), moreover, this Petri net does not allow for any execution sequences not present in the log. In this paper, we will quantify a notion of *fitness*. However, our primary objective is not to compare an event log and a process model, but to compare models in the presence of some event log as shown in Figure 1(f). Compare for example models (a) and (b): in a substantial number of cases (35) D precedes B or C. If we compare (a) and (c) based on the log, we can see that for 55 cases there is a difference regarding the presence of B. We will show that we can *quantify* these differences using the event log. It is important to note that we do not only consider full traces, e.g., if we compare Figure 1(a) with a Petri net where D is missing in the model, there is still some degree of similarity although none of the traces still fits (they all contain D).

The remainder is organized as follows. After providing a brief overview of related work, we introduce some preliminaries required to explain our approach.

Although we use Petri nets to illustrate our approach, any other process model with some local execution semantics (e.g., EPCs, activity diagrams, BPMN, etc.) could be used. In Section 4, we present two naive approaches (one based on the static structure and one based on a direct comparison of all possible behaviors) and discuss their limitations. Then, in Section 5 we present the core results of this paper. We will show that we can define *precision* and *recall* measures using event logs containing typical behavior. These notions have been implemented in ProM [9]. Finally, we conclude the paper.

2 Overview of Various Equivalence Notations and Related Work

In the literature, many equivalence notions have been defined for process models. Most equivalence notions focus on the dynamics of the model and not on the syntactical structure (e.g., trace equivalence and bisimulation [1,11,13]).

This paper uses Petri nets as a theoretical foundation [16]. In [15] an overview is given of equivalence notions in the context of Petri nets. See also [5] for more discussions on equivalence in the context of nets. Most authors translate a Petri net to a transition system to give it semantics. However, there are also authors that emphasize the true-concurrency aspects when giving Petri nets semantics. For example, in [7] the well-known concept of occurrence nets (also named runs) are used to reason about the semantics of Petri nets.

Any model with formal/executable semantics (including Petri nets) can be translated to a (possibly infinite) transition system. If we consider transition systems, many notions of equivalence have been identified. The weakest notion considered is *trace equivalence*: two process models are considered equivalent if the sets of traces they can execute are identical. Trace equivalence has two problems: (1) the set of traces may be infinite and (2) trace equivalence does not capture the moment of choice. The first problem can be addressed in various ways (e.g., looking at finite sets of prefixes or comparing transition systems rather than traces). The second problem requires stronger notions of equivalence. Bisimulation and various kinds of observation equivalence [13] attempt to capture the moment of choice. For example, there may be different processes having identical sets of traces $\{ABC, ABD\}$, e.g., the process where the choice for C or D is made after executing A or the process where the same choice is made only after executing B. Branching bisimilarity [11] is a slightly finer equivalence notion than the well-known observation equivalence [13]. A comparison of branching bisimilarity, observation equivalence, and a few other equivalences on processes with silent behavior can be found in [11]. Based on these equivalence relations also other relations have been introduced, e.g., the four inheritance relations in [1] are based on branching bisimilarity.

All references mentioned so far, aim at a "true/false" answer. Moreover, they do not take into account that some parts of the process may be more important than others. Few people (e.g., Prakash Panangaden and Jose Desharnais [8]) have been working on probabilistic bisimulation using labeled Markov processes rather than labeled transition systems. See [8] for an excellent overview of this work and also links to the probability theory community working on metrics on spaces of measures. In this paper, we use a different approach. We do not assume that we know any probabilities. Instead we assume that we have some example behavior than can serve as a basis for a comparison of two models. Also related is the work on metric labeled transition systems where the "behavioral difference" between states is a non-negative real number indicating the similarity between those states [6]. This way one can define a behavioral pseudometric to compare transition systems as shown in [6]. Note that this approach very much depends on an explicit notion of states and it is not clear how this can be applied to a practical, mainly activity oriented, setting.

As far as we know, this paper is the first to propose the use of "typical behavior" recorded in event logs as an aid for comparison. This makes the work quite different from the references mentioned in this section. Moreover, we show that this can be used in the context of process mining [2,4].

3 Preliminaries

This section introduces some of the basic mathematical and Petri-net related concepts used in the remainder.

3.1 Multi-sets, Sequences, and Matrices

Let A be a set. $\mathbb{B}(A) = A \rightarrow \mathbb{N}$ is the set of multi-sets (bags) over A, i.e., $X \in \mathbb{B}(A)$ is a multi-set where for each $a \in A$: $X(a)$ denotes the number of times a is included in the multi-set. The sum of two multi-sets $(X + Y)$, the difference $(X - Y)$, the presence of an element in a multi-set $(x \in X)$, and the notion of subset $(X \leq Y)$ are defined in a straightforward way and they can handle a mixture of sets and multi-sets. The operators are also robust with respect to the domains of the multi-sets, i.e., even if X and Y are defined on different domains, $X+Y$, $X-Y$, and $X \leq Y$ are defined properly by extending the domain where needed. $|X| = \sum_{a \in A} X(a)$ is the size of some multi-set X over A.

For a given set A, A^* is the set of all finite sequences over A. A finite sequence over A of length n is a mapping $\sigma \in \{1,\ldots,n\} \rightarrow A$. Such a sequence is represented by a string, i.e., $\sigma = \langle a_1, a_2, \ldots, a_n \rangle$ where $a_i = \sigma(i)$ for $1 \leq i \leq n$. $hd(\sigma, k) = \langle a_1, a_2, \ldots, a_k \rangle$, i.e., the sequence of just the first k elements. Note that $hd(\sigma, 0)$ is the empty sequence.

Every multi-set can be represented as a vector, i.e., $X \in \mathbb{B}(A)$ can be represented as a row vector $(X(a_1), X(a_2), \ldots, X(a_n))$ where a_1, a_2, … ,a_n enumerate the domain of X. $(X(a_1), X(a_2), \ldots, X(a_n))^T$ denotes the corresponding column vector (^{T} transposes the vector). Assume X is an $k \times \ell$ matrix, i.e., a matrix with k rows and ℓ columns. A row vector can be seen as $1 \times \ell$ matrix and a column vector can be seen as a $k \times 1$ vector. $X(i, j)$ is the value of the element in the ith row and the jth column. Let X be an $k \times \ell$ matrix and Y an $\ell \times m$ matrix. The product $X \cdot Y$ is the product of X and Y yielding a $k \times m$ matrix, where $X \cdot Y(i,j) = \sum_{1 \leq q \leq \ell} X(i,q)Y(q,j)$. The sum of two matrices having the same dimensions is denoted by $X + Y$.

For any sequence $\sigma \in \{1,\ldots,n\} \to A$ over A, the Parikh vector $\overrightarrow{\sigma}$ maps every element a of A onto the number of occurrences of a in σ, i.e., $\overrightarrow{\sigma} \in \mathbb{B}(A)$ where for any $a \in A$: $\overrightarrow{\sigma}(a) = \sum_{1 \leq i \leq n}$ if $\sigma(i) = a$ then 1 else 0.

3.2 Petri Nets

This subsection briefly introduces some basic *Petri net* terminology [16] and notations used in the remainder.

Definition 1 (Petri net). *A Petri net is a triple (P, T, F). P is a finite set of places, T is a finite set of transitions ($P \cap T = \emptyset$), and $F \subseteq (P \times T) \cup (T \times P)$ is a set of arcs (flow relation).*

Figure 1 shows four Petri nets. Places are represented by circles and transitions are represented by squares.

For any relation/directed graph $G \subseteq A \times A$ we define the preset $\bullet a = \{a_1 \mid (a_1, a) \in G\}$ and postset $a\bullet = \{a_2 \mid (a, a_2) \in G\}$ for any node $a \in A$. We use $\overset{G}{\bullet} a$ or $a \overset{G}{\bullet}$ to explicitly indicate the context G if needed. Based on the flow relation F we use this notation as follows. $\bullet t$ denotes the set of input places for a transition t. The notations $t\bullet$, $\bullet p$ and $p\bullet$ have similar meanings, e.g., $p\bullet$ is the set of transitions sharing p as an input place. Note that we do not consider multiple arcs from one node to another. In the Petri net shown Figure 1(d): $p5\bullet = \{E, F\}$, $\bullet p5 = \{D\}$, $A\bullet = \{p2, p3\}$, $\bullet A = \{p1\}$, etc.

At any time a place contains zero or more *tokens*, drawn as black dots. The state of the Petri net, often referred to as *marking*, is the distribution of tokens over its places, i.e., $M \in \mathbb{B}(P)$. In each of the four Petri nets shown in Figure 1 only one place is initially marked ($p1$). Note that more places could be marked in the initial state and that places can be marked with multiple tokens.

We use the standard *firing rule*, i.e., a transition t is said to be *enabled* if and only if each input place p of t contains at least one token. An enabled transition may *fire*, and if transition t fires, then t *consumes* one token from each input place p of t and *produces* one token for each output place p of t. For example, in Figure 1(a), A is enabled and firing A will result in the state marking place $p2$ and $p3$. In this state both B, C, and D are enabled. If B fires, C is disabled, but D remains enabled. Similarly, if C fires, B is disabled, but D remains enabled, etc. After firing 4 transitions in Figure 1(a) the resulting state marks $p6$ with one token (independent of the order of B or C). In the following definition, we formalize these notions.

Definition 2 (Firing rule). *Let $N = (P, T, F)$ be a Petri net and $M \in \mathbb{B}(P)$ be a marking.*

- *$enabled(N, M) = \{t \in T \mid M \geq \bullet t\}$ is the set of enabled transitions,*
- *$result(N, M, t) = (M - \bullet t) + t\bullet$ is the state resulting after firing $t \in T$,*

- $(N, M)[t\rangle(N, M')$ *denotes that* t *is enabled in* (N, M) *(i.e.,* $t \in$ *enabled* (N, M)*) and that firing* t *results in marking* M' *(i.e.,* $M' = result(N, M, t)$*).*

$(N, M)[t\rangle(N, M')$ defines how a Petri net can move from one marking to another by firing a transition. We can extend this notion to firing sequences. Suppose $\sigma = \langle t_1, t_2, \ldots, t_n\rangle$ is a sequence of transitions present in some Petri net N with initial marking M. $(N, M)[\sigma\rangle(N, M')$ means that there is also a sequence of markings $\langle M_0, M_1, \ldots, M_n\rangle$ where $M_0 = M$, $M_n = M'$, and for any $0 \leq i < n$: $(N, M_i)[t_{i+1}\rangle(N, M_{i+1})$. Using this notation we define the set of reachable markings $R(N, M)$ as follows: $R(N, M) = \{M' \in \mathbb{B}(P) \mid \exists_\sigma (N, M)[\sigma\rangle(N, M')\}$. Note that $M \in R(N, M)$ because M is reachable via the empty sequence.

Note that *result*(N, M, t) does not need to yield a multi-set if t is not enabled in marking M because some places may have a negative number of tokens. Although this is not allowed in a Petri net (only enabled transitions can fire), for technical reasons it is sometimes convenient to use markings that may have "negative tokens". This becomes clear when considering the incidence matrix of a Petri net.

Definition 3 (Incidence matrix). *Let* $N = (P, T, F)$ *be a Petri net and* $M \in \mathbb{B}(P)$ *be a marking.*

- $\tilde{N}$ *is the incidence matrix of* N*, i.e.,* $\tilde{N}$ *is a* $|P| \times |T|$ *matrix with* $\tilde{N}(p, t) = 1$ *if* $(p, t) \notin F$ *and* $(t, p) \in F$*,* $\tilde{N}(p, t) = -1$ *if* $(p, t) \in F$ *and* $(t, p) \notin F$*, and* $\tilde{N}(p, t) = 0$ *in all other cases,*
- *result*$(N, M, \sigma) = M + \tilde{N} \cdot \vec{\sigma}$ *is the state resulting after firing* $\sigma \in T^*$*,*[1]
- *enabled*$(N, M, \sigma) =$ *enabled*$(N,$ *result*$(N, M, \sigma))$ *is the set of enabled transitions after firing* $\sigma \in T^*$*.*

The incidence matrix of a Petri net can be used for different types of analysis, e.g., based on $\tilde{N}$ it is possible to efficiently calculate place and transition invariants and to provide minimal (but not sufficient) requirements for the reachability of a marking. It is important to see that *result*(N, M, σ) does not need to yield a valid marking, i.e., there may be a place p such that *result*$(N, M, \sigma)(p) < 0$ indicating a negative number of tokens. If $(N, M)[\sigma\rangle(N, M')$, then *result*$(N, M, \sigma) = M'$. However, the reverse does not need to be the case. *enabled*(N, M, σ) calculates which transitions are enabled *after* firing each transition $\vec{\sigma}$ times using function *result* and the earlier defined function *enabled* (cf. Definition 2). It may be the case that while executing σ starting from (N, M), transitions were forced to be fired although they were not enabled. As a result, places may get a negative number of tokens. The reason we need such concepts is because we will later compare Petri nets with some observed behavior. In such situations, we need to be able to deal with transitions that were observed even if they were not enabled.

[1] Note that σ does not need to be enabled, i.e., transitions are forced to fire even if they are not enabled. Also note that we do not explicitly distinguish row and column vectors.

4 Naive Approaches

In this paper we propose to compare two processes on the basis on some event log containing typical behavior. However, before presenting this approach in detail, we first discuss some naive approaches.

4.1 Equivalence of Processes Based on Their Structure

When humans compare process models they typically compare the graphical structure, i.e., do the same activities (transitions in Petri net terms) appear in both models and do they have similar connections. Clearly, the graphical structure may be misleading: two models that superficially appear similar may be very different. Nevertheless, the graphical structure is an indicator that may be used to quantify similarity. Let us abstract from the precise split and join behavior (i.e., we do not distinguish between AND/XOR-splits/joins). In other words, we derive a simple graph where each node represents an activity and each arc some kind of connection. For example, the Petri net shown in Figure 1(a) is reduced to a graph with nodes A, B, C, D and E, and arcs (A, B), (A, C), (A, D), (B, E), (C, E) and (D, E). For the other Petri nets models in Figure 1 a similar graph structure can be derived. It is easy to see that each of the four process models has a different graph structure. However, there are many overlapping connections, e.g., all models have arc (A, C). This suggests that from a structural point of view the models are not equivalent but similar. When quantifying the overlap relative to the whole model we can take the perspective of the first model or the second model. This leads to the definition of *precision* and *recall* as specified below.[2]

Definition 4 (Structural Precision and Recall). *Let $N_1 = (P_1, T_1, F_1)$ and $N_2 = (P_2, T_2, F_2)$ be two Petri nets. Using $C_1 = \{(t_1, t_2) \in T_1 \times T_1 \mid t_1 \overset{N_1}{\bullet} \cap \overset{N_1}{\bullet} t_2 \neq \emptyset\}$ and $C_2 = \{(t_1, t_2) \in T_2 \times T_2 \mid t_1 \overset{N_2}{\bullet} \cap \overset{N_2}{\bullet} t_2 \neq \emptyset\}$, we define:*

$$precision^S(N_1, N_2) = \frac{|C_1 \cap C_2|}{|C_2|} \qquad recall^S(N_1, N_2) = \frac{|C_1 \cap C_2|}{|C_1|}$$

$precision^S(N_1, N_2)$ is the fraction of connections in N_2 that also appear in N_1. If this value is 1, the precision is high because all connections in the second model exist in the first model. $recall^S(N_2, N_1)$ is the fraction of connections in N_1 that also appear in N_2. If this value is 1, the recall is high because all connections in the first model appear in the second model. Note that here we think of N_1 as the "original model" and N_2 as some "new model" that we want to compare with the original one.

Let N_a, N_b, N_c, and N_d be the four Petri nets shown in Figure 1. $precision^S(N_a, N_b) = \frac{3}{5} = 0.6$. $recall^S(N_a, N_b) = \frac{3}{6} = 0.5$. Note that $precision^S(N_1, N_2) = recall^S(N_2, N_1)$ by definition for any pair of Petri nets N_1 and N_2. Therefore,

[2] These metrics are an adaptation of the precision and recall metrics in [14].

we only list some precision values: $precision^S(N_a, N_b) = 0.6$, $precision^S(N_a, N_c) = 4/4 = 1.0$, $precision^S(N_a, N_d) = 6/8 = 0.75$, $precision^S(N_b, N_a) = 3/6 = 0.5$, $precision^S(N_b, N_c) = 2/4 = 0.5$, $precision^S(N_b, N_d) = 3/8 = 0.375$, etc. If we consider N_a to be the initial model, then N_c has the best precision of the other three models because all connections in N_c also appear in N_a. Moreover, if we consider N_a to be the initial model, then N_d has the best recall because all connections in N_a also appear in N_d.

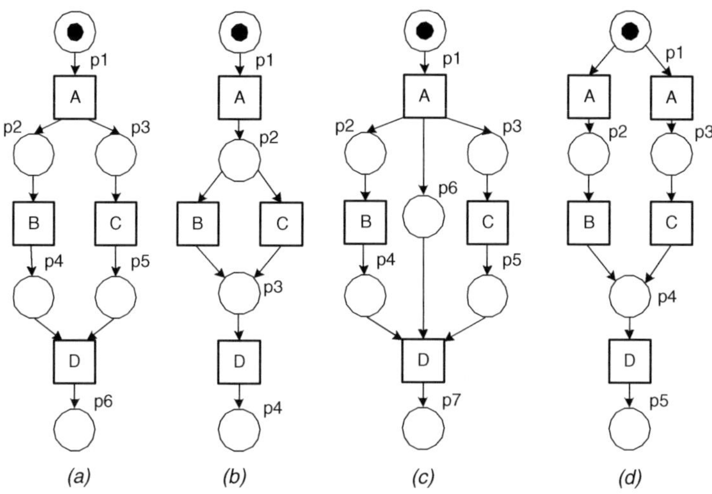

Fig. 2. Although the connection structures of (a) and (b) are similar they are quite different in terms of behavior. Moreover, the connection structure of (a) and (c) differs while the corresponding behaviors are identical.

The precision and recall figures for the four process models in Figure 1 seem reasonable. Unfortunately, models with nearly identical connections may be quite different as is shown in Figure 2. Let N_a, N_b, N_c, and N_d be the four Petri nets shown in Figure 2.[3] Although $precision^S(N_a, N_b) = recall^S(N_a, N_b) = 1$, N_a and N_b are clearly different. In N_a transitions B and C are executed concurrently while in N_b a choice is made between these two transitions. However, although N_a and N_c are structurally different ($precision^S(N_a, N_c) = 4/5 = 0.8$), they have identical behaviors. These examples show that Definition 4 does not provide a completely satisfactory answer when it comes to process equivalence. Nevertheless, $precision^S(N_1, N_2)$ and $recall^S(N_1, N_1)$ can be used as rough indicators for selecting a similar model, e.g., in a repository of reference models.

[3] Note that strictly speaking N_d does not correspond to a Petri net as defined in Definition 1, because there are two transitions A. However, it is easy to extend Definition 1 to so-called labeled Petri nets where different transitions can have the same label.

4.2 Equivalence of Processes Based on Their State Space or Traces

Since process models with a similar structure may have very different behaviors and models with different structures can have similar behaviors, we now focus on *quantifying the equivalence of processes based on their actual behaviors.* We start with a rather naive approach where we define recall and precision based on the *full firing sequences* of two marked Petri nets.

Definition 5 (Naive Behavioral Precision and Recall). *Let $N_1 = (P_1, T_1, F_1)$ and $N_2 = (P_2, T_2, F_2)$ be two Petri nets having initial markings M_1 and M_2 respectively. Moreover, let the corresponding two sets of possible full firing sequences be finite:*
$S_1 = \{\sigma \in T_1^* \mid \exists_{M' \in \mathbb{B}(P_1)} (N_1, M_1)[\sigma\rangle(N_1, M') \wedge enabled(N_1, M') = \emptyset\}$ *and*
$S_2 = \{\sigma \in T_2^* \mid \exists_{M' \in \mathbb{B}(P_2)} (N_2, M_2)[\sigma\rangle(N_2, M') \wedge enabled(N_2, M') = \emptyset\}$.

$$precision^B((N_1, M_1), (N_2, M_2)) = \frac{|S_1 \cap S_2|}{|S_2|}$$

$$recall^B((N_1, M_1), (N_2, M_2)) = \frac{|S_1 \cap S_2|}{|S_1|}$$

Clearly, the initial markings of N_1 and N_2 are highly relevant. However, if these are clear from the context, we do not explicitly mention these, i.e., $precision^B(N_1, N_2) = precision^B((N_1, M_1), (N_2, M_2))$ and $recall^B(N_1, N_2) = recall^B((N_1, M_1), (N_2, M_2))$.

Let N_a, N_b, N_c, and N_d be the four Petri nets shown in Figure 2 and S_a, S_b, S_c, and S_d their corresponding full firing sequences. $S_a = \{\langle A, B, C, D\rangle, \langle A, C, B, D\rangle\}$, $S_b = \{\langle A, B, D\rangle, \langle A, C, D\rangle\}$, $S_c = S_a$, and $S_d = S_b$. Hence, $precision^B(N_a, N_b) = 0$ and $recall^B(N_a, N_b) = 0$, i.e., the models are considered to be completely different because there are no identical full firing sequences possible in both models. However, $precision^B(N_a, N_c) = 1$ and $recall^B(N_a, N_c) = 1$ and $precision^B(N_b, N_d) = 1$ and $recall^B(N_b, N_d) = 1$.

We can also consider the four process models in Figure 1. The fourth model (N_d) has an infinite set of full firing sequences. Therefore, we focus on the first three models: N_a, N_b, and N_c. Let us first compare N_a and N_b: $precision^B(N_a, N_b) = 2/2 = 1$ and $recall^B(N_a, N_b) = 2/4 = 0.5$, i.e., all full firing sequences in N_b are possible in N_a but not the other way around. Although N_c differs from N_b, the precision and recall values are identical when comparing with N_a, i.e., $precision^B(N_a, N_c) = 1$ and $recall^B(N_a, N_c) = 0.5$.

These examples show that Definition 5 provides another useful quantification of equivalence quite different from Definition 4. However, also this quantification has a number of problems:

1. The set of full firing sequences needs to be *finite*. This does not need to be the case as is illustrated by the Petri net shown in Figure 1(d).

2. The models need to be *terminating*, i.e., it should be possible to end in a dead marking representing the completion of the process. Note that models may have unintentional livelocks or are designed to be non-terminating. For such models, we cannot apply Definition 5 in a meaningful way.
3. Definition 5 does not take into account differences in importance (i.e., frequently visited parts of the model are probably more important). For example, certain full firing sequences may have a very *low probability* in comparison to other sequences that occur *more frequent*. Clearly this should be taken into account.
4. Fourth, Definition 5 appears to be too *rigid*, i.e., one difference in a full firing sequence invalidates the entire sequence. In Figure 2 $precision^B(N_a, N_b) = 0$ and $recall^B(N_a, N_b) = 0$ although both models always start with A and end with D.
5. The *moment of choice* is not taken into account in Definition 5, i.e., essentially trace equivalence is used as a criterion. Many authors [1,11,13] have emphasized the importance of preserving the moment of choice by defining notions such as observation equivalence, bisimilarity, branching/weak bisimilarity, etc. To illustrate the importance of preserving the moment of choice, consider N_b and N_d depicted in Figure 2. Although $precision^B(N_b, N_d) = 1$ and $recall^B(N_b, N_d) = 1$, most environments will be able to distinguish both processes. In N_b in Figure 2(b) there is no state where only B or just C is enabled. However, such states exist in N_d in Figure 2(d), e.g., there can be a token in $p2$ enabling only B. Suppose that B and C correspond to the receipt of different messages sendt by some environment. In this case, N_d potentially deadlocks, e.g., a message for B cannot be handled because the system is waiting for C (i.e., $p3$ is marked). Such a deadlock is not possible in N_b.

The problems listed above show that similarity metrics based on criteria directly comparing all possible behaviors in terms of traces are of little use from a practical point of view. An alternative approach is to compare the state spaces rather than the sets of traces. For example, trying to establish a bisimulation relation where states are related in such a way that any move of one process model can be followed by the other one and vice versa [1,11,13]. However, this would only solve some of the problems listed above. Moreover, the notion of state often only exists implicitly and it is very difficult to extend more refined equivalence notions to include probabilities (cf. [6,8]). Therefore, we propose another approach as presented in the next section.

5 Equivalence of Processes in the Context of Observed Behavior

To overcome the problems highlighted so far, we propose an approach that uses *exemplary behavior* to compare two models. This exemplary behavior can be obtained on the basis of real process executions (in case the process already exists), user-defined scenarios, or by simply simulating one of the two models (or both). We assume this exemplary behavior to be recorded in an *event log*.

Definition 6 (Event log). *An event log L is a multi-set of sequences on some set of T, i.e., $L \in \mathbb{B}(T^*)$.*

An event log can be considered as a multi-set of full firing sequences (cf. Definition 5). However, now these sequences may exist independent of some model and the same sequence may occur multiple times.

Before comparing two process models using an event log, we first define the notion of *fitness*. This notion is inspired by earlier work on genetic mining and conformance checking [12,17].

Definition 7 (Fitness). *Let (N, M) be a marked Petri net and let $L \in \mathbb{B}(T^*)$ be a multi-set over T.*[4]

$$fitness((N, M), L) =$$
$$\left(\sum_{\sigma \in L} \frac{L(\sigma)}{|\sigma|} \; |\{i \in \{0, |\sigma| - 1\} \mid \sigma(i+1) \in enabled(N, M, hd(\sigma, i))\}| \; \right)/|L|$$

$fitness((N, M), L)$ yields a number between 0 and 1. Note that per sequence $\sigma \in L$ we calculate the number of times that a transition that was supposed to fire according to σ was actually enabled. This is divided by $|\sigma|$ to yield a number between 0 and 1 per sequence. This number shows the "fit" of σ. This is repeated for all $\sigma \in L$. Since the same sequence may appear multiple times in L (i.e., $L(\sigma) > 1$), we multiply the result for σ with $L(\sigma)$ and divide by $|L|$. Definition 7 assumes that $|L| > 0$ and $|\sigma| > 0$. This is not a fundamental restriction, if such strange cases occur (empty event log or an empty sequence), then we can simply assume that $0/0 = 0$.

As an example, consider the event log L shown in Figure 1(f) containing 160 traces. Clearly, $fitness(N_a, L) = 1$ because all sequences in L can be reproduced by N_a.[5] Moreover, $fitness(N_b, L) = (40 + 85 + (15 * 3/4) + (20 * 3/4))/160 = 0.945$, $fitness(N_c, L) = ((40 * 1/2) + 85 + (15 * 1/2) + 20)/160 = 0.828$, and $fitness(N_d, L) = 1$. These examples show that Definition 7 matches our intuitive understanding of fitness. *It is important to note that transitions are "forced" to fire even if they are not enabled*, cf. Definition 3. Moreover, a particular sequence can be "partly fitting", e.g., if we parse sequence $\langle A, B, D, E\rangle$ using N_c in Figure 1(c), half of the sequence fits. When forcing the execution of $\langle A, B, D, E\rangle$ using N_c, A is initially enabled. However, B is not enabled and does not even exist in the model. Nevertheless, in the resulting state D is still enabled. However, after firing D, the last event in the sequence (E) is not enabled. Hence, only two of the four events in $\langle A, B, D, E\rangle$ are actually enabled,

[4] Note that not all events in the log need to correspond to actual transitions. These events are simply ignored, i.e., we assume $enabled(N, M, \sigma)$ to be defined properly even if not all transitions in σ actually appear in N.

[5] Note that again we omit the initial marking if it is clear from the context, i.e., $fitness(N_a, L) = fitness((N_a, [p1]), L)$.

resulting in a fitness of 0.5. Note that it is better to look at individual events rather than considering whole sequences like in Definition 5. Using Definition 7, $fitness(N_c, L) = 0.828$. However, if we would focus on completely fitting sequences, $fitness(N_c, L) = (0 + 85 + 0 + 20)/160 = 0.656$, i.e., considerably lower because partly fitting are ignored.

Inspired by the definition of fitness, we would like to compare *two* models on the basis of a log. A straightforward extension of Definition 7 to two models is to compare the overlap in fitting or partially fitting sequences. However, in this case one only considers the actual behavior contained in the log. Therefore, we go one step further and look at the *enabled transitions* in both models and compare these, i.e., we do not just check whether an event in some sequence is possible, but *also take into account all enabled transitions at any point in the sequence.* This idea results in the following definition of precision and recall.

Definition 8 (Behavioral Precision and Recall). *Let* (N_1, M_1) *and* (N_2, M_2) *be marked Petri nets and let* $L \in \mathbb{B}(T^*)$ *be a multi-set over* T.[6]

$$precision((N_1, M_1), (N_2, M_2), L) =$$

$$(\sum_{\sigma \in L} \frac{L(\sigma)}{|\sigma|} (\sum_{i=0}^{|\sigma|-1} \frac{|enabled(N_1, M_1, hd(\sigma, i)) \cap enabled(N_2, M_2, hd(\sigma, i))|}{|enabled(N_2, M_2, hd(\sigma, i))|}))/|L|$$

$$recall((N_1, M_1), (N_2, M_2), L) =$$

$$(\sum_{\sigma \in L} \frac{L(\sigma)}{|\sigma|} (\sum_{i=0}^{|\sigma|-1} \frac{|enabled(N_1, M_1, hd(\sigma, i)) \cap enabled(N_2, M_2, hd(\sigma, i))|}{|enabled(N_1, M_1, hd(\sigma, i))|}))/|L|$$

To explain the concept consider a log $L = \{(\langle A, B, C, D\rangle, 2), (\langle A, C, B, D\rangle, 1)\}$ and the first three Petri nets shown in Figure 2. $precision(N_a, N_b, L) = ((2/4 * (1/1 + 2/2 + 0/1 + 1/1)) + (1/4 * (1/1 + 2/2 + 0/1 + 1/1)))/3 = 0.75$ and $recall(N_a, N_b, L) = ((2/4 * (1/1 + 2/2 + 0/1 + 1/1)) + (1/4 * (1/1 + 2/2 + 0/1 + 1/1)))/3 = 0.75$. $precision(N_a, N_c, L) = recall(N_a, N_c, L) = 1$.

We can also consider the four process models in Figure 1 with respect to the logs shown in Figure 1(f). $precision(N_a, N_b, L) = ((40/4 * (1/1 + 2/2 + 1/1 + 1/1)) + (85/4 * (1/1 + 2/2 + 1/1 + 1/1)) + (15/4 * (1/1 + 2/2 + 2/3 + 1/1)) + (20/4 * (1/1 + 2/2 + 2/3 + 1/1)))/160 = 0.98$ and $recall(N_a, N_b, L) = ((40/4 * (1/1 + 2/3 + 1/1 + 1/1)) + (85/4 * (1/1 + 2/3 + 1/1 + 1/1)) + (15/4 * (1/1 + 2/3 + 2/2 + 1/1)) + (20/4 * (1/1 + 2/3 + 2/2 + 1/1)))/160 = 0.92$. Note that both numbers would be lower if the sequences starting with $\langle A, D, \ldots\rangle$ would be more frequent. Let us now compare N_a and N_d in Figure 1 using L. $precision(N_a, N_d, L) = ((40/4*(1/1+3/3+1/1+1/2))+(85/4*(1/1+3/3+1/1+1/2))+(15/4*(1/1+3/3+2/3+1/2))+(20/4*(1/1+3/3+2/3+1/2)))/160 = 0.75$

[6] Note that the two denominators $|enabled(N_2, M_2, hd(\sigma, i))|$ and $|enabled(N_1, M_1, hd(\sigma, i))|$ may evaluate to zero. In these case, the numerator is also zero. Again, we assume in such cases that $0/0 = 0$.

and $recall(N_a, N_d, L) = ((40/4*(1/1+3/3+1/1+1/1))+(85/4*(1/1+3/3+1/1+1/1))+(15/4*(1/1+3/3+2/2+1/1))+(20/4*(1/1+3/3+2/2+1/1)))/160 = 1$. Note that N_d allows for behavior not present in log L (i.e., executing F). Nevertheless, as we can see from $precision(N_a, N_d, L) = 0.75$, the enabling of F is taken into account. It is also easy to see that Definition 8 takes into account the moment of choice, i.e., the enabling of set of transitions is the basis of comparison rather than the resulting sequences. Hence, we can distinguish N_b and N_d in Figure 2.[7]

In Section 4.2 we listed five problems related to the use of Definition 5. It is easy to see that Definition 8 addresses each of these problems:

1. Even models with an infinite set of firing sequences can be compared using a finite, but representative, set of traces.
2. Models do not need to be terminating.
3. Differences between frequent and infrequent sequences can be taken into account by selecting a representative log.
4. Partial fits are taken into account, i.e., small local differences do not result in a complete "misfit".
5. The moment of choice is taken into account because the focus is on enabling.

Given the attractive properties of the precision and recall metrics defined in Definition 8, we have implemented these metrics in the ProM framework [9].[8] Here it has been applied to a variety of process models. In particular the context of genetic mining [3].

One the of critical success factors is the availability of some log L that can serve as a basis for comparison. We propose to use *existing event logs* or to generate *artificial logs using simulation.*

Existing logs can be extracted from information systems but can also be obtained by manually describing some typical scenarios. It is important to realize that today's information systems are logging a wide variety of events. For example, any user action is logged in ERP systems like SAP R/3, workflow management systems like Staffware, and case handling systems like FLOWer. Classical information systems have some centralized database for logging such events (called transaction log or audit trail). Modern service-oriented architectures record the interactions between web services (e.g., in the form of SOAP messages). Moreover, today's organizations are forced to log events by national or international regulations (cf. the Sarbanes-Oxley (SOX) Act that is forcing organizations to audit their processes).

An example application scenario where existing event logs are used is the comparison of an existing process and a set of possible redesigns. For each of the redesigns, we can measure the precision and recall taking an event log of the existing information system as a starting point. First of all, the existing process

---

[7] Note that N_d contains duplicate labels, i.e., two transitions with label A. However, it is possible to extend Definition 8 and the resulting approach for such models.

[8] ProM and the analysis plug-in implementing the precision and recall metrics can be downloaded from www.processmining.org.

can be compared with this event log using the fitness notion presented in this section. This gives an indication of the quality of the initial model. Then, if the quality is acceptable, each of the redesigns can be compared with the existing process using this log.

Another approach would be to use simulation. This simulation could be based on both models or just the initial model. Note that the generated logs do not need to be complete, because Definition 8 also takes the enabling into account. It is more important that the probabilities are taken into account, because differences in the frequently visited parts of the model are of less importance than differences in rarely visited parts of the model.

6 Conclusion

This paper presented a novel approach to compare process models. Existing approaches typically do not quantify equivalence, i.e., models are equivalent or not. However, for many practical applications such an approach is not very useful, because in most real-life settings we want to distinguish between marginally different processes and completely different processes. We have proposed and implemented notions of *fitness*, *precision*, and *recall* in the context of the ProM framework. The key differentiator is that these notions take an event log with typical execution sequences as a starting point. This allows us to overcome many of the problems associated with approaches directly comparing processes at the model level. Although our approach is based on Petri nets, it can be applied to other models with executable semantics, e.g., formalizations of EPCs, BPMN, or UML activity diagrams.

Future work will focus on the application of the concepts and tools presented in this paper. We have already applied the approach in the context of process mining. Genetic algorithms have been evaluated using notions of precision and recall [3]. However, these notions can be applied in a wide variety of situations, e.g., to measure the difference between an organization specific process model and a reference model, to select a web service that fits best based on some description (e.g., PIPs or abstract BPEL), to compare medical guidelines, or to compare an existing process model with some redesign.

References

1. W.M.P. van der Aalst and T. Basten. Inheritance of Workflows: An Approach to Tackling Problems Related to Change. *Theoretical Computer Science*, 270 (1-2):125–203, 2002.
2. W.M.P. van der Aalst, A.K. Alves de Medeiros, and A.J.M.M. Weijters. Genetic Process Mining. In G. Ciardo and P. Darondeau, editors, *Applications and Theory of Petri Nets 2005*, volume 3536 of *Lecture Notes in Computer Science*, pages 48–69. Springer-Verlag, Berlin, 2005.
3. W.M.P. van der Aalst, A.K. Alves de Medeiros, and A.J.M.M. Weijters. Process Equivalence in the Context of Genetic Mining. BPM Center Report BPM-06-15, BPMcenter.org, 2006.

4. W.M.P. van der Aalst, A.J.M.M. Weijters, and L. Maruster. Workflow Mining: Discovering Process Models from Event Logs. *IEEE Transactions on Knowledge and Data Engineering*, 16(9):1128–1142, 2004.
5. E. Best and M.W. Shields. Some equivalence results for free choice nets and simple nets, and on the periodicity of live free choice nets. In W. Brauer, W. Reisig, and G. Rozenberg, editors, *Proceedings of CAAP '83*, volume 159 of *Lecture Notes in Computer Science*, pages 141–154. Springer-Verlag, Berlin, 1987.
6. F. van Breugel. A Behavioural Pseudometric for Metric Labelled Transition Systems. In *16th International Conference on Concurrency Theory (CONCUR 2005)*, volume 3653 of *Lecture Notes in Computer Science*, pages 141–155. Springer-Verlag, Berlin, 2005.
7. J. Desel. Validation of Process Models by Construction of Process Nets. In W.M.P. van der Aalst, J. Desel, and A. Oberweis, editors, *Business Process Management: Models, Techniques, and Empirical Studies*, volume 1806 of *Lecture Notes in Computer Science*, pages 110–128. Springer-Verlag, Berlin, 2000.
8. J. Desharnais, V. Gupta, R. Jagadeesan, and P. Panangaden. Metrics for labelled Markov processes. *Theoretical Computer Science*, 318(3):323–354, 2004.
9. B. van Dongen, A.K. Alves de Medeiros, H.M.W. Verbeek, A.J.M.M. Weijters, and W.M.P. van der Aalst. The ProM framework: A New Era in Process Mining Tool Support. In G. Ciardo and P. Darondeau, editors, *Application and Theory of Petri Nets 2005*, volume 3536 of *Lecture Notes in Computer Science*, pages 444–454. Springer-Verlag, Berlin, 2005.
10. M. Dumas, W.M.P. van der Aalst, and A.H.M. ter Hofstede. *Process-Aware Information Systems: Bridging People and Software through Process Technology.* Wiley & Sons, 2005.
11. R.J. van Glabbeek and W.P. Weijland. Branching Time and Abstraction in Bisimulation Semantics. *Journal of the ACM*, 43(3):555–600, 1996.
12. A.K.A. de Medeiros, A.J.M.M. Weijters, and W.M.P. van der Aalst. Genetic Process Mining: A Basic Approach and its Challenges. In C. Bussler et al., editor, *BPM 2005 Workshops (Workshop on Business Process Intelligence)*, volume 3812 of *Lecture Notes in Computer Science*, pages 203–215. Springer-Verlag, Berlin, 2006.
13. R. Milner. *A Calculus of Communicating Systems*, volume 92 of *Lecture Notes in Computer Science.* Springer-Verlag, Berlin, 1980.
14. S.S. Pinter and M. Golani. Discovering Workflow Models from Activities Lifespans. *Computers in Industry*, 53(3):283–296, 2004.
15. L. Pomello, G. Rozenberg, and C. Simone. A Survey of Equivalence Notions of Net Based Systems. In G. Rozenberg, editor, *Advances in Petri Nets 1992*, volume 609 of *Lecture Notes in Computer Science*, pages 420–472. Springer-Verlag, Berlin, 1992.
16. W. Reisig and G. Rozenberg, editors. *Lectures on Petri Nets I: Basic Models*, volume 1491 of *Lecture Notes in Computer Science.* Springer-Verlag, Berlin, 1998.
17. A. Rozinat and W.M.P. van der Aalst. Conformance Testing: Measuring the Fit and Appropriateness of Event Logs and Process Models. In C. Bussler et al., editor, *BPM 2005 Workshops (Workshop on Business Process Intelligence)*, volume 3812 of *Lecture Notes in Computer Science*, pages 163–176. Springer-Verlag, Berlin, 2006.

Investigations on Soundness Regarding Lazy Activities

Frank Puhlmann and Mathias Weske

Business Process Technology Group
Hasso-Plattner-Institute for IT Systems Engineering
at the University of Potsdam
D-14482 Potsdam, Germany
{puhlmann, weske}@hpi.uni-potsdam.de

Abstract. Current approaches for proving the correctness of business processes focus on either soundness, weak soundness, or relaxed soundness. Soundness states that each activity should be on a path from the initial to the final activity, that after the final activity has been reached no other activities should become active, and that there are no unreachable activities. Relaxed soundness softens soundness by stating that each activity should be able to participate in the business process, whereas weak soundness allows unreachable activities. However, all these kinds of soundness are not satisfactory for processes containing discriminator, n-out-of-m-join or multiple instances without synchronization patterns that can leave running (lazy) activities behind. As these patterns occur in interacting business processes, we propose a solution based on lazy soundness. We utilize the π-calculus to discuss and implement reasoning on lazy soundness.

1 Introduction

Business Process Management (BPM) aims at designing, enacting, managing, analyzing, and adapting business processes [1]. A key technology for implementing BPM systems are service-oriented architectures (SOA). These aim at supporting business processes within and between companies [2]. However, they also increase the complexity to be modeled, especially regarding interacting business processes. Thus, special care has to be taken during the design phase to avoid errors leading to deadlocks or livelocks. The former leads to processes stopping execution and interaction with their environment, whereas the latter might continue working but the process is never finished. Three major approaches for analyzing the correctness of business processes have been published: *Soundness* [3], *Relaxed Soundness* [4], and *Weak Soundness* [5]. All three approaches operate on a special type of business processes, called workflow nets [6] but they can be adapted to graph-based approaches like BPMN, EPC, or UML Activity Diagrams.

However, soundness, relaxed soundness, and weak soundness are not satisfactory for processes containing discriminator, n-out-of-m-join or multiple instances

S. Dustdar, J.L. Fiadeiro, and A. Sheth (Eds.): BPM 2006, LNCS 4102, pp. 145–160, 2006.

without synchronization patterns. These patterns are required in interacting business processes for representing interaction patterns [7], as *Racing Incoming Messages* (discriminator), *One to many Send/Receive* (n-out-of-m-join) or execute secondary tasks (multiple instances without synchronization). All of these patterns can leave activities behind that are or can become active after the final activity has been reached. Thereby, all processes containing these patterns are not sound per definition (i.e. in terms of Petri nets they leave tokens in the net). One example is a business process where three experts are asked to write an expertise each. The process can continue after two expertises have been received. Only in certain cases a follow up activity has to wait for all three expertises to continue, e.g. if the first two expertises are very different. As the experts need different time for responding, the business process could have been already finished while the last expert is still writing her expertise. However, all three experts have to be paid after delivering their work. In this case, there is a *clean-up* or *lazy-activitiy* remaining (pay the last expert) that does in certain cases not directly contribute to the successful execution of the business process, but is an integral part of it.

Nevertheless, the given example might be relaxed sound. Relaxed sound processes, in turn, might contain deadlocks or livelocks that should be avoided. Weak soundness in contrast allows no activities to be active after the final activity has been reached. To overcome the limitations of soundness and weak soundness regarding these patterns, and to go beyond relaxed soundness by proving deadlock and livelock freedom, we propose a solution based on lazy soundness. Lazy soundness will be derived, discussed and implemented based on business processes formalized in the π-calculus, thus extending our prior work [8].

The paper is structured as follows. We first extend our motivation and discuss related work, followed by the preliminaries required for formal process representation and analysis. The main part introduces lazy soundness for formalized business processes, also including a running example. A tool support section shows how the theoretical results can be applied practically and also takes a look at performance. The paper concludes with an outlook of future work.

2 Motivation and Related Work

During our research on soundness for business processes defined in the π-calculus [9], a process algebra that can formally represent all Workflow patterns [8] as originally described in [10], we analyzed the soundness of discriminator, n-out-of-m-join and multiple instances without synchronization patterns (denoted as critical patterns in the remainder). These patterns can leave activities behind that are or can become active after the final activity has been reached. Soundness, in contrast, states that no activities are or can become active after a final activity has been reached. Thus, all processes containing these patterns are not sound per definition.

We investigated weak and relaxed soundness for supporting the critical patterns [4,5]. Relaxed soundness indeed supports the patterns but relaxed sound

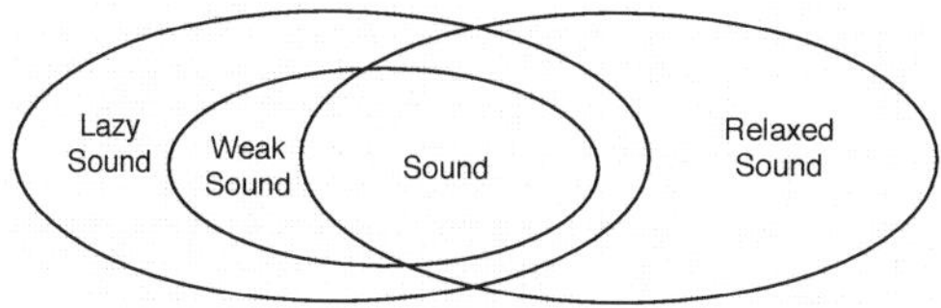

Fig. 1. A classification for different kinds of soundness

processes might contain livelocks and deadlocks. Weak soundness proves processes to be free of locks, but also forces all activities to finish before the final one. Thus, it does not support the critical patterns. To overcome these limitations we propose lazy soundness, complementing relaxed soundness by covering livelocks and deadlocks, and extending weak soundness by allowing activities to become active after the final activity has been reached. Unreachable activities are not covered. However, by combining relaxed and lazy soundness we can prove processes to be free of deadlocks, livelocks, and dead activities.

Figure 1 gives a classification of the different kinds of soundness. Lazy soundness states that if an activity is reachable from the initial activity, then the final activity is always reachable from this activity. (guarantees deadlock and livelock freedom). Furthermore, the final activity will only be reached once to denote the successful execution of the business process. *Clean-up* or so called *lazy-activities* might still be or become active. Relaxed soundness states that all activities of a business process participate in it (dead activity freedom). A relaxed sound process might contain deadlocks or livelocks. Weak soundness is a subset of lazy soundness by prohibiting lazy-activities, but still permitting dead activities. The rules for soundness are fullfilled by the intersection of weak and relaxed soundness, representing deadlock, livelock, and dead activity free processes without lazy activities. The intersection of relaxed and lazy soundness without soundness will not be investigated in this paper. Nevertheless, it offers interesting properties.

An important piece of related work is YAWL [11]. YAWL claims to support all workflow patterns, but actually redefines some of them to fit the YAWL semantics. Actually, the semantics of the critical workflow patterns has been changed.[1] A YAWL discriminator cancels all other tasks before the discriminator. A YAWL n-out-of-m-join only joins instances of the same activity, using a multiple instance pattern. Finally, a multiple instances without synchronization task has to be joined by an OR-join. All three solutions contradict the original workflow patterns but allow a YAWL net to be sound. In [12], an approach of reasoning in YAWL focusing on relaxed soundness is introduced, i.e. it requires all activities of a business process to be on a path from the initial to the final activity. However, this kind of reasoning also allows deadlocks and livelocks in the process, which is too relaxed regarding formal analysis. Lazy soundness, in contrast, is based on π-calculus formalizations of the workflow pattern [8], that

[1] See `http://www.yawl.fit.qut.edu.au/about/patterns/` for details.

capture the original semantics of the critical patterns, as these is required for interacting business processes and even special cases of traditional ones.

3 Preliminaries

This section introduces the π-calculus and the representation of business processes in it. Our motivation on using the π-calculus rather than other formalisms like Petri nets is discussed in [13].

3.1 The π-Calculus

The π-calculus is an algebra for the formal description and analysis of concurrent, interacting processes with support for link passing mobility. It is based on names and interactions used by processes defined according to [14].

Definition 1 (Pi Calculus). *The syntax of the π-calculus is given by:*

$$\begin{aligned} P &::= M \mid P|P' \mid \mathbf{v}zP \mid !P \\ M &::= \mathbf{0} \mid \pi.P \mid M + M' \\ \pi &::= \overline{x}\langle\tilde{y}\rangle \mid x(\tilde{z}) \mid \tau \mid [x = y]\pi \ . \end{aligned}$$

The informal semantics is as follows: $P|P'$ is the concurrent execution of P and P', $\mathbf{v}zP$ is the restriction of the scope of the name z to P, and $!P$ is an infinite number of copies of P. $\mathbf{0}$ is inaction, a process that can do nothing, $M + M'$ is the exclusive choice between M and M'. The output prefix $\overline{x}\langle\tilde{y}\rangle.P$ sends a sequence of names $\tilde{y}$ over the co-name $\overline{x}$ and then continues as P. The input prefix $x(\tilde{z})$ receives a sequence of names over the name x and then continues as P with $\tilde{z}$ replaced by the received names (written as $\{^{\tilde{name}}/_{\tilde{z}}\}$). Matching input and output prefixes might communicate, leading to an interaction. The unobservable prefix $\tau.P$ expresses an internal action of the process, and the match prefix $[x = y]\pi.P$ behaves as $\pi.P$, if x is equal to y.

Throughout this paper, upper case letters are used for process identifiers and lower case letters for names. Furthermore defined processes from the original paper on the π-calculus are used for parametric recursion, that is $A(y_1, ..., y_n)$ [9]. The formal semantics of the π-calculus is based on transition systems. We only give short definitions of the required concepts and refer to [14,15] for details.

Definition 2 (Transition Sequence). *A sequence of interactions on names or unobservable actions is denoted as $P \xrightarrow{\alpha} P'$, where α describes the sequence of actions required to transform a process P to P'.* □

Definition 3 (Context). *A* context *is a process term with a hole, denoted as $[\cdot]$. The hole can be filled with a process other than* $\mathbf{0}$. □

We write $C[P]$ for a context C with $[\cdot]$ replaced by P. The replacement is literal, which means that names free in P may be bound in $C[P]$. For example, let $C = \mathbf{v}x(\overline{x}a.\mathbf{0} \mid [\cdot])$, then $C[x(y).\mathbf{0}] = \mathbf{v}x(\overline{x}a.\mathbf{0} \mid x(y).\mathbf{0})$.

Definition 4 (Observability Predicate). Observability predicate $\downarrow_\mu$ *on names or co-names* μ *is defined by:*

1. $P \downarrow_x$ *if* P *can perform an input action with subject* x *and*
2. $P \downarrow_{\overline{x}}$ *if* P *can perform an output action with subject* x. □

The observables of a processes are then the free (unrestricted) names it can use for receiving and sending. For example, $P \stackrel{def}{=} \mathbf{v}z(!\overline{x}z.\mathbf{0} \mid \mathbf{v}z(\overline{w}a.\mathbf{0} \mid w(v).\mathbf{0} + y(u).\mathbf{0})))$, contains $P \downarrow_y$ and $P \downarrow_{\overline{x}}$ as the observables of P.

Definition 5 (Weak Open Bisimulation Equivalence). *Informally, two* π*-calculus processes* P *and* Q *are* weak open bisimulation equivalent *if they have the same observable behavior regarding the observability predicates* $\downarrow_{\tilde{s}}$. □

Thus, regarding weak open bisimulation, we abstract from all other internal actions. Formal details can be found in [15].

3.2 Business Process Patterns in the Pi-Calculus

Business processes in the π-calculus have been introduced in [8], by giving a collection of all workflow patterns [10] in their respective π-calculus formalization. An additional pattern common in interacting business processes, called *Event-based Rerouting*, has been presented in [16]. All pattern representations are based on events rather then states. A π-calculus process representing an activity waits for its required events (preconditions), does some internal action (functional part), and thereafter generates new events (postconditions). A business process formalized in the π-calculus consists of π-calculus processes representing different workflow patterns and a set of names, used for representing events.

During our investigations on lazy soundness, some pattern formalizations from [8] had to be refined since their original definitions are erroneous under certain circumstances.

Deferred Choice. As the π-calculus supports no transactional transitions, we need to make the choices in the preceding process to support loop behavior:

$$A = \tau_A.(b_{env}.\overline{b}.\mathbf{0} + c_{env}.\overline{c}.\mathbf{0}) \qquad B = b.\tau_B.B' \qquad c.\tau_C.C' \ .$$

MI without Synchronization. B has to continue immediately, however instances of B may still be active. This formalization gives a more applicable semantics to the pattern while still corresponding to [10]:

$$A = \tau_A.\overline{b}.\mathbf{0} \qquad B = b.((\prod_{i=1}^{n} \tau_B.\mathbf{0}) \mid B') \ .$$

Cancel Activity. Cancel activity has to accept a cancel event even after the functional part τ has been executed to provide correct routing:

$$\begin{aligned} A =& a.env_A(test_1).[test_1 = \bot].\tau_A.env_A(test_2).[test_2 = \bot].A' \\ \mathcal{E}_A =& \overline{env_A}\langle\bot\rangle.\mathcal{E}_A + \overline{env_A}\langle\top\rangle.\mathcal{E}_A{}' \ . \end{aligned}$$

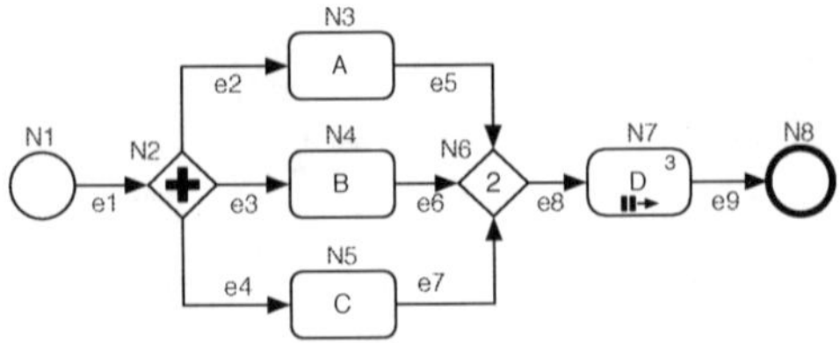

Fig. 2. A process containing a N-out-of-M-Join and a Multiple Instances without Synchronization pattern

4 Process Graphs

This section defines how business processes are formalized in terms of set theory and process algebra. It grounds structural correctness, that in turn is required for behavioral analysis discussed later on.

4.1 Structure

We start with the definitions of a *Process Graph*, a data structure that represents the behavioral aspects of a business process. Process graphs provide us with a uniform semi–formal representation of business processes regardless of their actual notations.

Definition 6 (Process Graph). *A process graph is a four-tuple consisting of nodes, directed edges, types and attributes. Formally:* $P = (N, E, T, A)$ *with*

- N *is a finite, non-empty set of nodes.*
- $E \subseteq (N \times N)$ *is a set of directed edges.*
- $T : N \to 2^{TYPE}$ *is a function mapping nodes to types.*
- $A : N \to KEY \times VALUE$ *is a function mapping key/value pairs to nodes.*□

The nodes N of a process graph define the activities of a process, and the directed edges E define dependencies between activities. Each node can have none, one, or more types assigned by the function T. Furthermore, each node can hold optional attributes represented by key/values pairs assigned by the function A. Sub-Processes are represented by a node N of the special type $Reference$, that references another process graph, i.e. $T(N) = \{Reference\}$. As such composed process graphs can always be flattened, we only consider flat process graphs. Some additional functions for accessing the sets of a process graph are given by:

- $source : E \to N$ returns the source node of a directed edge.
- $target : E \to N$ returns the target node of a directed edge.
- $type : N \to T$ returns the types of a node (same as $T(N)$).

To show the coherence between a process graph and a graphical notation, we give an example of how to map the structurally relevant parts of a business process to a process graph. We consider business processes given as a *Business Process Diagram* (BPD) of the *Business Process Modeling Notation* (BPMN) [17]. Other graph-based notations like EPCs or UML2 Activity Diagrams can be mapped in a similar manner.

Example 1 (Partly Mapping of a BPD to a Process Graph). A BPD is exemplary mapped to a process graph $P = (N, E, T, A)$ by the following steps:

1. N is given by all flow object of the BPD.
2. E is given by all sequence flows of the BPD.
3. T is given by the corresponding types of the flow objects.
4. A is given by additional attributes of flow objects, e.g.:
   (a) The number of incoming sequence flows for an n-out-of-m-join node;
   (b) The number of instances to be created for an activity;
   (c) The nodes to be canceled for a cancel event. □

An actual example of a business process modeled in BPMN is given in Figure 2. The process contains a n-out-of-m-join pattern, modeled by a gateway with the number of required sequence flows inside, as well as a multiple instances without synchronization pattern, modeled by activity D. The activities A, B, and C can represent sub-processes for contacting three different experts for writing an expertise. After two of them are ready, the process continues. However, some cleanup work is left for the remaining activity, e.g. receiving the last expertise and paying the expert. Although this does not directly contribute to the process, it is still required. Activity D send the accepted expertises to three different involved persons. This is again a lazy activity, as the business process can actually finish, even while the documents are actually in delivery. The complete business process diagram is mapped to a process graph according to the mapping rules given in Example 1.

Example 2 (Expertise Process). The process graph $P = (N, E, T, A)$ of the example from Figure 2 is given by:

1. $N = \{N1, N2, N3, N4, N5, N6, N7, N8\}$
2. $E = \{\ (N1, N2),\ (N2, N3),\ (N2, N4),\ (N2, N5),\ (N3, N6),\ (N4, N6),$ $(N5, N6),\ (N6, N7),\ (N7, N8)\ \}$
3. $T = \{(N1, StartEvent), (N2, ANDGateway), (N3, Task), (N4, Task),$ $(N5, Task), (N6, N\text{-}out\text{-}of\text{-}M\text{-}Join), (N7, MIwithoutSync),$ $(N8, EndEvent)\}$
4. $A = \{(N6, (continue, 2)), (N7, (count, 3))\}$ □

4.2 Semantics

We now give formal semantics to a process graph by mapping it to π-calculus processes according to the following algorithm.

Algorithm 1 (Mapping Process Graphs to π-Calculus Processes). A process graph $P = (P_N, P_E, P_T, P_A)$ is mapped to π-calculus processes as follows:

1. Assign all nodes of P an unique π-calculus process identifier $N1 \cdots N|P_N|$.
2. Assign all edges of P an unique π-calculus name $e1 \cdots e|P_E|$.
3. Define the π-calculus processes according to the behavioral patterns found in [8,16] as given by the type of the corresponding node. Take care of recursive definitions for supporting loop behavior, under the restrictions that:
   (a) All processes representing a node with no incoming edges do not support re-execution, and
   (b) All processes representing a node with no outgoing edges support re-execution by recursion.
4. Replace each functional part τ of the behavioral patterns mapped before with $[\cdot]$, thus constructing a context of each node.
5. Define a global process $N = (\mathbf{v}e1, \cdots, e|P_E|) \prod_{i=1}^{|P_N|} Ni$. This process can contain further components or restricted names according to the contained patterns. □

A node of a process graph is *executed* if the context of the corresponding π-calculus process is reached. We can now map the process graph from Example 2 to π-calculus processes.

Example 3 (π-calculus Process for Expertise Process).

$$\begin{aligned}
\mathit{Tasks}: \quad & N3 = e2.[\cdot].(\overline{e5}.\mathbf{0} \mid N3)\ , \quad N4 = e3.[\cdot].(\overline{e6}.\mathbf{0} \mid N4) \\
& N5 = e4.[\cdot].(\overline{e7}.\mathbf{0} \mid N5) \\
\mathit{ANDGateway}: \quad & N2 = e1.[\cdot].(N2 \mid \overline{e2}.\mathbf{0} \mid \overline{e3}.\mathbf{0} \mid \overline{e4}.\mathbf{0}) \\
\mathit{N\text{-}out\text{-}of\text{-}M\text{-}Join}: \quad & N6 = (\mathbf{v}h, run)(N6_1 \mid N6_2) \\
& N6_1 = e5.\overline{h}.\mathbf{0} \mid e6.\overline{h}.\mathbf{0} \mid e7.\overline{h}.\mathbf{0} \\
& N6_2 = h.h.\overline{run}.h.N6 \mid run.[\cdot].\overline{e8}.\mathbf{0} \\
\mathit{MIwithoutSync}: \quad & N7 = e8.([\cdot].\mathbf{0} \mid [\cdot].\mathbf{0} \mid [\cdot].\mathbf{0} \mid \overline{e9}.\mathbf{0} \mid N7) \\
\mathit{StartEvent}: \quad & N1 = [\cdot].\overline{e1}.\mathbf{0} \\
\mathit{EndEvent}: \quad & N8 = e9.[\cdot].N8 \\
\mathit{Global}: \quad & N = (\mathbf{v}e1, \cdots, e9) \prod_{i=1}^{8} Ni
\end{aligned}$$

A task waits for preconditions (the incoming edges), executes the functional perspective abstracted by a context, and generates postconditions (i.e. co-names). Although not required for the example, the processes use recursion to support loop behavior. Note that a BPMN AND Gateway combines two patterns, parallel split and synchronization, into one node. The process $N1$ representing a Start Event does not support re-execution by recursion. If a whole process should be executed another time, a new instance of it has to be created. □

5 Structural and Lazy Soundness

This section introduces correctness criteria for process graphs. We distinguish between structural and behavioral criteria. The former is denoted by *structural soundness*, whereas the latter is given by soundness, relaxed soundness, and lazy soundness. We focus on lazy soundness in this paper, although weak soundness can be defined and proved in a similar manner.

5.1 Structural Soundness

Structural soundness for process graphs is based on the concepts introduced in the following paragraphs.

Definition 7 (Path). *A path in a process graph $P = (N, E, T, A)$ is a sequence of directed edges leading from one node to another. Formally, a path ϵ from n_1 to n_2 is written as: $n_1 \xrightarrow{\epsilon} n_2$ with $n_1, n_2 \in N$ and $\epsilon \in E^*$, where we allow an empty sequence. An arbitrary path from n_1 to n_2 is denoted as $n_1 \xrightarrow{*} n_2$.* □

Definition 8 (Reachability). *A node of a process graph $P = (N, E, T, A)$ is reachable from another node if and only if there exist a path leading from the first to the second node. Formally: $n_2 \in N$ is reachable from $n_1 \in N$, iff $\exists \epsilon \in E^* : n_1 \xrightarrow{\epsilon} n_2$.* □

Definition 9 (Defined Process Graph). *A process graph $P = (N, E, T, A)$ is defined if and only if there is exactly one node of the type* Initial Node, *denoted as N_i, that is not the target of any edge and exactly one node of the type* Final Node, *denoted as N_o, that is not the source of any edge. Formally: $\exists n \in N : InitialNode \in type(n) \wedge \forall n_1, n_2 \in N : InitialNode \in type(n_1) \wedge InitialNode \in type(n_2) \Rightarrow n_1 = n_2$ and $\exists n \in N : FinalNode \in type(n) \wedge \forall n_1, n_2 \in N : FinalNode \in type(n_1) \wedge InitialNode \in type(n_2) \Rightarrow n_1 = n_2$. Furthermore: $\forall n \in N : InitialNode \in type(n) \Rightarrow \nexists e \in E : target(e) = n$ and $\forall n \in N : FinalNode \in type(n) \Rightarrow \nexists e \in E : source(e) = n$.* □

Definition 10 (Strongly Connected Process Graph). *A defined process graph $P = (N, E, T, A)$ is strongly connected, if and only if for all nodes exists a path from the initial to the final node. Formally: $\forall n \in N$ with $N_i \xrightarrow{*} n \Rightarrow n \xrightarrow{*} N_o$* □

This definition is in contrast to common definitions of a strongly connected directed graph, e.g. by Knuth [18]. We do not require a graph to be short circuited for analysis.

Lemma 1. *$P_{MIN}(N, E, T, A) = (\{N1\}, \emptyset, \{(N1, InitialNode), (N1, Final Node)\}, \emptyset)$ is the smallest strongly connected process graph.*

Proof (Lemma 1). Direct proof. $P_{MIN}(N, E, T, A)$ is strongly connected as it is defined by exactly one initial and final node, and the only node lies on an (empty) path from the initial to the final node. Formally: $\exists n_1 \in N : InitialNode \in type(n_1) \wedge \exists n_2 \in N : FinalNode \in type(n_2)$. $\forall n_1, n_2 \in N : n_1 \xrightarrow{\emptyset} n_2$. All components of P_{MIN} have the lowest possible count of elements for a strongly connected process graph. Formally: $|P_{MIN}(N, E, T, A)| = (1, 0, 2, 0)$ following from Definition 6 and 9. □

Definition 11 (Structural Sound). *A process graph $P = (N, E, T, A)$ is structural sound if and only if:*

1. *There is exactly one initial node $N_i \in N$.*
2. *There is exactly one final node $N_o \in N$.*
3. *Every node is on a path from N_i to N_o.* □

Structural soundness for process graphs adapts the definition of a workflow net as a special kind of Petri net introduced in [6].

Lemma 2. *A strongly connected process graph is structural sound.*

Proof (Lemma2). Direct proof. Criterion 1 and 2 from Definition 11 are fulfilled, as a strongly connected process graph is defined. Criterion 3 follows directly from Definition 10. □

Lemma 3. *$P_{MIN}(N, E, T, A)$ is structural sound.*

Proof (Lemma 3). Follows directly from Lemma 1. □

Algorithm 2 (Deciding Structural Soundness). We describe an algorithm for deciding structural soundness of a process graph $P(N, E, T, A)$:

1. Check if P is defined, i.e. has exactly one initial and exactly one final node (see Definition 9).
2. Check if P is strongly connected, i.e. if every node is on a path from the initial to the final node (see Definition 10). □

5.2 Lazy Soundness

Lazy soundness extends structural soundness by taking the semantics of the process nodes into account. Therefore it considers the π-calculus representation of a process graph, which includes semantics for the types of the process nodes. Lazy soundness states that there are no livelocks or deadlocks in the process graph regarding the semantics of the nodes. Furthermore, the final node will be executed exactly once, while other nodes representing activities can still be or become executed. However, they must not trigger the final node again. To define lazy soundness, we need the definition of *semantic reachability*, i.e. if a node lies on a path from the initial to the final node according to the semantics of all nodes.

Definition 12 (Semantic Reachability). *A node of a process graph $P = (N, E, T, A)$ is semantically reachable from another node if and only if there exists a path leading from the first to the second node according to the semantics of all nodes.* □

Regarding the mapping of a π-calculus process from a process graph, a π-calculus process representing a node is semantically reachable from another π-calculus process representing a node, if and only if there exists a transition sequence from the functional abstraction τ of the first process to the functional abstraction τ of the second process. Lazy soundness is then defined as follows.

Definition 13 (Lazy Sound). *A structural sound process graph $P = (N, E, T, A)$ is lazy sound if it represents a business process that is deadlock free and livelock free, as long as the final node has not been reached. Once the final node has been reached, other nodes might still be executed, however the final node is not enacted again. Formally:*

1. *The final node N_o must be semantically reachable from every node $n \in N$ semantically reachable from the initial node N_i until N_o has been reached for the first time.*
2. *The final node N_o is reached exactly once.* □

To be able to trace the transition sequences required for semantics reachability, we annotate the π-calculus mapping of a process graph with two observability predicates $\downarrow_i$, and $\downarrow_{\overline{o}}$. Using these predicates, we can observe the execution of the initial activity by $\downarrow_i$, and the final activity by $\downarrow_{\overline{o}}$.

Algorithm 3 (Lazy Soundness Annotated π-calculus Process). To annotate a π-calculus process representing a process graph for reasoning on lazy soundness, we need to fill the holes, i.e. $[\cdot]$,of the process definitions with:

- τ, if the the corresponding process graph node has incoming and outgoing edges,
- $i.\tau$, if the corresponding process graph node has only outgoing edges,
- $\tau.\overline{o}$, if the corresponding process graph node has only incoming edges, and
- $i.\tau.\overline{o}$ if the corresponding process graph node has no incoming or outgoing edges. □

An example can be found in Example 4. Due to the fact of being able to observe the initial and the final activity, we can prove lazy soundness for process graphs. Thus, for every activity reachable after the initial activity has been observed, we must always be able to observe the final activity exactly once if the process graph if lazy sound. If we observe the final activity more then once or never at all, the process graph contains a deadlock or livelock. We derive this theorem by constructing the smallest lazy soundness annotated π-calculus mapping of a process graph and prove it to be lazy sound.

Lemma 4. *$S_{LAZY} = i.\tau.\overline{o}.\mathbf{0}$ with the observability predicates $\downarrow_i$ and $\downarrow_{\overline{o}}$ is the smallest lazy soundness annotated π-calculus mapping of a process graph satisfying lazy soundness.*

Proof (Lemma 4). The proof consists of two parts. We first show that S_{LAZY} is the smallest lazy soundness annotated π-calculus of P_{MIN}. Secondly, we prove that S_{LAZY} is lazy sound by constructing all transitions.

1. Direct proof. S_{LAZY} is the smallest lazy soundness annotated π-calculus mapping of P_{MIN}. It has exactly one node denoted by τ and no pre- or postconditions. The initial node is exactly the final node, denoted by i before and $\overline{o}$ after τ.

2. Direct proof. Lazy soundness for S_{LAZY} is proved by constructing all transitions: $i.\tau.\overline{o}.\mathbf{0} \xrightarrow{i} \tau.\overline{o}.\mathbf{0} \xrightarrow{\tau} \overline{o}.\mathbf{0} \xrightarrow{\overline{o}} \mathbf{0}$. The transition trace proves that the initial node is always executed once (observability predicate $\downarrow_i$), all possible transitions are executed thereafter (one τ-transition), and eventually the final node is executed (observability predicate $\downarrow_{\overline{o}}$) before S_{LAZY} reaches inaction. □

Now we are ready to introduce the theorem for proving lazy soundness on structural sound process graphs mapped to a lazy sound π-calculus representation.

Theorem 1. *Each structural sound process graph P more complex then P_{MIN} is mapped to a lazy soundness annotated π-calculus process D, so that $D \sim^{o}_{i,\overline{o}} S_{LAZY}$ if and only if P is lazy sound.* □

Proof (Theorem 1). Direct proof. Each structural sound process graph more complex then P_{MIN} is mapped to a lazy soundness annotated π-calculus process D with $\downarrow_i$ as the observability predicate of the initial node and $\downarrow_{\overline{o}}$ as the observability predicate of the final node. The observability predicates are thus the invariants of the π-calculus processes. If a lazy soundness annotated π-calculus process $D \sim^{o}_{i,o} S_{LAZY}$, the corresponding process graph P of D must then be lazy sound. □

Algorithm 4 (Deciding Lazy Soundness). We describe an algorithm for deciding lazy soundness of a structural sound process graph mapped to π-calculus processes.

1. Map the structural sound process graph to π-calculus processes, following Algorithm 1.
2. Annotate the π-calculus processes for lazy soundness, following Algorithm 3.
3. Check the annotated definition for weak open bisimulation equivalence with S_{LAZY} concerning $\downarrow_i$ and $\downarrow_{\overline{o}}$. □

This algorithm has already been implemented and will be discussed in the next section.

6 Tool Support and Discussion

This section evaluates how the theoretical results achieved can be applied and verified using existing tools such as Mobility Workbench (MWB), Advanced Bisimulation Checker (ABC), or Open Bisimulation Checker (OBC) for deciding weak open bisimulation equivalence on π-calculus processes [19,20,21].

6.1 Tool Integration

To be able to integrate these tools into our theoretical framework, we have created a tool chain consisting of several scripts. The first script is written in

AppleScript and exports a graphical BPMN business process diagram from OmniGraffle[2] to a process graph. We had to use a slightly modified BPMN notation to support all workflow pattern, as can been see in Figure 2 were we introduced an n-out-of-m-gateway. We created Ruby scripts for deciding structural soundness of process graphs, as well as mapping process graphs to lazy and weak soundness annotated π-calculus processes. The generated π-calculus processes are then used as input to the tools MWB and ABC for deciding lazy or weak soundness. We illustrate lazy soundness by example in the corresponding input style for MWB or ABC:

Example 4 (Lazy Soundness annotated π-calculus process of Example 3 for Tool Analysis).

```
agent N8(e9,o)=e9.t.'o.N8(e9,o)
agent N7(e8,e9)=e8.(t.0 | t.0 | t.0 | 'e9.0 | N7(e8,e9))
agent N6(e5,e6,e7,e8)=(^h,run)(N6_1(e5,e6,e7,e8,h,run) | N6_2(e5,e6,e7,e8,h,run))
agent N6_1(e5,e6,e7,e8,h,run)=e5.'h.0 | e6.'h.0 | e7.'h.0
agent N6_2(e5,e6,e7,e8,h,run)=h.h.'run.h.N6(e5,e6,e7,e8) | run.t.'e8.0
agent N5(e4,e7)=e4.t.('e7.0 | N5(e4,e7))
agent N4(e3,e6)=e3.t.('e6.0 | N4(e3,e6))
agent N3(e2,e5)=e2.t.('e5.0 | N3(e2,e5))
agent N2(e1,e2,e3,e4)=e1.t.(N2(e1,e2,e3,e4) | 'e2.0 | 'e3.0 | 'e4.0)
agent N1(e1,i)=i.t.'e1.0
agent N(i,o)=(^e1,e2,e3,e4,e5,e6,e7,e8,e9)(N8(e9,o) | N7(e8,e9) | N6(e5,e6,e7,e8) |
      N5(e4,e7) | N4(e3,e6) | N3(e2,e5) | N2(e1,e2,e3,e4) | N1(e1,i))
agent S_LAZY(i,o)=i.t.'o.0
```

We can ask ABC for deciding weak open bisimulation equivalence on N and S_{LAZY}, thus deciding lazy soundness for the process graph from Example 2:

```
abc > weqd (i,o) N(i,o) S_LAZY(i,o)
The two agents are weakly related (315).
Do you want to see the core of the bisimulation (yes/no) ? no
```

Since $N(i, o)$ is weak open bisimulation equivalent to S_{LAZY}, the corresponding process graph is lazy sound. By simply modifying the AND Gateway of the example given in Figure 2 to an XOR Gateway in the corresponding lazy soundness annotated π-calculus process, we can prove the corresponding process graph to be not lazy sound:

```
abc > agent N2(e1,e2,e3,e4)=e1.t.(N2(e1,e2,e3,e4) | ('e2.0 + 'e3.0 + 'e4.0))
Agent N2 is defined.
abc > weqd (i,o) N(i,o) S_LAZY(i,o)
The two agents are not weakly related (9).
Do you want to see some traces (yes/no) ? no
```

Obviously, the modified process graph is not lazy sound as it contains a deadlock.

6.2 Supported Patterns and Performance

Tool support for reasoning on lazy soundness is still limited by the supported patterns as well as performance. Multi merge and simple merge patterns behave the same (indeed, same π-calculus representation). Since the π-calculus has a blocking semantics, parallel activation will be queued until the merge activity is ready again. The synchronizing merge pattern in the π-calculus has non local

[2] http://www.omnigroup.com/applications/omnigraffle/

Table 1. Performance results for deciding lazy soundness

	Fig. 2	**Fig. 2 mod.**	**Fig. A6 [6]**	**Fig. 2 [16]**	**Bookstore [24]**
Nodes	8 nodes	8 nodes	10 nodes	15 nodes	21 nodes
MWB	$10s$	$< 1s$	$< 1s$	$15s$	$6s$
ABC	$40s$	$2s$	$6s$	$275s$	$167s$
ABC.opt	$13s$	$< 1s$	$2s$	$55s$	$50s$
Lazy Sound?	Yes	No	Yes	Yes	Yes

semantics and is thus only supported by workarounds ranging from introducing a local semantics (true/false token passing, corresponding split/choice and synchronizing merge patterns, where the split/choice informs the corresponding merge about the number of incoming arcs) to global analysis (e.g. delay synchronizing merge while other transitions are possible). Further discussions regarding the synchronizing merge pattern can be found in [22,23]. Arbitrary cycles are only partly supported in MWB as well as ABC. These tools fail at deciding processes with loops generating an infinite number of $\downarrow_{\overline{o}}$. This is indeed a tool related issue, as the reasoning could be stopped immediately after more then one $\overline{o}$ has been observed, instead of creating the full space state. A related issue concerns multiple instances with a dynamic number of instances, either runtime or without a priori knowledge. MWB as well as ABC fail for unknown reasons at detecting the contained cycles, while they work at simple loops. However, both issues are tool related and do not disturb the theory. For all patterns containing cancellation, i.e. cancel activity, cancel case, event-based rerouting, we can not actually stop the unobservable action τ, only immediately reroute the control flow and cancel all related outgoing flows.

Regarding the performance of deciding weak open bisimulation, we are currently investigating existing tools. First practical results for business processes containing different patterns have been collected in table 1.[3] Some processes have been converted to BPMN and can be found in the cited references. Figure 2 and the modified version have been discussed in this paper. Figure A6 from [6] contains arbitrary cycles. Figure 2 from [16] contains event-based rerouting and deferred choice patterns. The bookstore process from [24] contains multiple deferred choices and arbitrary cycles.

7 Conclusion

In this paper, we introduced and discussed a new correctness criterion for business processes, called lazy soundness. Lazy soundness proves a business process to be deadlock and livelock free, but does not cover dead activities, or requires all activities to be finished when a final activity is reached. It can be classified below weak soundness and soundness, i.e. all sound and all weak sound business processes are lazy sound, and beside relaxed soundness, i.e. a relaxed sound

[3] Rough estimations measured on an Apple PowerBook G4 1.5GHz with 1.25GB RAM.

business process can be lazy sound. A stronger kind of lazy soundness is weak soundness, forcing all activities to finish before the final activity is reached.

Lazy soundness is an important correctness criterion for business processes, as it supports reasoning on deadlock and livelock freedom without being to restrictive regarding so called *clean-up* or *lazy-activities* that can be left behind. Our reasoning framework presented supports the original semantics of the workflow patterns discriminator, n-out-of-m-join, and multiple instances without synchronization. It achieves this by utilizing the π-calculus as formal foundation. All existing workflow patterns [8] as well as new routing patterns [16] can be represented in this calculus. It has strong theoretical reasoning capabilities based on different kinds of bisimulation [14,15], that can be used to prove lazy soundness. We already achieved first feasibility results using a tool chain for converting BPMN business process diagrams to π-calculus processes that can be analyzed using existing π-calculus tools. Obviously, the underlying concepts of lazy soundness as discussed in section 2 can also be adapted to other formalizations like workflow nets.

Further work will focus on complete support for soundness and relaxed soundness, as well as reasoning on interacting business processes. Therefore, a special capability of the π-calculus, namely *channel-passing*, will be of special interest as it allows support for dynamic routing patterns [7]. Alongside, we will improve tool development focusing on weak open bisimulation for π-calculus processes representing workflow patterns.

References

1. van der Aalst, W.M.P., ter Hofstede, A.H., Weske, M.: Business Process Management: A Survey. In van der Aalst, W.M.P., ter Hofstede, A.H., Weske, M., eds.: Proceedings of the 1st International Conference on Business Process Management, volume 2678 of LNCS, Berlin, Springer-Verlag (2003) 1–12
2. Burbeck, S.: The Tao of e-business services. Available at: `http://www-128.ibm.com/developerworks/library/ws-tao/` (2000)
3. van der Aalst, W.M.P.: Verification of Workflow Nets. In Azéma, P., Balbo, G., eds.: Application and Theory of Petri Nets, volume 1248 of LNCS, Berlin, Springer-Verlag (1997) 407–426
4. Dehnert, J., Rittgen, P.: Relaxed Soundness of Business Processes. In Dittrich, K., Geppert, A., Norrie, M.C., eds.: CAiSE 2001, volume 2068 of LNCS, Berlin, Springer-Verlag (2001) 157–170
5. Martens, A.: On Compatibility of Web Services. Petri Net Newsletter **65** (2003) 12–20
6. van der Aalst, W., van Hee, K.: Workflow Management. MIT Press (2002)
7. Barros, A., Dumas, M., ter Hofstede, A.: Service Interaction Patterns. In van der Aalst, W., Benatallah, B., Casati, F., eds.: Proceedings of the 3rd International Conference on Business Process Management, volume 3649 of LNCS, Berlin, Springer-Verlag (2005) 302–318
8. Puhlmann, F., Weske, M.: Using the Pi-Calculus for Formalizing Workflow Patterns. In van der Aalst, W., Benatallah, B., Casati, F., eds.: Proceedings of the 3rd International Conference on Business Process Management, volume 3649 of LNCS, Berlin, Springer-Verlag (2005) 153–168

9. Milner, R., Parrow, J., Walker, D.: A Calculus of Mobile Processes, Part I/II. Information and Computation **100** (1992) 1–77
10. van der Aalst, W.M.P., ter Hofstede, A.H.M., Kiepuszewski, B., Barros, A.: Workflow Patterns. Technical Report BETA Working Paper Series, WP 47, Eindhoven University of Technology (2000)
11. van der Aalst, W.M.P., ter Hofstede, A.H.M.: YAWL: Yet Another Workflow Language (Revised version. Technical Report FIT-TR-2003-04, Queensland University of Technology, Brisbane (2003)
12. Verbeek, H., van der Aalst, W., ter Hofstede, A.: Verifying Workflows with Cancellation Regions and OR-joins: An Approach based on Invariants, BETA Working Paper Series, WP 156. Technical report, Eindhoven University of Technology, Eindhoven, The Netherlands (2006)
13. Puhlmann, F.: Why do we actually need the Pi-Calculus for Business Process Management? In: Proceedings of the 9th International Conference on Business Information Systems. (2006) (to appear)
14. Sangiorgi, D., Walker, D.: The π-calculus: A Theory of Mobile Processes. Paperback edn. Cambridge University Press, Cambridge (2003)
15. Sangiorgi, D.: A Theory of Bisimulation for the Pi-Calculus. In: CONCUR '93: Proceedings of the 4th International Conference on Concurrency Theory, Berlin, Springer-Verlag (1993) 127–142
16. Overdick, H., Puhlmann, F., Weske, M.: Towards a Formal Model for Agile Service Discovery and Integration. In Verma, K., Sheth, A., Zaremba, M., Bussler, C., eds.: Proceedings of the International Workshop on Dynamic Web Processes (DWP 2005). IBM technical report RC23822, Amsterdam (2005)
17. BPMI.org: Business Process Modeling Notation. 1.0 edn. (2004)
18. Knuth, D.E.: The Art of Computer Programming. 3rd edn. Volume 1. Addison–Wesley (1997)
19. Björn Victor, Faron Moller, M.D., Eriksson, L.H.: The Mobility Workbench. Available at: `http://www.it.uu.se/research/group/mobility/mwb` (2005)
20. Briais, S.: ABC Bisimulation Checker. Available at: `http://lamp.epfl.ch/~sbriais/abc/abc.html` (2003)
21. Frendrup, U., Jensen, J.N., Hüttel, H.: OBC Workbench. Available at: `http://www.cs.auc.dk/research/FS/ny/PR-pi/` (2001)
22. Wynn, M., Edmond, D., van der Aalst, W., ter Hofstede, A.: Achieving a General, Formal and Decidable Approach to the OR-join in Workflow using Reset nets (2005)
23. Kindler, E.: On the Semantics of EPCs: A Framework for Resolving the Vicious Circle. In Desel, J., Pernici, B., Weske, M., eds.: Proceedings of the 2nd International Conference on Business Process Management, volume 3080 of LNCS, Berlin, Springer-Verlag (2004) 82–97
24. van der Aalst, W.M.P., Weske, M.: The P2P Approach to Interorganizational Workflow. In Dittrich, K., Geppert, A., Norrie, M., eds.: Proceedings of the 13th International Conference on Advanced Information Systems Engineering (CAiSE'01), volume 2068 of LNCS, Berlin, Springer-Verlag (2001) 140–156

On the Suitability of BPMN for Business Process Modelling*

P. Wohed[1,**], W.M.P. van der Aalst[2,3], M. Dumas[3], A.H.M. ter Hofstede[3], and N. Russell[3]

[1] The Department of Computer and Systems Sciences, SU/KTH, Sweden
petia@dsv.su.se
[2] Faculty of Information Technology, QUT, Australia
{m.dumas, a.terhofstede, n.russell}@qut.edu.au
[3] Department of Technology Management, TU/e, The Netherlands
w.m.p.v.d.aalst@tm.tue.nl

Abstract. In this paper we examine the suitability of the Business Process Modelling Notation (BPMN) for business process modelling, using the Workflow Patterns as an evaluation framework. The Workflow Patterns are a collection of patterns developed for assessing control-flow, data and resource capabilities in the area of Process Aware Information Systems (PAISs). In doing so, we provide a comprehensive evaluation of the capabilities of BPMN, and its strengths and weaknesses when utilised for business process modelling. The analysis provided for BPMN is part of a larger effort aiming at an unbiased and vendor-independent survey of the suitability and the expressive power of some mainstream process modelling languages. It is a sequel to previous work in which languages including BPEL and UML Activity Diagrams were evaluated.

Keywords: BPMN, Business Process Modelling, Workflow Patterns.

1 Introduction

The focus on Process-Aware Information Systems (PAISs) during the last decade has led to a new generation of languages and tools for process modelling. Existing languages for process description have been enhanced, e.g. UML 2.0 Activity Diagrams (AD), while new languages like BPMN and BPEL have been developed and have experienced rapid take-up. The common feature of these three languages is their focus on providing a comprehensive, integrated notation for (business) process modelling. Despite their common aims, these languages operate at different levels: UML AD and BPMN are graphical and informal notations targeted at analysts while BPEL is a textual and executable language targeted at application developers.

This broad characterisation does not, however, provide insights into the suitability of these languages for (business) process modelling, or how they actually relate to each other. To address these issues, a thorough analysis of each of the languages is necessary.

* This work is funded in part by VR 621-2001-2768 and by ARC DP0451092.

** Research conducted during a visit to the Queensland University of Technology.

S. Dustdar, J.L. Fiadeiro, and A. Sheth (Eds.): BPM 2006, LNCS 4102, pp. 161–176, 2006.

In this paper we focus on BPMN. Through a detailed examination, we aim to expose advantages and shortcomings of BPMN and to critically question its suitability for business process modelling. This analysis is part of a broader survey of mainstream process modelling languages and is a companion to earlier analysis of UML 2.0 AD [17,9] and BPEL [15,1]. The overarching goal of the survey is to provide comparative insights, which is achieved by analysing the languages using a common framework, namely the *Workflow Patterns* (`www.workflowpatterns.com`).

The Workflow Patterns Framework is a collection of generic, recurring constructs originally devised to evaluate workflow systems, but also suitable to evaluate workflow standards, business process languages and PAISs in general. Following Jablonski and Bussler's classification [3], these patterns span the *Control-flow*, *Data* and *Resource* perspectives of PAISs. Our choice of this evaluation framework is based on the fact that it is: (1) widely used; (2) well accepted; (3) comprehensible to IT practitioners; and (4) sufficiently detailed to provide a comprehensive basis for assessing the capabilities of process modelling languages.

In essence, the contributions of this paper are as follows:

- It is the first multi-perspective evaluation of the expressive capabilities of BPMN;
- It provides an assessment of the overall suitability of BPMN for process modelling;
- It identifies areas for possible improvement of BPMN;
- It provides a basis for comparing BPMN with related languages.

Previous efforts [11,7] have analysed the quality and ontological standard of BPMN. The evaluation in [11] is based on the *Semiotic Quality Framework*. It is positioned by its authors as a more general than and complementary to the evaluation in [7], which relies on the *Bunge Wand and Weber (BWW) Framework*. Based on an ontology for Information Systems, the BWW Framework is at a higher abstraction level and less specialised compared to the Workflow Patterns Framework. Lastly, a review of the capabilities of BPMN from a control flow perspective based on the Workflow Patterns is provided in [14]. However, the evaluation in [14] has a limited focus as well as ambiguities which we have identified in [16].

In the remainder of the paper we evaluate BPMN from the Control-flow, the Data and the Resource perspectives. Then we discuss our findings and compare these with earlier evaluations of UML 2.0 AD and BPEL.

2 The Control-Flow Perspective in BPMN

In this section we examine the control-flow perspective of BPMN and its ability to represent a series of twenty common control-flow modelling requirements that occur when defining process models. These requirements are described in terms of the Workflow Control-flow Patterns [2]. The material in this section summarises the findings reported in a technical report [16]. There has also been a review of this perspective of BPMN by White [14], who is one of BPMN's developers. The results reported here differ from those in [14], however due to space limitations we refer to [16] for a detailed discussion on the differences and the flaws identified in [14].

2.1 Basic Control-Flow Patterns

The basic control-flow patterns define elementary aspects of process control. These are analogous to the definitions of elementary control-flow concepts laid down by the Workflow Management Coalition [12]. There are five of these patterns:

- WCP1: *Sequence* – the ability to depict a sequence of activities;
- WCP2: *Parallel split* – the ability to capture a split in a single thread of control into multiple threads of control which can execute in parallel;
- WCP3: *Synchronisation* – the ability to capture a synchronisation of multiple parallel subprocesses/activities into a single thread;
- WCP4: *Exclusive choice* – the ability to represent a decision point in a workflow process where one of several branches is chosen;
- WCP5: *Simple merge* – the ability to depict a point in the workflow process where two or more alternative branches come together without synchronisation.

All these five patterns can be captured in BPMN. *Sequence* corresponds directly to the "sequence flow" construct, while the other four patterns are illustrated in Figure 1.

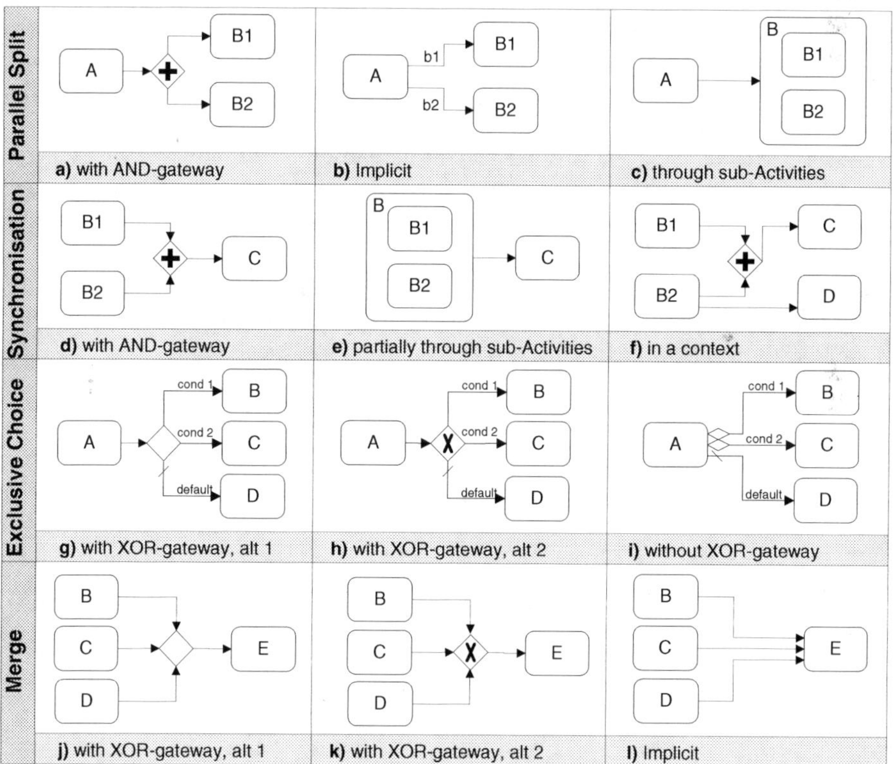

Fig. 1. Basic control-flow patterns in BPMN

2.2 Advanced Branching and Synchronisation Patterns

This class of patterns corresponds to advanced branching and synchronisation scenarios that often do not have direct realisations in PAISs but are relatively common in real-life business processes. There are four of these patterns:

- WCP6: *Multiple choice* – the ability to represent a divergence of the thread of control into several parallel branches on a selective basis;
- WCP7: *Synchronising merge* – the ability to depict the synchronised convergence of two or more alternative branches;
- WCP8: *Multiple merge* – the ability to represent the unsynchronised convergence of two or more distinct branches. If more than one branch is active, the activity following the merge is started for every activation of every incoming branch;
- WCP9: *Discriminator* – the ability to depict the convergence of two or more branches such that the first activation of an incoming branch results in the subsequent activity being triggered and subsequent activations of remaining incoming branches are ignored. It is a special case of *N-out-of-M* pattern, where N is equal to one.

The solution for the *Multiple merge* pattern is identical to the solution for the *Simple merge* pattern (see figures 1j, 1k and 1l). The solutions for the *Multiple choice* pattern are illustrated in figures 2a, 2b and 2c. The *Discriminator* pattern is captured for the case when it joins the instances of a Multiple Instances task, see Figure 2d. A work-around generalising this solution to the N-out-of-M join is shown in Figure 2e and a work-around for the N-out-of-M join pattern for distinct activities is presented in Figure 2f. The *Synchronising merge* pattern is captured partially through the OR-join gateway. The solution is partial because it assumes a structured workflow context.

2.3 Structural Patterns

Structural patterns identify whether the modelling formalism has any restrictions in regard to the way in which processes can be structured (particularly in terms of the type of loops supported and whether a single terminating node is necessary).

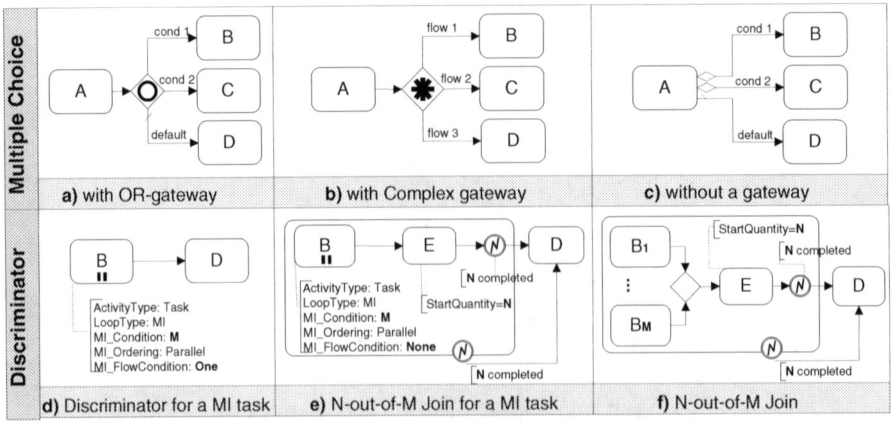

Fig. 2. Advanced branching and synchronisation patterns in BPMN

- WCP10: *Arbitrary cycles* – the ability to represent loops that have multiple entry or exit points;
- WCP11: *Implicit termination* – the ability to depict the notion that a given subprocess should be terminated when there are no remaining activities to be completed (i.e. no explicit unique termination node is needed).

Both of these patterns are directly supported in BPMN.

2.4 Multiple Instances (MI) Patterns

This category encompasses situations where is more than one instance of an activity active at the same time for the same process instance. There are four such patterns:

- WCP12: *MI without synchronisation* – the ability to initiate multiple instances of an activity within a given process instance;
- WCP13: *MI with a priori design time knowledge* – the ability to initiate multiple instances of an activity within a given process instance. The number of instances is known at design time. Once all instances have completed, a subsequent activity is initiated;
- WCP14: *MI with a priori runtime knowledge* – the ability to initiate multiple instances of an activity within a given process instance. The number of instances varies but is known at runtime before the instances must be created. Once all instances have completed, a subsequent activity is initiated;
- WCP15: *MI without a priori runtime knowledge* – the ability to initiate multiple instances of an activity within a given process instance. The number of instances varies but is not known at design time or at runtime before the instances must be created. Once all instances have completed, a subsequent activity is initiated. New instances can be created even while other instances are executing or have already completed.

The first three of these patterns can be captured in BPMN as illustrated in Figure 3. The *MI without a priori runtime knowledge* pattern is not directly supported in BPMN because it is not possible to add instances on-the-fly.

2.5 State-Based Patterns

This class of patterns characterise scenarios in a process where subsequent execution is determined by the state of the process instance. There are three such patterns:

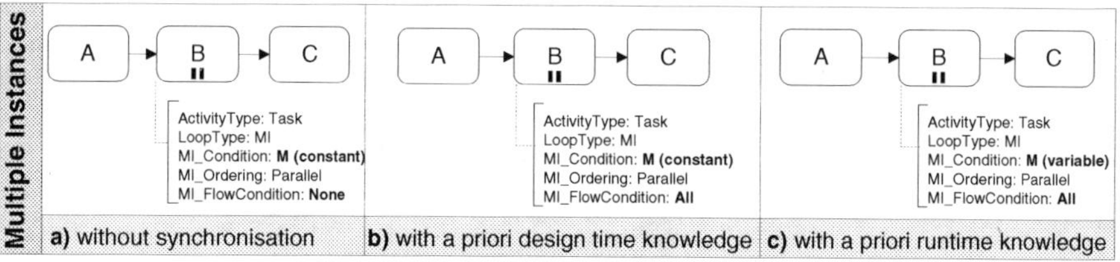

Fig. 3. Multiple Instances patterns in BPMN

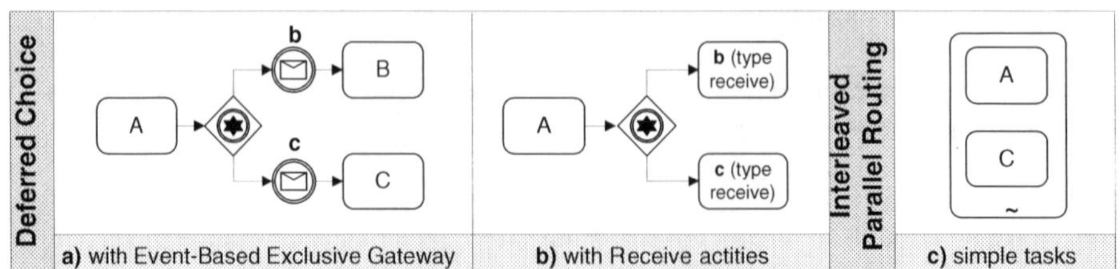

Fig. 4. State-based patterns in BPMN

- WCP16: *Deferred choice* – the ability to depict a divergence point in a process where one of several possible branches should be activated. The actual decision on which branch is activated is made by the environment and is deferred to the latest possible moment;
- WCP17: *Interleaved parallel routing* – the ability to depict a set of activities that can be executed in arbitrary order;
- WCP18: *Milestone* – the ability to depict that a specified activity cannot be commenced until some nominated state is reached which has not expired yet.

Owing to the absence of the notion of state, only the *Deferred choice* pattern can be fully captured in BPMN. This is illustrated in figures 4a and 4b. The *Interleaved parallel routing* pattern is captured for the case when the activities to be interleaved are simple tasks. This solution is illustrated in Figure 4c. The *Milestone* pattern is not supported.

2.6 Cancellation Patterns

Cancellation patterns characterise the ability of the modelling formalism to represent the potential termination of activities and process instances in certain (specified) circumstances. There are two such patterns:

- WCP19: *Cancel activity* – the ability to depict that an enabled activity should be disabled in some nominated circumstance;
- WCP20: *Cancel case* – the ability to represent the cancellation of an entire process instance (i.e. all activities relating to the process instance) in some nominated circumstance.

Both of these patterns can be captured in BPMN. The solutions are shown in Figure 5.

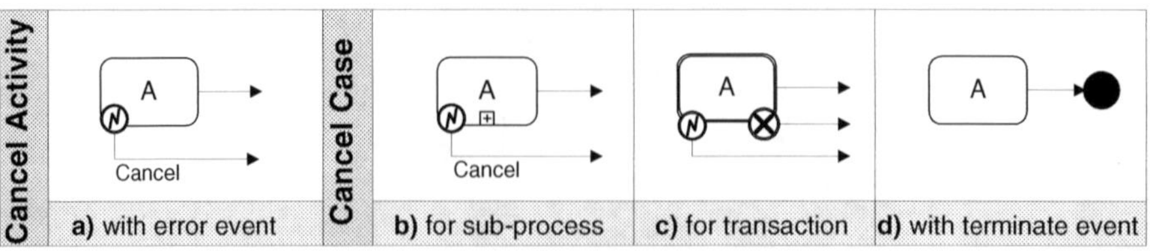

Fig. 5. Cancellation patterns in BPMN

Table 1 summarises the results from this part of the evaluation. The table also shows the results from the evaluations of UML 2.0 AD, BPEL, and a concrete system based on the latter language Oracle BPEL Process Manager (PM) Version 10.1.2. In the conclusion we will compare BPMN with these other languages.

3 The Data Perspective in BPMN

Extensions [10] to the *Workflow Patterns Initiative* have focused on identifying and defining generic constructs that occur in the data perspective of PAISs. In total forty data patterns have been delineated in four distinct groups – data visibility, data interaction, data transfer and data-based routing. In this section, an analysis of BPMN is presented using the data patterns described in [10].

3.1 Data Visibility Patterns

Data visibility patterns seek to characterise the various ways in which data elements can be defined and utilised within the context of a process. In general, this is determined by the main construct to which the data element is bound as it implies a particular scope in which the data element is visible and capable of being utilised. There are eight patterns which relate to data visibility:

- WDP1: *Task data* – data elements defined and accessible in the context of individual execution instances of a task or activity;
- WDP2: *Block data* – data elements defined by block tasks (i.e. tasks which can be described in terms of a corresponding decomposition) and accessible to the block task and all corresponding components within the associated decomposition;
- WDP3: *Scope data* – data elements bound to a subset of the tasks in a process instance;
- WDP4: *Multiple instance data* – data elements specific to a single execution instance of a task (where the task is able to be executed multiple times);
- WDP5: *Case data* – data elements specific to a process instance which are accessible to all components of the process instance during execution;

Table 1. Support for the Control–flow Patterns in **1**–BPMN, **2**–UML2.0 AD [17,9], **3**–BPEL [15,1], and **4**–Oracle BPEL PM v.10.1.2 [5]

	1	2	3	4		1	2	3	4
Basic Control–flow					11. Implicit Termination	+	+	+	+
1. Sequence	+	+	+	+	Multiple Instances Patterns				
2. Parallel Split	+	+	+	+	12. MI without Synchronization	+	+	+	+
3. Synchronisation	+	+	+	+	13. MI with a priori Design Time Knowledge	+	+	+	+
4. Exclusive Choice	+	+	+	+	14. MI with a priori Runtime Knowledge	+	+	–	+
5. Simple Merge	+	+	+	+	15. MI without a priori Runtime Knowledge	–	–	–	+/–
Advanced Synchronisation					State-Based Patterns				
6. Multiple Choice	+	+	+	+	16. Deferred Choice	+	+	+	+
7. Synchronising Merge	+/–	–	+	+	17. Interleaved Parallel Routing	+/–	–	+/–	–
8. Multiple Merge	+	+	–	–	18. Milestone	–	–	–	+/–
9. Discriminator	+/–	+	–	–	Cancellation Patterns				
Structural Patterns					19. Cancel Activity	+	+	+	+/–
10. Arbitrary Cycles	+	+	–	–	20. Cancel Case	+	+	+	+

- WDP6: *Folder data* – data elements bound to a subset of the tasks in a process definition but accessible to all task instances regardless of the case to which they correspond;
- WDP7: *Workflow data* – data elements accessible to all components in all cases;
- WDP8: *Environment data* – data elements defined in the operational environment which can be accessed by process elements.

BPMN supports several of these patterns. *Task*, *Block* and *Case data* are supported through the attribute Properties of Task, Sub-Process and Process elements, respectively. *Scope data* is not supported as the Group construct does not offer any data handling for the elements it groups together.

Multiple instance data is partially supported. There are three situations where multiple instances of a given task may arise: (i) Where a task is specifically designated as having multiple instances in the process model. The lack of an attribute "Properties" for the distinct instances of a multiple instances activity (akin to the attribute Properties of Activity) eliminates the possibility to handle any instance specific data for a multiple instances task; (ii) Where a task can be triggered multiple times, e.g., it is part of a loop or it is a task following a multiple merge construct. These situations are allowable in BPMN; (iii) Where two tasks share the same decomposition. This is supported. An activity decomposition can be captured through the notion of an Independent Sub-Process. Several Independent Sub-Processes can invoke one and the same Process.

Folder, *Workflow* and *Environment data* patterns are not supported in BPMN.

3.2 Data Interaction Patterns

Data interaction patterns deal with the various ways in which data elements can be passed between components within a process instance and also with the operating environment (e.g. data transfer between a component of a process and an application, data store or interface that is external to the process). They examine how the characteristics of the individual components can influence the manner in which the trafficking of data elements occurs. There are six internal data interaction patterns:

- WDP9: *Data elements flowing between task instances*;
- WDP10: *Data elements flowing to a block*;
- WDP11: *Data elements flowing from a block*;
- WDP12: *Data elements flowing to a multiple instance task instance*;
- WDP13: *Data elements flowing from a multiple instance task instance*;
- WDP14: *Data elements flowing between process instances or cases.*

Data interaction between tasks (WDP9) can be utilised in three different ways: (i) through integrated control and data channels; or (ii) through distinct control and data channels; or (iii) through the use of global shared data. BPMN supports global shared data (through the Properties attribute for a Process), hence the third alternative is clearly supported. It also appears that the first two alternatives are supported. Data interaction through distinct control and data channels is supported through the notion of Data Object. Data interaction through integrated control and data channels is supported through the construct of Data Objects associated with sequence flows.

Furthermore, the *Data interactions block task to and from sub-workflow* (WDP10 and WDP11) are directly supported. One of the means of doing this is via parameters, i.e., through the Input- and OutputPropertyMaps attributes. This is relevant for cases where the decomposition is defined through an Independent Sub-Process. Another way of doing this is through the global shared data defined for a process. This is relevant for the cases when the decomposition is defined through an Embedded Sub-Processes.

Data interaction to and from multiple instance task instances (WDP12 and WDP13) and data interaction between cases (WDP14) are not supported in BPMN.

In addition to the internal data interaction patterns, there are 12 external data interaction patterns. These are characterised by three dimensions:

- The type of process element – task, case or complete process – that is interacting with the environment;
- Whether the interaction is push or pull-based;
- Whether the interaction is initiated by the process component or the environment.

The patterns *Task to Environment, Push* and *Pull*, and *Environment to Task, Push* and *Pull*, (i.e., WDPs 15, 16, 17 and 18) are supported in BPMN. They are captured through one or a pair of message flow(s) flowing to, from, or to and from a task and the boundary of a pool representing the environment. Note that for these patterns the environment is modelled explicitly.

The patterns *Case to Environment, Push and Pull*, as well as *Environment to Case, Push and Pull* (i.e., WDPs 19–22) are not supported. Message flows can indeed be drawn between the boundaries of two pools where one of the pools represents a process and the other one the environment. However, "If the Message Flow is connected to the boundary to the Expanded Sub-Process, then this is equivalent to connecting to the Start Event for incoming Message Flow or the End Event for outgoing Message Flow." ([13], p. 117). Hence, this construct does not provide support for data exchange of case data at *any* moment during the execution of a case.

Finally, the *Workflow to Environment, Push* and *Pull*, and *Environment to Workflow, Push* and *Pull* patterns (i.e., WDPs 23-26) are not supported, as workflow data is not supported in BPMN (see WDP7 above).

3.3 Data Transfer Patterns

Data transfer patterns focus on the way in which data elements are actually transferred between one process element and another. They aim to capture the various mechanisms by which data elements can be passed across the interface of a process element. There are seven distinct patterns in this category:

- WDP27: *Data transfer by value – incoming* – incoming data elements passed by value;
- WDP28: *Data transfer by value – outgoing* – outgoing data elements passed by value;
- WDP29: *Data transfer – copy in/copy out* – where a process element synchronises data elements with an external data source at commencement and completion;

- WDP30: *Data transfer by reference – without lock* – data elements are communicated between components via a reference to a data element in some mutually accessible location. No concurrency restrictions are implied;
- WDP31: *Data transfer by reference – with lock* – similar to WDP30 except that concurrency restrictions are implied with the receiving component receiving the privilege of read-only or dedicated access to the data element;
- WDP32: *Data transformation – input* – where a transformation function is applied to a data element prior to it being passed to a subsequent component;
- WDP33: *Data transformation – output* – where a transformation function is applied to a data element prior to it being passed from a previous component.

In BPMN, the WDP27 and WDP28 patterns are supported through the notion of the Input and OutputSets. WDP29 *Data transfer – copy in/copy out* is partially supported. It occurs when a decomposition is realised with Independent Sub-Processes. The data attributes to be copied into/out of the Independent Sub-Process are specified through the Input- and OutputPropertyMaps attributes. As these PropertyMaps are in the form of Expressions we assume that also different transformation functions can be captured through them. Transformation functions can also be defined through Expression Assignments of Gates. This implies that the patterns WDP32 and WDP33 are partially supported as well. The support is partial because it only applies to data transfer to and from Independent Sub-Processes or to Activities subsequent to a Gateway, and not between any pair of Activities.

Finally, the WDP31 *Data transfer by reference – with lock* is supported. As BPMN adopts a token-oriented approach to data passing, the parameters – which typically relate to objects – are effectively consumed at activity commencement and only become visible and accessible to other activities once the specific activity to which they were passed has completed and returned them.

3.4 Data-Based Routing Patterns

Data-based routing patterns capture the various ways in which data elements can interact with other perspectives and influence the overall execution of the process. There are seven (relatively self-explanatory) patterns in this category:

- WDP34: *Task precondition – data existence*;
- WDP35: *Task precondition – data value*;
- WDP36: *Task postcondition – data existence*;
- WDP37: *Task postcondition – data value*;
- WDP38: *Event-based task trigger*;
- WDP39: *Data-based task trigger*;
- WDP40: *Data-based routing*.

BPMN does not directly support pre- and postcondition definitions. Hence, the patterns 35 and 37 are not supported. In the cases data transfer is realised though Data Objects, the boolean attributes RequiredForStart and ProducedAtCompletion capture the *Pre- and postconditions for data existence* (i.e., WDP34 and WDP36).

The Message, Timer, Error and Cancel Event constructs provide direct support for the *Event-based task triggering* pattern (WDP38). The Rule Event construct provides

Table 2. Support for the Data Patterns in **1**–BPMN, **2**–UML2.0 AD [17,9], **3**–BPEL [15,1], and **4**–Oracle BPEL PM v.10.1.2 [5]

Data Visibility	1	2	3	4	Data Interaction (External) (cont.)	1	2	3	4
1. Task Data	+	+/–	+/–	+/–	21. Env. to Case – Push-Oriented	–	–	–	–
2. Block Data	+	+	–	–	22. Case to Env. – Pull-Oriented	–	–	–	–
3. Scope Data	–	–	+	+	23. Workflow to Env. – Push-Oriented	–	–	–	–
4. Multiple Instance Data	+/–	+	–	+/–	24. Env. to Workflow – Pull-Oriented	–	–	–	–
5. Case Data	+	–	+	+	25. Env. to Workflow – Push-Oriented	–	–	–	–
6. Folder Data	–	–	–	–	26. Workflow to Env. – Pull-Oriented	–	–	–	–
7. Workflow Data	–	+	–	–	Data Transfer				
8. Environment Data	–	–	+	+	27. by Value – Incoming	+	–	+	+
Data Interaction (Internal)					28. by Value – Outgoing	+	–	+	+
9. between Tasks	+	+	+	+	29. Copy In/Copy Out	+/–	–	–	+
10. Block Task to Sub-wf Decomp.	+	+	–	–	30. by Reference – Unlocked	–	–	+	+
11. Sub-wf Decomp. to Block Task	+	+	–	–	31. by Reference – Locked	+	+	+/–	–
12. to Multiple Instance Task	–	+	–	+/–	32. Data Transformation – Input	+/–	+	–	–
13. from Multiple Instance Task	–	+	–	+/–	33. Data Transformation – Output	+/–	+	–	–
14. Case to Case	–	–	+/–	–	Data-based Routing				
Data Interaction (External)					34. Task Precondition – Data Exist.	+	+	+/–	–
15. Task to Env. – Push-Oriented	+	–	+	+	35. Task Precondition – Data Val.	–	+	+	+
16. Env. to Task – Pull-Oriented	+	–	+	+	36. Task Postcondition – Data Exist.	+	+	–	–
17. Env. to Task – Push-Oriented	+	–	+/–	+	37. Task Postcondition – Data Val.	–	+	–	–
18. Task to Env. – Pull-Oriented	+	–	+/–	+	38. Event-based Task Trigger	+	+	+	+
19. Case to Env. – Push-Oriented	–	–	–	–	39. Data-based Task Trigger	+	–	+/–	–
20. Env. to Case – Pull-Oriented	–	–	–	–	40. Data-based Routing	+	+	+	+

support for the *Data-based task trigger* pattern (WDP39). Finally, the *Data-based routing* (WDP40) is supported, as Condition Expressions are possible to specify for Sequence Flows.

Table 2 shows a summary of the results from the Data perspective.

4 The Resource Perspective in BPMN

Recent work [8] has focused on the resource perspective and the manner in which work is distributed amongst and managed by the resources associated with a business process. Our investigations have indicated that these patterns are relevant to all forms of PAISs including modelling languages such as XPDL and business process enactment languages such as BPEL. In this section, we examine the resource perspective of BPMN and its expressive power in regard to work distribution. Forty three workflow resource patterns have been identified in seven distinct groups:

- *Creation patterns* – which correspond to restrictions on the manner in which specific work items can be advertised, allocated and executed by resources;
- *Push patterns* – which describe situations where a PAIS proactively offers or allocates work to resources;
- *Pull patterns* – which characterise scenarios where resources initiate the identification of work that they are able to undertake and commit to its execution;
- *Detour patterns* – which describe deviations from the normal sequence of state transitions associated with a business process either at the instigation of a resource or the PAIS;
- *Auto-start patterns* – which relate to situations where the execution of work is triggered by specific events or state transitions in the business process;

- *Visibility patterns* – which describe the ability of resources to view the status of work within the PAIS;
- *Multiple resource patterns* – which describe scenarios where there is a many-to-many relationship between specific work items and the resources undertaking those work items.

In BPMN, the association of a particular action or set of actions with a specific resource is illustrated through the use of the Pool and Lane constructs, commonly called Swimlanes. "A Pool represents a Participant in the Process. A Participant can be a specific business entity (e.g. a company) or can be a more general business role." ([13], p. 103). "A Lane is a sub–partition within a Pool..." ([13], p. 106). Hence, the *Direct allocation* pattern (WRP1) as well as the *Role–based allocation* pattern (WRP2) are directly supported. Furthermore, a partitioning of a Process into Pools and Lanes is not required, i.e., the resource allocation for the different activities is not necessarily done during design time. Hence the *Automatic execution* pattern (WRP11) is also supported.

None of the other Creation Patterns are supported within BPMN. This is a consequence of the restrictive manner in which Swimlanes are specified (i.e., only by specifying their Names, and in case of sub-division, the sub-division hierarchy) and the lack of support for relationships between distinct Swimlanes. Lack of a capability specification, integrated authorisation framework, organisational model and access to some execution history, rules out any form of support for *Capability–based allocation* (WRP8), the *Authorisation* (WRP4), *Organisational allocation* (WRP10) and *History-based allocation* (WRP9) patterns respectively.

In a BPMN model activities become "live" once they receive the specified StartQuantity control-flow tokens. The resource associated with a given Swimlane can have multiple activities executing at the same time. There is no notion of scheduling work execution or of resources selecting the work (i.e. the activity) they wish to undertake, hence there is minimal support for the Push, Auto-start or Multiple Resource patterns. The following patterns from these classes are directly supported:

- WRP14: *Distribution by allocation - single resource* – the resource(s) associated with a given Swimlane is immediately allocated a Task/Sub-Process once it is triggered.
- WRP19: *Distribution on enablement* – all activities in a Swimlane are associated with the resource responsible for the Swimlane when they are triggered.
- WRP36: *Commencement on creation* – an activity is assumed to be live as soon as it receives the specified StartQuantity control-flow tokens.
- WRP39: *Chained execution* – once an activity is completed it "sends" a control-flow token to every subsequent activity. A subsequent activity is triggered when it receives the specified StartQuantity of tokens.
- WRP42: *Simultaneous execution* – there are no constraints on how many instances of a task specified for one Swimlane can be active at any time.

None of the Pull, Detour or Visibility patterns are supported. The results from this part of the evaluation are summarised in Table 3[4] and clearly reveal that BPMN provides little support for the resource patterns.

[4] Since BPEL does not cover the resource perspective, Table 3 does not include a BPEL column.

Table 3. Support for the Resource Patterns in **1**–BPMN, **2**–UML2.0 AD [17,9], and **4**–Oracle BPEL PM v.10.1.2 [5]

Creation Patterns	1	2	4	Pull Patterns (cont.)	1	2	4
1. Direct Allocation	+	+	+	24. System-Determ. Work Queue Content	–	–	–
2. Role-Based Allocation	+	+	+	25. Resource-Determ. Work Queue Content	–	–	+
3. Deferred Allocation	–	–	+	26. Selection Autonomy	–	–	+
4. Authorization	–	–	–	Detour Patterns			
5. Separation of Duties	–	–	–	27. Delegation	–	–	+
6. Case Handling	–	–	+	28. Escalation	–	–	+
7. Retain Familiar	–	–	+	29. Deallocation	–	–	+
8. Capability-based Allocation	–	–	+	30. Stateful Reallocation	–	–	+
9. History-based Allocation	–	–	+/–	31. Stateless Reallocation	–	–	–
10. Organizational Allocation	–	–	+/–	32. Suspension/Resumption	–	–	+
11. Automatic Execution	+	+	+	33. Skip	–	–	+
Push Patterns				34. Redo	–	–	–
12. Distribution by Offer-Single Resource	–	–	+	35. Pre-Do	–	–	–
13. Distribution by Offer-Multiple Resources	–	–	+	Auto-start Patterns			
14. Distribution by Allocation-Single Resource	+	+	+	36. Commencement on Creation	+	+	–
15. Random Allocation	–	–	+/–	37. Commencement on Allocation	–	–	–
16. Round Robin Allocation	–	–	+/–	38. Piled Execution	–	–	–
17. Shortest Queue	–	–	+/–	39. Chained Execution	+	+	–
18. Early Distribution	–	–	–	Visibility Patterns			
19. Distribution on Enablement	+	+	+	40. Config. Unallocated Work Item visibility	–	–	–
20. Late Distribution	–	–	–	41. Config. Allocated Work Item visibility	–	–	–
Pull Patterns				Multiple Resource Patterns			
21. Resource-Init. Allocation	–	–	–	42. Simultaneous Execution	+	+	+
22. Resource-Init. Exec. - Allocated Work Item	–	–	+	43. Additional Resources	–	–	+
23.Resource-Init. Execution - Offered Work Item	–	–	+				

5 Discussion and Conclusion

There are inherent difficulties in applying the Workflow Patterns Framework for assessing a language that does not have a commonly agreed-upon formal semantics nor an execution environment. The BPMN specification [13] provides a mapping from BPMN to BPEL, for which execution engines and formalisations exist. Closer inspection however shows that the mapping to BPEL in [13] is only partial, leaving aside models with unstructured topologies as well as constructs such as OR-join and complex gateways (see [6] for a discussion). Moreover, since the mapping is described in prose, it is subject to interpretations. More generally, many ambiguities can be found in the BPMN specification due to the lack of formalisation. In our work, we documented some of these ambiguities as well as assumptions that we made to circumvent them.

The results of the Workflow Patterns analysis of BPMN are presented in tables 1, 2 and 3. A "+" indicates direct support, a "+/–" partial support, and a "–" lack of support. These tables also contain results from previous pattern-based evaluations of UML 2.0 AD [17,9], BPEL [15,1] and an implementation of BPEL, namely Oracle BPEL PM Version 10.1.2 [5]. It can be seen from these tables that BPMN provides direct support for the majority of the control-flow patterns and for nearly half of the data patterns, while support for the resource patterns is scant.

Along the control-flow perspective (Table 1), BPMN lacks support for the *Multiple Instances without a priori runtime knowledge* and for the *Milestone* patterns while the *Synchronising merge*, *Discriminator* and *Interleaved parallel routing* patterns are only partially supported. The limitations in capturing the *Milestone* and *Interleaved parallel routing* patterns stem from the lack of an explicit notion of "state". As for the *Synchronising merge*, partial support is provided by BPMN's OR-join Gateway but the semantics of this construct needs generalisation to cover unstructured process models (see [18] for a general treatment of the OR-join). Finally, the concepts available to describe discriminator and tasks and sub-processes with multiple instances require extensions.

An outcome of the analysis of the Control-flow perspective that is not visible from Table 1 is that many patterns have multiple representations. The simpler patterns have as many as three different representations in BPMN. On the other hand, detailed knowledge of the attributes associated to BPMN's modelling constructs is required to capture some of the more advanced patterns.

Regarding BPMN's support for the Data patterns (Table 2) it can be seen that *Workflow* and *Environment data* patterns are not supported. *Data interaction to and from a Multiple Instances task* is not supported because any instance-specific data for a task or sub-process with a "multiple instance" marker can not be specified. Also support for the external data interaction patterns is limited. Only the patterns capturing the interaction between tasks and the environment are supported, as they can be captured by modelling the environment as a separate process which may be represented in full, as an abstract/public process, or implicitly through references in send and receive tasks/events.

Finally, BPMN's support for the Resource perspective is minimal (Table 3). It is acknowledged in the specification ([13], p. 22) that the modelling of organizational structures and resources is outside the scope of BPMN. However, the presence of the concepts Lane and Pool for representing parties and roles gives a contradictory impression. It is obvious though that Pools and Lanes do not provide a means for representing the subtleties associated with selective work allocation across a range of possible resources and the management of the resulting work items at run-time.

The tables also compare BPMN with UML 2.0 AD and BPEL. Along the Control-flow perspective, BPMN and UML 2.0 AD are largely overlapping. BPMN is slightly stronger when it comes to capturing the *Interleaved parallel routing* and the *Synchronising merge* patterns and slightly weaker in its support for the *Discriminator* pattern, but these differences are minor. It can also be seen from Table 1 that some Control-flow patterns are supported in BPMN but not in BPEL and vice-versa. Thus, manifestations of these patterns in a BPMN model would require special care when translating the model into BPEL. A translation from BPMN to BPEL is hence not as straightforward as it is often purported to be.

For the Data perspective the support for the patterns in BPMN and UML 2.0 AD is slightly different. UML 2.0 AD is stronger in capturing *Multiple instances data* as well as *Data interaction to and from multiple instances tasks*, while BPMN is stronger in the *Data interaction between task and environment*, due to the fact that the environment can be explicitly modelled. There are further differences for the patterns in the Data transfer and Data-based routing categories, as well as differences from the patterns captured by BPEL. However, even if the set of patterns captured in this perspective is distinct for every language and even if none of the languages fully captures all the patterns, it can be argued that the Data perspective is reasonably well covered.

Unfortunately, the same can not be said for the Resource perspective. The presence of the concepts Lane and Pool in BPMN reveals the need (and an intention) to support this perspective. However, providing support for a minimal set of resource patterns only exposes the immaturity of the language along this perspective. To the benefit of BPMN, it can be said that support for the resource perspective is also minimal in UML 2.0 AD and out of the scope of the upcoming BPEL standard. At the same time, extensions of BPEL to cover the resource perspective have been proposed (e.g. BPEL4People [4]) and some of these extensions are implemented in commercial tools such as Oracle BPEL PM, thus highlighting even further the necessity of capturing this perspective. More generally, the lack of support in BPMN and UML 2.0 AD for the resource perspective, contrasted to the ongoing efforts in the BPEL community to address this perspective, exposes a gap between contemporary process modelling tools and process execution engines (the latter generally support the resource perspective in one way or another). To achieve a consistent and coherent use of process models, from analysis down to implementation and enactment, it is important that the Resource perspective is more widely acknowledged as an integral part of business process modelling. Instead of creating new process modelling notations that largely overlap with existing ones along the control-flow perspective, the focus should rather be on further refining the existing notations to satisfactorily cover all aspects relevant to PAISs.

Acknowledgments. We thank Chun Ouyang for valuable discussions on BPMN and Nataliya Mulyar for her analysis of Oracle BPEL.

References

1. W.M.P. van der Aalst, M. Dumas, A.H.M. ter Hofstede, N. Russell, H.M.W Verbeek, and P. Wohed. Life After BPEL? In *Proc. of the 2nd Int. Workshop on Web Services and Formal Methods (WS-FM)*, volume 3670 of *LNCS*, pages 35–50. Springer Verlag, 2005.
2. W.M.P. van der Aalst, A.H.M. ter Hofstede, B. Kiepuszewski, and A.P. Barros. Workflow Patterns. *Distributed and Parallel Databases*, 14(1):5–51, 2003.
3. S. Jablonski and C. Bussler. *Workflow Management: Modeling Concepts, Architecture, and Implementation.* International Thomson Computer Press, London, UK, 1996.
4. M. Kloppmann, D. Koenig, F. Leymann, G. Pfau, A. Rickayzen, C. von Riegen, P. Schmidt, and I. Trickovic. WS-BPEL Extension for People – BPEL4People. `http://www.ibm.com/developerworks/webservices/library/specification/ws-bpel4people`, July 2005. accessed 16 March 2005.
5. N.A. Mulyar. Pattern-based Evaluation of Oracle-BPEL (v.10.1.2). Technical report, Center Report BPM-05-24, BPMcenter.org, 2005.
6. C. Ouyang, M. Dumas, S. Breutel, and A.H.M. ter Hofstede. Translating Standard Process Models to BPEL. To appear in *Proceedings of 18th International Conference on Advanced Information Systems Engineering (CAiSE 2006)*, June 2006.
7. J. Recker, M. Indulska, M. Rosemann, and P. Green. Do Process Modelling Techniques Get Better? A Comparative Ontological Analysis of BPMN. In *16th Australasian Conference on Information Systems*.

8. N. Russell, W.M.P. van der Aalst, A.H.M. ter Hofstede, and D. Edmond. Workflow Resource Patterns: Identification, Representation and Tool Support. In *Proc. of 17th Int. Conf. on Advanced Information Systems Engineering (CAiSE05)*, volume 3520 of *LNCS*, pages 216–232. Springer, 2005.
9. N. Russell, W.M.P. van der Aalst, A.H.M. ter Hofstede, and P. Wohed. On the Suitability of UML 2.0 Activity Diagrams for Business Process Modelling. In *Third Asia-Pacific Conference on Conceptual Modelling (APCCM2006)*, volume 53 of *CRPIT*, pages 95–104, Hobart, Australia, 2006. ACS.
10. N. Russell, A.H.M. ter Hofstede, D. Edmond, and W.M.P. van der Aalst. Workflow Data Patterns. In *Proc. of 24th Int. Conf. on Conceptual Modeling (ER05)*, volume 3716 of *LNCS*, pages 353–368. Springer Verlag, Oct 2005.
11. T. Wahl and G. Sindre. An Analytical Evaluation of BPMN Using a Semiotic Quality Framework. In *CAiSE'05 Workshops. Volume 1*, pages 533–544. FEUP, Porto, Portugal, 2005.
12. WfMC. Workflow Management Coalition Terminology & Glossary, Document Number WFMC-TC-1011, Document Status - Issue 3.0. Technical report, Workflow Management Coalition, Brussels, Belgium, 1999.
13. S. White. Business Process Modeling Notation (BPMN). Version 1.0 - May 3, 2004, BPMI.org, 2004. `www.bpmi.org`.
14. S. White. Process Modeling Notations and Workflow Patterns. In *Workflow Handbook 2004*, pages 265–294. Future Strategies Inc., Lighthouse Point, FL, USA, 2004.
15. P. Wohed, W.M.P. van der Aalst, M. Dumas, and A.H.M. ter Hofstede. Analysis of Web Services Composition Languages: The Case of BPEL4WS. In *Proc. of 22nd Int. Conf. on Conceptual Modeling (ER 2003)*, volume 2813 of *LNCS*, pages 200–215. Springer, 2003.
16. P. Wohed, W.M.P. van der Aalst, M. Dumas, A.H.M. ter Hofstede, and N. Russell. Pattern-based Analysis of BPMN - an extensive evaluation of the Control-flow, the Data and the Resource Perspectives. BPM Center Report BPM-05-26, BPMcenter.org, 2005.
17. P. Wohed, W.M.P. van der Aalst, M. Dumas, A.H.M. ter Hofstede, and N. Russell. Pattern-Based Analysis of the Control-Flow Perspective of UML Activity Diagrams. In *Proc. of 24th Int. Conf. on Conceptual Modeling (ER05)*, volume 3716 of *LNCS*, pages 63–78. Springer Verlag, 2005.
18. M.T. Wynn, D. Edmond, W.M.P. van der Aalst, and A.H.M. ter Hofstede. Achieving a General, Formal and Decidable Approach to the OR-Join in Workflow Using Reset Nets. In *Proc. of 26th Int. Conf. on Applications and Theory of Petri Nets 2005*, volume 3536 of *LNCS*, pages 423–443. Springer, 2005.

Workflow Model Compositions Preserving Relaxed Soundness

Juliane Siegeris (born Dehnert)[1] and Armin Zimmermann[2]

[1] Fraunhofer ISST Berlin
juliane.siegeris@isst.fraunhofer.de
[2] Technische Universität Berlin
azi@cs.tu-berlin.de

Abstract. Very often, e.g. in the context of inter-organizational Workflow or web services, it is necessary to merge existing business process descriptions. It is clear that correctness criteria valid for the single process descriptions should remain valid also for the combined model. However, looking at the popular soundness criterion this can not always be guaranteed. In this paper various composition alternatives are summarized and their ability to preserve relaxed soundness (in contrast to soundness) is investigated.

Keywords: Workflow, Composition, Inter-organizational Workflow, Validation, Petri nets.

1 Introduction

Process-aware information systems are an important aid in the design, improvement and execution of complex business processes. An important support for the modeling of complex business processes is provided by composition techniques. There are different scenarios for their application. The first are modular modeling and the combination of workflow patterns or building blocks. Other scenarios fall in the context of inter-organizational workflows or web services. Here it is essential to combine existing process descriptions on the basis of information exchange. Division of labor in general requires workflow composition, also inside one organization. Efficient use of available resources is an issue here.

The significance of composition within workflow modeling is reflected in the literature by numerous related publications, see e.g. [KMR00, AH02, AHT02] [HB03, CWBH$^+$03]. Different composition variants are described and the result is checked for structural and behavioral properties. So far, the focus was put on the soundness property, i.e liveness and boundedness of the composed process model.

The aim of this paper is to analyze a list of significant composition techniques in terms of WF-nets and to check whether the composition of relaxed sound models is again relaxed sound. We will see that in comparison to soundness, relaxed soundness is preserved by additional composition techniques.

S. Dustdar, J.L. Fiadeiro, and A. Sheth (Eds.): BPM 2006, LNCS 4102, pp. 177–192, 2006.

For the modeling we refer to WF-nets, a variant of Petri nets, that have been successfully used for the description and analysis of business processes. Their formal and furthermore operational semantics allows to use the process model as input for a workflow engine directly. In order to do this, the process description should be sound [Aal98]. *Soundness* guarantees that there are no dead tasks and that the process will always terminate properly, i.e. achieve the required result. *Relaxed soundness* has been proposed as a weaker property than soundness, thus allowing more workflow structures. In a relaxed sound WF-net, not all but only so many execution sequences must terminate properly, that every transition (task) is visited at least once. In [DZ04, DvdA04] it was shown how methods from Petri net controller synthesis can be applied to transform a relaxed sound and bounded WF-net into a sound model. Advantages and disadvantages w.r.t. the modeling and analysis of workflows are discussed for the two mentioned properties and well-structuredness in [DZ05].

The aim of this paper is to emphasize the benefit of relaxed soundness against the background of composition. Therefore, we will investigate a list of significant composition techniques and check whether relaxed soundness is preserved. The following techniques are covered:

- Refinement of a task by another workflow (or *subcontracting* in an interorganizational workflow): An atomic task is split into substeps that are described by another workflow in a hierarchical fashion. This technique goes back to [Val79] and was redefined for WF-nets in [AH02].
- Combinations of workflows as a whole: the simplest case is *chained execution* or sequential, but other options include iterative, parallel, alternative, discriminative (race condition), and multi merge composition, see e.g. [AH02, HB03, CWBH$^+$03].
- Client-server-like asynchronous composition with information exchange during concurrent execution (similar to *loosely coupled*). Parts of the workflow are executed concurrently after the invocation of a service, and arbitrary information exchange may take place between the partners during the service execution, see e.g. [Aal99, KMR00, AHT02, Mar05].
- Parallel composition with mutual use of restricted resources or *capacity sharing*: Two or more workflows operate distributed and need to be synchronized because of common resources.

We will prove that all of the above composition techniques in fact preserve relaxed soundness. This is important because it guarantees that by starting with simple relaxed sound building blocks and combining them following the given composition rules, ill-formed workflows are avoided. The resulting complex WF-nets can thus be made sound automatically following [DZ04, DvdA04], and executed on a workflow management system afterwards.

The remainder of the paper is structured as follows. Necessary basics are briefly revisited first. The main part of the paper recalls the mentioned set of composition techniques in terms of WF-nets and provides proofs for the fact that the composition types preserve relaxed soundness. Some concluding remarks are given finally.

2 Preliminaries

For the modeling of business processes we refer to Place/Transition nets[3] and use the more specific class of WF-nets as introduced in [Aal98]. A WF-net (P, T, F) is briefly characterized by a source place $({}^\bullet i = \emptyset)$ and a sink place o $(o^\bullet = \emptyset)$. Furthermore, it must hold that for any node $n \in (P \cup T)$ there is a path from i to n and from n to o. This ensures that every task (transition) or condition (place) contributes to the processing of cases.

Considering the behavior of a WF-net, we will always investigate the life-cycle of a single case, thus consider systems where initially only the source place i is marked ($M_i(i) = 1$ and for all $p \in P \setminus \{i\} : M_i(p) = 0$). Figure 1 (i) shows a simple WF-net with two parallel threads.

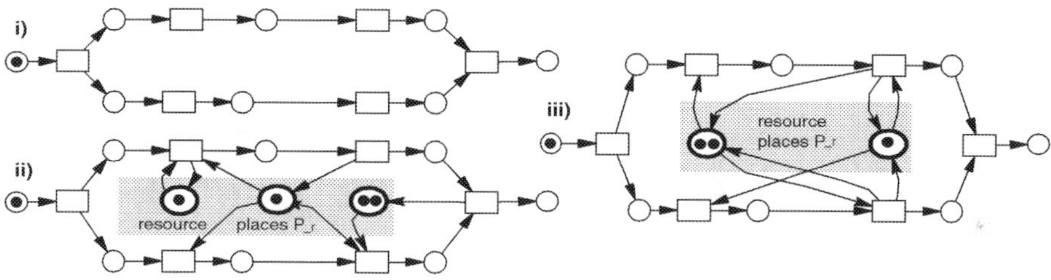

Fig. 1. A standard WF-net (i) and two resource constrained derivatives (ii) and (iii)

In the standard definition of WF-nets, resources are not explicitly characterized. According to [vHSSV05] we extend the notion of WF-nets to include information about the use of resources in the model. A resource belongs to a type. For every type a new place is introduced in the net, where resource tokens are located when they are available. The resources become part of the case-modeling tokens when they are occupied. Resources are assumed to be durable, i.e. they are used (blocked) and released later on. Resources are never created nor destroyed.

Definition 1 (Resource constrained WF-net). *A WF-net $PN = (P, T, F)$ becomes a resource constrained WF-net (P_{rc}, T, F_{rc}) by enhancing the set of places P with the set P_r of resource places ($P_{rc} = P \cup P_r, P \cap P_r = \emptyset$) and the flow relation F by corresponding arcs F_r ($F \cup F_r, F_r \subseteq (P_r \times T) \cup (T \times P_r)$).*

A standard WF-net can thus be interpreted as a special case of a resource-constrained one, where $P_r = \emptyset$. Different examples, illustrating the use of resources, are provided in the resource constrained WF-nets of Figure 1 (i-iii).

Resources are neither created nor destroyed during the processing. Therefore they are part of the initial marking M_i of the corresponding resource-constrained

[3] An introduction to Place/Transition nets is e.g. given in [DR98], where the concepts of pre- and postset ${}^\bullet x$ and $x^\bullet$, marking M, firing rule and firing sequence are defined among others.

WF-system, and their initial number is specified by $R : P_r \longrightarrow I\!N$. Formally, M_i is defined as:

$$\forall p \in P \cup P_r : M_i(p) = \begin{cases} 1 & \text{if } p = i \\ R(p) & \text{if } p \in P_r \\ 0 & \text{otherwise} \end{cases}$$

An important property in the context of workflow management is soundness [Aal98]. A WF-net is sound if termination in a final marking M_f is always possible. Furthermore, there are no dead transitions and neither deadlocks nor live-locks.

This definition was enhanced for resource constrained WF-nets with multiple cases (k-soundness [vHSSV05]). In this paper we only consider single cases (the special case of 1-soundness), for which the definition reads as below. For notational convenience we introduce a *final marking* M_f such that

$$\forall p \in P \cup P_r : M_f(p) = \begin{cases} 1 & \text{if } p = o \\ R(p) & \text{if } p \in P_r \\ 0 & \text{otherwise} \end{cases}$$

Definition 2 (Soundness of resource constrained WF-nets). *A resource constrained WF-net PN with input place i is sound for some $R \in I\!N^{P_r}$ iff*

1. *For every state M reachable from state M_i it holds that the number of tokens in each resource place is less than or equal to its initial number: $\forall M \in R_{PN}(M_i), \forall p \in P_r : M(p) \leq R(p)$ (resources are durable).*
2. *For every state M reachable from state M_i, there is a firing sequence leading from state M to state M_f: $\forall M : (M_i \xrightarrow{*} M) \Rightarrow (M \xrightarrow{*} M_f)$ (proper termination).*
3. *In addition to [vHSSV05] we require that there are no dead transitions in PN: $\forall t \in T\ \exists M, M' : (M_i \xrightarrow{*} M \xrightarrow{t} M')$.*

Enhancing the definition of a sound firing sequence accordingly, we get

Definition 3 (Sound firing sequence). *Let PN be a resource-constrained WF-net initially marked with M_i. A firing sequence σ is sound iff it leads from M_i to M_f and does not violate the durability property: $M_i \xrightarrow{\sigma} M_f \wedge \forall M \in Visited_{PN}(M_i, \sigma)$ [4], $\forall p \in P_r : M(p) \leq R(p)$.*

The set of sound firing sequences of a WF-net PN with initial marking M_i is denoted by Σ^{sound}_{PN,M_i} in the following. If the initial marking is implicitly clear, we just write Σ^{sound}_{PN}.

In a sound WF-net all firing sequences beginning in M_i can be continued until M_f (i.e. terminate properly), resulting in a sound firing sequence. The resource

[4] With $Visited_{PN}(M, \sigma)$ we denote the set of markings visited during a firing sequence $\sigma = t_1, t_2, \ldots, t_n$ starting in M.

constrained WF-nets of Figure 1 are all sound in the shown initial marking. However, if the resource places of net (iii) are initially only marked with one token, soundness of the corresponding WF-system would be violated.

Another important property for the modeling of business processes is *relaxed soundness*. A WF-system is relaxed sound iff each transition is contained in at least one sound firing sequence of the system.

Definition 4 (Relaxed soundness of resource constrained WF-nets). *A process specified by a (resource-constrained) WF-system* (PN, M_i) *is relaxed sound iff every transition of* PN *is contained in a sound firing sequence:* $\forall t \in T\, \exists \sigma \in \sigma_{sound}(PN, M_i) : t \in \sigma$.

Relaxed soundness poses weaker requirements to a process description than soundness. In contrast to a sound WF-net, a relaxed sound WF-net may have firing sequences which do not terminate properly. These firing sequences possibly deadlock in a marking other than M_f or do not terminate at all (livelock). Consider again the resource constrained WF-net from Figure 1 (iii). The net is relaxed sound, also if there is initially only one token per resource place.

From the given definitions it can easily be seen that a *sound* WF-net (either resource constrained or not) will also necessarily be *relaxed sound.* Note that if there are no resource places, the definitions of soundness and relaxed soundness coincide with the classical soundness notion [Aal98] and the primary notion of relaxed soundness [DR01], respectively.

3 Composition Techniques

In this section, different composition techniques are considered and interpreted in terms of WF-nets. Moreover, it is shown that their application to relaxed sound WF-nets leads to composed models that are again relaxed sound. The results presented in the first two subsections mainly transfer well-known results to the class of relaxed sound WF-nets.

To start with, net composition via transition refinement is considered. This method was first introduced in [Val79], where it was used to enhance Petri nets by well-formed blocks. In [AH02] the method was adapted for WF-nets.

3.1 Composition Via Transition Refinement

Two WF-nets are composed by replacing a transition of the first WF-net (A) by a transition-surrounded second WF-net (B). Figure 2 illustrates this kind of composition. It is easy to see that the resulting net is again a WF-net.

Refining a transition t of a sound WF-net A by a transition surrounded sound WF-net B, the composed WF-net is not necessarily sound. If the main WF-net (here WF-net A) is not safe, proper termination is not guaranteed. We refer again to Figure 2. The result of the illustrated composition is not sound[5]. This

[5] Note, here the counterexample from [HSV03] was slightly changed, as the refining WF-net (here WF-net B) was primarily not sound.

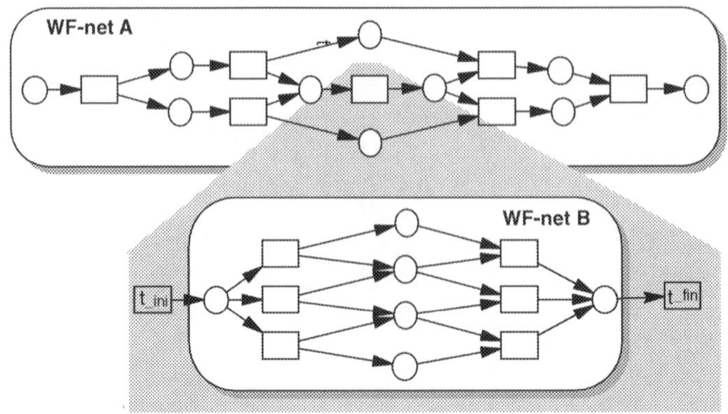

Fig. 2. Not sound WF-net composed by transition refinement

goes back to the fact that the refining WF-net becomes initiated with two tokens in i. This caused a deadlock, as B was in fact 1- but not 2-sound. However, if the two WF-nets are sound[6] and the main WF-net is additionally safe, the composed WF-net is always sound [AH02]. We will now investigate the property for relaxed sound WF-nets which are not necessarily safe.

Theorem 1. *When a transition t of a relaxed sound WF-net A is refined by a relaxed sound WF-net B, the resulting WF-net C is again relaxed sound.*

Proof. To prove that C is relaxed sound, we have to show that every transition t_i of C is contained in at least one sound firing sequence of C[7]. We construct a set of sound firing sequences of C as follows. First, all sound firing sequences of A that do not contain t are considered (this set may be empty). Second, we take all sound firing sequences of A that do contain t (there must be at least one of them) and replace t by one of the (always existing) sound firing sequences of B. Third, we select one of the sound firing sequences of A containing t, and form a set of new firing sequences by substituting t in it by elements of a set of sound firing sequences of B. This set is chosen such that all transitions of WF-net B are contained in it (which is always possible because B is relaxed sound). The union of these three sets is a set of sound firing sequences of C by construction. It remains to be shown that each transition of C is contained in at least one of them, which is obvious because A and B are relaxed sound and all their "local" sound firing sequences are contained in the constructed set. □

3.2 Combinations of Workflows as a Whole

Within this paragraph we consider purely structural composition techniques that define the interaction of two WF-nets A and B by the use of workflow pattern.

[6] We again refer to the classical soundness definition here, i.e. 1-soundness.

[7] Except for $t_i = t$, which is replaced by B.

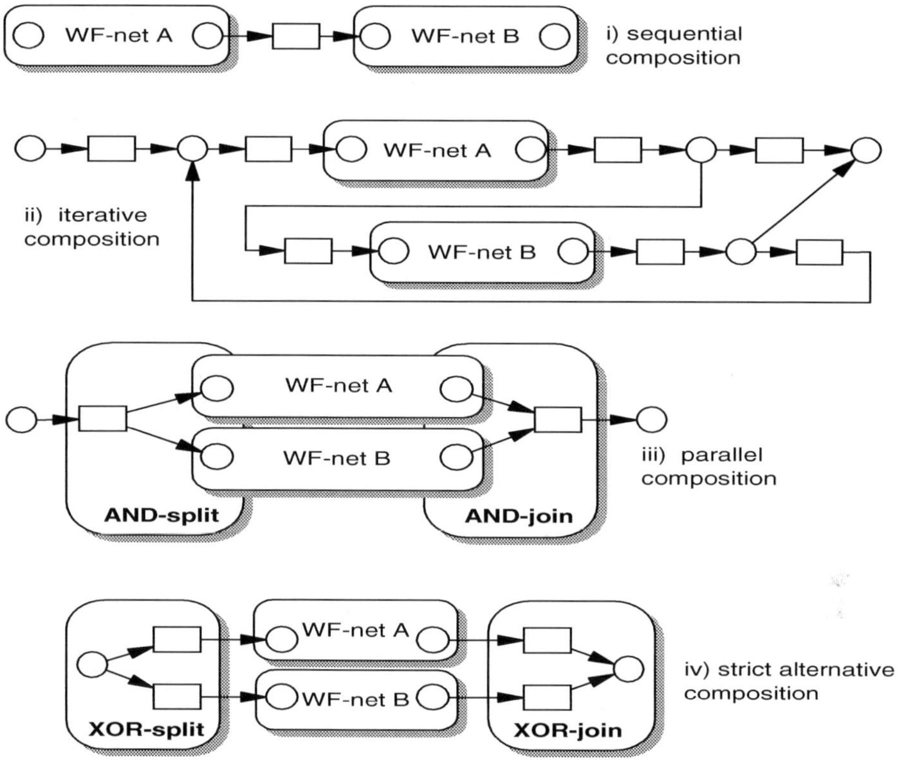

Fig. 3. Structural composition rules using basic WF-pattern

The following basic and advanced pattern will be used: sequence, structured cycle, parallel split (AND-join), synchronization (AND-join), exclusive choice (XOR-split), simple merge (XOR-join) multiple choice (OR-split), synchronizing merge (OR-join), discriminator and multi merge.

Sequential composition of WF-nets. One workflow process is enabled after the completion of the other. Within the proposed composition technique this was implemented linking two WF-nets with a transition connecting the sink of the first with the source of the second WF-net, cf. Figure 3 (i).

Iterative composition of WF-nets. Two workflow processes can repeatedly be executed after one another, where the loop can be abandoned after termination of one of the processes. The composition technique, implementing this pattern of a structured cycle in terms of WF-nets, is provided in Figure 3 (ii).

Parallel composition of WF-nets. Two workflow processes are routed in parallel. This composition technique was implemented accommodating the parallel split and the synchronization pattern as shown in Figure 3 (iii).

Alternative composition of WF-nets. Two workflow process are activated alternatively. There are two implementations possible. Applying the basic WF-

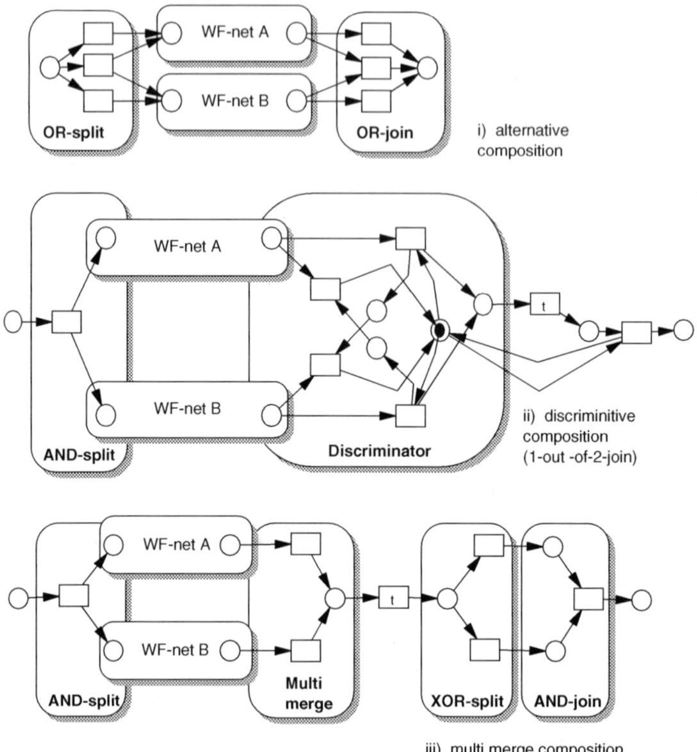

Fig. 4. Structural composition rules using advanced WF-pattern

pattern exclusive choice and simple merge two WF-nets are composed, such that only one of them is executed, cf. Figure 3 (iv). The second possibility of conditional routing is implemented accommodating the advanced WF-pattern multiple choice and synchronizing merge. Here, the two WF-nets can be used either in parallel or alternatively, cf. Figure 4 (i).

Discriminative composition of WF-nets. Two workflow processes are enabled at the same time. After the first terminates, subsequent tasks are activated. Termination of the second process is awaited but ignored, i.e. no subsequent tasks are triggered. This behavior was implemented using a parallel split and a discriminator pattern. Figure 4 (ii) illustrates this composition technique. The subsequent task is modeled by transition t. The privilege to activate the subsequent task is modeled by a semaphore, i.e. a resource place initially marked with one token.

Multi merge of WF-nets. Two workflow processes are activated in parallel. If one of them terminates the subsequent task is activated. In contrary to the previous composition technique, the subsequent task is not activated once, but twice. In order to unify the two threads again, the proposed composition technique uses an exclusive choice and a synchronization pattern. Figure 4 (iii) illustrates this composition technique.

When applying the proposed set of composition techniques, it is guaranteed that the resulting net is always a WF-net, which can hence again be used for composition. This follows from the fact that the WF-nets are only composed via their source and there sink place. Note that the proposed composition techniques only represent a choice. There are other combinations of WF-pattern possible, providing meaningful compositions of two or more workflow processes.

We will now investigate whether the proposed composition techniques maintain relaxed soundness. Therefore we will prove the following statements.

1. A sequence of relaxed sound WF-nets is relaxed sound.
2. The result of the iterative composition of two relaxed sound WF-nets is again relaxed sound.
3. A parallel composition of relaxed sound WF-nets is relaxed sound.
4. An alternative composition of relaxed sound WF-nets is relaxed sound.
5. The proposed discriminative composition of two relaxed sound WF-nets yields again a relaxed sound WF-net.
6. The proposed multi merge composition of two relaxed sound WF-nets yields again a relaxed sound WF-net.

Proof. The proof argumentation is for all statements the same. Replacing every placeholder for the WF-nets A and B in the composition rules with a single transition with one input and one output place, we gain a set of WF-nets. All these WF-nets are relaxed sound. We exploit the previous result, concluding that refining the transitions by relaxed sound WF-nets, the resulting nets are again relaxed sound. □

Note that this result cannot be transferred for soundness, as some of the gained WF-nets are not sound, namely the ones described in Figure 4 (i) and 4 (iii).

The following two composition techniques are somehow more complex than the previous ones. The difference is that the interaction of the two WF-nets now goes beyond the use of the source and the sink place but comprises additional elements.

3.3 Combination of WF-Nets Due to Information Exchange

The fact that e.g. two organizations interact on some purpose is mostly reflected in the exchange of data or flow of information. In terms of WF-nets this is modeled by interface places. Typical examples include sending and reception of data or documents.

The corresponding composition technique assumes two independent WF-nets A and B, where B provides a service that A needs (client-server pattern). Figure 5 illustrates this type of combination. Some information must be passed between A and B to facilitate their interaction. Therefore the server WF-net B has to be invoked by a request, and an interface for the exchange of results and possible further data/information must be available.

This composition technique is similar to the approach proposed in [AHT02], where C-nets modeling the behavior of SW-components are composed to form

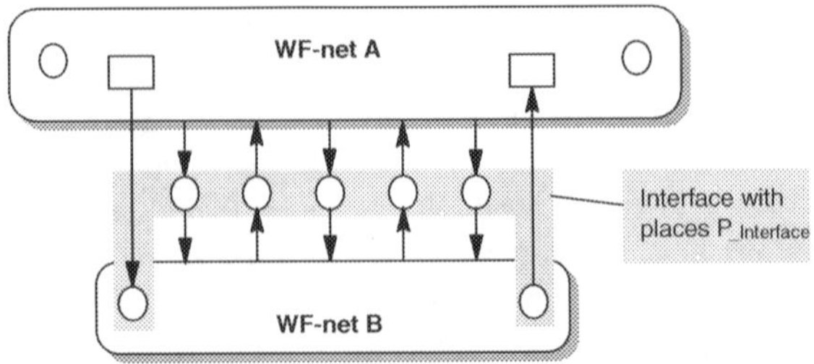

Fig. 5. Combination of WF-nets via interface places

complex architectures. Therefore a set of interface places was introduced, connecting transitions of the two WF-nets. This set is denoted by $P_{interface}$ in the following, and shown in the figure.

As in [AHT02] we assume the interaction to be always executed within the scope of the client (WF-net A). That is, the client starts the interaction (marks the initial place of B) and the server always reports back to the client when it finished the interaction (marks the final place of B). The combined workflow model C comprises the client model A, interface places $P_{interface}$, and server workflow B. Therefore, initial and final places of the client i_A and o_A are the respective places of the combined model. The initial and final place of the server are part of the interface ($i_B, o_B \in P_{interface}$).

There are two further assumptions on this composition type: First, every place of the interface connects exactly one pair of transitions: the introduced interface places thus have exactly one transition in their preset and one transition in their postset, out of which obviously exactly one belongs to each WF-net A or B. Formally, $\forall p \in P_{interface} : |{}^\bullet p| = |p^\bullet| = 1, {}^\bullet p \in T_A \Leftrightarrow p^\bullet \in T_B$ and vice versa. We denote by the set of synchronization transitions T_{sync} the ones that are connected to an interface place, $T_{sync} = \{t \in T_A \cup T_B | \exists p \in P_{interface} : t \in {}^\bullet p \cup p^\bullet\}$.

Moreover, we require every synchronization transition to be connected to only one interface place $\forall t \in T_{sync} : |{}^\bullet t \cap P_{interface}| = |t^\bullet \cap P_{interface}| = 1$. There is thus a one-to-one correspondence between synchronization transitions in A and B, which is formally captured by relation $sync(t_1, t_2) \Leftrightarrow \exists p \in P_{interface} : t_1 \in {}^\bullet p, p \in {}^\bullet t_2 \vee t_2 \in {}^\bullet p, p \in {}^\bullet t_1$.

It has been shown in [AHT02] that the combined net C is again a WF-net. However, it is not clear whether the (relaxed) soundness of C follows from the soundness properties of A and B. In the general case (without further restrictions) the combination does not preserve soundness nor relaxed soundness which is illustrated in Figure 6 (i).

For sound WF-nets there are two alternative additional requirements that are sufficient conditions for a soundness-preserving composition of this type. It was shown in [AHT02] that the global model C is sound if the local workflow nets are branching bisimular. Its informal meaning for the workflow is that the behavior of A is not restricted by adding B and the interface. A structural property that is a sufficient condition which is simpler to check is a *request-response-pattern* defined in the same paper. However, it restricts the allowed interactions significantly.

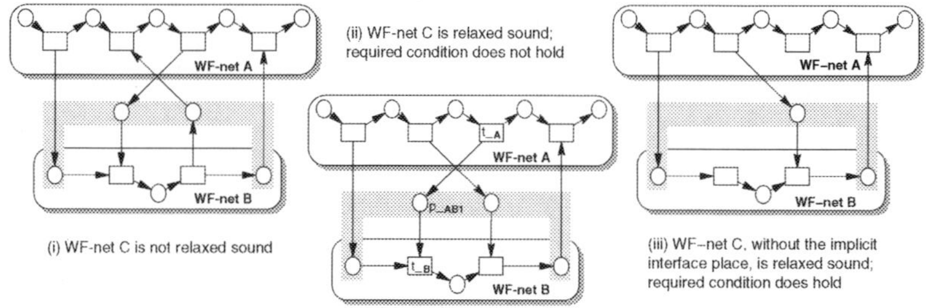

Fig. 6. Examples for the combination of WF-nets via interface places

We will show in the following that C is relaxed sound if A and B are, provided that there are pairs of sound firing sequences in A and B such that the synchronization transitions appear in the same order and multiplicity in them.

A minor additional requirement is an upper bound on the number of occurrences of every synchronization transition in any local firing sequence (in an isolated A and B). This is done only to prevent infinitely many invocations of B. Transitions other than the synchronizing ones may still occur infinitely often.

The idea behind the proof is to look at the local sound firing sequences of A that have some interaction with B, and to consider those that "match" some local firing sequence of B. Two firing sequences match if they describe an interleaving of transition firings that may be executed concurrently without a deadlock. The non-synchronization transitions are obviously not an issue here, we only have to consider the interactions between the two models. Each of the firing sequences in A and B can be executed locally until the next synchronization transition appears. Here come the structural restrictions into play: because of the one-to-one relationship between synchronization transitions in A and B, their sequence is defined by the way they are connected with an interface place. If we imagine all matching firing sequences constructed in this way, we only have to make sure that every transition of A and B appears in one of them to know that C is relaxed sound.

To improve readability of the following theorem we introduce the notion of an abstracted firing sequence to filter out non-synchronization transitions. A firing sequence $\sigma^{abstract}$ of a WF-net $PN = (P, T, F)$ w.r.t. the transition subset $T_{sync} \subseteq T$ is denoted as an abstraction of a firing sequence σ of PN iff $\sigma^{abstract}$ is derived from σ by deleting every occurrence of all $t \in T \setminus T_{sync}$.

We say that two abstracted firing sequences $\sigma_A^{abstract}$ and $\sigma_B^{abstract}$ of WF-nets A and B match if their lenghts are equal, $\left|\sigma_A^{abstract}\right| = \left|\sigma_B^{abstract}\right|$, and the transition steps are pairwise connected by interface places[8]: $\forall i \in 1, \ldots \left|\sigma_A^{abstract}\right| :$ $sync(\sigma_A^{abstract}[i], \sigma_B^{abstract}[i])$.

Theorem 2. *Let WF-net C be the composition of relaxed sound WF-nets A and B as described above, and $P_{interface}$ their set of interface places. Consider the two sets of all abstracted sound firing sequences for A and B, denoted by $\Sigma_A^{sound,abstract}$ and $\Sigma_B^{sound,abstract}$.*

[8] $\sigma[i]$ denotes the i-th transition in the sequence.

The composed WF-net C is relaxed sound if every synchronization transition of A is contained in an abstracted sound firing sequence of A for which there is a matching abstracted sound firing sequence of B (and vice versa). Formally, $\forall t \in T_A \cap T_{sync} : \exists \sigma_A \in \Sigma_A^{sound,abstract}$ *such that* $t \in \sigma_A$ *and* $\exists \sigma_B \in \Sigma_B^{sound,abstract}$ *with* σ_A *matching* σ_B.

Proof. To prove that the composed WF-net C is relaxed sound, we have to show that there are sound firing sequences of C such that all transitions of C are contained in at least one of them. We consider two cases for transition $t \in T_A \cup T_B$:

1. There is no sound firing sequence containing t with a matching sequence: Thus there is no synchronization transition contained in the sound firing sequences visiting t, and hence B is not invoked; therefore $t \in T_A$. As WF-net A was relaxed sound, there is a sound firing sequence $\sigma \in \Sigma_A^{sound}$ containing t. The firing sequences visiting t are not influenced by the introduction of the additional interface places (otherwise t would have been part of such a related pair of firing sequences), concluding that σ must also be a sound firing sequence of the composed WF-net C.

2. There is a sound firing sequence containing t with a matching firing sequence: Assume w.l.o.g. that $t \in T_A$, and denote the sound firing sequence containing t by σ_A. We may then safely assume from the theorem that there is at least one sound firing sequence σ_B of B that matches σ_A.

It remains to be shown that t is contained in a sound firing sequence of C. Such a firing sequence is constructed by an interleaving of σ_A and σ_B with the following rules.

- In every step, select either σ_A or σ_B to be progressed, such that every transition firing follows the local sequence in A or B.
- Transitions from σ_B may only be selected in the time span between an invocation of B, i.e. when a token is added to $i_B \in P_{interface}$, until B has terminated, i.e. when a token is added to o_B.
- If at least one of the next transitions in the sequences σ_A and σ_B is not a synchronization transition, select it to be fired. This is always possible in any order because there are no synchronization dependencies.
- In the case that both next transitions are in T_{sync}, fire them one after the other in the sequence that is specified by their postset or preset relation with the connecting interface place. This ordering is unique because of the restrictions on the interface.
- Continue until both sequences σ_A and σ_B have been fully executed, which is the case when o_A is marked.

The local order of the transitions in σ_A and σ_B remains the same in the constructed firing sequence of C, and all dependencies between A and B are observed. The effect of the introduced interface places comes down to a synchronization of the connected transitions. Because σ_A and σ_B were sound, we can conclude that also their constructed interleaving is sound. □

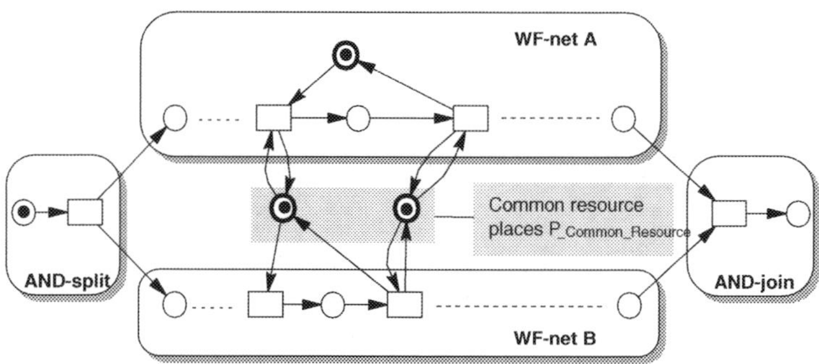

Fig. 7. Composition of WF-nets via common resource places

Note that our additional requirement is much weaker than the one given in [AHT02]. It is in fact sufficient to require bisimulation only for a set of firing sequences covering all transitions, to ensure that a composition of relaxed sound WF-nets preserves this property. The consequence of the fewer restrictions is that WF-net A may not only postpone but possibly also restrict the behavior of WF-net B and vice versa.

Although the above requirement is sufficient for a preservation of relaxed soundness, there are other cases in which C is relaxed sound as well. Figure 6 (ii) shows an example. In the shown case the problem stems from an unnecessary synchronization between transitions t_A and t_B, which is overspecified because of their indirect causal dependency. Such cases can be easily detected and avoided based on the notion of *implicit places* [Ber87]. A place is implicit if its removal does not change the overall behavior, i.e. does not enable additional firing sequences. As a consequence, we remove all implicit places from the interface, which possibly extends the set of synchronization patterns for which the above proof applies.

Removing the implicit place p_{AB1} from Figure 6 (ii) leads to the model given in Figure 6 (iii) where our condition holds. It can therefore be concluded that the composed WF-net from Figure 6 (ii) is relaxed sound.

3.4 Parallel Composition with Mutual Use of Restricted Resources

For this composition technique we explicitly refer to resource-constrained WF-nets. Remember that resources were typed via resource places. If two processes request the same type of resources it is useful to compose the two nets by merging the resource places.

In the presence of shared resources it has to be investigated whether there are any bad interactions, e.g. leading to a deadlock. Therefore the two nets are always composed in parallel, i.e. initiated at the same time. Figure 7 illustrates this kind of composition. It is obvious that the resulting net again fulfills the requirements of a WF-net.

Starting from two sound WF-nets this composition technique does not maintain soundness. A counterexample is given in Figure 8. Still, we will show that starting with relaxed sound WF-nets the resulting net is again relaxed sound.

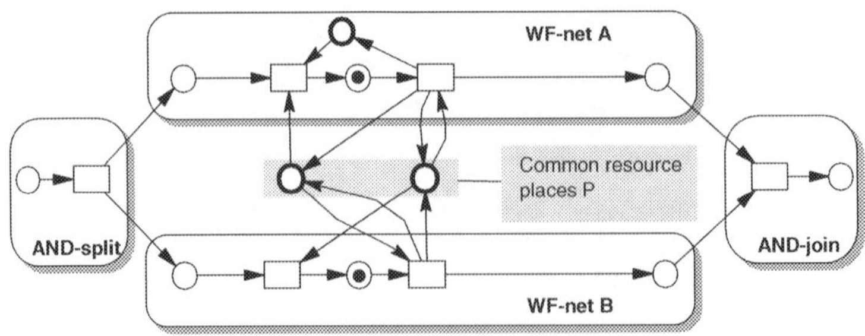

Fig. 8. Deadlock in a WF-net, composed by joining common resource places

Theorem 3. *Composing relaxed sound resource constrained WF-nets A and B at common resource places, the resulting WF-net C is relaxed sound.*

Proof. We only have to show that there are enough sound firing sequences in C such that all transitions of C are contained in at least one of them. We know the primary WF-nets contained enough sound firing sequences to cover the set T_A or T_B, respectively. These two nets are now composed in parallel. It is nevertheless possible to execute A completely first, and then B as a whole because of their relaxed soundness property. The resulting firing sequences are obviously sound sequences of C and cover all transitions of A and B by construction. □

4 Conclusion

This paper investigated whether typical composition techniques for Petri net workflow models preserve relaxed soundness. We have shown that (under additional restrictions in some cases) any two relaxed sound WF-nets can be composed, leading to a WF-net that is again relaxed sound. The application of previous results drawing on Petri net controller synthesis [DZ04, DvdA04] extend such a net to a sound one with an automated algorithm.

The presented results allow to construct WF-nets by combining basic patterns in a stepwise composition or hierarchical refinement approach. Any combination of the described compositions is possible in sequential steps. Such a composition always leads to a relaxed sound model if the initial building blocks were relaxed sound. The only restriction is that common resources and interface places may not be used at the same time for the proofs to hold. The controller generated by [DvdA04] guarantees a sound result to be derived from the final composition.

For the resource composition technique this means that the presented result is not as trivial as one may think from the proof. If the possibility of mutual waiting for the release of resources exist, it is not required to fully sequentialize the executions of A and B. Parts of the execution may allow interleaving without running into a deadlock. None of the possible concurrent behavior is deleted, because the controller algorithm always computes the maximally permissive behavior. Applying the algorithm to a relaxed sound model with shared resources thus results in scheduling resource accesses such that no deadlock will occur.

Although it is guaranteed that the composed WF-net is relaxed sound, it may be unbounded. That is the case if one of the initial WF-nets was unbounded; unboundedness is never introduced by the application of the presented rules. As the used controller algorithm only works on the basis of a finite reachability graph, it cannot be applied in these cases.

A side effect of the presented results is the following. Relaxed soundness can be shown in finite time if it holds, while the check for not being relaxed sound takes infinite time for unbounded nets [Deh03]. The set of compositions preserving relaxed soundness of this paper may offer a better possibility to check relaxed soundness for unbounded WF-nets. If subnets can be identified in a model such that it can be interpreted as the result of a composition, relaxed soundness has to be checked for the subnets only. The problem is thus cut back in size, which can be done repeatedly until a set of submodels is derived that are known to be relaxed sound.

References

[Aal98] W.M.P. van der Aalst. The Application of Petri Nets to Workflow Management. *The Journal of Circuits, Systems and Computers*, 8(1):21–66, 1998.

[Aal99] W.M.P. van der Aalst. Interorganizational Workflows: An Approach based on Message Sequence Charts and Petri Nets. *Systems Analysis - Modelling - Simulation*, 34(3):335–367, 1999.

[AH02] W.M.P. van der Aalst and K.M. van Hee. *Workflow Management: Models, Methods, and Systems.* MIT press, Cambridge, MA, 2002.

[AHT02] W.M.P. v.d. Aalst, K.M. van Hee, and R.A. v.d. Toorn. Component-based software architectures: a framework based on inheritance of behavior. *Science of Computer Programming*, 42(2–3):129–171, 2002.

[Ber87] G. Berthelot. Transformations and decompositions of nets. In G. Rozenberg, editor, *Advances in Petri Nets*, volume 266 of *LNCS*. 1987.

[CWBH+03] P. Chrzastowski-Wachtel, B. Benatallah, R. Hamadi, M. O'Dell, and A. Susanto. A Top-Down Petri Net-Based Approach for Dynamic Workflow Modeling. In W. van der Aalst, A. ter Hofstede, and M. Weske, editors, *Int. Conf. on BPM*, volume 2678 of *LNCS*, pages 336–353, 2003.

[Deh03] J. Dehnert. *A Methodology for Workflow Modeling - From business process modeling towards sound workflow specification.* PhD thesis, TU Berlin, 2003.

[DR98] J. Desel and W. Reisig. Place/Transition Petri Nets. volume 1491 of *LNCS*. Springer, 1998.

[DR01] J. Dehnert and P. Rittgen. Relaxed Soundness of Business Processes. In K.L. Dittrich, A. Geppert, and M.C. Norrie, editors, *Advanced Information System Engineering, CAISE 2001*, volume 2068 of *LNCS*, pages 157–170. Springer, 2001.

[DvdA04] J. Dehnert and W.M.P. van der Aalst. Bridging the Gap Between Business Models and Workflow Specifications. *Int. Journal of Cooperative Information Systems (IJCIS)*, 13(3):289–332, 2004.

[DZ04] J. Dehnert and A. Zimmermann. Making Workflow Models Sound Using Petri Net Controller Synthesis. In R. Meersman and Z. Tari et.al., editors, *Int. Conf. Cooperative Information Systems (CoopIS) 2004*, volume 3290 of *LNCS*, pages 139–154, Cyprus, 2004.

[DZ05] J. Dehnert and A. Zimmermann. On the Suitability of Correctness Criteria for Business Process Models. In W.M.P. van der Aalst and B. Benatallah et.al., editors, *Int. Conf. Business Process Management, BPM 2005*, volume 3649 of *LNCS*, pages 386–391, France, 2005.

[HB03] R. Hamadi and B. Benatallah. A Petri Net-based Model for Web Service Composition. In X. Zhou and K.-D. Schewe, editors, *14th Australasian Database Conference (ADC2003)*, volume 17 of *Conferences in Research and Practice in Information Technology*, Australia, 2003.

[HSV03] K.M. van Hee, N. Sidorova, and M. Voorhoeve. Soundness and Separability of Workflow Nets in the Stepwise Refinement Approach. In W.M.P. van der Aalst and E. Best, editors, *24th Int. Conf. on Application and Theory of Petri Nets*, LNCS, pages 337–356. Springer, 2003.

[KMR00] E. Kindler, A. Martens, and W. Reisig. Inter-Operability of Workflow Applications: Local Criteria for Global Soundness. In W.M.P. van der Aalst, J. Desel, and A. Oberweis, editors, *BPM: Models, Techniques, and Empirical Studies*, volume 1806 of *LNCS*, pages 235–253. Springer, 2000.

[Mar05] Martens, A. Analyzing web service based business processes. In M. Cerioli, editor, *8th Int. Conf. on Fundamental Approaches to Software Engineering (FASE 2005)*, volume 3442 of *LNCS*, pages 19–33. Springer Verlag, 2005.

[Val79] R. Valette. Analysis of Petri nets by stepwise refinements. *Journal of Computer and System Sciences*, 18:35–46, 1979.

[vHSSV05] K. M. van Hee, A. Serebrenik, N. Sidorova, and M. Voorhoeve. Soundness of resource-constrained workflow nets. In *ICATPN*, pages 250–267, 2005.

Semantic Correctness in Adaptive Process Management Systems

Linh Thao Ly, Stefanie Rinderle, and Peter Dadam

Dept. DBIS, University of Ulm, Germany
{thao.ly, stefanie.rinderle, peter.dadam}@uni-ulm.de

Abstract. Adaptivity in Process Management Systems (PMS) is key to their successful applicability in pratice. Approaches have already been developed to ensure the system correctness after arbitrary process changes at the syntactical level. However, still errors may be caused at the semantical level. Therefore, the integration of application knowledge will flag a milestone in the development of process management technology. In this paper, we introduce a framework for defining semantic constraints over processes in such a way that they can express real-world application knowledge. On the other hand, these constraints are still manageable concerning the effort for maintenance and semantic process verification. This can be used, for example, to detect semantic conflicts when applying process changes (e.g., drug incompatibilities). In order to enable the PMS to deal with such semantic conflicts we also introduce a notion of semantic correctness and discuss how to (efficiently) verify semantic correctness in the context of process changes.

Keywords: Semantic Correctness, Semantic Process Verification, Semantic Constraints, Adaptive Process Management Systems.

1 Introduction

Due to steadily changing conditions at the global market, companies are forced to frequently adapt their business processes [1–4]. Therefore, adaptivity is the key factor for the successful application of process management technology in practice. Generally, process changes can take place at two levels – process type and instance level [5, 6]. Therefore, it is crucial for an adaptive process management system (PMS) to support both kinds of changes. However, it is still not sufficient to support process type and instance changes in an isolated manner. An adaptive PMS must also allow for the *interplay* between process type and instance changes [7]. A framework for the support of process type and instance changes as well as for their interplay (i.e., the support of change propagation to already individually modified instances) has been developed [3, 8]. Within this framework the structural (syntactical) correctness of the system is always preserved after arbitrary process changes. For example, it is automatically checked by the PMS whether process changes will lead to structural errors, like deadlock-causing cycles or not properly supplied input parameters, or to inconsistent instance states. However, the framework abstracts from semantical aspects. Thus,

S. Dustdar, J.L. Fiadeiro, and A. Sheth (Eds.): BPM 2006, LNCS 4102, pp. 193–208, 2006.

semantic errors may arise, especially in the context of process changes intitiated under time pressure. Consider, for example, process instance I reflecting the treatment process for patient Smith as depicted in Fig. 1. Assume that, due to suddenly arising headache, the drug Aspirin is administered to patient Smith. This is achieved by inserting activity `Administer Aspirin` into instance I in an ad-hoc manner by, for example, a nurse at her workplace.

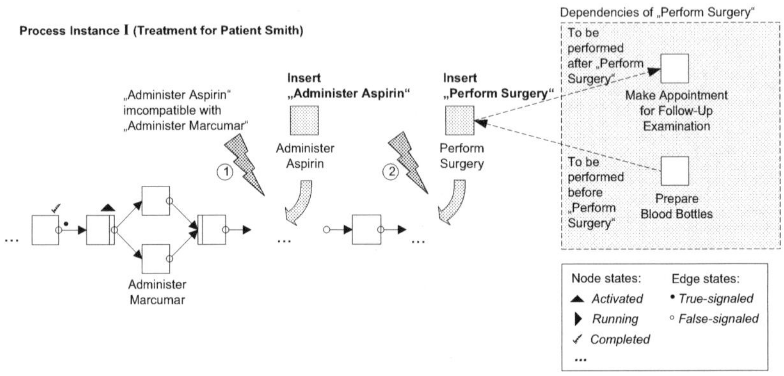

Fig. 1. Semantic conflicts after process changes due to drug incompatibility and dependencies between activities

However, in this treatment process, the drug Marcumar, which is not compatible to Aspirin, is already administered some activities ahead (*semantic conflict*). Even if the process change is syntactically correct, it is not semantically. Especially when the process instance is often modified in an ad-hoc manner (for instance, `Administer Marcumar` was previously inserted as an ad-hoc modification) or when process changes at scheme level and at instance level occur together, it is likely that those conflicts remain undetected by users. If the PMS was aware of the incompatibility of these activities, it could prevent the user from causing semantic conflicts by, for example, warn the user accordingly. In Fig. 2, the user (a doctor with the appropriate authorization) still performs the change operation but has to document the reason for overriding the semantic constraint. Thus, it is possible to trace back semantic conflicts.

As motivated, it is crucial to be able to also integrate application knowledge (i.e., *semantic knowlegde*) within the process change framework in order to avoid semantic conflicts. In this context, many challenging questions arise:

- How to formalize and integrate application knowledge within an adaptive PMS?
- How to define a notion of semantic correctness of processes after changes?
- How to support the efficient verification of the semantic correctness?
- How to maintain the knowledge base?

Fig. 2. Interaction scenario when a semantic conflict occurs

In this paper, we extend the framework presented in [3, 8] by integrating application knowledge into adaptive PMS. First of all, we provide a formalization for semantic constraints imposed on business processes. In particular, we introduce two fundamental kinds of semantic constraints (mutual exclusion constraints and dependency constraints) which serve as a basis for the following considerations. However, the set of semantic constraints can be easily extended. Based on the notion of semantic constraints, a general criterion for the semantic correctness of business processes (independently from the underlying process meta model) is provided. We show how to verify semantic correctness of processes based on this criterion, in particular in the context of process changes. For this, we exploit the semantics of the applied change operations, for example when applying single change operations (e.g., adhoc changes of process instances), or when applying concurrent changes (e.g., propagating process schema changes to biased process instances). Afterwards, we discuss different possibilities to realize verification of semantic process correctness in an efficient manner. One way based on exploiting certain process meta-model properties is discussed in more detail. Finally, we show how the semantic constraints can be organized within a domain repository.

This paper is structured as follows. In Sect. 2, a framework for the definition of semantic constraints and the notion of semantic correctness are introduced. In Sect. 3, we show how the semantic correctness of processes can be verified. In Sect. 4, we show the application of the criterion when, for example, a block-structured process model is used. In Sect. 5, a framework for organizing semantic constraints is introduced. Related work is discussed in Sect. 6. Finally, Sect. 7 concludes with a summary and an outlook on future research.

2 Semantic Constraints and Semantic Correctness in Adaptive Process Management Systems

As motivated in Sect. 1, it is desirable to integrate (semantic) application knowledge in the PMS in order to avoid semantic conflicts. It is in principle possible to integrate even very complex application knowledge in adaptive PMS. By connecting the PMS with a knowledge-based system or an expert system (e.g. [9, 10]), for instance, application knowledge maintained in the external system can be used by the PMS to avoid semantic conflicts. However, two important aspects influence the possibilities of integrating application knowledge in adaptive PMS. First of all, it is an important question how and by whom the knowledge base is maintained. The more application knowledge, and in particular the more complex the knowledge, the greater is the effort to keep the knowledge base up-to-date. Thus, there is a risk that the knowledge, according to which the semantic checks are performed, is outdated. In fact, this might be even more dangerous than not performing semantic checks at all. Users might rely on the semantic checks to ensure the semantic correctness of the process not knowing that the knowledge base is outdated. As a consequence, it seems reasonable to only integrate that kind of application knowledge which is really important and which will really be kept up-to-date. Second, the goal of integrating application knowledge is to enable the PMS to also perform process checks at the semantic level. However, the effort to perform these semantic checks must not lead to a bottleneck, especially when changes on process schemes are propagated to many running (and possibly ad-hoc modified) instances. This restricts the complexity of application knowledge to be integrated in adaptive PMS.

The two aspects mentioned above need to be kept in mind when thinking about integrating application knowledge in adaptive PMS. In future work, we will investigate the influence of these aspects in more detail. In this paper, we introduce two fundamental kinds of semantic constraints which can be imposed on processes: mutual exclusion constraints and dependency constraints. These constraints refer to activities and impose certain conditions on how these activities can be used in the process. By enabling the PMS to be aware of these fundamental constraints, many semantic errors, for example the ones depicted in Fig. 1, can be avoided. On the other hand, the introduced kinds of constraints are still manageable regarding the effort for maintenance and for semantic verification.

Mutual exclusion constraints express that two activities are not compatible and should not be executed together, for instance administering two incompatible drugs. Please note, that this does not mean that these activities must not occur in the same process. Due to the process structure, it depends on the position of the activities whether the constraint is satisfied or not. In Fig. 3, a semantic conflict occurs in the first process fragment while the second process fragment is semantically correct. Mutual exclusion constraints are symmetric.

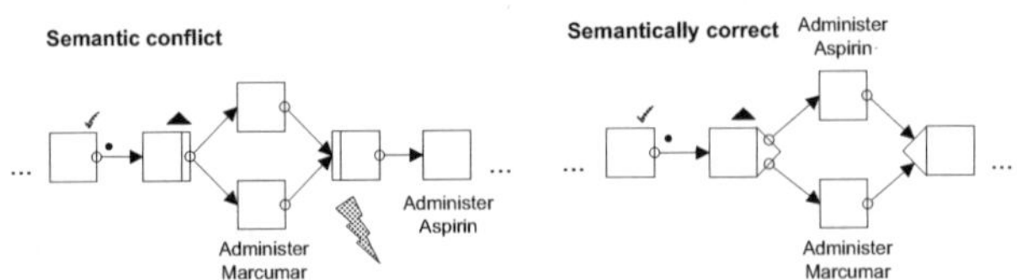

Fig. 3. Semantic conflict dependent of process structure

Dependency constraints express that an activity is dependent of another activity, i.e. these activities need to occur together in the process. In Fig. 1 for instance, activity `Perform Surgery` is added to the process. However, in the treatment process the activity `Prepare Blood Bottles` needs to be performed before and `Make Appointment for Follow-Up Examination` needs to be performed after `Perform Surgery`. These semantic dependencies of `Perform Surgery` cause a semantic conflict, when only `Perform Surgery` is inserted to the process.

Whether a process change can be applied to a concrete process is, therefore, not only a question of structural correctness or data flows but also a question of whether the semantic constraints over the process are violated by the process change. For our following considerations we assume the uniqueness of activities in a process (i.e. each activity may occur only once in a business process).

Definition 1 (Semantic constraint). *Let $\mathcal{A}$ be a set of activities*[1]. *A semantic constraint c is defined as a tuple (type,source,target,position,userDefined) whereas*

- $type \in \{Exclusion, Dependency\}$
- $source, target \in \mathcal{A}$, $source \neq target$
- $position \in \{pre, post, notSpecified\}$
- $userDefined$ *is a user-defined parameter*

The parameter *type* denotes whether the semantic constraint is a mutual exclusion constraint or a dependency constraint. The second parameter *source* denotes the source activity the constraint refers to while *target* denotes the target activity related to the source activity. Parameter *position* specifies the order the source and target activity are to be related to each other within the process (e.g., the surgery depends on the preparation of blood bottles and the bottles have to be prepared before (*pre*) the surgery). The last parameter $userDefined$ can be used for several purposes, for instance for additionally describing the constraint. Furthermore, it might also be used to indicate the importance of the constraint. For instance, to indicate whether a constraint is merely a recommendation or whether it is more severe. This information can be used by the PMS client to create an appropriate feedback for the user. As an example, the constraint mentioned above would look like this:

(`Dependency`, `Perform surgery`, `Prepare blood bottles`, `pre`,
`Blood bottles need to be prepared for the patient and stored in the surgery room before the surgery can take place`)

In Def. 2, the satisfaction of semantic constraints is defined taking the notion of execution trace as a basis. According to Def. 2, the constraint above, for example, is satisfied over a process if the source activity (`Perform surgery`) is not included in this process. In case it is, the constraint is satisfied, if `Prepare blood bottles` is always performed before `Perform surgery` in each possible execution trace of the process, in which `Perform surgery` appears.

Definition 2 (Satisfaction of semantic constraints). *Let $\mathcal{A}$ be a set of activities which can be used to specify a process p of type T. Let $\mathcal{Q}$ be the set of all possible execution traces of p. A trace $q \in \mathcal{Q}$ is defined by $q := < e_1, \ldots, e_k >$ with events e_i = End(t)*[2], *$t \in \mathcal{A}$. Then, we define the following functions:*

[1] Within the ADEPT framework, for example, $\mathcal{A}$ refers to the activity repository containing all relevant activities in the context of a certain process type T.

[2] We abstract from start events in the traces.

- *activities:* $\mathcal{Q} \mapsto \mathcal{A}$ *with activities(q):=* $\{t_1, \ldots, t_n\}$ *with* $q = < e_1, \ldots, e_k > \wedge \forall\, t_l\ \exists\, e_i$ *with* $e_i = End(t_l)$*, l = 1, ..., n; i = 1, ..., k (i.e., activities denotes a function that returns the set of all activities included in an execution trace q).*
- *processActs(p):=*$\{t_1, \ldots, t_n\}$ *with* $\forall\, t_l\ \exists\, q \in \mathcal{Q}$ *with* $t_l \in activities(q)$*, l = 1, ..., n (i.e., processAtcs returns all activities included in the process p).*
- *traceSucc:* $\mathcal{A} \times \mathcal{Q} \mapsto \mathcal{A}$ *with* $traceSucc(t, \sigma) := \{t_1, \ldots, t_n\}$ *with* $\sigma = < e_1, \ldots, e_k >$, $t_1, \ldots, t_n \in activities(\sigma) \wedge \forall\, t_l :\ \exists\, e_i,\ e_j \in \sigma$ *with* $e_i = End(t_l)$, $e_j = End(t)$, *l = 1, ..., n; i, j = 1, ..., k* $\wedge\ i < j$ *(i.e., traceSucc denotes a function which returns all direct or indirect successors of a given activity t within an execution trace* σ*).*
- *tracePred:* $\mathcal{A} \times \mathcal{Q} \mapsto \mathcal{A}$ *with* $tracePred(t, \sigma) := \{t_1, \ldots, t_n\}$ *with* $\sigma = < e_1, \ldots, e_k >$, $t_1, \ldots, t_n \in activities(\sigma) \wedge \forall\, t_l :\ \exists\, e_i,\ e_j \in \sigma$ *with* $e_i = End(t_l)$, $e_j = End(t)$, *l = 1, ..., n; i, j = 1, ..., k* $\wedge\ i > j$ *(i.e., tracePred denotes a function which returns all direct or indirect predecessors of a given activity t within an execution trace* σ*).*

Let $a_1, a_2 \in \mathcal{A}$ *be two activities,* $a_1 \neq a_2$*. Then, a semantic constraint c = (type, source, target, position, userDefined) with source=*a_1 *and target=*a_2 *is* `satisfied` *over process p (formally: satisfied(c, p) =* `True`*) iff one of the following conditions holds:*

- *type* $\in$ *{Exclusion,Dependendency} and* $a_1 \notin processActs(p)$
- *type = Exclusion, position = pre and* $\forall$ *execution traces* $\phi \in \mathcal{Q}$*:* $a_1 \in activities(\phi) \Rightarrow a_2 \notin tracePred(a_1, \phi)$
- *type = Exclusion, position = post and* $\forall$ *execution traces* $\phi \in \mathcal{Q}$*:* $a_1 \in activities(\phi) \Rightarrow a_2 \notin traceSucc(a_1, \phi)$
- *type = Exclusion, position = notSpecified and* $\forall$ *execution traces* $\phi \in \mathcal{Q}$*:* $a_1 \in activities(\phi) \Rightarrow a_2 \notin traceSucc(a_1, \phi)$ *and* $a_2 \notin tracePred(a_1, \phi)$
- *type = Dependendency, position = pre and* $\forall$ *execution traces* $\phi \in \mathcal{Q}$*:* $a_1 \in activities(\phi) \Rightarrow a_2 \in tracePred(a_1, \phi)$
- *type = Dependendency, position = post and* $\forall$ *execution traces* $\phi \in \mathcal{Q}$*:* $a_1 \in activities(\phi) \Rightarrow a_2 \in traceSucc(a_1, \phi)$
- *type = Dependendency, position = notSpecified and* $\forall$ *execution traces* $\phi \in \mathcal{Q}$*:* $a_1 \in activities(\phi) \Rightarrow (a_2 \in tracePred(a_1, \phi)$ *or* $a_2 \in traceSucc(a_1, \phi))$

Otherwise, c is `violated` *over p (formally: satisfied(c, p) =* `False`*).*

For a process type (e.g., the treatment process), many constraints might be relevant. Even if the process was modelled semantically correct at buildtime, due to possible (unforeseen) process changes, activities might be deleted from or added to the process at runtime. Furthermore, mutual exclusion constraints cannot be modelled in the control-flow of a process. In these cases, the constraints imposed on the process will help to ensure a semantically correct execution. Now, based on the notion of satisfaction of constraints, a semantic correctness criterion for business processes can be defined.

Definition 3 (Semantic correctness of business processes). *Let T be a process type and let p be a process of type T. Let further C_p be the set of all semantic constraints defined over p. Process p is semantically correct* $\Longleftrightarrow$

$$\forall c \in C_p\text{: } satisfied(c,p) = \texttt{True}$$

Using Def. 1–3, it is possible to state for each business process whether the business process is semantically correct or not.

3 On Preserving Semantic Correctness of Processes

As specified in Def. 3, a process (no matter whether it is a process instance or a process schema) is semantically correct only if all of its semantic constraints are satisfied. Consequently, the semantic constraints of the process need to be analyzed when checking the process' semantic correctness. Not all the constraints on a process, however, are relevant. Depending on the situation in which the semantic check is initiated, it is possible to restrict the set of relevant constraints to be verified and thus to reduce the effort for semantic process verification. We now have a closer look on that.

In Sect. 3.1, we show how the semantic correctness of process schemes can be verified. In Sect. 3.2, we show how to ensure the semantic correctness of a process when ad-hoc process adaptations are carried out. In Sect. 3.3, we consider how to maintain the semantic correctness when schema evolution is performed. For the remainder of this section, let p be the process to be verified and let C_{vp} be the set of the constraints to be verified in the respective situation.

3.1 Semantic Correctness of Process Schemes

Basically, there are two ways of ensuring the semantic correctness of process schemes depending on the way the process models are constructed. If a process model is built by applying process changes to an "empty" schema the PMS might perform a semantic check each time a change operation is applied and check whether the semantic correctness of the process is still preserved after the change or not (cf. 3.2). The second possibility is to take an already existing process model[3] and to verify the correctness of the complete process schema at once. In this case, it is necessary to verify, whether the constraints imposed on the process are satisfied or not. However, constraints, for which the source activity is not included in the process, are always satisfied over this process by definition. Thus, these constraints need not be considered.

More formally: $C_{vp\ Schema}=\{c \in C_p;\ c(source)^4 \in processActs(p)\}$

3.2 Semantic Correctness After Applying Ad-Hoc Process Changes

In our framework, an ad-hoc process change is considered *semantically applicable* to a process if its application still preserves the semantic correctness of the

[3] This is, for instance, relevant when a process model is imported to the PMS or the process schema is obtained by applying process mining techniques.

[4] $c(source)$ denotes the source parameter of the constraint c.

process. The naive way of verifying the semantic correctness of a process after a process change is to verify the complete process model, as described in Sect. 3.1. However, this effort can be reduced by exploiting the semantics of the applied change operations (e.g., which activity has been inserted at which position). Thus, depending on which change operation is requested, only a smaller subset of constraints on the process needs to be verified. In the following, we discuss the interplay between change operations of type *Insert*, *Delete* and *Move* and the set of constraints to be verified.

When **inserting** an activity t into process p, all semantic constraints over p which have t as source parameter need to be verified since they might be violated. However, since dependency constraints which do not have t as source parameter cannot be violated by the addition of t, only mutual exclusion constraints with t as target parameter need to be considered. We can even further restrict the set of interesting exclusion constraints to those constraints whose source parameter is among the activities of p and whose target parameter corresponds to the inserted activity t. That is because all exclusion constraints, whose source parameter are not included in the process, are satisfied by definition.

More formally: $C_{vp\ Insertion}=\{c \in C_p;\ (c(source)=t)$ or $(c(type)^5=$Exclusion and $c(source) \in processActs(p)$ and $c(target)^6=t)\}$.

When **deleting** an activity t from process p, all semantic constraints over p with t as source parameter are satisified by definition. Similar to the insertion of activities, all constraints for which t occurs as target parameter are potentially interesting for correctness checks. However, mutual exclusion constraints with t as target parameter cannot be violated by the deletion of t. Only dependency constraints with t as target parameter and for which the source parameter is included in p might be violated by the deletion operation and therefore need to be verified.

More formally: $C_{vp\ Deletion}=\{c \in C_p;\ c(type)=$Dependency and $c(source) \in processActs(p)$ and $c(target)=t\}$.

The **moving** of an activity t from its original position within process p to a new position *pos* can be understood as being equivalent of deleting t and inserting t at *pos* afterwards[7]. Consequently, all constraints that which might be violated after applying deletion and insertion operations need to be verified.

More formally: $C_{vp\ Move} = C_{vp\ Deletion} \cup C_{vp\ Insertion}$.

3.3 Semantic Correctness for Process Schema Evolution

In addition to ad-hoc changes at the instance level, adaptive PMS must support the modification of process schemes at the type level followed by the migration of running instances to the modified process schema as well. The semantic correctness of the process schema after applying the changes can be verified

[5] $c(type)$ denotes the type of the constraint c (Dependency or Exclusion).

[6] $c(target)$ denotes the target parameter of the constraint c.

[7] In conjunction with data flow aspects, moving is not always equivalent to deleting and inserting. However, this assumption can be used to derive statements about possible semantic conflicts here.

by using the considerations for ad-hoc changes made in Sect. 3.2. In case the schema change is semantically correct, it will also be semantically correct when being applied to *unbiased* instances (i.e., instances which still run according to the process schema they have been started on). However, the direct application of the schema change to *biased* instances (i.e., instances which have already been individually modified) might lead to semantic conflicts between type and instance changes. Assume that at instance level drug Marcumar has been administered for process instance I as an ad-hoc change. Afterwards, at process type level, activity `Administer Aspirin` is inserted into the associated process schema and is to be propagated to I. Migrating I to the modified process schema then causes a semantic conflict, even though the migration can be performed in a syntactically correct manner. Therefore, we have to check whether the process changes at type level are semantically applicable to the biased instances. We assume that the biased instances are semantically correct after the individually applied process instance changes. The propagation of changes at type level to a biased instance is semantically correct if the type changes are *semantically applicable* to the biased instance as ad-hoc instance change or vice versa (cf. Sect. 3.2).

Due to only considering *biased* instances, the number of instances to be checked is highly decreased. However, it is possible to further decrease the number of instances and relevant constraints to be verified. For example, if the change operations applied to a process instance constitute a superset of the change operations applied to the process schema (or vice versa), no semantic conflicts can occur. Due to space restrictions, we omit further details. For details on superset relations between change operations we refer to [8, 11].

For an efficient implementation of the considerations in Sect. 3, employing indexing techniques in order to easily access the relevant constraints in the respective situations seems very useful. After having considered, which constraints need to be verified in different situations, in the next section we consider how to verify those constraints.

4 On Optimizing Semantic Process Verification

The semantic correctness criterion for business processes defined in Sect. 2 is generic and can be applied to any process meta-model (e.g., Petri Nets [1] or BPEL4WS Nets [12]). For verifying the criterion, reachability analysis can be applied (i.e., by calculating all possible execution traces and checking them for certain order relations between activities according to the semantic constraints) which might be very costly. Therefore, we want to investigate different methods to ensure the semantic correctness criterion which are less expensive. In this paper, we present an approach which makes use of certain properties of the underlying process meta-model, namely block-structuring (e.g., WSM Nets [3]). However, we intend to also develop model-independent methods in future work.

4.1 Background Information

This section summarizes background information on WSM Nets [13, 14] as process description formalism in order to present an optimized verification method for semantic correctness.

A *process schema* is represented by a WSM Net which defines the *process activities* as well as the *control* and *data flow* between them. When using WSM Nets the control flow schema can be represented by attributed, serial-parallel graphs. In order to synchronize activities from parallel paths additional links can be used [15]. In this paper we abstract from cyclic structures within the process meta model in order to provide a fundament for an optimized semantic correctness verification. Further on, a WSM Net comprises a set of *data elements* and a set of *data edges.* A data edge links an activity with a data element and either represent a read access of this activity or a write access. The total set of data edges constitutes the data flow schema.

Definition 4 (WSM Net). *A tuple S = (N, D, NT, CtrlEdges, SyncEdges, DataEdges, BC) is called a WSM Net, if the following holds:*

- *N is a set of process activities and D a set of process data elements*
- *NT: N* $\mapsto$ {`StartFlow`, `EndFlow`, `Activity`, `AndSplit`, `AndJoin`, `XOrSplit`, `XOrJoin`, `StartLoop`, `EndLoop`}
  NT assigns to each node of the process schema a respective node type.
- *CtrlEdges* $\subset N \times N$ *is a precedence relation definining the valid order of activities (notation:* $n_{src} \rightarrow n_{dst} \equiv (n_{src}, n_{dst}) \in$ *CtrlEdges)*
- *SyncEdges* $\subset N \times N$ *is a precedence relation between activities of parallel branches*
- *DataEdges* $\subseteq N \times D \times$ *{read, write} is a set of read/write data links between activities and data elements*
- *BC: N* $\mapsto$ *Conds(D) where Conds(D) denotes the set of all valid transition conditions on data elements from D. BC(n) is undefined for nodes n with NT(n)* $\neq$ `XOrSplit`.

Which constraints have to hold such that a process schema S is well-structured is summarized in [15, 8] (e.g., absence of deadlock–causing cycles and correctly supplied input parameters). In the context of this paper, the block-structuring property is important, i.e., for all activities of node type `AndSplit` (`XOrSplit`) there is a unique activity of node type `AndJoin` (`XOrJoin`) and blocks (sequences as well as parallel and alternatives branchings can be nested but must overlap).

In this paper we abstain from defining process instances (see [3]) since this is not relevant for the following considerations.

4.2 On Exploiting Process Meta Model Properties

From the general constraint satisfaction criteria presented in Sect. 2 we derived meta-model specific conditions on WSM Nets. Using these meta-model specific criteria the satisfaction of semantic constraints and thus the semantic correctness of a process can be verified in an optimized way. For all semantic constraints in

Def. 1, such meta-model specific criteria can be derived. Due to space restrictions, however, we abstain from presenting all the criteria. Instead, as an example, we show how a particular meta-model specific criterion can be derived. Consider the following semantic constraint over the treatment process from Sect. 1:

c_1: (`Dependency`, `Perform surgery`, `Prepare blood bottles`, `pre`, ...)

If `Perform surgery` does not occur in the treatment process, then c_1 is satisfied by definition and consequently not of further interest for semantic process verification (cf. Sect. 3). In case `Perform surgery` occurs in the process, it is necessary that `Prepare Blood Bottles` is a direct or indirect predecessor of `Perform surgery` in the treatment process for c_1 to be satisfied. Otherwise, it is not possible that `Prepare Blood Bottles` is performed before `Perform Surgery`, each time `Perform Surgery` is performed. However, this is not sufficient, since this execution order is not guaranteed. When verifying semantic constraints, it is necessary to also take the process structure into account. If `Prepare Blood Bottles` is contained in the inner part of an XOR-block while `Perform Surgery` is not, `Prepare Blood Bottles` is not sure to be performed each time `Perform Surgery` is performed. Therefore, c_1 is not satisfied over the process depicted in Fig. 4.

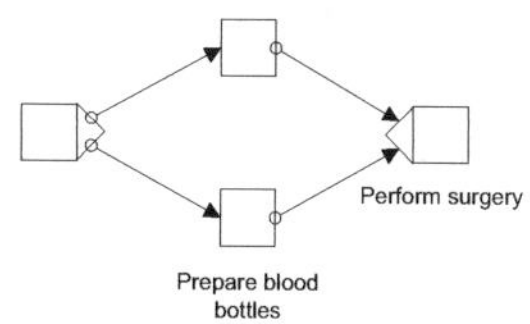

Fig. 4. `Prepare blood bottles` is not sure to be performed each time `Perform surgery` is performed

From this example we conclude the following conditions for the satisfaction of that kind of dependency constraints over block-structured meta models:
A semantic dependency constraint c_{dep}= $(Dependency, source, target, pre, ...)$ over a process p represented by a WSM Net $S = (N, D, NT, ...)$ with $source \in N$ (i.e. $source \in processActs(p)$) is satisfied (i.e., $satisfied(c_{dep}, p)$ = `True`) if and only if the two following conditions hold:

- $target \in pred^*(S, source)$ (*necessary condition*)
- $\forall s \in N$ with $NT(S)$ = `XOrSplit`: $target \in inBlock(S, s) \Rightarrow source \in inBlock(S, s)$ (*sufficient condition*), where:
  - $pred^*(S, n)$ $(succ^*(S, n))$ denotes the set of all direct and indirect predecessors (successors) of n in S[8]
  - $inBlock(S, s) := succ^*(S, s) \cap pred^*(S, join(S))$
  - $join(S, s)$ yields the unique associated join for split node s

[8] Note that $pred^*$ $(succ^*)$ refers to structural predecessors (successors) whereas $tracePred$ $(traceSucc)$ refers to predecessors (successors) within execution traces.

In the following we show that these conditions ensure the semantic correctness.

Proof sketch. Let c_{dep}= $(Dependency, source, target, pre, userDefined)$ be a semantic dependency constraint over a process p represented by a WSM Net $S = (N, D, NT, ...)$ with the set of all execution traces Φ for which $source \in N$ holds. Then, the following proposition $\bowtie$ is to be proven (cf. Def. 2):

$satisfied(c_{dep}, p) = \texttt{True} \Longleftrightarrow$
$(target \in pred^*(S, source)) \wedge$
$(\forall s \in N \text{ with } NT(S) = \texttt{XOrSplit}: target \in inBlock(S, s) \Rightarrow$
$source \in inBlock(S, s))$
$\bowtie \Longleftrightarrow$
$\forall \phi \in \Phi: source \in activities(\phi) \Rightarrow target \in tracePred(source, \phi)$ (i) $\Longleftrightarrow$
$(target \in pred^*(S, source)) \wedge$
$(\forall s \in N \text{ with } NT(S) = \texttt{XOrSplit}: target \in inBlock(S, s) \Rightarrow$
$source \in inBlock(S, s))$ (ii)
"$\Longrightarrow$": Proof by contradiction (i.e. ((i) $\Longrightarrow$ (ii)) $\Longleftrightarrow$ ($\neg$(ii) $\Longrightarrow$ $\neg$(i)))

Let us assume that (ii) does not hold (i.e. $\neg$(ii) holds). Let us first assume that the necessary condition does not hold, i.e. $target \notin pred^*(S, source)$. This means that there is no path from $source$ to $target$ in p. Then, there are four possibilities:

1. $target \notin N \Longrightarrow source \notin tracePred(target, \Phi)$
2. $target \in succ^*(S, source) \Longrightarrow source \notin tracePred(target, \Phi)$
3. $target$ and $source$ are in an parallel block
4. $target \in N$ and $target$ in an XOR-path while $source$ is in the other XOR-path

Possibilities 1 and 2 are clear. If the third possibility is true, then c_{dep} is also violated since, due to the interleavings of parallelly executed activities, there might be at least one trace, where $target$ and $source$ do not occur in the required ordering relation. If the fourth possibility is true, then either $source$ or $target$ are executed during an process execution. Thus c_{dep} is violated as well. As shown, all possibilites that are left when the necessary condition is not true lead to the violation of c_{dep} ($\neg$(i)).

Now let us assume that the necessary condition holds, but not the sufficient condition. This means: $\exists s, NT(S) = \texttt{XOrSplit}$ with $target \in inBlock(S, s) \wedge source \notin inBlock(S, s)$. Since $target \in pred^*(source)$) holds (necessary condition), we can construct an execution trace of p by not chosing the XOR-path which $target$ is on while still executing $source$. This leads to $\neg$(i). □

The reverse direction "$\Longleftarrow$" can be proven analogously.

The satisfaction criterion for dependency constraints for block-structured process meta-models presented above can be verified very efficiently. Special constructs of the meta-models, for instance references to the split and join nodes, can be exploited by the PMS in order to find out whether the respective constraint is satisfied or not. However, using the meta-model specific criterion it is also possible to leave the verification to an external reasoning system (e.g. RACER [9]). In this case, information about the process structure need to be mapped to rules in the reasoning system in order enable it to apply inference techniques. We intend to further investigate these implementation alternatives in future work.

5 A Framework for Semantic Constraints

In our approach, a set of semantic constraints is assigned to a process. However, several processes may share constraints. In this section, we present a framework for organising semantic constraints such that they can be reused easily.

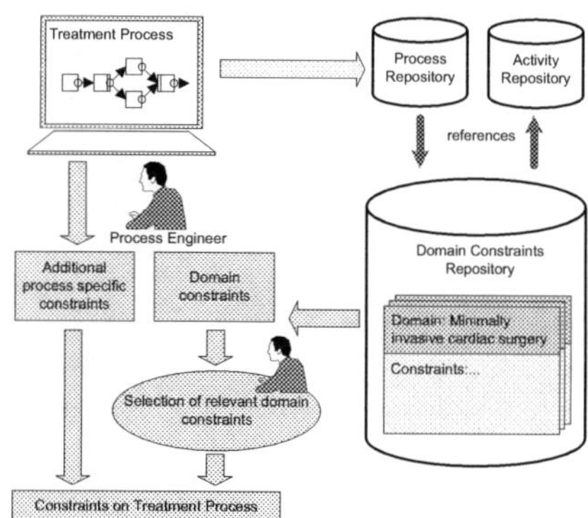

Fig. 5. Organisation of constraints in a domain constraints repository

The three main components of the framework are the *domain repository*, the *process repository*, and the *activity repository* (cf. Fig. 5). Semantic constraints are organised in the domain repository. In particular, constraints are assigned to domains, for instance the domain *Minimally invasive cardiac surgery*. Thus, a domain contains a set of constraints that are typical of this domain. The constraints presented in this paper refer to activities which are organized in an activity repository. For future work, we also plan to introduce constraints that refer to other abstraction levels, for instance abstraction levels in the activity repository. Process types (process schemes) are organized in a process repository. Each process type is assigned a domain of the domain repository. Thus, it is possible to assign a default set of domain constraints to a process. However, processes that are assigned to the same domain might still have different semantic constraints that are not captured in the domain. Therefore, for each process type, the process designer can specify additional semantic constraints for the process or leave out some unnecessary domain constraints.

6 Related Work

The issue of integrating semantics in process management systems has often been adressed in literature. In particular, there are interesting approaches from the clinical domain concerning the formalization of clinical guidelines in a computer-readable way, e.g. [16, 17] and GLIF3 [18] or GUIDE [19]. However, so far, this information cannot be directly used for automatical analyses by the PMS.

Current approaches on adaptive PMS mainly focus on structural aspects (e.g., [3, 4, 8, 20]) or have a different notion of semantic correctness (e.g., [21, 1]). Many related approaches focus on the aspect of integrating heterogenous resources. In particular, activities and their parameters are often described using ontologies, e.g. [22–24] and also many approaches concerning semantic web service composition, for instance [25, 26]. When a process is composed, the PMS can check, whether the activities and their parameters semantically fit together. However, these approaches do not consider semantic constraints over processes, for instance mutual exclusion constraints, the way we do.

As discussed in Sect. 2, approaches from the field of *Artificial Intelligence*, in particular knowledge-based systems, e.g. [27, 10, 9], can be used to integrate application knowledge in PMS. This is also closely related to approaches concerning the integration of business rules in PMS. Application knowledge can be sourced out into a *Business Rule Engine*, e.g. commercially available systems like ILOG [28]. Thus, decision processes, for instance, which outgoing paths of an activity to follow, can be supported taking also background knowledge into account. This approach, however, is not directly suitable for situations like the one outlined in our example scenario since this situation concerns not only the occurrence of an activity in the process but also the relations between activities (cf. Fig. 3). In [29, 30], an approach to ensure the integrity of processes is introduced. Rules, realized as database triggers, are applied, when certain data conditions occur. Using the change framework presented in [3, 8] the process is adapted in an ad-hoc manner according to the triggered rule. Our approach, however, goes further since for the semantic verification, structural information about the process is needed.

In [31] van der Aalst et al. introduced an approach for verifying given properties of past processes by applying process mining techniques. This approach can help detecting constraint violations. However, the approach introduced in [31] is orthogonal to our work because it aims on analysing past processes on certain aspects while our intention is to ensure the semantic correctness of running processes. Thus, these two approaches can complement each other.

We consider our approach to be orthogonal to the approaches mentioned in this section.

7 Conclusion and Outlook

In this paper, we introduced a framework for the integration of application knowledge within an adaptive PMS by using semantic constraints. Based on these constraints, a generic criterion for semantic correctness of processes has been provided. We have shown how this criterion can be generally ensured. Furthermore, we have addressed the issue of verifying semantic correctness after process changes. Exemplarily for block-structured process meta-models, we have shown how semantic process verification can be realized in an efficient manner.

Finally, an architecture for the integration of semantic constraints within an adaptive PMS has been presented.

Using our approach, all semantic conflicts caused by violation of dependency and mutual exclusion constraints can be avoided. However, the expressiveness of the presented constraints is limited. Therefore, in future work we will extend our framework, e.g. by introducing context restrictions on constraints concerning their validity (e.g., time or location) or by introducing constraints on other levels of granularity than the activity level (e.g. data). Furthermore, we want to develop further methods to efficiently verify semantic correctness within an adaptive PMS. For example, we want to analyze how the information referred to by semantic constraints can be organized (e.g., within an ontology) in order to decrease evaluation effort. All considerations are to be implemented within the adaptive PMS ADEPT (e.g. [15]).

Acknowledgement. We thank Michael Nahler for the valuable results of his Master thesis ([32]) which have partially been incorporated in this paper.

References

1. v.d. Aalst, W., Basten, T.: Inheritance of workflows: An approach to tackling problems related to change. Theoret. Comp. Science **270** (2002) 125–203
2. Casati, F., Ceri, S., Pernici, B., Pozzi, G.: Workflow evolution. Data and Knowledge Engineering **24** (1998) 211–238
3. Rinderle, S., Reichert, M., Dadam, P.: Flexible support of team processes by adaptive workflow systems. DPD **16** (2004) 91–116
4. Weske, M.: Formal foundation and conceptual design of dynamic adaptations in a workflow management system. In: HICSS-34. (2001)
5. Kochut, K., Arnold, J., Sheth, A., Miller, J., Kraemer, E., Arpinar, B., Cardoso, J.: IntelliGEN: A distributed workflow system for discovering protein-protein interactions. DPD **13** (2003) 43–72
6. Reichert, M., Rinderle, S., Dadam, P.: On the modeling of correct service flows with BPEL4WS. In: EMISA'04. (2004) 117–128
7. Rinderle, S., Reichert, M., Dadam, P.: Correctness criteria for dynamic changes in workflow systems – a survey. DKE **50** (2004) 9–34
8. Rinderle, S.: Schema Evolution in Process Management Systems. PhD thesis, University of Ulm (2004)
9. Haarslev, V., Möller, R.: Description of the racer system and its applications. In: Proceedings International Workshop on Description Logics (DL-2001), Stanford, USA, 1.-3. August. (2001) 131–141
10. Hayes-Roth, F.: Rule-based systems. Commun. ACM **28** (1985) 921–932
11. Rinderle, S., Weber, B., Reichert, M., Wild, W.: Integrating process learning and process evolution - a semantics based approach. In: BPM'05. (2005)
12. Andrews, T., Curbera, F., Dholakia, H., et al., Y.G.: BPELWS - Business Process Execution Language for Web Services. (2003) BEA Systems, International Business Machines Corporation, Microsoft Corporation, SAP AG, Siebel Systems.
13. Rinderle, S., Reichert, M., Dadam, P.: On dealing with structural conflicts between process type and instance changes. In: BPM'04. (2004) 274–289
14. Rinderle, S., Reichert, M., Dadam, P.: Disjoint and overlapping process changes: Challenges, solutions, applications. In: CoopIS'04. (2004) 101–120

15. Reichert, M., Dadam, P.: ADEPT$_{flex}$ - supporting dynamic changes of workflows without losing control. JIIS **10** (1998) 93–129
16. Maviglia, S., Zielstorff, R., Paterno, M., Teich, J., Bates, D., Kuperman, G.: Automating complex guidelines for chronic disease: Lessons learned. Journal of American Medical Inf. Ass. **10** (2003) 154–165
17. Blaser, R., Schnabel, M., Heger, O., Opitz, E., Lenz, R., Kuhn, K.: Improving pathway compliance and clinician performance by using information technology. In: MIE'05. (2005)
18. Boxwala, A., Peleg, M., Tu, S.: GLIF3: a representation format for sharable computer-interpretable clinical practice guidelines. Biomed Inform. **37** (2004) 147–61
19. Quaglini, S., Stefanelli, M., Cavallini, A., G, G.M., Fassino, C., C, C.M.: Guideline-based careflow systems. Artif Intell Med **20** (2000) 5–22
20. Weske, M.: Flexible modeling and execution of workflow activities. In: Proc. Hawaii Int'l Conf. on System Sciences, Hawaii (1998) 713–722
21. van der Aalst W. M. P., Basten, T., Verbeek, H.M.W., Verkoulen, P.A.C., Voorhoeve, M.: Adaptive workflow: On the interplay between flexibility and support. Interprise Information Systems (2000) 63–70
22. Pathak, J., Caragea, D., Honovar, V.: Ontolgy-extended component-based workflows: A framework for constructing complex workflows from semantically heterogeneous software components. In: SWDB'04. (2005) 41–56
23. Bowers, S., Lin, K., Ludäscher, B.: On integrating scientific resources through semantic registration. In: SSDBM'04. (2004)
24. Kim, J., Gil, Y., Spraragen, M.: A knowledge-based approach to interactive workflow composition. In: ICAPS 04. (2004)
25. Cardoso, J., Sheth, A.: Semantic e-workflow composition. JIIS. **21** (2003) 191–225
26. Zhang, R., Arpinar, I.B., Aleman-Meza, B.: Automatic composition of semantic web services. In: Intl. Conf. on Web Services, Las Vegas NV, June 2003. (2003)
27. Hayes-Roth, F., Jacobstein, N.: The state of knowledge-based systems. Commun. ACM **37** (1994) 26–39
28. Ader, M.: Ilog components for business process management solutions (2002)
29. Greiner, U., Ramsch, J., Heller, B., Löffler, M., Müller, R., Rahm, E.: Adaptive guideline-based treatment workflows with adaptflow. In: CGP 2004. (2004) 113–117
30. Müller, R., Greiner, U., Rahm, E.: Agentwork: A workflow system supporting rule-based workflow adaption. DKE **51** (2004) 223–256
31. v. d. Aalst, W., de Beer, H., van Dongen, B.: Process mining and verification of properties: An approach based on temporal logic. In: CoopIS'05. (2005) 130–147
32. Nahler, M.: Semantical conflicts in adaptive process managament systems (2005) (in german).

A Framework for the Development and Execution of Horizontal Protocols in Open BPM Systems*

J. Fabra, P. Álvarez, J.A. Bañares, and J. Ezpeleta

Instituto de Investigación en Ingeniería de Aragón (I3A)
Department of Computer Science and Systems Engineering, University of Zaragoza,
María de Luna 3, E-50018 Zaragoza, Spain
{jfabra, alvaper, banares, ezpeleta}@unizar.es

Abstract. A new generation of open *Business Process Management* (BPM) systems based on the service-oriented architecture and Web service technologies has recently emerged. The general tendency for these systems should be governed by the integration of independent Web-service specifications. Web services requirements guide the description, execution and choreography of business process and the implementation of frameworks for supporting the coordination, synchronization and creation of business transactions. However, a wide variety of open research issues related to the lack of maturity of the involved specifications makes the development of standard-based BPM systems difficult. In this paper we propose an abstract architecture inspired by Web service specifications to overcome these difficulties. Also, a particular implementation based on the *Nets-within-Nets* paradigm and the Renew tool is presented. The result is an executable infrastructure able to run business processes (their workflows and coordination protocols) as well as the horizontal protocols that guarantee a coherent outcome of their whole execution, such as the *WS-Atomic Transaction* protocol.

Keywords: SOA and Process Management, Formal models in BPM, Horizontal protocols, Petri nets, Nets-within-Nets paradigm.

1 Introduction

In [1] a *Business Process Management* (BPM) system is defined as a middleware system that provides a central point of control for the definition and orchestration of business processes. Regardless of the technologies used in its implementation, these systems integrate a set of software tools for the definition of business processes, an engine able to run the tasks described by the process descriptions and frameworks for the creation and execution of business transactions involving a set of processes. New business opportunities offered by the

* This work has been supported by the research project PIP086/2005, granted by the Government of Aragón.

S. Dustdar, J.L. Fiadeiro, and A. Sheth (Eds.): BPM 2006, LNCS 4102, pp. 209–224, 2006.

Internet have motivated the development of a new generation of open BPM systems oriented towards inter-organization business processes. In this context, different initiatives inspired by the service-oriented architecture and Web service technologies [2] have been launched with industry-wide support with the aim of promoting common frameworks for open solutions, such as the *Workflow Management Coalition*, *RosettaNet* and *ebXML*. In parallel, other independent initiatives have published their standard specifications for the description of business processes (BPEL4WS [3]) and their protocols and allowed conversations (WCSI [4], WS-CDL [5] and OWL-S [6]) with the objective of helping organizations to coordinate their business processes and transactions in a Web service environment (the *horizontal protocols* [2] described by *Web Service Coordination* and *Web Service Transactions* specifications [7] or the *Web Service Composite Application Framework* [8], for instance).

Nevertheless, despite of these standardization efforts, many open issues must be considered as research targets. Let us, for instance, to adopt the software developer point of view. When building an open and standard-based BPM system many problems must be dealt with. Among the most important ones, the following must be considered: 1) the standards involved have different levels of maturity; 2) there are duplicated standardization initiatives dealing with the same aspect (such as WCSI and WS-CDL for the description of the external behavior of business processes or *Web Service Transactions* and *Web Service Composite Application Framework* for managing business transactions); 3) there is a lack of a global vision of different involved standards and a clear methodology to develop complex Web-based solutions by means of their integration; and 4) the analysis and verification of the different distributed components that compose a system is a very difficult task.

Recently, a very interesting research work is being carried out to apply the well-developed theory and tools of Petri nets to the world of Web services, where Petri nets are the tool to model and analyze the behavior of Web services, allowing to alleviate some of the lacks just described. In some cases, the models are obtained from a translation process, taking some standard descriptions as the input; in other cases, the Petri net model is directly generated by the engineer. In [9], WS-BPEL descriptions are translated into Petri nets to provide that formalism with a formal semantics; [10] generates High Level Petri net models from DAML-S specifications, as is the case in [11]. With a different point of view, [12] focuses on the analysis of Web service's properties (such as compatibility and equivalence between Web services) based on a Petri net model translated from a BPEL4WS service's specification.

In [13] we proposed a system infrastructure, based on the Nets-within-Nets paradigm [14] and the Renew tool [15], for the design and execution of Web services, which can be understood as an instance of the more abstract and general approach presented in [16]. In this paper, an evolution of this infrastructure is introduced, which supports the execution of business processes (their workflows and conversations) and provides a standard-based framework for the coordination, synchronization and the creation of business transactions. This flexibility is shown by means of the implementation of a particular horizontal protocol, as is the case of *WS-AtomicTransaction* [7]. Besides, this implementation allows us to show how the main open issues described above can be dealt with the proposed Web services infrastructure.

The paper is organized as follows. Section 2 presents the current approaches for Web service composition and coordination and shows some of its lacks. Section 3 introduces an evolution of the original model presented in [13], an infrastructure for Web service development and execution based on the Nets-within-Nets paradigm and the Renew tool, for the design and execution of Web services. This infrastructure is applied to the design and implementation of the *WS-Atomic Transaction* [7] horizontal protocol in Section 4. Finally, Section 5 contains some concluding remarks and future work directions.

2 Current Approaches for Web Service Composition and Coordination

Service composition is an aspect related to the implementation of a Web service whose internal logic involves the invocation of operations offered by other Web services. It is then clear that Web services composition requires different Web services to interact. A *conversation* is a dialog among two or more Web services participating in these complex interactions, whereas a *coordination protocol* describes a set of acceptable conversations (the external observable behavior of involved Web services) [2].

In order to be able to compose general Web services, which can require complex interactions, service invocation has to be provided with a long-lasting conversation where several messages are exchanged before the service is completed [17].

The following elements are necessary when Web service compositions must be considered: 1) a *high-level composition language*, enabling the specification of the way services have to be combined, the order in which they must be invoked and the way in which service invocation parameters are determined; 2) a *development environment*, typically characterized by a graphical user interface, for the design of schemas denoting the order constraints imposed to the way services are invoked; and 3) a *composition engine*, able to execute the business logic imposed by the composite service [2]. Different proposals are available in the marketplace, most of them offering some type of modeling mechanism based on the BPEL4WS specification [3].

As stated before, a composite service must interact with other Web services by invoking the operations they publish. BPEL4WS uses WSDL interfaces to describe the functionality it offers and also to invoke functionalities required from other Web services [18,19]. As a consequence, the management of interactions provided by BPEL4WS is based on one-shot interactions instead of a long-lived conversational approach, causing business and conversation logics to be highly-coupled. Nevertheless, a natural evolution of the BPEL4WS specification should replace current WSDL-based abstractions with new conversation models such as WCSI [4], WS-CDL [5] and OWL-S [6].

On the other hand, a composite service must deal with the (possible) failure of some participating Web services, guaranteeing a coherent outcome of the whole business process [18]. Actually the *Web service Coordination* (WS-Coordination) specification [20] provides a mechanism for initiating and agreeing on the outcome of a multiparty interaction. Being WS-Coordination a general coordination framework, different protocols can be used to define specific ways of reaching a global agreement, as it is the case of *WS-AtomicTransaction* [7] for ACID transactions or *WS-BusinessActivity* [21] for long-running and compensation-based transaction protocols.

As an alternative to WS-Coordination, the *Web Service Composite Application Framework* (WS-CAF) [22] supports the coordinated and transactional composition of multiple Web services, whose most emphasized contribution is to consider *coordination contexts* [23] as a first-class architectural entities, facilitating the management of large-scale environments.

3 An Infrastructure for Web Service Development and Execution

In [13] we proposed a basic model, based on the Nets-within-Nets paradigm and the Renew tool, for the design and execution of Web services, which can be understood as an instance of the more abstract and general approach presented in [16]. An evolution of that original model which maintains its main components is presented in this section.

Firstly let us briefly introduce a top-level view of the abstract architecture we are proposing for the development of Web service execution environments, and then a particular infrastructure implemented in accordance with its architectural rules.

3.1 High-Level Components of an Architecture for Web Service Execution Environments

Figure 1 outlines the main components of an architecture able to execute Web services and interpret their conversations.

The *composition component* integrates a workflow engine that executes the business logic of composed services. Some of these services are exposed to external consumers as WSDL-described services and other provide operational support, for example, for the execution of transactions. In any case, a workflow-based language, such as BPEL4WS, can be used to describe the business logic of the mentioned services.

In order to make possible service executions, even when the involved providers require complex interactions, service invocations have to be modeled as conversations. In the proposed architecture, the management of conversations is kept separated from the business logic. In fact, these are complementary one to each other.

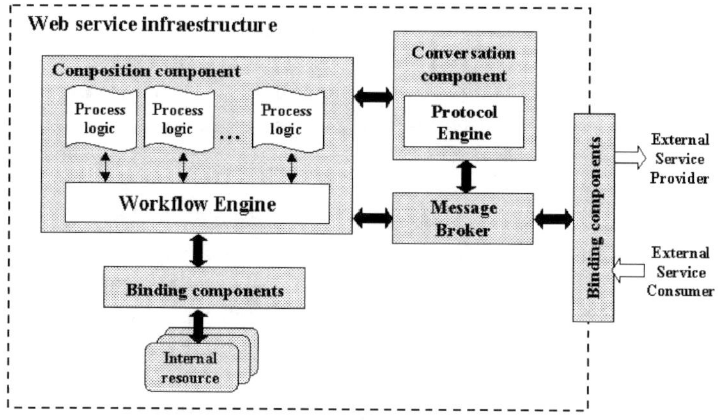

Fig. 1. Top-level view of the architecture

The *conversation component* interprets the coordination protocols; more specifically, the role-specific view of a protocol played by the service. A protocol defines the interactions among services, the way sending/receiving operations must be ordered, the format and encoding of messages, etc. Different approaches have been considered to move from one-shot service invocations towards more powerful and flexible ways of defining the valid sequences of messages and the coordination protocols or conversation policies, as proposed in [24,25], or, alternatively, WSCI or WS-CDL.

Messages exchanged among services are dispatched by the *message broker* component. Messages generated by the conversations must be routed to either external or internal service providers. On the other hand, incoming messages must be dispatched to a conversation or to the composition component. These messages may cause the execution of a new service instance or the start of a new conversation for a running service.

The last link in this chain corresponds to the *binding components*. They serve as the bridge between the proposed architecture and the external world, allowing the communication with external entities that use a wide variety of communication technologies, such as SOAP, JMS, HTTP, SMTP, etc. These components understand messages in the message broker requiring some interaction with a given external entity and with some specific communication technology, and are able to execute such communication. They are also able to receive incoming invocations and to translate them into the adequate messages to be put into the message broker.

3.2 Initial Design Considerations

In order to make the paper as self-contained as possible, let us remember here the main design aspects involved in the participant model presented in [13], which are strongly related to the components of Figure 1. The proposal was based on the following facts:

1. Both, Web service composition and coordination have quite similar aspects, which are strongly related to concurrent elements, and for which (the different families of) Petri nets are very adequate tools. Composition aspects are related to the way the involved Web services are organized, while coordination elements are related to the way interactions (conversation protocols) must be arranged.
2. Interactions among Web services have an inherent asynchronous nature and are organized by means of global agreed protocols, in which involved services accept to play different roles. Service architects can logically group one or more exchanged messages (like units of communication between services) to form interaction patterns (MEPs, *Message Exchange Patterns* of WSDL); or alternatively to form complex conversations and protocols grouping several messages, which are associated with some well-defined behavior for the participating services. In this sense, the adopted approach is quite similar to the one proposed in [24].
3. An asynchronous standard-independent coordination language as an intermediate language for the definition and execution of coordination protocols can be an interesting approach (the same as defining intermediate code when implementing compilers). We have considered the Linda [26] coordination model as intermediate language for the modeling of conversations among Web services [13]. This choice is motivated because its communication primitives are particulary well-suited for Web service environments allowing an uncoupled communication and requiring a minimum prior knowledge between the cooperating peers. Besides, a Linda-based coordination space is used as the repository where conversations and Web processes write/read messages in an implementation-independent way. In this sense, it can be interpreted as a *message broker*.
4. *Binding components* must be implemented to send and receive messages by the different standardized transport protocols (SOAP, JMS, RMI, etc.). In this sense, they are responsible of inserting the information coded in received messages into the Linda-based coordination space, and recovering from the coordination space (and optionally formatting) messages to be sent to external services.
5. The fact of having the models corresponding to composition and coordination aspects to be executed in a collaborative way in a instance of the architecture makes the Nets-within-Nets based approach to be quite natural. Another reason is the fact of the existence of the Renew tool, which facilitated an easy definition and execution of our participant model, together with the easy interaction between the Petri net models and Java code.

3.3 The *Nets-Within-Nets* Paradigm

Let us now briefly remember some definitions about Reference nets [27]. Reference nets is a subclass of the *Nets-within-Nets* family of Petri nets [14]. *Nets-within-Nets* are an extension of the Colored Petri net formalism. They fall into the set of object oriented approaches. In classical Petri nets, the net structure is static, and tokens move inside the net. *Nets-within-Nets* have a static part (the environment, also called *system net*) and a dynamic part, composed of instances of *object nets* that move inside the system net. These instances can be created in a dynamic way. Each object net can have its own internal dynamic behavior and can also interact with the system net by means of *interactions*. The system net can also move (*transport*) object nets by its own.

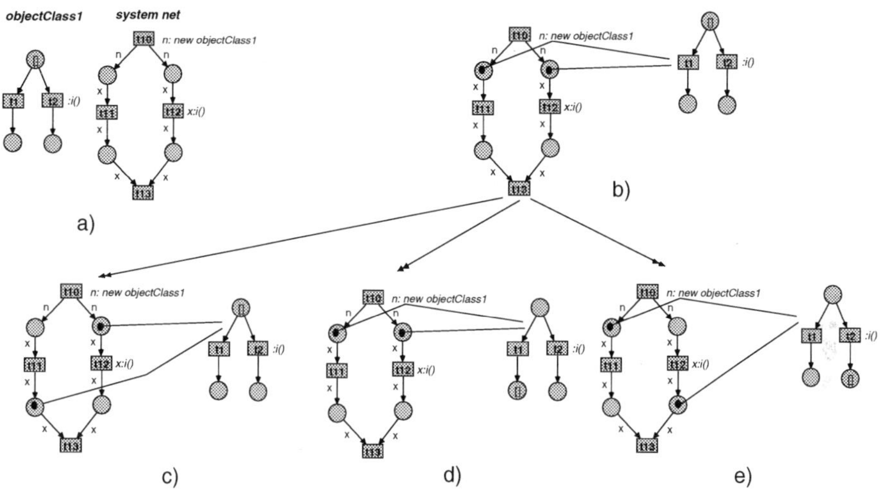

Fig. 2. a) A reference Net-within-Net example with the *system net* and an *object net*. b) The previous systems once transition t10 has been fired. c) Evolution from the state in Figure-b) when t11 fires (*transport*). d) Evolution from the state in Figure-b) when t1 fires (*autonomous object event*). e) Evolution from the state in Figure-b) when the synchronized firing of t12 and t2 occurs (*interaction*).

Reference nets are a special subclass of *Nets-within-Nets* in which tokens in the system net, instead of object nets, are references to object nets, so that it is possible for different tokens to refer to the same object net. Figure 2-a) depicts a system net and an object net class. Firing transition t10 creates two references to a new instance of objectClass1, moving the system to the state in Figure 2-b). In *Nets-within-Nets* three different types of transition firings are possible. The first one corresponds to the case in which an object instance executes an *object autonomous action*: in the state in Figure 2-b), transition t1 of the object net is enabled, and can fire independently of the system net, leading to the state in Figure 2-d). The second one corresponds to the initiative of the system net: in the state in Figure 2-b), transition t11 of the system net is enabled, and can fire moving the reference from the input place of transition t11 to its output place, leading to the state in Figure 2-c) (notice that nothing has changed in the internal state of the object net). This is the reason why these firings are called *transports*. The last case corresponds to the synchronized firing of a transition of the system net with a transition of an object: in the state in Figure 2-b), transitions `t12` and `t2` can synchronize their firings (this is indicated by the common part in their inscriptions, `:i()`), whose firing will give the state in Figure 2-e). This way of firing is called an *interaction.*

A powerful tool called `Renew` [28] allows to execute reference nets. It is developed in Java, and allows an easy integration of reference nets and Java code associated to transitions (it is possible to access Java code from the net, but also to access the net from Java code). This makes Renew to become a very interesting and useful tool to work on Web services environments.

3.4 Implementation Details

Figure 3 shows our proposal of Web service execution infrastructure, based on the Nets-within-Nets paradigm and the Renew tool. It corresponds to what in Nets-within-Nets terminology is called the *system net.* Service compositions are modeled as Petri nets (workfows) which stay in place `work-space`. Conversations, also modeled as Petri nets, stay in place `conversation-space`. Both are modeled as *object nets*, as defined in the Nets-within-Nets paradigm.

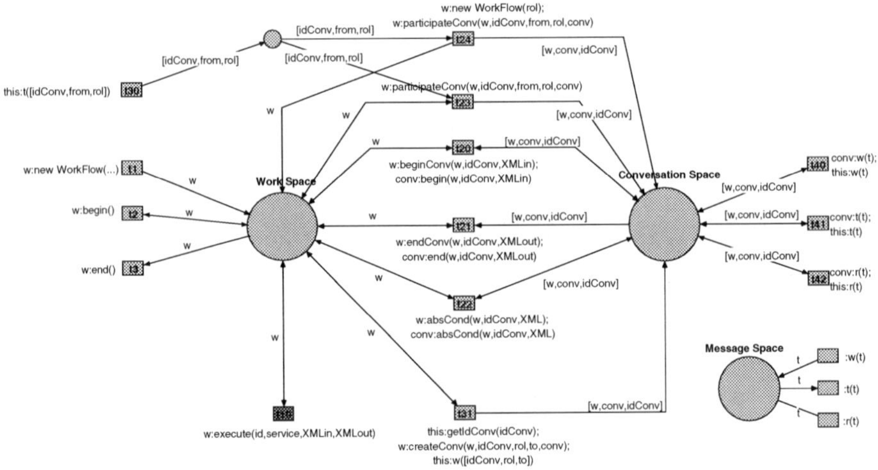

Fig. 3. A Nets-within-Nets Web service execution infrastructure

A new composition to be executed in the infrastructure can start as either, its own initiative (firing transition `t1`, which implies to create a new conversation, to adopt a role in this conversation and to ask the Web service community for candidates interested in adopting the rest of needed roles (firing of transition `t31`) or as a response to some request put by another participant into the `message space` (transition `t30` once the adequate message has been put there by a binding component of an external Web service, as it is described below). This last case is the symmetric of the previous one: a service accepts to play a role in a conversation created by another Web service, which implies to create the inner workflow and the conversation necessary to play the accepted role (transition `t24`). A running composition may also participate on a conversation, and consequently, an inner workflow does not have to be created (transition `t23`).

Different interactions can be necessary between a workflow and a conversation resulting from the conversation execution; these interactions are executed by firing transitions `t20, t21, t22`. The execution of a workflow in a participant may also require to call some internal services (as querying a database or launching a manufacturing process, for instance); this is accomplished by firing transition `t10`. The easy interaction between Renew and Java code associated to transitions facilitates this task.

On the other hand, the place `message-space` is the internal repository for incoming/outgoing messages. This place, together surrounding elements, forms our message broker. The place and the associated transitions form a Linda-like coordination system. We have also implemented it in the Renew tool [29], which has made its integration in our participant model an easy task. With its current implementation, it is possible to use one broker per participant, to share the same broker for a set of participants of the same organization and also to use it as an external service, shared by a set of inter-organizational services. Besides, binding components have been implemented for executing the real interactions across the Internet using particular protocols. They are the bridge between the external world and our message-space.

Figure 4 is an abstract view of the infrastructure, to show it as an instance of the architecture described by Figure 1. Place *work-space*, together surrounding elements and the workflows modeled as Petri nets match the *composition component*. In a similar way place `conversation-space` and conversations match the *conversation component*. To conclude, as it was mentioned above, place `message-space` and the associated transitions form the *message broker*, and the *binding components* the interface to provide communication with external entities.

4 An Implementation of Horizontal Protocols as Web Services

In this section we present a working implementation of the *WS-Atomic Transaction* [7] horizontal protocol (a standard transaction service based on the Two-Phase Commitment transaction protocol commonly used in database systems). For such purpose, the involved operations must be published as Web services (a similar consideration is contained in the IBM Web Services Toolkit [30]). This model provides an example integrating WS-Coordination [20] and WS-Transaction [7] on the partner infrastructure explained in Section 3.

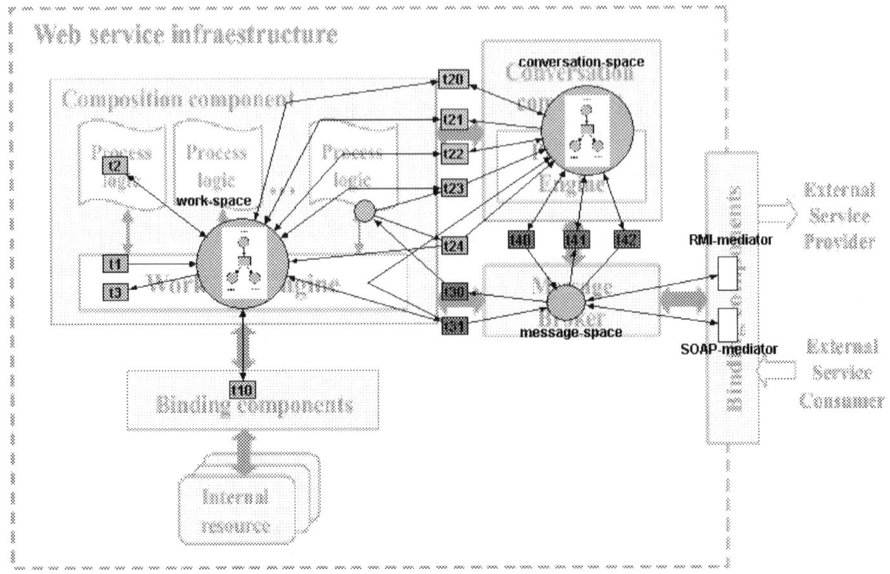

Fig. 4. An abstract view of the model in Figure 3

4.1 Description of a Standard Transaction Service

Figure 5 shows the scenario of the Atomic transaction protocol in a trace chart and depicts the architectural overview at the top of the figure. First, we consider the existence of a *Director*, who is responsible of performing the transactional process when an application requires to execute a set of operations under a coordination context. Second, a *Coordination Framework*, which represents the core of the transaction protocol, composed of: the *Registration service*, which registers the participants in the transaction; the *Activation service*, which creates the coordination context and informs the coordinator about the participants; and the *Coordinator*, which performs the Two-Phase Completion protocol. Finally, the involved resources, being each one managed by the corresponding *Resource manager*, which serves as a bridge between the Director or the Coordination framework and the resource, publishing its access methods as Web services [30]. Thus, a Participant is represented as a pair composed of a resource and its corresponding Resource manager.

The presented architecture allows an easy integration on a distributed schema, where each service can be executed on different physical hosts.

The execution of the *Atomic Transaction protocol*, following the specifications described in [7], can be divided into three phases. The *Activation phase*, in which the application requiring to perform an atomic Web service operation under the Completion protocol (this is, under the WS-Atomic transaction protocol) delegates the execution of the protocol to the Director, which creates a transactional activity context using the WS-Coordination Framework Activation service (step 1a). The Activation service notifies the Coordinator about the created context

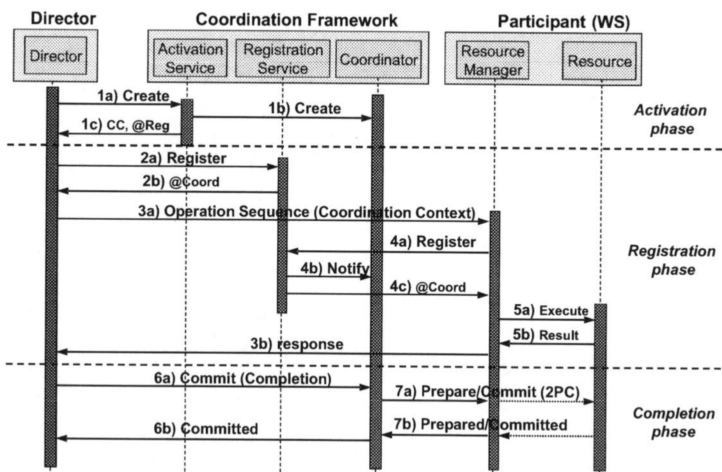

Fig. 5. A scenario of Atomic transactions

(1b) and returns to the Director a coordination context identifier (CC) and the address of the Registration service (1c). Note that the CC identifier is used during the rest of the protocol execution to uniquely identify the transaction and also to specify the protocol type (in this case, the Atomic transaction).

In the *Registration phase* the Director interacts with the Registration service with a request-response protocol (steps 2a and 2b) to obtain the address of the Coordinator. Then, the Resource managers of the involved resources are demanded to perform the corresponding operations (3a). The first time a Resource manager receives and processes an activity context, it must access the WS-Coordination Registration service using the address provided by the Director (4a). Then, the Registration service notifies the Coordinator that a new participant is going to perform an operation under the given `CoordinationContext` (4b), and sends back the address of the Coordinator (4c). The resource executes the requested operation (5a) and the results are returned to the Director through the manager (steps 5b and then 3b). Subsequent operations on the same participant do not require to repeat the registration steps (4a to 4c).

Finally, once all participants have executed the requested operations the *Completion/Coordination phase* is performed. The Director sends a `commit` message to the Coordinator (6a) and blocks until it receives a response. The Coordinator is responsible of performing the agreement protocol with each participant that was previously registered. First, a `prepare` message is sent to solicit the resource status and collect the votes (7a). When all votes have been collected a final outcome is transmitted sending a `commit/rollback` message (7a) depending on whether the transaction can be committed or not. As soon as all resources have performed their commit actions (7b), the Coordinator sends a `committed` notification to the Director (6b). Then, the Application is notified that the transactional operation has been performed successfully.

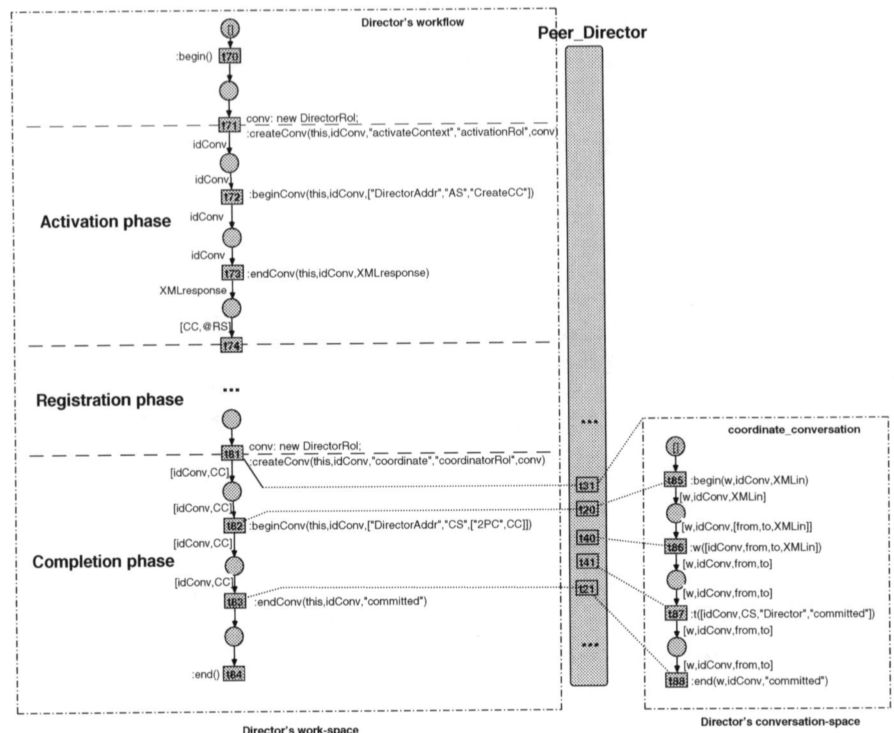

Fig. 6. The (partial) Director workflow and conversation(s) interaction

4.2 Modelling and Implementation of the Involved Entities

According to our proposal, the involved entities in the Atomic transaction protocol (Director, Coordination framework and participants) must be described by means of their workflows and coordination protocols. Interactions between these entities are modeled using an intermediate Linda-like conversation language, which is independent of the deployment scenario of entities and the underlying communication technologies. Binding components are responsible for considering these communication details.

From the modelling/implementation point of view, the approach we propose allows the separation of workflows and conversations. From a methodological point of view different perspectives can be adopted. On the one hand, one can use very simple conversations (using, for instance, simple `in/out` and `out/in` conversation patterns). The main drawback of this approach is that it produces too complex workflow models, highly-coupled with the involved protocols, in the same way some languages as BPEL4WS do. On the other hand, our proposal also allows the use of complex conversations as a modeling approach, which produces simpler workflows. This approach provides a clear separation of the business logic (implemented by the workflow) and the needed interactions, implemented

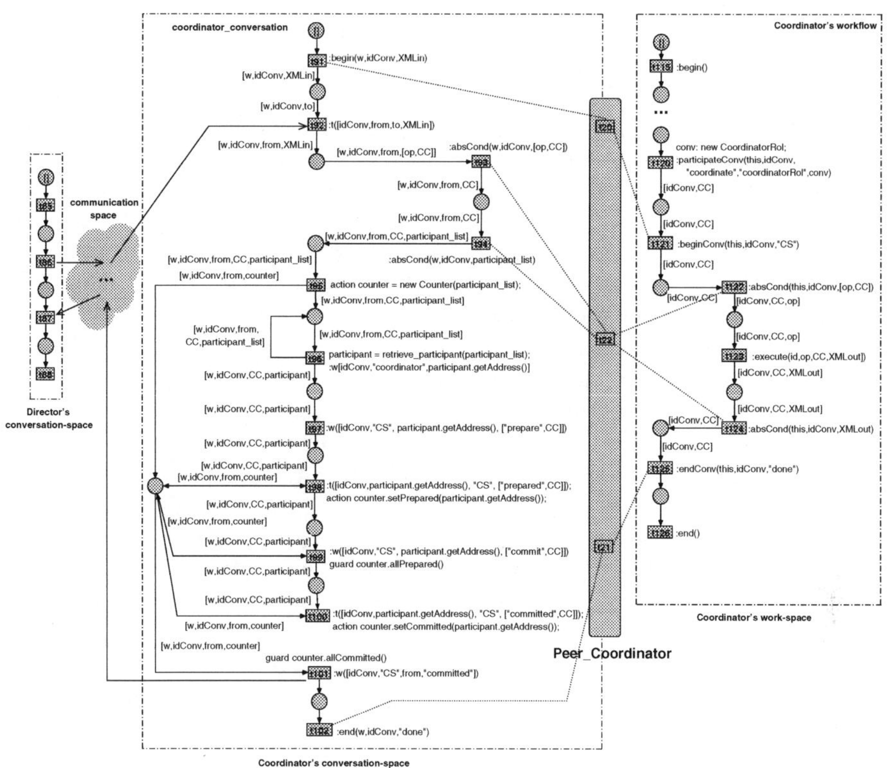

Fig. 7. Coordinator overview

by means of the conversation(s) the workflow is involved in. These conversations can be started either by the service itself or by another Web service. This second approach is the one adopted in the following to implement the transactions service.

Left part of Figure 6 shows a partial representation of the workflow corresponding to the previously described Director. The workflow stays in the `work-space` place of the peer executing it (`Peer_Director`). It manages the composition of the services required to perform the atomic transaction creating three conversations, one for each phase. Let us now concentrate on the *Completion* phase that is executed between transitions `t81` and `t83`. `t81` creates the conversation and places on the communication-space a request for the `CoordinationRol` synchronizing with `t31`. Right part in Figure 6 represents the request-response interaction. Transition `t86` corresponds to the request, while transition `t87` performs the reception of the response. These transitions synchronize, respectively, with `t40` and `t41` in the peer infrastructure to access to the communication space. The synchronized firing of `t83`, `t88` and `t21` means that the protocol conversation has finished.

On the other hand, right part of Figure 7 corresponds to the (partial) workflow executing the coordinator part.

From the Coordinator's point of view, the *Completion* phase corresponds to the transitions between `t120` and `t125`. Transition `t120` takes, from the communication space, the request for participating in the *Completion* phase and creates the Coordinator's conversation. The interactions needed to execute this phase are more complicated, and require to create and execute a complex conversation involving the Coordinator, the Director, and the participants.

Firing transition `t92` the Coordinator's conversation takes the input parameters from the communication space. These parameters are passed to the workflow through the abstract condition by the synchronized firing of `t93`, `t122` and `t22`. Then, the workflow executes a local query to retrieve a list with the registered participants under the given coordination context identifier (`t123`). The synchronized firing of transitions `t124`, `t94` and `t22` the workflow returns to the conversation the list of involved participants (variable `participant_list`). With this information, the Coordinator initiates a parallel set of conversations corresponding to the completion protocol, one with each participant (transitions `t95` to `t100`). Once the completion messages have arrived from all the participants (firing of transition `t101`), the `committed` message is returned to the Director firing transition `t101`. The conversation is then terminated by means of the synchronized firing of transitions `t125`, `t102` and `t21`.

5 Conclusions

Developing and using business processes is a complex task, which requires the help of both, formal methods for the specification, modeling and analysis, and also flexible and powerful tools for their execution and monitoring.

In the context of Web services, the authors adopted high level Petri nets as the formalism for the first aspect, and Renew as the tool for the implementation issues. In this paper we have shown how these tools can be adapted to work on the domain of business processes. In a previous work, the authors provided a prototype of framework able to run workflows and coordination protocols and the related horizontal protocols. As an application case, the paper details an executable implementation of the *WS-Atomic Transaction* protocol.

Our future work will concentrate on different aspects. First, on the implementation of some new Web service-related (horizontal) protocols. And second, on the study of the application of Petri net based analysis techniques to the checking of desired behavioral properties, such as compatibility or deadlock freeness, for instance.

Acknowledgements

The authors want to thank the three anonymous referees, whose remarks helped us to improve this paper.

References

1. U. Dayal, M. Hsu, and R. Ladin: Business Process Coordination: State of the Art, Trends and Open Issues. In: Proceedings of the 2th Very Large Databases Conference (VLDB 2001), Roma, Italy. (2001)
2. G. Alonso, F. Casati, H. Kuno, and V. Machiraju: Web Services. Concepts, Architectures and Applications. Springer Verlag (2004)
3. T. Andrews, F. Curbera, H. Dholakia, Y. Goland, J. Klein, F. Leymann, K. Liu, D. Roller, D. Smith, S. Thatte, I. Trickovic, and S. Weerawarana: Business Process Execution Language for Web Services (BPEL4WS). Technical report, BEA Systems, IBM Corp., Microsoft Corp., SAP AG, and Siebel Systems (2003)
4. A. Arkin, S. Askary, S. Fordin, K. Kawaguchi, D. Orchard, S. Pogliani, K. Riemer, S. Struble, P. Takacsi-Nagy, I. Trickovic, and S. Zimek: Web Service Choreography Interface (WSCI). Technical report, World Wide Web Consortium (W3C) (2002)
5. N. Kavantzas, D. Burdett, G. Ritzinger, T. Fletcher, and Y. Lafon: Web Service Choreography Description Language (WS-CDL). Technical report, World Wide Web Consortium (W3C) (2004)
6. D. Martin, M. Paolucci, S. McIlraith, M. Burstein, D. McDermott, D. McGuinness, B. Parsia, T. Payne, M. Sabou, M. Solanki, N. Srinivasan, and K. Sycara: Bringing Semantics to Web Services: The OWL-S Approach. Number 3387 in Lecture Notes in Computer Science. In: First International Workshop, SWSWPC 2004. Revised Selected Papers. Springer Verlag (2004) 26–42
7. IBM, BEA Systems, Microsoft, Arjuna, Hitachi, IONA: Web Services Transactions specifications. Technical report, IBM (2005)
8. Arjuna, Fujitsu Software, IONA Technologies, Oracle and Sun Microsystems: Web Service Coordination Framework(WS-CF). Technical report (2004)
9. C. Ouyang, W.M.P. van der Aalst, S. Breutel, M. Dumas, A.H.M. ter Hofstede, and H.M.W. Verbeek: Formal Semantics and Analysis of Control Flow in WS-BPEL (Revised version). Research Report BPM-05-15, Business Process Management (BPM) Center, BPMcenter.org (2005)
10. D. Moldt and J. Ortmann: Dagen: A tool for automatic translation from DAML-S to high-level petri nets. In: Fundamental Approaches to Software Engineering: 7th International Conference, FASE 2004, Springer-Verlag (2004) 209–213
11. Srini Narayanan and Sheila A. McIlraith: Simulation, verification and automated composition of web services. In: WWW '02: Proceedings of the 11th international conference on World Wide Web, New York, NY, USA, ACM Press (2002) 77–88
12. A. Martens: Analyzing web service based business processes. In: Fundamental Approaches to Software Engineering: 8th International Conference, FASE 2005. (2005)
13. P. Álvarez, J. A. Bañares, and J. Ezpeleta: Approaching Web Service Coordination and Composition by Means of Petri Nets. The Case of the Nets-Within-Nets Paradigm. Number 3826 in Lecture Notes in Computer Science. In: Third International Conference on Service Oriented Computing –ICSOC 2005. Springer Verlag (2005) 185–197
14. R. Valk: Petri Nets as Token Objects - An Introduction to Elementary Object Nets. Lecture Notes in Computer Science: 19th Int. Conf. on Application and Theory of Petri Nets, ICATPN'98, Lisbon, Portugal, June 1998 **1420** (1998) 1–25
15. L. Cabac, M. Duvigneau, D. Moldt, and H. Rölke: Modeling Dynamic Architectures Using Nets-within-Nets. In: 26th International Conference On Application and Theory of Petri Nets and Other Models of Concurrency, Miami, Florida (2005)

16. D. Moldt, S. Offermann, and J. Ortmann: Proposal for Petri Net Based Web Service Application Modeling. Number 3140 in Lecture Notes in Computer Science. In: Web Engineering: 4th International Conference, ICWE 2004. Springer Verlag (2004) 93–97
17. L. Ardissono, G. Petrone, and M. Segnan: Enabling flexible interaction with web services. In: Extending Web Service Technologies: The use of Multi-Agent approaches. Springer Verlag (2004) 187–208
18. S. Weerawarana, F. Curbera, F. Leymann, T. Storey, and D. Ferguson: Modeling Business Processes: BPEL. In: Web services platform architecture. Prentice Hall (2005) 313–340
19. F. Curbera, R. Khalaf, N. Mukhi, S. Tai, and S. Weerawarana: The next step in web services. Communications of the ACM **46** (2003) 29–34
20. Arjuna Technologies, BEA Systems, Hitachi, IBM, IONA Technologies & Microsoft: Web service coordination (ws-coordination). Technical report (2005)
21. Arjuna Technologies, BEA Systems, Hitachi, IBM, IONA Technologies & Microsoft: Web Services Business Activity Framework (WS-BusinessActivity). Technical report (2005)
22. Arjuna Technologies, Fujitsu Limited, IONA Technologies, Sun Microsystems and Oracle Corporation: Web Services Composite Application Framework (WS-CAF). Technical report (2003)
23. Arjuna Technologies, Fujitsu Limited, IONA Technologies, Sun Microsystems and Oracle Corporation: Web Services Context (WS-Context). Technical report (2003)
24. J. E. Hanson, P. Nandi, and S. Kumaran: Conversation Support for Business Process Integration. In: Proceedings of the 6th International Enterprise Distributed Object Computing Conference (EDOC2002). (2002) 65–74
25. G. Petrone: Managing flexible interaction with Web Services. In: AAMAS-03 Workshop on Web-services and Agent-based Engineering (WSABE 2003), Melbourne (2003) 41–47
26. N. Carriero and D. Gelernter: Linda in context. Communications of the ACM **32** (1989) 444–458
27. O. Kummer: Introduction to Petri Nets and Reference Nets. Sozionik Aktuell **1** (2001) 1–9
28. O. Kummer and F. Wienberg: Renew - the reference net workshop. In: Tool Demonstrations, 21st International Conference on Application and Theory of Petri Nets, Computer Science Department, Aarhus University, Aarhus, Denmark (2000) 87–89
29. J. Fabra, P. Álvarez , J. A. Bañares, and J. Ezpeleta: RLinda: a Petri net based implementation of the Linda coordination paradigm for Web services interactions. In: To appear in Proceedings of the 7th International Conference on Electronic Commerce and Web Technologies (EC-Web 2006), Vienna, 5.-7. September (2006)
30. Alphaworks: Web Services Toolkit (WSTK). Technical report, IBM (2005)

History-Based Joins: Semantics, Soundness and Implementation

Kees van Hee, Olivia Oanea*, Alexander Serebrenik, Natalia Sidorova, and Marc Voorhoeve

Department of Mathematics and Computer Science,
Eindhoven University of Technology
P.O. Box 513, 5600 MB Eindhoven, The Netherlands
{k.m.v.hee, o.i.oanea, a.serebrenik, n.sidorova, m.voorhoeve}@tue.nl

Abstract. In this paper we study the use of case history for control structures in workflow processes. In particular we introduce a history-dependent join. History dependent control offers much more modeling power than classical control structures and it solves several semantical problems of industrial modeling frameworks. We study the modeling power by means of workflow patterns. Since proper completion (i.e. the ability of any configuration reachable from the initial one to reach the final one) is always an important "sanity check" of process modeling, we introduce a modeling method that guarantees this property for the new control structures. Finally we consider an implementation of the proposed control structures on top of an existing workflow engine.

Keywords: Business process modeling and analysis—Formal models in business process management—Process patterns—Process verification and validation—Workflow management systems.

1 Introduction

There is a variety of process modeling frameworks and tools available. A modeling framework for processes consists of a syntax and semantics. The syntax is often a graphical notation of a diagram language. Semantics concern the behavior of the processes.

We may distinguish industrial frameworks, such as EPCs [12,17], UML activity diagrams [8], BPMN [22] and BPEL4WS [6,21], and the more academic frameworks like Petri nets and process algebras. In industry there is a tendency to standardize the frameworks and the late three frameworks are in fact standards. The academic frameworks have several variants. Petri nets variants include, among others, place-transition nets, predicate-transition nets [9] and colored Petri nets [16]. For process algebras we have such formalisms as pi-calculus [20], CSP [15] and CCS [19].

* Supported by the NWO Open Competitie project "Modeling and Verification of Business Processes" (MoveBP), Project number 612.000.315.

S. Dustdar, J.L. Fiadeiro, and A. Sheth (Eds.): BPM 2006, LNCS 4102, pp. 225–240, 2006.

Most of the industrial frameworks suffer from the fact that they have no formally defined semantics which causes many problems when applying them. The only analysis facilities these frameworks offer is syntax checking and sometimes simulation of modeled processes. The academic frameworks have exact formal semantics and they offer besides syntax checking, methods for the analysis of the behavior of the modeled processes. The industrial frameworks offer more "modeling power" than the academic frameworks, which means that they offer more modeling primitives and modeling patterns that can easily be applied to practical situations. It is obvious that many research has been devoted to link the two types of frameworks. The industrial frameworks are mapped onto the academic frameworks in order to provide them with formal semantics and the accompanying analysis methods [4,12,21,23]. These mappings are far from straightforward and sometimes impossible, see for instance [17].

The industrial frameworks cover most of the *control structures* (connectors and patterns) needed for modeling workflow processes in practice. Typical examples of *connectors* are the XOR-split, XOR-join, AND-split and AND-join. But there are many others like the implicit-OR split and the m-out-of-n split and join. The YAWL language [4] is an attempt to incorporate most of them. For YAWL formal semantics are defined in the form of a transition system.

In this paper we study the use of the *case history* as a way to obtain more flexible control structures. In workflow management systems the concept of a *case* is very important. A case is the object that is treated by the *tasks* of the workflow process. (Note that it is allowed that two or more tasks work in parallel on the same case.) The case history is the set of all *events* a case was engaged in. The case history offers the possibility to express all kind of preconditions for tasks or connectors (see [11] for a history-based logics). From the experiments we have done so far with the control structures of BPMN, UML activity diagrams and EPC's we have seen that semantics for the control structures can easily be formulated using the case history.

We have three objectives. Firstly we will introduce new split and join connectors that are based on the case history. Based on the case data the split connector may produce as many case tokens as it likes for each outgoing arc. In the tasks the case data can be updated by a user or a software agent. We do not consider the case data here. The new join connector should be able to deal with all possible decisions made in split connectors, just by inspection of the case history. These new connectors provide more modeling power than the usual ones. In order to do so we introduce a simple modeling framework that covers most of the control structures of the existing industrial frameworks. The framework is only meant to define and analyze the new control structures and not as a new modeling language. The syntax is very easy so it is not difficult to translate models in our framework into the industrial ones. We consider three types of connectors: the *split* connector, the *transfer* connector and the *join* connector. The split connector consumes one object, called *case token* and may produce as many case tokens as necessary for all its outgoing arcs. The transfer connector is consuming one case token from one of its inputs and producing exactly one for one of the output arcs. It is in fact a combination of a classical XOR split and XOR join [4]. The join connector is special: it waits for all case tokens that may arrive as its inputs and then it consumes them all and produces one output case token. The modeling engineer should understand the semantics of the join connector well in order to make correct process models.

Secondly we want to be able to guarantee the *proper completion* property of processes, which is normally called *soundness* for workflow nets. We will give sufficient conditions for processes in our framework to satisfy this property. Proper completion requires that a workflow is always able to finish without leaving "garbage". This generic property could be considered as a "sanity check" that should hold for all workflow applications. Our goal is to have a modeling method that guarantees soundness by construction.

Thirdly we consider the implementation of the new control structures. Instead of constructing a new workflow engine we propose to build an add-on for an existing workflow engine. The only requirement is that the workflow engine will log the events and that this event log is accessible.

In section 2 we introduce the syntax of our framework, whereas in section 3 we describe the semantics. In section 4 we introduce soundness and describe "soundness by construction" rules. In section 5 we consider an implementation of the new control structures for an existing workflow engine. In section 6 we consider the modeling power of the proposed control structures by comparison with the well-known workflow patterns. In section 7 we consider future work.

2 Syntax

It is not our intention to define "yet another workflow language", like the successful YAWL, but to give a simple language that expresses the most essential elements of workflow languages, the control structures. We believe that our control structures are as flexible as possible and therefore our approach provides semantics that can be applied to other frameworks as well.

The modeling framework comprises the following concepts:

Process is a graph with two kinds of nodes: *tasks* and *connectors.*
A *workflow* process has one initial task (without inputs) and one final task (without outputs), and each node is on a path from the initial to the final task.

Task is a unit of activity. A task has one input and one output node, except for the initial and the final one. Tasks usually correspond to activities carried out by users, such as registering a patient or prescribing medication.

Connector is either a split, a join or a transfer connector. A *split connector* has one input arc and n ($n \geq 1$) output arcs. A *join connector* has n input arcs ($n \geq 1$) and one output arc. A *transfer connector* has one or more input arcs and one or more output arcs.

Case is an entity to be treated by the process. A case has a documented history that reflects the tasks performed and the choices made. We may have several active cases in a process. We consider them independently of each other.

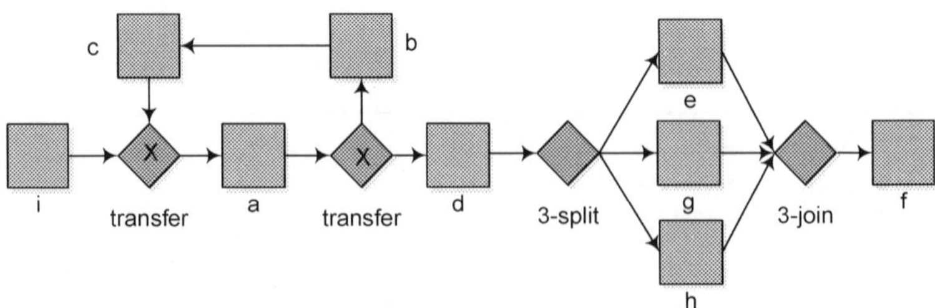

Fig. 1. An example of a workflow process

Next we formalize these concepts. A graph is a tuple $G = (N, A)$, where N is the set of nodes and $A \subseteq N \times N$ is the set of arcs. Given a node n in G, the preset ${}^{\bullet}n$ of n, and the postset $n^{\bullet}$ of n are $\{m \mid (m, n) \in A\}$ and $\{m \mid (n, m) \in A\}$, respectively. Given a set S, $|S|$ denotes the cardinality of S.

Definition 1 (workflow process). *A workflow process P is defined by a graph (N, A) where:*

- *N, called the set of* nodes, *is a union of pairwise disjoint sets: a set of tasks T, a set of split connectors S, a set of join connectors J and a set of transfer connectors X;*
- *$A \subseteq N \times N$ is a set of* arcs;
- *the* initial task *$i \in T$ and the* final task *$f \in T$ satisfy ${}^{\bullet}i = f^{\bullet} = \emptyset$ and $|i^{\bullet}| = |{}^{\bullet}f| = 1$;*
- *$|{}^{\bullet}t| = |t^{\bullet}| = 1$ for all $t \in T \setminus \{i, f\}$;*
- *$|{}^{\bullet}s| = 1$ and $|s^{\bullet}| \geq 1$ for all $s \in S$;*
- *$|{}^{\bullet}j| \geq 1$ and $|j^{\bullet}| = 1$ for all $j \in J$;*
- *$|{}^{\bullet}x| \geq 1$ and $|x^{\bullet}| \geq 1$ for all $x \in X$;*
- *$\forall x \in N : \mathrm{path}(i, x) \wedge \mathrm{path}(x, f)$, where the predicate* path *is defined by: $\mathrm{path}(x, y) = \exists n \geq 0 : \exists z_0, \ldots, z_n \in N : x = z_0 \wedge y = z_n \wedge (\forall k : 0 \leq k < n : (z_k, z_{k+1}) \in A)$.*

We denote the outgoing arc of i by a_i and the incoming arc of f by a_f. Graphically, we represent tasks by rectangles and connectors by diamonds. Transfer connectors are marked with an X.

Fig. 1 gives an example of a process. In the example we can see an *iteration* between the transfer nodes, and *parallel threads*, between the 3-split and 3-join. It is possible to have just one thread active, but two or three threads can execute concurrently. In this particular example the set T consists of tasks a, b, c, d, e, g and h, the set S of the 3-split, the set J of the 3-join, and the set X of the transfer connectors.

3 Semantics

A workflow system over a workflow process consists of the workflow process and cases in execution. Cases are identified by means of case identities (ids), which are assumed to be positive integers. Cases are represented by means of tokens that either are engaged in an activity performed by the user (task) or can be waiting for an activity performed by the user (task) or by the system (connector). The connectors, the initial and the final tasks are activities carried out instantaneously by the workflow management system. One case may be represented by a number of tokens. Placement of tokens in the workflow system is called a *marking*.

As already mentioned in the introduction we explicitly store the case history. To this end we keep a global *history log*, being a sequence of events, where an event is the consumption or the production of tokens after the firing of a rule. Thus, a *state* of the workflow system is a pair (m, h) where m is a marking and h is a history log. Using the notion of state we define the semantics of a workflow system as a transition system.

In order to formalize these notions we need a well-known concept of a *multiset*. Let B be a set. A *multiset* m over B is a mapping $m : B \to \mathbb{N}$. The set of all multisets over B is $\mathbb{N}^B$. We use $+$ and $-$ for the sum and the difference of two multisets and $=, <, \leq$ for comparisons of multisets, which are defined in a standard way. We say that a multiset m over B is non-empty is there exists $b \in B$ such that $m(b) > 0$. We also use $\mathbb{N}^+$ to denote $\mathbb{N} \setminus \{0\}$.

We introduce first the notions of a token and a marking.

Definition 2. *Let P be a workflow process. A* token *is a pair (n, k), where $n \in A \cup T \setminus \{i, f\}$ is an arc or a task and $k \in \mathbb{N}^+$ is a case id. A* marking *m is a multiset of tokens, $m \in \mathbb{N}^{(A \cup T \setminus \{i,f\}) \times \mathbb{N}^+}$.*

Unlike in the case of markings the history logs do not record actions performed by the user but only those performed by the workflow management system. To this end events logged are transfers of tokens from one multiset of arcs to another multiset of arcs. For the sake of simplicity we distinguish between *productions* and *consumptions*.

Definition 3. *Let P be a workflow process.*

- *An* event *is a triple (l, k, λ), where $l \in \{\text{prod}, \text{cons}\}$, k is a case id and λ is a multiset of arcs.*
- *A state σ is a pair (m, h), where m is a marking, and h, called a* history log, *is a sequence of events.*
- *The* initial state *σ_0 is $(\emptyset, \epsilon)$, where $\emptyset$ denotes the empty marking and ϵ—the empty history log.*

Adding an event (l, k, λ) to a history log h is denoted by $h \cdot (l, k, \lambda)$. This notation can be easily generalized to concatenation of logs.

As we are going to see, for states reachable from the initial state, history log determines uniquely the corresponding marking. Therefore, the use of marking is for presentation purposes only: actual workflow management systems do not need to have a global look at the marking but will make use only of the history log. We describe the semantics of a workflow system by means of a transition relation between states as follows:

Definition 4. *Let P be a workflow process. The semantics of the workflow system over P is given by a transition system $\mathcal{T} = (\Sigma, \rightarrow, \sigma_0)$, where Σ is the set of states of the workflow system, σ_0 is the initial state and $\rightarrow \subseteq \Sigma \times \Sigma$ is the transition relation defined by the rules $(a - g)$ below. Let $\sigma = (m, h)$.*

(a) case creation rule *(creates a token with a new id on the outgoing arc of the initial task) $\sigma \rightarrow \sigma'$ if $\sigma' = (m + (a_i, k), h \cdot (\text{prod}, k, a_i))$, where $k = \max_{(n_1,k_1) \in m} k_1 + 1$. We define $\max_{(n_1,k_1) \in \emptyset} k_1$ as 0.*

(b) start task rule *(transfers a token from the incoming arc of a task to the task) $\sigma \rightarrow \sigma'$ if $(a, k) \in m$, where a is the incoming arc of a task $t \in T \setminus \{i, f\}$ and $\sigma' = (m + (t, k) - (a, k), h \cdot (\text{cons}, k, a))$;*

(c) complete task rule *(transfers a token from a task to the outgoing arc of the task) $\sigma \rightarrow \sigma'$ if $(t, k) \in m$ for some $t \in T \setminus \{i, f\}$ and $\sigma' = (m + (a, k) - (t, k), h \cdot (\text{prod}, k, a))$, where a is the outgoing arc of the task t.*

(d) complete case rule *(removes a token from the incoming arc of the final task) $\sigma \rightarrow \sigma'$ if $(a_f, k) \in m$ and $\sigma' = (m - (a_f, k), h \cdot (\text{cons}, k, a_f))$.*

(e) split rule *(removes a token from the incoming arc and puts at least one token on the outgoing arcs of the split connector) $\sigma \rightarrow \sigma'$ if*
- *$(a, k) \in m$, where a is the incoming arc of a split node $s \in S$;*
- *$\sigma' = (m - (a, k) + m', h')$, where*
  - *m' is a finite non-empty multiset of tokens with the case id k on the outgoing arcs of s, i.e., $m' \in \mathbb{N}^{\{(s,n) | n \in N\} \times \{k\}}$;*
  - *$h' = h \cdot (\text{cons}, k, a) \cdot (\text{prod}, k, m_a)$, where m_a is a multiset of outgoing arcs of s occupied by the tokens of m', i.e., $m_a \in \mathbb{N}^{\{(s,n) | n \in N\}}$ and for any $n \in N$, $m_a((s, n)) = m'(((s, n), k))$;*

(f) transfer rule *(removes one token from an incoming arc of a transfer node and puts one token on an outgoing arc of the transfer node) $\sigma \rightarrow \sigma'$ if*
- *$(a, k) \in m$, where a is an incoming arc of a transfer node $x \in X$;*
- *$\sigma' = (m - (a, k) + (a', k), h')$, where a' is an outgoing arc of x and $h' = h \cdot (\text{cons}, k, a) \cdot (\text{prod}, k, a')$;*

(g) join rule *(removes tokens with the same id from the incoming arcs of a join node and puts one token on the outgoing arc) $\sigma \rightarrow \sigma'$ if*
- *a condition $\mathcal{C}(j, k, (m, h))$, requiring that all tokens with the id k that could potentially arrive to the join j have already arrived. We postpone discussion of this condition.*
- *$\sigma' = (m + (a', k) - m^k_j, h \cdot (\text{cons}, k, m^k_a) \cdot (\text{prod}, k, a'))$, where a' is the outgoing arc of the join connector j and $m^k_j \leq m$ is the multiset of tokens on the incoming arcs of the join connector j having the id k, and m^k_a is the set of arcs corresponding to m^k_j.*

We further assume that the *transfer* connectors are *fair*. Formally, let x be a transfer connector and let $\sigma_0 \rightarrow \sigma_1 \rightarrow \ldots \rightarrow \sigma_n \rightarrow \ldots$ be an infinite firing sequence containing infinitely many applications of the (f)-rule for x. Assume that in this firing sequence tokens arrive infinitely many times on x. Then, we require that tokens are produced infinitely often for each outgoing arc of x.

We write $\sigma \xrightarrow{*} \sigma'$ if there is a sequence of rules that lead from σ to σ'. In this case we also say that σ' is *reachable* from σ.

Next we formalize the condition $\mathcal{C}$ above. A join connector should wait for all possible incoming tokens, i.e., it is allowed to fire when at least one token is present on one of the incoming arcs, and there is evidence that no other tokens with the same case id can possibly arrive unless the join itself fires. Straightforward formalization of this intuition is impossible since producing more tokens on the incoming arcs of some join j_1 might require reasoning on fireability of some another join j_2 which in its turn might involve reasoning on firings of j_1 (the so-called "vicious circle", see [17]). To resolve this circular definition problem we introduce a *tentative firing relation* with respect to a join j. Using this notion we say that a join can fire, if no additional tokens on the incoming arcs are produced by any sequence of tentative firings.

We say that tasks, split and transfer connectors fire tentatively with respect to j if they fire according to Definition 4; join j cannot fire tentatively with respect to itself; any other join can fire tentatively whenever there is at least one token present at one of its incoming arcs.

Definition 5. *For each join connector j, we define a* tentative firing relation *$\rightarrow_j$. Let $\sigma = (m, h)$ be a state. Then $\sigma \rightarrow_j \sigma'$ if*

- *$\sigma \rightarrow \sigma'$ by firing rules $(a - f)$ of Definition 4;*
- *$\sigma' = (m+(a', k)-m^k_{j'}, h\cdot(\text{cons}, k, m^k_a)\cdot(\text{prod}, k, a'))$, where a' is the outgoing arc of the join connector $j' \neq j$ and $m^k_{j'} \leq m$ is the multiset of tokens on the incoming arcs of j' having the id k, and m^k_a is the set of arcs corresponding to $m^k_{j'}$.*

We write $\sigma \xrightarrow{*}_j \sigma'$ if there is a sequence of firings that lead from σ to σ'.

We now define the condition $\mathcal{C}$ for the *join* connector. Let (m, h) be a state, $m^k_j \leq m$ the non-empty multiset of tokens on the incoming arcs of a join connector j, having the same id k and a_j the outgoing arc of j. The condition $\mathcal{C}$ states that there is no state (m', h') reachable from (m, h) by a series of tentative firings for which the number of tokens on the incoming arcs increases:

$$\mathcal{C}(j, k, (m, h)) ::= \forall (m', h') : ((m, h) \xrightarrow{*}_j (m', h')) \Rightarrow {m'}^k_j \leq m^k_j.$$

Consider now the workflow process in Figure 2 which is taken from [17]. The process is in a state in which the join connectors j_1, j_2, and j_3 have a token on an incoming arc. The join rule connector for j_1 needs to consider its own tentative firing where the other join connectors, j_2, j_3 and j_4 fire using the transfer rule. Thus we have the following tentative firing sequence $(((s_1, j_1), k) + ((s_1, j_2), k) + ((s_1, j_3), k), h) \rightarrow_{j_1} (((s_1, j_1), k) + ((s_1, j_2), k) + ((j_3, s_4), k), h') \rightarrow_{j_1} (((s_1, j_1), k) + ((s_1, j_2), k) + ((s_4, j_1), k), h'')$, which violates the condition $\mathcal{C}$, i.e. we reach a state in which the number of tokens on the incoming arcs of the join connector has increased. In fact, none of the join connectors can fire since the condition $\mathcal{C}$ is violated for all of them. Hence, the process deadlocks.

States reachable from σ_0 in $\mathcal{T}$ have an important property: for any such state (m, h) the marking m can be uniquely derived from the history log h. Intuitively,

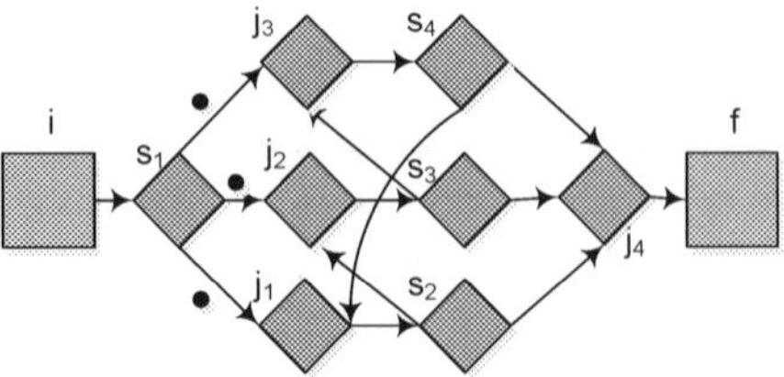

Fig. 2. Vicious loop

this means that the states are consistent and that by "playing the log", i.e., producing and consuming the tokens as recorded in the log, one obtains the corresponding multiset of tokens m. The converse is clearly not true as more than one history log may result in the same multiset of tokens.

Lemma 6. *Let P be a workflow process and let $\mathcal{T} = (\Sigma, \rightarrow, \sigma_0)$ be the transition system giving the semantics of the workflow system over P. Then, for any (m_1, h_1) and (m_2, h_2) such that $\sigma_0 \stackrel{*}{\rightarrow} (m_1, h_1)$ and $\sigma_0 \stackrel{*}{\rightarrow} (m_2, h_2)$, $h_1 = h_2$ implies $m_1 = m_2$. Moreover, for any (m_1, h_1) and (m_2, h_2) such that $\sigma_0 \stackrel{*}{\rightarrow}_j (m_1, h_1)$ and $\sigma_0 \stackrel{*}{\rightarrow}_j (m_2, h_2)$, $h_1 = h_2$ implies $m_1 = m_2$.*

Proof. The proof is done by induction on the length of the history log.

The most important corollary of this Lemma states that the condition $\mathcal{C}$ can be verified based solely on the knowledge of the history.

Corollary 7. *For any states (m_1, h_1) and (m_2, h_2) reachable from σ_0 it holds that $\mathcal{C}(j, k, (m_1, h_1))$ is logically equivalent to $\mathcal{C}(j, k, (m_2, h_2))$ whenever $h_1 = h_2$.*

4 Soundness

In this section we define soundness, introduce a class of well-structured processes and show that well-structured processes are sound. A process is *sound* (cf.[14,3]) if and only if after the initial task created a new case, it is possible for each reachable state to continue the process such that the final task can be executed and that after that execution, no tokens of that case are left on the arcs or tasks of the process. To formalize this intuitive requirement we restrict the transition relation $\rightarrow$ to applications of rules $(b), (c), (e-g)$ of Definition 4, i.e., we do not allow creating new tokens (rule (a)) and destroying tokens (rule (d)). We denote this restricted transition relation $\rightharpoonup$.

Definition 8 (Soundness). *A workflow process P is called* sound *if for any case id k and for all σ such that $((a_i, k), (\text{prod}, k, a_i)) \stackrel{*}{\rightharpoonup} \sigma$*

- *there exists a history log h_f such that $\sigma \stackrel{*}{\rightharpoonup} ((a_f, k), h_f)$, and*
- *$\sigma \stackrel{*}{\rightharpoonup} (m + (a_f, k), h_f)$ implies $m = \emptyset$.*

Next we formulate a structural condition implying soundness of a process. To this end we introduce task refinement. The general idea of refinement consists in replacing a basic element in a structure by a more elaborate one. In our case one can replace a task in a workflow process by another workflow process. Refinement is formalized in the following definition.

Definition 9. *Let P_1 and P_2 be workflow processes defined by (N_1, A_1) and (N_2, A_2), respectively, with $N_1 = T_1 \cup S_1 \cup J_1 \cup X_1$ and $N_2 = T_2 \cup S_2 \cup J_2 \cup X_2$, and i_1, f_1 and i_2, f_2 are the initial and final tasks of P_1 and P_2, respectively. Let $t \in T_1$. Then, the* refinement of t in P_1 by P_2, $\mathrm{ref}(t, P_1, P_2)$, *is a graph (N, A), where $N = T \cup S \cup J \cup X$ and $i, f \in T$ such that:*

- *if $t = i_1$ then $i = i_2$, else $i = i_1$;*
- *if $t = f_1$ then $f = f_2$, else $f = f_1$;*
- *$T = T_1 \cup T_2 \backslash \{t\}$, $S = S_1 \cup S_2$, $J = J_1 \cup J_2$, $X = X_1 \cup X_2$;*
- *$(n, n') \in A$ if one of the following holds:*
  - *$n, n' \in N_2$ and $(n, n') \in A_2$;*
  - *$n, n' \in N_1 \backslash \{t\}$ and $(n, n') \in A_1$;*
  - *$t \neq i_1$ and ${}^\bullet t = \{n\}, n' = i_2$;*
  - *$t \neq f_1$ and $n = f_2, t^\bullet = \{n'\}$.*

The following lemma establishes correctness of refinement as an operation.

Lemma 10. *Let P_1, P_2 be workflow processes as in Definition 9 and let $t \in T_1$. Then, $\mathrm{ref}(t, P_1, P_2)$ is a workflow process.*

Proof. Immediate by checking the definitions.

Using the notion of refinement we present a class of processes that are sound by construction. We start with two basic types of workflow processes, called acyclic and cyclic blocks. Then we introduce well-structured workflow processes (cf. [7,18]) that can be built by means of refinement using these blocks. We pose two additional requirements on an acyclic block. The first connector, i.e., the connector closest to i, should be a split connector, while the last connector, i.e., the connector closest to f, of an acyclic block should be a join connector. Note that the first and the last connectors are unique.

Definition 11. *A* well-structured *workflow process is defined recursively using two kinds of blocks:*

1. *An* acyclic *block is an workflow process $P = (N, A)$ such that*
   - *for all $n_1, n_2 \in N$, $\mathrm{path}(n_1, n_2) \wedge \neg\mathrm{path}(n_2, n_1)$, and*
   - *if $S \cup J \cup X \neq \emptyset$ then*
     - *there exists $j \in J$ such that for all $n \in N$, $n \neq j$ and $\mathrm{path}(j, n)$ implies $n \in T$ and*
     - *there exists $s \in S$ such that for all $n \in N$, $n \neq s$ and $\mathrm{path}(n, s)$ implies $n \in T$.*
2. *A* cyclic *block is presented in Figure 3, where $T = \{i, f, t_1, t_2\}$, $S = J = \emptyset$, $X = \{x_1, x_2\}$ and $A = \{(i, x_1), (x_1, t_1), (t_1, x_2), (x_2, f), (x_2, t_2), (t_2, x_1)\}$;*

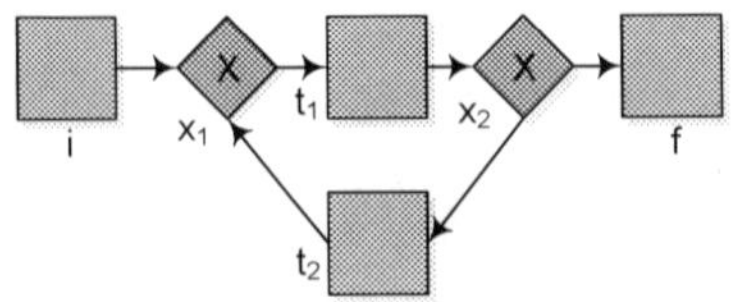

Fig. 3. Cyclic block

3. *A well-structured workflow process P is an acyclic block, a cyclic block or $P = \text{ref}(t, P_1, P_2)$ where P_1 is a well-structured workflow process, P_2 is a cyclic or an acyclic block, and t is a task in P_1.*

Observe that the requirement that P_2 is a block rather than an arbitrary well-structured process does not influence the set of well-structured processes: any process that can be obtained by a series of refinements of *two* well-structured processes can be also obtained with series of refinements where P_2 is a block.

The workflow process P from Figure 1 is well-structured. To see this, observe that it can be obtained by the following steps. First, take a cyclic block with tasks a and t_1. Refine this workflow process with respect to t_1 and the acyclic block with two distinct tasks (the initial task and the final task). By doing this one obtains the left part of the process from Figure 1 starting with i and going up to d where d serves as the final task. Refine this process with respect to the final task and the acyclic net corresponding to the right part of from Figure 1 starting from d and leading to f. The right part of Figure 1 is a valid acyclic block since it does not contain cycles, the first connector is a split and the last connector is a join.

Lemma 12. *An acyclic block is sound.*

Proof (Sketch). Use induction on the number of joins preceding the current one. If there are no preceding joins, the join can fire, since real firings coincide with the tentative firings. Moreover, after the firing of this join there are no tokens in the preceding part of the process. Assume by induction that all joins having no more than n preceding joins can fire and no tokens are present after the firing in the part of the process that precedes them. Joins having $n+1$ predecessor joins depend either on non-joins that cannot deadlock by their semantics or on joins with no more than n predecessors that cannot deadlock by the inductive assumption. Hence joins of depth $n+1$ also can fire and after the firing the corresponding part of the process is empty.

Theorem 13. *A well-structured workflow process is sound.*

Proof (Sketch). Let P be a well-structured process. By Definition 11, P is either an acyclic block, a cyclic block or it has been obtained as the result of the refinement operation. The proof is done by induction on construction of P.

- If P is an acyclic block then it is sound by Lemma 12.
- Assume that P is a cyclic block. This block does not contain joins so firings cannot deadlock. Semantics of the transfer rule implies that at each firing

exactly one token will be produced. Fairness assumption for transfer nodes guarantees that the output token will be eventually placed on a_f.

- Let P be obtained as the result of refinement of a sound process P_1, a block P_2 and a task t. If P_2 is a cyclic block than the fairness assumption guarantees that tokens eventually leave it. P_2 consumes and produces the same tokens as t. Hence, soundness of P_1 implies soundness of P. Let P_2 be an acyclic block. If exactly one token arrives at the input arc of P_2, it will also leave P_2 (by Lemma 12). Hence, P_2 again behaves exactly as t and soundness of P_1 implies soundness of P. If multiple tokens with the same case id arrive at the input arc of P_2 then t was preceded by a split connector. Thus, t is followed by a corresponding join connector. Since join does not depend on the number of incoming tokens but on their presence or absence, P is sound.

5 Implementation

In this section we discuss how an existing workflow engine (WE) can be extended to support workflow processes as defined above. To this end, we define an *activation control* extension called (AC).

We describe the communication protocol between the AC and the WE. The WE sets up the static structure of the AC by creating nodes and arcs connecting them. Then it communicates the tokens received and sent, and the activation of the various nodes. The AC keeps track of the number of tokens waiting at each input arc. A node is *enabled* if there are tokens on some input arc; for enabled nodes except join nodes the WE must communicate their firing to the AC. Enabled join nodes only fire if the condition $\mathcal{C}$ holds, i.e., all its indirect predecessor arcs are empty; this is the task of the AC to report this to the WE. By firing, tokens are consumed and produced.

The implementation of the protocol is as follows. Nodes and arcs are objects of classes `Node`, `Arc` respectively. The static structure of the process is established by entering the predecessor and successor node (`from`/`to`) of an arc and the direct predecessor and successor arcs (`dpred`/`dsucc`) of each node. By computing the transitive closure, the indirect successor join nodes of an arc and the indirect predecessor arcs of a join node are computed.

The dynamic structure is maintained by keeping track for each arc of the number of tokens of a given case k (`pending`(k)). Pending tokens can be produced, consumed or emptied. For all nodes except join nodes, the WE report the firing by calling the `repf` method with as parameters the case k, the input arc c (which should satisfy `self.dpred` $= \{c\}$) and a list of arcs for the produced tokens (the arcs should be contained in `self.dsucc`). For join nodes, the AC induces the firing by calling `indf`(k), signaling the WE. Both the `repf` and `indf` methods update the state by producing, consuming or emptying tokens from arcs.

After having consumed tokens from the input arc, the `repf` method will search whether enabled successor join nodes may fire; if so, the `indf` method of that join node is called. The consumption of tokens induced by the `indf` method of some join node j will not lead to the firing of another join node, since every enabled successor join node of j has the direct successor arc of j as indirect predecessor.

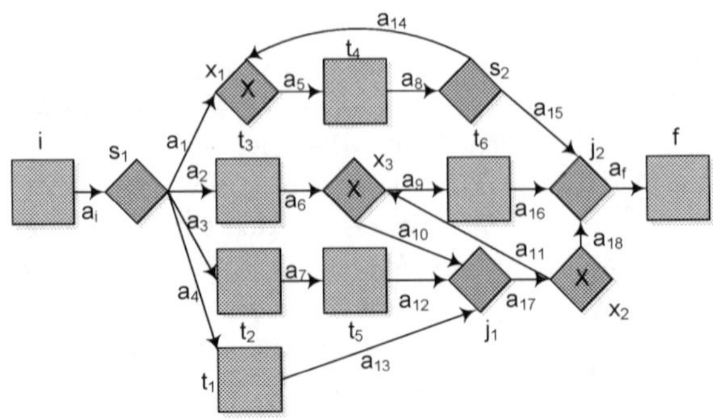

Fig. 4. Example workflow process

In Figure 5, a trace is shown for the AC in Figure 4, except for the initial and final firing, the handling of which has been left to the WE. The initial split node s_1 starts by producing two tokens on a_4, then node t_1 fires twice. After the first firing, the successor node j_1 cannot fire because the indirect predecessor arc a_4 possesses a token. After a second firing of t_1, all indirect predecessor arcs of j_1 are empty, so j_1 is triggered, the a_{13} tokens are consumed and an a_{17} token is produced. Then x_2 fires, producing a a_{11} token, after which x_3 fires, producing an a_{10} token. Now j_1 is triggered again, after which x_2 and j_2 fire, leaving the network empty. The firing for case k, thus, terminated successfully.

Below an implementation of the AC in object-oriented pseudo-code is given.

```
class Arc
attr from, to: Node;
func pending(k:caseID): Nat;
     isucc: setof(Node); /* indirect successor join nodes */
meth prod(k:caseID); /* pending(k) := pending(k) + 1 */
     cons(k:caseID); /* pending(k) := pending(k) - 1 */
     empty(k:caseID) /* pending(k) := 0 */
end;

class Node
attr dpred, dsucc, ipred: setof(Arc): /* (in)direct predecessors/successors */
meth repf(k:caseID, c: Arc, l: listof(Arc)); /* report firing: tasks, splits, transfers */
     indf(k:caseID); /* induce firing: joins */

method repf(k:caseID, c: Arc, l: listof(Arc)) ::=
f: Bool;
while l!= empty do head(l).prod(k); l := tail(l) od;
c.cons(k);
if c.pending(k) = 0
then for j in c.isucc with (j.dpred).pending>0 do
         f = true;
         for a in j.ipred while f do f := a.pending=0 od;
         if f then j.indf(k) od;

method indf(k) ::=
/* trigger firing of self in WE */
for a in dpred do a.empty(k) od;
dsucc.prod(k);
end;
```

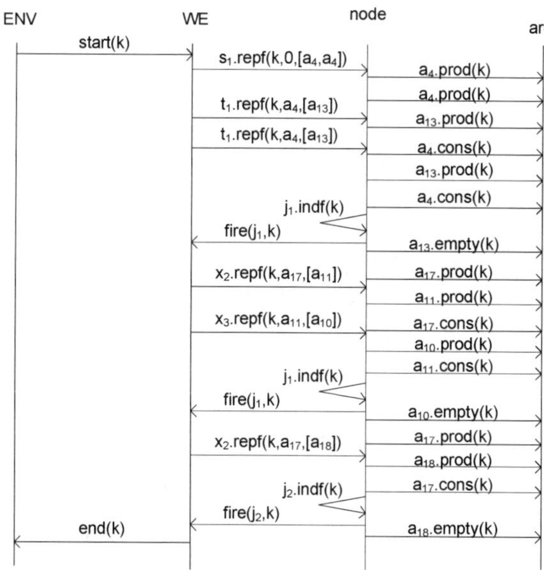

Fig. 5. Message sequence chart of AC implementation

6 Workflow Patterns

In order to evaluate the expressive power of the framework we consider the well-known collection of twenty-one workflow patterns used for benchmarking the functionality of formalisms and tools [5]. For the sake of brevity we do not describe the patterns.

The first category consists of *basic control patterns*. Sequence pattern corresponds to an arc; parallel split to a split connector that puts tokens at all outgoing arcs; synchronization to a join that assumes that exactly one token arrives on each of the incoming arcs; exclusive choice to a transfer connector with one incoming and multiple outgoing arcs; and simple merge to a join connector with multiple incoming and one outgoing arc under assumption that not more than one token arrives on the incoming arcs. Next *advanced branching and synchronization patterns* are considered. Multiple choice corresponds to a split connector; synchronizing merge to a join; multiple merge to a transfer connector with multiple incoming and one outgoing arc. Discriminator and n-out-of-m join cannot be expressed in the basic formalism but they can be expressed with history-dependent preconditions. *Structural patterns* include arbitrary cycles and implicit termination. Arbitrary cycles can be imitated by transfer connectors in a way similar to the cyclic block (Figure 3). Implicit termination can be modeled by adding a final join. The next group of patterns involves *multiple instances* (MI). MI without synchronization can be mimicked by using a split connector with one outgoing arc that can produce an arbitrary number of tokens. MI with a priori known design time knowledge and MI with a priori known runtime knowl-

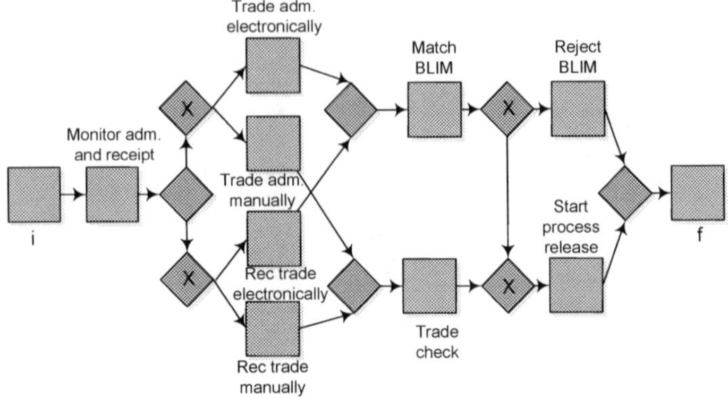

Fig. 6. Acyclic workflow process

edge correspond to a split-join pair enclosing a task where both connectors can produce and, respectively, consume n tokens where n is known at design time or at runtime. MI with no a priori runtime knowledge can also be imitated by a split-join pair such that join is has one incoming arc coming from split (via a task) and another one(s) coming from a different part of the process. *State-based patterns* include deferred choice, interleaved parallel routing and milestone. We cannot model the deferred choice as our formalism is not concerned with environment. Interleaving parallel routing can be imitated by split, followed by a set of tasks and then by a join. Implementing the milestone pattern demands history-based preconditions. The last group of patterns is dedicated to *cancellation*: we cannot model these patterns. Summarizing the discussion above we observe that our formalism is powerful enough to express eighteen out of twenty-one patterns of [5].

Figure 6 shows an acyclic workflow process corresponding to the event-driven process chain example in [12] in which XOR nodes have been transformed into transfer nodes, AND splits into split connectors and AND joins into join connectors. While in [12] we have added "color" (data attributes) to synchronize the choices made by the transfer connectors, here we can add preconditions for such transfer connectors based on the history log. Note that we have added a final join connector for the final events that makes the workflow process sound.

7 Conclusions and Future work

In this paper we have investigated application of case history to controlling workflow processes. We have seen that constructs such as join that usually require elaborate semantics [17] can be easily expressed if case history is included in the model. We have further defined an appropriate notion of soundness and provided a sufficient condition for it. We further reported on implementation of the framework and its application in YasperWE.

We intend to apply and extend the results of this study in two directions. Firstly we will implement the algorithms in our experimental workflow engine, called YasperWE [2]. YasperWE is an extension of a modeling tool, called Yasper (Yet Another Smart Process EditoR) that is developed at our institute [1,10,13] and the document manager InfoPath of MicroSoft. Yasper supports workflow design, simulation and analysis. In particular Yasper supports the case concept and the use of resources. The extension (WE) of Yasper is the workflow engine. With Infopath it is possible to design an XML document and to define different views on that document. These views have can be displayed as forms with the usual user interface facilities, such as tables, list boxes, check boxes and radio buttons. For each case type (i.e. each process) a document type in the form of an XML schema is designed with InfoPath. Also a set of forms is defined, one for each view. In YasperWE each task is connected to a view. As soon as the initial task for a process is executed, a case document is created and all resources that can handle the case receive an alert (a work item in the input basket of the resource). The workflow engine has very little knowledge of the cases: only the case identity is known and this identity can be passed to InfoPath. The workflow engine obtains messages from InfoPath about the branch to be chosen in a split connector or the readiness of a task or join connector. So the data manipulation is in fact "outsourced" to InfoPath. In InfoPath the whole case history is memorized. So to implement the control structures we have to build a component that inspects the case history and determines the control actions for the workflow engine. The second line of work is the formalization of the concept of *local history*, i.e. the history of the case restricted to the block it is in. This will allow for compositionality results which make verification easier.

References

1. Yasper. Petri net editor. `www.yasper.org`.
2. Yasper workflow engine (YasperWE). `www.yasper.org/we`.
3. W.M.P. van der Aalst and K. van Hee. *Workflow Management: Models, Methods, and Systems.* MIT Press, 2002.
4. W.M.P. van der Aalst and A. H. M. ter Hofstede. YAWL: yet another workflow language. *Inf. Syst.*, 30(4):245–275, 2005.
5. W.M.P. van der Aalst, A. H. M. ter Hofstede, B. Kiepuszewski, and A. P. Barros. Workflow patterns. *Distributed and Parallel Databases*, 14(1):5–51, 2003.
6. T. Andrews, F. Curbera, H. Dholakia, Y. Goland, J. Klein, F. Leymann, K. Liu, D. Roller, D. Smith, S. Thatte, I. Trickovic, and S. Weerawarana. Business process execution language for web services. version 1.1, 2003. Available at ftp://www6.software.ibm.com/software/developer/library/ws-bpel.pdf.
7. P. Chrzastowski-Wachtel, B. Benatallah, R. Hamadi, M. O'Dell, and A. Susanto. A top-down petri net-based approach for dynamic workflow modeling. In *Business Process Management*, volume 2678 of *Lecture Notes in Computer Science*, pages 336–353, 2003.
8. M. Dumas and A. H. M. ter Hofstede. UML activity diagrams as a workflow specification language. In M. Gogolla and C. Kobryn, editors, *UML*, volume 2185 of *Lecture Notes in Computer Science*, pages 76–90. Springer, 2001.

9. H. J. Genrich and K. Lautenbach. System modelling with high-level Petri nets. *Theor. Comput. Sci.*, 13(1):109–136, 1981.
10. K. van Hee, O. Oanea, R. Post, L. Somers, and J. M. van der Werf. Yasper a tool for workflow modeling and analysis. In *Proceedings of the 5th International Conference on Application of Concurrency to System Design (ACSD 2006)*, 2006. accepted.
11. K. van Hee, O. Oanea, A. Serebrenik, N. Sidorova, and M. Voorhoeve. Modelling History-Dependent Business Processes. In *Proc. of the Workshop on Modelling, Simulation, Verification and Validation of Enterprise Information Systems (MSVVEIS06)*, 2006. to appear.
12. K. van Hee, O. Oanea, and N. Sidorova. Colored Petri nets to verify extended event-driven process chains. In *OTM Conferences (1)*, volume 3760 of *Lecture Notes in Computer Science*, pages 183–201. Springer, 2005.
13. K. van Hee, R. Post, and L. Somers. Yet Another Smart Process Editor. In *Proc. of European Simulation and Modelling Conference (ESM 2005), EUROSIS, Porto, Portugal*, 2005.
14. K. van Hee, N. Sidorova, and M. Voorhoeve. Soundness and separability of workflow nets in the stepwise refinement approach. In *Proc. of ICATPN'2003*, volume 2679 of *LNCS*, pages 337–356, 2003.
15. C. A. R. Hoare. Communicating sequential processes. *Commun. ACM*, 21(8):666–677, 1978.
16. K. Jensen. *Coloured Petri Nets - Basic Concepts, Analysis Methods and Practical.* Springer-Verlag, 1992.
17. E. Kindler. On the semantics of EPCs: Resolving the vicious circle. *Data Knowl. Eng.*, 56(1):23–40, 2006.
18. R. Liu and A. Kumar. An analysis and taxonomy of unstructured workflows. In *Business Process Management*, volume 3649 of *Lecture Notes in Computer Science*, pages 268–284, 2005.
19. R. Milner. *A Calculus of Communicating Systems.* Springer-Verlag New York, Inc., Secaucus, NJ, USA, 1982.
20. R. Milner. *Communicating and Mobile Systems: The Pi Calculus.* Cambridge University Press, 1999.
21. C. Ouyang, E. Verbeek, W. van der Aalst, S. Breutel, M. Dumas, and A. H. M. ter Hofstede. WofBPEL: A tool for automated analysis of BPEL processes. In *ICSOC*, volume 3826 of *Lecture Notes in Computer Science*, pages 484–489. Springer, 2005.
22. S. A. White. Workflow patterns with BPMN and UML. Technical report, IBM, 2004. Available at: http://www.bpmn.org/Documents/Notations
23. M. T. Wynn, D. Edmond, W. M. P. van der Aalst, and A. ter Hofstede. Achieving a general, formal and decidable approach to the OR-join in workflow using reset nets. In *Proc. of ATPN*, volume 3536 of *Lecture Notes in Computer Science*, pages 423–443. Springer, 2005.

On Representing, Purging, and Utilizing Change Logs in Process Management Systems

Stefanie Rinderle[1], Manfred Reichert[2], Martin Jurisch[1], and Ulrich Kreher[1]

[1] Dept. DBIS, University of Ulm, Germany
{stefanie.rinderle, martin.jurisch, ulrich.kreher}@uni-ulm.de
[2] Informations Systems Group, University of Twente, The Netherlands
m.u.reichert@utwente.nl

Abstract. In recent years adaptive process management technolgy has emerged in order to increase the flexibility of business process implementations and to support process changes at different levels. Usually, respective systems log comprehensive information about changes, which can then be used for different purposes including process traceability, change reuse and process recovery. Therefore the adequate and efficient representation of change logs is a crucial task for adaptive process management systems. In this paper we show which information has to be (minimally) captured in process change logs and how it should be represented in a generic and efficient way. We discuss different design alternatives and show how to deal with noise in process change logs. Finally, we present an elegant and efficient implementation approach, which we applied in the ADEPT2 process management system. Altogether the presented concepts provide an important pillar for adaptive process management technology and emerging fields (e.g., process change mining).

1 Introduction

The management of log information is crucial in different areas of information systems. One prominent example are transaction logs in database systems which allow to restore a consistent database state after transaction abortions or system crashes. Log information is also exploited for analysis in fields like data mining [1], online analytical processing [2], and process mining [3]. Current process management systems (PMS) maintain comprehensive *execution logs* which capture events related to the start and completion of process activities [4,5].

A key requirement for BPM technology becoming more and more important in practice is (runtime) adaptivity; i.e., the ability of the PMS to support (dynamic) changes at the process type as well as the process instance level. Several approaches have been discussed in literature (e.g. [6,4,5]), and a number of prototypes demonstrating the high potential of adaptive PMS have emerged [7,8]. Obviously, with the introduction of adaptive PMS we obtain additional runtime information about process executions not explicitly captured in current execution logs. This information can be useful in different context and should therefore be managed in respective *change logs*. Change log entries may contain

S. Dustdar, J.L. Fiadeiro, and A. Sheth (Eds.): BPM 2006, LNCS 4102, pp. 241–256, 2006.

information about the type of a change, the applied change operations and their parameterizations, the time the change happened, etc. (cf. Fig. 1).

The kind of change information being logged and the way this information is represented are crucial for the usefulness of change logs. To our best knowledge there has been no profound work related to these fundamental issues so far. Several use cases appear when dealing with change log management. First, execution logs themselves are not sufficient to *restore* the logical structure of a process instance to which ad-hoc changes have been applied (e.g., insertion or deletion of activities). Instead, additional information from change logs is needed. Second, *change traceability* is an important requirement for any adaptive information system. In the medical domain, for example, all deviations from standard procedures have to be recorded for legal reasons. Third, the logged information can be utilized if similar situations re-occur and a previous process change shall be *reused*. Fourth, conflicts between changes concurrently applied to the same process (instance) can be detected based on change log information [9]; i.e., *conflict analyses* can be based on the logged information.

Traceability and change reuse are requirements mainly related to the user level since change information is then presented to and possibly used by human actors. By contrast, restoring process structures after changes and analyzing concurrent changes for the absence of conflicts concern the system level and usually do not involve user interaction. Furthermore, comparable to the use of execution logs in connection with process mining, we must be able to deal with noise in change logs, i.e., information which is unnecessary, irrelevant, or even wrong. Purging change logs from such noise is an important prerequisite, for example, for comparing (conflicting) changes, for reasoning about change effects, and for change mining. However, providing specific *views* on change logs, which hide noisy information, is useful for better user assistance as well, e.g., by providing a homogeneous view on process changes or facilitating their reuse. In summary, the following challenges emerge with respect to change log management:

- How shall change log information be represented in order to meet the described requirements? Which representation form is appropriate at the user level and which one is needed at the system level?
- How can we create purged views on change logs at the *user level* (e.g., to hide 'noise' from users)?
- How can we efficiently store and manage change log information at the *system level*?

In our previous work on adaptive process management (e.g., [10,5]) we have introduced a theoretical framework for dealing with changes at both the process type and the process instance level. In particular we have put emphasis on formal correctness issues arising in connection with dynamic process changes at different levels. In this paper we tackle the above mentioned challenges and introduce a mature approach for representing change information in adaptive PMS. This approach is based on a set of well-defined change operations (applicable at different levels), on change transactions, and on change logs. Further we describe how to create special views on change logs which purge these logs from noisy

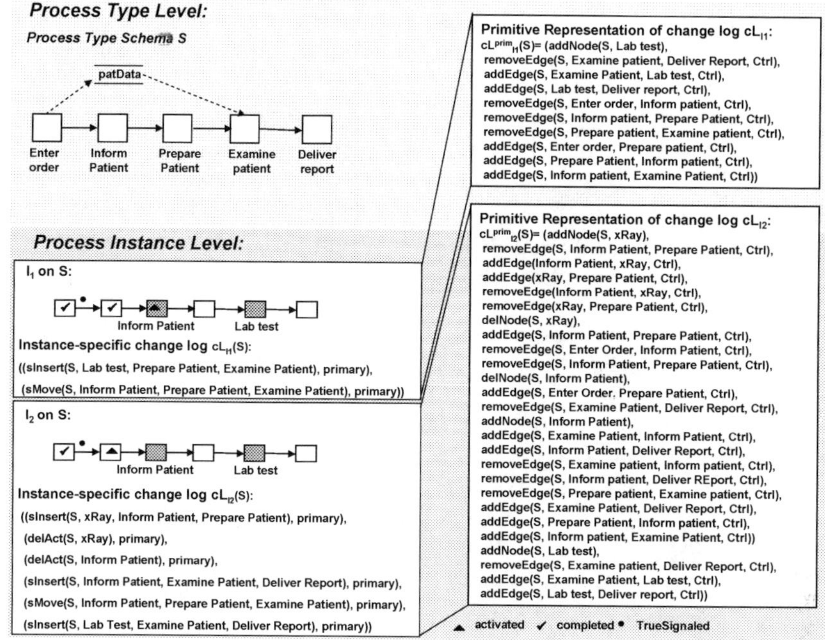

Process Type Level:
Process Type Schema S
patData
Enter order
Inform Patient
Prepare Patient
Examine patient
Deliver report
Primitive Representation of change log cL_{I1}:
cL^{prim}_{I1}(S)= (addNode(S, Lab test),
removeEdge(S, Examine patient, Deliver Report, Ctrl),
addEdge(S, Examine Patient, Lab test, Ctrl),
addEdge(S, Lab test, Deliver report, Ctrl),
removeEdge(S, Enter order, Inform patient, Ctrl),
removeEdge(S, Inform patient, Prepare Patient, Ctrl),
removeEdge(S, Prepare patient, Examine patient, Ctrl),
addEdge(S, Enter order, Prepare patient, Ctrl),
addEdge(S, Prepare Patient, Inform patient, Ctrl),
addEdge(S, Inform patient, Examine Patient, Ctrl))
Process Instance Level:
I_1 on S:
Inform Patient
Lab test
Instance-specific change log cL_{I1}(S):
((sInsert(S, Lab test, Prepare Patient, Examine Patient), primary),
(sMove(S, Inform Patient, Prepare Patient, Examine Patient), primary))
I_2 on S:
Inform Patient
Lab test
Instance-specific change log cL_{I2}(S):
((sInsert(S, xRay, Inform Patient, Prepare Patient), primary),
(delAct(S, xRay), primary),
(delAct(S, Inform Patient), primary),
(sInsert(S, Inform Patient, Examine Patient, Deliver Report), primary),
(sMove(S, Inform Patient, Prepare Patient, Examine Patient), primary),
(sInsert(S, Lab Test, Examine Patient, Deliver Report), primary))
Primitive Representation of change log cL_{I2}:
cL^{prim}_{I2}(S)= (addNode(S, xRay),
removeEdge(S, Inform Patient, Prepare Patient, Ctrl),
addEdge(Inform Patient, xRay, Ctrl),
addEdge(xRay, Prepare Patient, Ctrl),
removeEdge(Inform Patient, xRay, Ctrl),
removeEdge(xRay, Prepare Patient, Ctrl),
delNode(S, xRay),
addEdge(S, Inform Patient, Prepare Patient, Ctrl),
removeEdge(S, Enter Order, Inform Patient, Ctrl),
removeEdge(S, Inform Patient, Prepare Patient, Ctrl),
delNode(S, Inform Patient),
addEdge(S, Enter Order. Prepare Patient, Ctrl),
removeEdge(S, Examine Patient, Deliver Report, Ctrl),
addNode(S, Inform Patient),
addEdge(S, Examine Patient, Inform Patient, Ctrl),
addEdge(S, Inform Patient, Deliver Report, Ctrl),
removeEdge(S, Examine patient, Inform patient, Ctrl),
removeEdge(S, Inform patient, Deliver REport, Ctrl),
removeEdge(S, Prepare patient, Examine patient, Ctrl),
addEdge(S, Examine Patient, Deliver Report, Ctrl),
addEdge(S, Prepare Patient, Inform patient, Ctrl),
addEdge(S, Inform patient, Examine Patient, Ctrl))
addNode(S, Lab test),
removeEdge(S, Examine patient, Deliver Report, Ctrl),
addEdge(S, Examine Patient, Lab test, Ctrl),
addEdge(S, Lab test, Deliver report, Ctrl))
activated
completed
TrueSignaled

Fig. 1. Change Logs for Modified Process Instances

information (at the user level). Finally, we show how noise-free change logs can be efficiently implemented at the system level.

Sect. 2 deals with basic issues related to change log representation. In Sect. 3 we present an approach for (logically) purging change logs from noise. Sect. 4 shows how change information can be efficiently handled at the system level. Sect. 5 gives an illustrating example. In Sect. 6 we discuss related work and in Sect. 7 we conclude with a summary and an outlook on future work.

2 On Representing Change Logs

We assume a graph–based meta model for defining process templates and representing changes on them. For the sake of simplicity, we restrict our considerations to Activity Nets as, for example, used in MQSeries Workflow [11]. However, our approach can be easily adapted to other process meta models as well.

Logically, a process change is accomplished by applying a sequence of change primitives or operations to the respective process graph (i.e., *process template*). In principle, the change information to be logged can be represented in different ways, which more or less affect the use cases described in Sect. 1. To meet the requirements of these use cases we must find an adequate representation for change log information and appropriate methods for processing it. Independent from the applied (high–level) change operations, for example, we could translate the change into a set of basic change primitives (i.e., graph primitives like `addNode` or `deleteEdge`). This would still allow us to restore process structures, but also result in a loss of information about change semantics. Consequently, change traceability and conflict analyses would be limited. As an alternative we can explicitly store the applied high–level change operations (incl. their parameterization). We will illustrate both approaches (see also Fig. 1) and discuss their strengths and drawbacks.

We first define the notion of *process template*. For each business process to be supported a process type T is defined. It is represented by a *process template* of which different versions may exist.

Definition 1 (Process Template). *A tuple S with S = (N, D, CtrlEdges, DataEdges, EC) is called a process template, if the following holds:*

- *N is a set of process activities and D a set of process data elements*
- *CtrlEdges* $\subset N \times N$ *is a precedence relation (notation:* $n_{src} \rightarrow n_{dst} \equiv (n_{src}, n_{dst}) \in$ *CtrlEdges)*
- *DataEdges* $\subseteq N \times D \times \{read, write\}$ *is a set of read/write data links between process activities and process data elements*
- *EC: CtrlEdges* $\mapsto$ *Conds(D)* $\cup$ $\{TRUE\}$ *where Conds(D) denotes the set of all valid transition conditions on data elements from D.*

For a process template several correctness constraints exist, e.g., (N, CtrlEdges) must be an acyclic graph to ensure the absence of deadlocks (for details see [10,9]).

For definining changes on a process template two basic approaches (cf. Fig. 2) exist. One approach is to define changes by applying a sequence of basic graph primitives (e.g., inserting or deleting nodes and edges) to the process graph (template). Whether the resulting graph is correct (e.g., does not contain deadlock-causing cycles) or not can be checked, for example, by analyzing the resulting process graph. Tab. 1 summarizes selected change primitives.

Table 1. Examples for Change Primitives on Process Templates

Change Primitive Applied to S	Effects on S
addNode(S,X)	adds node X to template S
delNode(S,X)	deletes node X from template S
addEdge(S,A,B,Ctrl)	adds control edge (A, B) between activities A and B to S
removeEdge(S,A,B,Ctrl)	removes edge (A, B) from S

The other possibility is to use high-level change operations each of which combining change primitives in a certain way (cf. Fig. 2a), e.g., to insert an activity and embed it into the process context. High-level operations comprise more semantics and are characterized by formal pre- and post-conditions. The latter can be used, for example, to ensure correctness when applying a set of operations to a process template. Table 2 presents selected *high-level change operations*. These operations can be applied at the process type as well as the process instance level in order to create or modify process templates. For the

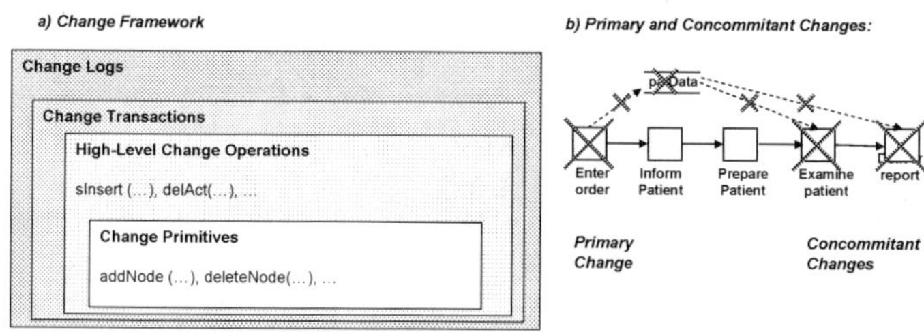

Fig. 2. (a) Overview Change Framework (b) Primary and concomitant Changes

Table 2. Examples for High-Level Change Operations on Process Templates

Change Operation *op* **Applied to S**	opType	subject	paramList	**Effects on S**
		Additive Change Operations		
sInsert(S,X,A,B)	Insert	X	S, A, B	adds activity X between two directly succeeding activities A and B
cInsert(S,X,A,B,c)	Insert	X	S, A, B, sc	adds activity X between two directly succeeding activities A and B as a conditional branch with transition condition c.
		Subtractive Change Operations		
delAct(S,X)	Delete	X	S	deletes activity X from template S and relinks context activities
		Order-Changing Operations		
sMove(S,X,A,B)	Move	X	S, A, B	moves activity X from its current position to the position between directly succeeding activities A and B

two operations *serial move* and *serial insert* Fig. 3 gives more details (incl. pre- and post-conditions and used change primitives).

In order to express more complex changes, high-level change operations can be combined within change transactions (cf. Fig. 2a). This might be needed, for example, if the application of a single change operation would lead to an incorrect process template, but this problem can be overcome by applying a set of concomitant change operations. As example consider the scenario from Fig. 2b). Assume that activity `Enter order` shall be deleted. Due to the existence of data-dependent activities either this change has to be rejected or the two data-dependent activities have to be concomitantly removed to preserve data flow correctness [10]. These concomitant changes must then be carried out within the same change transaction. For change analysis it makes sense to distinguish between such *primary* changes (i.e., changes which initiate the change transactions) and secondary (i.e., *concomitant*) changes (i.e., operations preserving process template correctness afterwards).

As mentioned, process changes may be conducted at the type as well as the instance level. In both cases, several change transactions may be applied during the lifecycle of the process instance or process type respectively. These

sMove(S, X, A, B) with S = (N, D, CtrlEdges, ...)	
Pre-conditions (structural)	- X, A, B ∈ N - ∃ (A, B) ∈ CtrlEdges
Pre-Conditions (state-related)	$NS^S(X)$, $NS^S(B)$ ∈ {NotActivated, Activated}
Change Primitives	- removeEdge(S, A, B, Ctrl) - removeEdge(S, pred(X), X, Ctrl) - removeEdge(S, X, succ(X), Ctrl) - addEdge(S, pred(X), succ(X), Ctrl) - addEdge(S, A, X, Ctrl) - addEdge(S, X, B, Ctrl)
Post-Conditions	- $NS^S(B)$ = Activated → $NS^S(B)$ = NotActivated and $NS^S(X)$ = Activated - $NS^S(B)$ = NotActivated and $NS^S(X)$ = Activated → $NS^S(X)$ = NotActivated

sInsert(S, X, A, B) with S = (N, D, CtrlEdges, ...)	
Pre-conditions (structural)	- X ∉ N - A, B ∈ N - ∃ (A, B) ∈ CtrlEdges
Pre-Conditions (state-related)	$NS^S(B)$ ∈ {NotActivated, Activated}
Change Primitives	- addNode(S, X) - removeEdge(S, A, B, Ctrl) - addEdge(S, A, X, Ctrl) - addEdge(S, X, B, Ctrl)
Post-Conditions	$NS^S(B)$ = Activated → $NS^S(B)$ = NotActivated and $NS^S(X)$ = Activated

delAct(S, X) with S = (N, D, CtrlEdges, ...)	
Pre-conditions (structural)	X ∈ N
Pre-Conditions (state-related)	$NS^S(X)$ ∈ {NotActivated, Activated}
Change Primitives	- removeEdge(S, pred(X), X, Ctrl) - removeEdge (S, X, succ(X), Ctrl) - delNode(S, X) - addEdge(S, pred(X), succ(X), Ctrl)
Post-Conditions	$NS^S(X)$ = Activated → $NS^S(succ(X))$ = Activated
pred(X) (succ(X)) denotes all direct predecessors (successors) of X in S	

Fig. 3. Serial Move/ Serial Insert Operation with Pre- and Post-Conditions (when applying it to a process instance; NS: activity state)

transactions are logically grouped in the *change log* of the instance or type.[1] In Def. 2 we formally define *change transaction* and *change log*. We base this definition on the notion of a process template independent from whether this template is related to a process type or process instance.

Definition 2 (Change Transaction, Change Log). *Let S = (N, D, ...) be a process template. A sequence of change transactions* $cL = < \Delta_1, ..., \Delta_k >$ *applied to S is denoted as process change log. Thereby each change transaction* $\Delta_j :=\, < (op_1^j, cK_1^j), ..., (op_{n_j}^j, cK_{n_j}^j) >$ *(j = 1, ... , k) consists of a sequence of high-level change operations* $op_1^j, \ldots, op_{n_j}^j$ *where either all operations were successfully applied or none of them (atomicity). Flag* $cK_k^j \in \{primary, concomitant\}$ *indicates whether* op_k^j *is a primary change operation or a concomitant one*[2].

In our implementation we maintain additional attributes for change log entries (e.g., time stamps). However this is outside the scope of this paper.

[1] For the sake of readability we use single process instances or process types as granule for a change log.

[2] A change transactions Δ may also consist of exactly one change operation *op*. In this case we write *op* instead of Δ for short and set cK to primary.

Since all transactions Δ_j preserve correctness, the intermediate process templates S_j resulting after the application of change Δ_j are correct. Formally: S + Δ_1:= S_1, S_1 + Δ_2 := S_2, ... , S_{k-1} + Δ_k := S_k are correct process templates. In addition state-related correctness is checked when applying instance changes [5]. However these checks are not based on change logs but on execution logs.

For several reasons it makes sense to maintain both of the aforementioned representation forms for changes in respective logs; i.e., representation of the change as a set of high-level operations and as a set of low-level change primitives. On the one hand, high-level operations are user-friendly and capture more change semantics, on the other hand low-level change primitives enable efficient conflict checks (as we will discuss later on). Therefore, in addition to change log cL (cf. Def. 2) we introduce cL^{prim} which comprises the primitive represenation of cL, i.e., in cL^{prim} the high-level operations from cL are replaced by the change primitives of the respective high-level operations (cf. Fig. 3). As example take the change scenario from Fig. 1 where both representation forms are depicted.

At runtime new *process instances* can be created and executed based on a process template S. Logically, each instance I is associated with an instance-specific process template $S_I := S + cL_I$[3]. S = S(T,V) denotes the original process template from which I was derived, whereby T denotes the process type and V the version of the process type template; cL_I constitutes the instance-specific change log which contains all changes applied to I so far.

The current execution state of I is represented by a marking (NS^{S_I}, ES^{S_I}). It assigns to each activity n and to each control edge e its current status $NS(n)$ or $ES(e)$ respectively. Further, execution history $\mathcal{H}_\mathcal{I}$ captures events related to the start and completion of activities. Based on S, $\mathcal{H}_\mathcal{I}$ and cL^I the current structure and state of instance I can be restored at any point in time.

Definition 3 (Process Instance). *A process instance I is defined by a tuple (T, V, cL^I, M^{S_I}, $\mathcal{H}_\mathcal{I}$, Val^{S_I}) where*

- *T denotes the process type and V the version of the process template S := S(T,V) = (N, D, CtrlEdges, ...) instance I was derived from. We call S the original template of I.*
- *Change log cL^I captures the instance-specific change transactions Δ_i^I (i = 1, ..., n) applied to I so far. We also denote cL^I as bias of I. $S_I := S + cL^I$ (with $S_I = (N_I, D_I, \ldots)$) resulting from the application of cL^I to S is called instance-specific template of I.*
- *M^{S_I} = (NS^{S_I}, ES^{S_I}) describes node and edge markings of I:*
  NS^{S_I}: $N_I \mapsto$ {`NotActivated`, `Activated`, `Running`, `Completed`, `Skipped`}
  ES^{S_I}: ($CtrlEdges_I$) $\mapsto$ {`NotSignaled`, `TrueSignaled`, `FalseSignaled`}
- *$\mathcal{H}_\mathcal{I}$ denotes the execution history of I which captures events related to the start and completion of activities*
- *Val^{S_I} is a function on D_I. It reflects for each data element $d \in D_I$ either its current value or the value* `UNDEFINED` *(if d has not been written yet).*

[3] For unchanged instances $cL_I = \emptyset$ and consequently $S_I = S$ holds.

3 The Logical View – On Purging Change Logs

After having defined the notion of change log we now have a closer look at the information captured by such logs. This makes sense since changes with same effects can be expressed in different ways and therefore be represented by different sets of change operations. As example consider Fig. 1 (left side). Though the changes captured by cL_{I_2} and cL_{I_2} comprise different operations, at the end they have resulted in equal schemes for instances I_1 and I_2. When analyzing cL_{I_2} we can observe that this change log contains operations which do not have any effect (e.g., insertion and immediate deletion of activity `xRay`). Reason for the presence of such changes can be that users either do not act in a goal-oriented way (i.e., they "try out" the change) or, e.g. in the medical domain, certain possible steps (treatments) are first considered and discarded later.

For the mentioned use cases (e.g., change mining, conflict checking) logs should only provide relevant information (about those changes which actually have had effects). By contrast, irrelevant or noisy information make checks or the comparison of changes (as necessary when propagating a process type change to biased process instances) difficult. For traceability reasons, by contrast, the logs should exactly reflect the change transactions as applied (independent from their actual effects). Consequently, change log management should provide different *views* on the stored information depending on the respective use case. In this paper we consider two views, the original change log view (containing all change transactions) and the *purged* change log which only reflects change transactions which actually had an effect on the affected process template.

1. Let S be a process template which is transformed into template S' by applying the operations from change log cL. The first group of changes without any effect on S' are *compensating changes*, i.e., changes mutually compensating their effects. Consider the change log as depicted in Fig. 4: activity `xRay` is first inserted (between `Inform Patient` and `Prepare Patient`) and afterwards deleted by the user. Therefore the associated operations `sInsert(S, xRay, Inform Patient, Prepare Patient)` and `delete(S, xRay)` have no visible effects on S'.
2. The second category of noise in change logs comprises changes which only have hidden effects on S'. Such *hidden changes* always arise when deleting an activity which is then re-inserted at another position. This actually has the effect of a move operation. Consider again Fig. 4 where activity `Inform Patient` is first deleted and then inserted again between `Examine Patient` and `Deliver Report`. The effect behind this is the same as of the move operation `sMove(S, Inform Patient, Examine Patient, Deliver Report)`.
3. There are changes overriding effects of preceding ones (note that a change transaction is an <u>ordered</u> set of operations). Fig. 4 depicts a change log where the effect of the hidden move operation `sMove(S, Inform Patient, Examine Patient, Deliver Report))` is overwritten by operation `sMove (S, Inform Patient, Prepare Patient, Examine Patient)`, i.e., in S' `Inform Patient` is finally placed between `Prepare Patient` and `Examine Patient`.

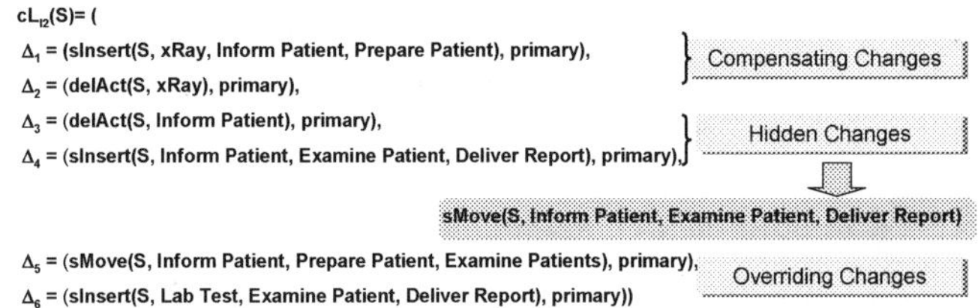
cL12(S)= (
Δ1 = (sInsert(S, xRay, Inform Patient, Prepare Patient), primary),
Δ2 = (delAct(S, xRay), primary),
Δ3 = (delAct(S, Inform Patient), primary),
Δ4 = (sInsert(S, Inform Patient, Examine Patient, Deliver Report), primary),
sMove(S, Inform Patient, Examine Patient, Deliver Report)
Δ5 = (sMove(S, Inform Patient, Prepare Patient, Examine Patients), primary),
Δ6 = (sInsert(S, Lab Test, Examine Patient, Deliver Report), primary))
Compensating Changes
Hidden Changes
Overriding Changes

Fig. 4. Different Types of Noise within Change Log

In order to purge a change log from such noise we provide an algorithm for detecting and removing irrelevant or noisy information from change logs. Let $cL =< \Delta_1, ..., \Delta_n >$ be a change log whose application to template $S = (N, D, ..)$ has resulted in template $S' = (N', D', ...)$. We call N_{cL}^{add} := N' \ N the set of all added activities in S' and N_{cL}^{del} := N \ N' the set of all deleted activities.

For the sake of readability and without loss of generality we assume that all change transactions Δ_j (j = 1, ..., n) consist of exactly one (primary) change operation op_j (formally: $\forall \Delta_j : \ \Delta_j =< (op_j, \ primary) >$); i.e., we abstain from change transactions comprising multiple operations. However, the algorithm presented in the following can be applied to most complex change transactions as well. Exceptional are only very special cases as the following example shows. Assume that an activity is deleted (primary change) followed by the concomitant deletion of data-dependent steps (e.g., deletion of `Enter order` as depicted in Fig. 2b). Assume further that this activity is re-inserted afterwards, but not all of the other deleted steps. Taking the scenario from Fig. 2b), for example, activities `Enter order` and `Examine` might be re-inserted, but activity `Deliver report` not. Though the primary changes override each other (deletion and insertion of `Enter order`) there is a remaining effect. Consequently the associated change transactions cannot be completely purged from the change log.

Informally the algorithm for purging change logs works as follows: First of all, sets N_{cL}^{add} and N_{cL}^{del} are determined. Taking this information change log cL can be purged. This is accomplished by scanning cL in reverse direction and by determining whether change transaction (operation) $\Delta_j = op_j$ $(j = 1, \ldots, n)$ actually has any effect on S. If so we incorporate $\Delta_j = op_j$ into another – intially empty – change log cL^{purged}. Finally, in order to reduce the number of necessary change log scans to one we use auxiliary sets to memorize which activities, control edges, data elements and data edges have been already treated. The following informal description focuses on the insertion, deletion, and moving of activities in order to get the idea behind the respective algorithm. However, the used methods can be also applied to purge logs capturing information about insertion and deletion of, for example, data elements.

– Assume that we find a log entry $\Delta_j = op_j$ for an operation inserting activity X between activities src and $dest$ into S and that X is not yet present in A (let A be an auxiliary set for which $A = \emptyset$ holds at the beginning), i.e., $\Delta_j = op_j$ is the last change operation within cL which manipulates X. If

X has been already present in S ($X \notin N_{cL}^{add}$) a *hidden change* is found. Consequently, a respective log entry for an operation moving X between *src* and *dest* is created and written into cL^{purged}.

- If log entry $\Delta_j = op_j$ denotes an operation deleting X from S, $X \notin A$, and X is still present in S' ($X \notin N_{cL}^{del}$) we have found a *compensating change*. Therefore $\Delta_j = op_j$ (and the respective insert op.) are left outside cL^{purged}.
- If log entry $\Delta_j = op_j$ denotes an operation moving X to a position between activities *src* and *dest* and $\Delta_j = op_j$ is the last operation within cL having effects regarding X ($X \notin A$) we have to distinguish two cases: If X has been inserted before $\Delta_j = op_j$ ($X \in N_{cL}^{add}$) we write a new log entry in cL^{purged} denoting an operation inserting X between *src* and *dest*. If X has been also present in S ($X \notin N_{cL}^{add}$) we write $\Delta_j = op_j$ unalteredly into cL^{purged}.

A formalization of the method described above is given in Alg. 1. Due to lack of space we restrict this description to serial insert operations. However adopting parallel and branch insertions runs analogously and has been considered in our approach (see [9] for details).

Definition 4 (Purged Change Log). *Let S = (N, D, ...) be a (correct) process template. Let further cL be a change log whose application transforms S into another (correct) process template S' = (N', S', ...). Let (N_{cL}^{add} := $N' \setminus N$ and N_{cL}^{del} := $N \setminus N'$. Algorithm 1 determines the purged change log cL^{purged}.*

Algorithm 1. PurgeConsolidate(S, N, N', $cL = (\Delta_1 = op_1, \ldots, \Delta_n = op_n)$) $\longrightarrow cL^{purged}$

```
A:=∅; cL^purged = ∅;
N_cL^add := N' \ N; N_cL^del := N \ N';
for i = n to 1 do {
  if (Δ_j = op_j = serialInsert(S, X, src, dest)) {
   if (X ∉ A) {
    A := A ∪ {X}; //X not considered so far
    if(X ∉ N_Δ^add){ //X actually not inserted ⟶ hidden move
     if (src ≠ c_pred(S, X) ∧ dest ≠ c_succ(S, X)⁴){ //X moved to another position?
      cL^purged.addFirst(serialMove(S, X, src, dest))//adds entry at beginning of cL^purged;
    }} else {
     cL^purged.addFirst(serialInsert(S, X, src, dest));}} continue};
  if (Δ_j = op_j = serialMove(S, X, src, dest)) {
   if (X ∉ A) {
    A := A ∪ {X};
    if (X ∈ N_cL^add) {
     cL^purged.addFirst(serialInsert(S, X, src, dest)); } else {
     if (src ≠ c_pred(S, X) ∧ dest ≠ c_succ(S, X)) {
      cL^purged.addFirst(serialMove(S, X, src, dest));}} continue;}
  if (Δ_j = op_j = delete(S, X)) {
   if (X ∉ A) {
    A := A ∪ {X};
    if(X ∈ N_cL^del){
      cL^purged.addFirst(delete(S, X));}}}
   cL^purged.addFirst(op_i);
}
return cL^purged;
```

[4] c_pred(S, X) (c_succ(S, X)) denotes all direct predecessors (successors) of X in S.

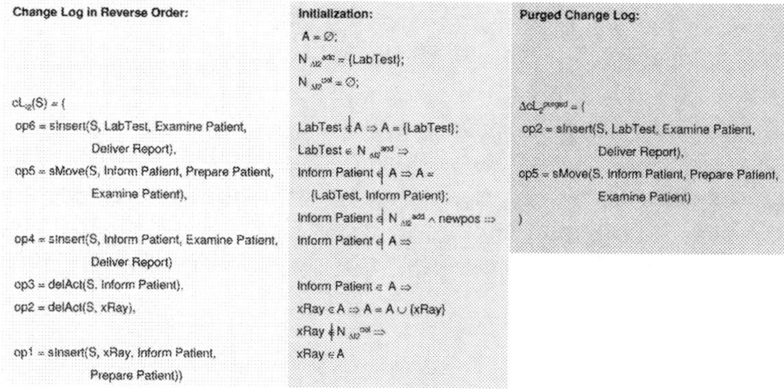
Change Log in Reverse Order:
op6 = sInsert(S, LabTest, Examine Patient, Deliver Report),
op5 = sMove(S, Inform Patient, Prepare Patient, Examine Patient),
op4 = sInsert(S, Inform Patient, Examine Patient, Deliver Report)
op3 = delAct(S, Inform Patient),
op2 = delAct(S, xRay),
op1 = sInsert(S, xRay, Inform Patient, Prepare Patient))
Initialization:
A = ∅;
LabTest ∉ A ⇒ A = {LabTest};
{LabTest, Inform Patient};
Inform Patient ∉ A ⇒
Inform Patient ∈ A ⇒
xRay ∈ A ⇒ A = A ∪ {xRay}
xRay ∈ A
Purged Change Log:
op2 = sInsert(S, LabTest, Examine Patient, Deliver Report),
op5 = sMove(S, Inform Patient, Prepare Patient, Examine Patient)
)

Fig. 5. Purging the Change Log of Instance I_2 (cf. Fig. 4)

Figure 5 depicts how change log cL_{I2} from Fig. 4 is purged resulting in purged change log cL^{purged}. This view just contains those change transactions (operations) which actually have had an effect on the instance-specific template.

Altogether purging change logs in the described way results in a specific, logical view on the conducted changes. This view may, for example, be presented to users if an overview on the actual change effects on the original process template is required. As we will discuss in the next section, at the system level a more efficient approach becomes necessary.

4 The Implementation View – The Delta Layer Concept

In this section we present concepts for representing changes at the system level which have been implemented within the ADEPT prototype. Before presenting the delta layer concept in more detail, some background information on the general representation of process type and process instance templates is needed. Fig. 6a illustrates an approach which has been implemented by several adaptive PMS [8,12]. The *process logic* (e.g., control and data flow) is encapsulated within object *process template* which represents the *process type*. *Instance objects* representing process instances solely contain runtime information (like activity execution states or – logically – the content of data elements). The associated process type is expressed by a reference to the respective process template object. Following this approach, all instances of a given process type reference the same template object. We chose this representation since the necessary storage space is significantly reduced – especially for a large number of running instances – compared to storing a process description for each instance in a redundant way.

In order to reflect the difference between template and instance objects (e.g., after instance changes) we introduced the delta layer concept (cf. Fig. 6b). The delta layer is represented by an object which has the same interfaces as the process template object and therefore offers the same operations. As difference between the delta layer object and the template object the delta layer object does not reflect the whole process graph but only those parts of the process template which have been changed by instance-specific modifications. Therefore, together with the template object the delta layer object allows to restore the instance-specific template of biased instances. The instance object which represents a biased instance does no longer reference the associated template object but the delta layer object. The delta layer object itself references the original template object and therefore preserves the assocation between instance and process type. Unchanged instances directly reference the original process template object further on.

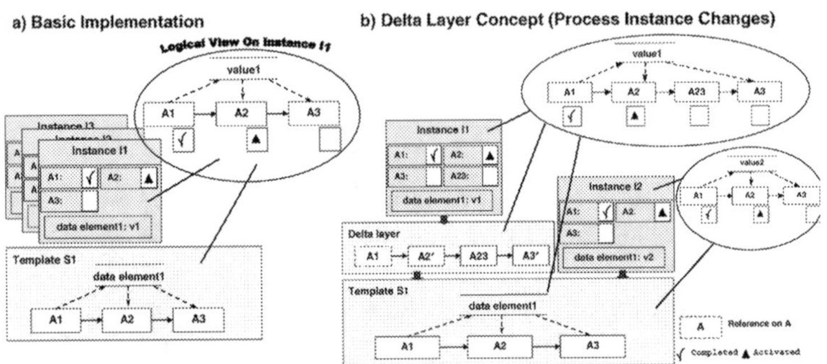

Fig. 6. On Representing Process Template and Process Instance Objects

Fig. 7 depicts how the delta layer concept is realized. As discussed in Sect. 2, at the system level, the (high-level) change operations are translated into change primitives which directly operate on node and edge sets. We represent change information by change log cL and its primitive representation cL^{prim}. The change primitives captured by cL^{purged} are directly stored within the delta layer (e.g., information about added and deleted nodes and edges). For change log cL_{I1}, for example, the set of added nodes and edges as well as the set of deleted edges exactly reflect the "difference" between templates S_{I1} and S'_{I1}.

The "self-purging" effect of storing changes within a delta layer is illustrated by Fig. 8. Change log cL_{I2} contains noise, i.e., information which has to be purged from the change log in order to obtain a "minimal" view on the change effects. Using the delta layer this purging effect is automatically achieved since the change primitives overwrite unnecessary information automatically. For compensating change operations `sInsert(S, xRay, Inform Patient, Prepare Patient)` and `delAct (S, xRay)`, for example, first control edge `(Inform Patient, Prepare Patient)` is removed and re-inserted afterwards such that this change has no effect within the delta layer.

5 Illustrating Example

We illustrate the different concepts presented in this paper by means of an example – a process template evolution with related instance migrations. Consider

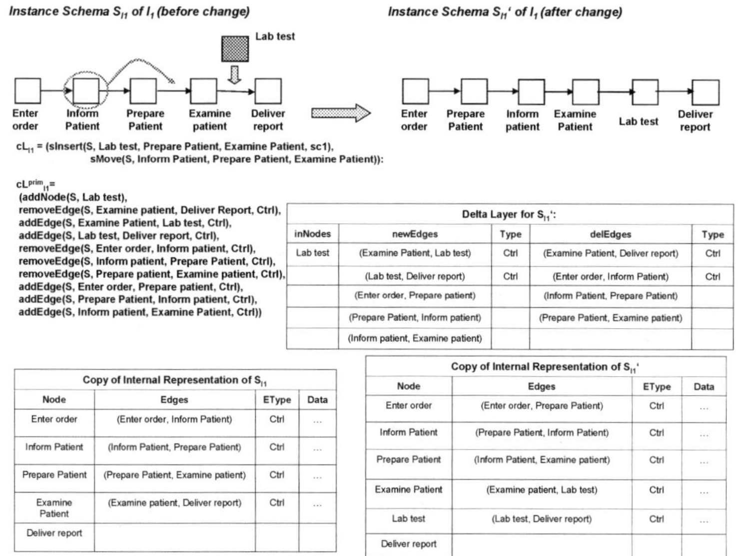
Instance Schema S_{I1} of I_1 (before change)
Instance Schema S_{I1}' of I_1 (after change)
Lab test
Enter order
Inform Patient
Prepare Patient
Examine patient
Deliver report
Enter order
Prepare Patient
Inform patient
Examine Patient
Lab test
Deliver report
cL$_{I1}$ = (sInsert(S, Lab test, Prepare Patient, Examine Patient, sc1),
sMove(S, Inform Patient, Prepare Patient, Examine Patient)):
cL$^{prim}_{I1}$=
(addNode(S, Lab test),
removeEdge(S, Examine patient, Deliver Report, Ctrl),
addEdge(S, Examine Patient, Lab test, Ctrl),
addEdge(S, Lab test, Deliver report, Ctrl),
removeEdge(S, Enter order, Inform patient, Ctrl),
removeEdge(S, Inform patient, Prepare Patient, Ctrl),
removeEdge(S, Prepare patient, Examine patient, Ctrl),
addEdge(S, Enter order, Prepare patient, Ctrl),
addEdge(S, Prepare Patient, Inform patient, Ctrl),
addEdge(S, Inform patient, Examine Patient, Ctrl))

Delta Layer for S_{I1}':

inNodes	newEdges	Type	delEdges	Type
Lab test	(Examine Patient, Lab test)	Ctrl	(Examine Patient, Deliver report)	Ctrl
	(Lab test, Deliver report)	Ctrl	(Enter order, Inform Patient)	Ctrl
	(Enter order, Prepare patient)		(Inform Patient, Prepare Patient)	
	(Prepare Patient, Inform patient)		(Prepare Patient, Examine patient)	
	(Inform patient, Examine patient)			

Copy of Internal Representation of S_{I1}

Node	Edges	EType	Data
Enter order	(Enter order, Inform Patient)	Ctrl	...
Inform Patient	(Inform Patient, Prepare Patient)	Ctrl	...
Prepare Patient	(Prepare Patient, Examine patient)	Ctrl	...
Examine Patient	(Examine patient, Deliver report)	Ctrl	...
Deliver report			

Copy of Internal Representation of S_{I1}'

Node	Edges	EType	Data
Enter order	(Enter order, Prepare Patient)	Ctrl	...
Inform Patient	(Prepare Patient, Inform Patient)	Ctrl	...
Prepare Patient	(Inform Patient, Examine patient)	Ctrl	...
Examine Patient	(Examine patient, Lab test)	Ctrl	...
Lab test	(Lab test, Deliver report)	Ctrl	...
Deliver report			

Fig. 7. Process Instance Changes Stored within Delta Layer

the scenario depicted in Fig. 8: Instances I_1, I_2 and I_3 were derived from process type template S and have been individually modified. For I_1 and I_2 activity `Lab test` was inserted between `Examine patient` and `Deliver report`, and activity `Inform patient` was moved to the position between `Prepare patient` and `Examine patient`. For I_3 activity `Inform patient` was moved to the same position as for I_1 and I_2 but, by contrast, activity `Deliver report` was deleted. The instance changes are captured by the logs cL_{I_1}, cL_{I_2}, and cL_{I_3} where cL_{I_2} contains noisy information. The purged view on cL_{I_2} as well as the primitive representations of all change logs are depicted in Fig. 8 as well.

Taking this scenario assume that the process type template S is modified by inserting activity `Lab test` between activities `Examine patient` and `Deliver report` and by moving activity `Inform patient` to the position between `Prepare patient` and `Examine patient`. The associated change log cL^{T1} and the delta layer for the new template version S' capture these changes. When migrating I_1, I_2, and I_3 to S' (after performing required correctness checks [5]) the delta layers of I_1, I_2, and I_3 are purged by the delta layer of S'. This becomes necessary since the instance delta layers must not capture information about changes which are already reflected by the delta layer of the new template version after their migration. For I_1 and I_2, for example, all instance-specific changes are already captured by the delta layer of S'. Thus the delta layer and the resulting change log based on S' become empty. For I_3 the already captured move operation of `Inform patient` is purged from the delta layer of I_3 on S', but the change primitives reflecting the deletion of activity `Deliver report` are still kept. With this the delta layer of I_3 on S' exactly represents the difference between the instance-specific template of I_3 and S'.

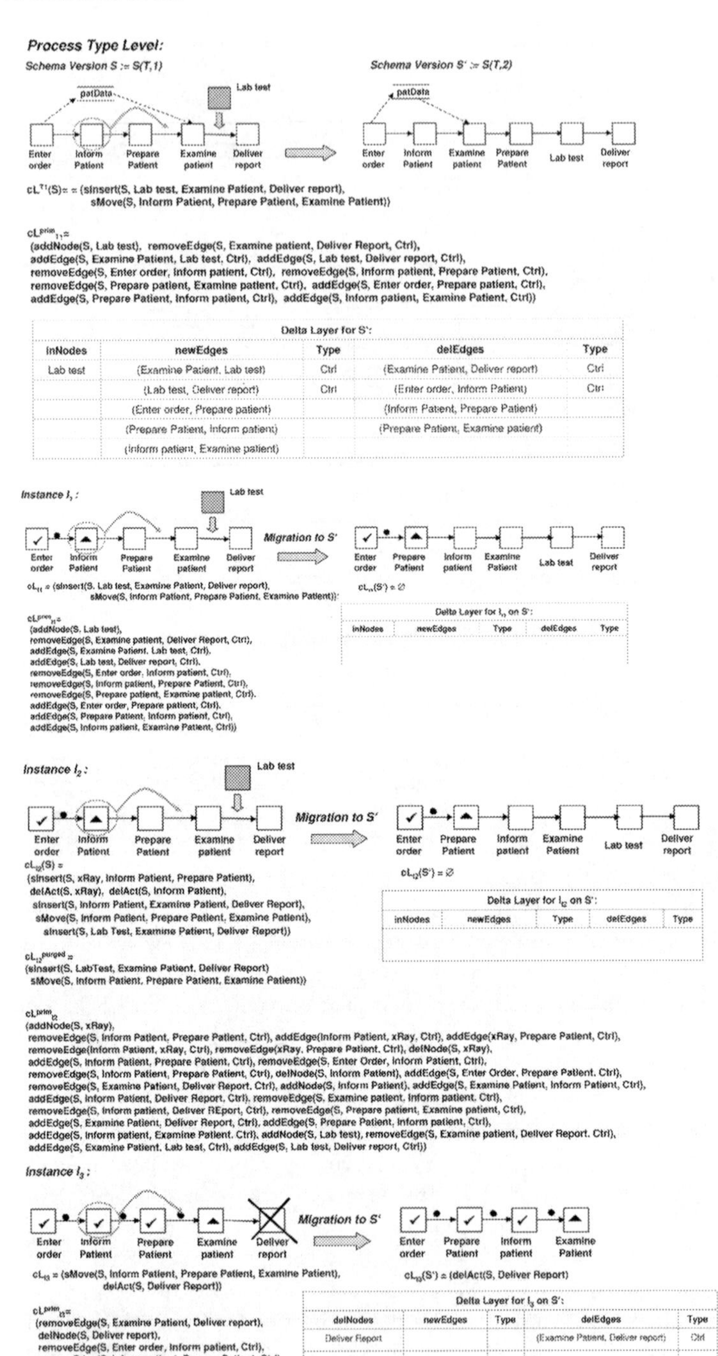

Process Type Level:
Schema Version S := S(T,1)
Schema Version S' := S(T,2)
patData
Lab test
Enter order
Inform Patient
Prepare Patient
Examine patient
Deliver report
Lab test
cL^T1(S)= = (sInsert(S, Lab test, Examine Patient, Deliver report),
sMove(S, Inform Patient, Prepare Patient, Examine Patient))
cL^prim_T1 =
(addNode(S, Lab test), removeEdge(S, Examine patient, Deliver Report, Ctrl),
addEdge(S, Examine Patient, Lab test, Ctrl), addEdge(S, Lab test, Deliver report, Ctrl),
removeEdge(S, Enter order, Inform patient, Ctrl), removeEdge(S, Inform patient, Prepare Patient, Ctrl),
removeEdge(S, Prepare patient, Examine patient, Ctrl), addEdge(S, Enter order, Prepare patient, Ctrl),
addEdge(S, Prepare Patient, Inform patient, Ctrl), addEdge(S, Inform patient, Examine Patient, Ctrl))
Delta Layer for S':
inNodes | newEdges | Type | delEdges | Type
Lab test | (Examine Patient, Lab test) | Ctrl | (Examine Patient, Deliver report) | Ctrl
(Lab test, Deliver report) | Ctrl | (Enter order, Inform Patient) | Ctrl
(Enter order, Prepare patient) | (Inform Patient, Prepare Patient)
(Prepare Patient, Inform patient) | (Prepare Patient, Examine patient)
(Inform patient, Examine patient)
Instance I1 :
Migration to S'
cL_I1 = (sInsert(S, Lab test, Examine Patient, Deliver report),
sMove(S, Inform Patient, Prepare Patient, Examine Patient)):
cL_I1(S') = ∅
cL^prim_I1 =
(addNode(S, Lab test),
removeEdge(S, Examine patient, Deliver Report, Ctrl),
addEdge(S, Examine Patient, Lab test, Ctrl),
addEdge(S, Lab test, Deliver report, Ctrl),
removeEdge(S, Enter order, Inform patient, Ctrl),
removeEdge(S, Inform patient, Prepare Patient, Ctrl),
removeEdge(S, Prepare patient, Examine patient, Ctrl),
addEdge(S, Enter order, Prepare patient, Ctrl),
addEdge(S, Prepare Patient, Inform patient, Ctrl),
addEdge(S, Inform patient, Examine Patient, Ctrl))
Delta Layer for I1 on S':
inNodes | newEdges | Type | delEdges | Type
Instance I2 :
Migration to S'
cL_I2(S) =
(sInsert(S, xRay, Inform Patient, Prepare Patient),
delAct(S, xRay), delAct(S, Inform Patient),
sInsert(S, Inform Patient, Examine Patient, Deliver Report),
sMove(S, Inform Patient, Prepare Patient, Examine Patient),
sInsert(S, Lab Test, Examine Patient, Deliver Report))
cL_I2(S') = ∅
Delta Layer for I2 on S':
inNodes | newEdges | Type | delEdges | Type
cL_I2^purged =
(sInsert(S, LabTest, Examine Patient, Deliver Report)
sMove(S, Inform Patient, Prepare Patient, Examine Patient))
cL^prim_I2
(addNode(S, xRay),
removeEdge(S, Inform Patient, Prepare Patient, Ctrl), addEdge(Inform Patient, xRay, Ctrl), addEdge(xRay, Prepare Patient, Ctrl),
removeEdge(Inform Patient, xRay, Ctrl), removeEdge(xRay, Prepare Patient, Ctrl), delNode(S, xRay),
addEdge(S, Inform Patient, Prepare Patient, Ctrl), removeEdge(S, Enter Order, Inform Patient, Ctrl),
removeEdge(S, Inform Patient, Prepare Patient, Ctrl), delNode(S, Inform Patient), addEdge(S, Enter Order, Prepare Patient, Ctrl),
removeEdge(S, Examine Patient, Deliver Report, Ctrl), addNode(S, Inform Patient), addEdge(S, Examine Patient, Inform Patient, Ctrl),
addEdge(S, Inform Patient, Deliver Report, Ctrl), removeEdge(S, Examine patient, Inform patient, Ctrl),
removeEdge(S, Inform patient, Deliver REport, Ctrl), removeEdge(S, Prepare patient, Examine patient, Ctrl),
addEdge(S, Examine Patient, Deliver Report, Ctrl), addEdge(S, Prepare Patient, Inform patient, Ctrl),
addEdge(S, Inform patient, Examine Patient, Ctrl), addNode(S, Lab test), removeEdge(S, Examine patient, Deliver Report, Ctrl),
addEdge(S, Examine Patient, Lab test, Ctrl), addEdge(S, Lab test, Deliver report, Ctrl))
Instance I3 :
Migration to S'
cL_I3 = (sMove(S, Inform Patient, Prepare Patient, Examine Patient),
delAct(S, Deliver Report))
cL_I3(S') = (delAct(S, Deliver Report)
cL^prim_I3 =
(removeEdge(S, Examine Patient, Deliver report),
delNode(S, Deliver report),
removeEdge(S, Enter order, Inform patient, Ctrl),
removeEdge(S, Inform patient, Prepare Patient, Ctrl),
removeEdge(S, Prepare patient, Examine patient, Ctrl),
addEdge(S, Enter order, Prepare patient, Ctrl),
addEdge(S, Prepare Patient, Inform patient, Ctrl),
addEdge(S, Inform patient, Examine Patient, Ctrl))
Delta Layer for I3 on S':
delNodes | newEdges | Type | delEdges | Type
Deliver Report | (Examine Patient, Deliver report) | Ctrl

Fig. 8. Process Template Evolution (Example)

Altogether, the change log management illustrated by this example meets all imposed requirements. The applied changes are still traceable at type and instance level due to the full change logs being kept (e.g., change log for I_2). The purged view on, for example, change log cL_{I_2} may be helpful for reusing the change operation. At the system level, the delta layers provide the information necessary for restoring instance-specific templates at any point in time. Furthermore, they constitue the basis for checks (e.g., regarding possible overlaps between changes) and for correctly determining the resulting delta layers and instance-specific changes after instance migration.

6 Related Work

As discussed the management of log information plays an important role in different areas. Examples are recovery in DBMS or data analyses in the context of data mining [1], online analytical processing [2], and process mining [3]. For process mining a meta model representation for execution logs based on MXML format has been developed [13]. In particular, for OLAP and process mining views on logs are built as well (e.g., by clustering [1] or filtering [14]). However, none of these approaches has dealt with change logs so far. Therefore the framework for change log management presented in this paper can be used as basis for an optimized mining of advanced aspects in adaptive PMS (e.g., change mining).

In general, adaptivity in PMS has been a hot topic in literature for many years. Most approaches have focussed on process instance or process type changes and related correctness issues [6,4]. Some approaches have also dealt with both kinds of changes in one system [7,5,8]. However, the representation and organization of the changes themselves has been left pretty vague so far. The approach presented in this paper is complementary to this work.

There are only few approaches dealing with an efficient implementation of advanced process management functionality, [15,7]. So far, they have neglected issues related to change log management. The functionality of existing prototypes are mostly restricted to buildtime and runtime simulations. Using such simulations it can be shown that the particular functionality is realized in principle, but not how it can be implemented in a performant way in practice. Our ADEPT system is one of the very few available research prototypes for adaptive, high-performance process management [12].

7 Summary and Outlook

We have presented an approach for the management of change logs in PMS facing requirements of different uses cases. In order to meet these requirements we have distinguished between the representation of change information at the user and the system level (high-level operations vs. primitives). Based on this we have defined change primitives and operations as well as change transactions. A special view on change logs, the so called purged change logs, has been introduced in order to present the actual change effects to users (e.g., for reuse purposes). For the system level, we have presented the counterpart based on change primitives stored within a delta layer. An example on correctness checks in the context of process template evolution and individually modified process instances has illustrated the presented concepts.

In future we want to use our change management approach for advanced application scenarios. One example is the mining of change logs in order to, for example, derive process type changes from process instance logs. Furthermore, the presented results are to be transferred to other types of change logs (e.g., logs capturing information on changes of organizational models [16]) as well. Finally we intend to formalize our approach to derive change logs from delta layer information which can be used, for example, to calculate differences between changes. This is necessary, for example, to store correct instance-specific changes after migration to a changed process type template.

References

1. Han, J., Kamber, M.: Data Mining: Concepts and Techniques. Academic Press (2001)
2. Bauer, A., Günzel, H.: Data Warehouse Systems. dpunkt (2004)
3. v.d. Aalst, W., van Dongen, B., Herbst, J., Maruster, L., Schimm, G., Weijters, A.: Workflow mining: A survey of issues and approaches. DKE **27** (2003) 237–267
4. Casati, F., Ceri, S., Pernici, B., Pozzi, G.: Workflow evolution. DKE **24** (1998) 211–238
5. Rinderle, S., Reichert, M., Dadam, P.: Flexible support of team processes by adaptive workflow systems. Distributed and Parallel Databases **16** (2004) 91–116
6. v.d. Aalst, W., Basten, T.: Inheritance of workflows: An approach to tackling problems related to change. Theoret. Comp. Science **270** (2002) 125–203
7. Kochut, K., Arnold, J., Sheth, A., Miller, J., Kraemer, E., Arpinar, B., Cardoso, J.: IntelliGEN: A distributed workflow system for discovering protein-protein interactions. DPD **13** (2003) 43–72
8. Weske, M.: Formal foundation and conceptual design of dynamic adaptations in a workflow management system. In: HICSS-34. (2001)
9. Rinderle, S.: Schema Evolution in Process Management Systems. PhD thesis, University of Ulm (2004)
10. Reichert, M., Dadam, P.: ADEPT$_{flex}$ - supporting dynamic changes of workflows without losing control. JIIS **10** (1998) 93–129
11. Leymann, F., Altenhuber, W.: Managing business processes as an information ressource. IBM Systems Journal **33** (1994) 326–348
12. Reichert, M., Rinderle, S., Kreher, U., Dadam, P.: Adaptive process management with ADEPT2. In: ICDE'05. (2005) 1113–1114
13. van Dongen, B., van der Aalst, W.: A meta model for process mining data. In: CAiSE'05 Workshops. (2005) 309–320
14. van Dongen, B., de Medeiros, A., Verbeek, H., Weijters, A., van der Aalst, W.: The ProM framework: A new era in process mining tool support. In: ICATPN'05. (2005) 444–454
15. Weske, M.: Object-oriented design of a flexible workflow management system. In: ADBIS98. (1998) 119–131
16. Rinderle, S., Reichert, M.: On the controlled evolution of access rules in cooperative information systems. In: CoopIS'05. (2005) 238–255

Towards Formal Verification of Web Service Composition

Mohsen Rouached, Olivier Perrin, and Claude Godart

LORIA-INRIA-UMR 7503
BP 239, F-54506 Vandœuvre-les-Nancy Cedex, France
{mohsen.rouached, olivier.perrin, claude.godart}@loria.fr

Abstract. Web services composition is an emerging paradigm for enabling application integration within and across organizational boundaries. Current Web services composition proposals, such as BPML, WS-BPEL, WSCI, and OWL-S, provide solutions for describing the control and data flows in Web service composition. However, such proposals remain at the descriptive level, without providing any kind of mechanisms or tool support for analysis and verification. Therefore, there is a growing interest for the verification techniques which enable designers to test and repair design errors even before actual running of the service, or allow designers to detect erroneous properties and formally verify whether the service process design does have certain desired properties.

In this paper, we propose to verify Web services composition using an event driven approach. We assume Web services that are coordinated by a composition process expressed in WSBPEL and we use Event Calculus to specify the properties and requirements to be monitored.

1 Introduction

In 2001, Gartner defined Business Process Management as *a general term describing a set of services and tools that provide for explicit process management (e.g. process modeling, analysis, simulation, execution, monitoring and administration), ideally including support for human and application-level interaction.* Five years later, Service Oriented Architectures (SOA) seems to be a key architecture to support BPM. With SOA, an application can be now considered as a composition of services, Workflow Management Systems (WfMSs), or legacy applications. Thus, a business process becomes a set of composed services that are shared across business units, organizations, or outsourced to partners.

Currently many products that offer modeling, analysis, and simulation facilities for business processes exist. However, one of the great advantages offered by the coupling of BPM and SOA is that designers can not only model, analyze, simulate, but they can also use the result directly for deployment, using WS-BPEL for instance. Functions at the modeling layer can be linked to required services at the architecture level, and engines can now manage the resulting business process. This is a great improvement, and it clearly shows that BPM over SOA can add value over traditional WfMSs for instance. However, there are many challenges for trully realizing BPM over SOA.

S. Dustdar, J.L. Fiadeiro, and A. Sheth (Eds.): BPM 2006, LNCS 4102, pp. 257–273, 2006.

A first challenge deals with the ability to offer self-management of the designed processes [18]. This is an important topic since these processes are quite complex and dynamic, and deviations from the expected behavior may be highly desirable. In fact, one may want to adapt the process due to changes in the way the process is actually used, as it sometimes exists a gap between the designed process and the observed behavior. Then, once a deviation is found, it is important to dynamically adapt either the process, either the services that render the functions of the process. For that, it is important to collect information about business process activities, and to modify the process (at the design layer) and/or the services used by the process (at the execution layer). A second challenge is the need for checking the consistency of the process. This can be done either statically, i.e. at design time, or dynamically, i.e. at runtime. For the static part of the work, we should be able to express the business process using a formalism on which we can reason on. As business processes are quite huge and complex, proving the correctness of the composed business process is not an easy task, and it is hard to find their potential bottlenecks: livelocks, deadlocks, unused activities, inaccurate activities, inaccurate flows, inaccurate wiring between functions in the model and services in the SOA, etc. For the dynamic part of the verification, the business process should be auditable. For that, we can use process mining techniques, because processes (and their associated services) leave many traces of their behavior in the underlying systems they used to be executed. In our approach, we use mining techniques not for discovery but for dynamic verification of the execution of the process, i.e. requirements associated with the process. The verification deals with two kind of requirements: the functional requirements, and the non-functional requirements, such as security for instance.

In this paper, we propose an event-based approach for checking consistency of a business process, for mining the business process events, and for analyzing the process execution. It appears that using events is very attractive when compared to other approaches, as stated in [18]. Main advantages are: (i) business processes leave their business events in so-called event logs,(ii) it exists various works for checking event-based specifications consistency. Our proposition provides a formal framework for modeling and checking the consistency of WSBPEL compositions. We use the Event Calculus (EC) of Kowalski and Sergot [7], and an extension proposed by Mueller on Discrete EC [12]. Compared to other works, the choice of EC is motivated by both practical and formal needs, and it gives three major advantages. First, in contrast to pure state-transition representations, the EC ontology includes an explicit time structure that is independent of any (sequence of) events under consideration. This helps for managing event-based systems where a number of input events may occur simultaneously (risk of non-deterministic behavior [11]). Second, the EC ontology is close enough to the WSBPEL specification to allow it to be mapped automatically into the logical representation. Thus, we use the same logical foundation for verification at both design time (static analysis) and runtime (dynamic analysis). Third, the semantics of non-functional requirements can be represented in EC, so that verification is once again straightforward.

The paper is structured as follows. Section 2 introduces a scenario used to illustrate our approach. Section 3 rapidly presents WSBPEL and EC, and describes how to transform WSBPEL into EC. Section 4 studies the EC checking and indicates how the proposed formalism can verify and detect some examples of inconsistencies that may arise in the running scenario. The related work is discussed in Section 5, and Section 6 concludes and outlines future directions.

2 Case Study

Throughout this article, we will illustrate our ideas using a running example of Web services composition. We consider a car rental scenario that involves four services. A Car Broker Service (CBS) acts as a broker offering its customers the ability to rent cars provided by different car rental companies directly from car parks at different locations. CBS is implemented as a service composition process which interacts with Car Information Services (CIS), and Customer Management Service (CMS). CIS services are provided by different car rental companies and maintain databases of cars, check their availability and allocate cars to customers as requested by CBS. CMS maintains the database of the customers and authenticates customers as requested by CBS. Each Car Park (CP) also provides a Car Sensor Service (CSS) that senses cars as they are driven in or out of car parks and inform CBS accordingly. The end users can access CBS through a User Interaction Service (UIS). Typically, CBS receives car rental requests from UIS services, authorizes customers contacting CMS and checks for the availability of cars by contacting CIS services, and gets car movement information from CSS services. However, due to the autonomous nature of services and the run-time monitoring of requirements, many complications may arise. For example, CBS can accept a car rental request and allocate a specific car to it if, due to the malfunctioning of a CSS service, the departure of the relevant car from a car park has not been reported and, as a consequence, the car is considered to be available by the UIS service. Through this example, we aim to demonstrate how Web services interactions can be specified and formalized using events, and how this specification could facilitate their monitoring at run-time.

3 Transforming BPEL into Event Calculus

3.1 Overview of BPEL

WSBPEL [1] introduces a stateful model of Web services interacting by exchanging sequences of messages between business partners. The major parts of a BPEL process definition consist of (1) partners of the business process (Web services that the process interacts with), (2) a set of variables that keep the state of the process, and (3) an activity defining the logic behind the interactions between the process and its partners. Activities that can be performed are categorized into *basic*, *structured*, and *scope-related* activities. Basic activities perform simple operations like receive, reply, invoke and others. Structured activities impose an execution order on a collection of activities and can be nested. Then, scope-related activities enable defining logical units of work and delineating the reversible behavior of each unit. Below, we describe the main activities (basic and structured).

Basic Activities. Basic activities in a WSBPEL process support primitive functions (e.g. invocation of operations and assignments of variable values):

(i) the *invoke* activity calls an operation in one of the partner services of the composition process.
(ii) the *receive* activity makes the composition process to wait for the receipt of an invocation of its operations by some of its partner services.
(iii) the *reply* activity makes the composition process to respond to a request for the execution of an operation previously accepted through a receive activity.
(iv) the *assign* activity is used to copy the value from a variable to another one.
(v) the *throw* activity is used to signal an internal fault.
(vi) the *wait* activity is used to specify a delay in the process that must last for a certain period of time.

Structured Activities. Structured activities provide the control and data flow structures that enable the composition of basic activities into a business process:

(i) the *sequence* activity includes an ordered list of other activities that must be performed sequentially in the exact order of their listing.
(ii) the *switch* activity includes an ordered list of one or more conditional branches that include other activities and may be executed subject to the satisfiability of the conditions associated with them.
(iii) the *flow* activity includes a set of two or more activities that should be executed concurrently. A flow activity completes when all these activities have completed.
(iv) the *pick* activity makes a composition process to wait for different events (expressed by onMessage elements) and perform activities associated with each of these events as soon as it occurs.
(v) the *while* activity is used to specify iterative occurrence of one or more activities as long some condition holds true.

3.2 Event Calculus

The Event Calculus [7] is a temporal formalism designed to model and reason about scenarios characterized by a set of events, whose occurrences have the effect of starting or terminating the validity of determined properties. Given a (possibly incomplete) description of when events take place and a description of the properties they affect, EC is able to determine the maximal validity intervals over which a property holds uninterruptedly. The reasoning is based upon the hypothesis that all changes must be due to a cause, and properties of the world can only change at particular time points when events happen.

Language. The ontology of the event calculus comprises *fluents*, *events* (or actions) and *timepoints*. Events are the fundamental concept that brings about changes to the world. Any property of the world that can change over time is known as a fluent. A fluent is a function of the timepoint. The Event Calculus uses predicates to specify actions and their effects. Then, the following predicates define fluents' initiation, state, and termination, and events happening:

- $HoldsAt(f, t)$ is true iff fluent f holds at timepoint t.
- $Happens(a, t)$ is true iff action a happens at timepoint t.
- $Initiates(a, f, t)$ expresses that fluent f holds after timepoint t if action a happens at t.
- $Terminates(a, f, t)$ expresses that fluent f does not hold after timepoint t if action a happens at t.
- $InitiallyTrue(f)|InitiallyFalse(f)$ define if f holds or not at timepoint 0.

Axiomatics. The four axioms below capture the behavior of fluents once intiated or terminated by an action.

- $Clipped(t1, f, t2) \longleftarrow Happens(a, t1) \wedge (t1 \leq t < t2) \wedge Terminates(f, t2)$
- $Declipped(t1, f, t2) \longleftarrow Happens(a, t1) \wedge (t1 \leq t < t2) \wedge Initiates(f, t2)$
- $HoldsAt(f, t2) \longleftarrow Happens(a, t1) \wedge Initiates(a, f, t1) \wedge (t1 < t2) \wedge \neg Clipped(t1, f, t2)$
- $\neg HoldsAt(f, t2) \longleftarrow Happens(a, t1) \wedge Terminates(a, f, t1) \wedge (t1 < t2) \wedge \neg Declipped(t1, f, t2)$

Clipped expresses if fluent f was terminated during time interval $[t1, t2[$. Similarly, *Declipped* expresses if fluent f was initiated during time interval $[t1, t2[$. Fluents which have been initiated by event continue to hold until it occurs an event which terminates them ($HoldsAt$). Similarly, fluents which have been terminated by an event continue not to hold until an event which initiates them.

Then, we need to describe fluents' behavior before the occurrence of any actions which affect them:

- $HoldsAt(f, t) \longleftarrow InitiallyTrue(f) \wedge \neg Clipped(0, f, t)$
- $\neg HoldsAt(f, t) \longleftarrow InitiallyFalse(f) \wedge \neg Declipped(0, f, t)$
- $InitiallyTrue(f)|InitiallyFalse(f)$

Using these predicates, a fragment of the event log of the car rental scenario introduced in Section 2 is shown in Figure 1. Variables loc_i, veh_i, and car_i represent respectively the park number, the car number, and the customer identifier.

3.3 Our Approach: BPEL2EC

We now focus on how to transform WSBPEL activities into EC formulas in order to formally specify services behavior and therefore facilitate their analysis and verification.

L1 : $Happens(CSS.Enter(op1), 1)$
L2 : $InitiatesCSS.Enter(op1), equalTo(v1, veh1), 1)$
L3 : $Initiates(CSS.Enter(op1), equalTo(p1, loc1), 1)$
L4 : $Happens(CSS.Enter(op2), 27)$
L5 : $Initiates(CSS.Enter(op2), equalTo(v1, veh1), 27)$
L6 : $Initiates(CSS.Enter(op2), equalTo(p1, loc3), 27)$
L7 : $Happens(UIS.RelKey(op3, veh2), 28)$
L8 : $Happens(UIS.RelKey(op3), 29)$
L9 : $Happens(UIS.CarRequest(op4), 49)$
L10: $Initiates(UIS.CarRequest(op4), equalTo(p, loc2), 49)$
L11: $Happens(CIS.FindAvailable(op5, loc2), 50)$
L12: $Happens(CIS.FindAvailable(op5), 51)$
L13: $Initiates(CIS.FindAvailable(op5), equalTo(Res, veh2), 51)$
L14: $Happens(UIS.CarHire(op6, veh2, loc2), 52)$
L15: $Happens(CSS.Enter(op7), 53)$
L16: $Initiates(CSS.Enter(op7), equalTo(v1, veh2), 53)$
L17: $Initiates(CSS.Enter(op7), equalTo(p1, loc4), 53)$
L18: $Happens(UIS.RetKey(op8), 54)$
L19: $Initiates(UIS.RetKey(op8), equalTo(v, veh2), 54)$
L20: $Happens(UIS.CarRequest(op9), 69)$

Fig. 1. The CRS Event Log

Mapping of Basic Activities. Basic WSBPEL activities are transformed into their EC counterparts according to the transformations shown in Figure 2.

The EC representation of an *invoke* activity that calls an operation O in a service P consists of a literal such that it exists an event of calling O (i.e., $inv{:}P.O(vID, vX)$) and an event notifying the reception of the execution of O by the service composition (i.e., $rec{:}P.O(vID)$). The variable vID takes as value a unique identifier that represents the exact instance of the operation invocation and the variable vX takes the value that the input variable X of O has at the time of the invocation. The value of the output variable Y of O is represented by the fluent $equalTo$[1](Y, vY) initiated by the $Initiates$ predicate.

The EC representation of a *receive* activity in a service P that receives an invocation of its operation O by other partner service consists of a literal such that it exists an event of receipt of an invocation of O (i.e. $rec{:}P.O(vID)$), where the variable vID represents the exact instance of the operation invocation by other partner. The value of the variable X of O on message receipt is represented by the fluent $equalTo(X, vX)$ initiated by the $Initiates$ predicate.

A *reply* activity in a service P that respond to a previously accepted request for the execution of the operation O is represented in EC using a literal such that it exists the completion of the execution of O (i.e. $rep{:}P.O(vID, vX)$), where the variable vID represents the exact instance of the operation invocation and the variable vX represents the value of the output variable X of O.

[1] The fluent $equalTo(VarName, val)$ signifies that value of $VarName$ is equal to val.

Sample BPEL Code	Sample EC Specification
<invoke partnerLink="P" portType= "a:Pport" operation= "O" inputVariable= "X" outputVariable= "Y"/>	$Happens(\text{inv}{:}P.O(vID,vX),t1)\wedge(\exists t2)$ $Happens(\text{rec}{:}P.O(vID),t2)\wedge(t1\leq t2)\wedge$ $Initiates(\text{rec}{:}P.O(vID),equalTo(Y,),t2)$
<receive partnerLink="P" portType= "a:Pport" operation="O" variable="X"/>	$Happens(\text{rec}{:}P.O(vID),t)\wedge Initiates(\text{rec}{:}$ $P.O(vID),equalTo(X,vXc),t)$
<reply partner="P" portType = "a:Pport" operation= "O" variable="X"/>	$Happens(\text{rep}{:}P.O(vID,vX),t)\wedge Happens$ $(\text{rec}{:}P.O(vID,vX),t1)\wedge(t1<t)$
<assign name ="A"> <copy><from variable ="X" part="a"/> <to variable="Y" part="b"/> </copy> </assign>	$Happens(\text{as}{:}A(vID),t1)\wedge(\exists t2)(t1<t2)\wedge$ $Initiates(\text{as}{:}A(vID),equalTo(Y.b,vX.a),$ $t2)$
<actType name="A">...</actType> <wait for = "T"/> <actType name="B">...</actType>	$EC(A,\mathcal{T})\wedge EC(B,\mathcal{T})\wedge max_t(A)<$ $(min_t(A)-T)$
<throw faultName="faultname" faultVariable="X"/>	$Happens(th:faultname(vID,vX),t)$

Fig. 2. Mapping of Basic activities

Then, the EC representation of a *throw* activity that signals internal fault $faultName$ in a service P consists of a literal such that it exists a throwing event, (i.e. $th{:}faultName(vID,vX)$), where the variable vID represents the exact instance of the *throw* activity and the variable vX represents the value of the $faultVariable$ being thrown.

Mapping of Structured Activities. After transforming the basic activities, it is also important to specify their temporal relationships. That is the case for the *sequence* and the *flow* constructs. The translation scheme of the EC formulas for the *squence* and *switch* activities is given in Figure 3.

In these patterns, (i) actType can be any type of a basic or structured WS-BPEL activity; (ii) EC(A,$\mathcal{T}$) represents the EC formulas where A is an activity and $\mathcal{T}$ a temporal domain (we use an ordered set ($\mathbb{T}$,$\prec$), and the natural numbers $\mathbb{N}$ with their usual ordering); (iii) $min_t(A)$ represents the time variable of the earliest predicate in the formulas of activity A (i.e., the predicate that is expected to occur the first given the constraints between the time variables of the predicates representing A), and (iv) $max_t(B)$ represents the time variable

Sample BPEL Code	Sample EC Specification
<sequence> <actType name="A"> ... </actType> <pick> <onMessage partner="P" portType= "a:Pport" operation="O" variable="X"> <actType name="B">...</actType> </onMessage> <onAlarm for="T"> <actType name="C">...</actType> </onAlarm> </pick> </sequence>	$EC(A,T) \wedge Happens(\text{om:}O(vID,vX),t2) \wedge (max_t(A) \leq \text{t2} \leq (max_t(A)+\text{T})) \wedge Initiates(\text{om:}O(vID,vX), equalTo(X,vX),t2) \Longrightarrow EC(B,[min_t(B)]) \wedge t1 < min_t(B)$ $EC(A,T) \wedge \neg Happens(\text{om:}O(vID,vX),t2) \wedge (max_t(A) \leq \text{t2} \leq (max_t(A)+\text{T})) \Longrightarrow \text{EC}(C,[min_t(C)]) \wedge max_t(A)+\text{T} < min_t(C)$
<switch> <case condition=" P=v1"> <actType name="A">...</actType> </case> <otherwise> <actType name="C">...</actType> </otherwise> </switch>	$HoldsAt(equalTo(P,v1),t1) \Longrightarrow \text{EC}(A,[min_t(A)]) \wedge (t1 < min_t(A))$ $\neg HoldsAt(equalTo(P,v1),t1) \Longrightarrow \text{EC}(C,[min_t(C)]) \wedge \text{t2} < min_t(C)$

Fig. 3. Mapping of *pick* and *switch* activities

of the latest predicate in the formulas of activity B (i.e., the predicate that is expected to occur the lastest given the constraints between the time variables of the predicates representing B). The rest of the transformations are analogous to the transformation of *switch* and *pick* activities, and are presented in Figure 4.

Let us now give an example of EC formulas extracted according to the above patterns. We show an extract of the WSBPEL specification of the car rental scenario introduced in section 2, and the EC formula extracted from it. This fragment refers to the part of process that receives a request for a car and checks for available cars. It is presented in Figure 5.

The first implication in the EC formula represents the link $rec-to-auth$ in the flow activity of the process. Conditions of this implication represent the receive activity *receiveRequest*, and its consequence represents the sequence activity in the process. The second implication represents the ordering of the constituent activities of the *sequence* activity: its conditions represent the *assign* activity $a1$ and its consequence represents the *invoke* of activity $findCar$.

4 EC Checking

In the previous section, we showed how to translate the WSBPEL constructs into their Event Calculus predicates counterparts. The objective of this section is to show how we offer reasoning about a WSBPEL process represented as a set

Sample BPEL Code	Sample EC Specification
<sequence> <actType name="A">...</actType> <actType name="B"> ...</actType> </sequence>	$EC(A,T) \Longrightarrow EC(B,T) \wedge max_t(A) < min_t(B)$
<while condition="P=v1"> <actType name="A">... </actType> </while>	$HoldsAt(equalTo(P,v1),t1) \Longrightarrow EC(A,[min_t(A)]) \wedge t1 < min_t(A)$
<flow> <links> <link name="AtoB"/> <link name="AtoC"/> ... </links> <actType name="A"> <source linkName="AtoB" transitionCondition="P=v1"/> <source linkName="AtoC" /> ... <actType name="B"> <target linkName="AtoB" /> ... <actType name="C"> <target linkName="AtoC" /> ... </flow>	$EC(A,T) \wedge HoldsAt(equalTo(P,v1),t1) \wedge max_t(A) < t2 \Longrightarrow EC(B,[min_t(B)]) \wedge t2 < min_t(B)$ $EC(A,T) \Longrightarrow EC(C,[min_t(c)]) \wedge max_t(A) < min_t(C)$

Fig. 4. Mapping of Structured activities

of EC predicates in order to check its consistency in three cases: the first case is a static check, before running the process, the second case is at runtime, and the third case is the ability to check the process execution against non-functional requirements.

4.1 Static Verification

The need for static verification is important for composite processes which coordinate a set of autonomous Web services because these processes can be very complex processes, and that we need to check if a WSBPEL process is consistent, which is not a trivial task as soon as a WSBPEL process manages concurrency, distribution and long-duration activities. Transforming WSBPEL constructs into EC predicates gives the opportunity to model-check such a process, with respect to temporal constraints, and to verify that processes satisfy certain properties.

For instance, let us suppose a process including a flow construct. This construct allows to specify one or more activities to be performed concurrently. The EC specification on this construct is given in Figure 4. Once it is rewritten using EC predicates, we propose a solution for verifying a WSBPEL process instance against its temporal constraints. For instance, we can express that, given a sequence of two services, the second service will be executed only once the first one is completed (see Figure 3 for the EC specification of WSBPEL sequence). This very basic example shows that it is possible to formally check the control flow of

Part of WSBPEL composition process for CRS

```
<process name="CRS">
<partners> ... </partners>
 <flow>
 <links>
 <link name="rec-to-auth"/>
 </links>
 <receive name="receiveRequest"
  partner="UIS"
  portType="sns:UISPT"
  operation="CarRequest"
  variable="Req"
  createInstance="yes">
<sourcelinkName="rec-to-auth"/>
<sequence>
<target linkName="rec-to-auth"/>
<assign name="a1">
<copy><from variable="Req" part="Loc"/>
<to variable="Q" part="Loc"/>
</copy>
</assign>
<invoke name="findCar"
 partner="CIS"
 portType="crns:CISPT"
 operation="FindAvailable"
 inputVariable="Q"
 outputVariable="Res"/>
</sequence>
</flow>
</process>
```

EC formulas

$Happens(\text{rec:}UIS.CarRequest(oID1), t1) \wedge Initiates(\text{rec:}UIS.CarRequest(oID1),$
$\text{equalTo } (Req.Loc, vReq.Loc), t1) \wedge Initiates(\text{rec:}UIS.CarRequest(oID1),$
$equalTo(Req.CId, vReq.CId), t1) \Longrightarrow$
$(\exists \text{t2})(\text{t1}<\text{t2}) \wedge Happens(\text{as:}a1(aID), t2) \wedge (\exists t3)(\text{t2}<\text{t3}) \wedge Initiates(\text{as:}a1(aID),$
$equalTo(Q.Loc, vReq.loc), t3) \Longrightarrow$
$(\exists \text{t4}) Happens(\text{inv:}CIS.FindAvailable(oID2, vQ), t4) \wedge (t3 \leq \text{t4}) \wedge (\exists \text{t5})$
$Happens(\text{rec:}CIS.FindAvailable(oID2, vQ), t5) \wedge (\text{t4} \leq \text{t5}) \wedge Initiates(\text{rec:}CIS.$
$FindAvailable(oID2, vQ), equalTo(Res, vRes), t5))$

Fig. 5. Example of EC formulas extracted from the WSBPEL process for CRS

a WSBPEL process (and the interactions between the Web services) using the EC predicates, and this offers the ability to discover the potential flaws of such a process such as livelocks, deadlocks, or unused branches in the control flow.

4.2 Dynamic Verification

A second aspect of verification is the runtime verification. This kind of verification is welcome since some interactions between Web services that constitute a process may be dynamically specified at runtime, causing unpredictable interactions with other services, and making the previous verification method (static) unusable. This dynamic behavior can not be model-checked, but it remains important to be sure that the execution of the process remains consistent. This is the reason why we offer the possibility to verify a process at runtime. As the verification occurs in real-time, it becomes possible to handle deviations wrt. the observed behavior of the process. To provide this verification, we use logical predicates (as in the previous method), but we compare these predicates with the events that occur and are recorded during the process execution. When one or several predicates are unsatisfied, this means that something wrong occurs in the execution, and it is possible to exactly point out what happens.

For instance, in our example, the CSS and the CIS services won't be owned by the owner of CBS. Moreover, new instances of the CSS and CIS services may be deployed when new car rental companies and car parks make their offerings available to the CBS, and existing instances may be withdrawn when companies and car parks stop their collaboration with CBS. When such conditions occur, services monitoring has to be based on events and state information that can be reasonably assumed to be in the ownership of the service provider and is fixed at runtime. Requirements for individual services are still to be specified and monitored but only if this is possible through events that are known to the composition process, or events that can be derived from them.

4.3 Non-functional Requirements Verification

Another interest is the ability to model non-functional requirements using the EC, and to check a process against these properties. Let us consider an example on policies (security policies for instance). We consider a WSBPEL process that expect to enforce some high-level authorization policies. The specifications of these authorization policies are separated from the process code, and they should be carefully audited. Using the EC, we are able to formalize these policies by embedding logical predicates, and to check if a process complies with the policies.

4.4 Example

Let us suppose the following CRS requirements, represented as rules.

R1) The rule R1 expresses an assumption about the behavior of the CSS sensoring services: $(\forall t1, t2) Happens(inv : CSS.Enter(oID1), t1) \wedge Initiates (inv : CSS.Enter(oID1), equalTo(v1, vID), t1) \wedge Initiates(inv : CSS.Enter (oID1), equalTo(p1, pID1), t1) \wedge Happens(inv : CSS.Enter(oID2), t2) \wedge (t1 + {t_m}^2 \leq t2) \wedge Initiates(inv : CSS.Enter(oID2), equalTo(v2, vID), t2) \wedge Initiates(inv : CSS.Enter(oID2), equalTo(p2, pID2), t2) \Longrightarrow (\exists t3) Happens(inv : CSS.Depart(oID3), t3) \wedge (t1 + t_m \leq t3 \leq t2 - t_m) \wedge Initiates (inv : CSS.Depart(oID3), equalTo(v3, vID), t3) \wedge Initiates(inv : CSS. Depart(oID3), equalTo(p3, pID1), t3)$.

According to this rule, if a car vID is sensed to enter a car park $pID1$ at time $t1$ and later, at time $t2$, the same car is sensed to enter the same or a different car park, then a *Depart* event (signifying the departure of vID from $pID1$) must have also occurred between the two *enter* events. The *Happens* predicates in R1 represent the invocation of the operations *Enter* and *Depart* in CBS by CSS following the entrance and departure of cars in car parks. The *Initiates* predicates initiate fluents that represent the specific value bindings of the input parameters *vi* and *pi* (i=1,2,3) of the operations *Enter* and *Depart*. R1 represents a composite requirement whose satisfiability depends on the availability of CSS services and their

[2] t_m refers to the minimum time between the occurrence of two events.

ability to correctly execute. This requirement is an example of requirement that cannot be statically verified and that must be monitored at runtime.

R2) The rule R2 defines the behavior of CIS services:
$(\forall t1, t2) Happens(inv : CIS.FindAvailable(oID, pID), t1) \wedge Happens(rec : CIS.FindAvailable(oID), t2) \wedge (t1 \leq t2) \wedge HoldsAt(equalTo(availability (vID1), "not\ avail"), t2 - t_m) \implies \neg Initiates(rec : CIS.FindAvailable (oID), equalTo(vID2, vID1), t2)$.

According to this rule, the operation *FindAvailable*, which is provided by the CIS service and searches for available cars at specific car parks, should not return the identifier of a car to CBS unless this car is available.

R3) The rule R3 states that whilst a customer has the key of a car, this car cannot be available for rental:
$(\forall t1, t2, t3) Happens(inv : UIS.RelKey(oID1, vID), t1) \wedge Happens(rec : UIS.RelKey(oID1), t2) \wedge (t1 \leq t2) \wedge Happens(inv : UIS.RetKey(oID2), t3) \wedge (t2 \leq t3) \wedge Initiates(inv : UIS.RetKey(oID2), equalTo(v, vID), t3) \implies (\forall t4)(t1 < t4) \wedge (t4 < t3) HoldsAt(equalTo(available(vID), "not\ avail"), t4)$.

Detecting Some Deviations. Assuming the log of events of the car rental scenario (see Figure 1), we now show how we can detect some deviations:

D1) The behavior of CBS violates the requirement R1. This occurs because there are two *enter* events that signify the entrance of *veh*1 first to car park *loc*1 at T=1 (see literals L1-L3 in Figure 2) and, subsequently, to car park *loc*3 at T=27 (see literals L4- L6 in Figure 2) but no *depart* event to signify the departure of *veh*1 from *loc*1 between these *enter* events.

D2) The requirement R2 is violated by the behavior of CBS. The violation of R2 in this case occurs since we can derive from the requirement R3 that *veh*2 could not be available from T=30 when its key was released (see literals L7 and L8 in Figure 1) until T=53 (that is one time unit before its key was returned back). Nevertheless, the execution of the operation *FindAvailable* of the CIS service at T=51 reports that vehicle *veh*2 is available (see literal L13 in Figure 1).

5 Architecture and Implementation

To support the verification and the consistency checking of the behavior of a Web service composition, we propose the framework shown in Figure 6.

The EC checker processes the events which are recorded in the event log by the event extractor in the order of their occurrence, identifies other expected events that should have happened but have not been recorded (these events can be derived from the composition requirements by deduction), and checks if these events are compliant with the behavioral properties and assumptions of the composition. When events are not consistent with specified requirements, the EC checker records the deviation in a deviations log.

Non-functional requirements are additional constraints about the behavior of partners, or their individual services. These constraints are specified by service

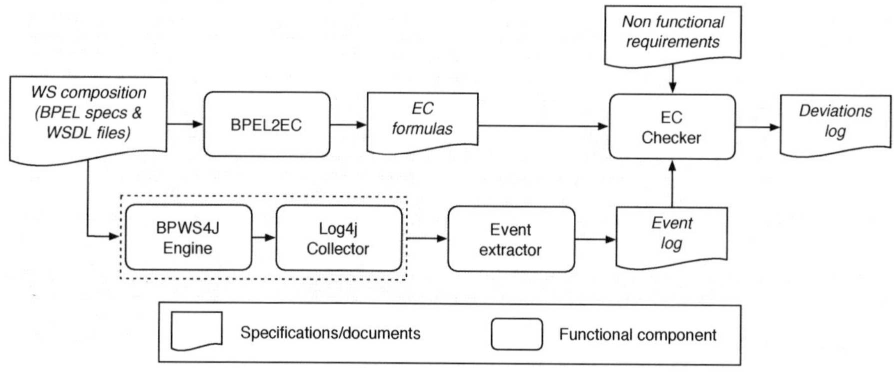

Fig. 6. Monitoring framework

providers and must be expressed in terms of events, effects and state variable conditions which are used in the behavioral properties directly or indirectly, and are formalized in terms of EC predicates. They may include, for example, security and control access policies.

The BPEL2EC tool is built as a parser that can automatically transform a given BPEL process into EC formulas according to the transformation scheme detailed in Section 3.3. It takes as input the specification of the Web service composition as a set of coordinated web services in WSBPEL and produces as output the behavioral specification of this composition in Event Calculus. This specification can be amended by the service providers, who can also use the atomic formulas of the extracted specification to specify additional assumptions about the operations if appropriate.

While executing the Web service composition, the process execution engine generates events which are sent as string streams to the event extractor of our framework. In our implementation, we have used the engine bpws4j[3] and log4j[4] to generate logging events. The event extractor (which is implemented as a remote log4j server) sets some log4j properties of the bpws4j engine to specify level of event reporting (INFO, DEBUG etc.). The logging events from bpws4j that corresponds respectively to the invocation of an operation in some external service and its *receive* activity look as follows:

```
2006-03-13 11:41:59,714[Thread-34]
     DEBUG  bpws.runtime.bus Invoking external service with[WSIFRequest:se
     rviceID='{http://tempuri.org/services/CarReg}CarRegServicefb0b0-fbc59
     65758-8000'operationName='isAvailable'incomingMessage='org.apache.wsi
     f.base.WSIFDefaultMessage@155423name:nullparts[0]:[JROMString:loc:One
     ]'contextMessage='null']
2006-03-13 11:42:00,724[http8080-Processor25]
     INFO   bpws.runtime- Incoming request:[WSIFRequest:serviceID='{http:
     //carservice.org/wsdl/OnlineRenter}carServiceBP'operationName='receiv
```

[3] http://alphaworks.ibm.com/tech/bpws4j

[4] http://logging.apache.org/log4j/docs/

```
e Request'incomingMessage='org.apache.wsif.base.WSIFDefaultMessage@25
491dname:null parts[0]:[JROMString:loc:One]parts[1]:[JROMString:custI
d:km r]'Context-Message='org.apache.wsif.base.WSIFDefaultMessage@1e32
382 name:null parts[0]:http://xml.apache.org/soap/v1parts[1]:{http://
carservice.org/wsdl/OnlineRenter}CarRenter parts[2]:CRS']
```

The [Thread-34] is the unique ID assigned by the bpws4j engine to the invocation of the external service of this instance of the invoke activity and the corresponding response from the external service. The [http8080-Processor25] is the unique ID assigned by the bpws4j engine to this instance of the *receive* activity and its corresponding *reply* activity. These events are then converted to EC events to be checked by the EC checker, which uses the Discrete Event Calculus Reasoner[5].

6 Related Work

It exists various research activities to formally define, analyze, and verify Web services orchestration languages. A group at Humboldt University is working on formalizations of BPEL for analysis, graphics and semantics [9], using Petri-nets and ASMs to formalize the semantics of BPEL. However, the pattern-based Petri-Net semantics of BPEL [16] does not capture fault handling, compensation handling, and timing aspects. Moreover, the feasibility of verifying more complex business processes is not clear and still subject to future work.

Additionally, there are some attempts based on finite state machines [5], and process algebras [3]. Although all of them are successful in unraveling weaknesses in the informal specification, they are of different significance for formal verification. Like abstract state machines, these approaches typically do not support some of BPEL's most interesting features such as fault and event handling.

Work concerning the area of adapting Golog for composition of semantic web services is carried out by McIlraith and others [10]. They have shown that Golog might be a suitable candidate to solve the planning problems occurring when services are to be combined dynamically at run-time. Additionally they related their work [8] to WSBPEL explicitly by stating that the semantic web efforts in the research area are disconnected from the seamless interaction efforts of industry and thus propose to take a bottom-up approach to integrating Semantic Web technology into Web services. But they mainly focus on introducing a semantic discovery service and facilitating semantic translations.

Formal verification of Web Services is addressed in several papers. The SPIN model-checker is used for verification [13] by translating Web Services Flow Language (WSFL) descriptions into Promela. [6] uses a process algebra to derive a structural operational semantics of BPEL as a formal basis for verifying properties of the specification. In [4], BPEL processes are translated to Finite State Process (FSP) models and compiled into a Labeled Transition System (LTS)

[5] http://decreasoner.sourceforge.net

in inferring the correctness of the Web service compositions which are specified using message sequence charts. In [14], Web services are verified using a Petri Net model generated from a DAML-S description of a service.

One common pattern of the above attempts is that they adapt static verification techniques and therefore violations of requirements may not be detectable. This is because Web services that constitute a composition process may not be specified at a level of completeness that would allow the application of static verification, and some of these services may change dynamically at run-time causing unpredictable interactions with other services.

Unlike these earlier verification efforts, we consider the correctness of the individual peer implementations as well as the verification of the global properties of the composite Web services. Verification of the communication flow does not guarantee that the composition behaves according to the specification unless we ensure that each individual service obeys its published contract.

The Event Calculus has been theoretically studied. Denecker et al. [2] use the Event Calculus for specifying process protocols using domain propositions to denote the meanings of actions. In [17] the Event Calculus has been used in planning. Planning in the Event Calculus is an abductive reasoning process through resolution theorem prover. [19] develops an approach for formally representing and reasoning about business interactions in the Event Calculus. The approach was applied and evaluated in the context of protocols, which represent the interactions allowed among communicating agents. Our previous work [15] is close enough to the current work. It presents an event-based framework associated with a semantic definition of the commitments expressed in the Event Calculus, to model and monitor multi-party contracts. This framework permits to coordinate and regulate Web services in business collaborations.

7 Conclusion and Future Directions

In this paper, we have presented a formal framework for checking both functional and non-functional requirements of Web service composition. The properties to be monitored are specified using the Event Calculus formalism. Functional requirements are initially extracted from the specification of the composition process that is expressed in WSBPEL. This ensures that they can be expressed in terms of events occurring during the interaction between the composition process and the constituent services that can be detected from the execution log. Non-functional requirements to be checked are subsequently defined in terms of the identified detectable events by service providers.

The framework is still under development. Ongoing work on it is concerned with: (1) the implementation of the EC checker since until now we have used the Mueller's Discrete EC Reasoner, (2) the study of the correctness requirements in Web service coordination protocols, and their specification in terms of events expressed in the Event Calculus in order to facilitate their integration in our framework, (3) the study of alternatives to establish links with other process algebra in order to import process algebra specific verification techniques such as axiomatizations of behavioral equivalences.

References

1. A. Arkin, S. Askary, B. Bloch, and F.Curbera. Web services business process execution language version 2.0. Technical report, OASIS, December 2004.
2. M. Denecker, L. Missiaen, and M. Bruynooghe. Temporal reasoning with abductive event calculus. In *Proceedings of the 10th European Conference and Symposium on Logic Programming (ECAI)*, pages 384–388, 1992.
3. A. Ferrara. Web services: a process algebra approach. In *ICSOC '04: Proceedings of the 2nd international conference on Service oriented computing*, pages 242–251, New York, NY, USA, 2004. ACM Press.
4. H. Foster, S. Uchitel, J. Magee, and J. Kramer. Compatibility verification for web service choreography. In *ICWS '04: Proceedings of the IEEE International Conference on Web Services (ICWS'04)*, page 738, Washington, DC, USA, 2004. IEEE Computer Society.
5. X. Fu, T. Bultan, and J. Su. Analysis of interacting bpel web services. In *WWW '04: Proceedings of the 13th international conference on World Wide Web*, pages 621–630, New York, NY, USA, 2004. ACM Press.
6. M. Koshina and F. van Breugel. Verification of business processes for web services. Technical report, New York University, SFUCMPT-TR-2003-06.
7. R. Kowalski and M. J. Sergot. A logic-based calculus of events. *New generation Computing 4(1)*, pages 67–95, 1986.
8. M. S. Mandell, D.J. Adapting bpel4ws for the semantic web: The bottom-up approach to web service interoperation. In *Proc of the 2nd Int. Semantic Web Conf. (ISWC)*, 2003.
9. A. Martens. Analysis and re-engineering of web services. In *ICEIS (3)*, pages 419–426, 2004.
10. S. McIlraith and T. Son. Adapting golog for composition of semantic web services. In *Proc of the 8th International Conference on Principles of Knowledge Representation and Reasoning*, 2002.
11. R. Miller and M. Shanahan. The event calculus in classical logic - alternative axiomatisations, 1999.
12. E. T. Mueller. Event calculus reasoning through satisfiability. *J. Log. and Comput.*, 14(5):703–730, 2004.
13. S. Nakajima. Verification of web service flows with model-checking techniques. In *CW*, pages 378–385, 2002.
14. S. Narayanan and S. A. McIlraith. Simulation, verification and automated composition of web services. In *WWW '02: Proceedings of the 11th international conference on World Wide Web*, pages 77–88, New York, NY, USA, 2002. ACM Press.
15. M. Rouached, O. Perrin, and C. Godart. A contract-based approach for monitoring collaborative web services using commitments in the event calculus. In *Sixth International Conference on Web Information Engineering System (WISE05)*, pages 426–434, 2005.
16. K. Schmidt and C. Stahl. A petri net semantic for BPEL4WS validation and application. In *Proceedings of the 11th Workshop on Algorithms and Tools for Petri Nets (AWPN 04) / Ekkart Kindler (Ed.)*, pages 1–6. Bericht tr-ri-04-251, Universitt Paderborn, Sept. 2004.

17. M. Shanahan and M. Witkowski. Event calculus planning through satisfiability. *J. Log. and Comput.*, 14(5):731–745, 2004.
18. W. M. P. van der Aalst, H. T. de Beer, and B. F. van Dongen. Process mining and verification of properties: An approach based on temporal logic. In *OTM Conferences (1)*, pages 130–147, 2005.
19. P. Yolum and M. P. Singh. Reasoning about commitments in the event calculus: An approach for specifying and executing protocols. *Annals of Mathematics and Artificial Intelligence*, 42(1-3):227–253, 2004.

E-Service/Process Composition Through Multi-agent Constraint Management

Minhong Wang [1,2], William K. Cheung[2], Jiming Liu [3,2], Xiaofeng Xie [2], and Zongwei Luo[4]

[1] Division of Information and Technology Studies, The University of Hong Kong
maggie_mh_wang@yahoo.com
[2] Department of Computer Science, Hong Kong Baptist University
william@comp.hkbu.edu.hk, xiexf@ieee.org
[3] School of Computer Science, University of Windsor
jiming@uwindsor.ca
[4] E-Business Technology Institute, The University of Hong Kong
zwluo@eti.hku.hk

Abstract. E-service/process composition requires allocating suitable resources to a set of services that constitute a composite service/process. The problem is complicated due to undetermined constraints of each component service and unpredictable solutions contributed by service providers. It needs the ability to rapidly identify the suitable solutions as well as effectively coordinate them under various constraints. In this paper, an agent-mediated coordination framework for e-service/process composition is proposed. Each agent works as a broker for each service type, posting service constraints, searching suitable solutions and refining the constraints for achieving coherence among the decisions of each service. Based on the framework, a prototype of multi-agent supported e-supply chain composition is implemented. The experimental results indicate the significant effectiveness of the approach.

1 Introduction

A composite service is a set of services together with the control and data flow among the services, which is similar to a workflow or process [1, 9]. Service composition contains two main stages, planning and scheduling. In the planning stage, a plan of a composite service is generated or a process of the service is determined to achieve the goal; in the scheduling stage, real services are searched, selected and bound to fulfill the plan [16]. Although planning and scheduling seem similar, they are different. Planning tackles the problem of finding plans to achieve goals; scheduling deals with the exact allocation of resources to activities over time precedence, duration, capacity, and incompatibility. To date, the methods of automated service composition have been studied with growing interests, particularly focusing on plan generation in AI approaches or process modeling in workflow approaches [26, 30]. While e-service/process composition is similar to traditional workflow or process composition, it is more complex as a result of a huge amount of web service resources to be searched, scheduled and coordinated, especially in a real-time fashion [4]. Therefore, consideration of the complexity, such as dynamic availability of web services and large number of alternative combinations of service choices is essential to

S. Dustdar, J.L. Fiadeiro, and A. Sheth (Eds.): BPM 2006, LNCS 4102, pp. 274 – 289, 2006.

e-service/process composition [24, 5]. In relation to the two stages of service composition -- planning and scheduling, this work will particularly focus on service scheduling, dealing with the assignment of services or tasks to appropriate service providers where a set of constraints has to be regarded.

After a composite service is decomposed into a set of component services with a plan generated, real-time selection, coordination and aggregation of partial solutions to component services is crucial for building a global solution to the composite service. Partial solutions may not have a complete view of the global solution, and very often generate incoherent and contradictory hypotheses and actions [24]. If a service is scheduled to start before its preceding service is completed, it may fail for lack of prerequisite resources from the preceding service. From the viewpoint of service scheduling, the complexity of e-service composition is mainly from the uncertainty in determining the constraints (referring to start time, execution duration, cost, destination, etc.) of component services, and the unpredictability (referring to availability, capacity, price, location, etc.) of partial solutions to the component services. As a result, there maybe no feasible global solution achieved based on tentative constraints of services, and it needs a series of adjustments of these requests to achieve the goal. Given this observation, a critical problem of e-service/process composition is to find a way to achieve coordination and coherence among decisions of component services in a real-time and adaptive fashion [24].

To this end, this paper considers an agent mediated approach to e-service/process composition. Automated coordination by software agents is a key enabling technology for e-commerce. Considering the large-scale and dynamic settings in web-based environments, business services can be delegated to a number of autonomous problem solving agents, which are enabled to manage complex activities based on continuous awareness of situations and real-time decisions of activities [23]. Agents can be viewed as entities that act flexibly in modern computing environment by coping with various constraints [12]. It offers a new perspective of autonomous activity, interactivity, reactivity and proactivity as a result of the attempt to handle local and global constraints [25]. To deal with the uncertainties and dynamics in e-service/process composition, we introduce a dynamic constraint-based and agent mediated coordination framework. In this framework, coordination among services is modeled as a distributed constraint optimization problem (DisCOP) in which solutions and constraints are distributed into a number of component services and to be solved by a group of agents. Each agent works as a broker of each service type, managing tentative service request as well as identifying suitable solutions from service providers. Based on real-time local information and information inferred from communication with others, each agent may refine its constraints for achieving compatibility of solutions with other agents.

The remainder of the paper is organized as follows. We first outline the constraint problem to be solved in e-service/process composition in Section 2. Section 3 presents the multi-agent framework, and elaborates the mechanism of agent-mediated constraint management for e-service/process composition. The effectiveness of the approach is demonstrated by simulated experiments in Section 4. The related work in terms of web service composition, constraint programming, and workflow & supply chain scheduling is discussed in Section 5. Finally, we conclude the work in Section 6.

2 Constrain Management in E-Service/Process Composition

To enable e-service/process composition, research efforts have been put on improving workflow technologies for supporting cross-enterprise workflows. While most work has focused on workflow modeling, constraint management is crucial to designing and managing workflows for allocating and scheduling activities to appropriate resources. Time/temporal constraints were addressed as a critical component early in workflow systems in [7, 13, 29, 31]; resource constraints (related to people, machine, and software issues) were investigated lately in [10, 20]. Most work has concentrated on scheduling and run-time checking of workflows, especially in the context where the requirements of each activity are determined and all available resources are known in advance. As discussed, e-service/process composition is more complex than traditional process composition by virtue of undetermined constraints of component services and unpredictable solutions from service providers. Furthermore, in addition to time and resource constraints, other type of constraints such as cost, location, etc. should be taken into account as well.

To this end, e-service composition is mapped as an agent-based DisCOP. A DisCOP consists of a set of variables, each assigned to an agent, where the values of the variables are taken from finite and discrete domains. Finding a solution to a DisCOP requires that all agents find the values for their variables that satisfy not only their own constraints but also interagent constraints [27, 11]. In this work, component services are mapped to variables, and solutions of component services are mapped to values.

In web service composition, a composite service consists of:

(1) A finite set of component services involved in the composite service $\boldsymbol{S}$,

$$\boldsymbol{S} = \{S_1, S_2, \ldots, S_n\}.$$

(2) A domain set, containing a finite domain of solutions to each component service:

$$\boldsymbol{D} = \{D_1, D_2, \ldots, D_n\},\ \forall i \in [1, n], S_i \in D_i.$$

(3) A constraint set, $\boldsymbol{C} = \{C(R_{C1}), \ldots, C(R_{Ci}), \ldots, C(R_{CI})\}$, where each R_{Ci} is an ordered subset of the services, and each constraint $C(R_{Ci})$ is a set of tuples indicating the mutually consistent solutions to the services in R_{Ci}.
(4) An objective set, $\boldsymbol{F} = \{F(R_{F1}), \ldots, F(R_{Fj}), \ldots, F(R_{FJ})\}$, where each R_{Fj} is an ordered subset of the services, and each objective function $F(R_{Fj})$ indicates the objective value to be minimized for the mutually consistent solutions to the component services in R_{Fj}.

The feasible solution, L, for the composite service is an assignment to all services such that the assignment satisfies all given constraints. Specially,

$$L = \langle V_1, V_2, \ldots, V_n \rangle \qquad L \in D_1 \times D_2 \times \ldots \times D_n$$

where $V_i \in D_i$ is a specified domain member of D_i, so called as a partial solution.

If there is no objective function, the constrain optimization problem is degenerated into the constrain satisfaction problem, where any feasible solution is a solution to problem. If there is only one objective function, the feasible solution with minimized objective value is considered as the solution. If there are multiple objective functions, all the solutions in the Pareto set are recognized.

For each component service, its domain is contributed by corresponding service providers. Unlike traditional situation, e-service is complex in that the domain members in each domain D_i are unpredictable in advance and varied throughout the composition process. It is mainly due to: a) a service provider may be reluctant to report its all solutions for commercial privacy; b) to list all possible partial solutions in advance may make the solving intractable; c) solutions are explored based on updated service request. Hence, each component service may have to maintain its service requests for collecting required partial solutions from service providers.

With regard to service request, the issues of time, cost and location are concerned as important attributes of quality of service [16, 2, 6]. Normally, a composite service should be completed before the due date and be delivered to the location required by the customer; a feasible solution with the lowest cost will be accepted. For each component service, it should be scheduled to start after its preceding service is completed, and to end before its succeeding service starts. Moreover, when the customer and component service providers are distributed in different locations, one or more delivery services are embedded into the composite service. Furthermore, the cost issue in service composition is dealt with as a constraint optimization problem to identify the best composite solution (the one of the lowest cost). To manage these constraints, we take time and location as the issues to be constrained, and the global cost as the issue to be optimized. Hence each domain member has multiply feature values to answer for different issues, with each constraint or objective applied on certain feature value.

Given these observations, the main problem discussed in this work is to find an appropriate solution from each domain that can be integrated to form a composite service satisfying the above constraints. The difficulty is that the available solutions to each service type are unknown in advance. To find them, we need send service requests to service providers. However, we only have the constraints of the composite service instead of the constraints of each component service. To solve the problem, we may first estimate the constraints of each component service, and then refine them based on real-time responses from service providers and send out again for achieving more compatible solutions.

3 Agent-Based E-Service/Process Composition

In this section, we outline the framework of e-service/process composition through multi-agent constraint management by taking e-Supply Chain Management (e-SCM) as an example. A supply chain is a network of suppliers, manufactories, distribution centers, and retailers. Conventional supply chains are based on tight and long-term integration of partners. Such kind of close and static relationship among partners makes the integration cost high and makes it impractical to dynamically integrate partners in an on-demand manner [22]. The advent of web-based technologies will allow low cost and instant integration of supply chain partners. Compared with traditional supply chains, supply chains established via e-service/process composition are characterized by large number of service resources to be selected and aggregated. The ability to rapidly identify suitable resources and effectively coordinate them across the chain is a key to e-supply chain success [18].

3.1 Multi-agent Framework

As shown in Fig.1, a society of software agents, including a Service Dispatcher Agent, and a set of Service Broker Agents and Service Provider Agents is proposed. It is corresponding to a composite service depicted in Fig.2, where a product service is fulfilled through a set of services including procuring components, preprocessing components, assembling components into products, postprocessing products[1], and delivering components or products whenever the customer and service providers are distributed in different locations. Once receiving a request (e.g. 1000 products to XYZ Plaza before 25-02-2006) from a customer, the Service Dispatcher will generate a service plan/process with constraints estimated for each component service. Accordingly, a set of Service Brokers are deployed, each for a specific component service. To decrease the complexity of the composition process caused by adding deliver services on demand, we treated delivery as a type of standard service that could be provided by a certain global delivery company (e.g. DHL), and could be bound with any component service when necessary (refer to more details in Section 3.2.2).

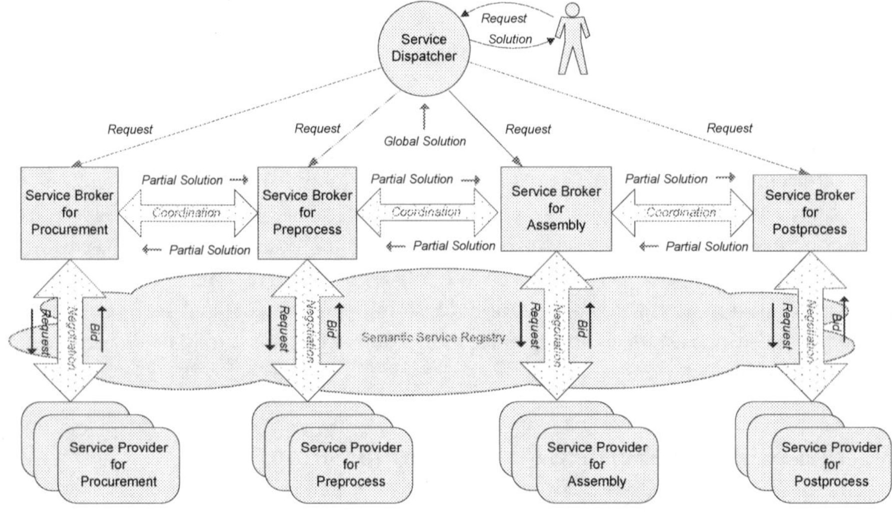

Fig. 1. An agent-mediated service composition framework

After receiving service requests from the Service Dispatcher, Service Brokers will send them to Service Providers for collecting suitable solutions to each service. However, the available bids or solutions may not be compatible with each other to form a global solution. A Service Broker needs coordinate with its neighbouring brokers to refine the constraints for achieving new bids that could be involved in a global solution. For the sake of simplicity, we ignore the situations that there are more than one preceding or succeeding service of a component service in this paper.

---

[1] This work focuses on the discussion of service scheduling in service composition, therefore how to generate or predefine a plan or flow for a composite service is beyond the scope of this work.

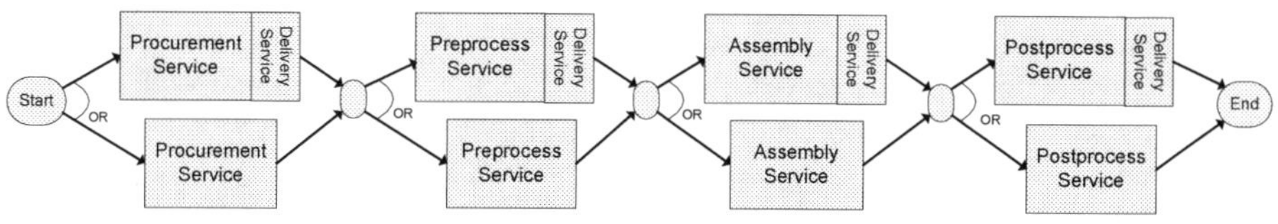

Fig. 2. A composite service process

3.2 Agent-Mediated Constraint Management

E-service/process composition requires a set of agents to allocate suitable resources/web services to a set of services. We define the *i*th service to be performed in a composite service as follows:

$$S_i = [S_u, S_v, Rq_i]$$

where S_u denotes the preceding service of S_i; S_v denotes the succeeding service of S_i; Rq_i denotes the requirement of S_i , defined as follows:

$$Rq_i = [st_i, et_i, loca_i, dest_i]$$

It consists of four parts: st_i denotes the start time scheduled for S_i; et_i denotes the end time expected for S_i; $loca_i$ denotes the location of S_i; $dest_i$ denotes the destination of S_i. For different service type, the requirement constitution can be different. For example, while the end time is to specify the available time of a material procurement service, the start time of such type of service is not meaningful and will not be specified.

In this work, each Service Broker is designed as a dynamic constraint-based agent. The detail how they interact with each other to achieve coherence among decisions of component services is discussed as follows.

3.2.1 Initialize Service Requests

The requirement Rq_i is initially estimated by the Service Dispatcher, and then be refined by Service Brokers throughout the composition process. The estimation is based on the customer's request as well as the history information of the component services. The estimation of time constraints is based on the average percentage of time spent on the services. For example, a composite service S is requested to start on July 1, and to finish by July 20. It is composed of three services, S_1, S_2 and S_3, respectively taking 25%, 50% and 25% of the time on average. Accordingly, S_2 can be scheduled to start on July 6 and to end by July 15. Moreover, the start time of the first service and the end time of the last service are fixed, as required by the customer. Similarly, the locations and destinations of component services are also initially specified by the Service Dispatcher, and then be tuned by Service Brokers, with the destination of the final service to be fixed.

3.2.2 Collect Solutions from Service Providers

Each Service Broker then forwards its service request to Service Providers for collecting bids of each service, where a bid is defined as follows.

$$Bid_{ij} = [b\_id_{ij}, s\_t_{ij}, e\_t_{ij}, c_{ij}, loc_{ij}, des_{ij}]$$

Bid_{ij}, the *j*th bid sent to Service Broker *i* for service *i* contains five parts: b_id_{ij} denotes the ID number of the bid, which is associated with the private details of a bid; s_t_{ij} and

e_t_{ij} denote the start time and end time respectively scheduled for the service; c_{ij} denotes the cost claimed by the service provider; loc_{ij} denotes the location of the service; des_{ij} denotes the destination of the service. Each provider may generate a bid satisfying the request with the lowest cost. In case of no bid generated due to the time constraints, the provider may relax the constraints as less as a bid generates. If the provider cannot make the service reach the destination by itself, a standard delivery service could be bound to the service with delivery cost and delivery time taken into account.

3.2.3 Filter Out Dominated Solutions

For all bids received from service providers, the Service Broker will filter out dominated bids before posting them as candidate solutions. A newly received bid, $Bid_{i\beta}$ (bid β for service i), is identified as a dominated bid if it is worse than or the same with an existing candidate solution Bid_{ij} by satisfying the following condition.

$$c_{i\beta} \geq c_{ij} \text{ AND } s\_t_{i\beta} \leq s\_t_{ij} \text{ AND } e\_t_{i\beta} \geq e\_t_{ij} \text{ AND } loc_{i\beta} = loc_{ij} \text{ AND } des_{i\beta} = des_{ij}$$

On the other hand, any existing candidate solution Bid_{ij} will be filtered out if it is dominated by a new bid $Bid_{i\beta}$ by satisfying the following condition.

$$c_{i\beta} < c_{ij} \text{ AND } s\_t_{i\beta} \geq s\_t_{ij} \text{ AND } e\_t_{i\beta} \leq e\_t_{ij} \text{ AND } loc_{i\beta} = loc_{ij} \text{ AND } des_{i\beta} = des_{ij}$$

After a bid is removed as a dominated bid, its connections with other bids are removed as well. By filtering out dominated solutions, the number of partial solutions, i.e. domain members can be controlled in a reasonable scale.

3.2.4 Identify Compatible Solutions

Each Service Broker will report its newly posted bids to its preceding and succeeding Service Broker, so that each broker may identify its solutions that are compatible with the solutions of its neighbours. We denote service u and service v as the preceding and succeeding service of service i, and $Bid_{i\beta}$, $Bid_{u\alpha}$, $Bid_{v\gamma}$ as a bid of service i, service u, service v respectively. After posting $Bid_{i\beta}$, Service Broker i will connect it with $Bid_{u\alpha}$, an existing bid of its preceding service if the two bids are compatible by satisfying the following condition.

$$s\_t_{i\beta} > e\_t_{u\alpha} \text{ AND } loc_{i\beta} = des_{u\alpha}$$

The Service Broker will also link $Bid_{i\beta}$ with $Bid_{v\gamma}$, an existing bid of its preceding service if the two bids are compatible by satisfying the following condition.

$$e\_t_{i\beta} < s\_t_{v\gamma} \text{ AND } des_{i\beta} = loc_{v\gamma}$$

3.2.5 Identify Promising Solutions

In service composition, each Service Broker may utilize its own information and limited information from its neighbours for coordination and achieving coherence among the solutions. To achieve this, a Service Broker needs identify a promising solution of its preceding and a promising solution of its succeeding service, based on which it can refine the constraints of its own service to seek new bids that would be compatible with the promising solutions of its neighbours. A solution to a component service is more promising to be involved in a global solution if it connects with more existing solutions to its preceding or succeeding service, as well as leaves more free time to its succeeding or preceding or service. As an example shown in Fig.3, each bid is posted with its start time, end time, and connections with other bids. Bid_{b5} is identified as the most **promising preceding solution** from the viewpoint of S_c. It is because Bid_{b5} is connected with more bids of its preceding service, S_a as well as leaving more time to its succeeding service S_c than any other bid of S_b. On the other hand, Bid_{b5} is also identified as the most **promising succeeding solution** from the viewpoint of S_a. It is because Bid_{b5} is connected with more bids of its succeeding service S_c as well as leaving more free time for its preceding service S_a than any other bid of S_b. In this way, each Service Broker may identify a promising preceding solution among all the solutions of its preceding service, and a promising succeeding solution from all the solutions of its succeeding neighbour. A new bid of a service will be more probably involved in a global solution if it is compatible with both the promising preceding solution and the promising succeeding solution.

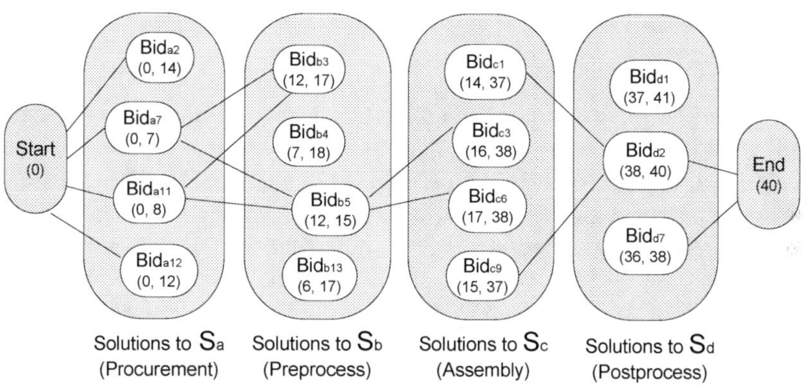

Fig. 3. Solutions to component services and their connections

A promising solution is identified based on its promising value. The promising value is measured by its connectivity with its neighbour solutions and the free time it leaves for its neighbour solutions. In detail, the preceding promising value (*Pre_prom*) of Bid_{ij} is measured by the following function.

$$Pre\_prom\ (Bid_{ij}) = w\_conn * Pre\_conn\ (Bid_{ij}) + w\_tf * Pre\_tf\ (Bid_{ij})$$

where $Pre\_conn\ (Bid_{ij})$ measures the connectivity of Bid_{ij} with its preceding solutions; $Pre\_tf\ (Bid_{ij})$ measures the free time Bid_{ij} leaves for its succeeding solutions; w_conn and w_tf denote the weight of *Pre_conn* and *Pre_tf* respectively. $Pre\_conn\ (Bid_{ij})$ and $Pre\_tf\ (Bid_{ij})$ are further detailed as follows.

$$Pre\_conn\ (Bid_{ij}) = (pre_{ij} - MINPRE_i) / (MAXPRE_i - MINPRE_i)$$

where pre_{ij} denotes the number of the preceding bids that connect with Bid_{ij}; $MAXPRE_i$ denotes the maximum value of pre_{ij} for $\forall j$; $MINPRE_i$ denotes the minimum value of pre_{ij} for $\forall j$.

$$Pre\_tf\ (Bid_{ij}) = (MAXET_i - e\_t_{ij}) / (MAXET_i - MINET_i)$$

where e_t_{ij} denotes the end time of Bid_{ij}; $MAXET_i$ is the maximum value of e_t_{ij} for $\forall j$; $MINET_i$ is the minimum value of e_t_{ij} for $\forall j$.

Similarly, the succeeding promising value (*Suc_prom*) of Bid_{ij} can be measured by the following function.

$$Suc\_prom\ (Bid_{ij}) = w\_conn * Suc\_conn\ (Bid_{ij}) + w\_tf * Suc\_tf\ (Bid_{ij})$$

where $Suc\_conn\ (Bid_{ij})$ denotes the function to measure the connectivity of Bid_{ij} with its succeeding solutions; $Suc\_tf\ (Bid_{ij})$ measures the free time Bid_{ij} leaves for its preceding solutions; *w_conn* and *w_tf* denote the weight of *Suc_conn* and *Suc_tf* respectively. $Suc\_conn\ (Bid_{ij})$ and $Suc\_tf\ (Bid_{ij})$ are further detailed as follows.

$$Suc\_conn\ (Bid_{ij}) = (suc_{ij} - MINSUC_i) / (MAXSUC_i - MINSUC_i)$$

where suc_{ij} denotes the number of succeeding solutions that connect with Bid_{ij}; $MAXSUC_i$ is the maximum value of suc_{ij} for $\forall j$; $MINSUC_i$ is the minimum value of suc_{ij} for $\forall j$.

$$Suc\_tf\ (Bid_{ij}) = (MAXST_i - s\_t_{ij}) / (MAXST_i - MINST_i)$$

where s_t_{ij} denotes the start time of Bid_{ij}; $MAXST_i$ denotes the maximum value of s_t_{ij} for $\forall j$; $MINST_i$ denotes the minimum value of s_t_{ij} for $\forall j$.

Based on the promising value, a promising bid can be selected using different strategies, such as random selection strategy, elitist strategy and tournament selection strategy. The **random selection strategy** chooses a bid at random. The **elitist strategy** selects the best bid, i.e. the bid with the largest promising value. **Tournament selection** is one of many methods of selection in genetic algorithms which runs a "tournament" among a few individuals chosen at random from the population and selects the winner (the one with the best fitness) for crossover. Selection pressure can be easily adjusted by changing the tournament size. If the tournament size is higher, weak individuals have a smaller chance to be selected. Tournament selection is equivalent to random selection when the tournament size is 1, and equivalent to elitist strategy when the tournament size is the population size. As shown in Fig.3, by using the elitist strategy, the Service Broker of S_c may choose Bid_{b5} as its most promising preceding solution, and Bid_{d2} as its most promising succeeding solution.

3.2.6 Refine Constraints Towards a Global Solution

Based on the promising preceding solution $Bid_{u\alpha}$ (a solution of the preceding service S_u) and the promising succeeding solution $Bid_{v\gamma}$ (a solution of the succeeding service S_v), the Service Broker of S_i may refine its service constraints Rq_i as follows.

$$Rq_i = [st_i, et_i, loca_i, dest_i]$$

where $st_i = e\_t_{u\alpha} + 1$; $et_i = s\_t_{v\gamma} - 1$; $loca_i = des_{u\alpha}$; $dest_i = loca_{v\gamma}$

In this way, Service Brokers may achieve coordination and coherence among decisions of component services through a series of adjustments on constraints that are individually made but interact with each other.

Furthermore, Service Brokers may communicate for figuring out a global solution at regular intervals. One or more feasible global solutions could be generated, and the one of the lowest cost will be reported to the Service Dispatcher as a bid for the customer. The main activities involved in the proposed approach are summarized as a flow chart in Fig. 4.

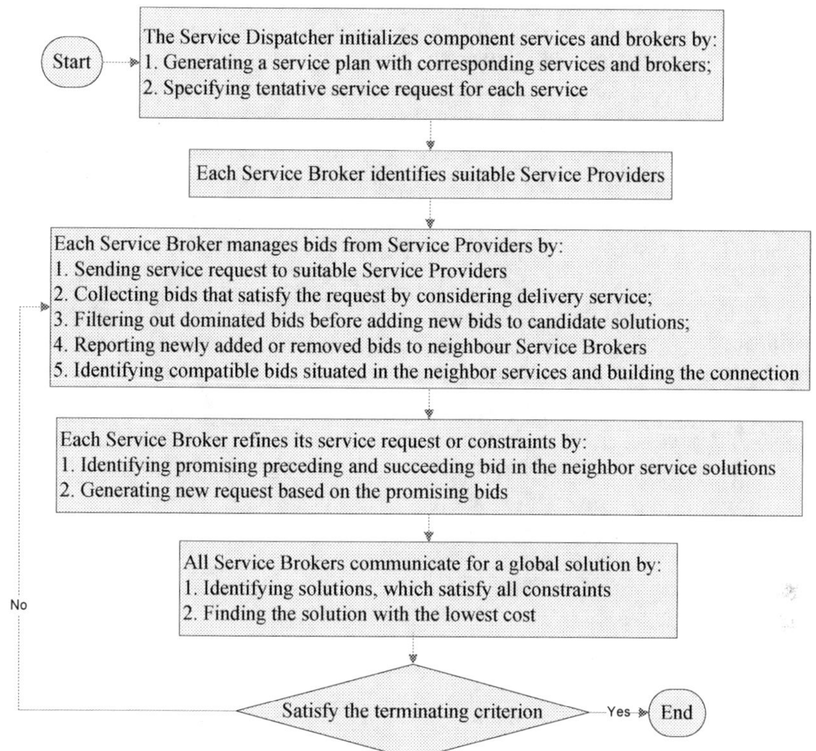

Fig. 4. A flow chart of agent-mediated e-service composition

4 Experiments

A number of experiments have been run to evaluate the performance of the proposed approach. A service network is randomly initialized by varying the distribution of price, stock, deliverable time, and location of the procurement service providers, as well as varying the distribution of price, overall load, available time periods, and location of the providers of production services such as preprocess, assembly and postprocess. Furthermore, each procurement service provider may have more than one service options associated with different price, stock and deliverable time, e.g. the earlier deliverable time the higher price. For a procurement request, a supplier may generate a bid based on a pack of options to satisfy the time constraint at the lowest cost. The experiments simulate the agent-mediated coordination in supply chain composition by associating 24 providers of each service type, and going through 50 cycles of constraint refinement for each problem. Each problem is tested 500 times to calculate the success rate, average cost, and average time used to achieve a global solution. Results are reported for two suites of problems to see the impact of number of services involved in a composite service: 1) problems of four component services involved, where the composite service chain is relatively short; 2) problems of seven component services involved, where the composite service chain is relatively long.

Each suite is made of five sets of problems obtained by varying due time of the composite service as very tight, tight, average, loose, and very loose.

Furthermore, as discussed, a key to this approach is to identify promising solutions of component services, based on which the constraints of component services can be refined towards a global solution. Accordingly, the method of evaluating the promising value of a solution as well as the strategy of choosing a promising solution are regarded as the important factors of success of the approach, hence tested in the experiments. The results are further detailed below.

1) Weights of Connectivity and Time Freedom in Evaluating a Promising Solution

From the viewpoint of generating a global solution, a partial solution to a component service is more promising to be involved in a global solution if it is more connective with its neighbour service solutions and leaves more free time to neighbour solutions. Accordingly, we test how the weigh of connectivity and time freedom used for measuring the promising value may impact the performance of the approach.

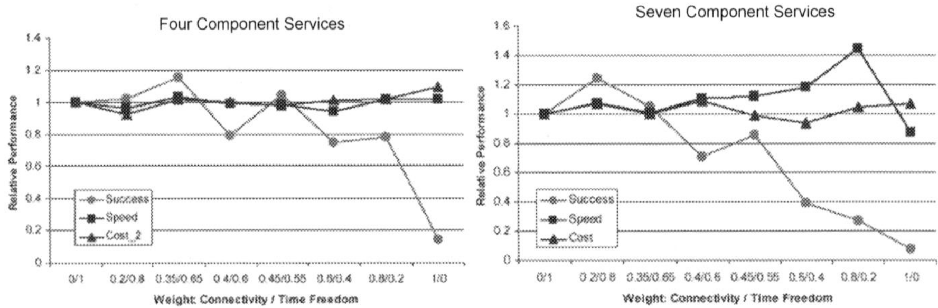

Fig. 5. Weights of connectivity and time freedom in measuring the promising value

As shown in Fig.5, either connectivity only (1/0) or time freedom only (0/1) cannot perform better than their mixed form in certain weight. Especially, the performance is better when the weight is about 0.35 for connectivity and 0.65 for time freedom, when the due time of the composite service is tight. This weight structure also yields better results in other situations of due time, and we choose it for further experiments.

2) Impact of Three Strategies of Selecting a Promising Solution

As a key step in agent-mediated constraint management, promising solutions to component services are identified for constraint refinement. Fig.6 summarizes the performance of three strategies used for selecting a promising solution, i.e. random selection strategy, elitist strategy, and tournament selection strategy. It is shown that the tournament selection strategy performs better than the other two by a higher success rate in most situations of due time. The results also show a faster speed and similar cost as a result of this strategy. The elitist strategy yields poor results, mainly due to the premature convergence caused by the greedy nature.

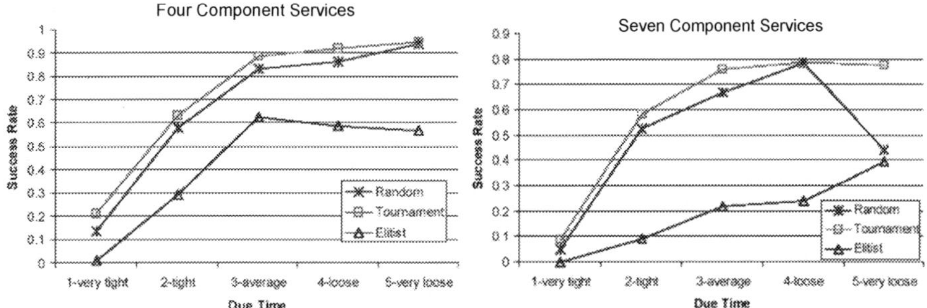

Fig. 6. Success rates of three selection strategies

3) Tournament Size of the Tournament Selection Strategy

For selecting an appropriate tournament selection strategy, different tournament sizes are tested. In doing so, we compare the tournament selection strategy with the random selection strategy by calculating their relative performance in success rate, cost and speed with the change of tournament size. As shown in Fig.7, the success rate of the tournament selection strategy is about 10% higher than that of the random selection strategy when the tournament size is 5, in the situation of average due time. Furthermore, the experiments indicate that the tournament selection strategy yields an overall better performance when the tournament size is 4 or 5 in all situations of due time.

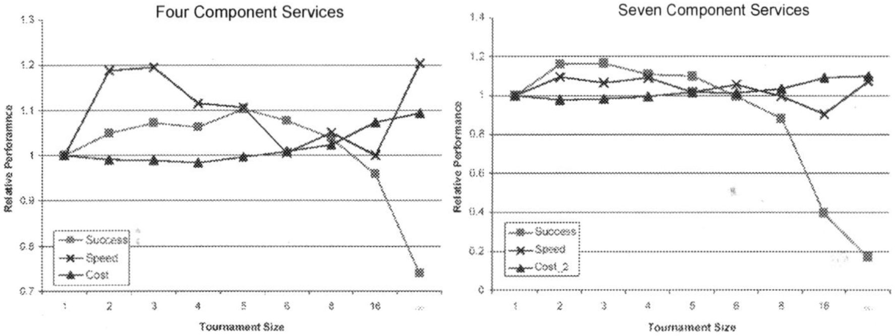

Fig. 7. Tournament selection strategy with tournament size

4) Tournament Selection Versus Random Selection

Setting the tournament size as 4, we compare the tournament selection strategy with the random selection strategy by calculating their relative performance in Fig.8. It is shown that the success rate of the tournament selection strategy is 58% higher than that of the random selection strategy in very tight due time situation. The speed of the tournament selection strategy is 11% faster than that of the random selection strategy in average due time situation. These results also indicate that the tournament selection strategy yields an overall better performance by more successfully generating a global solution with less time in most situations of due time, however with less difference in cost.

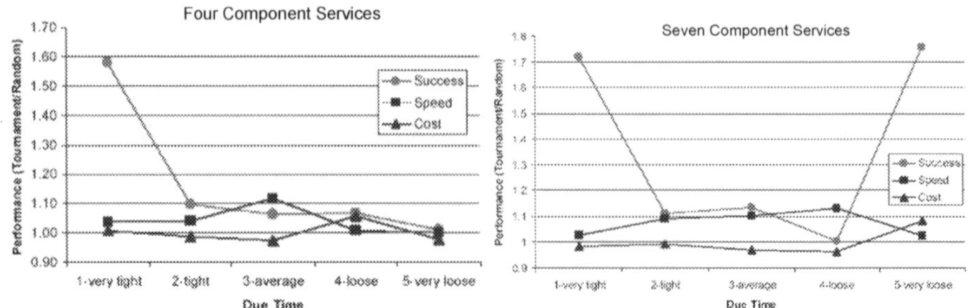

Fig. 8. Tournament selection versus random selection: relative performance

5 Related Work

The emergence of web services has received many interests to support the interaction of business partners and their processes by inter-connecting web services. There are abundant literatures of web services, mainly on the description of web services, the syntax of their flows, and how they could be executed [15]. With regard to web service composition, most researches have fallen in the realm of workflow/process composition and AI planning [21, 17].

AI planning and scheduling techniques have been playing an essential role in managing workflows of web services, including their composition, resource allocation, execution and repair [9]. However, many issues remain to be resolved on how to identify the most appropriate ways to formalize service composition as a planning and scheduling problem. Most ongoing studies have made efforts on service planning, i.e. working out a sequence in which services are invoked. With respect to the major difference between web service composition from workflow composition, there is a need on how to identify appropriate service candidates from a number of resources, especially by addressing non-functional properties, such as cost, timeliness, security, and dependability [14, 28]. From this point of view, service scheduling, the exact allocation of activities or services to appropriate resources has become critical to ensuring reliable web service composition. There have been growing attention paid to this field in terms of constraint driven web service composition and QoS aware web service composition (e.g. [2], [3], [6]), where web service compositions have been translated into a certain type of constraint satisfaction and optimization problem. However, existing methods require a completely specified problem as input and have not been able to deal with uncertainties and dynamics of the environment. In more detail, they did not solve the problem where only the constraints of the composite service are specified, with the constraints and available solutions of component services not completely known. Moreover, there have been fewer efforts on managing the dynamics inside a scheduling process, e.g. changes of service offerings and service constraints. Indeed, we face the ambiguity in determining the constraints of specific services involved in a composite service, which may further result in the uncertainties and dynamics throughout the composition process. Furthermore, although there are a number of service providers available for each service type, they may be engaged in various composite services at different time. Therefore, it is not necessary that every service request can be allocated to an appropriate service resource at one time. To this end, our approach aims to handle such over-constrained problem and handling uncertainties and dynamics by using dynamic constraint-based agents that dynamically and interactively tune the constraints of services involved in a composite service.

This work is also related to workflow scheduling, resource management and constraint analysis in workflow modeling. In addition to those mentioned in Section 2, other relevant work includes job-shop scheduling in production and supply chains, where constraint logic programming has been used to deal with scheduling problems. In many of these studies, agents have been used to represent physical resources for solving resource scheduling problems [8, 19]. However, most approaches rely on complete information of all available resources, such as cost, location, and available time. They suffer from uncertain and dynamic information of resources and tasks. Instead of using conventional job scheduling approaches, more robust and adaptive strategies should be adopted in dynamic web-based environments [5].

6 Conclusions

E-service/process composition is a complex task that coordinates the flow of information among services and links their business processes under various constraints. Existing constraint programming methods require a completely specified problem as input. They can not solve the problem of e-service composition where only the constraints of the composite service are specified, with the constraints and available solutions of component services not completely known. In this paper, we have described a multi-agent formulation that can be used to deal with uncertainties and dynamics of service composition especially in web-based environments. The key idea behind the approach lies in a distributed multi-agent system, in which autonomous agents have to make choices of component services to undertake within a composite service. Coordination among agents is modeled as a distributed constraint satisfaction problem in which solutions and constraints are distributed into specific services. This system can self-organize itself, where each individual agent explores its own solution, coordinates with other agents and gradually evolves towards a global solution state. Although presented in the context of supply chain management, this approach is appropriate to other situations where a set of services are to be composed as a result of a large amount of resources to be searched, scheduled and coordinated, especially in a real-time fashion.

Acknowledgement

The authors thank the reviewers of BPM 2006, and Mr. Haijing Jiang for their constructive comments on this paper. This work was supported by a RGC Central Allocation Group Research Grant (HKBU 2/03/C) from Hong Kong Government.

References

1. Aalst, W.M.P., Dumas, M., and Hofstede, A.H.M., Web Service Composition Languages: Old Wine in New Bottles? 29th EUROMICRO Conference, 2003, 298-305
2. Ardagna, D. and Pernici, B., Global and Local QoS Guarantee in Web Service Selection, Business Process Management Workshops, LNCS 3812, 2006, 32-46
3. Canfora, G., Penta, M., Esposito, R., and Villani, M.L., QoS-Aware Replanning of Composite Web Services, 2005 IEEE International Conference on Web Services (ICWS 2005), 2005
4. Casati, F. and Shan, M., Dynamic and adaptive composition of e-services, Information Systems, 26(3), 2001, 143-163
5. Cheung, W.K. and Liu, J., On Knowledge Grid and Grid Intelligence – A Survey, Computational Intelligence - An International Journal, 21(2), 2005, 111-129
6. Claro, D.B., Albers, P., and Hao, J.K., Selecting web services for optimal composition, ICWS 2005 Second International Workshop on Semantic and Dynamic Web Processes, 2005
7. Eder, J., Panagos, E., and Rabinovich, M., Time Constraints in Workflow Systems, 11th International Conference on Advanced Information Systems Engineering (CAiSE), LNCS 1626, 1999, 286-300
8. Fox, M.S., Barbuceanu, M., and Teigen, R., Agent-Oriented Supply-Chain Management, International Journal of Flexible Manufacturing Systems, 12(2/3), 2000, 165-188
9. Kumar, A. and Zhao, J.L., Workflow support for electronic commerce applications, Decision Support Systems, 32(3), 2002, 265-278
10. Li, H., Yang, Y., and Chen, T.Y., Resource constraints analysis of workflow specifications, Journal of Systems and Software, 73, 2004, 271-285
11. Liu, J., Jing, H., and Tang, Y.Y., Multi-agent oriented constraint satisfaction, Artificial Intelligence, 136(1), 2002, 101-144
12. Liu, J., Jin, X.L., and Tsui, K.C., Autonomy Oriented Computing (AOC): Formulating computational systems with autonomous components, IEEE Transactions on Systems, Man, and Cybernetics, Part A: Systems and Humans, 35(6), 2005, 879- 902
13. Marjanovic, O. and Orlowska, M.E., On modeling and verification of temporal constraints in production workflows, Knowledge Information Systems, 1(2), 1999, 157-192
14. Menasce, D.A., Composing Web Services: A QoS View, IEEE Internet Computing, 8(6), 2004, 88-90
15. Milanovic, N. and Malek, M., Current Solutions for Web Service Composition, IEEE Internet Computing, 8(6), 2004, 51-59
16. Muscettola, N., Integrating Planning and Scheduling, in Zweben, M., and Fox, M.S. (eds), Intelligent Scheduling, Morgan Kaufmann, 1994, 169-212
17. Rao, J. and Su, X., A Survey of Automated Web Service Composition Methods, First International Workshop on Semantic Web Services and Web Process Composition (SWSWPC), 2004, 43-54
18. Sadeh, N.M., Arunachalam, R., Eriksson, J., Finne, N., and Janson, S., TAC-03 - A Supply-Chain Trading Competition, AI Magazine, 24(1), 2003, 92-94
19. Sauer, J. and Appelrath, H., Scheduling the Supply Chain by Teams of Agents, 38th Hawaii International Conference on System Sciences (HICSS), 2003.
20. Senkul, S. and Toroslu, I.H. An architecture for workflow scheduling under resource allocation constraints, Information Systems, 30(5), 2005, 399-422
21. Srivastava, B. and Koehler, J., Web Service Composition - Current Solutions and Open Problems, ICAPS 2003 Workshop on Planning for Web Services, 2003.

22. Subramani, M., How Do Suppliers Benefit from Information Technology Use in Supply Chain Relationships? MIS Quarterly, 28(1), 2004, 45-73
23. Wang, M. and Wang, H., From Process Logic to Business Logic -- A Cognitive Approach to Business Process Management, Information & Management, 43(2), 2006, 179-193
24. Wang, M., Cheung, W.K., Liu, J., and Luo, Z., Agent-based Web Service Composition for Supply Chain Management, IEEE Joint Conference on E-Commerce Technology (CEC' 06) and Enterprise Computing, E-Commerce and E-Services (EEE' 06), 2006
25. Weiß, G., Cognition, Sociability, and Constraints, ECAI 2000 Workshop on Balancing Reactivity and Social Deliberation in Multi-Agent Systems, LNCS 2103, 217-236
26. Weske, M., Aalst, W.M.P., and Verbeek, H.M.W., Advances in Business Process Management, Special Issue of Data and Knowledge Engineering, 50(1), 2004, 1-8
27. Yokoo, M., Distributed Constraint Satisfaction: Foundation of Cooperation in Multi-agent Systems, 2001, Springer, Berlin, New York
28. Zeng, L., Benatallah, B., Ngu, A.H.H., Dumas, M., Kalagnanam, J., and Chang, H., QoS-Aware Middleware for Web Services Composition, IEEE Transactions on Software Engineering, 30(5), 2004, 311-327
29. Zhao, J. and Stohr, E., Temporal workflow management in a claim handling system, Proceedings of Work Activities Coordination and Collaboration (WACC'99), 1999, 187–195.
30. Zhao, J.L. and Cheng, H.K., Web services and process management: a union of convenience or a new area of research? Decision Support Systems, 40(1), 2005, 1-8
31. Zhuge, H., Cheung, T., and Pung, H., A timed workflow process model, Journal of Systems and Software, 55(3), 2001, 231-243

Web Service E-Contract Establishment Using Features

Marcelo Fantinato[1], Itana Maria de S. Gimenes[2], and Maria Beatriz F. de Toledo[1]

[1] Institute of Computing, University of Campinas, Brazil
[2] Department of Computer Science, University of Maringá, Brazil
mfantina@ic.unicamp.br, beatriz@ic.unicamp.br, itana@din.uem.br

Abstract. Electronic contracts describe inter-organizational business processes in terms of supply and consumption of electronic services (commonly Web services). In a given contract domain, it is usually possible to identify a set of well-defined common and variation points. Feature modeling is an ontology-like technique that has been widely used for capturing and managing commonalities and variabilities of product families in the context of software product line. This paper proposes a feature-based approach in order to decrease the complexity in Web service e-contract establishment. The feasibility of the approach is shown by a case study carried out within the telecom context and based on experimental software engineering concepts.

1 Introduction

The Internet and Business Process Management Systems (BPMS) are major steps towards improving inter-organizational cooperation [1], [2]. Moreover, service-oriented computing [3] helps the integration among applications executed by BPMS. The main type of electronic service (e-service) being used currently for this purpose are the web services [4]. Web services are an emergent and promising technology for the effective automation of inter-organizational interactions. They are a specific type of e-service based on industry standard technologies such as WSDL [5], UDDI [6], and SOAP [7] – all of them based on XML. The use of these standards makes easier service automatic publication, discovery and invocation.

E-contracts are used to describe the supply and the consumption details of electronic services within a business process [8]. E-contracts concerned with Web services are normally called Web service e-contracts. There is a complexity involved in e-contract establishment that may hinder new business partnerships. This complexity is due to: the amount of information necessary in e-contract establishment; the potential long-duration of complex electronic negotiations; and the involvement of different profiles (business and development teams) from distinct organizations.

To deal with these drawbacks, many approaches to e-contract establishment achieve information structure and reuse using contract templates [8]-[14]. In most of them, templates are normally treaded as simple documents that have empty fields to be fulfilled. In general, the existent approaches do not offer suitable mechanisms to manage common and variable elements in similar contracts. Although they contribute with a series of advances in the area of e-contract elaboration and enactment, they provide a limited potential for information reuse.

S. Dustdar, J.L. Fiadeiro, and A. Sheth (Eds.): BPM 2006, LNCS 4102, pp. 290–305, 2006.

In this paper, a new approach to e-contract establishment is proposed. It is based on software product line concepts and mainly in feature modeling. Its main contribution is to offer a principled and efficient way for information reuse, optimizing the Web service e-contract establishment process. More than offering contract templates, it intends to manage more efficiently the mandatory, optional and alternative parts of them. A similar but partial approach has already been presented [15], but it is not concerned with the specific Web service context besides other new extensions.

Product Line (PL) promotes the generation of specific software products from a product family based on the reuse of a well-defined infrastructure [16]. PL exploits common points among systems in the same domain and manages variabilities among them in a systematic way [17]. Both software development and e-contract establishment demand an efficient information reuse. Thus, both may take profit of the PL approach to achieve a better understanding of domains and reduce time-to-market [18].

Most of the PL methodologies uses feature modeling [19] to capture and manage common points and variabilities [17], [18], [20]-[23]. Feature models are a kind of computing ontology [24], [25] used to describe properties of entities at different levels of abstraction. They constitute a simple, structured and easy to understand representation of information that may be used in different phases of the software development cycle. These facilities may also be helpful in e-contract establishment making contracts easier to understand and improving information reuse.

In brief, the proposed approach consists of some stages derived from a specific PL process, making use of feature modeling to allow the generic representation of e-services by features. The e-contract establishment activities (including negotiation between involved parties) will be oriented by the feature model and feature model configurations. The contracted generic e-services will be mapped to the Web services implementing them, which are referenced in the resulting e-contract. Applying this approach, the management of commonalities and variabilities will make the reuse of e-services and the establishment of new e-contracts easier.

The paper is organized as follows. Section 2 presents related works. Section 3 and 4 present an overview of e-contracts and feature modeling respectively. Section 5 introduces the proposed approach for Web service e-contract establishment. The case study is described in Section 6 and some lessons learned are discussed in the following section. Finally, conclusions and future work end the paper.

2 Related Work

CrossFlow project [8] is one of the precursor projects to treat e-contracts systematically through contract templates. CrossFlow allows template creation using pre-existent e-contracts that are often used in some business domain. Its reuse approach allows that fields with variable values are kept blank to be filled later, for each specific contract. CrossFlow last papers already indicated the necessity of more systematic ways to deal with templates. Chiu et. al. [9] advance towards this direction. Templates are treated as new entities in contract metamodels and may contain template variables whose values are defined during e-contract establishment. Variable values are defined and changed in a controlled way. Other similar approaches, which make use of e-contract metamodels, are presented in [10]-[12]. Some papers treat specifically the negotiation process to establish e-contracts, such as [26]-[28]. However, in these and other similar approaches, there is little emphasis in information reuse. It is expected that with the use of feature modeling, as proposed in this paper, better reuse be achieved. This new approach can be understood as a contract parameterization way that must be improved during the several e-contract instantiations that can take place with a same contract type.

There is some research concerned with the description of Web service properties in the e-contract context. The WSLA framework [13] supports the creation and use of QoS attributes for Web services in e-contract templates. This approach facilitates automatic matchmaking in the Internet. In a more recent work [14], it is presented a unified framework for comprehensive contractual description of Web services. Moreover, two complimentary standards are proposed to treat policy guarantees for Web services: WS-Agreement [29], [30] and WS-Policy [31], [32]. In this context, the approach proposed here is just interested in how to manage the mandatory, optional and alternative QoS levels in a high-level way. Therefore, the feature-based approach to Web service e-contract establishment can be potentially used in association with any of these standards.

3 Electronic Contracts

E-contracts [8] consist of: *parties* representing organizations involved in a business process, *activities* representing e-services to be executed during process enactment, and *contractual clauses* describing restrictions on the execution of activities. There are three types of clauses [33]: *obligations* (what parties should do), *permissions* (what parties are allowed to do) and *prohibitions* (what parties should not do). Obligations may include QoS clauses associated with e-services. These clauses define attributes such as performance, availability, security and reply time [13], 34, [35].

E-contracts may be derived from models or templates. Models are instances of metamodels for a specific application domain. Templates are partially-filled contracts. To facilitate the specification of e-contracts and their transfer between BPMSs, XML-based languages have been developed. Either DTD or, more recently, XML Schemas can be used in the specification of metamodels.

The e-contract metamodel used in the proposed approach is based on the one developed within the CrossFlow project [8] for its significance in the area [1] and wide coverage of essential aspects. The original metamodel, which does not take into account Web services, is presented in the next section.

3.1 CrossFlow e-Contract Metamodel

CrossFlow e-contracts are established between two parties: the provider and the consumer of an e-service. According to the metamodel in Fig. 1 (presented as an Entity-Relationship Diagram), an e-contract has five sections described below. The refinement of each section by other metamodels is presented in [36].

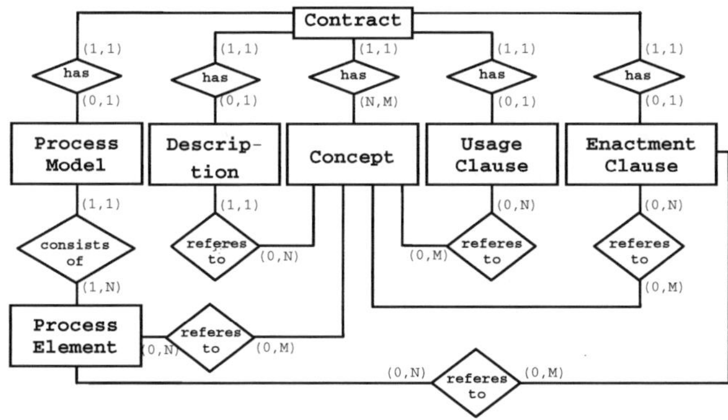

Fig. 1. CrossFlow e-contract metamodel [8]

- Concept: contains the terminology used in the e-contract. This section consists of a list of parameters formed by name, type and description. They receive a value during contract establishment or execution time.
- Process Model: defines the inter-organizational business process between the parties. It is based on the Process Description Language (PDL) by Workflow Management Coalition (WfMC) [37]. Processes are constituted by the Process Elements – Activities and Transitions. The other elements in the language are not used in this context.
- Enactment Clause: specifies clauses related to operations. There are three types of operations: control (e.g. suspend, abort), monitoring (e.g. operations to consult process status), QoS (e.g. operations that check if QoS attributes are satisfied).
- Usage Clause: defines how the contract must be used. Among required conditions, it can be cited the maximum number of process instances to be created at a time.
- Description: contains text in natural language for human readers.

CrossFlow contracts are specified in XML. The specification for a complete metamodel is available at the CrossFlow project site [36].

4 Feature Modeling

Feature modeling is an important technique that has been applied for capturing and managing commonalities and variabilities in PL [17]. It has been originally proposed in the domain engineering context, as part of the Feature-Oriented Domain Analysis (FODA) method [19], and has been applied in a range of domains including telecom systems, template libraries, networks protocols, and embedded systems.

In general, a feature model is a description of the relevant characteristics of some entity of interest. A feature can be defined as a system property that is relevant to some stakeholder and is used to capture commonalities or discriminate systems in a family. They may denote any functional or non-functional characteristic at the requirement, architectural, component, platform, or any other level [17]. According to the original FODA method, features can be mandatory, optional or alternative.

Features can be organized in a feature diagram, which is a tree-like structure where each node represents a feature and each feature may be described by a set of sub-features represented as children nodes [21]. Feature diagrams offer a simple and intuitive notation to represent variation points without using implementation mechanisms such as inheritance or aggregation. A set of feature diagrams and additional information – such as descriptions, binding times and priorities – forms a feature model [17].

A feature model can describe the configuration space of a system family. A member of the system family can be specified by selecting the desired features from the feature model within the variability constraints defined by the model (e.g., the choice of exactly one feature from a set of alternative features). This process is called feature configuration [17].

Due to its high level of abstraction, feature modeling has been used with other goals besides PL, such as: encapsulating system requirements, driving marketing decisions, future planning and communication between system stakeholders [22]. Some development tools have facilitated the use of feature model concepts in the industry. For instance, RequisitePro [38] already supports feature modeling, although without any graphical representation.

Feature models can be understood as a kind of computing ontology [24], [25]. Ontologies have been often used in computer science to capture knowledge about some domain of interest, enabling its sharing and reuse – e.g. in Semantic Web [39]. Both techniques are used to represent concepts in a particular domain and relationships between them. Despite some similarities, there are differences between them. Ontology languages and tools commonly offer reasoning facilities to check consistency and completeness, and inference engines to enhance rules processing. On the other hand, feature modeling offers facilities to capture and manage common and variable concepts. Both could be extended to incorporate characteristics offered by the other one.

The feature metamodel used here is the one proposed by Czarnecki et. al. [17]. Its main advantages are: integration of previous extensions and balance between simplicity and conceptual completeness. The metamodel is presented in the next section.

4.1 Cardinality-Based Feature Metamodel

The cardinality-based feature metamodel involves the concepts of attributes, feature groups, diagram modularization, and feature and feature group cardinalities. The metamodel is presented as a Class Diagram in Fig. 2.

There are three kinds of *features* in a *feature model*: *root feature* that forms the root of the different feature diagrams in a model; *grouped feature* that can only occur in a feature group; and *solitary feature* that is, by definition, not grouped in a *feature group*. Many features in a typical feature model are solitary. Features can have an *attribute* with a *typed value* – *string value* or *integer value*. The abstract classes *ContainableByFG* and *ContainableByF* stand for those kinds of objects that can be contained by a feature group and a feature, respectively. A feature group contains grouped features or diagram references, whereas a feature can include solitary features, feature groups and references. Diagram modularization is achieved by using the *FDReference* class, which stands for a feature diagram reference. It can refer to only one root feature, but a root feature can be referred by several references.

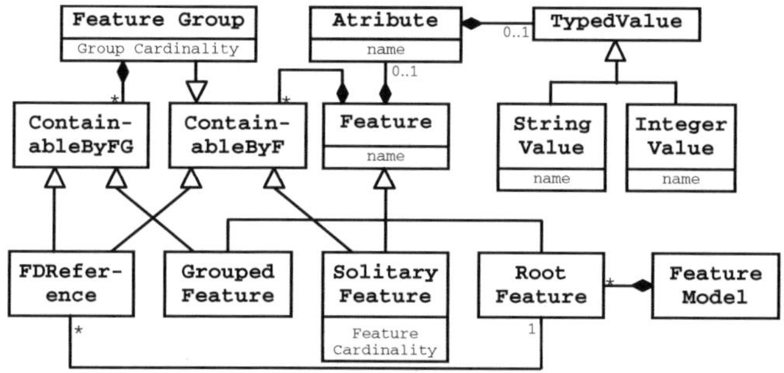

Fig. 2. Cardinality-based feature metamodel [17]

Feature and feature group cardinalities are represented as attributes in the feature metamodel. *Feature cardinality* defines how often a solitary sub feature (and possible subtrees) can be cloned as a child of its parent feature. Similarly, *group cardinality* is a property of the relationship between a parent and a set of sub features. A feature group expresses a choice over the grouped features in the group.

5 Modeling Web Service e-Contracts Based on Features

This section presents an overview of Web service e-contract establishment based on feature modeling. More details about the approach are found in the next section where the case study is presented. The proposed approach consists of five stages according to the FORM process (A Feature-Oriented Reuse Method with Domain-Specific Reference Architectures) [20] used in PL. The stages are the following:

1. E-service feature model elaboration: A feature model is elaborated to represent e-services and further related information (such as QoS attributes) from each organization willing to provide services for others. All possible e-services are represented by features in a high-level way, without considering technical details;
2. Web service e-contract template creation: Having an e-service feature model as the basis, a Web service e-contract template is created. It will contain basic information that can be used in any e-contract to be established from this feature model. Here, all the high-level e-services are mapped to Web services implementing them;
3. Web service development and publication: Web services that implement the e-services to be electronically contracted must be developed to be available during e-contract establishment. They may have been developed before and just reused;
4. E-service feature model configuration: The e-service feature model is configured to represent the exact e-services, from each organization, and QoS attributes to be used in a specific integration between systems from two cooperative organizations;
5. Web service e-contract establishment: Using the e-service feature model configuration, a Web service e-contract is defined by refining an e-contract template.

Stages 1, 2 and 3 are entirely carried out just once for the same contract domain, i.e. preparing the integration between two types of organizations (or systems). Stages 4 and 5 are carried out entirely for each instance of a Web service e-contract between two specific organizations (or systems). During the execution of the last two stages, the first three stages can be partially carried out again, when appropriate, to manage further information not treated previously. The last two stages are executed knowing the involved partners; therefore, this approach is not intended for dynamically established business relationships.

Fig. 3 represents, by a class diagram, the artifacts produced and the relationship between them. The E-service feature model is the basic artifact from which a unique Web service e-contract template is created and one or more E-service feature model configurations (one for each desired integration between systems) are derived. The e-contract template is created based also on the Support information artifact. For each E-service feature model configuration, a specific Web service e-contract is established. All the e-contracts are established based on the same e-contract template. All the Web services implementing e-services of the feature model are referenced by the Web service e-contract template. Only the Web services implementing e-services of the feature model configuration are referenced by the corresponding e-contract.

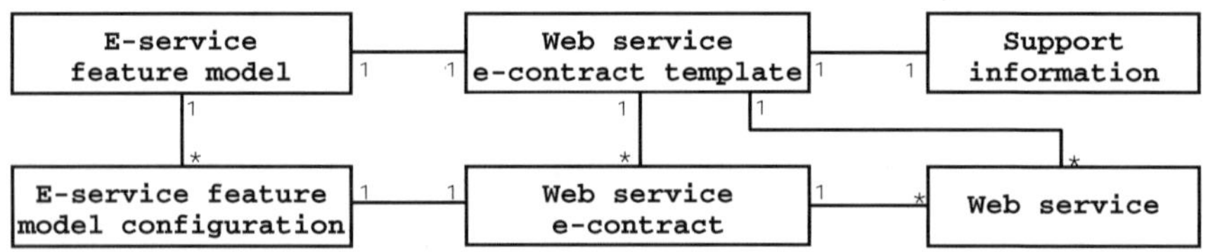

Fig. 3. Artifacts relationship

The feature model represents only the e-services required for the integration between two systems. Further information for the creation of the e-contract template, such as activities belonging to a single system that take part into the process and the activity transitions, is grouped in the Support information artifact.

6 Case Study

This section presents a summary of a case study undertaken on a pseudo-real scenario (i.e., not in a real organizational settings) to evaluate the approach above. In addition, more details about each stage are discussed in the context of the case study. This case study is based on the concepts of experimental software engineering and the evaluation of software engineering methods and tools [40], [41].

6.1 Application Domain

The case study object is the integration between two Business and Operation Support Systems (BOSS) [42] in the telecom context [43]. The systems are the following:

- Customer Relationship Management (CRM): System that manages the relationship between customers and a telecom company. Its execution requires the integration with other telecom BOSS systems such as: asset management, outside plant management, workforce management, service rating, service billing, collection, dunning and accounting;

- Dunning: System that supports customer debit charging which can involve actions such as debit notification (by mail or by phone), service supply suspension (partial or total) and legal actions.

The case study has considered that a telecom company (operating the CRM system) outsourced the charging activities to another company (operating the Dunning system) – creating an inter-organizational business process. Each system provides a set of e-services to be used by the other and an e-contract is established to define the details about the business agreement.

6.2 E-Service Feature Model Elaboration

In this stage, a feature model for each system involved in the collaboration is developed. In addition to high-level e-services, the feature model should describe QoS attributes and functional specifications for each e-service. Fig. 4-a and Fig. 4-b show the partial feature diagram representing e-services provided by the Dunning system to the CRM system. These diagrams have been produced by the FeaturePlugin tool [44].

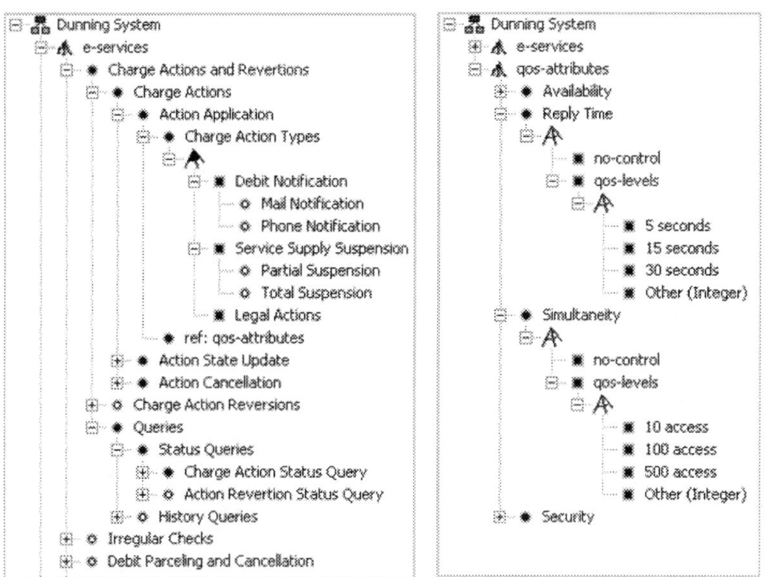

Fig. 4. Dunning e-service feature model. a) Dunning e-services / b) Dunning QoS attributes.

Mandatory, optional and alternative features specify common points and variabilities related to e-service provision. The inherent flexibility of the feature metamodel allows the definition of e-services in different ways. Rules have been defined to make e-service specifications always uniform. These rules are described below and are presented as a Class Diagram in Fig. 5. Actually, Fig. 4-a and Fig. 4-b represent an in stance of meta- model presented in Fig. 5.

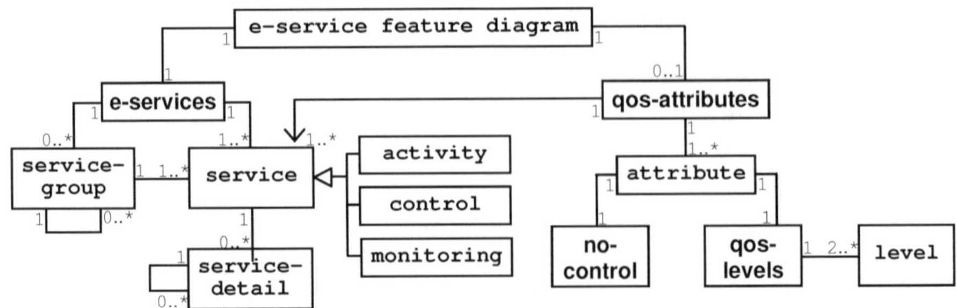

Fig. 5. Hierarchical rules for e-service specification using features

1. Each e-service feature diagram consists of one root feature named e-services (Fig. 4-a) and, optionally, one root feature named qos-attributes (Fig. 4-b);
2. Features below e-services must be created using the three following types:
   - *service-group* feature: represents a group or sub-group of e-services in the service hierarchy – used to structuralize service information (e.g. Charge Actions);
   - *service* feature: represents an e-service, which can be one of three subtypes: *activity* – services representing business actions of the process (e.g. Action Application), *control* – services representing process management actions (e.g. Action Cancellation) and *monitoring* – services representing process query actions (e.g. Charge Action Status Query);
   - *service-detail* feature: represents additional information of an e-service (e.g. Charge Action Types and its grouped features and sub-features).
3. Features below qos-attributes must be created using the three following types:
   - *attribute* feature: represents a QoS attribute that must be set by e-services (e.g. Reply Time). An *attribute* feature must have a feature group to contain only two grouped features – no control and qos-levels;
   - no-control feature: represents the option in which QoS attribute may be undefined to a specific QoS attribute for a specific e-service;
   - qos-levels feature: represents the QoS levels that can be defined for a specific QoS attribute of a given e-service. A qos-levels feature must have a feature group to contain its QoS level options;
   - *level* feature: represents a specific QoS level that can be defined for one QoS attribute (e.g. 15 seconds). One of the *level* features for a qos-levels feature can have no predefined value, being represented by a TypedValued.

The qos-attributes root feature must be referenced by all the features of the *service* type below the e-services root feature using the modularization mechanism (e.g., ref: qos-attributes associated with Action Application). The original feature metamodel has been extended to include an attribute that identifies the feature type according to the previous two categories. Feature types are not noticeable in the diagram (Fig. 4-a and Fig. 4-b) but they are presented elsewhere within the tool. The names given to features may suggest their type.

6.3 Web Service e-Contract Template Creation

In this stage, the Web service e-contract template associated with the e-service feature model is created. The CrossFlow e-contract metamodel (Section 2.1) has been extended to incorporate the Web service technology. Process Description Language (WfMC PDL) used in Process Model section was substituted by BPEL4WS (Business Process Execution Language for Web Services) [45], a XML-based language. As CrossFlow e-contracts are also based on XML, this change has been easily applied. Other CrossFlow e-contract metamodel sections have not been changed.

Most of the information required to create the template comes directly from the feature model, whereas any further information comes from the Support information artifact. There is a guideline for the mapping between entities in the feature metamodel and entities in the e-contract metamodel (in a one-to-one mapping basis). As this mapping is not automatic yet, human support is needed to complete it. A brief description of this mapping guideline is described below.

- Concepts: major parameters defining contract concepts are based on features of the *service-detail* type. Other parameters may be created using information from the Support information artifact;
- Process Model: most of the activities in the business process are created from features of the *service* type and *activity* subtype. Other activities (such as those belonging to a single system) and the activity transitions may be created using information from the Support information artifact;
- Enactment Clauses: control and monitoring clauses are also created from features of the *service* type, and *control* and *monitoring* subtypes – respectively, whereas QoS clauses are created from features of the *attribute* type and its sub-features (no-control, qos-level and *level*);
- Usage Clause: section not used in this case study;
- Description: section for free text.

All features in the feature model are considered when creating the e-contract template (mandatory, optional and alternatives). As a result, a possibly large and generic business process will be created, in which several integration types between the systems are considered. This generic process will be specialized during e-contract establishments according to the feature model configuration. The business process may begin with a basic version and evolve while the e-contract template is used.

Fig. 6 presents two small parts of the template produced by the case study. The first part belongs to the BPEL4WS-adapted Process Model section in which two activities, applyChargeActions and revertChargeActionApplication (which are mapped to the respective Web services defined elsewhere by WSDL descriptions), are defined from the respective features in the feature model. The other part belongs to the Enactment Clause section in which the QoS clause is defined (the QoS Reply Time is defined for the applyChargeActions activity). All the possible QoS levels for this attribute are presented in the template, as they have not been selected yet.

Fig. 7 presents a graphical view of the generic business process defined in the Web service e-contract template. Activities (and transitions) represented by solid elements are related to mandatory features whereas the dashed ones are related to optional or alternative features. Activities represented by gray-colored elements are internal activities that are never invoked by other systems (not represented in the feature model). Each feature of the *service-group* type can derive a process section. Only the Charge Actions and Reversions are detailed whereas others, such as Irregular Checks and Debit Parceling and Cancellation are just pointed out as other process sections.

```
<invoke  partner="dunning"
         portType="actionApplierPT"
         operation="applyChargeActions"
         inputContainer="customerInDebit"
   <target linkName"crm-to-dunning"/>
   <source linkName"dunning-to-crm"/>
</invoke>

<invoke  partner="dunning"
         portType="actionReversionApplier"
         operation=" revertChargeActionApplication "
         inputContainer="actionToRevert"
   <target linkName"crm-to-dunning"/>
   <source linkName"dunning-to-crm"/>
</invoke>

(...)

<GoalExpression>
   <Condition>
      <ActRef ActID="applyChargeActions"/>
      <ParamRef ParamID="REPLY_TIME"/>None|5|15|30|Other
   </Condition>
</GoalExpression>
```

Fig. 6. Partial CRM-Dunning Web service e-contract template

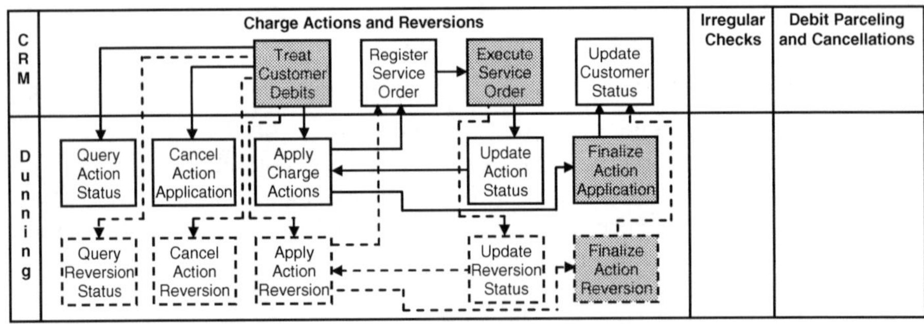

Fig. 7. Partial CRM-Dunning generic business process

6.4 E-Service Feature Model Configuration

The two previous stages are executed before Web service e-contract establishment. These produced artifacts may be reused in several situations involving business partners with similar characteristics. These next two steps are executed for each specific e-contract to be established.

The current stage corresponds to the main negotiation phase in which e-services and related contractual details are chosen. Negotiation is carried out according to configuration techniques for feature modeling [17]. Features representing mandatory e-services are kept whereas optional and alternative features are chosen according to the negotiation between the involved parts. Cardinalities restrictions must be satisfied.

Fig. 8-a and Fig. 8-b show the partial configuration of the e-service feature model corresponding to the diagrams in Fig. 4-a and Fig. 4-b. Mandatory features reappear selected whereas some optional and alternative features have been selected and others have not. For example, Action Application (of *service* type) must be selected whereas Charge Action Reversions (of *service-group* type) and, consequently, its sub-features, are not selected, although they could have been. Moreover, only some features of the Charge Action Types (of *service-detail* type) have been selected as they correspond to the types of charging actions to be contracted.

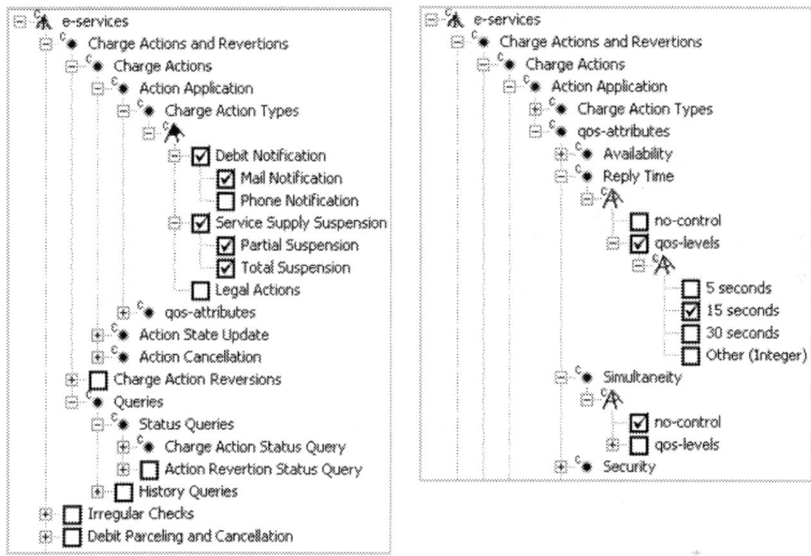

Fig. 8. Dunning e-service feature model configuration a) E-services / b) QoS attributes

Features representing QoS attributes should also be configured. References to the qos-attributes root feature are created the features of *service* type (Fig. 8.b). QoS attribute configuration is carried out for all features that have this reference. For example, the QoS level "15 seconds" has been chosen for the Action Application e-service.

6.5 Web Service e-Contract Establishment

In this stage, the Web service e-contract template is refined to completion considering the e-service feature model configured in the previous stage. In this stage, pending details are defined and information not required are removed from the contract.

Fig. 9 shows the partial Web service e-contract corresponding to the template in Fig. 6. Considering that the feature Charge Action Reversions has not been selected in the e-service feature model configuration, the corresponding activity (RevertCharge-

ActionApplication) does not appear in the e-contract. For the QoS Reply Time attribute, only the selected level during the configuration ("15 seconds") appears in the established e-contract.

```
<invoke  partner="dunning"
         portType="actionApplierPT"
         operation="applyChargeActions"
         inputContainer="customerInDebit"
   <target linkName"crm-to-dunning"/>
   <source linkName"dunning-to-crm"/>
</invoke>
(...)
<GoalExpression>
   <Condition>
      <ActRef ActID="applyChargeActions"/>
      <ParamRef ParamID="REPLY_TIME"/>15
   </Condition>
</GoalExpression>
```

Fig. 9. Partial CRM-Dunning Web service e-contract

Fig. 10 presents a graphical view of the specific business process defined in the Web service e-contract. It has been created based on the generic process (Fig. 7). This process contains only the activities related to the mandatory features or the optional and alternative features that have been selected during feature model configuration.

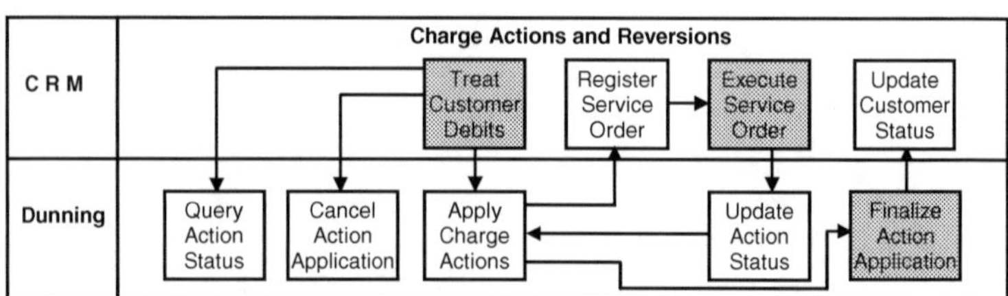

Fig. 10. Partial CRM-Dunning specific business process

During Web service e-contract establishments, unforeseen information such as new activities, new e-services or transitions might be required. In this case, artifacts used in the establishment of e-contracts (feature model and e-contract template) may be updated to include this information. This facility allows reuse during the establishment of other e-contracts. After the last stage, the established Web service e-contract may be released and used by BPMSs.

7 Lessons Learned

This section presents the lessons learned from the development and the exercising of the feature-based approach to e-contract establishment.

- E-service representation: The feature modeling technique has been considered suitable for the representation of e-services and QoS attributes. The metamodel flexibility has allowed the use of specific rules for e-services specification. Modularization facilities have been particularly useful for QoS attributes specification. Even if the produced artifacts are not reused, the application of feature models to e-service allows structured representation that is useful per se. With the support tool it has been possible to add new properties into the feature model and extend the metamodel used in the case study.

- Web service e-contract establishment: The metamodel used includes the most relevant items required in an e-contract. The e-contract well-defined structure shows the potential reuse in this application domain. The metamodel has been easily extended to incorporate the Web service technology since the metamodel and BPEL4WS are both XML-based. BPEL4WS has been considered rather complete and consistent, simplifying the e-contract template creation. Some restrictions have been found in the QoS attributes subsection of the XML specification, which have been adapted to make possible a better interpretation by BPMS.
- Metamodels mapping: It has been identified a direct mapping between elements in feature and e-contract metamodels. Some rules have been defined to map the features representing e-service information to elements in e-contract sections. These rules have proved to be suitable. However, human intervention has been necessary to complete the mapping.
- Approach contributions: The case study has demonstrated that the use of feature models during the establishment of Web service e-contracts makes them easier to understand, simple and systematic. The approach improves information and artifact reuse; and allows a quicker contract establishment. Common points and variabilities provided by feature modeling represent e-services in a controlled and structured way. Distinct stakeholders, at different levels, can benefit from the proposed approach. The e-service feature model can be understood as a Web service e-contract configuration space – depending on the choices made during feature model configurations, different and specific e-contracts are established.

8 Conclusions and Future Work

In this paper, a new approach to e-contract establishment based on feature modeling is proposed. Its main contribution is allowing a better management of common and variable points found in similar Web service e-contracts and information reuse in a systematic way. Such improvement is achieved by the use of e-contract templates associated with feature models. Inspired by the software product line context, the proposed approach can be seen as a kind of e-contract product line. The feasibility of the proposed approach has been shown by a case study carried out within the telecom context and based on experimental software engineering concepts.

Future work includes: a detailed evaluation of the actual possibilities and advantages in extending feature models to incorporate some characteristics offered by computing ontologies, in the e-contract context; the automated support for the elaboration of Web service e-contract templates and e-contracts based on e-service feature models and feature model configurations (mainly for the automatic mapping between metamodels); and the adoption of specific QoS mechanisms applied to Web services – such as WS-Agreement or WS-Policy standards, aiming at enhancing the adherence between e-contract metamodels subsections.

Acknowledgements

This work was partially supported by CAPES, CNPq, FAPESP and Araucaria Foundation.

References

[1] U. Dayal, M., and R. Ladin, "Business Process Coordination: State of the Art, Trends, and Open Issues", VLBD 2001, Morgan Kaufmann, Italy, 2001, pp. 3-13.
[2] F. Leymann, D. Roller, and M.-T. Schmidt, "Web services and business process management", *IBM Systems Journal*, 41(2), IBM Press, 2002, pp. 198-211.
[3] M. Papazoglou, and D. Georgakopoulos, "ServiceOriented Computing", *Communications of the ACM: ServiceOriented Computing*, 46(10), ACM Press, 2003, pp. 24-28.
[4] Web Services. http://www.w3.org/2002/ws/.
[5] Web Services Description Language (WSDL). http://www.w3.org/TR/wsdl.
[6] UDDI.org. http://www.uddi.org.
[7] SOAP Specifications. http://www.w3.org/TR/SOAP.
[8] Y. Hoffner, S. Field, P. Grefen and H. Ludwig, "Contract-Driven Creation and Operation of Virtual Enterprises", Computer Networks, The International Journal of Computer and Telecommunications Networking, North Holland, Volume 37, pp. 111-136, September 2001.
[9] D.K.W. Chiu, S-C Cheung, and S. Till, "A Three Layer Architecture for E-Contract Enforcement in an E-Service Environment", HICSS 2003, USA, 2003.
[10] M. Rouached, O. Perring and C. Godart, "A Contract Layered Architecture for Regulating Cross-Organisational Business Processes", BPM 2005, Springer, 2005, pp. 410-415.
[11] P.R. Krishna, K. Karlapalem, A.R.Dani, "From Contract to E-Contracts: Modeling and Enactment", Information Technology and Management, 6(4), 2005, pp. 363-387.
[12] O. von Susani and P. Dugerdil, "Contract-Based Cross-Organizational Automated Processes", IEEE CEC 2005, IEEE Computer Society, 2005, pp. 540-543.
[13] A. Keller and H. Ludwig, "The WSLA Framework: Specifying and Monitoring Service Level Agreements for Web Services", Journal of Network and Systems Management, 11(1), Springer, 2003, pp. 57-81.
[14] V. Tosic, "On Comprehensive Contractual Descriptions of Web Services", IEEE Int. Conf. On e-Technology, e-Commerce and e-Service, 2005, pp.444-449.
[15] M. Fantinato, M.B.F. de Toledo and I.M.S. Gimenes, "A Feature-based Approach to Electronic Contracts", IEEE Joint Conference on E-Commerce Technology (CEC'06) and Enterprise Computing, E-Commerce and E-Services (EEE'06), 2006.
[16] SEI – Software Engineering Institute, "A Framework for Software Product Line Practice" Version 4.2, http://www.sei.cmu.edu/productlines/framework.html, Pittsburgh.
[17] K. Czarnecki, S. Helsen, and U. Eisenecker, "Staged Configuration through Specialization and Multi-Level Configuration of Feature Models", Software Process Improv. and Practice, 10(2), John Wiley & Sons, 2005, pp. 143-169.
[18] E.A. Oliveira Junior et. al., "A Variability Management Process for Software Product Lines", CASCON 2005, IBM Press, Canada, 2005.
[19] K. Kang et. al., "Feature-Oriented Domain Analysis (FODA) Feasibility Study", Technical Report CMU/SEI-90-TR-021, SEI/CMU, Pittsburgh, 1990.
[20] K.C. Kang et. al., "FORM: A Feature-Oriented Reuse Method with Domain-Specific Reference Architectures", Annals of Soft. Engin., Vol. 5, Springer, 1998, pp. 143-168.
[21] V. Cechticky et. al., "XML-Based Feature Modelling", ICSR 2004, Springer, Spain, 2004, pp. 101-114.

[22] P. Sochos, I. Philippow, and M. Riebisch, "Feature-Oriented Development of Software Product Lines: Mapping Feature Models to the Architecture", Net.ObjectDays 2004, 2004.
[23] M. Griss. "Implementing Product-Line Features with Component Reuse", ICSR 2000, Springer, Austria, 2000, pp. 137-152.
[24] T. R. Gruber. "A translation approach to portable ontologies". *Knowledge Acquisition*, 5(2):199-220, 1993.
[25] OWL Web Ontology Language Overview Web site. http://www.w3.org/TR/owl-features/.
[26] W. Streitberger, "Framework for the Negotiation of Electronic Contracts in E-Business on Demand", IEEE CEC 2005, IEEE Computer Society, 2005, pp. 370-373.
[27] S. Rinderle and M. Benyoucef, "Towards the Automation of E-Negotiation Processes Based on Web Services - A Modeling Approach", WISE 2005, Springer, 2005, pp. 443-453.
[28] A. Jertila and M. Schoop, "Electronic Contracts in Negotiation Support Systems: Challenges, Design and Implementation", IEEE CEC 2005, IEEE Comp.Soc., 2005, pp. 396-399.
[29] A. Andrieux et. al., "Web Services Agreement Specification (WS-Agreement). https://forge.gridforum.org/projects/graap-wg/document/WS-AgreementSpecificationDraft. doc/en/10. 2006.
[30] N. Oldham et. al., "Semantic WS-Agreement Partner Selection", 15th International World Wide Web Conference (WWW2006), ACM, 2006.
[31] S. Bajaj et. al., "Web Services Policy Framework (WS-Policy)", http:// download.boulder.ibm.com/ibmdl/pub/software/dw/specs/ws-polfram/ws-policy-2006-03-01.pdf.
[32] L. Baresi, S. Guinea and P. Plebani, "WS-Policy for Service Monitoring", 6th VLDB Workshop on Technologies for E-Services (VLDB-TES'05), 2005.
[33] O. Marjanovic and Z. Milosevic, "Towards Formal Modeling of e-Contracts", EDOC 2001, IEEE Computer Society, USA, 2001, pp. 59-68.
[34] A. Sahai et. al., "Automated SLA Monitoring for Web Services", DSON 2002, Springer, Canada, 2002, pp. 28-41.
[35] D.A. Menasce, "QoS Issues in Web Services", IEEE Internet Computing, 6(6), pp. 72-75, Nov/Dec, 2002.
[36] CrossFlow Web site. http://www.crossflow.org.
[37] WfMC Web site. http://www.wfmc.org.
[38] IBM Rational RequisitePro Web site. http://www-306.ibm.com/software/awdtools/ reqpro.
[39] H. Wang, L. Y. Fang, J. Sun, H. Zhang and J. Z. Pan. "A Semantic Web Approach to Feature Modeling and Verification", SWESE, 2005.
[40] B. Kitchenham, L. Pickard, and S. Lawrence Pfleeger, "Case Studies for Method and Tool Evaluation", IEEE Software, 12(4), IEEE Computer Society, 1995, pp. 52-62.
[41] S.L. Pfleeger, "Experimental design and analysis in software engineering: Part 2: how to set up and experiment", ACM SIGSOFT Soft. Eng. Notes, 20(1), 1995, pp. 22-26.
[42] K. Terplan, "OSS Essentials: Support System Solutions for Service Providers", John Wiley & Sons, USA, 2001.
[43] J. Hunter and M. Thiebaud, "Telecommunications Billing Systems – Implementing and Upgrading for Profitability", McGraw-Hill, USA, 2003.
[44] M. Antkiewicz and K. Czarnecki, "FeaturePlugin: Feature Modeling Plug-in for Eclipse", Workshop on Eclipse Technology Exchange, ACM Press, Canada, 2004, pp. 67-72.
[45] Business Process Execution Language for Web Services (BPEL4WS). http://www-128. ibm.com/developerworks/library/specification/ws-bpel/.

A Redesign Framework for Call Centers

M.H. Jansen-Vullers, M. Netjes, H.A. Reijers, and M.J. Stegeman

Department of Technology Management, Eindhoven University of Technology
P.O. Box 513, NL-5600 MB, Eindhoven, The Netherlands
{m.h.jansen-vullers, m.netjes, h.a.reijers}@tm.tue.nl,
m.j.stegeman@student.tue.nl

Abstract. An important shortcoming in the Business Process Redesign (BPR) literature is the lack of concrete guidance on how to improve an existing business process. Our earlier work has aimed at filling this gap by identifying a set of BPR *best practices*. This paper takes a further step by showing how a set of best practices can be used to derive a redesign framework for a specific domain, in this case for *call centers*. Such a framework identifies the various available design options and specifies the relevant performance characteristics. To evaluate concrete design configurations (i.e., coherent combinations of design choices) we use a formal modelling approach based on Petri nets and the simulation tool CPN-Tools. An industrial case study is used to gather relevant context data. We expect that this work helps researchers and practitioners to optimize the performance of actual call centers and to set up similar frameworks for other domains.

Keywords: Business Process Redesign, Call centers, Simulation, Petri nets.

1 Introduction

There is a strong movement in BPM research to identify recurring problems and their solutions, e.g. with respect to process modelling [1] and data processing [22]. Earlier, similar explorations of *patterns* and *best practices* have taken place in architecture [2], business planning [13], health care [8], software development [5], and manufacturing [7]. It could be argued that such attempts are signs of a research field to become more mature, as its shifts attention from the specific and concrete to the general and abstract.

One particular research field within BPM that would be served by a more scientific approach is that of Business Process Redesign (BPR). BPR is concerned with optimizing the structure of a business process and exploiting the opportunities that IT provides hereto [4]. As many authors have argued [16,24,28], there is little concrete guidance to be found in the great numbers of BPR publications on how to actually turn an existing process into a better performing one. "Given the prominence of BPR in recent years", say Melao and Pidd [15], "such superficiality is a little puzzling."

S. Dustdar, J.L. Fiadeiro, and A. Sheth (Eds.): BPM 2006, LNCS 4102, pp. 306–321, 2006.

In our earlier work, we presented a set of 29 best practices for process redesign [21], as distilled from documented cases (e.g. [9]), earlier approaches towards identifying best practices (e.g. [18], and our own BPR experience (see [20]). For example, the 'order assignment' best practice states that a worker should perform as many steps as possible for the same order, as this will positively affect the quality of the work. The set of best practices was validated through case studies and a large survey among experienced BPR practitioners [12].

Although such a collection of BPR best practices fits the desirable trend to identify solutions for recurring problems, it has some limitations. First of all, the best practices concerned are evaluated with respect to rather abstract notions of cost, quality, flexibility, and time. This makes it difficult to predict the impact of applying a best practice in a concrete situation. Moreover, skilful efforts are still required to adapt best practices to make them fit a particular context of the recurring problem. For example, the options for one particular worker to execute a number of steps in a financial business process are different from those in a health care setting.

In this paper we will demonstrate how this generic list of best patterns can be used to develop a domain-specific *redesign framework*. Such a framework offers:

1. the relevant *process design options* that are available for generating specific designs in such a domain
2. the concrete *performance characteristics* that are considered relevant in this domain,
3. the means to accurately *predict the actual performance* for a specific design configuration with respect to such characteristics.

For the development of a redesign framework, we turn towards the field of *call centers*. Call centers have received a wide share of research attention [6,14,23,25,26,27,30,31]. A very apparent best practice that is relevant in this domain is that of finding the right mix of specialists and generalists. Compared to generalists, specialists are expected to be fast and reliable, deliver good quality, etc. On the other hand, it takes time and cost to become a specialist, and a specialist can handle only particular types of cases or perform only particular tasks of an individual case.

For the evaluation component of the framework, we propose the use of discrete event simulation. In particular, we used the software package CPN Tools version 2.0.0 [10,29]. Literature revealed that both queueing theory and simulation models are applied in this area [6]. Queueing models have the advantage of being able to find optimal staffing levels, but the disadvantage that a realistic call center process is too complex to be modelled in an adequate manner. Simulation models can be arbitrarily complex while yielding good results. The price to be paid, however, is that the result is merely a comparison of several scenarios instead of the optimal scenario.

Our research method has been to first study the wide field of literature related to the subject of optimizing call centers. Our set of best practices was then used as a lens to consider the recurring solutions from the various specific redesign actions. This has led to a number of best practices with their specific application in the domain. Next, we enriched this selection (1) by extending the observed ways of adapting best practices towards a wider set of conceivable solutions and (2) by incorporating best practices that we did not see applied in the call center domain so far (but seem attractive). In taking these steps, a list of domain-specific design options emerged that sets the stage for creating concrete design configurations, i.e. a combination of concrete choices with respect to the design options. Independent from this path, we identified important performance characteristics from the call center literature, e.g. abandonment rates and numbers of handled calls. Finally, we used simulation to determine the performance of several design configurations under some realistic scenarios. To give the design configurations a realistic content, we used the actual data we gathered from a case study we performed at a large Dutch call center (e.g. intensity of calls, staffing levels, etc.). Obviously, these data could be replaced with information from other concrete call centers.

The structure of our paper is now as follows. In Section 2, we review the existing literature on call centers. This review results in an overview of best practices that can be observed in call center settings and a set of relevant performance characteristics. In Section 3, we present the various design options that result from a wider consideration of the various best practices. Next, in Section 4, we describe an industrial call center, which is used to provide the context information for the redesign framework. In Section 5, we will present a set of design configurations, which are being evaluated using simulation. Finally, we will present our conclusions and ideas for future work.

2 Related Work

In this section we describe the related work to redesign call center processes. We first provide an overview of call centers in literature. Then we elaborate the call center processes from the viewpoint of redesign best practices. We conclude this section with an overview of performance management in call centers.

2.1 Call Centers in Literature

Call centers are a fruitful domain for many research disciplines. Mandelbaum published an extensive overview of call center literature in many different areas, such as operations research, consumer and agent psychology, management models, etc. [11]. Starting from this overview, we researched literature on staffing levels in multiple skill inbound call centers [27]. In the area of analytical models, a lot of models have been developed for generalists, specialists and cross-trained workers. An example of this type of models is the gatekeeper model [25].

Figure 1 represents this call center model that uses the principles of gatekeepers and referrals to characterize the difference between generalists and specialists. The authors conclude that the performance of a call center and the behavior of an agent (gatekeeper) mainly depend on the prescribed referral rate (the rate at which work is routed from generalists to specialists). If a call is too difficult to

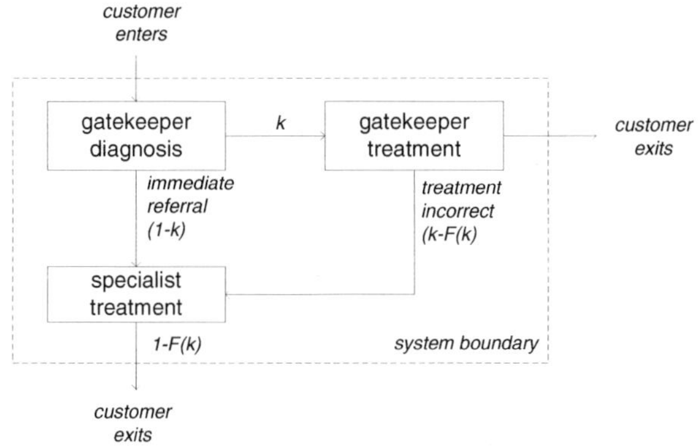

Fig. 1. Gatekeeper and referral configuration of a call center [25]

be handled and solved by the gatekeeper, he or she refers the call to a specialist. The authors call it a triage system, because customers first interact with a generalist who determines whether the attention of a specialist is required.

Another view on the call center process is provided, e.g., by Zapf [30,31]. He uses a Petri-net kind of model to represent the process in a call center, see Figure 2. Calls flow from left to right through the model, being processed by tasks *R*egister, *C*lassify and *H*andle. Resources are assigned to (a set of) tasks, and are either *G*eneralists or *S*pecialists with skill *i*. The difference with the previous representation of a call center process is the distinction between two types of requests (standard and special) which are handled both in a different way. The difficulty of a service request is known upfront in this case. Standard requests are classified and handled by generalists and special requests are first classified by generalists and then handled by specialists.

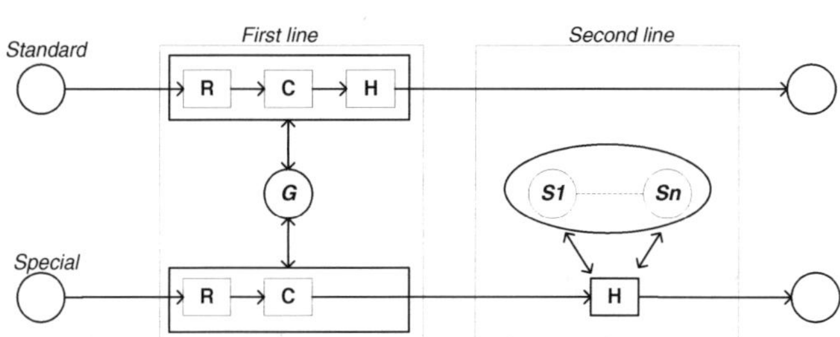

Fig. 2. Two-level design of a call center process, based on [31]

2.2 Redesign Best Practices in Call Centers

The literature on call centers revealed a number of design options, which we now describe from a best practices viewpoint. The best practices are given in italics.

The distinction between standard and special *case types* [21] is quite common but may not be that strict for the incoming calls at a call center and may be unknown upfront. Some calls can be classified as standard calls because they are relatively easy to solve by the generalists in the 1st line. Some calls are sent straight away to the 2nd line. In addition to this distinction of case types, a distinction between synchronous and asynchronous requests can be defined [30]. The notion of different case types enables a distinction of different routings per case type. This kind of specialization of a more general routing is called *triage* [21].

The distinction of 1st line and 2nd line operations is based on the principle of *task composition* [21] and refers to one of the two basic designs of a call center: the one-level design and the two-level design. These designs come from the fact that the process in a call center consists of a limited number of steps: registration, classification and handling of requests. This does not leave much room for variation in task composition, if one considers that registration and classification may be done implicitly when (trying to) handle the case.

The application of *task automation* [21] is encountered in the form of automated call distributers (ACDs). Application of ACD tools and techniques supports or even executes the task of classification of a call, which may also lead to *contact reduction* [21].

Finally, the distinction between *generalists and specialists* [21] is frequently encountered. A generalist is considered to be able to handle all standard calls whereas a specialist can handle all calls. Note that also other definitions exist, e.g. a generalist can handle all calls whereas a specialist can handle only one particular type of calls. In this context, also cross-trained workers can be recognized, being able to handle a set of call types.

Summarizing, when looking to call center literature from the viewpoint of redesign best practices, we found the following best practices (though never combined in one approach):

- case types: standard/special and synchronous/aynchonous
- triage: based on the two kinds of case types, different routings may be defined
- task composition: one level and two-level designs
- task automation, i.e. an ACD menu
- generalist/specialist: consider different skill sets for cross-trained workers.

2.3 Performance Measurement in Call Centers

A last topic we would like to highlight is related to performance characteristics in call centers. Many papers in call center literature focus on specific performance characteristics, e.g. the number of lost calls or the throughput time. Generally, four main dimensions are distinguished in the effects of (re)design measures: time, cost, quality and flexibility. The trade-off that has to be made between the different dimensions is often difficult. Usually, an improvement along one dimension comes at the expense of another. Brand and Van der Kolk clarify this with the devil's quadrangle [3].

Amongst others, Zapf and Heinzl provide an extensive overview on performance characteristics for call centers [31]. They distinguish quality objectives and efficiency objectives. Based on their paper, we defined the following performance characteristics:

- Service level, i.e. the number of answered calls divided by the sum of the numbers of answered and lost calls.
- Speed of answer, i.e. the average time before a call can be accepted.
- Throughput time, i.e. the overall time a call is 'open', including both service time and waiting time. We distinguish throughput time of standard requests and special requests.
- Labor costs, i.e. resource allocation times salary. Labor costs may account up to 60 percent of a call center's total operating costs.

3 Mapping onto Process Designs

In the previous section we have seen that several papers focus on the redesign of call centers, though a structured approach is lacking here. Elements in existing approaches are the distinction of one-level and two-level designs on the one hand and synchronous and asynchronous requests on the other. Furthermore, some authors distinguish standard and special requests, and some distinguish several case types. However, a combination and integration of those approaches is lacking. In this section, we will look at the redesign best practices as already encountered in literature, extend them in a wider set of solutions and finally incorporate other fruitful best practices [12].

Task Composition
Starting point of our redesigns is the distinction between one-level designs and two-level designs. On top of this, we are able to add a number of best practices, which are elaborated below.

Introduction of Case Types and Triage
The definition of standard versus special requests is usually defined based on the complexity of the request. This means that the required skill set is the same for both standard and special requests, though the skills for special requests require a more advanced level. A more detailed classification of case types may be based on the content of a request, e.g., the ACD type in a call center. In many cases a strong correlation exists between complexity of the case and the case type based on contents. For one group, the referral rate may be more than 90% whereas the referral rate of the other group may be less than 10%. Finally, one can distinguish between synchronous and asynchronous requests. Both types can be subdivided into standard/special or per ACD type. Recognizing a division into case types, enables the consideration of alternative process designs per (group of) case type(s); this is called triage. This can be applied on all one-level and two-level designs.

Introduction of Generalist - Specialist Dilemma
An example of triage can be encountered when assigning generalists and specialists based on different case types, in this domain by (groups of) ACD type. A special case is the division into two groups: standard and special. Note that several definitions of 'specialist' exist. In some definitions or domains, a specialist has the same skills as a generalist, but on a more advanced level. In that case, specialists are homogeneous. In other cases or domains, a specialist implies that he has only one particular skill on an advanced level, whereas other specialists have different advanced skills. As a results, the specialists form an heterogeneous resource group. We may apply the generalist-specialist dilemma in a one-level design and in a two level design both in the 1st and 2nd line.

Introduction of Task Automation and Contact Reduction
If specialists are introduced in the 1st line or calls are directly forwarded to specialists in the 2nd line, a mechanism needs to be introduced in order to decide to which specialist queue the call should be added. One way to do so is by introducing automation. In the 1st line this is commonly known as the ACD menu, an alternative counterpart for the 2nd line should be introduced in addition to this automated menu. If calls are either completely handled in the 1st line or in the 2nd line, contact reduction has been realized as well.

Apart from a black and white division of those who can do all tasks and cases and those who can do only one task or case type, we introduce cross-trained workers. When considering Figure 2, this may include more generalist resources in the 2nd line, but we may also consider introducing more specialized workers in the 1st line.

Introduction of Flexibility
In a homogeneous setting, the selection of a suitable resource is trivial. However, in a heterogeneous setting, we may have a choice either to select a specialist or any of the cross trained workers for a particular task. Flexibility means that we want to keep as much options open as possible [17]. In a random assignment procedure for task A, one may assign a resource with skills A and B instead of a resource with only skill A. As a result, a subsequent assignment for task B is not possible anymore. Several strategies can be introduced to increase flexibility and to optimize process performance. In this paper, we assign the resource that has the required skill and is the most specialized resource available.

Introduction of Additional Resources
A very simple measure to improve process performance is to add resources to the existing staffing level. The additional costs can be calculated quite easily and the benefits in terms of time and flexibility can be determined. Apart from increasing the current staffing level, one may consider to move staff from one resource group to another, e.g., from the 2nd line to 1st line, or the other way around, or even to another group of cross trained workers. These movements may be permanent but also temporary, e.g. during peak hours.

By reviewing the redesign best practices, we are now able to create a large set of possible process designs which can be evaluated for any setting of a concrete call center. In addition to the individual best practices encountered in (both queuing theory and simulation!) literature, we contributed

- integration of currently applied best practices in one approach
- fine-grained application of generalist/specialist and triage best practices
- addition of flexibility best practice
- addition of additional resources best practice.

4 Case Study: The IT Help Desk

Within a large Dutch call center we have performed a case study at the IT help desk. The IT help desk provides IT support to 4,000 employees which contact the IT help desk when they have IT related problems or questions. The IT help desk can be described by some typologies or terminologies that are used in literature to characterize call centers [27]. In this section we will describe the process, the characteristics and the parameters of the IT help desk.

4.1 The Process

In this subsection the IT help desk process will be explained. As shown in Figure 3 the IT help desk process begins with the arrival of calls. The incoming communication channels are synchronous (telephone, personal contact) as well as asynchronous (mail, fax). Most calls enter the process by telephone and callers go through an Automated Call Distributor (ACD) before speaking to an agent. With the ACD, the caller chooses a type of problem from a menu, after which the ACD leads the call to a suitable agent. Callers have to wait for the availability of an agent and during this queueing process they may decide to hang up. The IT help desk consists of a 1st line and a 2nd line. All calls enter the 1st line which is taken care of by agents that can handle all ACD options from the menu. The 1st line agents are generalists and the ACD is just used as part of the communication infrastructure and a recording tool for historic data on calls and agents. The ACD database, AVAYA, allows for access to the database and designing all kinds of ACD types and call reports.

An incoming call will be classified by a 1st line generalist and served and solved right away if possible. If the call turns out to be too difficult, it will be forwarded to an agent in the 2nd line. The agents in the 2nd line are called specialists and can only handle specific tasks or problems. Specialists in the 2nd line are heterogeneous, a specialist with skill A cannot replace another specialist with skill B. This resembles the idea of process partitioning [31]. A specialist in the 2nd line may reroute the call to another specialist when necessary or send it to a 3rd line. This 3rd line is outside the scope of this case study.

4.2 The Characteristics and Parameters

The historic data present in the AVAYA database has been analyzed to make reliable estimations and predictions on the required input parameters for the

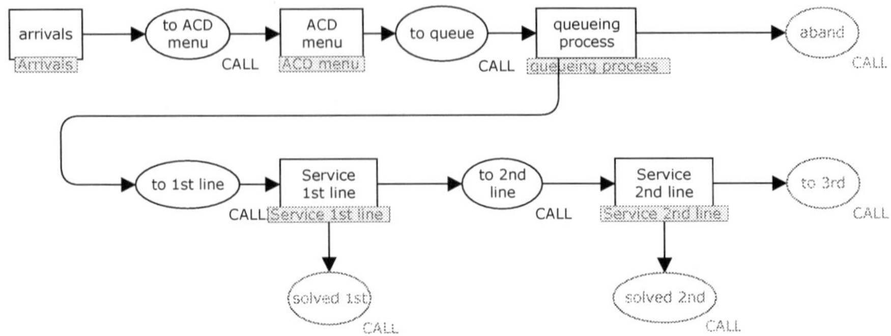

Fig. 3. Overview of the (executable) process model of the IT help desk

modelling of the IT help desk process. We analyzed the number of calls for each call type and the routing of calls through the process. We also analyzed arrival, waiting and service times and agent availability. One whole year of historic data has been used for these analyses.

Calls are routed through the IT help desk process as illustrated in Figure 3. The call center process starts with incoming calls. Based on our analyses we distinguish two basic types of calls: incidents and requests for information. The percentage of incident calls that was registered is determined at 72%. Furthermore 30% of incidents and 93% of information requests is solved immediately by a 1st line agent. From these percentages we derive that almost all information requests are handled in the 1st line which makes them standard calls. For similar reasons we perceive the incident calls as special calls which are classified in the 1st line and handled by the 2nd line. The inter-arrival rate of calls (the number of seconds between each call) is stored in the AVAYA database in time blocks of 30 minutes. Our analysis showed no patterns or trends over the months or the years in terms of incoming calls. However, the number of calls in the time blocks is different per day and week and this is modelled in detail.

Before a call is answered, the caller is waiting in a queue. While in the queue, the caller may become impatient, leading to an abandoned call. Approximately 80% of the callers is either not patient at all or, on the contrary, very willing to wait for service. The fact that calls are abandoned is represented in the simulation model by a function representing the patience of the caller. The abandonment of calls is implemented in the IT help desk model with a parameter representing the patience of the caller. When a call is serviced it will either be solved in the 1st line or it is forwarded to a specialist in the 2nd line. This specialist could redistribute the call to another specialist or to the 3rd line when he is unable to solve the problem or he could send the call back to the 1st line for further registration.

In the 1st line an agent answers, registers, classifies and if possible solves the call. The service of the call at the 1st line ends when an agent closes the call or when he sends the call through for further service in the 2nd line. The distribution of service times in the 1st line seems to be random. Every time block of the day and week may have a different number of available agents. Ten weeks of detailed time block data has been used to determine averages for every time block within the week. The time an agent is available to take a call is very likely to be less than the time for which he is scheduled [19], because of coffee breaks, trips to restrooms, etc. The detailed data of the ACD reports though, shows the average number of agents that has been logged on the ACD per time block.

In the 2nd line, the agents are specialists and can handle one type of special calls. Therefore, each specialist has its own capabilities and skills. We measured the time spent on a call by specialist type. Also work schedules, pauses and available time to handle calls have been collected to obtain the availability of the 2nd line agents.

5 Simulations

Based on the general redesigns defined in Section 3 and the case described in Section 4, this section focuses on the evaluation of particular redesigns. The general redesigns are formulated per best practice; for a particular redesign we combine these in an integrated set, e.g. we chose to apply cross-trained workers in a one level design instead of in any of the two level designs. To compare a particular redesign with an alternative, we use simulation. In this section, we first describe our simulation approach, followed by the evaluation of a number of process designs.

5.1 Simulation Scenarios

Each of the designs will be simulated for a number of scenario's, e.g. average arrival rate, overflow, etc. The previously defined designs have been implemented in a CPN model and run in CPN Tools 2.0.0 [10]. The models have been verified for structural correctness by a State space analysis, and have been validated by comparing the simulation results with current numbers of performance and output of the IT help desk. Current numbers were based on the design of the current situation with the current settings of the IT help desk. These settings included the arrival pattern, the distribution of case types and the number of resources for the 1st and 2nd line.

Although the current settings are interesting to be compared for the defined designs, we also added a number of different scenarios. In case the current settings may change, we can consider the impact of alternative scenarios on a particular design beforehand. We distinguished the following scenarios:

S1 current situation
S2 change in arrival pattern: number of cases increases with 75%
S3 number of special cases increases to 75%
S4 number of standard cases increases to 75%
S5 number of generalists has been reduced from 6 to 5
S6 number of specialists has been reduced from 16 to 15

All simulations are run with a warm-up period of 8 weeks and a run length of 4 weeks for measurement purposes. The analysis is based on a non-terminating simulation in a steady state, 30 replications per simulation. One simulation thus included 30 replications of 12 weeks, taking about 20 minutes of computer time. In total, we analyzed 6 scenarios for 10 different designs, i.e. 1800 replications.

Each of the performance characteristics has been implemented as a monitor in CPN Tools [29]. We calculated the 95% reliability intervals to be able to compare simulation results of different design/scenario combinations and to decide whether discovered process improvements were significant.

5.2 Specialization in a One-Level Design

In this section, we created process models based on a one level design and two request types: standard and special. We evaluate the generalist-specialist best practice in three different designs: (1) one-level with only generalists who can handle all requests, (2) one-level with only specialists who can handle only one request type and (3) one-level design with cross-trained workers. In the design with cross-trained workers, we created one group of heterogenous specialists (1 advanced skill, total 11 skills) and two groups with partly the same skills (standard requests) and partly different skills (5 resp. 6 advanced skills).

Comparison of the simulation results show that resource utilization is lower in design 2, which can be explained by (too) high a number of lost calls. Therefore design 2 is unacceptable in our case study. The service levels in design 1 and 3 are both within the service level agreements, even with an overload of calls (scenario 2) or with an unfavorable unbalance of request types (scenario 3 and 4). Differences between scenarios within a design are not significant, but differences in throughput time between the designs 1 and 3 for special calls are significant. For a final evaluation, management of the call center should balance the expensive design 1 with the less expensive design 3. Such a final assessment is based on salaries of generalists versus cross-trained workers. Based on resource utilization, the price of decreased throughput time can be calculated, especially for special calls (see Table 1).

5.3 Task Composition

In this subsection we play with different task compositions, which may have task automation or contact reduction as a side-effect. Simulation results are obtained for three designs. In each of these designs standard requests are being registered, classified and handled in the 1st line by generalists. Special requests in these designs are treated as follows: (1) register and classify in the 1st line, (2) only registration in the 1st line and (3) all steps are executed in the 2nd line. We observed that the latter design resulted in low service levels, outside the service level agreements. This can be explained by the relatively long service times in the second line, causing long waiting lines and lost calls. The other two designs have no significant difference in service levels, except for the overload scenario which is handled significantly better in design 2. Average speed of answer is best

Table 1. Simulation results of three one-level designs. Lower Bound (LB) and Upper Bound (UB) are given for 95% reliability intervals.

design	scenario	service level	resource utilization	speed of answer	throughput time special calls LB – AVG – UB	throughput time standard calls LB – AVG – UB
1	1	100	0.342	0.000	1472-1489-1506	143-144-144
1	2	100	0.431	0.005	1468-1482-1496	144-145-145
1	3	100	0.282	0.000	1484-1513-1542	147-148-148
1	4	100	0.403	0.002	1474-1488-1502	133-134-135
1	5	100	0.354	0.000	1461-1482-1503	144-145-145
2	1	89	0.286	2.292	2488-2533-2578	146-147-148
2	2	85	0.339	3.533	2602-2637-2672	148-149-150
2	3	89	0.228	4.786	2413-2465-2517	152-153-154
2	4	83	0.313	1.670	2595-2645-2696	133-134-135
3	1	99	0.307	0.067	2414-2457-2500	143-144-145
3	2	98	0.377	0.277	2396-2440-2485	144-145-145
3	3	100	0.235	0.010	2324-2390-2408	148-149-149
3	4	97	0.369	0.509	2398-2439-2484	132-133-134
3	5	99	0.315	0.084	2391-2437-2483	144-145-146
3	6	99	0.307	0.145	2383-2423-2463	143-144-145

in designs 2 and 3. In design 2 this can be explained by the fact that resources are no longer allowed to try to solve special requests, thus spending less time here. In design 3, this can be explained by the fact that resource utilization is much less than in other designs. This effect can also be observed in the throughput times of standard and special requests for the three designs. Management of the call center should decide whether the number of lost calls for design 3 can be acceptable given lower operation costs. If this is not acceptable, design 2 seems to be favorable over design 1.

5.4 Synchronous Versus Asynchronous Designs

When distinguishing synchronous requests from asynchronous requests, one needs to decide whether these types should be handled differently. To evaluate this effect we compare two designs. The first design is a two level design with standard and special requests, the current situation of the IT help desk as described in Section 4. In this design, synchronous and asynchronous requests are handled the same way. The second design differs only with respect to the treatment of asynchronous requests, see Figure 4. We stress that this particular comparison is merely an illustration; a similar distinction can be made in other designs, e.g. in a one-level design or a design including cross-trained workers. Simulation results and final assessment of trade-offs may be different due to different numbers of resources per resource class and different cost of resource classes.

In terms of service level, the two designs perform both quite well in all scenarios. The resource utilization in the 1st line is higher for design 2, resource

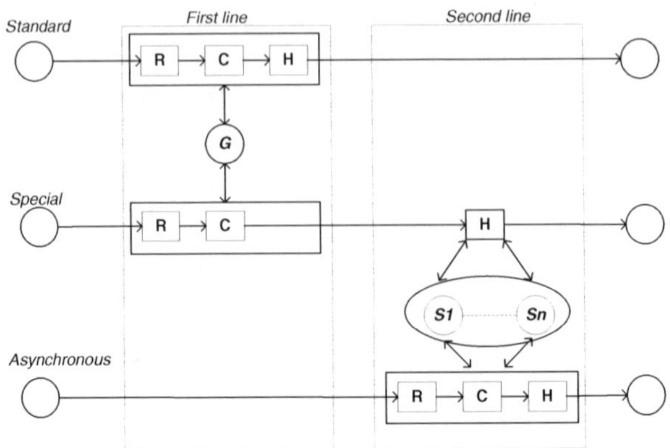

Fig. 4. Two-level process design, with different routing for asynchronous calls

Table 2. Comparison of two two-level designs for asynchronous requests: (1) design 1 performs better, (2) design 2 performs better and (*) no significant difference

scenario	service level	res. util. 1st line	res. util. 2nd line	speed of answer	throughput time (special)	throughput time (standard)
1	(*)	(2)	(1)	(2)	(*)	(2)
2	(*)	(2)	(1)	(2)	(*)	(2)
3	(*)	(2)	(1)	(2)	(*)	(2)
4	(*)	(2)	(1)	(2)	(*)	(2)
5	(*)	(2)	(1)	(2)	(*)	(2)

utilization in the 2nd line is higher for design 1. The average speed of answering is much better in design 2. Throughput times of special requests are a bit less in design 1 (not significant) and throughput times of standard requests are better in design 2 (significant). An overview is provided in Table 2.

5.5 Generalist-Specialist Dilemma and Flexibility

In Section 5.2 we compared three one-level designs to assess the added value of cross-trained workers and specialists. We concluded that advanced skilled generalists perform better but might be very expensive. We observed that (slightly less expensive) cross-trained workers already improved the call center performance. In this section, we elaborate on the assignment of cross-trained workers. We compare such assignments based on a random assignment procedure with those based on a more flexible assignment, i.e. we assign the most specialized resource.

For the one level design we simulate design 3 from Section 5.2 (random assignment) and compare the results with flexible assignment. For the two level design, we adapted the design of the case study (Figure 2): the 16 specialists with one skill are replaced by 8 specialists with 1 skill and 4 cross-trained workers with skills 1-4 and 4 cross-trained workers with skills 5-8. Again, we compared random assignment with flexible assignment.

When analyzing the simulation results, little differences can be observed in service level, resource utilization and speed of answer. An improvement, however, can be observed for the throughput time of special requests, especially in scenario's with an overload of special calls or with fewer resources.

6 Conclusion

In this paper, we had a look at call center design and redesign literature through the lens of redesign best practices. We aimed at defining domain specific best practices, thus supporting future redesigns in the domain. Call center literature revealed that several best practices have been applied, but in different kinds of approaches and without making use of structured integration of best practices. Our approach resulted in a redesign framework for call centers which includes a combination of best practices:

- task composition: one level and two-level designs
- case types: standard/special, synchronous/aynchonous and based on ACD types.
- triage: based on the case types defined above, different routings may be defined
- generalist/specialist: consider different skill sets, i.e. specialists (1 skill), cross-trained workers (set of skills) and generalists (all skills). This can be observed in one-level design and in a two-level design (2nd line) on an advanced level and in a two-level design (1st line) on a limited level.
- task automation: an ACD menu in the 1st line or an extended menu in the 2nd line may support optimal queuing, thus reducing redistribution in the 2nd line.
- flexibility: in any design with overlapping skill sets, a better algorithm than random selection may improve process performance.
- task addition: adding resources or moving resources from one resource class to another may reduce recource utilisation at particular moments and thus improve lead times.

Based on the framework, favorable designs can be developed and compared with discrete event simulation. In this way, trade-offs between operational costs (resource utilization times salaries), throughput times, and service levels can be quantified, in this way supporting management in making good redesign decisions.

In future, our research will focus on the further development of process designs. In the case study we showed that the application of cross-trained employees may be beneficial. It is obvious that a particular selection of skills for this resource group will perform much better than other selections, depending on the mix of request types that will enter the process. We aim to develop further guidelines, e.g. based on analytical models on skill based routing, that can be integrated in the redesign framework for call centers. In addition, we would like to extend our studies towards other domains, so that a deeper understanding of the application of redesign best practices can be accomplished.

Acknowledgement

This research is supported by the Technology Foundation STW, applied science division of NWO and the technology programme of the Dutch Ministry of Economic Affairs.

References

1. W.M.P. van der Aalst, A.H.M. ter Hofstede, B. Kiepuszewski, and A.P. Barros. Workflow Patterns. *Distributed and Parallel Databases*, 14(3):5–51, 2003.
2. C. Alexander, S. Ishikawa, and M. Silverstein. *A Pattern Language: Towns, Buildings, Construction.* Oxford University Press, New York, 1977.
3. N. Brand and H. van der Kolk. *Workflow Analysis and Design.* Kluwer Bedrijfswetenschappen, Deventer (in Dutch), 1995.
4. T.H. Davenport. *Process Innovation: Reengineering Work through Information Technology.* Harvard Business School Press, Cambridge, Mass., 1993.
5. E. Gamma, R. Helm, R. Johnson, and J. Vlissides. *Design Patterns: Elements of Reusable Object-Oriented Software.* Addison-Wesley, Boston, 1995.
6. N. Gans, G. Koole, and A. Mandelbaum. Telephone Call Centers: Tutorial, Review and Research Prospects. *Manufacturing & Service Operations Management*, 5(2):79–141, 2003.
7. J. Golovin. *Achieving stretch goals: best practices in manufacturing for the new millennium.* Prentice-Hall Editions, New York, 1997.
8. J.M. Grimshaw and I.T. Russell. Effect of clinical guidelines on medical practice: a systematic review of rigorous evaluations. *Lancet*, 342(8883):1317–22, 1993.
9. M. Hammer and J. Champy. *Reengineering the corporation:a manifesto for business revolution.* Harper Business Editions, New York, 1993.
10. L.M. Kristensen, S. Christensen, and K. Jensen. The Practicioner's Guide to Colored Petri Nets. *International Journal on Software Tools for Technology Transfer*, 2(2):98–132, 1998.
11. A. Mandelbaum. Call Centers. Research Bibliography with Abstracts. Download from http://iew3.technion.ac.il/serveng/References/references.html, most recent access March 25, 2006, Israel Institute of Technology (Technion), Haifa, 2004.
12. S. Limam Mansar and H.A. Reijers. Best Practices in Business Process Redesign: Validation of a Redesign Framework. *Computers in Industry*, 56(5):457–471, 2005.
13. J. Martin. *The best practice of business.* John Martin Publishing, London, 1978.
14. V. Mehrotra and J. Fama. Call center simulation modelling: methods, challenges and opportunities. In S. Chick, P.J. Sanchez, D. Ferrin, and D.J. Morrice, editors, *Proceedings of the 2003 Winter Simulation Conference*, pages 135–143, 2003.
15. N. Melao and M. Pidd. Use of business process simulation: a survey of practitioners. *Journal of the Operations Research Society*, 54(1):2–10, 2003.
16. J. Motwani, A. Kumar A, and J. Jiang. Business process reengineering: a theoretical framework and an integrated model. *International Journal of Operations & Production Management*, 18(9-10):964–77, 1998.

17. M. Netjes, W.M.P. van der Aalst, and H.A. Reijers. Analysis of resource-constrained processes with Colored Petri Nets. In K. Jensen, editor, *Sixth Workshop and Tutorial on Practical Use of Coloured Petri Nets and the CPN Tools (CPN' 05)*, volume 576. University of Arhus, Denmark, 2005.
18. J. Peppard and P. Rowland. *The essence of business process reengineering.* Prentice-Hall Editions, New York, 1995.
19. J. Pitchitlamken, A. Deslauriers, P. l'Ecuyer, and A.N. Avramidis. Modelling and simulation of a telephone call center. In S. Chick, P.J. Sanchez, D. Ferrin, and D.J. Morrice, editors, *Proceedings of the 2003 Winter Simulation Conference*, pages 1805–1812, 2003.
20. H.A. Reijers. *Design and Control of Workflow Processes: Business Process Management for the Service Industry*, volume 2617 of *Lecture Notes in Computer Science.* Springer-Verlag, Berlin, 2003.
21. H.A. Reijers and S. Limam Mansar. Best Practices in Business Process Redesign: An Overview and Qualitative Evaluation of Successful Redesign Heuristics. *Omega: The International Journal of Management Science*, 33(4):283–306, 2005.
22. N. Russell, A.H.M. ter Hofstede, D. Edmond, and W.M.P. van der Aalst. Workflow data patterns: Identification, Representation and Tool support. In L. Delcambre, H.C. Mayr, J. Mylopoulos, and O. Pastor, editors, *Proceedings of the 24th Int. Conf. on Conceptual Modeling (ER05)*, volume 3716 of *Lecture Notes in Computer Science*, pages 217–221. Springer-Verlag, Berlin, 2005.
23. A. Seidmann and A. Sundararajan. The effects of task and information asymmetry on business process redesign. *International Journal of Production Economics*, 50(2-3):117–128, 1997.
24. A. Sharp and P. McDermott. *Workflow modeling: tools for process improvement and application development.* Artech Prentice-Hall Editions, Boston, 1997.
25. S.Hasija, E.J. Pinker, and R.A. Shumsky. Staffing and routing in a two-tier call center. *International Journal of Operational Research*, 1(1-2):8–29, 2005.
26. R.A. Shumsky and E.J. Pinker. Gatekeepers and Referrals in Services. *Management Science*, 49(7):839–856, 2003.
27. M.J. Stegeman and M.H. Jansen-Vullers. Determining optimal staffing levels in multiple skill inbound call centers: a literature survey. Beta Reports 160, Eindhoven University of Technology, Eindhoven, 2006.
28. G. Valiris and M. Glykas. Critical review of existing BPR methodologies. *Business Process Management Journal*, 5(1):65–86, 1999.
29. L. Wells. Performance Analysis using Coloured Petri Nets. In A. Boukerche, S.K. Das, and S. Majumdar, editors, *Proceedings of the Tenth IEEE International Symposium on Modeling, Analysis and Simulation of Computer and Telecommunication Systems (MASCOTS'02)*, pages 217–221. IEEE Computer Society, 2002.
30. M. Zapf. From the customer to the firm: ealuating generic service process designs for incoming customer requests. *Computers in Industry*, 55(1):53–71, 2004.
31. M. Zapf and A. Heinzl. Evaluation of generic Process Design Patterns: an Experimental Study. In W.M.P. van der Aalst, J. Desel, and A. Oberweis, editors, *Business Process Management: Models, techniques and Empirical Studies*, volume 1806 of *Lecture Notes in Computer Science*, pages 83–98. Springer-Verlag, Berlin, 2000.

Building Business Process Driven Web Applications*

Victoria Torres and Vicente Pelechano

Department of Information System and Computation
Technical University of Valencia
Camí de Vera s/n 46022
Valencia, Spain
{vtorres, pele}@dsic.upv.es

Abstract. The Internet has turned to be one the most common platform for the development of applications. In addition, sometimes the specification of these applications is given to web developers in the form of Business Processes (BP), and from this specification they are asked to develop the corresponding Web Application. In this situation, Web Engineering Methods should provide a way in which these specifications could be taken and be transformed into a Web Application that gives support to the process execution. Furthermore, when we are talking about B2B applications, we have to take into account that these BP usually involve the use of distributed functionality where different partners collaborate to accomplish an agreed goal. Therefore, in this work we provide a method for the automatic generation of Web Applications that give support to BP specifications. For this purpose, we generate from a BP definition the Navigation (web pages) and the WS-BPEL executable description that implements the entire process.

1 Introduction

The Internet has turned to be the most common platform for the development of business applications. This is due to the fact that many organizations and companies are already providing their functionality by means of Web Service technology. Moreover, sometimes the description of these business applications is highly tied to a Business Process (BP) definition, and hence the objective of these applications is not only *information management* but also *process management*. Therefore, in these situations it is more natural to describe these processes in the most appropriate way, which is by means of workflow charts, activity diagrams or a similar notation.

Web Engineering Methods emerged to address some of the aspects that conventional software methods did not consider while generating Web applications. These aspects refer to Navigational and Presentation issues, and these became, within the Web Engineering methods, first-order citizens in the conceptual modelling step. Most well known Web Engineering Methods follow a Model Driven Development (MDD) approach in the sense that they are based on a set of models that cover those concerns that are necessary to specify a Web Application (structure, behaviour, navigation and presentation). In addition to this, when these models are unambiguously

* This work has been developed with the support of MEC under the project DESTINO TIN2004-03534 and cofinanced by FEDER.

S. Dustdar, J.L. Fiadeiro, and A. Sheth (Eds.): BPM 2006, LNCS 4102, pp. 322 – 337, 2006.

specified, with clear semantics, they can be (semi-)automatically transformed in order to obtain the equivalent solution in terms of an implementation technology. Therefore, Web Engineering Methods should now be adapted to accept BP definitions and by means of a set of transformations generate the appropriate software solution.

In addition, we should also take into account that real BPs do not only include automated activities and system participants, in fact, they can also include human participants (participants that require a user interface to interact with the process) and manual activities (activities that are not automated at all, for instance, "to make a phone call" or "to review a document"). Moreover, the kind of interaction that a human participant can have within a BP can range from simple decisions to the introduction of some required data through a user interface. Therefore, Web Engineering Methods should provide a mechanism that allows designers to define the necessary graphical interfaces (by means of their Navigational Model) that give support to the required interaction between human participants and the process.

The challenge pursued in this work is to extract from a BP definition the required navigation (user interaction) to execute the process via a Web Application. We have focused on those cases where the interaction with the user is crucial for the process to be accomplished.

The main contribution of this work is to provide a proposal for the automatic-generation of Web Applications that give full support to the execution of BPs. To achieve this goal we generate from a BP definition (1) the required graphical user interface to launch and complete process activities, as well as (2) the equivalent executable definition of the process. This proposal allows us to obtain BP implementations that are totally integrated within the Web Application. This integration is achieved at three levels, which are data/content, functionality and graphical user interface. This proposal is based on the OOWS [7] approach (a Model Driven Web Development Method that is an extension to the object-oriented software production method OO-Method [15])-OOWS introduces the required expressivity to capture the navigational and presentational requirements of web applications. For this purpose we have defined an extension to the OOWS Navigational Model that allows us to model the graphical interfaces that are necessary to allow interaction between human participants and the business process.

The rest of the paper is structured as follows. Section 2 makes an overview of the related work in both, the Web Engineering and the Business Process area. Section 3 provides an overview of the proposal presented in this work. In section 4 we introduce the example used to present the proposal. Section 5 presents the set of stereotypes added to the BPMN notation to allow us modelling the corresponding graphical user interfaces. Section 6 introduces the transformation approaches used in this work. In Section 7 we first provide an overview of the OOWS approach and then present the transformation rules for the generation of the OOWS Navigational Model that gives support to the BP execution. Section 8 provides an overview of the interaction schema followed to build the equivalent process defined in the Web Services Business Process Execution Language (WS-BPEL [4]). Finally, section 9 gives some conclusions and outlines some further work.

2 Related Works

Several Web Engineering methods have developed their own proposal for the systematic development of Web applications. Moreover, these methods have been extended to provide solutions to the new challenges that have come up in the Web application development. In particular, most of these proposals (UWE and OO-H [13], OOHDM [16], WebML [9] and WSDM [6]) have extended their methods in order to support the integration between Navigation and Business Processes. However, in some cases these extensions (1) do not consider the interaction of different business partners, (2) do not provide a process oriented user interface to guide the user for the accomplishment of their pending tasks or (3) do not take into account that real BPs entail sometimes the realization of manual tasks.

On the other hand, the solutions provided in the area of business processes (Oracle BPEL Process Manager[1], Active BPEL[2], etc.) are more centred on the orchestration of Web Services more than in providing a suitable user interface that solves the interaction between the user and the business process. In fact, as stated in [2], the WS-BPEL language does not consider people as a type of participant in a process definition. In this sense, the Oracle BPEL Process Manager has developed a solution to define this interaction. However, this solution is provided at the implementation level, what entails that Web Engineering Methodologies cannot take profit of these mechanisms at the modelling level.

3 Proposal Overview

As we have stated previously, Web Engineering Methods should allow us to specify the application functional requirements by means of BP definitions. Moreover, the BPs that we want to model, range from those that include human interaction for the realization of some activities to those that include activities that are performed by external partners. For this reason, we have included within the OOWS method a model that allows us to define a BP. This model is the *Business Process Model* (BPM). Fig. 1 provides a graphical overview that includes just the models involved in the proposal as well as the relationships defined between them. The purpose of the BPM is to describe by means of a graphical notation a set of activities performed by different agents and sequenced by means of a control flow. These activities invoke operations that have been modeled either in the *Class Diagram* (CD) or in the *Services Model* (SM). The existing relationship between the BPM and the CD and the SM is depicted graphically in Fig. 1 by means of an arrow stereotyped with the <<uses>> keyword. The set of operations defined in the CD include the functionality that is provided within the boundaries of our system. On the other hand, the functionality that is "lent" from external partners is defined in the SM. The SM was introduced in a previous work [18] in order to define the set of services (and operations provided by these services) that are supplied by external partners. The major benefit of having external functionality at the modeling level is twofold, (1) it

[1] http://www.oracle.com/technology/products/ias/bpel/index.html
[2] http://www.activebpel.org/

allows us to handle external functionality as if it was part of our system and (2) it facilitates the integration between external functionality and other models defined in our method.

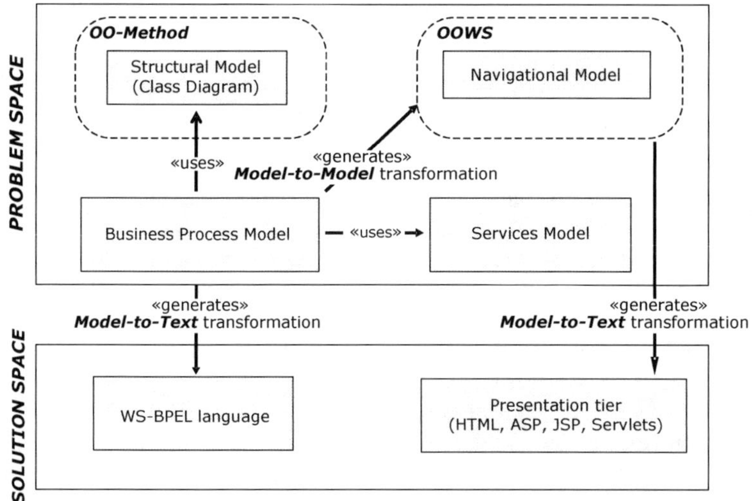

Fig. 1. Proposal Overview. Relationship between Models.

Some activities defined within the process definition require the existence of a user interface to be performed. These user interfaces are defined in the *Navigational Model* and allow the user to interact with the process by introducing some data, starting some activities or taking decisions over some displayed data. The relationship between the BPM and the Navigational Model is depicted in Fig. 1 as an arrow stereotyped with the "<<generates>> Model-to-Model transformation" keyword. This means that from a BP definition we are going to obtain, after applying a set of transformation rules, an initial version of the navigational model that will give support to the process execution. Then, once the Navigational model is completely defined, again, by means of model-to-text transformations we generate the equivalent graphical interfaces represented in a specific technology.

Finally, to execute the BP definition in a process engine, we transform the process definition into a target executable process language. This transformation is represented in Fig. 1 with an arrow stereotyped as "<<generates>> Model-to-Text transformation". Once we have the equivalent executable description we can execute the process in any engine capable of executing process definitions created in WS-BPEL [4].

As can be seen in Fig. 1, the OOWS/OOMethod approach, in the same direction as the MDA proposal, is based on the use of models to achieve software development. In fact, its models characterize the system domain at the problem space, independently of any particular implementation technology.

4 The e-Library Example

To illustrate the proposal, we include in this work an example based on a real scenario that has been identified in the Department of Information Systems and Computation at the Technical University of Valencia. The department has developed a web application (www.dsic.upv.es) following the OOWS approach. This application provides the typical information and functionality that a web site like this usually offers (access to personal directories, information about subjects given at the department, enrollment to seminars and so on). Moreover, this application supports the realization of a set of Business Processes. However, the activities that make up the BPs are hidden through the navigation of the application, and users usually have the feeling that they are executing operations individually and not as a part of a whole process. This fact can finally imply that users involved in the process get lost when they have to perform an activity (normally when the process takes a long time to be completed) because they do not have the process in mind (which is quite normal if we think that people usually have multiple and disparate responsibilities).

The BP that we have taken as the running example (Request Book Purchase Business Process) has as main goal to purchase a new book for the library of the department and to lend it to the purchase applicant after the book arrives to the department. This process involves the participation of different agents, which range from individuals (the secretary staff of the department, the department librarian, and the applicant member) to automated systems (the central library system and the department system). The graphical definition of the running example is shown and explained in the following section.

5 The Business Process Model. Defining the BP Example

There are available several notations (such as UML Activity Diagrams, UML EDOC Business Processes, IDEF, ebXML BPSS or BPMN among others) that can be used to model BPs. As it is stated in [3], there is a gap between a BP definition and its equivalent process definition that has to be bridged. On the one hand, a BP definition focuses on providing a high level view of the activities performed by different agents to accomplish a specific goal. On the other hand, a process definition is more focused on technical aspects that define how these activities are accomplished. In this work, we have skipped the high level definition of a process and have directly defined BPs as process models. In particular, we are going to use the Business Process Modeling Notation (BPMN) [5] because it provides a mapping between the graphics of the notation to the underlying constructs of an execution language, in particular to the WS-BPEL language, what makes this notation a good candidate to be used. This notation is designed to cover a wide range of type of diagrams. However, as our goal is to obtain those software components that implement these BP definitions, we are going to use the notation for the design of "detailed private business processes with interactions to one or more external entities". It is important to make this clear in order to obtain, after the application of the transformation rules, a correct Web Application solution.

As we have stated before, from a BPMN definition we want to obtain two different kinds of assets, one is the graphical interface that will allow the user to interact with the process, and the other one is the executable definition of the process.

Fig. 2 depicts the BP definition of the running example. In this figure we can see how participants are organized first in pools (to represent the different organizations that take part in the process) and then in lanes (to organize different roles within the same organization). Moreover, to differentiate when human participants behave as individuals or as members of a group we have refined the participant type *role* (type that represents human participants) into *role-one* (to refer to individuals) and *role-any* (to refer to a group). In the running example (see Fig. 2) we have defined two Pools, one for the DSIC organization and another for the Central Library (external system). For instance, within the DSIC organization we have included four lanes to organize responsibilities; three of them refer to human roles (Librarian, Secretary and Member) and the last one refers to an automated system.

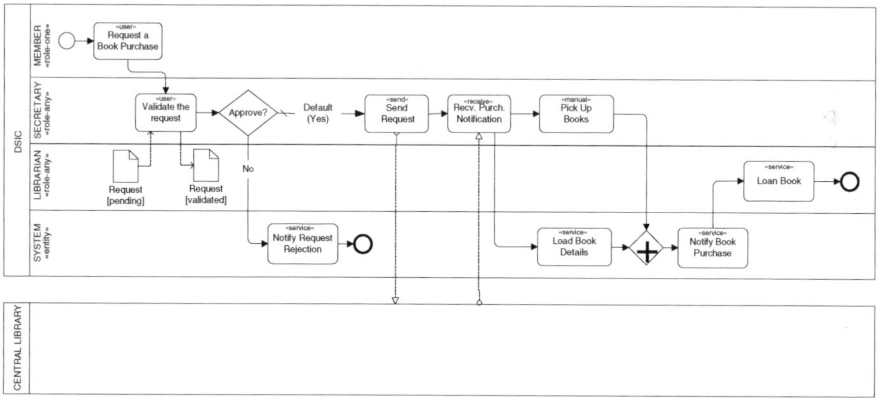

Fig. 2. Process Definition for the "Request Book Purchase" Business Process

The lanes that refer to human beings are stereotyped with the <<role>> keyword. On the other hand, automated participants are stereotyped with the <<entity>> keyword. Once Pools and Lanes are identified, we proceed to define the activities and the control flow that sequences them. We have stereotyped activities with the *manual*, *user*, *service*, *send* and *receive* keywords depending on the kind of activity that we want to represent. We want to note that the realization of a *manual* activity do not imply any change in the state of the automated system. For readability reasons, we have included a graphical definition that only displays the basic structure, control flow and data within the BP. However, this definition also includes a set of attributes that define completely each element of the process.

6 Transformation Techniques. Background

Currently, the Model Driven Architecture (MDA) is the most well known approach to achieve the Model Driven Development (MDD) and advocates for the use of models in software development. These models are defined at different levels of abstraction, which are (1) system requirements modelled in a computation independent model (CIM), (2) system description defined in a platform independent model (PIM) where details of its use of its platform are not shown and (3) a detailed system specification that specify how to use a particular type of platform, the platform specific model (PSM). The act of converting one model into another from the same system is called a Model transformation. Fig. 3 and Fig. 4 depict graphically the approach proposed by the MDA to achieve transformations. However, model transformation does not always refer to transformations between models defined at different levels of abstractions (see Fig. 3). In fact, the same approach can be used to transform any model into another related model (see Fig. 4).

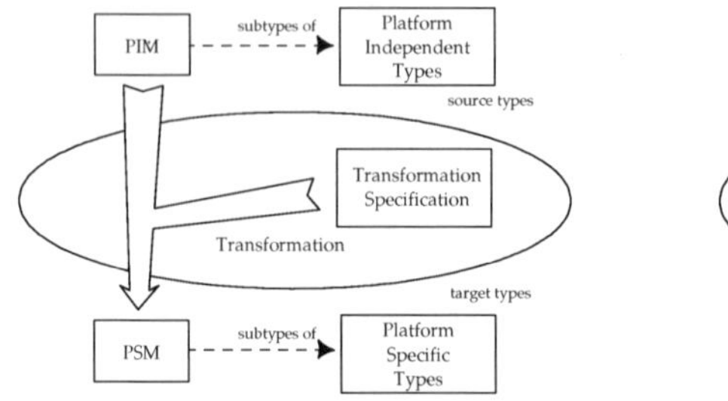

Fig. 3. PIM to PSM transformation approach

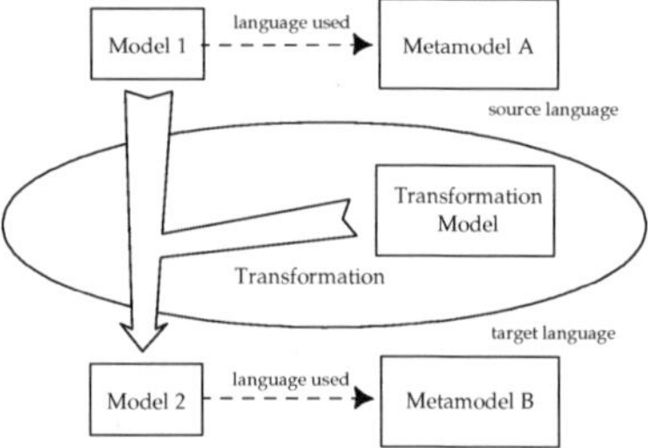

Fig. 4. Model to Model transformation approach

In particular, within the context of this work, we need to perform two different kinds of transformations, which are (1) model-to-model transformations (PIM-to-PIM transformations) to generate the Navigational Model from the BP definition and (2) model-to-text transformations (PIM-to-Code transformations) to generate an executable process definition in WS-BPEL.

7 Model-to-Model Transformations. From BPMN to OOWS

This section is divided into four subsections. In the first one, after providing a brief overview of the OOWS approach, we present the primitives that have been added to this method and the reasons why they are necessary. In the second subsection we provide an overview of languages and tools to achieve model-to-text transformations. Next, we define intuitively (and using the graphical notation of the MOF QVT Relations language) the transformation rules that generate the corresponding OOWS Navigational model. Finally, we include some of the generated user interfaces obtained after applying the transformations.

7.1 New Navigational Primitives for Business Process Support

The OOWS method extends OO-Method with three additional models (which are the *User*, *Navigation* and *Presentation* models) that allow us (1) to express what kind of users can interact with the system as well as the inheritance relationships between them, (2) to define the visibility and the navigational semantics of the system for each user and (3) to specify the presentational requirements for the user interfaces. However, the current primitives defined by the OOWS approach do not fit well to represent the Navigation required by BP execution. For this reason, we have defined a set of new primitives in order to (1) organize the way pending activities are displayed to the user, (2) guide the user in order to complete his/her pending tasks, and (3) to improve the user experience while performing the activities assigned to him/her. This improvement is achieved by providing him/her with additional information that will help the user to finish the activity.

The OOWS Navigational model allows us to define the navigational structure of a web application at the conceptual level. To do this, we associate a *navigational map* to each kind of user defined in the *User model*. A navigational map is represented by a directed graph whose nodes represent *navigational contexts* and whose arcs portray *navigational links* (see Fig. 5).

On the one hand, a navigational context defines a view over the class diagram (see Fig. 6) that allows us to specify an object population retrieval that defines the information that users can access. On the other hand, a navigational link defines a reachability relationship among contexts. There are two kinds of navigational links:

(1) *Exploration links* (targeted with dashed arrows and depicted with the "E" label in Fig. 5) that define a reachability relationship between every context of the navigational map and the target context. For instance, in Fig. 5 the Authors, Books and Members contexts can be accessed by the secretary user from any other navigational context.

(2) *Sequence link* (targeted with solid arrows and depicted with the "S" label in Fig. 5). These navigational links define a reachability relationship between two specific contexts. For instance, in Fig. 5 the Loans context can only be accessed either from the Books or Members contexts.

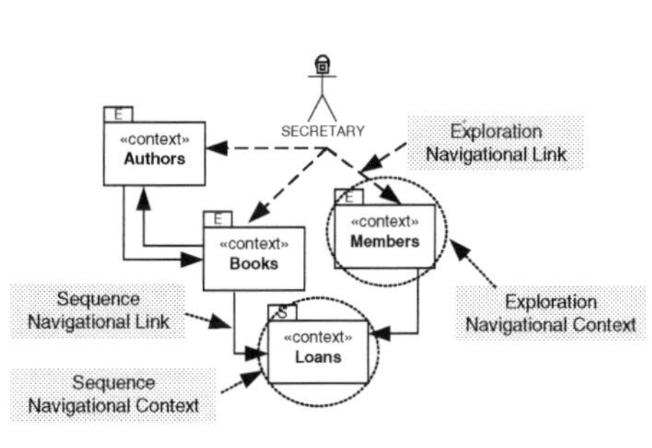

Fig. 5. Navigational Map for the secretary user

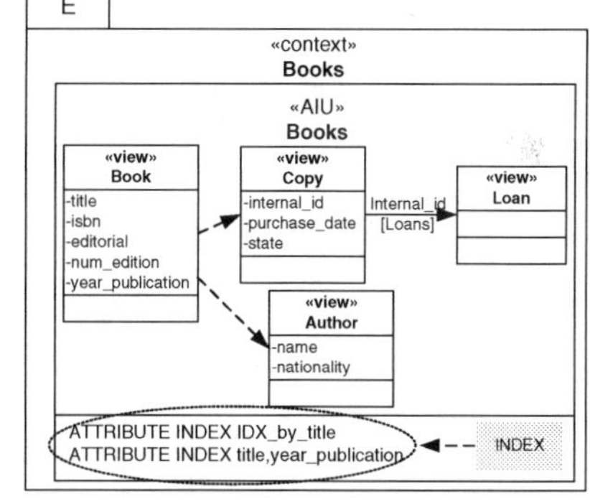

Fig. 6. Detailed view of the Books Navigational Context

Furthermore, this model includes mechanisms that facilitate users to access the information retrieved by the context (see bottom part of Fig. 6). We can define *indexes* to provide users with summarized information about the object population and *search filters*, which allow users to find specific objects.

In its current state, the OOWS method allows users to decide which paths, from those already defined in the navigational map (via Exploration and Sequence links), they want to follow. However, within the execution of a process, the user does not decide which contents navigate through; in fact, it is the process which should drive the user to the next contents to accomplish the process target goal. For this purpose, we have included a set of primitives to model the navigation that define business processes. These new primitives are *ProcessContext*, *ActivityContainer*, *Main-AIU*, *Complementary-AIU* and *Human-AIU* and they are explained in the following paragraphs.

Given a specific type of user, the *ProcessContext* primitive defines, in an abstract way, a process whose activities (or some of them) are assigned to this user. Each different activity is represented by means of the *ActivityContainer* primitive. An *ActivityContainer* is composed of a set of AIUs. An AIU (Abstract Information Unit) is an abstraction mechanism introduced to bring together a set of contents (class views) that are somehow related. Through the AIU primitive we can model contexts as an aggregation of contents, where no relationship between AIUs is expected at all.

The proposed extension includes three different new kinds of AIUs: *Main-AIU*, *Complementary-AIU* and *Human-AIU*. An *ActivityContainer* is defined as a set of AIUs which can include either a *Main-AIU* or a *Human-AIU* and optionally several *Complementary-AIU*. The *Main-AIU* primitive presents the data and functionality needed in order to perform certain task. The *Human-AIU* primitive provides the user with a mechanism to inform the process that a manual activity has been completed. Moreover, the graphical interface that implements a *Human-AIU* includes the description of the manual task (for instance "Send the document via fax" o "Make a phone call"). On the contrary, *Complementary-AIU* provides information that complements the one given by the *Main-AIU* and *Human-AIU*. Although the contents provided by a *Complementary-AIU* are not vital to accomplish a task, they really help the user to complete the task. For instance, this primitive gathers some information kept in the system avoiding the user to navigate through the web application to acquire it.

Regarding the *Main-AIU*, this abstraction mechanism provides the necessary data and functionality to perform the activity that it was designed for. On the other hand, a *Complementary-AIU* provides a mechanism to include a set of data that helps the user while performing an activity. Although the content supplied by a *Complementary-AIU* is not vital for the accomplishment of the activity (i.e. a list that provides the user with the necessary information to take a decision, avoiding the user to search for that information by navigating through the system) it helps the user in accomplishing it.

Finally, a *Human-AIU* provides the user with a mechanism to notify the process that he/she has already finished a manual activity (an activity that is not automated at all). This mechanism, at the implementation level (see Fig. 7), could be represented as a button whose effect after pressing it is to make the process continue. This graphical interface also includes a description of the manual activity to perform (i.e. "Send a report via fax" or "Prepare the meeting and make the necessary arrangements").

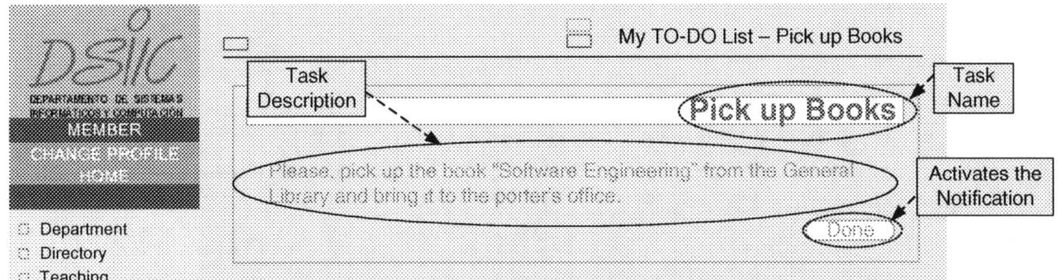

Fig. 7. Graphical Implementation of a Human-Activity Primitive

7.2 Model-to-Model Transformations Language/Tool Support

There are different techniques that can be used to define transformations between models. Among the most used (or popular) languages/techniques we find MOF 2.0 QVT [10], MTF (an IBM implementation of a subset of QVT) [11], ATL [1] or AGG [17]. In particular we have chosen to use the QVT specification because it has been adopted by the OMG as the MDA standard to achieve model-to-model transformations. The QVT specification has a hybrid declarative/imperative nature. The declarative part is made of two languages (*Relations* and *Core*) that embody the same semantics at two different levels of abstraction. On the other hand, the imperative part is represented by the *Operational* language.

In this work we have defined transformations using the *Operacional Mappings* imperative language. This language allows us to define unidirectional transformations between models, which are instances of MOF (Meta Object Facility) metamodels. We have used the Borland Together Architect 2006 for Eclipse that allows us to define transformations in this language and execute them over models defined by means of Ecore (a *MOF Core* implementation together).

7.3 Transformation Rules Definition

To define the rules that generate the associated GUI, we only take into account the elements defined within the lanes marked as «role» in the BP definition (tasks that are performed by people). Therefore, we apply the following rules to the elements defined within these lanes:

- *Process Context Definition*. For each lane defined in the process with its typed valued as «role» (human participant) we build a *Process Context in the Navigational Map*. We want to note that the roles used in the BP definition correspond to the type of users defined in the User Diagram modeled in the Navigational model. In the running example we build a Process Context called *Request Book Purchase* for the secretary user type (see Fig. 9).
- *Activity Container Definition*. Each «user» and «manual» tasks within the boundaries of a «role» (human participant) Lane are transformed into *Activity Containers*. For instance, in the running example we include two Activity Containers within the Request Book Purchase Process Context previously built, one for the *Validate Request* activity and another for the *Pick up Book* activity (see Fig. 9).

- *AIU Definition.*
  - For the tasks that are defined as «user» tasks include a *Main-AIU* within the *Activity Container*.
    - If the operation defined in the task refers to an operation modeled in the Class Diagram, then include a class view in the *Main-AIU* that references the class that contains the operation.
    - If the operation defined in the task refers to an operation modeled in a Service (from the SM), then include a service view [18] in the *Main-AIU* that references the service that offers this operation.
  - For the tasks defined as «manual» tasks include a *Human-AIU* within the *Activity Container*. In Fig. 9 the Pick up Books Human-AIU has been created for the Pick_up_books activity container.

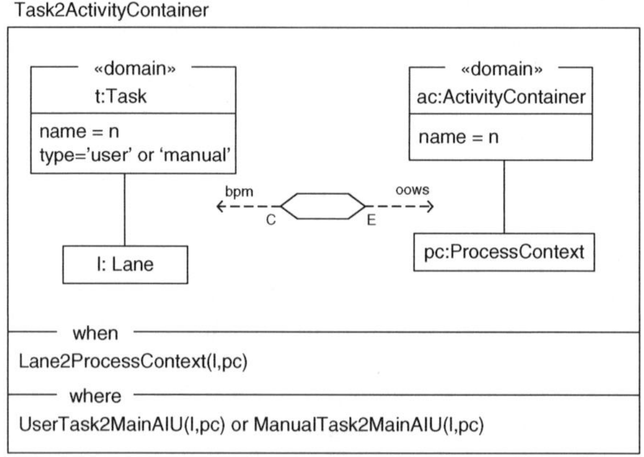

Fig. 8. QVT Transformation

As an example, and for readability reason, Fig. 8 depicts using the graphical notation of the QVT Relations language the second transformation rule presented above. This transformation rule builds activity containers for each user or manual task included within the role lanes of the BP definition.

In the MOF QVT specification, transformations can be invoked for two purposes, either to check the consistency between models or to modify one model to enforce consistency. In particular, the transformation depicted in Fig. 8 has been defined to modify the OOWS model (target model) to enforce consistency with the BPMN model. The "E" label under the right limb of the relation symbol (depicted as a hexagon) specifies that the OOWS domain is enforced to be consistent with the BPMN model. The *when* clause specifies the conditions under which the relationship needs to hold, so the relation *Task2ActivityContainer* needs to hold only when the *Lane2ProcessContext* relation holds between the lane containing the task and the process context containing the activity container. The *where* clause included in the above transformation specifies that the *relations UserTask2MainAIU(l,pc) and ManualTask2MainAIU(l,pc)* are going to be applied on every task within a lane.

After applying the transformation rules defined above we obtain the basic navigational model required to execute the process (process contexts, their activity containers, their Main-AIUs and so on). Fig. 9 depicts the process context obtained for the secretary role. Moreover, this context also includes a set of complementary content that the web designer should add. These included elements refer to Complementary-AIUs.

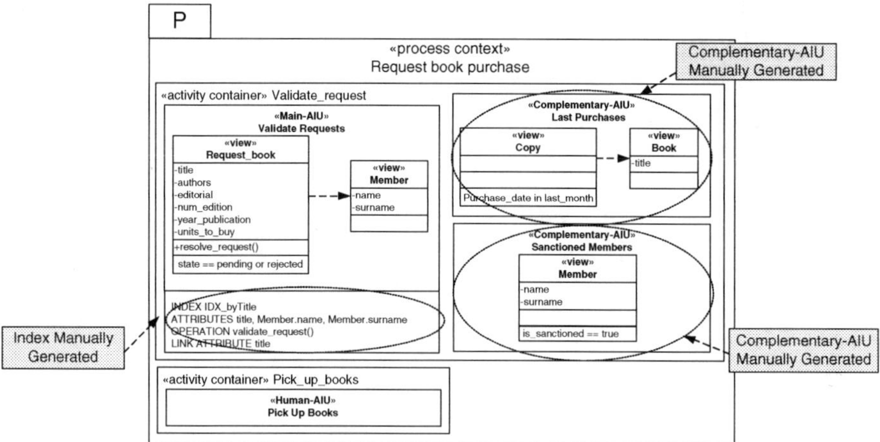

Fig. 9. Process Context for the Validate_request activity defined in the Request Book Purchase Process

For the Process Context depicted in Fig. 9 we have included manually (1) an index associated to the Validate Request Main-AIU and (2) two Complementary-AIUs associated to the Validate_Request activity container. The generated user interface is depicted in Fig. 10. On the one hand, the index defined for the Validate Request Main-AIU provides an indexed access to the population of the Request_book class. This index retrieves a list (just including the data defined in the ATTRIBUTES section of the index, which are the title of the book and the name and surname of the requester) where the user can chose one item (object) from the list. This selection makes the selected object to become active in the AIU. On the other hand, the complementary-AIUs added to the activity container provide the user with two lists that gather, the sanctioned members and the last purchased books. These lists will help the secretary user to decide about the acceptance or rejection of each request.

7.4 Generated User Interface

The implementation of the user interface of the web application is performed by the OOWS tool [19]. Given a Navigational Model, this tool generates the set of web pages that allow the user to interact with the application. Briefly, the procedure followed by the tool to obtain the implementation is the following:

(1) It creates a web page for each activity container included in a Process Context. These generated web pages are dynamic and retrieve the information, which is

generated by the ONME tool [14], and functionality that was defined in the corresponding AIUs.

(2) When an AIU includes an index, the tool generates an additional web page that retrieves as a list the information modelled in the AIU. (See the *Validate Requests* section in Fig. 10).

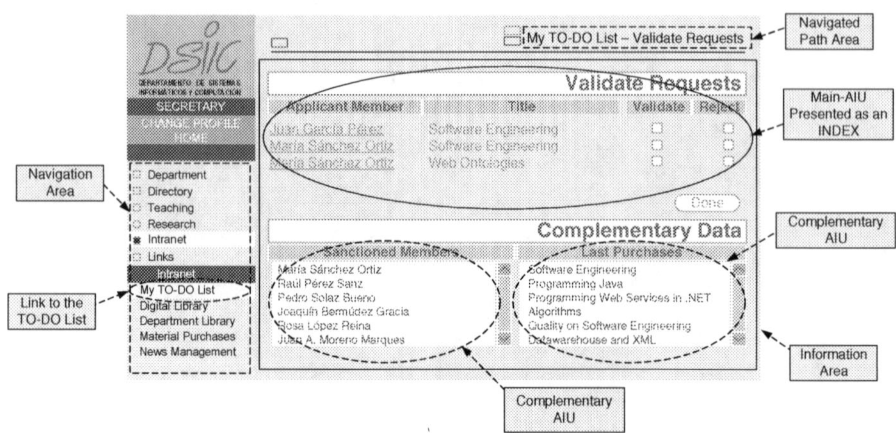

Fig. 10. Web page generated for the Validate Requests Activity

The set of web pages generated are made up of two different areas (see Figure 8), which are the *information* and the *navigation* area. On the one hand, the information area is where the contents (lists, forms and so on) are shown to the user. In particular, Fig. 10 includes the Validate activity container shown in Fig. 9. This activity container includes a Main-AIU (Validate Requests) and two Complementary-AIUs (Sanctioned members and Last Purchases). On the other hand, the navigation area is what allows the user to navigate through the web application. Moreover, the navigation area includes a new link where the user can access his/her TO-DO list. This list includes the activities that the logged user has pending to complete. This list is obtained by querying the workflow engine the state of the started process for a specific user.

8 Model-to-Text Transformations. From BPMN to WS-BPEL

This section is organized in two subsections. On the one hand, first subsection provides a brief overview about the language used to perform model-to-text transformations as well as the reasons that led us to take this decision. On the other hand, second subsection outlines the strategy followed to obtain the equivalent WS-BPEL process definition.

8.1 Model-to-Text Transformation Language/Tool Support

There are different alternatives to perform model-to-text transformations. Among the most well know techniques we find (1) XSLT [21], (2) Template Languages (as JET,

Velocity [20] or FreeMarker [8]) or (3) MOFScript [12]. The MOFScript language is currently a candidate in the OMG RFP process on MOF Model to Text Transformation (http://www.omg.org/docs/ad/05-11-03.pdf). To achieve this kind of transformation we have chosen the MOFScript model-to-text transformation language because (1) it is a language specifically designed for the transformation of models into text files, (2) it deals directly with metamodel descriptions, (3) its transformations can be directly executed in a tool (in particular within the Eclipse environment) and (4) it provides a file constructor for the creation of the target text file. The tool that we have used to implement the transformations is the MOFScript tool included within the Generative Model Transformer (GMT) project of Eclipse.

8.2 Obtaining Executable BP Descriptions

Model-to-text transformations have been organized in several modules. For instance, for each generated file (WSDL files and WS-BPEL) we have defined a specific transformation. The generated WSDL files define the interfaces of the functionality implemented within the boundaries of our system (defined in the CD) and that takes part in the process. On the other hand, the executable WS-BPEL description of the BP is obtained after applying the BPMN to WS-BPEL mappings outlined in [5].

Regarding the Web Services that take part in the process, we have organized them in three groups which are (1) services whose operations are implemented in our system, (2) services whose operations are provided by external partners and (3) services that simulate manual (non automated) activities. The reason why we build this third kind of service is that WS-BPEL does not provide support to human participation interaction. In fact, every participant included in the process must be a service. Therefore, we had to find a way in which human tasks could be "simulated" in order to generate executable definitions of the process. We need to define executable business processes that include activities that range from services provided via web services to activities that are not automated and that are performed by people.

In order to do this, we propose to build a module (called the Task Manager) in charge of managing the Web services that simulate the interaction between the process and the people involved in it. Among the responsibilities of this module we distinguish the two following:

- Collect the messages produced by service invocations launched by the process engine. These services refer to *user* and *manual* tasks defined in the process; this is, to tasks that involve participation with users.
- Listen to the requests received by the application layer and returning, given a user in particular and his/her role, the list with his/her pending tasks as well as the contexts that allow performing these tasks.

We want to note that all the services exposed by the Task Manager should be defined as asynchronous. This is because the process has to wait until the person in charge of doing this task notifies the process that the activity has been completely finished. This notification is performed by means of the corresponding user interface. As a result, once this notification is done, it is the Task Manager module that gathers and returns to the process the results of the activity.

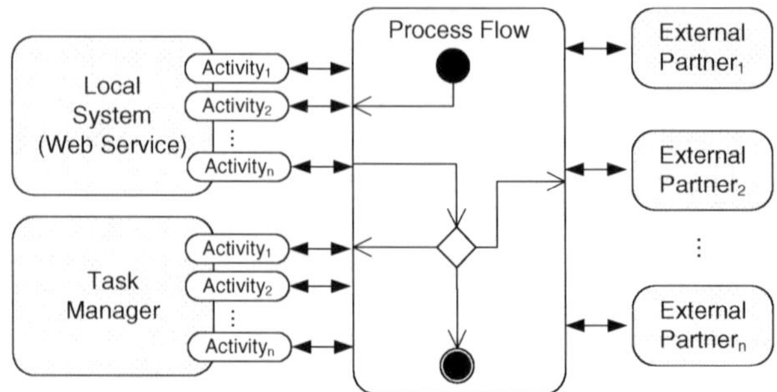

Fig. 11. Web Service Interaction schema

On the other hand, to define the interaction between the local system and the process, we have also defined a web service (Local System Web Service, see Fig. 11) whose operations refer to the activities that are implemented by the operations defined in our system. The schema that has been designed to build the interaction between the participating actors is depicted in Fig. 11. In this figure we also can see that the interaction with external partners is performed via Web services. The definition of these Web services was imported to the SM at the modelling level.

9 Conclusions and Further Work

In this work we have presented, based on a model transformation approach, a solution to generate Web Applications whose specification is highly tied to a BP description. In order to cover properly all kind of Web Applications, Web Engineering Methods should consider supporting BPs in an appropriate way, where not only automated participants are considered (in the form of Web Services) but also human participants. For this reason, we have tuned the OOWS approach in order to accept this kind of specifications and generate the appropriate Web solution.

For this purpose, we have defined a set of transformations, Model-to-Model and Model-to-Text depending on the origin and target artifacts that take part in the transformation. In particular, to obtain the WS-BPEL definition of the process we had to decide how to perform this transformation, as a model-to-model or model-to-text transformation. In the end, we opted for the model-to-text transformation because this approach allows us to develop, in a very short time, the BPMN to WS-BPEL generator. This speediness is due mainly to the fact that it is not necessary to realize the construction of the WS-BPEL metamodel.

As further work we have planned to integrate the solution presented in this work within the ONME tool [14]. This tool provides a conceptual modeling-based environment where the model becomes the program, and the code generation process is fully automated following a MDA based approach.

Moreover, we want to study the presentation patterns associated with the new primitives introduced to the Navigational model. In fact, the Presentation Model is strongly based on the navigational model and uses its navigational contexts to define the presentation properties.

References

1. Atlas Transformation Language (ATL). http://www.sciences.univ-nantes.fr/lina/atl/
2. A Joint White Paper by IBM and SAP: WS-BPEL Extension for People – BPEL4People. July 2005
3. Andersson, B., Bergholtz, M., Edirisuriya, A., Ilayperuma, T., Johannesson, P.: A Declarative Foundation of Process Models. CAiSE 2005: 233-247
4. Business Process Execution Language for Web Services Specification, version 1.1 dated May 5, 2003
5. Business Process Modeling Notation (BPMN) Version 1.0 - May 3, 2004
6. De Troyer, O., Casteleyn, S.: Modeling Complex Processes for Web Applications using WSDM, In Proceedings of the Third International Workshop on Web-Oriented Software Technologies, IWWOST2003
7. Fons, J, Pelechano, V., Albert, M., Pastor, O.: Development of Web Applications from Web Enhanced Conceptual Schemas. In Workshop on Conceptual Modeling and the Web, ER'03, volume 2813 of Lecture Notes in Computer Science. Springer, 2003.
8. Freemarker. http://freemarker.sourceforge.net/
9. Manolescu, I., Brambilla, M., Ceri, S., Comai, S., & Fraternali, P. (2005). Model-driven design and deployment of service-enabled web applications. ACM Trans. Inter. Tech. 5, 3, 439-479.
10. Meta Object Facility (MOF) 2.0 Query/View/Transformation Specification. Final Adopted Specification ptc/05-11-01.
11. Model Transformation Framework (http://www.alphaworks.ibm.com/tech/mtf)
12. MOFScript. http://www.eclipse.org/gmt/mofscript/
13. N. Koch, A. Kraus, C. Cachero and S. Meliá, "Integration of Business Processes in Web Application Models". Journal of Web Engineering. Vol. 3, No. 1 (2004)
14. OlivaNova Model Execution System. CARE Technologies (www.care-t.com).
15. Pastor, O., Gomez, J., Insfran, E., Pelechano, V. The OO-Method Approach for Information Systems Modelling: From Object-Oriented Conceptual Modeling to Automated Programming. Information Systems 26, pp 507–534 (2001)
16. Schmid, H. A., Rossi, G.: Modeling and Designing Processes in E-Commerce Applications. IEEE Internet Computing 8(1): 19-27 (2004)
17. The Attributed Graph Grammar System v1.2.4. http://tfs.cs.tu-berlin.de/agg/. 2004
18. Torres, V., Pelechano, V., Ruiz, M., Valderas, P.: A Model Driven Approach for the Integration of External Functionality in Web Applications. The Travel Agency System. MDWE 2005.
19. Valderas, P., Fons, J., Pelechano, V: Transforming Web Requirements into Navigational Models: AN MDA Based Approach. ER 2005: 320-336
20. Velocity. http://jakarta.apache.org/velocity/
21. XSL Transformations (XSLT) Version 1.0. http://www.w3.org/TR/xslt

A Proposal for an Open Solution Business Process Integration and Management Implementation Framework

Fathi M. Al-Ghaiati

Founder of GAIA Technology Innovation, Egypt
M.Sc. from Faculty of Engineering and Automatic Control, Alexandria University, Egypt
fathi.ghaiati@gaiati.com
www.gaiati.com

Abstract. SOA, Service Oriented Architecture, some people tightly couple this concept with some technologies, as some believes that SOA is about Web Services and its orchestrations. SOA, is the umbrella of "Business Services" and "Enterprise Architecture", meanwhile the technology evolves in the direction of building and sustaining both concepts; at early days it was tight to Enterprise Application Integration and vendor specific solutions, then Web Services and its orchestrations, and now Business Process Management is in the front with the WS-BPEL, WfMC-XPDL, ebXML-BP business integration open standards. However, Open Standards communities have helped a lot in understanding SOA concepts and building the base open standards for implementing SOA in right approaches, it is not providing an open solution implementation framework for SOA. This article proposes an Open Solution Business Process Integration and Management Implementation Framework based on technology open standards that we believe in its value for today and future. By this initiative article we are looking for examining and verifying this framework through SOA communities.

Keywords: Service-Oriented Architecture and Process Management, E-services Architectures and Technology, Workflow Management Systems.

1 The Business Problem and Business Case

Last four years, where the SOA open standards communities were not started or starting to evolve; the Enterprises' Business needs for Services Delivery to its customers through new channels such as Web, WAP, IVR, and B2B were huge and the competition was high especially in the Banking Industry. This lead some large organizations to go to non standards based customized EAI solution, using specific vendor oriented products (they locked into), and become an IT solution provider dependent.

Moreover, some organizations kept securing their internal infrastructure by up security (i.e. using only domain firewalls); ignoring the integrity, authenticity, confidentiality, non-repudiation, and accountability and violating its architecture policies in some cases to reach to the market on the targeted time.

S. Dustdar, J.L. Fiadeiro,and A. Sheth (Eds.): BPM 2006, LNCS 4102, pp. 338 – 347, 2006.

In the worst scenarios, integration projects are locked in by conflicts in conceptualization, an Enterprise failing to store its customers and users secure information in an LDAP e-Directory due to less integration capabilities of its EAI solutions with open standards is an example.

The chaos in EAI has lead to different integration frameworks that most of them are not based on standards.

In the Banking Industry, the integration concept is very old since the telefax (telex) days for operational banking; in the early days of SWIFT FIN messaging integration was mainly based on point to point forcing all legacy applications to talk the same language of the outside world to be able to integrate with it, while not speaking the business language. Now, many Banks are in the challenge of integrating its business to use the new evolving open standard "SWIFT XML".

A need for an Open Solution SOA framework based on open standards with large supporting communities is becoming a must; moreover this puts more challenges on Large Enterprises to invest in such framework. We acknowledge Open Application Group (OAG), SWIFT, and Open Mobile Alliance group (OMA) for their effort in e-business messaging standardization in various industries (*relatively manufacturing & e-commerce, banking, and telecommunication*).

Now Business Enterprises (small as well as large) are lacking a clear road map for its business strategy alignment with the technology for having a continuous business return all the time.

2 Towards a SOA Open Solution and Sustainability

Some people think that Java is competing with business process open standards WS-BPEL, WfMC … etc. This is not completely right, Java supports those standards. These standards are tools optimized for the orchestration of synchronous and asynchronous interactions into long running business flows, and are made open to help us talk the same language; i.e. to make "invisible contribution" by sharing the same vocabulary and concepts. Meanwhile, Java communities are advancing development tools for the sole purpose of leveraging sustainable industry advances in software engineering, for example the latest JBI, Java Business Integration (JSR 208), which defines the core component architecture for SOA Business Integration, has helped the eclipse community propose projects like Java Workflow Toolbox (JWT) and SOA Tools Project (STP).

We see such effort of open source development communities for open standards is a right path for Enterprises SOA open solution that is based on optimized integration of open source products for executing open standards.

For sustainability to be achieved, the framework of integrating such products together must be powerful enough in orchestrating these products, and to comply with the current research efforts that will guide the enhancement and change in the future. Some research points are Semantic Knowledge, Ontology based Information Assets Representation and Generation, Emulating Human Immune System in Systems Security, Cognitive Agents, Ontological Agents … etc.

3 Proposed Solution Framework

3.1 Philosophy

Back to the meaning of the SOA, Service Oriented Architecture is the umbrella of "Business Services" and "Enterprise Architecture"; the players of the Business Services are Service Consumer (could be intra-enterprise or extra-enterprise), Service Provider, and Services Orchestrator, meanwhile the Architecture must integrate them through the support of Services Registry, and Contracts management.

This scenario is like a hybrid of multi-distributed agents; each agent may be static or evolve acting as cognitive agent (i.e. human oriented agent). The communication framework between these agents is our challenge in this article to reach to the minimum or null effect of the evolution of any agent being in a sustainable world.

3.2 The Framework

The following diagram (Fig. 1.) illustrates the proposed framework high level architecture. This architecture is based on the N-tier application pattern that considered as the best pattern to articulate and design an application around the realities of managing state across great distances, multiple channels, complex transaction types executed with a good response time, and high-scalability requirements through the support of Service Based/Oriented Architecture with multiple access methods and application integration, also scalability on the level of network, server, and desktops.

The main objective of this framework is to be able to maintain the individuality of each application while enabling the sharing of enterprise data and linking of enterprise processes (i.e., ***enterprise applications are tightly integrated while being loosely coupled***) in a controlled environment.

In such types of solutions there are many factors (software system attributes) that affect the product and its quality, and make the solution accepted for evaluation. Such factors are

- Security considering data-integrity, accountability, confidentiality, authenticity, and non-reproduction on different domains (e.g. intra- and extra- the enterprise),
- Availability and Reliability, the system must be designed in a way that responds to the external and internal events that may require to have some sort of clustering, failover management, fault detection, …etc.
- Performance, the solution must guarantee minimum service level performance requirements,
- Modifiability and Maintainability, to keep extensions easier in such types of solutions requires basing the solution on international standards and supporting general interfacing schemas, and considering recommended features in coding considering modularity, reusability, extendibility, and simplicity of the code.
- Interoperability, using open standards for applications communication enables a high level of portability between them.

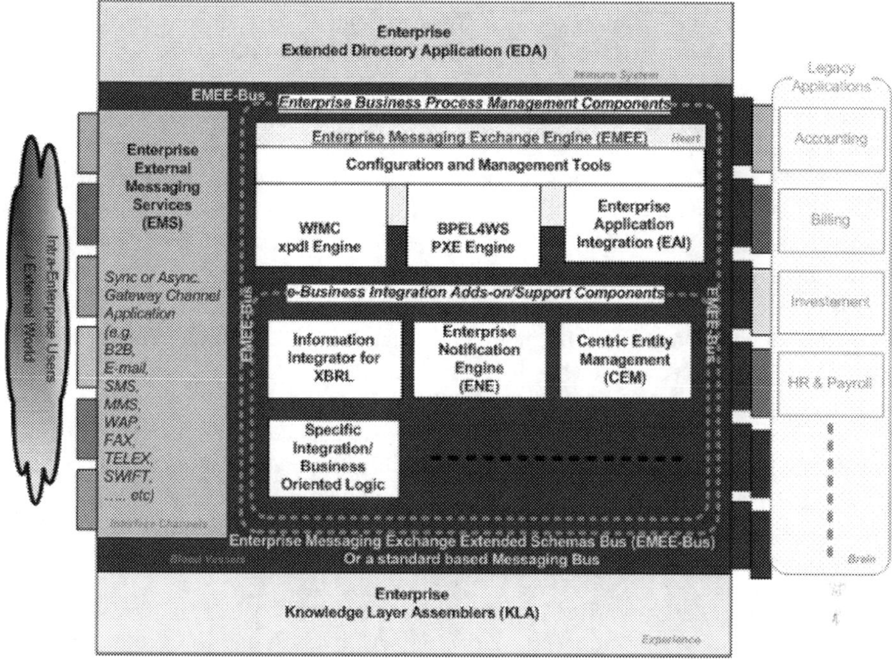

Fig. 1. Proposed Framework High Level Architecture

So that, the components of the framework are structured in a way to help achieving those mentioned challenges and more to act as an open solution for the SOA problem in the market. The next sections provide an overview for each component.

3.3 Framework Components Overview

In this framework, the Enterprise Business Process Management components plays the role of *Heart* of the solution that pumps the blood to all the body entities, the Extended Directory Application (EDA) plays the role of the *Immune System*, External Messaging Services (EMS) plays the role of the *Interfaces Channels*, the Knowledge Layer Assemblers (KLA) plays the role of the *Experience and Capabilities Dictionary and Discoverer*, the Enterprise Messaging Exchange Extended schema Bus (EMEE-Bus) the *Blood Vessels*, and the legacy application remains the *Brain* of the main logic (Business).

(Extra and Intra) Enterprise Messaging Services (EMS) Gateway

The EMS Gateway acts as a transparent synchronously and/or asynchronously two way ("push or publish" and "pull" or "Request/Response") messaging gate between the Enterprise EMEE middleware and its customers/users/agents for the purpose of external communication (e.g. *mobile messaging exchange (SMS or MMS), or e-mail messaging exchange, or telefax/telex, SWIFT, WAP, Web, Portal, XBRL*); it could be an advertisement, customer specific information, up to business transactions. The verification of the message content and authentication of the business message sender is a business service dependent so it must be a property of the EMEE engine.

This application is structured in a way that initiates a "*Channel Service Instance (CSI)*" for each external physical entity (delivery channel) for interfacing with (e.g. SMSc for Telecom A, SMSc for Telecom B, Mail Server for gaiati.com domain, mail server for gaiati.org domain, …etc). On the other side of the CSI, it interfaces with the inside enterprise over EMEE-Bus through a specific ports (i.e. *JMS queues*) or shared ports with another CSI using XML messaging.

The service engine of the EMS is designed to act as a technology standards integrator where it integrates the mobile messaging standard protocols (e.g. SMPP, MM7, MM1), or e-mail (SMTP or POP3 mime) messaging standard with an enterprise wide schema (EMEE schema) building factories.

Meanwhile the CSI gets its properties (e.g. external messaging center properties and its public key if exists, public key for EMEE engine , messaging ports ...etc) through EDA during startup process to initiate its binding components and links to a specific service engine (factory instance of a service engine component).

The major benefits of this architecture of EMS and CSI in general:

- It decouples the enterprise applications from the delivery channel specifications, makes the focus of the contents of the message not how and when to deliver it.
- Makes the enterprise independent of the changes of the standards in the delivery channels interfacing.
- Easy to extend the enterprise applications to support more delivery channels in future such as TV.
- Inherits all generic benefits of the proposed SOA Framework for Implementation.

Enterprise Extended Directory Application (EDA)

The EDA is here to play the role of a central point of applications configuration and security management (e.g. applications startup/stopping management processes). Also it plays a role of checking applications users provided security information.

Moreover, it plays the role of a guard between the inter-Enterprise applications and the Enterprise LDAP eDirectory.

The objective behind this is to achieve:

- A standard secure and controlled enterprise oriented messaging interface between the application and eDirectory, an EMEE for EDA schema provides this through encapsulating DSMLv2.0 requests within it.
- Loosely couple the inter-enterprise applications from the Enterprise continuous evolution of its Directory structure, and even standards in LDAP.
- To come-over the limitations of the LDAP protocol, that cannot query on multiple levels in one request.
- Central point of enterprise security information management (authentication and authorization).

Enterprise Knowledge Layer Assemblers (KLA)
The objective of this layer is to have a unique center of the Enterprise knowledge information; it is based on meta-data and meta-meta definition. It is supposed to hold services registry and its information, applications properties, legacy and enterprise message formats (note, for non xml message formats, a mapping to an xml schema definition is a must and to be stored as well in this layer), mapping rules between messages, validation and business rules dictionary, open standard business specific schemas (e.g. ebXML core components such as UN/CEFACT, and UN/EDIFACT) comprise a Universal Business Library (UBL), … etc.

We see in the coming years there will be a great evolution in the open standards that will support or be incorporated in this layer as the semantic, and ontology are opening more advanced approaches of knowledge representation and generation. So the decision to have one central layer of the Enterprise wide information is a right approach especially for future extensions.

The major objective of this layer is to achieve:

- Central point of the enterprise e-business knowledge (information) management
- One portable solution and place for enterprise knowledge management
- Enable easy to integrate ways between the EMEE engine tools and the enterprise knowledge
- To be ready for semantic web for web services and its discovery
- Being as a knowledge base for supporting system dynamics and/or inference engines

Enterprise Legacy Applications
The Brain
These are the Enterprise existing traditional applications that play the role of the core engines of the enterprise business. Specific adapters are needed to interface with these legacy applications; it can be encapsulated with the enterprise wide EMEE schema for communicating with EMEE engine in a secure and standard based approach. This concept will enable enterprises to build this adapter once for a domain or set of applications that shares the same runtime platform (e.g. MVS CICS 3270).

Enterprise Messaging Exchange Extended Schemas – Bus (EMEE-Bus)
The Blood Vessels
The EMEE schema provides a robust and scalable XML schema for messaging exchange between different applications in the enterprise controlled by the EMEE centralized middleware. The EMEE middleware Engine with the EMEE schema comprises a standard Service Oriented Architecture Framework for Integration between the different enterprise applications.

The main objective behind the EMEE schema is to have one enterprise wide core schema, that resolves the inter-enterprise security problems (data-integrity, accountability, confidentiality, authenticity, and non-reproduction) by implementing it once and deploying it at the connection points of all communicating applications (i.e. part of the interface or the adapter interface). Achieving this concept will enable interoperability between components, model expendability (e.g. easy integration with an *Intruder Detection System (IDS)*), and enable the enterprise to focus on its business functionality extension rather than on how to integrate each new business component.

This EMEE schema is an application integration schema that is built over the SOAP schema. Another alternative for EMEE schema could be the Web Services schemas over SOAP, but we see that the open standards in this area are focusing on solving the extra-enterprise integration problems rather than the inter-enterprise. Either a customized version of web service schemas or a new schema for encapsulation (*such as this proposed EMEE schema*) needs to be open standardized for a wide inter-enterprise generic and secure integration, also for monitoring of the performance and availability management.

Enterprise Business Process Management Components

The Heart

From the practice, an Enterprise SOA for a complete business process management solution cannot be achieved by one product or a single integration standard, such SOA solution must be like a suite of products that comprise integration engines and integration support/adds on products.

Now, the open standards work has identified three major standards for SOA engines that can work together to run the enterprise SOA; it is the WS-BPEL the Business Process Execution Language for Web Services open standard by OASIS, WfMC XPDL XML Process Definition Language for workflow management open standard by Workflow Management Coalition, and a need for an EAI that is based on the JBI the Java Business Integration standard. Integrating these engines together supports applications integration at the process as well as event level (human or application), and providing different levels of business process and end to end service assembling (Workflow, Business process, application integration) and service integration independent of its location.

The need for powerful configuration and management tools for the orchestration definition in these engines is a must, for the support of fast business process definition, integration and management. These tools could help the user by providing standard design patterns, act as a cognitive tool that guides and thinks with the user building its experience by international as well as enterprise local integration practices (i.e. extends and utilizes the information kept in the Knowledge Layer), and to provide solution total management tools (i.e. design, deploy, monitor, and optimize).

The suite of products that tights these engines and tools together, we called it the "*Enterprise Messaging Exchange Engine (EMEE management engine)*".

In e-business spectrum the need for supporting more integration components has become a fact, here are some examples for such needed components:

- When the existing legacy applications are being account based, a need for centric customer/entity management that integrates the enterprise with its customer/agents/users is a must.
- A need for an Enterprise central notification engine that manages the enterprise notifications between applications and users or event between applications and each other is a must.

More e-business Integration Adds on / Support components can be introduced today and in the future based on the business needs.

4 The Solution and Technology

JBI, the Java Business Integration Standard (JSR 208) is gaining more potential as a JCP approved standard that defines the core component architecture for SOA. Now we see the direction is moving towards emphasizing over this standard. We encourage the open source communities to propose more projects to fill the gap in the proposed framework, especially to see an open source project(s) for WfMC complete workflow architecture solution based on JBI. More interest and focus on the standardization of the knowledge layer is required.

4.1 Where Can Intellectual Property Software Products Fit in This Framework?

It can fit into any component in the model as it complies with open standards and has a good base for products supports and extensions such as IBM, and Microsoft.

Vendors provide superior value to their customers when supporting open standards in their products. Unfortunately, this is not true in most real world deployed systems where each vendor has his own proprietary integration interface or API. However, software engineers successfully utilized technologies like remote procedure call, reliable messaging and web services in their integration architecture, wrapping the legacy applications functions. Although standards are being used in these systems; the systems themselves are designers driven. New standards like JBI and SCA are trying to address this problem, providing implementations of a SOA approach for integration. Quoting from Dave Chappell's book "Enterprise Service Bus":

"*Because the ESB can support multiple ways of connecting into it, applications don't require any drastic changes to "get on the bus." The motto for ESB adoption is "If you can't bring the application to the bus, bring the bus to the application." This means that applications should be able to connect into the bus with as little modification as possible. It is the bus, not the applications, that provides the flexibility in connection technologies.*"

JBI, for example, allows an integrator to encapsulate the application into the JBI container acting as a service engine, or communicating with it over a specific protocol through a binding component. Either way an integrator was able to achieve, the communication, or "*message exchange*" in JBI terms, between service engines and binding components is part of the specification. Perhaps the closest concepts to this are the broker and router patterns, where applications are decoupled communicating through the broker and addressing each other through the router. Moreover, it is possible for a service provider inside a JBI container to describe and publish the service it provides, allowing a consumer to query, discover and consume the service.

5 Proposed Framework and Sustainability

When Sustainability is being checked a major question must be asked:

How Can This Architecture Fit into the Future Research and Technology Evolution?

The main objective of this framework is to decouple the business from the communication while it tightly couples the interface keeping components to virtually orchestrate.

With JBI, the binding component is virtually wires external services with internal service engine components; meanwhile each service engine evolves in its business domain irrespective of how, when, and where it will be used.

This gives the business logic a complete freedom to evolve and provide services to the market faster and in a stable way, meanwhile the communication (binding) is visited only for spreading the space of the framework or enhancing the communication between components.

From the research perspective, semantic web and anthologies are going to play major roles in both knowledge and logic engines where they turn information into useful knowledge, harness Enterprise knowledge assets (maintain and find the right information at the right time and place), and secure Enterprise competition as it efficiently release and reuse knowledge.

In the presented framework each component engine has specific domain of functions where it can evolve its way of thinking or doing the work meanwhile the base for the communication is not affected.

Examples for current research, the research of "Ontology Based Information Assets Representation and Generation" can help the Knowledge Layer component to provide its service (service engine) in a more advanced way meanwhile the underlying communication infrastructure between components is functioning.

Another example, the EDA engine component (service engine) can evolve to emulate the human immune system in its functionality meanwhile the same Blood Vessel is ruining the life over the EMEE-Bus.

And a third example is to have ontology based work list assignment to the right expert for problem solving in a human workflow, or dynamic ontology based service selection/execution.

We see the most sustainable framework in this life is Human structure, so we tried in this presented framework to emulate the human being, our logic and brain evolves, our communication ways evolves, ….etc meanwhile our core interface is being sustainable helping us to evolve as we are going; actually Humans make the civilization and cope with it, the civilization does not make us.

6 Conclusion

In this article, we explored SOA within current open standards and supporting open technologies, proposed an SOA Open Solution Business Process Integration and

Implementation Framework based on the current open standards and considering the impact of current research on it. The main objective of proposing this framework in this article is to examine and verify it with the SOA communities, hoping to share by this framework in the definition of "*Language of Sustainability in e-business*" and to become a "*Center Of Excellence (COE)*" as the effort takes on a larger, multi-process scope, and spanning multiple domains.

Experiences in Enhancing Existing BPM Tools with BPEL Import and Export

Jan Mendling[1], Kristian Bisgaard Lassen[2], and Uwe Zdun[1]

[1] Institute of Information Systems and New Media
Vienna University of Economics and Business Administration
Augasse 2-6, A-1090 Wien, Austria
{jan.mendling, uwe.zdun}@wu-wien.ac.at
[2] Department of Computer Science, University of Aarhus
IT-parken, Aabogade 34, DK-8200 Aarhus N, Denmark
k.b.lassen@daimi.au.dk

Abstract. The Business Process Execution Language for Web Services (BPEL) has become a de-facto standard for executable process specifications. The broad industry acceptance of BPEL forces workflow and BPM system vendors to consider respective import and export interfaces. Yet, several existing systems utilize graph-based BPM languages such as EPCs, Workflow Nets, UML Activity Diagrams, and BPMN in their modeling component while BPEL is rather a block-oriented language inspired by process calculi. In this paper we identify transformation strategies as reusable solutions for mapping control flow between graph-based BPM tools and BPEL. Furthermore, we present a case study in which we have applied these strategies in an industry project. This case study shows that transformation strategies are helpful for implementing import and export interfaces in a systematic way, and that they can easily be extended to address vendor-specific aspects of a graph-based BPM tool.

1 Introduction

The Business Process Execution Language for Web Services [1] (BPEL4WS or BPEL) has become a de-facto standard for executable process specifications. Although the BPEL 2.0 standard is not yet published by OASIS, there are already several systems that support BPEL, including Oracle BPEL Process Manager, IBM Websphere, or the open source system ActiveBPEL. For an overview of currently available BPEL implementations see [8]. This broad industry acceptance forces other BPM system vendors to consider BPEL support, too.

Basically, tool vendors have two options to approach this challenge: to provide a native BPEL implementation with a corresponding new modeling tool; or, to enhance the existing modeling tool with BPEL import and export. The import/export option might be preferable to vendors for several reasons. First, it is much quicker, easier, and cheaper to be implemented than a native BPEL component. Furthermore, the evolution of the vendor's tool is decoupled from potential modifications of the BPEL standard. Finally, the experiences that went

S. Dustdar, J.L. Fiadeiro, and A. Sheth (Eds.): BPM 2006, LNCS 4102, pp. 348–357, 2006.

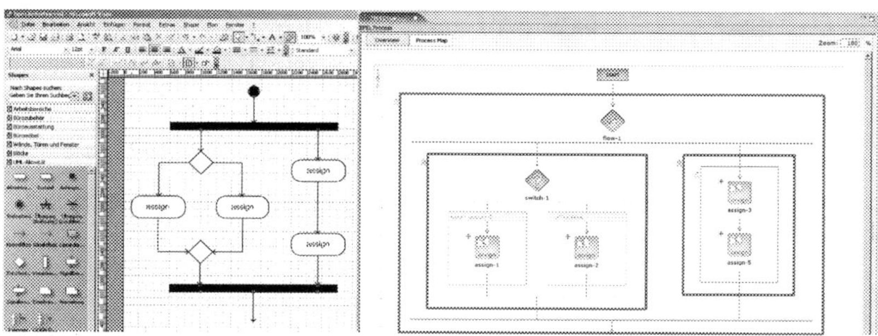

Fig. 1. Graph-based modeling with UML Activity Diagrams in MS Visio versus block-oriented modeling with BPEL in Oracle BPEL Designer

into the tool are a valuable asset for the vendor. Therefore, in the context of an existing industrial tool, it is often not an option to start yet another BPEL standard implementation from scratch. Rather it is desirable to enhance the existing tool with BPEL import and export. The trade-off of enhancing an existing tool with BPEL import and export is that conceptual mappings have to be identified between the modeling language of the BPM tool and BPEL. In particular, the mapping of control flow is a non-trivial task, especially if the BPM tool uses a graph-based language. Such graph-based languages like EPCs, UML Activity Diagrams, BPMN, or Workflow nets are used by many BPM modeling tools because they are handy in the analysis and design phase of a project. In the following, we will use the term *graph-based BPM tool* to refer to them. On the other hand, processes can be modeled in a block-oriented fashion, similar to process calculi. BPEL is in first place a block-oriented language, as the control flow can be defined by nesting structures, e.g. sequence, while, or flow structured activities. Yet, BPEL also includes graph-based links that can be used within a flow block. Figure 1 illustrates graph-based versus block-oriented process modeling.

The representational differences of control flow between graph-based BPM tools and rather block-oriented BPEL is a major problem for the implementation of BPEL import and export interfaces. In the following, we consider control flow transformation strategies as defined in [9] to solve this problem. Section 2 presents available transformation strategies for importing and exporting BPEL from graph-based BPM tools. In Section 3 we present our experiences of a case study where we utilized the transformation strategies for the implementation of an export interface for a commercial graph-based BPM tool. This tool uses UML Activity Diagrams in its modeling component. After discussing some related research in Section 4, we give a conclusion of the case study in Section 5.

2 Transformation Strategies for Graph-Based BPM Tools

In this section we describe transformation strategies for importing from and exporting to BPEL, respectively to and from a graph-based language such as EPCs,

BPMN, Workflow nets, and UML Activity Diagrams. Most of these languages support the definition of sub-processes, and we will take advantage of that fact in some transformation strategies. The idea of the strategies is to explicate mapping options between BPEL and graph-based languages and to provide formal algorithms that can be adapted to the specifics of any graph-based language. Formal definitions and algorithms for each strategy are available in [9].

One specific problem of the mapping between BPEL and graph-based languages is that a transformation is not always possible. Some strategies require structural properties of the input format to be satisfied. Table 1 distinguishes structured graphs and acyclic graphs. Essentially, a structured graph uses only control flow patterns that can be mapped to BPEL structured activities. This also includes a simple loop that can be mapped to a BPEL while. An acyclic graph can include any kind of split and join conditions as long as there is no cycle. This implies that an acyclic graph does not need to be structured. Such graphs can always be mapped to a BPEL flow that permits only acyclic links. Furthermore, a BPEL process is structured if it does not include any link elements. In the following, we briefly describe transformation strategies for the import of BPEL to a graph-based BPM tool (Section 2.2) and for the export of BPEL from (Section 2.1). Table 1 gives an overview of them and for which input they are applicable.

Table 1. Transformation strategies and applicable models

Transformation Strategy from Graph to BPEL	Structured Graph	Acyclic Graph	All Graphs	Transformation Strategy from BPEL to Graph	Structured BPEL	All BPEL
Element-Preservation	-	+	-	Flattening	+	+
Element-Minimization	-	+	-	Hierarchy-Preservation	+	-
Structure-Identification	+	-	-	Hierarchy-Maximization	+	+
Structure-Maximization	+	+	-			

2.1 Exporting BPEL from a Graph-Based BPM Tool

Transformation strategies in this section can be divided into two categories: Either they preserve the graph-based modeling paradigm by mapping to a BPEL flow (Element-Preservation, Element-Minimization) or they map to structured activities whenever possible (Structure-Identification, Structure-Maximization). The general idea of each strategy is illustrated in Figure 2.

Element-Preservation. This strategy maps all process graph elements to a flow construct and arcs to links. It is a prerequisite of this strategy that the process graph is acyclic. This is because a BPEL flow is not allowed to have cycles defined with links [1]. Routing elements of the graph-based language such as decision nodes and synchronization points are mapped to BPEL empty activities with respective join conditions and links carrying the appropriate split conditions (see Figure 2). The advantage of the Element-Preservation strategy is that it is simple to implement and the resulting BPEL will be very similar to the original process graph since there is a one-to-one correspondence between nodes and activities. As a drawback, the resulting BPEL control flow includes more

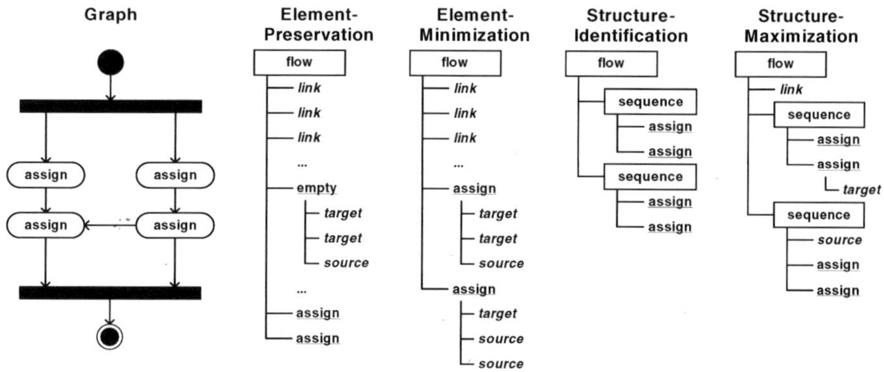

Fig. 2. Illustration of Transformation Strategies for Export

elements than actually needed: joins and splits are translated to separate empty activities in BPEL although split and join conditions could also be annotated to other activities. Furthermore, the resulting BPEL might be more difficult to read than structured activities, such as sequences. If the BPEL code is used in a scenario where readability is important, it should be applied for small process graphs since all elements of the process graph are mapped to one flow construct.

Element-Minimization. This strategy simplifies the generated BPEL code of the Element-Preservation strategy. The general idea is to remove the empty activities that have been generated from joins and splits and instead represent splitting behavior by transition conditions of links and joining behavior by join conditions of subsequent activities. As a prerequisite the process graph needs to be acyclic in order to make dead path elimination of BPEL work. The advantage of the resulting BPEL process is that it follows the semantics of the flow construct more closely than the Element-Preservation strategy, since it removes empty activities generated from joins and splits (see Figure 2). As a drawback, it is less intuitive to identify correspondences between the process graph and the generated BPEL specification. This strategy should be used in scenarios where the resulting BPEL code needs to have as few nodes as possible. This might be the case when runtime performance of the BPEL process matters. In contrast to the Element-Preservation strategy, the amount of nodes is decreased since all empty activities translated from join and split nodes are skipped.

Structure-Identification. The general idea of this transformation strategy is to identify structured activities in the process graph and apply structural reduction rules as defined in [9]. As a prerequisite the process graph needs to be structured according to a definition also described in [9]. The advantage of this strategy is that all control flow is translated into structured activities (see Figure 2). With regard to the readability of the resulting code, this is the most suitable strategy since it reveals the structured components of the process graph. As a drawback the relation to the original process graph might not be intuitive to identify. This transformation strategy is appropriate in a scenario when the BPEL should be

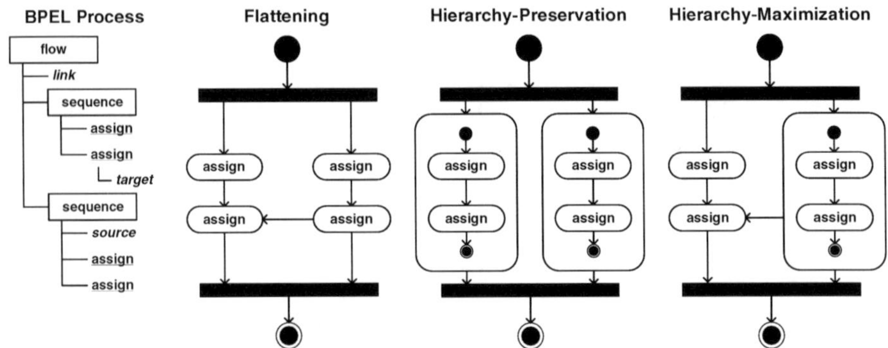

Fig. 3. Illustration of Transformation Strategies for Import

edited by a BPEL modeling tool such as Oracle BPEL designer that displays the process as a nesting of structured activities.

Structure-Maximization. The general idea of this strategy is to apply the reduction rules of the Structure-Identification strategy as often as possible to identify a maximum of structure (see Figure 2). The remaining annotated process graph is then translated following the element-preservation or Element-Minimization strategy. The advantage of this strategy is that it can be applied for arbitrary unstructured process graphs as long as its loops can be reduced via the reduction rules defined in [9]. Still this strategy is also not able to translate arbitrary cycles, i.e. cycles with multiple entrance and/or multiple exit points. A drawback of this strategy is that both Structure-Identification and at least Element-Preservation strategy need to be implemented. This strategy could be used in scenarios where models have to be edited by a BPEL modeling tool such as Oracle BPEL designer that uses structured activities as the primary modeling paradigm.

2.2 Importing BPEL into a Graph-Based BPM Tool

Transformation strategies for importing BPEL can be divided into two categories: Either the BPEL structure is transformed into a graph with no hierarchy (Flattening Strategy), or a graph where the BPEL structure is preserved as much as possible (Hierarchy-Preservation, Hierarchy-Maximization). The general idea of each strategy is illustrated in Figure 3.

Flattening. The general idea of this strategy is to map BPEL structured activities to respective process graph fragments. The nested BPEL control flow then becomes a flat process graph without hierarchy (see Figure 3). For this strategy, there are no prerequisites, both structured and unstructured BPEL control flow can be transformed according to this strategy. The advantage of flattening is that the behavior of the whole BPEL process is mapped to one process graph. Yet, as a drawback the descriptive semantics of structured activities get lost. Such a transformation strategy is useful in a scenario where a BPEL process has to be visually communicated to business analysts.

Hierarchy-Preservation. This strategy maps each BPEL structured activity to a sub-process in a hierarchy of nested graph-based processes (see Figure 3). The nesting of structured activities is preserved as nodes with sub-process relations. The algorithm can be defined in a top-down way similar to the Flattening strategy. Changes have to be defined for the transformation of structured activities as each is mapped to a new process graph. A prerequisite of this strategy is that the BPEL code is structured: links across the border of structured activities cannot the expressed by the subprocess relation. The advantage of this strategy is that the descriptive semantics of structured activities is preserved. Furthermore, such a transformation can correctly map the BPEL semantics of Terminate activities that are nested in Scopes. As a drawback, the model hierarchy has to be navigated in order to understand the whole process. This strategy might be useful in a scenario where process graphs are formally verified and then mapped back to BPEL structured activities.

Hierarchy-Maximization. One disadvantage of the Hierarchy-Preservation strategy is that it is bound to structured BPEL. The Hierarchy-Maximization strategy aims at preserving as much hierarchy as possible, and it is applicable to any (structured or unstructured) BPEL control flow. This strategy maps BPEL structured activities to sub-processes if there are no links nested that cross the border of the activity (see Figure 3). Accordingly, this strategy does not have any prerequisites regarding the BPEL code structure. The advantage of Hierarchy-Maximization is that as much structure as possible is preserved. Yet, the transformation logic of both previous strategies, Flattening and Hierarchy-Preservation, needs need to be implemented to realize Hierarchy-Maximization.

3 Case Study

In an industry project, we designed a BPEL export filter for a workflow designer that uses a graph-based notation based on UML activity diagrams including product-specific extensions. In essence, we followed the element-preservation strategy and deviated in order to capture specifics of the UML Activity Diagram variant of the workflow designer. These deviations related to start and end events, split elements, and a two-level modeling concept. Models built by the workflow designer have exactly one start node and end nodes with implicit termination semantics. As they do not need to be represented in the flow element, we decided not to transform them to BPEL. Accordingly, also arcs connected with start and end nodes are not mapped to BPEL links. The workflow designer offers two split elements that have semantics comparable to an XOR split; these are switch nodes (two alternatives) and decision nodes (multiple alternatives). We decided to map both of these elements to a BPEL switch that includes empty elements for each alternative that serves as a source for a link to the subsequent activity. This design has been chosen instead of a mapping to empty activities in order to easier distinguish different types of splits when the exported BPEL is re-imported. Furthermore, the workflow designer offers a two-level modeling approach: step nodes similar to process graph functions have to be specified by a sequence of one or multiple step actions. Step nodes are part of the UML model, step actions have no visual representation. As a consequence, we map step nodes to BPEL sequences that nest further BPEL activities corresponding to the semantics of the step actions.

The mapping of many proprietary concepts of the workflow designer turned out to be a problem. These proprietary concepts include sub-workflow elements, step actions, and properties of the individual visual elements:

- Regarding the sub-workflow concept, we decided to map each sub-workflow to a BPEL scope and a nested invoke. This allows us to define the input parameters of the sub-workflow as local variables in the scope and represent the invocation of the sub-process via a BPEL invoke. For a more appropriate mapping, the upcoming BPEL-SPE extension will be very helpful [7], especially for variable passing as well as fault and compensation handling.
- Step actions are defined in an abstract class, which is customized by a number of different possible step actions, such as defining a (local) variable, inline Java code, or mail sending. To map these steps, we first defined a generic mapping operation to BPEL in the abstract step action class which is used when no special class overrides the operation. In this case, a BPEL invoke is written to the output, containing the name of the step as a partner link. We also defined mappings for a number of concrete step actions. For instance, in the step action for invoking a form-based input, the partner link is set to the application receiving the form-based input. The inline Java code step action is transformed to a BPELJ snippet [3]. The variable setting step action is mapped to a BPEL assign activity.
- All visual elements of the workflow designer can have additional properties. Some of those, such as time-out conditions and escalations, might even have an influence on the control flow. We defined a special XML namespace for these properties and included them as attributes in the respective BPEL activity. Finally, we had to map step actions contained in the step nodes to BPEL basic activities.

Figure 4 illustrates the transformation with an example UML Activity Diagram and the generated BPEL export. The first step node *Step 103* contains two step actions: a send email task and Java inline code. The step node is mapped to a `sequence` containing basic activities for each of the step actions. The send email task maps to an invoke of the respective service, the Java inline code is mapped to a BPELJ snippet. The following decision node is transformed to a `switch`. The `empty` activity in its `case` branch serves as the source for a link to the subsequent `sequence` containing the `assign` activity (*Step 37*). The other branch links to the join node represented as an `empty` activity with `joinCondition` in BPEL. Afterwards there is a step node containing Java inline code (*Step 43*).

In conclusion, the transformation strategies have helped us to find a systematic, initial approach and process for the transformation of the workflow designer's notation to BPEL. They are also useful for explaining the overall

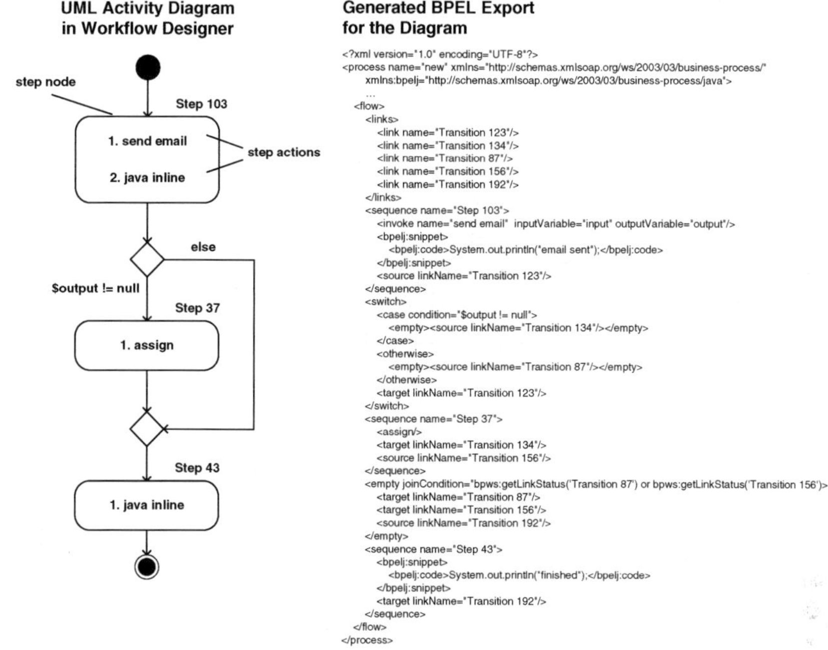

Fig. 4. UML Activity Diagram and generated BPEL export

design decisions. The case study also shows that the transformation strategies can be mixed. The strategies define ideal, prototypical mappings, but in a complex product like the workflow designer in our case study it is necessary to identify the most suitable transformation strategy for the different parts of the mapping. In addition, in a real-world industry product, there are proprietary extensions, such as step actions or properties in our case, and model elements with further semantics, such as sub-workflows, which are not addressed by the transformation strategies. These require further deviations from the general strategies.

4 Related Work

There have been several works on transformations between BPEL and graph-based process modeling languages. We highlight only some of them and refer to [9] for a more comprehensive overview.

The export of BPEL from a graph-based BPM tool can be related to work dedicated to *model-driven development* of executable BPEL process definitions. A conceptual mapping from *EPCs* to BPEL is presented in [13]. The authors choose a transformation based on the Element-Preservation strategy for the reason that it is easy to implement. In [11] a *Workflow-net*-based modeling approach for BPEL including a respective transformation is presented. Similar to the Structure-Identification strategy, Workflow nets are reduced by matching components that are equivalent to BPEL structured activities such as switch and pick. The Structure-Identification strategy has been chosen in order to generate readable BPEL template code and not executable BPEL processes.

Further work takes the modeling standards UML and BPMN as a starting point. In [4] a BPM-specific profile of *UML* is used to generate BPEL code. From the paper the transformation strategy is not clear, but the figures suggest that the author uses an Element-Preservation strategy and maps sequences to BPEL sequences. The *BPMN* specification [12] comes along with a proposal for a mapping to BPEL. As BPMN is a graph-based BPM language, the strategies of Section 2.1 can be applied. The subsection 6.17 of BPMN spec presents a mapping that is close to the Structure-Identification strategy. Yet, the mapping is given rather in prose, a precise algorithm and a definition of required structural properties is missing. Ouyang et al. [10] show a translation from so-called *Standard Process Models* (SPMs) [5] to BPEL. SPM basically reflects the commonalities of UML Activity Diagrams and BPMN. The authors generate Event-Condition-Action (ECA) rules for each activity in the SPM that describes what event must occur under what condition for an activity to become active. Each ECA is translated into BPEL as an event handler resulting in the entire BPEL process being a sequence of event handlers that invoke each other. To improve their result they only make ECAs for what they call Clusterable Activity Blocks (CABs), parts of an SPM that among other things do not contain AND-splits and AND-joins. This improves the readability of the resulting BPEL since nodes that are local in CABs are local in the BPEL. This approach can be regarded as an additional strategy for transforming graph-based process models to BPEL that is able to handle arbitrary cycles, too.

5 Conclusion

In this paper, we discussed import and export interfaces as a simple option for BPM tool vendors to provide BPEL support. We identified transformation strategies between graph-based BPM tools and BPEL as helpful predefined solutions to the problem of mapping control flow in this context. In a case study we applied transformation strategies in the implementation of an export interface of a commercial BPM tool that utilized UML Activity Diagrams for process modeling. The transformation strategies have helped us to find a systematic, initial approach for the export. Yet, several specifics of the tool required deviations and extensions to the strategies. Some of the mapping problems have already motivated to envision extensions to the new BPEL Version 2.0 [2]. While we could already utilize the BPEL-J specification for inline Java code, the envisioned BPEL-SPE extension would have been very helpful to map sub-processes. Maybe some of the vendor-specific activity properties like escalation would be considered in the future BPEL4People extension [6]. These extensions have the potential to facilitate a more straight-forward mapping and a simpler interchange of process definitions via BPEL in the future.

References

1. T. Andrews, F. Curbera, H. Dholakia, Y. Goland, J. Klein, F. Leymann, K. Liu, D. Roller, D. Smith, S. Thatte, I. Trickovic, and S. Weerawarana. Business Process Execution Language for Web Services, Version 1.1. Specification, BEA Systems, IBM Corp., Microsoft Corp., SAP AG, Siebel Systems, 2003.
2. Assaf Arkin, Sid Askary, Ben Bloch, Francisco Curbera, Yaron Goland, Neelakantan Kartha, Canyang Kevin Liu, Satish Thatte, Prasad Yendluri, and Alex Yiu. Web services business process execution language version 2.0. wsbpel-specification-draft-01, OASIS, September 2005.
3. Michael Blow, Yaron Goland, Matthias Kloppmann, Frank Leymann, Gerhard Pfau, Dieter Roller, and Michael Rowley. BPELJ: BPEL for Java. Whitepaper, BEA and IBM, 2004.
4. Tracy Gardner. UML Modelling of Automated Business Processes with a Mapping to BPEL4WS. In *Proceedings of the First European Workshop on Object Orientation and Web Services at ECOOP 2003*, 2003.
5. Bartek Kiepuszewski, Arthur H. M. ter Hofstede, and Wil M. P. van der Aalst. Fundamentals of control flow in workflows. *Acta Inf.*, 39(3):143–209, 2003.
6. Matthias Kloppmann, Dieter König, Frank Leymann, Gerhard Pfau, Alan Rickayzen, Claus von Riegen, Patrick Schmidt, and Ivana Trickovic. WS-BPEL Extension for People BPEL4People. Joint white paper, IBM and SAP, July 2005.
7. Matthias Kloppmann, Dieter König, Frank Leymann, Gerhard Pfau, Alan Rickayzen, Claus von Riegen, Patrick Schmidt, and Ivana Trickovic. WS-BPEL Extension for Sub-processes BPEL-SPE. Joint white paper, IBM and SAP, 2005.
8. Dieter König. WS-BPEL Standards Roadmap. Invited Talk at the 3rd GI-Workshop XML4BPM 2006, http://wi.wu-wien.ac.at/~mendling/XML4BPM2006/WS-BPEL%20Standards.pdf, February 2006.
9. J. Mendling, K. Lassen, and U. Zdun. Transformation strategies between block-oriented and graph-oriented process modelling languages. Technical Report JM-2005-10-10, WU Vienna, http://wi.wu-wien.ac.at/home/mendling/publications/TR05-Strategy.pdf, October 2005.
10. C. Ouyang, M. Dumas, S. Breutel, and A. H.M. ter Hofstede. Translating Standard Process Models to BPEL. In *Proceedings of the 18th International Conference on Advanced Information Systems Engineering (CAiSE)*, LNCS, 2006.
11. Wil M.P. van der Aalst, Jens Bæk Jørgensen, and Kristian Bisgaard Lassen. Let's Go All the Way: From Requirements via Colored Workflow Nets to a BPEL Implementation of a New Bank System. In R. Meersman and Z.Tari, editors, *Proceedings of CoopIS/DOA/ODBASE 2005, Cyprus*, LNCS 3760, pages 22–39, 2005.
12. S. A. White. Business Process Modeling Notation. Specification, BPMI.org, 2004.
13. J. Ziemann and J. Mendling. EPC-Based Modelling of BPEL Processes: a Pragmatic Transformation Approach. In *Proceedings of MITIP 2005, Italy*, 2005.

Introducing Case Management: Opening Workflow Management's Black Box

Kees Kaan[1], Hajo A. Reijers[2], and Peter van der Molen[1]

[1] Gyata BPI Consultants, P.O. Box 43, 4230 DJ Meerkerk, The Netherlands
{kkaan, pvandermolen}@gyatabpi.com
http://www.gyatabpi.com
[2] Technische Universiteit Eindhoven, Department of Technology Management,
Information Systems Group, P.O. Box 513, 5600 MB Eindhoven, The Netherlands
h.a.reijers@tm.tue.nl

Abstract. Workflow management systems are very adequate for supporting the flow of work through enterprises, but do not deliver coordination support to end-users *within* the work items they perform. In this paper, the concept of *case management* is introduced, which specifically targets this type of support. Its associated technology is intended to be used as a harmonious extension of workflow technology, instead of a competing system. A discussion in some depth is presented of the concept, methods, and technology of case management, as well as experiences with its application in industry.

1 Introduction

Technologies fight for survival, evolve, and undergo their own characteristic life cycle. They typically roam from an initial stage, where precursor technologies can be distinguished, through stages of development and maturity, towards finally becoming a relic [13]. It is safe to say that workflow technology has not quite reached that terminal stage. Throughout the introduction of office automation technology in the 70s, the rise of commercial systems during the 80s and 90s up till its recent re-branding as Business Process Management system, workflow technology is actively being researched and widely applied in industry (see e.g. [5,15,18]).

An interesting question is whether workflow technology should be considered as the final solution in providing support to people in coordinating their work. Workflow management systems (WfMSs) take care of the logistics of a workflow process by handing out work items to performers according to a predefined workflow plan [2,9,10]. What actually happens *within* the execution of a task for a particular case is of no concern to the WfMS. Aside from monitoring changes to case attribute values that may be of influence on further routing, the tasks in the workflow process are "black boxes" as far as the WfMS is concerned. And yet, in many settings it is hardly the case that people follow a strict sequence of operations to perform any but the simplest of tasks. In fact, one of the main reasons that a task cannot (or will not) be completely automated seems to be that it requires humans to skillfully adjust the contents of a task to fit the requirements of one case over the other.

S. Dustdar, J.L. Fiadeiro, and A. Sheth (Eds.): BPM 2006, LNCS 4102, pp. 358 – 367, 2006.

We can clarify this by the following example. Consider a single task in the processing of loan applications. Even though this task consists of several elementary parts (or *activities*), not all of these are relevant in every situation. If the application involves a new customer - that is, someone without an account - then the registration of its data and the preparation of a welcoming letter are relevant. Also, if a new customer requests a relatively high loan amount, some background investigation and the preparation of an additional appendix in the contract are relevant. In all cases where the loan amount is high (regardless of any account held by the customer), performing a risk analysis and informing the surveillance agency is relevant. Finally, for each application a contract is prepared. Clearly, this example shows how various activities exist within the scope *of a single task* which may or may not be applicable *for a specific case*.

While adequate for supporting the flow of work through enterprises (facilitating work distribution and task authorization), a WfMS is not very suitable to support the routing through activities within a single task. In an attempt to create such WfMS support nonetheless, a process designer may face the issues of "model explosion" and "self-routing" versus "lack of support". Striving to support the worker in a flexible way, one might end up adding as many possible routes between activities until the model becomes unmanageable (model explosion). Also, this will result in a solution where tiny work items are routed from and to the same resource (self-routing). When striving to keep models simple and maintainable on the other hand, one might end up with system imposing so many restrictions on the workers that it frustrates rather than supports their tasks ("lack of support").

In this paper, the concept of *case management* is introduced, which specifically aims at providing support within workflow's "black boxes". Case management is being supported by concrete methods, techniques, and tools and has been successfully applied in industry in over a dozen occasions. Despite other recent technologies which aim to bring a more fine-grained support to performers, e.g. case handling systems [1,3], case management is not advocated as a substitute for workflow management but as a harmonious extension. This can be clearly seen in industrial applications of case handling technology, where it is usually closely integrated with the operations of commercial workflow management systems (e.g. Tibco's Staffware Process Suite and FileNet's P8 platform).

The structure of this paper is as follows. In Section 2, the case management concept is clarified, together with its supporting methodologies and tools. In Section 3, a real-life application is described. Related work is reviewed shortly in Section 4. The paper ends with our conclusions in Section 5.

2 Case Management

2.1 Concept

Assuming that the workflow management paradigm is contingent with the support needs for work distribution and authorization, but not with the needs at the workplace, we introduce an architecture in which the processing of cases by individuals is decoupled from the routing of the cases through the enterprise. This decoupling allows the use of specialized process support paradigms for both aspects of the business process. As shown in Fig. 1, we propose the use of Workflow Management (including its methods, techniques and tools) on the *flow of control level* and introduce the case management paradigm on the *work contents level.*

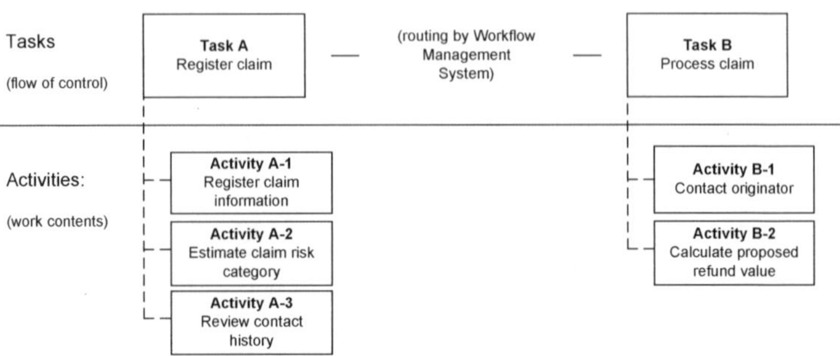

Fig. 1. Refining workflow tasks into activities

Within such a scope, it can be assumed that workers will receive *work items* from a WfMS, which are instantiations of particular tasks for particular cases. (Note that we use the terminology from [2] here). To complete a work item, a set of activities needs to be performed. A central element in case management is that the characteristics of the case determine what activities are considered to be relevant during case processing. This relevance is considered as the context of activities and expressed in terms of conditions on the case attributes. Fig. 2 shows the meta-model of process definition and enactment in workflow and case management. In this model, the left-hand side shows conceptual design-time elements, which result in run-time instantiations on the right-hand side.

As a work item is picked up at run-time, a list of all relevant activities is presented to the worker. An activity is contained in the list if the condition by which its context is specified in the process model is met by the case attributes at run-time. In the meta-model, this is expressed by the entity *Context evaluation*, which follows from the combination of a context definition and the run-time case attribute values. Unless otherwise specified (as we will describe in the next paragraph), the worker can perform any subset of the activities in any order to complete the work item. If the case characteristics change during the execution of an activity, the list of relevant activities is updated accordingly. Through this mechanism, the behavior can be achieved that activities are added and removed from the list while the case is being worked on. This resembles the real-life situation that changing a product while working on it also influences what operations can be performed on it.

Counterbalancing the freedom of the worker with respect to the activities that are carried out to complete a work item, some restrictions can be modeled. As a first construct, activities can be specified to be required in a certain context. This means that as long as this context applies and the activity has not been performed, the worker

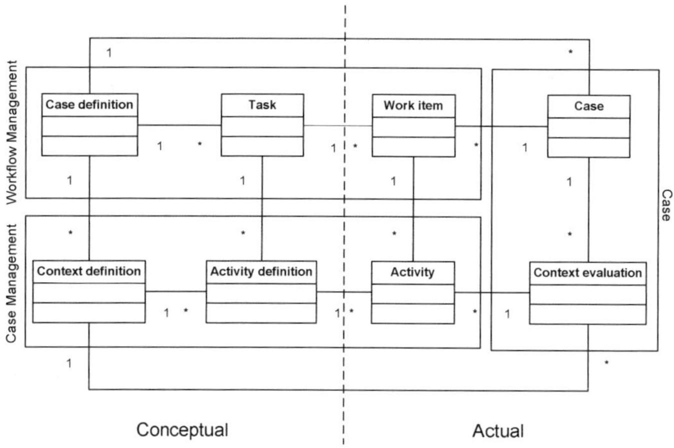

Fig. 2. Meta-model for the interplay between workflow management and case management

cannot complete the work item. However, 'relevance' takes precedence over 'being required', i.e., a required activity that is not relevant in some context, is treated as not being required to complete the work item. As a second construct, activities can be specified to be non-repeatable in a certain context. This means that the worker cannot perform the activity for a second time once it has been completed. As a third construct, an activity can be specified as being allowed to be performed only if another activity has already been completed.

2.2 Obtaining the View on Activities

Clearly, the case management concept presupposes a very fine-grained view on the activities that people perform within the context of carrying out a work item. This implies the need for methods to acquire relevant and valid information in terms of tasks, activities, contexts and restrictions. This section describes a bottom-up process analysis and design approach particularly suitable for situations in which case management is applied.

The key idea is that, in a session together with all workers (or representatives) that have a role in the process, the group is asked to collect all activities that are carried out in the process. Each activity has its name written on a small card and is grouped together with related activities. With the objective that groups of activities should form coherent tasks for individuals, the papers are rearranged until consensus is reached on the main flow of the process in terms of tasks. Each of these tasks has now already been decomposed into activities. This resulting model can be used to facilitate further steps in a business process management project and implementing case management.

2.3 Modeling

Activities and their relevance can be modeled graphically. In this case, relations between the relevance contexts of several activities are specified visually. In workflow

Management, graphical languages have been used extensively to model business processes, both in commercial products and in the academic field. Visual models can provide intuitive insight in the process and can facilitate the communication about models between stakeholders from different disciplines.

The idea of expressing the relevance of certain pieces of work in certain situations is to think of overlapping contexts surrounding one or more activities. If we refer back to the loan processing example of Section 1, six activities can be distinguished within the task of handling a new loan application. Together with their contexts, they are visualized in Fig. 3.

We assume that on the workflow management level, two case attributes are available: *cust_has_account* and *loan_amount* (see table B in the figure). These are used in the model to specify two situations: (1) the situation in which this case involves a customer without an account, and (2) the situation in which the loan amount is relatively high. Situation (1) corresponds with the predicate *not cust_has_account*; situation (2) corresponds with the predicate *loan_amount > 1000* (see table C in the figure).

The activities *Register customer data* and *Prepare welcome letter* are relevant in the context of situation (1). The activities *Perform risk analysis* and *Inform surveillance agency* are relevant in the context of situation (2). The activities *Investigate customer background* and *Prepare contract appendix* are relevant in the context where the two situations coincide. That is, they are relevant only if situations (1) and (2) both apply to the case. For this reason, they are drawn in the intersection of situation (1) and (2). Finally, *Prepare contract* is not restricted to any situation, because it is relevant at all times. As its context is universal, we draw it at some point outside situations (1) and (2).

2.4 Tool Support: Activity Manager

Activity Manager is a tool that supports case management. It has been applied in projects in the past years by the *Altran Group* member *Gyata BPI Consultants* in The Netherlands. It is being developed by *Workflow Management Solutions* and licensed by *BPI Products*. At the moment of writing, the most recent version was 1.2, with a version 2.0 under development.

From the perspective of the WfMS, the Activity Manager (AM) is an application instantiated when the user picks up a work item from the WfMS. Within the AM, various activities are presented to the user. Each activity is related to an application. Interfaces exist between AM and a large number of WfMSs, including FileNet, Staffware, Oracle Workflow, K2, COSA and IBM MQSeries. The interface between the WfMSs and the AM allows the AM to access the case variables defined in the WfMS.

To interface with other information system components (like databases, document management systems or transaction systems), small interface applications are used. These applications control the flow of information between the AM and the mentioned components. Some of these applications can be wrapper applications to interface with legacy systems. The AM toolbox provided by Gyata BPI Consultants contains a set of generic plug-in applications to interface with various 'off-the-shelf'

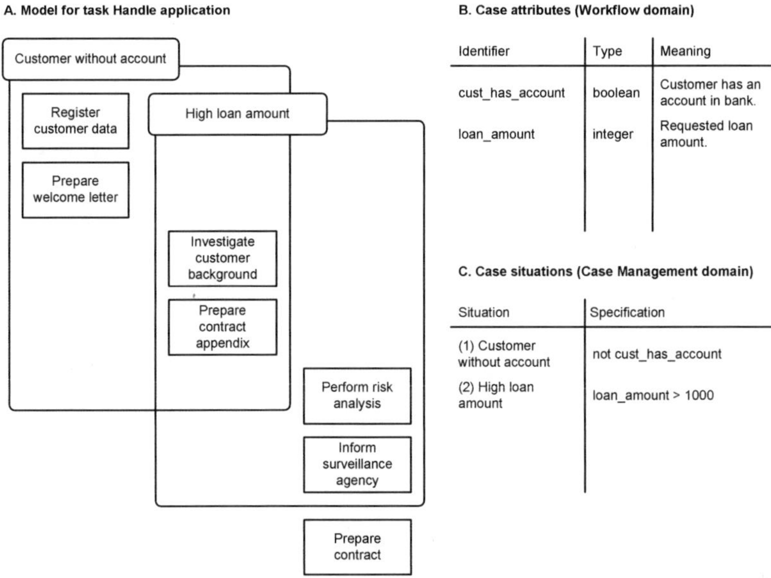

Identifier	Type	Meaning
cust_has_account	boolean	Customer has an account in bank.
loan_amount	integer	Requested loan amount.

Situation	Specification
(1) Customer without account	not cust_has_account
(2) High loan amount	loan_amount > 1000

Fig. 3. Modeling the example of handling a loan application

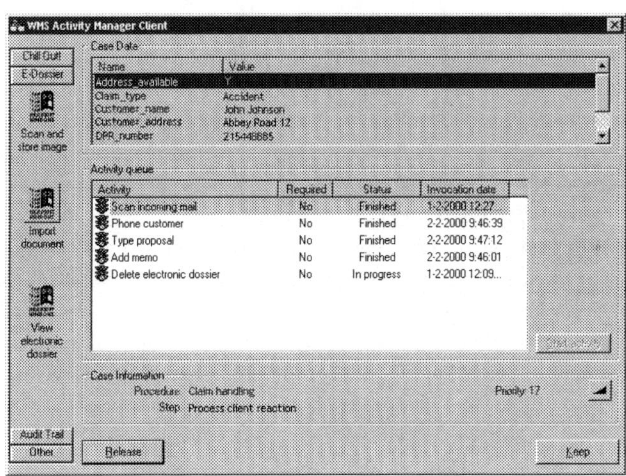

Fig. 4. Screen shot of the Activity Manager

system components. The functionality of these plug-ins varies from relatively 'lean' (transferring data back and forth) to relatively 'rich' (providing a user interface for viewing and modifying information from various systems). One example from the latter is a viewer application that enables users to view documents from the document management system, edit related case data, and provide decision information through an integrated user interface.

In addition to applying the case management concept as we describe it in this paper, the AM supports the use of time frames in which activities are relevant, the starting of activities in parallel, the definition of a repository of plug-ins to be started by the user and an ad-hoc taskbar for starting common functionality from anywhere in the process. The visual approach in modeling activities we described in the previous section is not supported yet in the current available version of the product.

3 Application

Only practice can prove a new concept's value in terms of feasibility and applicability. Case management originates from industry and has been applied in approximately 15 projects over the past years. Examples of implementations running today are in retail, government, insurance and international banking. One of these implementations will be discussed here in some more detail.

Our case involves a health insurance company for all active and retired employees of the Dutch national police. Starting in 2001, an existing WfMS solution based on Staffware was extended with case management. The reasons for this were a lack of user-friendliness and too high a dependency on custom-made applications. Some of the applications used to support the workflow tasks allowed access to as much as 100 data fields. For workers, it proved to be very hard to navigate through these applications to complete their tasks. On the level of workflow logistics however, the routing between the workers proved to be adequate.

Leaving the workflow model intact, case management was introduced at the workplace by means of the Activity Manager. After refining tasks into activities, a set of small-scale user interface components was designed to support the several kinds of operations performed by the workers. These components were then re-used extensively to support the activities performed by the workers.

In two years, two primary and six secondary processes have been analyzed and supported. The first process (addressing the handling of objections) took six months to implement, including the development of the required generic user interface components. A second process (handling the applications of withdrawal authorizations) took three months to implement. For subsequent processes, development lead times dropped below three months.

As an example of the benefits for the business processes themselves, the operational lead time of the second mentioned process dropped from 22 to 6 days by introducing workflow management technology and then dropped to 3 days by introducing case management. Case management in particular introduced the benefit of increased flexibility and uniformity in user interface presentation.

The case illustrates the use of case management to support the worker at a fine-grained level without the need to develop applications that incorporate knowledge of the business process. Also, it illustrates that the concept of activities enables us to re-use generic small-scale components for user interaction. At present, the described solution is still in use.

4 Related Work

Current WfMSs are by no means considered perfect. It has been argued that they fail to provide human actors two major things [4]: (1) awareness of the situation and (2) the flexibility to handle changes. Although some researchers have discussed the first issue (e.g. [12]), a large part of current research into workflow technology has focused on the issue of flexibility (e.g. [4,6,8,11,14]). It should be noted here that insufficient coordination support *within* task execution is not considered as one of the major lacks of workflow technology, although it is sometimes mentioned (e.g. [1]).

Highly relevant for the topic of this paper is the work on *case handling systems*, which are positioned as addressing both the awareness and flexibility issues [1,2]. The case handling solution consists of three parts: (1) the system's focus is on the case, (2) the process is data-driven, and (3) parts of the process are left implicit [1]. Through this combination, end users do receive fine-grained support in executing specific tasks, as the case handling system is involved at all times when case data is being manipulated. This is one of the problems we mentioned in the introduction. Moreover, the other problem we mentioned of potentially highly complex and unmaintainable workflow models is claimed to be countered by implicit modeling, i.e. only the normal process flow is modeled and the end user is provided with default mechanisms to deviate from this normal flow.

Therefore, case handling systems can be seen as dealing with exactly the same issues as case management, although addressing them from a different starting point, i.e. the issues of flexibility and awareness. However, case handling systems come with their own problems. In earlier work, we argued that the specific nature of a case handling system may actually impair the primary strengths of WfMSs with respect to coordination effort, maintainability, efficiency, and quality [16]. The use of a case management system in combination with a traditional WfMS is presented here as an alternative.

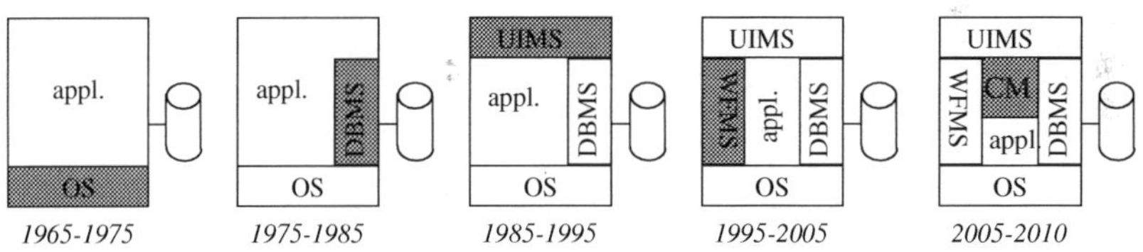

Fig. 5. Trends in information systems development (adapted from [2])

5 Conclusion

This paper introduces the concept of case management with its supporting technology. From a high-level perspective, case management can be seen as a next step in the evolution of information systems. Starting from the monolithic IT systems in the 50's, generic functionality has increasingly been taken out of applications and put into decomposed management systems, such as Operating Systems (OSs), Database Management Systems (DBMSs), User Interface Management Systems (UIMS), and

WfMSs [2]. Case management (CM) takes out the coordination logic *within* single tasks from the generic application (see Fig. 5). Instead, a generic system is available that offers both support and flexibility to the performer for executing a work item.

Clearly, there are open issues that need to be addressed. From a conceptual point, it is unclear where exactly the boundary lies between tasks and activities. This may sometimes hamper the decision where to place the right "split" between the support of the WfMS and the case management system. Although some notions have been suggested such as the Logic Unit of Work and the use of ACID properties from transaction processing to define task boundaries [2,7], the workflow management community has not delivered a concrete and definite distinction criterion yet. Our research into the clustering of related activities is related to this issue [17].

On a technical level, the visual modeling language that has been developed to capture the contexts of various activities needs yet to be integrated in the current software. We expect that a full graphical design environment will greatly add to the understandability and maintainability of case management models, in this way enhancing its value for delivering concrete support at the work floor.

References

1. van der Aalst, W.M.P., Berens, P.J.S.: Beyond Workflow Management: Product-Driven Case Handling. In Ellis, S. et al., (eds.): International ACM SIGGROUP Conference on Supporting Group Work (GROUP 2001). ACM Press, New York (2001) 42-51.
2. van der Aalst, W.M.P., van Hee, K.M.: Workflow Management: Models, Methods, and Systems. MIT Press, Cambridge (2002).
3. van der Aalst, W.M.P., Weske, M., Grünbauer, D.: Case Handling: A New Paradigm for Business Process Support. Data and Knowledge Engineering 53(2) (2005) 129–162.
4. Agostini, A., De Michelis, G.: A Light Workflow Management System using Simple Process Definitions. Computer Supported Cooperative Work 9(3) (2000) 335–363.
5. Cardoso, J., Bostrom, J.P., Sheth, A.: Workflow Management Systems and ERP Systems: Differences, Commonalities, and Applications. Information Technology and Management 5(3/4) (2004) 319-338.
6. Cugola, G.: Inconsistencies and Deviations in Process Support Systems. PhD thesis. Politecnico di Milano, Milan (1998).
7. Grefen, P.W.P.J., Pernici, B., Sanchez, G. (eds.): Database Support for Workflow Management : The Wide Project. Kluwer, Dordrecht (1999).
8. Heinl, P., Horn, S., Jablonski, S., Neeb, J., Stein, K., Teschke, M.: A Comprehensive Approach to Flexibility in Workflow Management Systems. Software Engineering Notes 24(2) (1999) 79-88.
9. Jablonski, S. Bussler, C.: Workflow Management: Modeling Concepts, Architecture, and Implementation. International Thomson Computer Press, London (1996).
10. Georgakopoulos, D., Hornick, M., Sheth, A.: An Overview of Workflow Management: From Process Modeling to Workflow Automation Infrastructure. Distributed and Parallel Databases 3(2) (1995) 119-153.
11. Kammer, P.J. , Bolcer, G.A., Taylor, R.N., Hitomi, A.S., Bergman, M.: Techniques for Supporting Dynamic and Adaptive Workflow. Computer Supported Cooperative Work 9(3/4) (2000) 269-292.

12. Kueng, P.: The Effects of Workflow Systems on Organizations: A Qualitative Study. In: Aalst, W.M.P. et al., (eds.): Business Process Management. Lecture Notes in Computer Science nr 1806. Springer Verlag, Berlin (2000) 301-316.
13. Kurzweil, R.: The Age of Spiritual Machines: When Computers exceed Human Intelligence. Viking, London (1999).
14. Reichert, M. Dadam, P.: ADEPTflex – Supporting Dynamic Changes of Workflows without Losing Control. Journal of Intelligent Information Systems 10(2) (1998) 93-129.
15. Reijers, H.A., Aalst, van der, W.M.P.: The Effectiveness of Workflow Management Systems: Predictions and Lessons Learned. International Journal of Information Management 56(5) (2005) 457-471.
16. Reijers, H.A., Rigter, J.H.M., Aalst, van der, W.M.P.: The Case Handling Case. International Journal of Cooperative Information Systems 12(3) (2003) 365-391.
17. Reijers, H.A., Vanderfeesten, I.T.P.: Cohesion and Coupling Metrics for Workflow Process Design. In: Desel, J., Pernici, B., Weske, M., (eds.): Proceedings of the 2nd International Conference on Business Process Management (BPM 2004). Lecture Notes in Computer Science 3080, Springer Verlag, Berlin (2004) 290-305.
18. zur Muehlen, M.: Workflow-based Process Controlling. Logos Verlag, Berlin (2004).

IT Support for Release Management Processes in the Automotive Industry*

Dominic Müller[1,2], Joachim Herbst[1], Markus Hammori[1], and Manfred Reichert[2]

[1] Dept. REI/ID, DaimlerChrysler AG Research and Technology, Germany
{uni-twente.mueller, joachim.j.herbst, markus.hammori}@daimlerchrysler.com

[2] Information Systems Group, University of Twente, The Netherlands
{d.mueller, m.u.reichert}@ewi.utwente.nl

Abstract. Car development is based on long running, concurrently executed and highly dependent processes. The coordination and synchronization of these processes has become a complex and error-prone task due to the increasing number of functions and embedded systems in modern cars. These systems realize advanced features by embedded software and enable the distribution of functionality as required, for example, by safety equipment. Different life cycle times of mechanical, software and hardware components as well as different duration of their development processes require efficient coordination. Furthermore, product-driven process structures, dynamic adaptation of these structures, and handling real-world exceptions result in challenging demands for any IT system. In this paper we elaborate fundamental requirements for the IT support of car development processes, taking release management as characteristic example. We show to which extent current product data and process management technology meets these requirements, and discuss which essential limitations still exist. This results in a number of fundamental challenges requiring new paradigms for the product-driven design, enactment and adaptation of processes.

1 Introduction

In the automotive industry, car development has been dramatically influenced by the introduction of electrical and electronic (E/E) systems. E/E-systems consist of electrical control units (ECUs), i.e., embedded systems containing hardware and software components. In modern cars, we can find up to 70 ECUs comprising more than 10.000.000 lines of code [1,2]. Several bus systems interconnect dependent ECUs realizing joint features like safety or multimedia functions. Car manufacturers expect shorter development cycles by faster implementation, bug fixing and installation of ECU software. Process support in E/E development shall accelerate product development and transfer of new technologies into the

* This work has been funded by *DaimlerChrysler Research and Technology* and has been conducted in the *COREPRO* (configuration based release processes) project.

S. Dustdar, J.L. Fiadeiro, and A. Sheth (Eds.): BPM 2006, LNCS 4102, pp. 368–377, 2006.

car. However, development processes must also meet the requirements of product liability laws and industrial standards, e.g., by adopting CMMI (Capability Maturity Model Integration) to achieve process maturity in car development or by implementing IEC 61508 to meet safety requirements. Altogether, mature processes shall contribute to realize strategic goals like high quality of the developed components and thus the whole car.

These expectations have raised new challenges for car development, particularly regarding the integrated support of engineering processes in the disciplines mechanics, electronics and software [3]. The synchronization of the different development life cycles is one challenge; another arises from the handling of the complex dependencies in E/E systems due to highly networked ECUs. Finally, different departments, engineering teams and external suppliers participating in the development processes have to be coordinated (cf. Fig. 1).

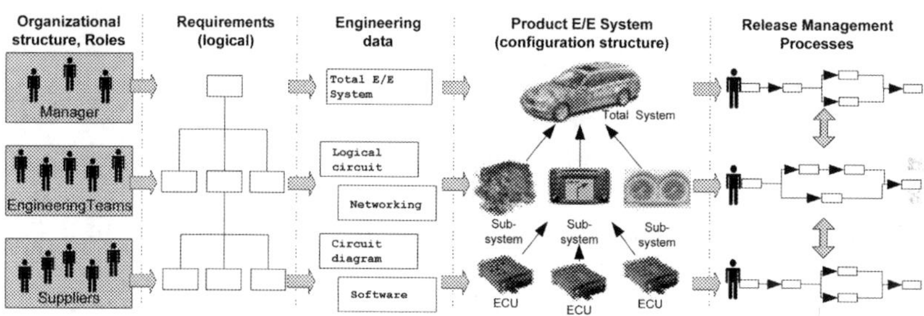

Fig. 1. E/E development with highly linked organizational structures, requirements, documents, product structures and processes [4]

The optimal coordination and synchronization of the development processes related to different car components is the key to adequate IT support. Fig. 1 illustrates the strong correlation between data and process structures. In particular, the structuring of the different development processes and their concrete dependencies are determined by the hierarchical structuring of the E/E system. Consequently, a process structure may have to be adapted if the corresponding product structure changes. For example, when adding a subsystem (e.g., a *navigation system*) to the product structure, new processes (e.g., for testing and releasing the new component) must be added and synchronized with the other ones. This is a complex task to be accomplished in a consistent and semantically correct manner. Finally, knowledge about the relations between process and data structures is helpful in the context of exception handling. When real-world exceptions related to a product component (e.g., failures in ECUs) occur, exception handling at the process level (e.g., abortion of the process) might become necessary.

This paper shows the high potential of BPM technology when being applied to product-driven processes in car development. We elaborate fundamental requirements for the IT support of automotive development processes taking *release management* (RLM) as characteristic example. To evaluate these requirements and to elaborate shortcomings of existing technology, we apply the process engine of a product data and process management system to RLM processes. We summarize the results of this evaluation and discuss which challenges remain with respect to the IT support of RLM processes.

Section 2 discusses characteristics of RLM processes and Section 3 elaborates basic requirements for their IT support. In Section 4 we highlight fundamental challenges based on the results of an implementation of RLM processes with the tool *UGS Teamcenter Engineering*. Section 5 discusses solution approaches in literature and Section 6 closes with a summary.

2 Release Management Processes

Release management (RLM) is an important part of the overall development process. Major goal of RLM is to systematically release the different product components at a specific point in time, for example, when a certain *quality gate* (i.e., milestone) or *production start* are reached. RLM covers *configuration management*, *testing* and finally the *release* of all necessary ECUs.

Different hardware and software versions as well as different variants of ECUs complicate RLM significantly. As an example for a product component with variants consider the *air condition unit*, where each variant is adapted to a specific climate region. These variants are realized by *ECU configurations* (when talking about ECUs we mean ECU configurations) consisting of different software or hardware. Fast implementation and change of ECU software result in about 100 changes of the total car system per day in early development phases [5]. However, proper functioning of every single variant as well as the total car system (based on combinations of all variants) have to be ensured. Thus, testing and release constitute complex tasks within the overall development process.

So far, ECUs often have been released without relying on a formal process that considers their complex dependencies. Due to the missing synchronization of the RLM processes for the different product components, costs as well as duration for integrating and testing have significantly increased. For this reason, configuration-based RLM has been introduced. The overall goal is to explicitly consider the dependencies between product components by defining hierarchical product configurations (cf. Fig. 2). These configurations represent the technical, logical, organizational or electrical view on the product [1]. The creation of configurations for E/E subsystems (e.g., the *air condition unit*) also helps encapsulating ECUs that realize functionality in common. As a result, we obtain a hierarchical configuration structure. Fig. 2 shows the encapsulation of the dependent ECUs 1, 2 and 3 by the configuration *Subsystem 2*.

Instead of performing RLM processes in an isolated fashion and solely at the level of single ECUs, we need improved process coordination and process synchronization. Case studies pointed out that the ordering structure of the RLM processes is determined by the configuration structure. We denote this phenomenon as *configuration-driven process structure*. The example in Fig. 2 shows a configuration-based release process. The creation of these RLM processes

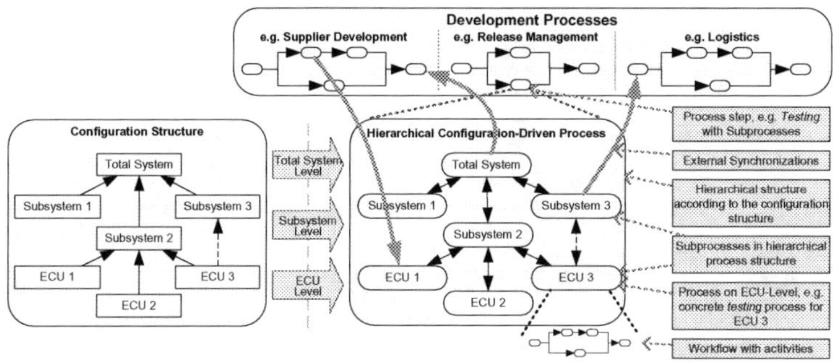

Fig. 2. Configuration-driven process structure

demands in-depth knowledge about the total car system and its configurations as well as existing dependencies between them [6]. Thus RLM processes cannot be fully automated, but consist of manually executed steps as well. The procedure to create a total system release (cf. Fig. 3), for example, starts with the following steps to gain the current ECU versions for a new release:

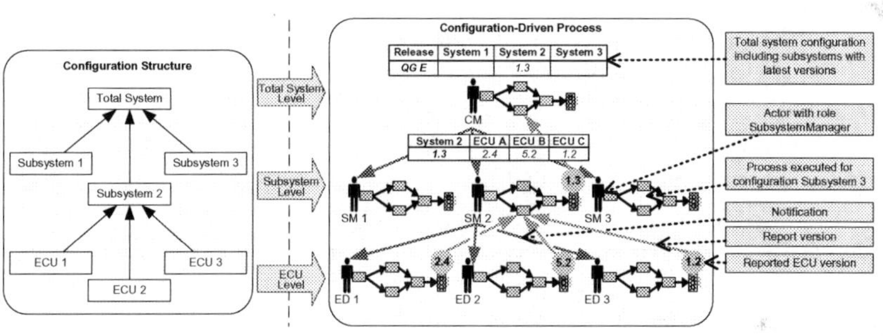

Fig. 3. Procedure to create a configuration-based release

1. With the given configuration structure, the actor with role *configuration manager* (CM) notifies the *subsystem managers* (SM) who are responsible for the subsystem level (e.g., SM1, SM2 and SM3 in Fig. 3).
2. All Actors with role *subsystem manager*(SM) also notify *ECU level actors* (ED) to retrieve the versions of their components (e.g., in Fig. 3 subsystem manager SM2 asks ECU level actors ED1, ED2 and ED3).
3. The actors working at the ECU level report the latest working ECU version to the corresponding SM (e.g., ED1 reports ECU version *2.4* in Fig. 3). After synchronizing the ECU versions, the SM generates a new version for the subsystem and reports it to the CM.
4. After completing the subprocesses and synchronizing the reported subsystem versions, further steps can be taken (e.g., triggering of external logistics processes for ordering the ECUs needed for testing).

The long duration of RLM processes amplifies the need for *flexible adaptation* of process structures during runtime. As an example, consider the removal of the configuration *Subsystem 2* from the configuration structure as shown in Fig. 2. Several adaptations of the process structure become necessary, such as the termination and removal of the processes for *Subsystem 2* as well as its subprocesses *ECU 1* and *ECU 2*. The process for *ECU 3* is still needed since this component is also linked with *Subsystem 3*. To ensure consistent and semantically correct process results, dependent processes in the process structure have to be notified (e.g., the superior process *Total System* in Fig. 2). In addition, also external processes, which are synchronized with the configuration-driven process structure have to be informed about the change (e.g., the *logistics* department might have to cancel orders for removed ECUs). Similar reactions will become necessary if the process structure is modified by changing the *process definition* (e.g., due to optimization) or when adapting the running processes to deal with exceptional events.

Adaptation procedures must enable adequate runtime reactions to external events as well. A process exception will occur, for example, if an actor on ECU level (e.g., ED1) does not report the ECU version the actor on the superior level (SM2) in time (cf. Fig. 3). Then the actor on the superior level (SM2) has to react, e.g., by sending a notification to ED1 or by exchanging this actor. Further, exceptions caused by exogenous events (e.g., failures found in ECUs) have to be handled by the process management (cf. Fig. 4). If a minor error appears, such as a failure in the multimedia component, one possible reaction will be to stop the execution in this subtree of the process structure, to fix the error at ECU level, and to continue (or restart) the execution of the dependent processes. By contrast, a severe fault in the braking subsystem has extensive consequences, necessitating, for example, the abortion of the complete process (including all dependencies) and marking the release as *faulty*. In this case, the RLM processes for the respective ECU, the encapsulating subsystem and the total car system have to be restarted after error correction (cf. Fig. 4).

The more complex configuration structures are the more difficult exception handling becomes. In case of an exception, all dependent processes have to be notified even if they have been already finished. The latter becomes necessary since external processes might also be affected by the exception. In large and

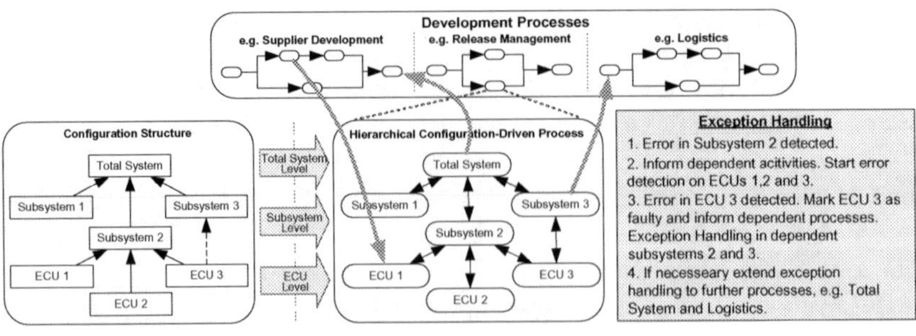

Fig. 4. Exception handling in configuration-driven process structures

highly coupled process structures, ad hoc reactions in conjunction with hierarchical and external dependencies may cause serious consequences up to deadlocks. Exception handling mechanisms must ensure process consistency as well as semantically correct and efficient process enactment.

3 Requirements for IT Support

The high number of product variants, versions and component dependencies as well as dynamic adaptations of product structures make manual synchronization of related RLM processes almost impossible. The major goal for the IT support of RLM processes is therefore to assist process participants in managing the complex dependencies among configuration-driven process structures at the different configuration levels (cf. Fig. 4); the focus is less on the complete automation of all activities of a particular RLM process. Based on the experience we gained during our case studies, we distinguish four categories of requirements as shown in Table 1.

Table 1. Requirements for IT support

A. IT Landscape	B. Process Control
A1) Product data and configuration management functionality A2) Process management and data exchange	B1) Configuration driven process structures B2) Flexible subprocess execution B3) External synchronizations
C. Process Enactment Support	**D. Usability**
C1) Flexible adaptation of process structures C2) Exception Handling	D1) Visualization D2) Logging, monitoring and forecasts D3) Semantical merge of processes

3.1 IT Infrastructure

IT support for RLM processes demands basic features and interfaces on IT infrastructure. First, there is a need for integrated product data management (PDM) in order to store and manage engineering data (e.g., component information, technical documents and software) and their dependencies in a consistent manner, and to make this information available for development processes (Req. A1). This includes support for product configuration management with the ability to manage a large number of product variants and versions [7]. Second, the IT system must also provide standard process management functions and support the controlled exchange of data between the PDM and the process management system (PMS) (Req. A2). This is required, for example, to transfer configuration-related results from the PMS to the PDM system (e.g., to flag a component as *released* after completing a RLM process). Further, user information needed for role resolution by the PMS is usually stored inside documents of the PDM system and therefore has to be made available for the PMS.

3.2 Process Control

To enable process control, we have to implement the configuration-driven process structures (Req. B1). First, standard modeling concepts are needed for describing the different aspects of a process (e.g., control and data flow, reuse of process fragments). Second, appropriate concepts for modeling hierarchical process structures become necessary to realize superior processes depending on the result of subprocesses; i.e., nested processes must fulfill a condition (e.g., provide a specified data quality or simply finish) until processes on higher levels are able to continue their execution. We call this mechanism *hierarchical synchronization* (cf. Fig. 4). As opposed to the common definition of hierarchical processes, where a subprocess is considered as a refinement of a superior process activity [8], we define a process activity as a placeholder for *a set of* subprocesses according to the configuration structure. These subprocesses constitute instances of different process definitions (e.g., different testing processes for multimedia and safety subsystems). Additional dependencies in hierarchical structures or exception handling constraints have to be applied to the hierarchical process structure.

Another requirement for synchronizing hierarchical processes concerns autonomy in terms of flexible execution of the subprocesses (Req. B2). As opposed to strict hierarchical process structures, there is a need to start single (and already instantiated) subprocesses independently of their superior processes. For example, the RLM process for *ECU 1* in Fig. 3 may be started independent from the RLM process of *Subsystem 2*. The synchronization of the hierarchical structure (cf. Req. B1) must be ensured for this case as well. In order to meet Req. B1 subprocesses have to fulfill the defined condition before superior processes can be started. Further, there are dependencies to external processes (e.g., *Subsystem 3* is connected to an independent process outside the hierarchical structure in Fig. 4), which we call *external synchronizations* (Req. B3).

3.3 Process Enactment Support

As described in Section 2, the *flexible adaptation* of configuration-driven process structures is a must. If a configuration change occurs, the hierarchical process structure has to be dynamically adapted (e.g., by adding or removing subprocesses) to ensure consistent results [9]. Thereby, hierarchical as well as external synchronizations have to be considered (irrespective of their execution state) and - if necessary - be adapted to ensure semantically consistent results (Req. C1). Changes of process definitions also affect running process instances. Due to the long execution time, proper adaptation might become necessary.

Further - and this is probably the most challenging issue - *exception handling*, in the sense of reacting on real-world exceptions, must be enabled. These exceptions are expected (to some extent), but require flexible handling mechanisms due to the large number of concurrently executed, dependent processes. Process reactions (executed automatically or by human interaction) depend on the error classification (comp. Section 2). Among other things, it must be possible to *abort*, *redo* and *restart* subprocesses in an efficient way. Thereby results of finished processes must be preserved, if they are not affected by the exception. Semantically consistent configuration structures and consistent process execution must be ensured in any case (Req. C2).

3.4 Usability

To enable the user-friendly execution of configuration-driven process structures, visualization support with partial, abstract, data- and process-centric views is required as well as the presentation of process changes and exceptions in a user friendly way (Req. D1). To ensure data privacy, authorization mechanisms with access control have to be implemented. For instance, engineers need technical views on configurations (and corresponding processes), while external suppliers shall only have restricted access to activities of assigned configurations (with exceptions being hidden). Managers want to have high-level views on the process, which are enriched with forecasts of process and product performance (e.g., execution duration, costs or the product quality). Basic to this kind of process intelligence is the creation and analysis of execution and change logs (Req. D2).

Regarding usability, we want to highlight the semantical merge of processes on ECU level (Req. D3). Generally, developers may be responsible for several ECUs. Considering the process in Fig. 3, the developer has to report the current version for every single ECU. From his point of view, it is sufficient to report all of his ECUs in one step. To realize this demand the execution of several processes has to be semantically merged.

4 Evaluation of Current Technology

The defined requirements in mind, we evaluated IT systems currently used in the automotive domain. For this purpose, we implemented the RLM process from Fig. 3 based on the PDM system *UGS Teamcenter Engineering* and its underlying process engine. This tool supports the management of engineering and product data, enables configuration management, and allows for process modeling and execution. Due to lack of space, we focus on the most important results of our evaluation (cf. Table 2).

Table 2. Summary rating of *Teamcenter Engineering*

A. IT Landscape	Rating	B. Process Control	Rating
A1) Product data and configuration management functionality	+	B1) Configuration driven processes structures	–
A2) Process management and data exchange	+	B2) Flexible subprocess execution	–
		B3) External synchronizations	o
C. Process Enactment Support	**Rating**	**D. Usability**	**Rating**
C1) Flexible adaptation of process structures	–	D1) Visualization	o
C2) Exception Handling	o	D2) Logging, monitoring and forecasts	o
		D3) Semantical merge of processes	–

+ = supported   o = partially supported   – = not supported

Teamcenter Engineering provides full product and configuration management support and meets the requirement for the exchange of data between PDM system and PMS (Req. A1 + A2). Basic mechanisms for modeling processes with sequential and parallel routing are available. Though hierarchical processes are supported, there is no possibility to create hierarchically synchronized processes as needed for configuration-driven process structures (Req. B1). Thus, flexible subprocess execution (Req. B2) also remains unsupported. Synchronization with external processes is enabled by a predefined activity (so called *sync task*). However this concept is too inflexible (e.g., synchronization based on data quality is unsupported) to meet Req. B3.

Adaptations of (hierarchical) process structures are not supported at all (Req. C1). The same applies to flexible exception handling (Req. C2). Though the process engine supports some ad hoc actions, like aborting the execution of an activity or revoking the whole process, the consideration of dependencies to realize exception handling in hierarchical process structures remains a challenge.

Visualization mechanisms like the ones set out by Req. D1 are also not provided. While basic logging mechanisms are available (Req. D2), further concepts like automatic evaluation of the derived data and forecasts based on this data stay unsupported. The realization of semantical merge of processes (Req. D3) is also not possible using standard features.

5 Related Work

Based on the described requirements and the results of our PDM system evaluation we have investigated solution approaches from literature.

Workflow systems define fixed control flows to manage the execution of activities. In contrast, *case handling* [10] describes the coordination based on data objects. This enables less rigid process execution and shall make dynamic changes obsolete. Case handling also provides a way to create direct links between data objects and processes (denoted as *product-driven case handling*). A commercial implementation is provided by the *FLOWer* system [11]. Data-driven process modeling is an interesting approach for development processes. However, our focus is on process synchronization rather than on the coordination of single activities. Further, we identified several approaches that handle parts of our requirements. A solution approach meeting Req. B1 is *product-based workflow design* [12], a method for redesigning process structures based on product structures. Further, approaches for adaptive process management enable flexible process changes during runtime [13].

Related approaches are provided by *AHEAD* and *SIMNET*. AHEAD [14] deals with dynamic (software) development processes. It offers dynamic support for project management, process management, and engineering data management. The authors assume that development processes cannot be planned in detail in advance. Based on the modeled relationships between data and processes, dynamic task nets are generated. Even though the goals of this approach are closely related to ours, there are many differences. In contrast to software processes, car development is more complex and needs fixed processes to guarantee evolving and mature processes and thus high quality.

SIMNET [4,15] is an approach for managing *engineering workflows*. Its goal is to enhance the communication between the participating parties in engineering processes by linking product data and workflow management (denoted as *product data-driven process*). SIMNET focuses on the provision of an evolutionary data model; extensive and flexible process control has not been considered.

6 Summary and Conclusion

Car manufacturers are more and more recognizing that process management is crucial not only for car production but also for the support of the complex development processes. Fast changes in technology and increasing complexity of development processes in the automotive domain are the challenges for an IT supported process management. As shown in this paper, current technology meets the requirements of car development processes only to a small degree. Especially the lack of flexibility and the non-availability of configuration-driven BPM tools prevent the usage of current process engines for development process support or necessitate a high degree of customization. New mechanism and paradigms for flexibility in configuration-driven process structures are required to enable IT support for process coordination not only in the automotive industry.

References

1. Knippel, E., Schulz, A.: Lessons learned from implementing configuration management within E/E development of an automotive OEM. In: INCOSE '04. (2004)
2. DaimlerChrysler AG, Research and Technology: Hightech report 01/2002 (2002)
3. VDI (Association of German Engineers): VDI 2006 - Design methodology for mechatronic systems. (2004)
4. Rouibah, K., Caskey, K.: A workflow system for the management of inter-company collaborative engineering process. Engineering Design **14**(3) (2003) 273–293
5. Wehlitz, P.: Nutzenorientierte Einführung eines Produktdatenmanagement-Systems. PhD thesis, TU Munich (2000)
6. Heinisch, C., Feil, V., Simons, M.: Efficient configuration management of automotive software. In: ERTS '04. (2004)
7. Crnkovic, I., Asklund, U., Dahlqvist, A.P.: Implementing and Integrating Product Data Management and Software Configuration Management. Artech House Publishers (2003) ISBN 1-58053-498-8.
8. Leymann, F., Roller, D.: Production Workflow: Concepts and Techniques. Prentice-Hall PTR (2000) ISBN 0-13-021753-0.
9. Müller, D., Reichert, M., Herbst, J.: Flexibility of data-driven process structures. In: DPM '06. (2006)
10. Aalst, W., Weske, M., Grünbauer, D.: Case handling: A new paradigm for business process support. DKE **53**(2) (2005) 129–162
11. Aalst, W., Berens, P.J.S.: Beyond workflow management: Product-driven case handling. In: GROUP 2001. (2001) 42–51
12. Reijers, H., Limam, S., Aalst, W.: Product-based workflow design. Management Information Systems **20**(1) (2003) 229–262
13. Reichert, M., Dadam, P.: ADEPTflex: Supporting dynamic changes of workflow without loosing control. JIIS **10**(2) (1998) 93–129
14. Jäger, D., Schleicher, A., Westfechtel, B.: AHEAD: A graph-based system for modeling and managing development processes. In: AGTIVE. (1999) 325–339
15. Goltz, M., Schmitt, R.: Simnet - workflow management for simultaneous engineering networks. IMV Institutsmitteilung **23** (1998) 97–100

Diagnosing SCA Components Using WOMBAT

Axel Martens[1] and Simon Moser[2]

[1] IBM TJ Watson Research Center
Component Systems Group
Hawthorne (NY), USA
amarten@us.ibm.com

[2] IBM Böblingen Laboratory
Business Process Solutions
Böblingen, Germany
smoser@de.ibm.com

Abstract. The Service Component Architecture (SCA) is a new technology aiming to simplify application development in a service-oriented architecture. Developing a SCA application basically consists of two major parts: The implementation or discovery of individual components, and the assembly of sets of components. Since each assembly itself might act as a component within a larger application, SCA obviously enables the construction of complex distributed systems that are hardly analyzable. Hence crucial questions like compatibility, consistency or soundness of components need to be answered early during the development process. This paper presents WOMBAT– an analysis tool that is integrated into IBM's development environment to perform on demand verification tasks. WOMBAT benefits from established formal methods for distributed systems. It tailors those methods to relevant use case and puts them into a context that directly supports the development of SCA applications.

Keywords: Business Process Modeling, SOA, Web service composition, Tool based Verification, BPEL, State Machine, Petri nets.

1 Introduction

The core idea of service-oriented architecture is to separate business functionality exposed as reusable components from business logic that orchestrates those components. This idea has been known to the workflow community at least for 15 years. Major software vendors like BEA, IBM, Oracle, SAP and others are now collaborating on specifications for actual business application development in accordance with this paradigm – called *Service Component Architecture (SCA)* [14]. SCA builds on open standards such as Web services and aims to provide developers with simpler and more powerful ways of constructing applications.

Simplifying the development process will encourage more and more companies to build their business critical applications based on SOA [1]. In this context, questions of *correctness* of applications, *compatibility* and *exchangeability* between components, and *generation* of partner or mediator components become

S. Dustdar, J.L. Fiadeiro, and A. Sheth (Eds.): BPM 2006, LNCS 4102, pp. 378–388, 2006.

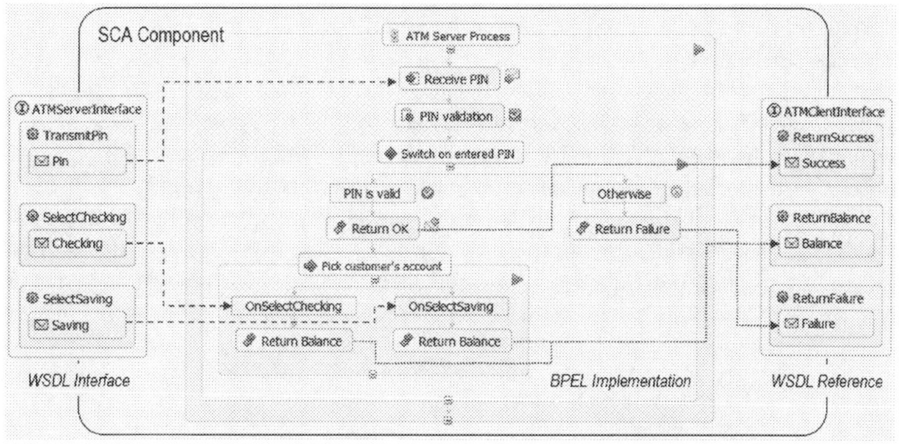

Fig. 1. A SCA component implemented by a BPEL process

more crucial than ever. Moreover, increasing complexity of applications requires the methodical support for those questions being closely tied to the development process. This paper presents WOMBAT – a tool that is integrated into IBM's SCA development environment. WOMBAT performs verification and generation tasks on demand – based on efficient formal methods that have been tailored to SOA relevant use cases – while only minimal additional user knowledge is required.

To motivate the focus of WOMBAT, the remainder of this section gives a short overview on SCA and describes the five major use cases. Section 2 delves into details of WOMBAT's architecture illustrated by an example. The employed formal methods are explained in Section 3. Since WOMBAT focusses on supporting the SCA developer, it puts a lot of effort into processing analysis results – as exposed in Section 4. Finally, Section 5 points to further steps of WOMBAT's evolution.

1.1 Overview on SCA

The Service Component Architecture [14] divides the development of application into two major parts: First, the implementation of components providing services and second, the wiring of components to build the business application through.

A SCA component is a generalization of a Web service. It can be *implemented* with different languages such as JAVA, BPEL, state machines or just by specifying message routing and mediation. That way, it is possible to easily integrate legacy applications. Each component provides standardized *interfaces* to the outside, and it might require others to implemented certain interfaces – called *references*. Figure 1 shows a the server component of an ATM protocol implemented as BPEL process. It provides the ATMServerInterface with three one-way operations, and it requires somebody to provide the ATMClientInterface with similar structure. The component awaits the PIN and evaluates it. If valid, the message Success is sent, and the server expects the account type selection whereupon it returns the associated Balance. Else, the message Failure is sent.

A SCA module (a. k. a. assembly) orchestrates a set of given components by wiring them together. Each wire connects a reference of one component with an interface of another component. Since not all interfaces are called from inside the module nor all references are resolved therein, a SCA module itself might provide interfaces to the outside – called *exports* or *entry points*, and it might require interfaces to be implemented somewhere else – called *imports* or *external services*. Thus, a SCA module can act as a component within a larger assembly.

1.2 SCA Relevant Use Cases

Giving the setting of SCA, we can assume there is a process designer who knows the components and defines the wiring. WOMBAT therefore supports currently five use cases, that seem most relevant to the development of SCA applications.

Final Correctness Check: While creating wires between components, the check of static type compatibility between required and provided interfaces can easily be performed. But considering especially stateful components like BPEL processes, this is not sufficient to ensure the *correctness* of the resulting SCA module as Figure 3 will later show. A development tool, however, should be able to answer the question whether its components really fit together with respect to the implemented behavior, i. e. control and data flow. *Correctness* in that sense is a necessary property of any useful SCA module.

Early Compatibility Check: If a fully specified SCA module has proven to be correct, obviously, all its components behave compatibly. On the other hand, if two wired components are not *behavioral compatible*, the resulting SCA module can not be correct at all. Given two components and the outlined wiring of the SCA module, a development tool should be able to answer the question whether the composition of those two components forms a useful building block for the further assembly of the SCA module. As exposed in Section 3.2, *behavioral compatibility* is closely related to the notions of correctness and controllability.

Component Template Generation: Lets assume, Component 1 and 2 have been developed and proven compatible, and the overall wiring has been outlined. Only the implementation of Component 3 missing. Obviously, there are many constraint to its behavior imposed by the context. Given the interfaces of a component and the behavior of its partners, a development tool should be able to *generate a template* of that component such that behavioral compatibility is guaranteed.

Component Exchangeability: Since SCA separates business logic from actual implementation, each component can be maintained independently as long as changes do not break the overall module. If a component in shall be *exchanged* by another component, a development tool should be able to decide whether this is possible in the given context. Unfortunately, this property is undecidable in general. But with respect to the pure control flow, *consistent* behavior of both components is a necessary condition for the required exchangeability.

Component Model Abstraction: Since a SCA module can become a component within a larger SCA module, complex systems can be built that are increasingly expensive to analyze. But, not all component details are necessary to reason about the properties of the module. A development tool should be able to generate a simplified, abstract model for a complex component in order to develop and analyze the larger SCA module.

2 Analysis Framework

Although SCA is a quite new technology, the core problem of service composition has been studied for almost decades. Hence, there is a huge theoretical background with a wide range of efficient algorithms. As shown in Figure 2(a), our approach is making this methods directly applicable to SCA in three steps.

1. Transformation of given component model of any supported component language into a common formal representation. Our approach is based on Petri nets because this method has been proven to be perfectly suited of formalizing and analyzing distributed business processes and Web services [3,5,9]. Currently, WOMBAT fully supports BPEL, state machines and human tasks. We are working on the extension to all IBM supported SCA modeling languages [10].

2. Analysis of structure and behavior of Petri net models to detect deadlocks, unbound loops, unreachable code, illegal states. Most algorithms generate either graphs of execution or communication traces [5]. While such a formal representation precisely describes the cases in which for example a certain property is violated, it is not well suited to communicate with the user.

3. Interpretation of analysis results is the most important part since the gained knowledge has to be mapped back into the original models. This is done by simulation of the original models or by generation of new component models [8].

2.1 Architecture

Our tool WOMBAT was designed as extension to the IBM's *WebSphere Integration Developer (WID)* – the eclipse based development environment for SCA. Figure 2(b) shows a high-level view on the architecture. On top, the WID layer provides access to the data model and the native editors for all SCA languages.

The Wombat.Core layer holds the Petri net data model and allows examination and manipulations of Petri nets. This component has been inspired by the PETRINETKERNEL [2]. As explained in Section 3.1, we have extended their Petri net data model to maintain the relation to the original component model.

The Wombat.UI component is closely tied to this layer. Besides providing a Petri net editor, this component enables visualization and simulation of SCA modules (cf. Sec. 4.1), and provides wizards guiding through the analysis process.

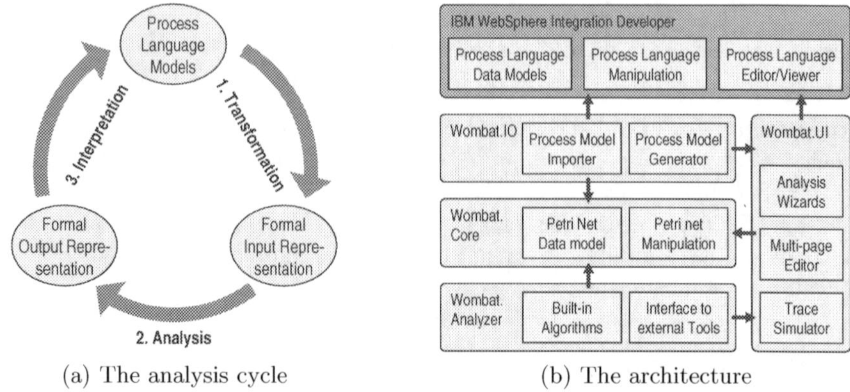

(a) The analysis cycle (b) The architecture

Fig. 2. Analysis framework WOMBAT

The Wombat.IO layer bridges the gap between the two worlds: It performs the mapping of a component model into a Petri net as well as the generation of new component model out of analysis results (cf. Sec. 4.2). Most of the mapping is done fully automatically. Nevertheless, at some points user interaction can yield to greater accuracy [4]. Finally, the extensible Wombat.Analyzer layer contains the actual analysis functions [5]. To enhance the performance it is planned to replace some of our own implementations by efficient model checking tools (e. g. [12]).

2.2 Example

WOMBAT provides on demand verification tasks according to the previously described use cases, e. g. correctness check. While executing this task, WOMBAT transforms each component of the SCA module into a Petri net, minimizes the results and composes all component Petri nets with respect to the specified wiring. This yields an integrated Petri net for the whole module – the *formal input representation*. For the correctness check, the reachability graph of the module net is generated – the *formal output representation* – to decide the correctness property. If proven correct, the user gets to see a report on the SCA module providing statistic information. Otherwise, the user can select and simulate a generated execution trace that violates the correctness property.

Figure 3 shows WOMBAT's Petri net editor simulating a SCA module consisting of two BPEL components: The ATMServerProcess (cf. Fig. 1) on the right and an ATMClientProcess on the left. There are two wires between the components, and the client is called from the outside via the ATMModuleExport. While simulating, the editor highlights step by step the active objects: After receiving the Request, the client process determines the account type and sends the selection to the server – in this case the message Checking. At this point the simulation stops since a *deadlock* state has been reached: While the client is waiting for the Success message the server has not even started working yet. As Section 4 will show, this is only one way to present analysis results to the user.

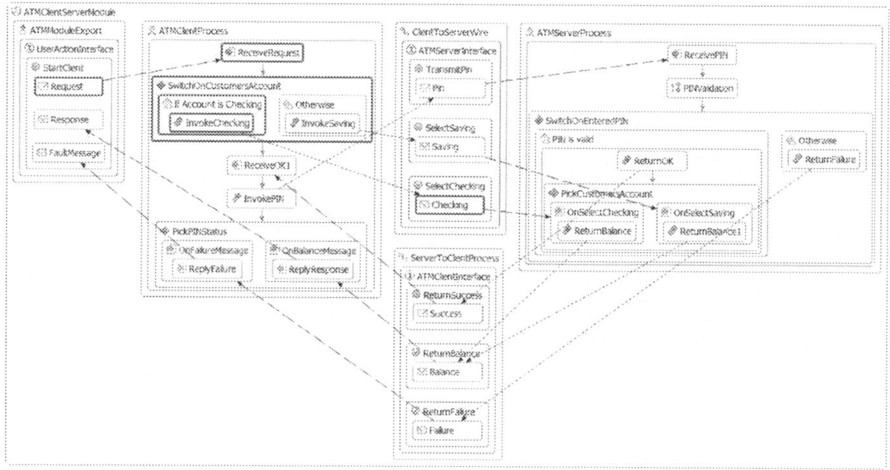

Fig. 3. Error trace simulation in WOMBAT's editor

3 Formalization

Since our goal was to apply available research results rather than reinventing the wheel, WOMBAT is based on Petri nets. There are efficient tools available for structural analysis [15] and model checking [12], and many other research projects also focus on Petri nets and Web Services, e. g. [3, 7, 9].

3.1 Formal Model

Basically, a *Petri net* is a bipartite directed graph. It consists of a set of *transitions* and a set of *places* that are the nodes of the graph. The *flow relation* is represented by arcs that always connect a place to a transition and vice versa [11]. A transition represents a dynamic element, i. e. an activity of a business process. A place represents a static element, i. e. the causality between activities or a message channel. The state of a Petri net is represented by black *tokens* distributed over the places. WOMBAT's Petri net representation shown in Figure 4(a). It is based on the generic Petri net data model described in [2] with two extensions.

Block Structures: While transforming a SCA component into a Petri net, each element of the source language is mapped into a modular Petri net pattern. A BlockStructure defines the boundary of such a pattern and keeps the correspondence to a source Language Element. A relation between different source language elements is represented either explicitly by a BlockArc or implicitly through the *parent-child-relation*. Hence, the component structure is still visible in the resulting net. Figure 3 actually shows a Petri net in WOMBAT's editor while hiding all Petri net nodes, i. e. showing only block structures and block arcs.

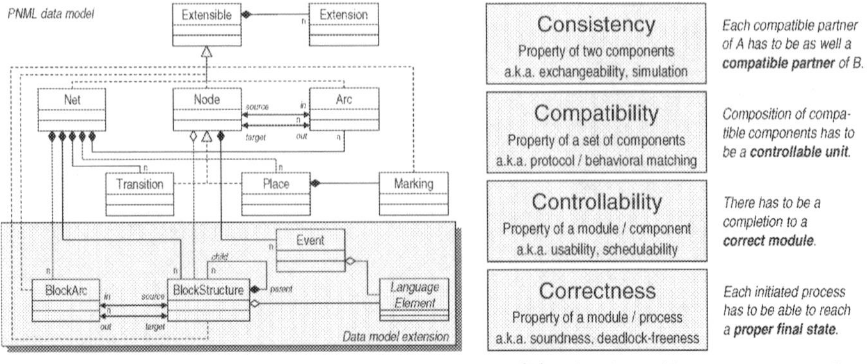

(a) Annotated Petri net data model (b) The four C's property stack

Fig. 4. WOMBAT's formal background

Events: An event represents a state change of a source language element, e. g. the activation of a task, the selection of a branch or the completion of a transaction. Mapping such an element into a block structure, each event is assigned to one embedded Petri net node. WOMBAT keeps track of those events while composing or simplifying Petri nets. That way, each execution trace of the Petri net contains sufficient information to simulate the original component model.

3.2 Properties

Given a formal representation of the original component languages, we need to define properties that can be verified automatically and that correspond with the questions raised while outlining the use cases. Figure 4(b) shows the stack of properties which forms the basis for WOMBAT's analyzer functionality.

Correctness is the core property of a SCA module's internal behavior. It forms the foundation for all further properties and basically stands for the absence of errors. While the classification may vary of what is considered to be an error and what not, the correctness definition has to be adjusted to the specific scenario. The *basic requirement* for correctness is the *proper termination* of all initiated processes in consideration of langauge requirements (e. g. for a BPEL component, a reply always has to follow receive for each two-way operation). *Additional requirements* might be possible *coverage* of all branches (i. e. no unreachable code), *clean* termination (i. e. no left-over messages), and *compliance* with globally specified policies (e. g. no outside propagation of confidential information). Specification and integration of policies into SCA and WOMBAT is the main focus of our ongoing research.

Controllability is a property of a single component or a SCA module that interacts to the outside. Besides the absence of internal control flow errors, controllability requires proper communication sequences. *Definition:* A component C is called *controllable* if there is at least one component E (for environment) such that the composition $C \oplus E$ yields a *correct* module. *Remark:* If a component or a module has no interface and no references, controllability equals correctness. More details about the implemented verification of correctness and controllability, the algorithms and the complexity can be found in [5, 13].

Compatibility is a property of a set of components and the necessary condition for their composition. *Definition:* Component $C_1 \ldots C_n$ are called *compatible* if the the composition $C_1 \oplus \ldots \oplus C_n$ yields a *controllable* component or module. *Remark:* If the the components $C_1 \ldots C_n$ are element of a correct SCA module, obviously those components are compatible. A detailed discussion on the verification of compatibility in WOMBAT can be found in [4].

Consistency is a property of two components and describes similarity of the components' observable behavior. One component specifies of the behavior and the other component has to implement it consistently. *Definition:* A component *Impl* is *consistent* to a component *Spec* if each component that is *compatible* to *Spec* is compatible to *Impl*, as well. *Remark:* Bidirectional consistency defines behavioral equivalence. For details on the consistency of BPEL processes see [6].

These four properties define necessary conditions for useful components and modules. Above that, the formal methods built into WOMBAT enable the verification of user defined properties like test for presences of all required and/or no prohibited execution traces – based on temporal logical formulas. Current research focusses on the integration of convenient specification techniques.

4 Interpretation

The most crucial part of building an integrated tool was to provide the interpretation of analysis results, i.e. the mapping back into the knowledge sphere of component designers. As shown in Figure 5, the user starts a verification task on the SCA module. Under the hood, the module is transformed and analyzed. Only the processed result is shown to the user – in this case as sequence diagram.

4.1 Simulation

An obvious way of visualizing the analysis results is simulating execution traces that yield to a desired or problematic states. WOMBAT provides three different kinds of simulation such that the user can look at his model from different angles.

Single Component Simulation: Each component model can be simulated in isolation using the native WID editor. WOMBAT uses a common mechanism to annotate the execution state step-by-step. In the state shown in Figure 1, the component awaits the selection of the account type. Three activities are running: the outer sequence, Switch on entered PIN, and Pick custermer's account. Three activities are completed: Receive PIN has received a message, PIN validation was successfully executed, and Return PIN has sent a message. The case branch PIN is valid was selected, and hence the otherwise branch was skipped.

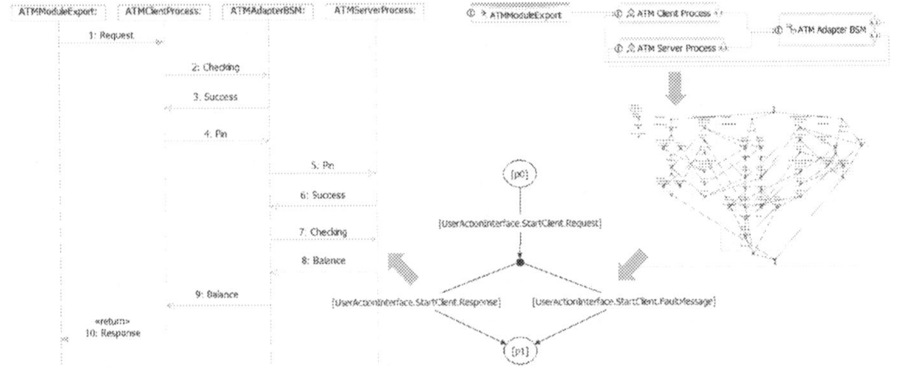

Fig. 5. Analysis cycle of ATM example with adapter component

Simulating a component in isolation does not require the user to understand any additional representation. But, it does not always give an adequate picture of the distributed state.

Petri Net Simulation: Since each SCA module is transformed into one composed Petri net, WOMBAT enables the simulation of the whole SCA module at once – using its Petri net editor. Figure 3 shows a screenshot of WOMBAT's Petri net editor simulating a deadlocking sequence. Since the editor provides the option to show the block structures only, the graphical representation comes close to the look of the native editors. The big advantage is that all involved components are shown at the same time. On the other hand, this makes the approach less suitable for SCA module with many components.

Message Trace Simulation: The third simulation approach tries also to capture all involved components at the same time, but without all details. To do so, it simulates the messages exchanged between the components only. Figure 5 shows the previously discussed SCA module extended by an adapter component (upper right corner) and the generated sequence diagram of one execution trace.

4.2 Generation

Beside simulation of execution traces, WOMBAT uses the analysis results to generate component models. Fully implemented at this time is the generation of BPEL process template that behaves as communication *partner* of one component or a group of components. Based on the *hybrid approach* [8] that incorporates the structure of the given components as well as the communication graph, the generation yields a new component model that is guaranteed to be compatible to the given components, and that can be further refined.

The most challenging generation task that we are currently working on is the generation of an *adapter* component to resolve behavioral incompatibilities as shown in Figure 3. In Figure 5, a manually designed adapter was added to the SCA module. The sequence diagram visualizes its behavior: First, it receives and acknowledges the account type selection of the ATMClientProcess. Then, it forwards the PIN to the ATMServerProcess and transmits the stored account type selection. Finally, it returns the Balance to the client. Obviously, an adapter between two components has to behave like a compatible partner of both components at the same time. The key to build an adapter automatically is to find an interleaving of the messages exchanged with both sides that respects the semantics of the communication: Some of the messages can be generated by the adapter, e. g. the acknowledgement towards the client, while other messages apparently can't, e. g. the PIN. The idea is use static analysis to discover such dependency and to provide a convenient way for the user to specify additional semantic constraints.

5 Conclusion

In this paper, the analysis framework Wombat was presented. It provides effective algorithms tailored to SOA relevant use cases. A prototype that supports a subset of the SCA implementation languages (BPEL, state machines and human tasks) exists as an plug-in to IBM's WebSphere Integration Developer (WID). Due to that integration, a user can perform generation/analysis tasks directly on the SCA modeling view, while the formal methods are hidden in the back-end. Ongoing research aims to determine the effectiveness in a field test.

In the current state, the verifications of controllability, compatibility and exchangeability [5] are largely realized. Moreover, Wombat offers capabilities to generate a guaranteed compatible BPEL partner processes [8]. The current implementation can handle larger examples, e.g. BPEL processes with more than hundred activities. Furthermore, Wombat's usability features include three different ways of presenting a verification result: directly in the SCA view, as an UML sequence diagram or in the Petri net representation. Upcoming work focusses on the integration of data aspects. Especially the dependencies between the content of incoming messages and internal decisions made by the components are of major interest. Applying technologies of static program analysis, it seems possible to achieve a higher level of precision in the mapping of SCA implementation languages to Petri nets, without loosing the possibility of efficient analysis. Another current field of research is to formalize the semantics of other SCA implementation languages with the goal of achieving greater language coverage. The initially implemented generation of an abstract BPEL model for a given process needs to be completed, especially in terms of tailoring the output to user's preferences and to reflect the final specification of abstract BPEL.

In the longer turn, verification of user-defined properties alongside with the existing verifications is a matter of interest. A user-defined property can be e.g. a requirement such as if an error occurs, the component always has to return an error-code. Such properties could be specified e.g. in temporal logic. Finally there is some room to improve the current implementation, for example, it might be worth re-implementing parts of the Wombat.Analyzer functionality in C/C++ in order to further increase analysis performance for large interaction scenarios.

Also, attaching efficient model checking tools, e. g. [12], to WOMBAT might help to increase the performance of computationally expensive analysis steps.

References

1. F. Curbera, D. Ferguson, M. Nally, and M. Stockton. Toward a Programming Model for Service-Oriented Computing. In *Proceedings of the 3rd International Conference on Service-Oriented Computing*, LNCS 3826. Springer, 2005.
2. E. Kindler and M. Weber. The Petri Net Kernel. *Software Tools for Technology Transfer (STTT)*, 3(4):486–497, September 2001.
3. N. Lohmann, P. Massuthe, Ch. Stahl, and D. Weinberg. Analyzing Interacting BPEL Processes. In *Proc. of Intl. Conference on Business Process Management (BPM'06)*, LNCS. Springer, 2006.
4. A. Martens, S. Moser, A. Gerhardt, and K. Funk. Analyzing Compatibility of BPEL Processes. In *Intl. Conf. Internet and Web Applications and Services (ICIW'06)*. IEEE Computer Society Press, February 2006.
5. Axel Martens. Analyzing Web Service based Business Processes. In Maura Cerioli, editor, *Proc. of Intl. Conf. on Fundamental Approaches to Software Engineering (FASE'05)*, LNCS 3442, Edinburgh, Scotland, April 2005. Springer.
6. Axel Martens. Consistency between Executable and Abstract Processes. In *Proc. of Intl. IEEE Conf. on e-Technology, e-Commerce, and e-Services (EEE'05)*, Hong Kong, March 2005. IEEE Computer Society Press.
7. P. Massuthe, W. Reisig, and K. Schmidt. An Operating Guideline Approach to the SOA. *Annals of Mathematics, Computing & Teleinformatics*, 1(3):35–43, 2005.
8. S. Moser, A. Martens, M. Häbich, and J. Mülle. A hybrid approach for generating guaranteed compatible WS-BPEL Partner Processes. In *Submitted to 4th Intl. Conf. on Business Process Management (BPM'06)*, September 2006.
9. C. Ouyang, W.M.P. van der Aalst, S. Breutel, M. Dumas, A.H.M. ter Hofstede, and H.M.W. Verbeek. Formal Semantics and Analysis of Control Flow in WS-BPEL. Bpm center report bpm-05-13, BPMcenter.org, 2005.
10. Barcia R and J. Brent. Building SOA solutions with the Service Component Architecture. *IBM WebSphere Developer Technical Journal*, 8.7:25–68, October 2005.
11. W. Reisig. *Petri Nets*. Springer, Berlin Heidelberg New York, 1985.
12. Karsten Schmidt. LoLA – A Low Level Analyser. In Nielsen and Simpson, editors, *Intl. Conf. on Application and Theory of Petri Nets*, LNCS 1825. Springer, 2000.
13. Karsten Schmidt. Controllability of Open Workflow Nets. In *Enterprise Modelling and Information Systems Architectures*, volume P-75 of *Lecture Notes in Informatics (LNI)*, pages 236–249, Bonn, 2005.
14. BEA Systems, IBM, IONA, Oracle, SAP AG, Siebel Systems, and Sybase. *Service Component Architecture*. Whitepaper, November 2005.
15. H. M. W. Verbeek, T. Basten, and W.M.P. van der Aalst. Diagnosing Workflow Processes using Woflan. *The Computer Journal*, 44(4):246–279, 2001.

Verifying Workflows with Cancellation Regions and OR-Joins: An Approach Based on Reset Nets and Reachability Analysis

M.T. Wynn[1], W.M.P. van der Aalst[1,2], A.H.M. ter Hofstede[1], and D. Edmond[1]

[1] Queensland University of Technology, Australia
{m.wynn, d.edmond, a.terhofstede}@qut.edu.au
[2] Eindhoven University of Technology, The Netherlands
w.m.p.v.d.aalst@tm.tue.nl

Abstract. When dealing with complex business processes (e.g., in the context of a workflow implementation or the configuration of some process-aware information system), it is important but sometimes difficult to determine whether a process contains any errors. The concepts such as cancellation and OR-joins occur naturally in business scenarios but the presence of these features in process models poses new challenges for verification. We take on the challenge of finding new verification techniques for workflows with cancellation regions and OR-joins. The proposed approach relies on reset nets and reachability analysis. We present these techniques in the context of workflow language YAWL that provides direct support for these features. We have extended the graphical editor of YAWL with these diagnostic features.

Keywords: Workflow verification, Cancellation, OR-joins, Reset nets, YAWL.

1 Introduction

Given that deployed workflows may execute for a long time and may take many actions that cannot be undone in a simple manner, it is desirable to detect errors at design time. Workflow verification is concerned with determining, *in advance*, whether a workflow exhibits certain desirable behaviours. In [9], verification of workflow nets is discussed in detail and Petri net analysis techniques are used to detect whether a workflow net is sound or not. Unfortunately, these results are not straight-forwardly transferable to situations where languages are involved that use concepts not easily expressed through Petri nets (e.g., cancellation and OR-joins).

Cancellation captures the interference of an activity in the execution of others in some circumstances. An *OR-join* is used in situations when we need to model "wait and see" behaviour for synchronisation. The OR-join and cancellation are two of the workflow patterns described in [4]. The workflow language YAWL provides direct support for all but one of these patterns [3] and in this paper, verification techniques are proposed in the context of this language. Due to limited space in this paper, we focus on the correctness notions for YAWL workflows and provide a brief discussion of our verification approach. A more complete discussion can be found in [11].

S. Dustdar, J.L. Fiadeiro, and A. Sheth (Eds.): BPM 2006, LNCS 4102, pp. 389–394, 2006.

2 Correctness Notions for YAWL Workflows

The workflow language YAWL is a general and powerful language grounded in workflow patterns and in Petri nets [3]. The introduction of new concepts such as cancellation regions or OR-joins in workflows requires the adaptation of existing verification techniques to determine the correctness of a workflow. In addition, it leads to new properties that need to be analysed. In this paper, we propose four desirable properties for YAWL workflows: *soundness*, *weak soundness*, *irreducible cancellation regions*, and *immutable OR-joins*. Using the notions of coverability and reachability, we will demonstrate how these properties are formulated and algorithmic approaches are derived.

A YAWL net is formally defined as an eYAWL-net and it is represented by the tuple $(C, \mathbf{i}, \mathbf{o}, T, F, \mathit{split}, \mathit{join}, \mathit{rem}, \mathit{nofi})$ where C is a set of conditions, T is a set of tasks, i and o are unique input and output conditions, F is the flow relation, split and join specify the split and join behaviours of each task, rem specifies the cancellation region for a task and nofi specifies the multiplicity of each task. Formal definitions and notations for YAWL can be found in [3]. In Figure 1, we present a YAWL net which describes the "lifecycle" of a student who is required to take an exam and in parallel may already book a flight to go on holidays after passing the exam. In this "holiday scenario", a student decides to reward himself/herself by going on holidays if he/she passes the exam and cancel the plans if he/she fails the exam. One of the fundamental properties

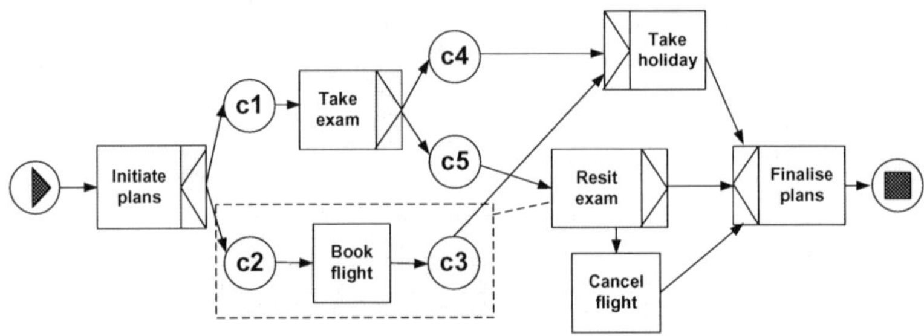

Fig. 1. Holiday scenario

of workflow is the soundness property and the soundness definition for YAWL is based on the definition for WF-nets [1].

Definition 1 (Soundness). *Let N be an eYAWL-net and M_i, M_o be the initial and end markings. N is sound iff: 1)* ***option to complete:*** *for every marking M reachable from M_i, there exists an occurrence sequence leading from M to M_o, and 2)* ***proper completion:*** *the marking M_o is the only marking reachable from M_i with at least one token in condition o, and 3)* ***no dead tasks:*** *for every task $t \in T$, there is a marking M reachable from M_i such that t is enabled at M.*

The concepts of reachability and coverability are defined using the YAWL semantics as defined in [3,12]. To detect the soundness property, all reachable markings need to be generated and it is not possible to generate reachable markings for a YAWL specification with infinite state space. Therefore, we propose a weaker property called the weak soundness property that describes the minimal requirements for the soundness property and that can be used for a YAWL specification with an infinite state space.

Definition 2 (Weak soundness). *Let N be an eYAWL-net and M_i, M_o be the initial and end markings. N satisfies the weak soundness property iff: 1)* ***weak option to complete:*** *M_o is coverable from M_i, and 2)* ***proper completion:*** *there is no marking M coverable from M_i such that $M > M_o$, and 3)* ***no dead transitions:*** *for every task $t \in T$, there is a marking M coverable from M_i such that t is enabled at M.*

Reducible elements in the cancellation region of a task represent elements that can never be active and therefore, can never be cancelled by the task. A net has the irreducible cancellation regions property if all elements in the cancellation regions are necessary and cannot be reduced.

Definition 3 (Irreducible cancellation regions). *Let N be an eYAWL-net. N has a reducible element x, if there is a task t such that $x \in rem(t)$ and x can never be cancelled when t is being executed. N satisfies the* ***irreducible cancellation regions*** *property iff for all $x \in ran\ (rem)$, x is not a reducible cancellation element.*

Non-local OR-join semantics in YAWL results in expensive runtime analysis. It is therefore desirable to determine in advance whether a more appropriate join structure could be found for a task modelled as an OR-join in a YAWL net.

Definition 4 (Immutable OR-joins). *Let N be an eYAWL-net and t be an OR-join task in N. OR-join task t is convertible to an XOR-join if only one condition in the input set of t is always marked in the enabling markings of t or to an AND-join if all conditions in the input set of t are always marked in the enabling markings of t. N satisfies the* ***immutable OR-joins*** *property iff for all $t \in T$, $join(t) = OR$ implies that t is not a convertible OR-join.*

In this section, we have presented the definitions of four structural properties for YAWL workflows. For verification purposes, YAWL specifications are divided into those with OR-joins and those without OR-joins. This distinction is necessary as a different verification technique is needed in each case. In the next two sections, we briefly describe how to detect these properties for YAWL nets with and without OR-joins.

3 Verifying YAWL Nets Without OR-Joins

We propose to transform an eYAWL-net (without OR-joins) into an RWF-net (a subclass of reset nets) to exploit the analysis techniques available for reset nets. This is achieved by first abstracting from multiple instances and hierarchy in YAWL and then applying the *transE2WF* function to transform an eYAWL-net into an RWF-net [12]. Figure 2 shows the RWF-net corresponding to the YAWL net in Figure 1. We have formulated the three criteria of the weak soundness property for an RWF-net using the notion of coverability. As coverability is decidable for a reset net using backwards firing rule [5,6,7,8], the three criteria of the weak soundness property are decidable. The **Coverable** procedure described in [12] is used to determine whether a marking is coverable

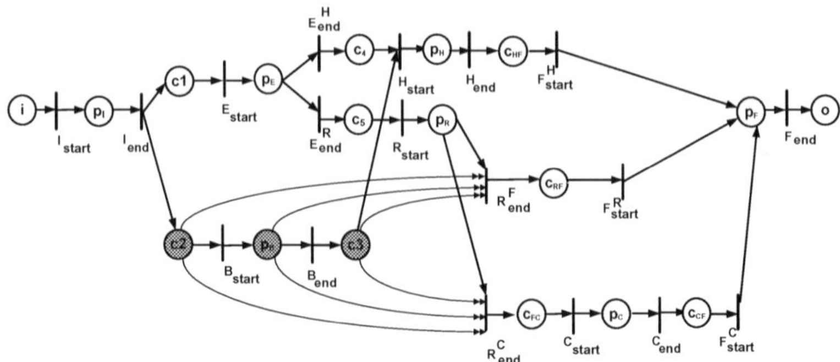

Fig. 2. Holiday scenario - RWF-net (Double-headed reset arcs from $c2$, $c3$ and p_B to R^F_{end} and R^C_{end})

from the initial marking in a reset net. We exploit these results to propose an algorithmic approach for deciding the weak soundness property and the irreducible cancellation regions property of an eYAWL-net without OR-joins.

Observation 1 (Weak soundness is decidable). *Given an eYAWL-net without OR-joins, 1) the weak option to complete can be decided by testing whether M_o is coverable from M_i in the corresponding RWF-net, 2) proper completion can be decided by testing whether $o + p$ is not coverable from M_i in the corresponding RWF-net for all $p \in P$, and 3) no dead transitions can be decided by testing whether p_t is coverable from M_i in the corresponding RWF-net for all $t \in T$.*

Observation 2 (Irreducible cancellation regions is decidable). *Given an eYAWL-net without OR-joins, 1) where a condition c is reducible in a cancellation region of t can be decided by testing whether $c + p_t$ is coverable from M_i in the corresponding RWF-net, and 2) where a task tx is reducible in a cancellation region of t can be decided by testing whether $p_{tx} + p_t$ is coverable from M_i in the corresponding RWF-net.*

As reachability is not decidable for reset nets [6] and its applicability is limited to reset nets with finite state space. As the soundness property definition relies on reachability results, the soundness property is only decidable for an RWF-net with a finite state space. For an eYAWL-net without OR-joins with a finite state space, it is possible to decide the soundness property by generating a reachability graph for the corresponding RWF-net.

Observation 3 (Soundness is decidable). *Given an eYAWL-net without OR-joins and a finite reachability graph, the soundness property can be decided by testing the three criteria on the corresponding RWF-netthrough its reachability graph.*

4 Verifying YAWL Nets with OR-Joins

Due to the non-local semantics of an OR-join [12], a net with OR-joins cannot be mapped directly onto a reset net. Hence, we propose to translate all OR-joins into XOR-joins first. The treatment of OR-joins in the YAWL net as XOR-joins is considered optimistic as it assumes an OR-join can be enabled if there is at least one token in its preset.

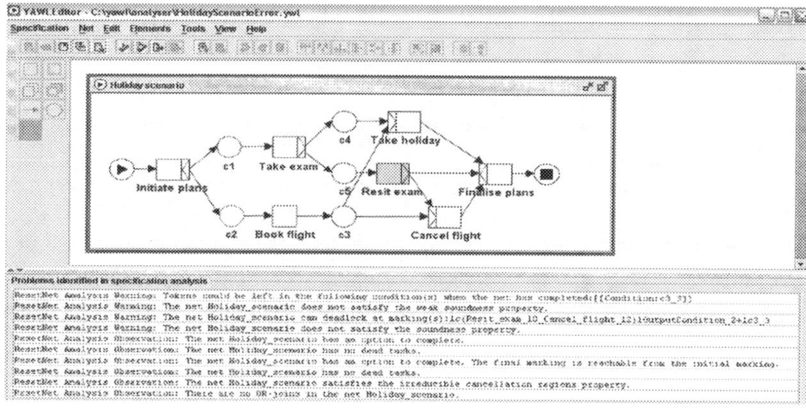

Fig. 3. Holiday Scenario with errors

After replacing all OR-joins with XOR-joins, it is now possible to transform the YAWL net into an RWF-net using the *transE2WF* function.

Observation 4. *Given an eYAWL-net N with OR-joins, let N' be the corresponding eYAWL-net without OR-joins where all OR-joins in N have been replaced by XOR-joins and RN be the equivalent RWF-net for N'. The following holds: 1) if RN does not have weak option to complete then N does not have weak option to complete, 2) if RN has dead transitions then N has dead transitions, and 3) if RN has proper completion, then N has proper completion.*

For a YAWL net with OR-joins that has a finite state space, we propose to create a reachability graph by taking into account OR-join semantics and using enabling and firing rules as defined in [3,12].

Observation 5. *Given an eYAWL-net with OR-joins and a finite reachability graph, soundness, irreducible cancellation regions and immutable OR-joins are decidable.*

5 Verification in YAWL

We have extended the YAWL editor to support the verification approach presented in this paper. The holiday scenario as modelled in Figure 1 satisfies both weak soundness and soundness properties. Figure 3 describes a slightly modified version that have neither the weak soundness nor the soundness property. There are two differences: $c3$ is not in the cancellation region of *Resit exam*, and *Cancel flight* is now an AND-join task. Consider the case where the student has failed the exam and has to resit, after booking the flights. The way this process is now modelled, it is possible for task *Finalise Plans* to be executed, without performing task *Cancel Flight* first. A token is left in condition $c3$ when a token is put into the output condition o which signals the end of the process. Therefore, the model does not satisfy the proper completion criterion. This example highlights how subtle differences in modelling business processes can adversely affect the correctness of a YAWL specification.

6 Conclusion

We have proposed four structural properties for workflows with cancellation regions and OR-joins together with new verification techniques based on reset nets and reachability analysis. The only other approach for YAWL verification can be found in [10]. The proposed approach transforms YAWL nets into Petri nets with inhibitor arcs to decide the relaxed soundness property. The use of inhibitor arcs instead of reset arcs means that this approach cannot detect problems in certain specifications with cancellation features. For example, this approach cannot detect problems in the erroneous holiday scenario described in Figure 3. On the other hand, approximation of OR-join semantics enables the verification of nets with OR-joins using invariants.

Acknowledgements. We like to thank Lindsay Bradford and Lachlan Aldred for their assistance with the integration of the verification techniques in the YAWL editor.

References

1. W.M.P van der Aalst. Verification of workflow nets. *Proceedings of Application and Theory of Petri Nets*, volume 1248 of *LNCS*, pages 407–426, 1997. Springer-Verlag.
2. W.M.P. van der Aalst. The Application of Petri Nets to Workflow Management. *The Journal of Circuits, Systems and Computers*, 8(1):21–66, 1998.
3. W.M.P. van der Aalst and A.H.M. ter Hofstede. YAWL: Yet Another Workflow Language. *Information Systems*, 30(4):245–275, June 2005.
4. W.M.P van der Aalst, A.H.M. ter Hofstede, B.Kiepuszewski, and A.P.Barros. Workflow Patterns. *Distributed and Parallel Databases*, 14:5–51, 2003.
5. C. Dufourd, A. Finkel, and Ph. Schnoebelen. Reset Nets Between Decidability and Undecidability. *Proceedings of the 25th International Colloquium on Automata, Languages and Programming*, volume 1443 of *LNCS*, pages 103–115, 1998. Springer-Verlag.
6. C. Dufourd, P. Jančar, and Ph. Schnoebelen. Boundedness of Reset P/T Nets. *Lectures on Concurrency and Petri Nets*, volume 1644 of *LNCS*, pages 301–310, 1999. Springer-Verlag.
7. A. Finkel, J.-F. Raskin, M. Samuelides, and L. van Begin. Monotonic Extensions of Petri Nets: Forward and Backward Search Revisited. *Electronic Notes in Theoretical Computer Science*, 68(6):1–22, 2002.
8. A. Finkel and Ph. Schnoebelen. Well-structured Transition Systems everywhere! *Theoretical Computer Science*, 256(1–2):63–92, 2001.
9. H.M.W. Verbeek. *Verification of WF-nets*. PhD thesis, Eindhoven University of Technology, The Netherlands, June 2004.
10. H.M.W. Verbeek, W.M.P. van der Aalst, and A.H.M ter Hofstede. Verifying Workflows with Cancellation Regions and OR-joins: An Approach Based on Invariants. Technical Report WP 156, Eindhoven University of Technology, The Netherlands, 2006.
11. M.T. Wynn, W.M.P. van der Aalst, A.H.M. ter Hofstede, and D. Edmond. Verifying workflows with Cancellation Regions and OR-joins: An Approach Based on Reset nets and Reachability Analysis (Revised version). Technical report BPM-06-16, bpmcenter.org, 2006.
12. M.T. Wynn, D. Edmond, W.M.P. van der Aalst, and A.H.M. ter Hofstede. Achieving a General, Formal and Decidable Approach to the OR-join in Workflow using Reset nets. *Proceedings of Application and Theory of Petri nets*, volume 3536 of *LNCS*, pages 423–443, 2005. Springer-Verlag.

Towards a Methodology for Deriving Contract-Compliant Business Processes

Zoran Milosevic[1,2], Shazia Sadiq[1], and Maria Orlowska[1]

[1] School of Information Technology and Electrical Engineering
The University of Queensland
Brisbane, Australia
{zoran, shazia, maria}@itee.uq.edu.au
[2] Also with Deontik Pty Ltd, Australia
zoran@deontik.com

Abstract. This paper presents a methodology for deriving business process descriptions based on terms in business contract. The aim is to assist process modellers in structuring collaborative interactions between parties, including their internal processes, to ensure contract-compliant behaviour. The methodology requires a formal model of contracts to facilitate process derivations and to form a basis for contract analysis tools and run-time process execution.

1 Introduction

Several types of requirements are to be considered in any business process management activity, be it a process design, process execution or process monitoring. Internal requirements reflect strategic goals for improving business outcomes, e.g. an increased efficiency. External requirements reflect constraints from outside world, e.g. contractual obligations with trading partners or regulatory policies with which parties need to comply. Future requirements address likely future states of affairs, e.g. organisational commitments from new contracts. This paper addresses contract-based requirements, namely how to design contract-compliant processes between parties.

Section 2 classifies legal statements in contracts into several types of contract conditions, described in a form suitable for translation into a formal contract expression. One such formalism is briefly discussed and the translation is illustrated by means of an example. Section 3 presents our methodology for deriving contract-compliant interactions between parties, covering cross-organisational interactions, internal processes and supplementary activities. Section 4 provides concluding remarks.

2 Transforming Legal Statements into Formal Representation

A contract is a legally enforceable agreement specifying mutual promises between legal entities, e.g. Subcontractor and Outback Water (OW) in the Maintenance Service Contract example below. Contracts are typically written using legally-centric contract statements, as illustrated through the following example.

S. Dustdar, J.L. Fiadeiro, and A. Sheth (Eds.): BPM 2006, LNCS 4102, pp. 395 – 400, 2006.

MAINTENANCE SERVICE CONTRACT

This agreement BETWEEN Outback Water (To be known as the OW) AND OZ Pumps (To be known as the Subcontractor) governs Maintenance Services (to be known as Service) subject to the following terms and conditions:

1 Definitions and Interpretations
1.1 Price is a reference to the currency of the Australia unless otherwise stated.
1.2 MTBF is Mean Time Between Failures and MTTR is Mean Time To Repair
2 Commencement and Completion
2.1 The commencement date is scheduled as January 30, 2006.
2.2 The completion date is scheduled as January 30, 2007.
2.3 The (OW) shall notify the (Subcontractor) of possibility of extension for 1 year by 3rd quarter of the contract
3 Service and QoS Delivery
3.1 The (Subcontractor) shall make its best efforts to ensure that the following QoS conditions are met:
- not exceed the maximum asset down time on any one asset
- average above the specified MTBF and below the MTTR over a month
The maximum or minimum values are provided in schedule A of the contract.
3.2 (Subcontractor must inform (OW) within 24 hours of any event that might affect the ability to achieve the quality of service
3.3. The (Subcontractor) shall not re-assign maintenance to another party, i.e. Sub-Subcontractor
3.4. The (OW) will provide access to all asset sites based on service requirements
4 Reports and notifications
4.1 The (Subcontractor) will submit monthly reports on all preventative maintenance activities and emergency events, including full timing details.
4.2 The (OW) will provide list of assets to be maintained, with clear instructions of the maintenance cycles required
4.3 The (OW) will provide clear MTBF and MTTR targets
4.4 The (OW) will provide feed back to the subcontractor of any information received about problems with the water supply, including emergencies reported by its customers within 24 hours
4.5 After each of the 1st and 2nd quarters, the (OW) will give guidance to the subcontractor on how any shortcomings in the service might be improved.
5 Payment
5.1 The (Subcontractor) shall submit monthly invoices to (OW) for services performed during that period
5.2. The (OW) shall make full payment of (Subcontractor) invoices within 30 days of receipt
6 Termination
6.1 The (OW) can terminate the contract after three QoS violations

Our analysis of many contracts suggests that legal statements can be classified into several groups whose structure is amenable for formal representation, namely:

1. The declaration of *pre-existing external constraints* from the environment which apply to the contract or to the variables in the contract, such as policies originating from taxation law or business contracts law (e.g. clause 1.1 in the example);
2. *Definitions*, explaining meaning of contracts terms (e.g. clause 1.2 in the example);
3. A *period of validity* when the contract is in effect (e.g. clauses 2 in the example);

4. The statement of *core normative policies*, i.e. obligations, permissions, prohibitions that apply to the parties (e.g. clauses 3, 4, 5 and 6); some obligation policies represent high-level constraints, stating a goal to be achieved (e.g. clause 3.1);
5. Other type of policies used in typical business/legal jargon, which can be reduced to the core policies; we call these *compound normative policies*; examples are rights, liabilities and responsibility (there are no such policies in our example);
6. Actions that cover transfer of normative modalities between principals and agents, as in delegation statements; we call these *policy-transfer actions* (e.g. clause 3.3);
7. Events that signify policy violations occurrence or situations potentially leading to future violations (e.g. clause 3.2 and 4.4); we call them *attention events*;
8. Second-effect policies to be invoked in cases of violations of any of the above policies; we call these *reparation policies* (see [1]), e.g. clause 6.1;
9. *Force-majeure* conditions, describing circumstances which are beyond control of either parties; (there are no such policies in our example);
10. A number of *structuring constructs*, e.g. clause groups 1-6.

We show through the example how the above structures can be mapped onto Formal Contract Language (FCL) [1]. FCL statements include triggering conditions for policy activation (e.g. *AccessSiteRequest* in clause 4.1) and deontic conditions. The latter consist of deontic modality (O for obligation, P for permission and F for prohibition) and the subject's behaviour expression (e.g. $O^{H}_{OW,\ Sub}$ *ProvideAccess* is OW's obligation to ensure Subcontractor's access). Note that 'H' superscript denotes a high-level policy, while 'D' denotes an action of delegation. The contract in FCL is:

2.3: 3rdQuarterEnd,ExtensionYes ⊢ OOW, Sub ExtensionNotification
3.1: ContractStart ⊢ O HSub EnsureBestQoS
3.2: OoSProblemEvent ⊢ OSub,OW InformWithin24hrs
3.3: ContractStart ⊢F DSub, Sub-Sub AssignMaintenance
3.4: AccessSiteRequest ⊢O HOW, Sub ProvideAccess
4.1: ContractStart,BeginMonth ⊢O Sub,OW SubmitMonthlyReport
4.2: ContractStart ⊢O HOW ProvideListOfAssets
4.3: ContractStart ⊢O HOW ProvideMTBFandMTTRTargets
4.4: ProblemOrEmergency ⊢O OW,Sub ProvideFeedback
4.5: EndOfFirstQuarter ⊢O OW,Sub GiveGuidance;
EndOfSecondQuarter ⊢O OW,Sub GiveGuidance;
5.1: BeginMonth ⊢O Sub,OW SubmitMonthlyInvoice
5.2: InvoiceReceipt ⊢O OW,Sub FullPaymentWithin30days
6.1: ThirdQoSViolation ⊢ POW TerminateContract

The FCL can express predicates such as those included under groups 1, 2 and 3 above, but they are not described in this paper. We plan to extend FCL in future to support complex contract conditions grouped under groups 5, 9 and 10.

3 Methodology

We exploit FCL contract form in initial steps of our methodology for constructing contract-compliant business processes (Fig. 1). This methodology is developed to cover various circumstances surrounding the establishment of contracts, as well as subsequent measures for ensuring contract-consistent behaviour. For example, parties may enter contract afresh, to reflect new collaboration opportunities and without limitations imposed by their established internal processes, policies or commitments to other parties. But it may be that their existing processes and policy present conflicting conditions with the new contract. These conflicts may require renegotiation of contract terms or adaptation of the existing processes or policies to align the existing and new policy spaces. In order to detect such conflicts, the first step is to undertake static analysis of contracts, possibly involving various types of simulations. Provided the conflicts are resolved, the problem of ensuring contract-consistent behaviour is reduced to first ensuring that each party formulates its *collaborative* interactions, directly reflecting contract conditions, and then ensuring that they formulate *internal* processes to fulfil contract constraints. Both collaborative interactions and internal processes may be augmented with *supplementary* processes that track interaction progress, detect potential future policy violations and send notifications to the parties to that effect. The methodology consists of several steps as described next.

In order to derive *collaborative* interactions, or a contract framing behaviour, directly reflecting constraints in contract conditions, one can start with the identification of the primitive actions that each party is *required* to carry out, as stated in the contract, i.e. obligation modalities. Typically, one would first consider (simple, but no high-level) obligation modalities in which both subject and beneficiary are explicitly mentioned. This helps identifying messages to be sent between partners and their direction. The messages either reflect consideration aspect of contract, or have purpose of sending notifications to the other party, e.g. about progress of some activity or a warning about likely or an occurring violation. In our example, one would go trough the FCL version of contract and identify modalities of the form $O_{OW,Sub}$ or $O_{OW,Sub}$, followed by the identification of the actions that may result in messages of some form, e.g. *Inform (Within24hrs), SubmitMonthlyInvoice, SubmitMonthlyReport, ProvideFeedback*. Some messages may be a result of complex internal processes. For example, *SubmitMonthlyReport* message can be a result of multiple internal process steps within the Subcontractor organisation. High-level obligations, e.g. O^{H}_{Sub} *EnsureBestQoS*, can be refined in terms of specific QoS indicators and the corresponding objectives. Similarly, one would also identify those actions that *must not* be carried out by the parties, e.g. $F^{D}_{Sub,\ Sub\text{-}Sub}$ *AssignMaintenance;* (superscript 'D' denotes that this prohibition applies to a delegation action). Note that the prohibition modalities will typically result in *supplementary* processes whose purpose is to realise mechanisms to prevent the occurrence of prohibited behaviour. Additionally, one would also identify compound normative concepts that have elements of obligations, such as duties and responsibilities and similarly, identify flow of messages or notifications.

Subsequent steps determine candidate *internal processes* for the parties, compliant with the contract framing behaviour. To this end, various heuristics can be applied to reflect different types of contract conditions, as proposed in [2]. Examples of such condition types are *exception conditions*, specifying actions to be done when a violation occurs and *quality oriented* conditions which imply some inspection stage. The respective heuristics are introduction of escalation branches in the internal process,

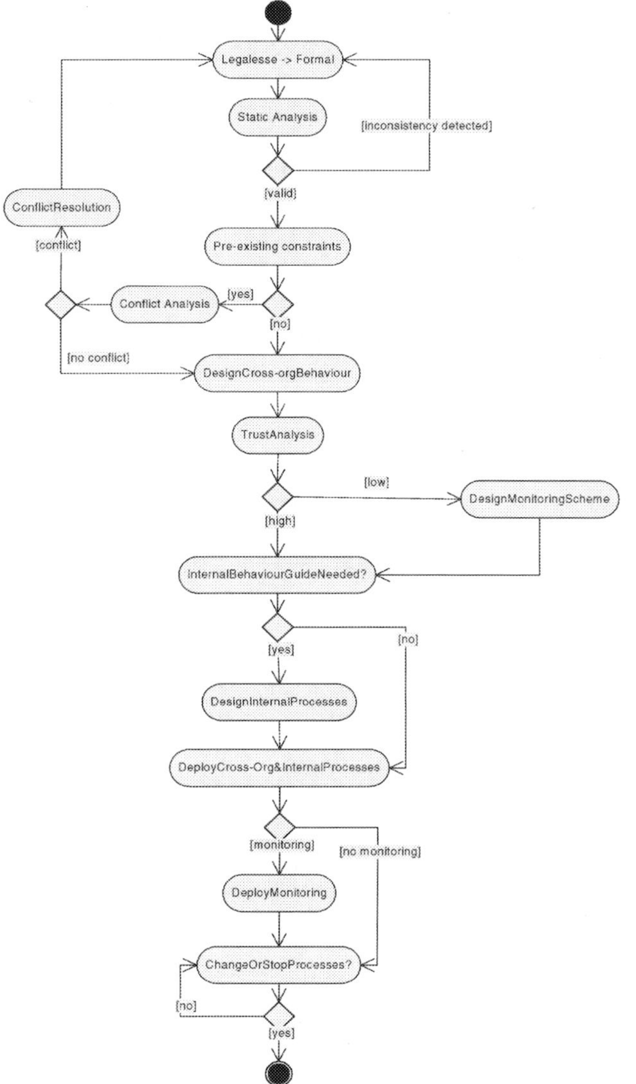

Fig. 1. Methodology for deriving contract-compliant processes

and introduction of loops to check deliverable. Such heuristics will be captured over time. For some conditions it may be impossible to determine any heuristic. In our example, the required action of the Subcontractor to send monthly report imply that the Subcontractor needs to structure own processes to accomplish this, e.g. they may introduce a Work Order processes, followed by an Assemble Report activity, the completion of which generates *SubmitMonthlyReport* event.

Further step is to design *supplementary* activities for the internal business processes, e.g. tracking of the progress of internal processes and checking whether there is a likelihood of contract violations. The aim is to provide early detection of significant state of affairs that need further attention about which parties need to be notified. Lastly, *policy checking procedures* step can be deployed in run-time to detect existing violations and activate fallback procedures; depending on the level of trust, this can be part of parties' internal processes or using trusted third party monitor.

This section focused on a methodology for creating new processes to be conformant with the contract. In many cases however, a contract will govern existing processes or augmented versions of those. The FCL formalism is applicable to both cases, and we expect that much of the methodology presented here can be reused.

4 Conclusions and Future Work

This paper presented a methodology for deriving business process descriptions based on business contract terms, to assist process modellers in constructing contract-compliant processes. The methodology provides guidelines for structuring collaborative interactions, internal processes and a number of supplementary processes. There are only few papers that dealt with links between contracts and business processes [3, 4, 5, 6]. To the best of our knowledge, the area of deriving contract-compliant processes has not been investigated so far, apart from some initial ideas presented in [2].

We hope that this paper opens new questions and stimulates further development in the area. Our own plans are to consider specific process specification languages as a target option for our derivation, in particular BPMN and BPEL, and to revise the methodology, in particular regarding the derivation of internal processes.

References

1. G. Governatori, Z. Milosevic, Dealing with contract violations: formalism and domain specific language Proc. of the 9th International Conference on Enterprise Distributed Object Computing, Enschede, The Netherlands, Sep. 2005
2. R. Tag, Z. Milosevic, S. Gibson, S. Kulkarni, Supporting Contract Execution through Recommended Workflows, DEXA04 Conference., Zaragoza, Spain, Sept. 2004.
3. W-Jan van den Heuvel, H. Weigand, Cross-Organisational Workflow Integration using Contracts, Decision Support Systems, 33(3): p. 247-265
4. P. F. Linington, Automating support for e-business contracts, International Journal of Cooperative Information Systems, 14(2&3):77-98, September 2005
5. R.M. Lee. A logic model for electronic contracting. Decision Support Systems, 4:27–44, 1988
6. A. Berry and Z. Milosevic. Extending choreography with contract constraints. Int. J. of Cooperative Inf. Syst., 14, 2005.

An AsmL Executable Model for WS-BPEL with Orthogonal Transactional Behavior

Luciano García-Bañuelos*

Universidad Autónoma de Tlaxcala
Calz. a Apizaquito s/n, 90300
Apizaco, Tlaxcala, MEXICO
lgbanuelos@gmail.com

Abstract. The current WS-BPEL specification is based on a textual description of the semantics of its constructs. This can raise some misunderstandings and difficults the development of tools for analysis and verification of WS-BPEL processes. To alleviate this lack, several groups have proposed formal models for WS-BPEL. Such models comprise more or less the full semantics in a tightly-coupled approach. We consider that WS-BPEL needs a more flexible fault handling model. This paper presents an executable model based on AsmL which allows to seamlessly add/modify behavior to implement new transaction models.

1 Introduction

WS-BPEL or BPEL for short [1] is the *de facto* standard for orchestration of Web Services. By the time of this writting, BPEL is being standardized by an OASIS committee, but the underlying semantics is described only in a textual document. This can raise some ambiguous interpretations. To alleviate this problem, some work has been devoted to provide a formal model for BPEL. All these works have been successful to some extent. However, the resulting models are tightly constructed so that it is not easy to modify the default behavior to accomodate new constructs or concepts.

Based on the ASM model for BPEL proposed in [4,3], we developped a framework written in AsmL [10]. This framework separates the underlying transactional behavior and allows to seamlessly acommodate new behavior to experiment with advanced models. AsmL is a software specification language based on the ASM (Abstract State Machines) formalism [9]. Specifications on AsmL are not only descriptive but they can be compiled, executed and used for simulating the target system.

This paper is organized as follows. Section 2 introduces structural aspects and process dynamics of BPEL as proposed in [4]. Section 3 presents our approach to separate the transactional behavior. Section 4 sketches how to extend the transactional behavior. Section 5 discuses about related work. We conclude and present future work in Section 6.

* The author thanks Microsoft Research for making available the AsmL workbench.

S. Dustdar, J.L. Fiadeiro, and A. Sheth (Eds.): BPM 2006, LNCS 4102, pp. 401–406, 2006.

2 BPEL Process Structure and Dynamics

Activities constituting a BPEL process can be structured in a process tree [3]: each leaf is a basic activity, the root of a non-trivial subtree is a structured activity. Other constructs, such as scopes and error/exception/event handlers are also included in the tree. The root of a tree will always be a scope node.

The dynamics of a BPEL process is captured within the process tree. Basic activities are executed at most once. Structured activities control the execution of their child activities (e.g. execution order, child instantiation). Control flow is done by message exchange. For instance, a structured activity starts the execution of a child by sending it down a signalEnable message. The structured activity will stay in a running state until every running child activity completes its execution and there is no other activity to enable. Each child activity notify its completion to its parent activity by sending it a signalComplete message.

Two types of control flow are identified in [3]. The *positive control flow* is related to message exchange used to control the normal execution of the process. The *negative control flow* in turn comprises message exchanges in the occurrence of a failure or for exception handling.

A distributed ASM (DASM) involves a collection of *agents* that perform their computation steps concurrently. BPEL activities can be modelled as DASM agents. The state of an agent evolves in sequential steps with the invocation to the execute() method. Agents interact by message interchange, so they provide at least a method to receive messages. The AsmL code in Figure 1 sketches these principles. Lines 15-17 allow simulating the system, by non-deterministically selecting agents and executing their behavior.

```
1 abstract enumerated class Agent
2   virtual execute()
3 enum SIGNALDOWN
4   enable
5 class Activity extends Agent
6   var channelDown as Set of SIGNALDOWN = {}
7   sendSignalDown(signal as SIGNALDOWN)
8     add signal to channelDown
9   override execute()
10    skip
11 Main()
12   step
13     var activity = new Activity()
14     activity.sendSignalDown(SIGNALDOWN.enable)
15   step until fixpoint
16     forall agent in enum of Agent
17       agent.execute()
```

Fig. 1. Activities as distributed ASM agents in AsmL

3 Our Approach to Separating Transactional Behavior

Our intend is to separate transaction support from the core behavior of BPEL. This is done by applying design patterns as shown in the following subsections.

3.1 Design Patterns

We use two Design Patterns to allow flexible compositions of behavior. First, we separate State and Behavior and use the Facade Pattern [8] to provide a single entry point. Second, we add/replace behavior by means of an adaption to the Interceptor Pattern [12].

(1) Facade Pattern. The separation of state and behavior is needed to use the Interceptor Pattern to seamlessly add behavior. To provide a unified interface to both state and behavior, we use the Facade Pattern [8]. Lines 1-21 in Figure 2 sketch the application of this pattern.

The State part handles the set of variables which are common to basic and structured activities (e.g. signalChannelDown). There are some other variables which are exclusive to structured activities. They are managed by a specialized class (i.e. StructuredState).

The general behavior for basic activities is enclosed in the Behavior class. For each type of basic activity there is a class which specializes the base behavior. There is another class called StructuredBehavior which is in turn extended with the specific behavior for each type of structured activity.

Lines 34-36 show how to "assemble" an Activity out of a State and a Behavior. Finally, lines 39-42 show that the resulting activity can be handled with a single reference.

```
1 class State
2   var signalChannelDown as Set of DOWNSIGNAL = {}
3   var activityState as ACTIVITYSTATE=disabled
4   sendSignalDown(s as DOWNSIGNAL)
5     add s to signalChannelDown
6 class Behavior
7   var state as State = null
8   virtual execute()
9     if signalEnable in state.signalChannelDown
10      remove signalEnable
11        from state.signalChannelDown
12      state.activityState := anabled
13    ...
14 class Activity
15   var state as State
16   var behavior as Behavior
17   ...
18   sendSignalDown(signal as DOWNSIGNAL)
19     state.sendSignalDown(signal)
20   execute()
21     behavior.execute()
22 class Interceptor extends Behavior
23   var interceptee as Behavior=null
24   setInterceptee(i as Behavior)
25     interceptee := i
26   override execute()
27     WriteLine("Before")
28     interceptee.execute()
29 class Activity
30   prependInterceptor(i as Interceptor)
31     i.setInterceptee(behavior)
32     behavior := i
33 Main()
34   step
35     var act as Activity =
36       new Activity(new State, new Behavior)
37   step
38     act.prependInterceptor(new Interceptor)
39   step
40     act.sendSignalDown(signalEnable)
41   step until fixpoint
42     act.execute()
```

Fig. 2. Applying Facade and Interceptor Design Patterns

(2) Interceptor Pattern. This pattern [12] enables functionality to be added seamlessly and transparently to components. Since functionality is added by delegation, the addition can be performed even at runtime.

The pattern chains a set of interceptors and then passes any request messages from interceptor to interceptor until it reaches one capable of handling the message. The interceptor is itself a specialization of Behavior, so the base behavior can be reached at the end of the chain. The AsmL sample code for interceptors is presented in Lines 22-42 within Figure 2.

An interceptor can be attached to an activity by calling the prependInterceptor() method to Activity [1]. For instance, the interceptor defined in Figure 2 "decorates" the execute() method of Behavior with a call to a WriteLine() method which will be executed before the base behavior. The step in lines 37-38 illustrates how to add the interceptor.

[1] AsmL supports complementing class definitions as shown in the example.

3.2 BPEL Fault Handling as an Orthogonal Behavior

We claim that the negative control flow can be handled orthogonally with respect to the positive control flow. We found in [3] that the only situation where there is an overlapping between negative and positive control flow is with the Terminate activity. Terminate uses the same signalStop message and stopped state as does the negative control flow. To clarify this situation, we propose to introduce signalTerminate and terminated for their usage by Terminate. Thus, signalStop and stopped may be exclusively used within the negative control flow.

In the occurrence of a fault, the faulty activity starts the propagation of a Fault object to its parent activity, and upwards. A skeleton for an interceptor to modify the base behavior is shown in Lines 1-17 within Figure 3.

```
1 structure FaultTriple
2   act1 as Activity
3   act2 as Activity
4   fault as Fault
5 class FaultChannel
6   var channel as Set of FaultTriple = {}
7 class FaultInterceptor extends Interceptor
8   var faultChannelUp as FaultChannel
9   override execute()
10    propagateFaultsActivity()
11    interceptee.execute()
12  virtual propagateFaultsActivity()
13    forall f in faultChannelUp.channel
14      if f.act2 = ME()
15        remove f from faultChannelUp.channel
16        if state.getParent() <> null
17          faultChannelUp.channel += {FaultTriple(ME(),state.getParent(),f.fault)}
```

```
1 class FaultChannel
2   var queue as Set of FaultTriple = {}
3 class FaultIntrV2 extends FaultInterceptor
4   override propagateFaultsActivity()
5     if exists ft in faultChannelUp.queue
6         where ft.act1 = ME()
7       forall f in faultChannelUp.queue
8         if f.act1 = ME()
9           faultChannelUp.channel +=
10            {FaultTriple(f.act1,f.act2,f.fault)}
11          remove f from faultChannelUp.queue
12        else
13          mybase.propagateFaultsActivity()
```

Fig. 3. Interceptors for fault handling

Note that faultChannelUp (line 8) is not part of the State class. faultChannelUp is a process-wide data structure, which is used to communicate faults. It is referenced explicitly within FaultInterceptor. If such a data structure is not useful for a new model, it can be easily eliminated.

FaultInterceptor class overrides the default execute() method and calls the propagateFaultsActivity () method. The latter implements the propagation of any eventual Fault to the parent activity (lines 12-17).

It has to be noted that a special ME() method is used. This method returns a reference to the enclosing Activity instance.

To modify the default transactional behavior, the delivery of the Fault object to the parent of the faulty activity must be delayed. To this end, the fault object is inserted into a queue. When an interceptor finds a fault in such a queue, it can process it as needed. If there is not an interceptor to modify the behavior, the fault can follow the default negative control flow, via the faultChannelUp. FaultIntrV2 in Figure 3 shows an interceptor that copies the fault from the delaying queue to the faultChannelUp, with no additional processing.

4 Extending Fault Handling

The default behavior for fault handling in BPEL is to compensate completed activities in reversal order. However, there are other extended transaction models that can be applied to BPEL. For instance, the Flexible Transactions model [14] provides several kinds of activity/transaction (i.e. *dummy*, *retriable*, *pivot* in addition to *compensatable*) and allows several alternative execution paths.

As a way of example, let us consider the behavior of a retriable activity. It supposed that such an activity is guaranteed to complete after retrying a finite number of times. A straightforward and simplistic way to implement such a behavior is to use a counter to control the reexecution of the activity. The specification for the corresponding behavior is presented in Figure 4.

```
class RetriableActInterceptor extends Interceptor
  var faultChannelUp as FaultChannel
  var counter as Integer = 3
  override execute()
    if exists f in faultChannelUp.queue
      where f.act1 = ME() and counter > 0
        forall ft in faultChannelUp.queue
          if ft.act1 = ME()
            remove ft from faultChannelUp.queue
            counter -= 1
            state.setActivityState(disabled)
            state.sendSignalDown(signalEnable)
    else
      interceptee.execute()
```

Fig. 4. Interceptor to implement the retriable behavior

5 Related Work

Some groups propose operational semantics for BPEL using Petri nets as the underlying formalism (see for instance [11,13]). The general approach is to translate each BPEL construct into a subnet, following a set of patterns and then composing them into a single net. The resulting Petri net can then be verified for relevant properties by using static analysis and model checking techniques.

Others use a sort of process algebra to model the behavior of BPEL processes. [6] presents a method to translate BPEL processes into LOTOS. Further, they discuse about the kind of analysis that can be carried out, such as temporal logic model checking, simulation and bisimulation. [2] describes the usage of a process algebra specially designed to model compensation related aspects.

Based on guarded finite state machines, [7] schetches how to translate BPEL constructs as well as partner web services into submachines. Then, the set of submachines for the entire system is composed and can be checked for some properties. However, this work is still incomplete, lacking for advanced features such as event and fault handling.

Others use ASM to model BPEL constructs. A complete BPEL process is modelled as a collection of interacting DASM agents. In this context, there are two major works: [5] which is still incomplete in some concerns such as Dead-Path Elimination, and [3] which is quite complete.

Our concern is not to develop a new model for BPEL, but to adapt one to accomodate extensions to the undelying transactional behavior. Our starting point was the ASM model described in [4,3]. We use AsmL as workbench to develop an executable specification suitable for simulation. Futher, such a workbench provides tools we want to explore for model-based testing and analysis.

6 Conclusions and Future Work

We have explored how to develop an executable model for BPEL using AsmL. This language, which reposes on the ASM theory, provides high-level, object-oriented constructs that allow us to use some Design Patterns to separate transaction behavior from the positive control flow inherent to BPEL. Based on this framework, we have shown how to modify the default transactional behavior.

Currently, we are completing the specification of the flexible transaction model so as to extend BPEL. This includes also proposing an extension to the syntax of the language so as to add means to specify alternative execution paths within BPEL scopes.

References

1. Andrews, T., Curbera, F., Dholakia, H., Goland, Y., Klein, J., Leymann, F., Liu, K., Roller, D., Smith, D., Thatte, S., Trickovic, I., Weerawarana, S.: Business Process Execution Language for Web Services, version 1.1 (2003)
2. Butler, M., Ferreira, C., Ng, M.: Precise Modelling of Compensating Business Transactions and its Application to BPEL. Journal of Universal Computer Science (2005)
3. Fahland, D.: Complete Abstract Operational Semantics for the Web Service Process Execution Language. Technical report, Humboldt-Universität zu Berlin (2005)
4. Fahland, D., Reisig, W.: ASM-based semantics for BPEL: The negative control flow. In: Proceedings of Abstract State Machines. (2005)
5. Farahbod, R., Glässer, U., Vajihollahi, M.: Abstract operational semantics of the Business Process Execution Language for Web Services. Technical Report SFU-CMPT-TR-2004-03, Simon Fraser University, Canada (2004)
6. Ferrara, A.: Web services: A process algebra approach. Technical Report 17-04, Università di Roma "La Sapienza" (2004)
7. Fu, X., Bultan, T., Su, J.: Analysis of Interacting BPEL Web Services. In: Proceedings of the 13th Inter. Conf. on World Wide Web, ACM Press (2004)
8. Gamma, E., Helm, R., Johnson, R., Vlissides, J.: Design Patterns: Elements of reusable object-oriented Software. Addison-Wesley (1995)
9. Gurevich, Y.: Evolving Algebras 1993: Lipari Guide. In: Specification and Validation Methods. Oxford University Press (1995)
10. Microsoft AsmL research team: (Asml web site) http://www.research.microsoft.com/foundations/asml/.
11. Ouyang, C., van der Aalst, W.M., Breutel, S., Dumas, M., ter Hofstede, A.H., Verbeek, E.: Formal Semantics and Analysis of Control Flow in WS-BPEL. Technical Report BPM-05-03, BPMcenter.org (2005)
12. Schmidt, D., Stal, M., Rohnert, H., Buschmann, F.: Pattern-Oriented Software Architecture: Patterns for concurrent and networked objects. Volume 2. Wiley & Sons (2000)
13. Stahl, C.: A Petri Net Semantics for BPEL. Technical Report 188, Humboldt-Universität zu Berlin, Institut für Informatik (2005)
14. Zhang, A., Nodine, M.H., Bhargava, B.K., Bukhres, O.A.: Ensuring Relaxed Atomicity for Flexible Transactions in Multidatabase Systems. In: Proc. of the 1994 ACM SIGMOD Inter. Conf. on Management of Data, ACM Press (1994)

Optimizing Exception Handling in Workflows Using Process Restructuring*

Mati Golani[1] and Avigdor Gal[2]

[1] Ort Braude College, Israel
matig@ort.org.il
[2] Technion - Israel Institute of Technology
avigal@ie.technion.ac.il

Abstract. Exception handling is the process by which a failure in a process is mitigated. Depending on the specifics of an exception, exception handers – specifications of exception handling processes – may range from halting a process, through attempts of activity reactivation, to an identification of an alternative path to successful completion of a process. Designing efficient exception handlers is not a simple task. By their very nature, exceptions are rare events that may result in poor design of exception handlers in terms of cost and logic. In this work we aim at improving exception handling performance in workflow management systems (WfMSs), a task which has been recognized as a fundamental component of WfMSs that is critical to their successful deployment in real-world scenarios. Our approach is based on the observation that when designing a business process as a workflow, a designer has some degree of freedom in streamlining actions. Therefore, we propose process model restructuring as a main tool in reducing the cost of exception handling. We believe that restructuring of a process model, based on exception efficiency consideration, can increase the overall productivity of the business process. Although the rarity of exceptions allows amortizing their costs over time we cannot ignore exception costs altogether. Therefore, we propose a cost-based approach to prioritize their impact on the workflow design. Our main contribution is the provision of a methodology for exception handling optimization at the workflow design phase.

1 Introduction

Exception handling is the process by which a failure in a process is mitigated. Depending on the specifics of an exception, exception handling may range from halting a process, through attempts of activity reactivation, to an identification of an alternative path to successful completion of a process. Exception handling is a crucial component in an efficient process management [1, 3] and has great impact on system performance.

Designing efficient exception handlers – specifications of exception handling processes – is not a simple task. By their very nature, exceptions are rare events

* We Thank Peter Dadam and Noa Kfir-Dahav for useful discussions.

S. Dustdar, J.L. Fiadeiro, and A. Sheth (Eds.): BPM 2006, LNCS 4102, pp. 407–413, 2006.

that do not enjoy the advantages of common processes, which are easily programmed with much expert information injected into them. Thus, exception handlers may well be ill-designed, affecting both the correctness and the efficiency of the process. Avoiding their design altogether is also not a valid option. During runtime, process operators see only a narrow perspective of the process, and given an exception, will not have sufficient information to effectively manage it. In those cases in which the operator mitigates the exception, the solution may be neither optimal nor effective.

Another aspect of exception handling involves the overwhelming amount of possible exceptions with respect to the "normal" process size. Clearly, for any "right" way of performing a process, there may be many things that could go wrong, each possibly requiring its own exception handling. Therefore, the modeling of exception handling routines, combined with the lack of expert support (due to the rarity of exceptions) would likely result in a poor design of exception handlers, both in terms of logic and in terms of cost.

In this work we we provide a methodology for exception handling optimization at the process design phase. As a modeling tool of choice we use workflows, which fundamental philosophy is to separate the description of a process flow from application functions. Workflows define a business process in terms of *activities* (also called actions or tasks). Activities, together with temporal constraints on execution ordering define a business process [6]. Workflow Management Systems (WfMSs) nowadays serve as the main process-based technology in enterprise environment, evolving in the past 10-15 years to support the design and execution of business processes. Efficient exception handling has been recognized as a fundamental component of WfMSs, critical to their successful deployment in real-world scenarios [1]. In this work, we formally define an exception handler as a workflow and discuss its combination with existing workflows.

Our approach is based on three basic observations. First, we observe that when designing a business process model, a designer has some degree of freedom in streamlining activities, and the decision on one specific design is typically based on organizational practices. Therefore, we propose process model restructuring as a main tool in reducing the cost of exception handling. Secondly, we observe that exception handling design is typically performed only after the "normal" process of execution has been designed. Clearly, current methodologies of process design are not geared towards exception handling. Therefore, restructuring of a process model, based on exception efficiency consideration, can increase the overall productivity of the business process. Nevertheless, we do not consider exceptions to be "first-class citizens." Our proposed methodology assumes that process design is indeed done first, followed by exception handler design and possible restructuring of the original design. Thirdly, it is clear that the rarity of exceptions requires amortizing their costs over time. This, however, is not parallel to ignoring exception costs altogether. Therefore, we use a cost-based approach to prioritize their impact on the process model design.

The rest of the paper is organized as follows: we start with presenting the workflow graph-based model (Section 2) andexception handlers (Section 3). In

Section 4 we provide the exception handler optimization methodology. We conclude in Section 5 with a short discussion of current achievements and future work.

2 Workflow Model

A workflow model can be described as a graph (ADEPT WSM net [5]) $G(V, E)$ $(V = (V_a \cup V_d);\ E = (E_c \cup E_d \cup E_s))$, combined of activity and data nodes, connected by control,data, and synchronization edges. Synchronizing edge are quite useful, allowing activities on parallel threads to be synchronized, even though they are not connected with control edges.

Control edges reflect temporal constraints on the ordering of activities. An ordering of (a_i, a_j) may reflect that a_j requires the input of a_i for its processing. Alternatively, if a_i and a_j make use of a common, limited resource, a designer may decide to avoid collisions by serializing their activation. Finally, such an ordering reflects the existing business process modeled by the workflow. Recall that one of our main observations is that when designing a business process, a designer has some degree of freedom in streamlining activities. Thus, we propose process model restructuring by possibly changing existing ordering in a workflow. Clearly, not all orderings are subject to change.

Given a workflow graph $G(V, E)$ we define for an activity $a \in V_a$, *The Nearest Xor split point of a* (denoted $NXSP(a)$) as the nearest Xor activity that provides an *alternative path* execution for a (path of execution that avoids a_i) [3]. In what follows, and following the WFMC definition (in interface 1) of *full-blocked workflows,* we assume the use of well structured processes.

3 Exception Handling

An *exception handler* is a workflow $X(V_X, E_X)$, executed in response to an occurrence of an exception for which it was defined. Given a workflow $G(V, E)$ and an exception handler $X(V_X, E_X)$, we define an operator *Apply* such that by applying $X(V_X, E_X)$ to $G(V, E)$ one receives a revised workflow model

$$G'(V', E') = \mathit{Apply}(G(V, E), X(V_X, E_X), v_s, V_e),$$

where $\{v_s\} \cup V_e \subseteq V$. v_s specifies the failing node in G and V_e is a set of nodes in G from which the normal operation of G will resume. Therefore, in G' there will be an edge $(v_s, root(X))$ connecting the failing activity with the exception handler. Also, any edge $(v_1, v_2) \in G'$ such that $v_1 \in V_X$ constrains v_1 to be in V_e. An exception handler can be schematically partitioned into two sections, namely *rollback* and *forward stepping.* A *rollback* section executes compensating activities and a *forward stepping* section activates and reactivates activities. For each exception handler we can define three reference activities. We denote by a_{sr} a *start activity,* the failing activity. a_{sp} is a stop activity, the activity where the control is returned to the original process. Finally, a target activity (a_{tr}) is the activity where the rollback section ends.

There are three types of activities an exception handler can use. The first type can activate activities in the workflow (for the first time), or reactivate them. The second type invokes *compensation* activities, also known as *undo* activities and *semantic rollback* activities [4, 2]. A compensating activity needs to be predefined, is associated with a single or combined set of workflow activities, and is typically used for reversing the impact of activities that were already performed for a given instance. Lastly, an exception handler can use activities that are not defined in the workflow altogether.

To illustrate the notion of exception handling further, we now present two types of exception handlers. We denote the first type a *repeat activation exception handler*. Such an exception handler attempts to repeat the activation of a subgraph of a workflow model by first applying compensating activities to the part that was already activated, followed by reactivation of activities. The second type is denoted an *alternative path exception handler* which was first introduced in [3]. Alternative path exception handlers combine the use of compensating activities, reactivation of activities and first-time activity activation. For an alternative path exception handler a_{sp} is always a *Xor split point.*

Several relationships between a_{sr}, a_{sp}, and a_{tr} warrant further attention. The case where $a_{sr}=a_{sp}=a_{tr}$ results in a degenerated exception handler, involving solely the reactivation of the failing activity. When $a_{sp}=a_{tr}$, the exception handler has a rollback section only with no reactivation. Finally, $a_{sr}=a_{tr}$ means that the exception handler compensates only the failing activity and begins the execution of alternative activities.

To establish a notion of optimality, we next discuss the various components of a cost model of an exception handler. To start with, there may be an initiation cost for starting a new exception handler instance. Then, given an activity a, we denote by $C(a)$ the cost of activating/reactivating a. Also, given a', a compensating activity of a, $C(a')$ is similarly defined to be the cost of compensating a using a'.

We distinguish between *actual* and *logical* execution in an exception handler. An actual activation of an activity a involves the invocation of a routine associated with a or performing a new work item in an item list of some role in the organization. A logical activation of a requires only recording its activation in the WfMS without actually activating it. $C(a)$ is set to 0 whenever a requires only a logical activation. If an actual activation is involved, then $C(a)$ is assigned with its full cost.

Finally, we assume costs are cumulative. Therefore, we define the cost of exception handler X to be the sum of costs of all activities in X.

4 Exception Handler Optimization

We now introduce a design time methodology for optimizing exception handler execution by avoiding possibly redundant activation of activities. Given a workflow graph G, and a set of corresponding exception handlers, each tagged with a frequency, and a cost, we would like to restructure G so as to minimize the weighted cost of exception handling.

We can reconstruct the process and reduce the exception handler costs by eliminating activities from the execution part which is before the target point activity as well as the execution section after this activity. By restructuring the process model, we may be able to shorten the rollback stage and minimize the number of rolled-back activities, and thus reactivated activities. Therefore, we could reconstruct the graph so that both the target activity and the start activity are moved as close as possible to the exception handler stop activity. We illustrate our approach via an example. A detailed description of our methodology is deferred to an extended version of this work.

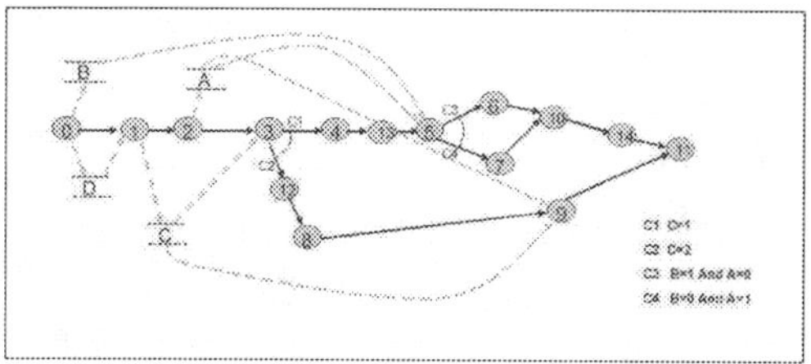

Fig. 1. An example process for propagation

Some of the activities in the exception handler, typically including the target activity, modify parameters to be used for either reactivation or the selection of an alternative path. Each such modifying activity must remain within the exception handler with its compensating activity in the rollback section of the exception handler. Other activities are candidates for removal. Iteratively, a modifying activity and its immediate successor are reordered unless there is a precedence constraint that prohibits this move. This iterative process continues until (a) reaching the stop activity, (b) reaching a dependent activity that does not allow reordering, or (c) reaching a sequence of activities that cannot be separated. A similar process is performed for the start activity, only this time moving backward and comparing it with its predecessors.

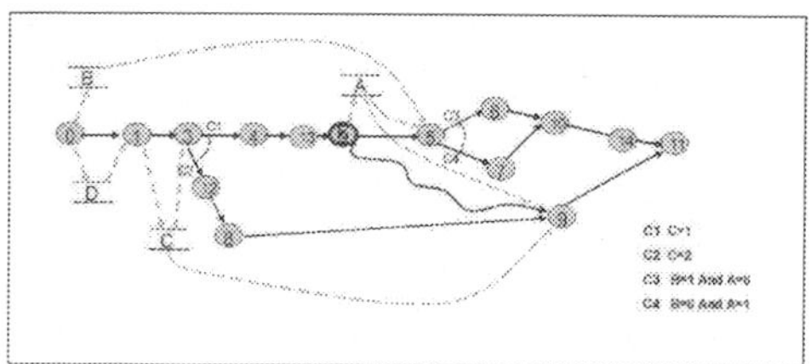

Fig. 2. Propagation into an And block

Given the example in Figure 1, consider an alternative path exception handler X for activity 13 that consists of compensating activities $13' - 4' - 3' - 2' - 1' - 1 - 2 - 3$. Recall that $a_{sr} = 13$, $a_{sp} = 3$,$a_{tr} = 1$. For each required compensating activity a' in X between a_{tr} and a_{sp}, we will try to reorder its corresponding activity a in G (activity 1 in the example), until reaching the stop activity $a_{sp} = 3$. Activities 1 and 2 are reordered. For each compensating activity a' in X between a_{sr} and a_{sp}, we will try to back-shift the failing activity 13 before a' corresponding activity a in G. Thus, activity 13 shifts back until switching places with activity 4.

Process models may contain blocks. When reaching such a block, instead of iterating over activities one at a time, we should check the dependencies of **all** block members with the propagated activity a_p. If there are no precedence constraints there and if a_{sp} is located beyond this block, a_p is propagated either after the join activity of this block or before its split activity.

An illustration for And blocks handling is presented in Figure 2 (assuming that activity 3 performs as an And split in Figure 1) .Given that all paths are executed, a propagated activity (activity 2 in Figure 1) is propagated to the path that contains activity 5 until reaching a dependent block member. If there is a dependent block memberon on other paths within the block (activity 9), a synchronization edge ($2 \rightarrow 9$) is added.

5 Conclusion

In this paper, we propose a methodology for design time optimization of exception handlers – in particular, by restructuring the process model. We show how changes in a process model can reduce the costs related to exception handler execution. Our goal is to develop an approach that allows interactive (semi-) automatic exception handler optimization for arbitrarily complex business processes, balancing the difficulties faced by current workflow models and the control of a designer over the business process.

Our specific contribution in this work is twofold. We provide a methodology for exception handling optimization and we also propose the modeling of an exception handler as a workflow by itself. The benefits of this approach has been discussed in this work.

One main avenue for a future research involves multiple exception handler optimization. We would also like to evaluate our cost heuristics on real-life cases, estimating the true gain of executing more complex optimizers. We shall also investigate efficient exhaustive approaches to achieve a better solution to the optimization problem and evaluate the trade-off between the benefit of optimized exception handling and the cost of multiple iterations with a designer.

References

1. A. Agostini and G. De Michelis. Improving flexibility of workflow management systems. In W. van der Aalst and J. Oberweis, editors, *BPM: Models, Techniques, and Empirical Studies*, pages 218–234. Springer Verlag, 2000.
2. H. Garcia-Molina and K. Salem. Sagas. In *Proceedings of the ACM SIGMOD Conference on Management of Data*, pages 249–259, May 1987.

3. M. Golani and A.Gal. Flexible business process management using forward stepping and alternative paths. In et al. W. van der Aalst, editor, *Lecture Notes on Computer Science, 3649*, pages 48–63. Springer Verlag, 2005. Proceedings of the Business Process Management International Conference, BPM 2005, Nancy, France, September 06-08, 2005.
4. C. Hagen and G. Alonso. Exception handling in workflow management systems. *IEEE Trans. Software Eng.*, 26(10):943–958, 2000.
5. M. Reichert and P. Dadam. Adept$_{flex}$-supporting dynamic changes of workflows without losing control. *Journal of Intelligent Information Systems (JIIS)*, 10(2):93–129, March-April 1998.
6. Workflow management coalition. the workflow reference model (wfmc-tc-1003), 1995. http://www.wfmc.org.

Formalizing Service Interactions

Gero Decker, Frank Puhlmann, and Mathias Weske

Business Process Technology Group
Hasso-Plattner-Institute for IT Systems Engineering
at the University of Potsdam
D-14482 Potsdam, Germany
{decker, puhlmann, weske}@hpi.uni-potsdam.de

Abstract. Cross-organizational business processes are gaining increased attention these days, especially with the service oriented architecture (SOA) as a realization for business process management (BPM). In SOA, interaction agreements between business partners are defined as choreographies containing common interaction patterns. However, complex interactions are difficult to specify, basically because a formal, common standard supporting all interaction patterns is missing. This paper motivates the use of the π-calculus for formally representing service interaction patterns.

1 Introduction

Service-oriented architectures (SOA) as a realization for business process management (BPM) aim at closely supporting business processes within a company and between business partners [1,2]. Services are employed to perform tasks within these processes and processes themselves can be exposed as services. It is distinguished between orchestrations where one business partner enacts a set of services in a given order and choreographies which represent the interaction protocols between several business partners [3]. In a setting where the different business partners encapsulate their business logic as services, service interactions are at the center of attention. A lot of effort has been undertaken to identify the most common interaction scenarios from a business perspective, which have been published as *Service Interaction Patterns* by Barros et al.[4]. Barros et al. categorize the patterns according to the number of participants in an interaction (bilateral vs. multi-lateral), the maximum number of exchanges (single-transmission vs. multi-transmission interactions) and whether the receiver of a response is necessarily the same as the sender of a request (round-trip vs. routed interactions).

The service interaction patterns are only described textually, together with business examples and design choices. The authors also come up with implementation examples using BPEL and other standards from the WS-* stack. However, the textual descriptions do not allow choreographies to be modeled else than by using textual descriptions again. The BPEL examples lack support for different service interaction patterns, thus leaving the modeler with only a subset

S. Dustdar, J.L. Fiadeiro, and A. Sheth (Eds.): BPM 2006, LNCS 4102, pp. 414–419, 2006.

of possibilities. Furthermore, both kinds of descriptions lack support for formal reasoning on interaction properties like conformance, reliability, or deadlock freedom.

To overcome the limitations of expressiveness in existing notations and to allow formal reasoning, we propose formal representations of service interaction patterns. When looking into BPM literature, Petri nets in all their different flavors dominate the research community. However, Petri nets lack the ability of easily representing *mobility*, a key feature for describing dynamic structures as required in SOA. Instead, we propose the use of a process algebra, π-calculus, for formalizing service interaction patterns. Interaction and mobility form the core aspects of π-calculus and are also at the heart of the service interaction patterns.

The remainder of this paper is organized as follows. It starts by investigating related work. This is followed by discussing a subset of interesting interaction patterns in the π-calculus. Finally, a conclusion is drawn and an outlook is given.

2 Related Work

Recently several papers have been published that deal with formalizing web service choreographies, e.g. [5,6], or Busi et al. [7]. All these approaches are based on process algebras other than π-calculus. Busi et al. argue that mobility, a key feature of the π-calculus, is not needed for describing service choreographies. They assume that all interaction participants are known at design-time. Petri net based approaches from Martens [8] or van der Aalst et al. [9] make the same assumptions. Moreover, Petri nets already fail in representing all workflow patterns [10], leading to the development of a new orchestration language called YAWL [11]. However, all these publications and standards like WS-CDL consider only one-way- and simple request-response-interactions. This is heavily criticized by Barros et al in [3]. Puhlmann and Weske have formalized all the workflow patterns [10] using the π-calculus [12]. This allows for translating service orchestrations into π-processes. Puhlmann et al. have already sketched in [13] how π-calculus can be used for formalizing service invocations and represent correlations. There has not been a formalization of the service interaction patterns so far.

3 Formalizing Interaction Patterns Using Pi-Calculus

At the center of π-calculus are processes that interact with each other. The communication channels as well as the messages sent over these channels are called names. Channels can be passed as messages to other processes and be used for interaction later on. This capability is called link passing mobility. It allows smart solutions for formalizing the service interaction patterns. The following subsections introduce how.

3.1 The Pi-Calculus

The π-calculus is an algebra for the formal description and analysis of concurrent, interacting processes with support for link passing mobility. It is based on names and interactions used by processes defined according to [14]. The syntax of the π-calculus processes is given by:

$$P ::= M \mid P|P' \mid \mathbf{v}zP \mid !P$$
$$M ::= \mathbf{0} \mid \pi.P \mid M + M'$$
$$\pi ::= \overline{x}\langle\tilde{y}\rangle \mid x(\tilde{z}) \mid \tau \mid [x = y]\pi \ .$$

The informal semantics is as follows: $P|P'$ is the concurrent execution of P and P', $\mathbf{v}zP$ is the restriction of the scope of the name z to P, and $!P$ is an infinite number of copies of P. $\mathbf{0}$ is inaction, a process that can do nothing, $M + M'$ is the exclusive choice between M and M'. The output prefix $\overline{x}\langle\tilde{y}\rangle.P$ sends a sequence of names $\tilde{y}$ over the co-name $\overline{x}$ and then continues as P. The input prefix $x(\tilde{z})$ receives a sequence of names over the name x and then continues as P with $\tilde{z}$ replaced by the received names (written as $\{^{\tilde{name}}/_{\tilde{z}}\}$). Matching input and output prefixes might communicate, thus leading to an interaction. The unobservable prefix $\tau.P$ expresses an internal action of the process, and the match prefix $[x = y]\pi.P$ behaves as $\pi.P$, if x equals y. We utilize upper case letters for process identifiers and lower case letters for names. The abbreviation $\sum_1^m(M)$ is used to denote the summation of m choices, $\prod_1^m(P)$ denotes the composition of m parallel copies of P, and $\{\pi\}_1^m$ denotes m subsequent executions of π. Furthermore defined processes are used for parametric recursion, that is $A(y_1, ..., y_n)$.

3.2 Interactions in the Pi-Calculus

In the pattern representations each interaction participant is modeled as a π-calculus process. In the case of bilateral interactions we named them A and B, in the case of multi-lateral interactions A, B_i and P where $i = 1, 2, \cdots$. Since timers and exception handling are explicitly called for in the patterns, we introduce an environmental process $\mathcal{E}_X$ per interaction participant ($X = A, B, B_i, P$). It is left open how timeouts and exception handling are implemented. $\overline{settimer_{\mathcal{E}_X}}\langle timer\rangle$ is supposed to set a new timer where a timeout is thrown by sending on channel $timer$. Exceptions can be thrown by sending on channel $\overline{fault_{\mathcal{E}_X}}$.

In the π-calculus a message represented by a name is synchronously sent and received, resulting in an interaction. I.e. if a process wants to send a message then it blocks until a receiver actually receives the message. Therefore, the π-calculus assumes synchronous communication as well as reliable and guaranteed delivery as the default case. The following subsections present formalizations for selected service interaction pattern. We omit the termination symbol $\mathbf{0}$ in process definitions for simplicity. The pattern descriptions can be found at [4].

3.3 Single-Transmission Bilateral Interaction Patterns

Send: A party sends a message to another party. The pattern definition distinguishes between blocking send and non-blocking send. In the case of blocking send the sending process cannot proceed until it can be sure that the message has been received. As already mentioned above this blocking behavior is inherent to π-calculus. Blocking send is given by:

$$A = \overline{b}\,\langle msg\rangle\,.A'$$
$$B = b(msg).B'\ .$$

This pattern formalization leaves it open if the receiver of the message is known at design-time or not. If the system is defined as

$$S = (\mathbf{v}\ b)(A \mid B)$$

then A knows the link to B at design-time. If it is defined as

$$S = (\mathbf{v}\ lookup)(lookup(b).A \mid (\mathbf{v}\ b)(B \mid D))$$

then A would get the link to B at run-time. In this case D could be something like a UDDI directory where the receiver can be looked up. A' and B' represent the so called continuations mentioned in the pattern descriptions. We continue with non-blocking send:

$$A = \overline{b}\,\langle msg\rangle\ \mid A'$$
$$B = b(msg).B'\ .$$

Strictly speaking, the formalization for B could be omitted. However, for illustration purposes one possible implementation for B is provided to have a valid choreography. Most interaction patterns describe the interactions from the perspective of one single participant. In order to get a minimal choreography, several patterns have to be plugged together (e.g. send for A and receive for B).

3.4 Single-Transmission Multilateral Interaction Patterns

Racing incoming messages: A party expects to receive one among a set of messages. These messages may be structurally different (i.e. different types) and may come from different categories of partners. The way a message is processed depends on its type and/or the category of partner from which it comes. Normally names are not typed in π-calculus. In order to retrieve the type of a message, a second name representing the type could be used. We opted for a more elegant way: for each type a channel is created and thus the channel a message is sent over determines the message's type. In the following formalization it is assumed that there are two different types of messages. Each B_i can send messages over channel a_1 if it is of the first type or over channel a_2 for the second type. Depending on the type of the message the continuation for A is either A'_1 or A'_2. The pattern distinguishes between discarding remaining messages and keeping them for further interactions. If remaining messages are not discarded, the patterns is defined by:

$$A = (a_1(msg).A'_1 + a_2(msg).A'_2)$$
$$B_i = (\overline{a_1}\langle msg\rangle.B'_i + \overline{a_2}\langle msg\rangle.B'_i) .$$

Once again the formalization for B_i is just an example. In this case every B_i can sent messages of every type. If it should be modeled that the continuation of A depends on the category of the sender, we could define $B_i = \overline{a_1}\langle msg\rangle.B'_i$ and introduce another category $C_i = \overline{a_2}\langle msg\rangle.C'_i$. A generic formalization for an arbitrary number of different types/categories would be $A = \sum_{i=1}^{n} a_i(msg).A'_i$.

3.5 Routing Patterns

Request with referral: Party A sends a request to party B indicating that any follow-up response should be sent to a number of other parties $(P1, P2, \cdots, Pn)$ *depending on the evaluation of certain conditions. While faults are sent by default to these parties, they could alternatively be sent to another nominated party (which may be party A).* While the pattern descriptions talks about a number of parties P_i, the following formalization only presents the case of one party P for better readability:

$$A = (\mathbf{v}\ a)\overline{b}\langle a, p, req\rangle.a(resp).A'$$
$$B = (\mathbf{v}\ msg)b(a, x, req).\tau_B.\overline{x}\langle a, msg\rangle.B'$$
$$P = p(a, msg).\tau_P.\overline{a}\langle resp\rangle.P' .$$

4 Conclusion and Outlook

In this paper we have shown how a selected subset of the service interaction patterns can be formalized. We investigated new directions based on mobile process algebra represented by the π-calculus. The concept of mobility is required if the receiver of a message is not known at runtime. Ten out of thirteen interaction patterns incorporate sending messages, where the receiver might not be known at design-time. In an extended research, we were able to express all service interaction patterns in π-calculus processes. Therefore, our final conclusion is that π-calculus is well suited for expressing the service interaction patterns. The full range of pattern formalizations as well as a direct comparison to Petri nets can be found at `http://pi-workflow.org`.

The formalizations presented in this paper can be the starting point for further work on a complete formal grounding of the intersection of the domains service oriented architectures and business process management using π-calculus. The very next step would be to show how the formalizations of the service interaction patterns can be integrated with the formalizations of the workflow patterns provided in [12]. Once we have both a choreography and corresponding orchestrations available as π-calculus processes we can proceed with introducing conformance checking, e.g. verifying if the behavior of individual orchestrations complies to the choreography. Another area of interest is the investigation of soundness criteria for choreographies.

References

1. IBM: Web Services Architecture Overview (2000) `http://www-128.ibm.com/developerworks/webservices/library/w-ovr/`.
2. van der Aalst, W.M.P., ter Hofstede, A.H., Weske, M.: Business Process Management: A Survey. In van der Aalst, W.M.P., ter Hofstede, A.H., Weske, M., eds.: Proceedings of the 1st International Conference on Business Process Management, volume 2678 of LNCS, Berlin, Springer-Verlag (2003) 1–12
3. Barros, A., Dumas, M., Oaks, P.: A Critical overview of the Web Services Choreography Description Language (WS-CDL). BPTrends Newsletter **3(3)** (2005)
4. Barros, A.P., Dumas, M., ter Hofstede, A.H.M.: Service Interaction Patterns. In: van der Aalst, W.M.P., Benatallah, B., Casati, F., Curbera, F., eds.: Business Process Management. Volume 3649. (2005) 302–318
5. Brogi, A., Canal, C., Pimentel, E., Vallecillo, A.: Formalizing Web Service Choreographies. In: Proceedings of First International Workshop on Web Services and Formal Methods, Elsevier (2004)
6. Gorrieri, R., Guidi, C., Lucchi, R.: Reasoning About Interaction Patterns in Choreography. In: M. Bravetti et al. (Eds.): Second International Workshop on Web Services and Formal Methods, LNCS 3670, Springer Verlag (2005) 333–348
7. Busi, N., Gorrieri, R., Guidi, C., Lucchi, R., Zavattaro, G.: Choreography and Orchestration: A Synergic Approach for System Design. In: B. Benatallah, F. Casati, and P. Traverso (Eds.): ICSOC 2005, LNCS 3826, Springer Verlag (2005) 228–240
8. Martens, A.: Analyzing Web Service based Business Processes. In Cerioli, M., ed.: Proceedings of Intl. Conference on Fundamental Approaches to Software Engineering (FASE'05). Volume 3442 of Lecture Notes in Computer Science., Springer-Verlag (2005)
9. van der Aalst, W.M.P., Weske, M.: The P2P Approach to Interorganizational Workflow. In Dittrich, K., Geppert, A., Norrie, M., eds.: Proceedings of the 13th International Conference on Advanced Information Systems Engineering (CAiSE'01), volume 2068 of LNCS, Berlin, Springer-Verlag (2001) 140–156
10. van der Aalst, W., ter Hofstede, A., Kiepuszewski, B., Barros, A.: Workflow Patterns. Distributed and Parallel Databases **14(3)** (2003) 5–51
11. van der Aalst, W.M.P., ter Hofstede, A.H.M.: YAWL: Yet Another Workflow Language (Revised version. Technical Report FIT-TR-2003-04, Queensland University of Technology, Brisbane (2003)
12. Puhlmann, F., Weske, M.: Using the π-Calculus for Formalizing Workflow Patterns. In: van der Aalst, W.M.P., Benatallah, B., Casati, F., Curbera, F., eds.: Business Process Management. Volume 3649. (2005) 153–168
13. Overdick, H., Puhlmann, F., Weske, M.: Towards a Formal Model for Agile Service Discovery and Integration. In Verma, K., Sheth, A., Zaremba, M., Bussler, C., eds.: Proceedings of the International Workshop on Dynamic Web Processes (DWP 2005). IBM technical report RC23822, Amsterdam (2005)
14. Sangiorgi, D., Walker, D.: The π-calculus: A Theory of Mobile Processes. Cambridge University Press, Cambridge (2003)

Decision Mining in ProM

A. Rozinat and W.M.P. van der Aalst

Department of Technology Management, Eindhoven University of Technology
P.O. Box 513, NL-5600 MB, Eindhoven, The Netherlands
{a.rozinat, w.m.p.v.d.aalst}@tm.tue.nl

Abstract. Process-aware Information Systems typically log events (e.g., in transaction logs or audit trails) related to the actual business process executions. Proper analysis of these execution logs can yield important knowledge that can help organizations to improve the quality of their services. Starting from a process model, which can be discovered by conventional process mining algorithms, we analyze how data attributes influence the choices made in the process based on past process executions. Decision mining, also referred to as decision point analysis, aims at the detection of data dependencies that affect the routing of a case. In this paper we describe how machine learning techniques can be leveraged for this purpose, and we present a *Decision Miner* implemented within the ProM framework.

Keywords: Business Process Intelligence, Process Mining, Petri Nets, Decision Trees.

1 Introduction

Process mining techniques have proven to be a valuable tool in order to gain insight into how business processes are handled within organizations. Taking a set of real process executions (the so-called "event logs") as the starting point, these techniques can be used for *process discovery* and *conformance checking*. Process discovery [2,3] can be used to automatically construct a process model reflecting the behavior that has been observed and recorded in the event log. Conformance checking [1,9] can be used to compare the recorded behavior with some already existing process model to detect possible deviations. Both may serve as *input* for designing and improving business processes, e.g., conformance checking can be used to find problems in existing processes, and process discovery can be used as a starting point for process analysis and system configuration. While there are several process mining algorithms that deal with the control flow perspective of a business process [2] *less attention has been paid to how the value of a data attribute may affect the routing of a case.*

Most information systems (cf. WFM, ERP, CRM, SCM, and B2B systems) provide some kind of *event log* (also referred to as transaction log or audit trail) [2] where an event refers to a case (i.e., process instance) and an activity, and, in most systems, also a timestamp, a performer, and some additional data. Nevertheless, many process mining techniques only make use of the first two

S. Dustdar, J.L. Fiadeiro, and A. Sheth (Eds.): BPM 2006, LNCS 4102, pp. 420–425, 2006.

attributes in order to construct a process model which reflects the causal relations that have been observed among the activities. In addition, machine learning algorithms have become a widely adopted means to extract knowledge from vast amounts of data [7,11]. In this paper we use the well-known concept of *decision trees* to carry out a *decision point analysis*, i.e., to find out which properties of a case might lead to taking certain paths in the process. Starting from a discovered process model (i.e., a model discovered by conventional process mining algorithms), we try to enhance the model by integrating patterns that can be observed from data modifications, i.e., every choice in the model is analyzed and, if possible, linked to properties of individual cases and activities.

Clearly, the application of (existing) data mining techniques in the context of business processes has the potential to gain knowledge, or to make tacit knowledge explicit. Besides data attributes, resource information, and timestamps, even more general quantitative (e.g., key performance indicators like waiting time derived from the log) and qualitative (i.e., desirable or undesirable properties) information could be included in the analysis if available. To directly support data analysis for business processes we have implemented a *Decision Miner* in the context of the ProM framework[1], which offers a wide range of tools related to process mining and process analysis.

The paper is organized as follows. First, the use of machine learning techniques in the context of the decision point analysis is described in Section 2. Section 3 presents the Decision Miner plug-in of the ProM framework. Finally, related work is discussed in Section 4, and the paper concludes by pointing out future research directions.

2 Using Decision Trees for Analyzing Choices

In order to analyze the choices in a business process we first need to identify those parts of the model where the process is split into alternative branches, also called decision points. Based on data attributes associated to the cases in the event log we subsequently want to find rules for following one route or the other.

In terms of a Petri net, a decision point corresponds to a place with multiple outgoing arcs. Since a token can only be consumed by one of the transitions connected to these arcs, alternative paths may be taken during the execution of a process instance. In order to analyze the choices that were made in past process executions we need to find out which alternative branch was taken by a certain process instance. Therefore, the set of possible decisions must be described with respect to the event log. Starting from the identification of a choice construct in the process model a decision can be detected if the execution of an activity in the respective alternative branch of the model has been observed, which requires a mapping from that activity to its "occurrence footprint" in the event log. So, if a process instance contains the given "footprint", this means that there was a decision for the associated alternative path in the process. For

[1] Both documentation and software (including the source code) can be downloaded from *www.processmining.org*.

simplicity we examine the occurrence of the *first* activity per alternative branch in order to classify the possible decisions. However, in order to make decision mining operational for real-life business processes several challenges posed by, for example, *invisible activities*, *duplicate activities*, and *loops* need to be met. Because of the limited space here we refer the interested reader to our technical report [10], where these issues are addressed.

After identifying a decision point in a business process, the next step is to determine whether this decision might be influenced by case data, i.e., whether cases with certain properties typically follow a specific route. The idea is to convert every decision point into a *classification problem* [7,11,8], where the *classes* are the different decisions that can be made. As training examples we use the process instances in the log (for which it is already known which alternative path they followed with respect to the decision point). The attributes to be analyzed are the case attributes contained in the log, and we assume that all attributes that have been written *before* the considered choice construct are relevant for the routing of a case at that point. In order to solve such a classification problem there are various algorithms available [7,11]. We decided to use decision trees (such as C4.5 [8]), which are among the most popular inductive inference algorithms, and which provide a number of extensions that are important for practical applicability. For example, they are able to deal with continuous-valued attributes, missing attribute values, and they include effective methods to avoid *overfitting* the data (i.e., that the tree is over-tailored towards the training examples). In [10] we show in detail how the training examples and the inferred decision rules look for each decision point in the example process.

3 Decision Mining with the ProM Framework

The approach presented in this paper was implemented as a plug-in for the ProM Framework. The *Decision Miner* plug-in determines the decision points contained in a Petri net model[2], and specifies the possible decisions with respect to the log while being able to deal with invisible and duplicate activities in the way described in [10]. Figure 1(a) shows the Model view of the Decision Miner, which provides a visualization of each decision point with respect to the given process model. The example process sketches the processing of a liability claim within an insurance company, and the depicted decision point relates to the choice of whether a full check or a policy-only check is to be performed. Only attributes of the activity "Register Claim" are within the analysis scope of this decision point. The Attributes view shown in Figure 1(b) allows for the selection of those attributes to be included in the analysis of each decision point. During the execution of activity "Register claim" information about the amount of money involved (*Amount*), the corresponding customer (*CustomerID*), and the type of policy (*PolicyType*) are provided. We retain all these attributes

[2] Note that although only Petri net process models are directly supported by the Decision Miner, various other process model types (EPC, YAWL, etc.) are indirectly supported via conversion tools available in ProM.

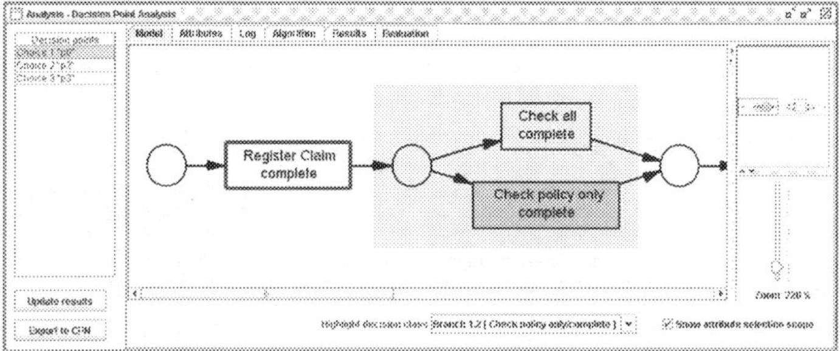

(a) Model view visualizes decision points in the process model

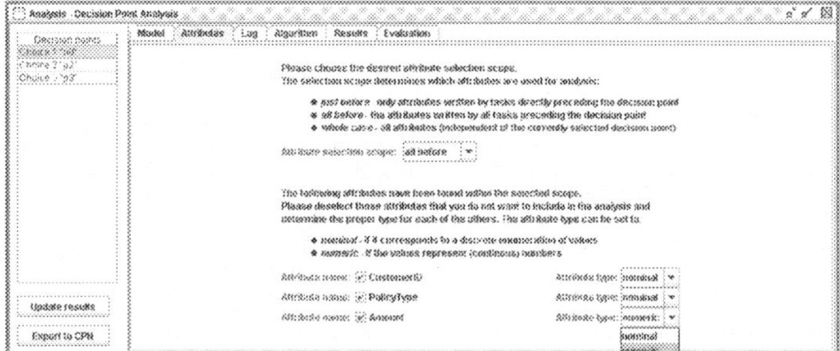

(b) Attributes view allows for selection of those attributes to be used for analysis

Fig. 1. Screenshots of the the Decision Miner in ProM

and set the type of the *Amount* attribute as numeric. Here the advantage of a tool suite like ProM becomes visible. The tight integration of further analysis components available in the framework can be used to add meta data to the event log before starting the actual decision point analysis. For example, a previous performance analysis evaluating the timestamps of each log event can provide additional attributes, such as the flow time and waiting time, to specific activities or to the whole process instance. These attributes then become available for analysis in the same way as the initial attributes.

While the Decision Miner formulates the learning problem, the actual analysis is carried out with the help of the J48 decision tree classifier, which is the implementation of the C4.5 algorithm [8] provided by the Weka software library [11]. The Algorithm view offers the full range of parameters that are available for the used decision tree algorithm from the Weka library. Figure 2(a) shows the decision tree result for the decision point *p0*, from which we can now infer the logical expressions that form the decision rules depicted in Figure 2(b) in the following way: If an instance is located in one of the leaf nodes of a decision tree, it fulfills all the predicates on the way from the root to the leaf, i.e., they are connected by a boolean AND operator; When a decision class is represented by multiple leaf nodes in the decision tree the leaf expressions are combined via a boolean OR operator. The discovered rules indicate that the extensive check (activity *B*) is only performed if the *Amount* is greater than 500 and the *PolicyType* is "normal", whereas a simpler coverage check (*C*) is sufficient if the

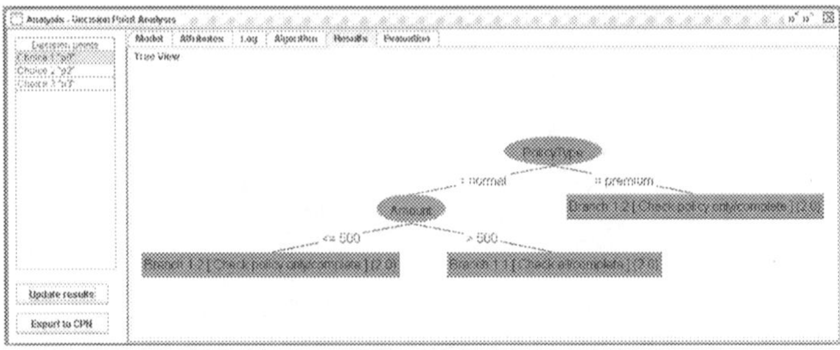

(a) Decision tree result for analysis of decision point "p0"

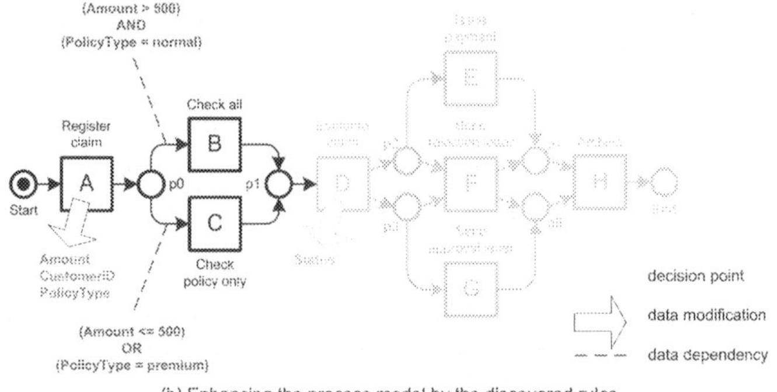

(b) Enhancing the process model by the discovered rules

Fig. 2. Interpreting the decision tree result

Amount is smaller than or equal to 500, or the *PolicyType* is "premium" (which may be due to certain guarantees from "premium" member corporations).

4 Related Work

The work reported in this paper is closely related to [5], in which the authors describe the architecture of the *Business Process Intelligence* (BPI) tool suite situated on top of the *HP Process Manager* (HPPM). Whereas they outline the use of data mining techniques for process behavior analysis in a broader scope, we show how a decision point analysis can be carried out in conjunction with process mining, i.e., we do not assume some a priori model. Another important difference, although not presented in this paper, is that we can also analyze models in the presence of duplicate and invisible activities. In [6] decision trees are used to analyze staff assignment rules. Additional information about the organizational structure is incorporated in order to derive higher-level attributes (i.e., roles) from the actual execution data (i.e., performers). In [4] the authors aim at the integration of neural networks into EPC process models via fuzzy events and fuzzy functions. While this approach may support, e.g., one concrete mortgage grant decision process, we focus on the use of machine learning techniques as a general tool to analyze business process executions.

5 Conclusion

In this paper we have presented a *Decision Miner* that analyzes the choice constructs of a (mined) Petri net process model in the context of the ProM framework. Future research plans include the support of further types of process models (such as EPCs), and the provision of alternative algorithms already available in the data mining field (and related software libraries). For example, sometimes it is better to directly capture a concept description in rules rather than in a decision tree. Finally, the application of data mining techniques in the context of business processes can be beneficial beyond the analysis of decisions that have been made. A free specification of the learning problem on the available data can be used to, for example, mine association rules, or to assess potential correlations to the fact that a case has a throughput time which exceeds some user-defined threshold value.

References

1. W.M.P. van der Aalst. Business Alignment: Using Process Mining as a Tool for Delta Analysis. In J. Grundspenkis and M. Kirikova, editors, *Proceedings of the 5th Workshop on Business Process Modeling, Development and Support (BPMDS'04)*, volume 2 of *Caise'04 Workshops*, pages 138–145. Riga Technical University, Latvia, 2004.
2. W.M.P. van der Aalst, B.F. van Dongen, J. Herbst, L. Maruster, G. Schimm, and A.J.M.M. Weijters. Workflow Mining: A Survey of Issues and Approaches. *Data and Knowledge Engineering*, 47(2):237–267, 2003.
3. W.M.P. van der Aalst, A.J.M.M. Weijters, and L. Maruster. Workflow Mining: Discovering Process Models from Event Logs. *IEEE Transactions on Knowledge and Data Engineering*, 16(9):1128–1142, 2004.
4. O. Adam, O. Thomas, and P. Loos. Soft Business Process Intelligence — Verbesserung von Geschäftsprozessen mit Neuro-Fuzzy-Methoden. In F. Lehner et al., editor, *Multikonferenz Wirtschaftsinformatik 2006*, pages 57–69. GITO-Verlag, Berlin, 2006.
5. D. Grigori, F. Casati, M. Castellanos, U. Dayal, M. Sayal, and M.-C. Shan. Business Process Intelligence. *Computers in Industry*, 53(3):321–343, 2004.
6. L. T. Ly, S. Rinderle, P. Dadam, and M. Reichert. Mining Staff Assignment Rules from Event-Based Data. In C. Bussler et al., editor, *Business Process Management 2005 Workshops*, volume 3812 of *Lecture Notes in Computer Science*, pages 177–190. Springer-Verlag, Berlin, 2006.
7. T. M. Mitchell. *Machine Learning.* McGraw-Hill, 1997.
8. J. R. Quinlan. *C4.5: Programs for Machine Learning.* Morgan Kaufmann, 1993.
9. A. Rozinat and W.M.P. van der Aalst. Conformance Testing: Measuring the Fit and Appropriateness of Event Logs and Process Models. In C. Bussler et al., editor, *Business Process Management 2005 Workshops*, volume 3812 of *Lecture Notes in Computer Science*, pages 163–176. Springer-Verlag, Berlin, 2006.
10. A. Rozinat and W.M.P. van der Aalst. Decision Mining in Business Processes. BPM Center Report BPM-06-10, BPMcenter.org, 2006.
11. I. H. Witten and E. Frank. *Data Mining: Practical machine learning tools and techniques, 2nd Edition.* Morgan Kaufmann, 2005.

Managing Process Variants as an Information Resource*

Ruopeng Lu and Shazia Sadiq

School of Information Technology and Electrical Engineering,
The University of Queensland, Brisbane, QLD, 4072, Australia
{ruopeng, shazia}@itee.uq.edu.au

Abstract. Many business solutions provide best practice process templates, both generic as well as for specific industry sectors. However, it is often the variance from template solutions that provide organizations with intellectual capital and competitive differentiation. In this paper, we present a modeling framework that is conducive to constrained variance, by supporting user driven process adaptations. The focus of the paper is on providing a means of utilizing the adaptations effectively for process improvement through effective management of the process variants repository (PVR). In particular, we will provide deliberations towards a facility to provide query functionality for PVR that is specifically targeted for effective search and retrieval of process variants.

1 Introduction

It is evident that work practices at the operational level are often diverse, incorporating the creativity and individualism of knowledge workers and potentially contributing to the organization's competitive advantage. This diversity needs to be both encouraged and controlled. A major difficulty in this issue lies in the fact that the requisite knowledge, that drives the diverse practices at an operational level, is only tacitly available. This knowledge constitutes the corporate skill base and is found in the experiences and practices of individual workers, who are domain experts in a particular aspect. There is significant evidence in literature on the difficulties in mapping process logic to process models. We believe that this is a limitation in current solutions, and part of the modeling effort needs to be transferred to domain experts who make design decisions based on (1) their expertise and (2) case specific conditions.

In this paper, we utilize a framework for process modeling and deployment [1, 2] that harnesses successful work practice and provides the ability to build a valuable information resource from them. The framework consists of: (1) A constraint-based process modeling approach, namely Business Process Constraint Network (BPCN); and (2) a repository for case specific process models, called Process Variant Repository (PVR). It is the last aspect which forms the focus of this paper. The aim of this paper is to provide an effective approach for structuring and querying PVR.

* This work is partially supported by the Australian Research Council funded Project DP0558854.

S. Dustdar, J.L. Fiadeiro, and A. Sheth (Eds.): BPM 2006, LNCS 4102, pp. 426 – 431, 2006.

2 Background

Business Process Constraint Network (BPCN) [1] has been developed to provide formal underpinning to the notion of **process templates**. BPCN relaxes rigid process specification to a set of minimal constraints. It provides the ability to accept a set of various constraint types; and provides methods for checking constraint network consistency [2]. These details are not included in this paper, but we will utilize BPCN concepts as background. We refer to the individually tailored process instances as **process variants**, each of which represent the preferred work practice, but are also valid in terms of process constraints as defined by the BPCN. Although all process variants satisfy the same set of constraints, they may vary significantly. Over time, the repository of such process variants can build into an immense corporate resource. We argue that such a resource can provide valuable insight into work practice, help externalize previously tacit knowledge, and provide valuable feedback on subsequent process design and improvement (cf. Fig.1).

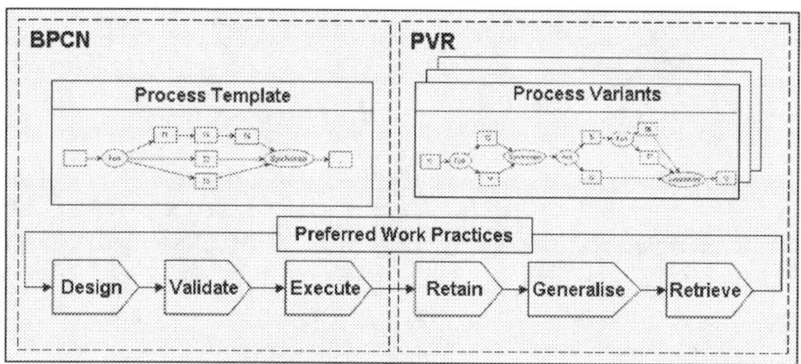

Fig. 1. Framework overview

3 Repository for Process Variants

When a process template completes execution, the model corresponding to the process variant as well as essential execution properties are stored in the PVR. A **query** is a statement of information needs, which is formulated according to one or more aspects of process variants. We are specifically interested in complex (structural) criteria.

The schema of the repository defines the structure according to which process variants are stored. Confining description of process variants to essential structural aspect, we can define a process variant V by the process model W, where $W = (N, F)$ is defined through a directed graph consisting N: Finite Set of Nodes, F: Flow Relation $F \subseteq N \times N$. Nodes are classified into tasks (T) and coordinators (C), where $C \cup T$, $C \cap T = \emptyset$. Task nodes represent atomic manual / automated activities or sub processes that must be performed to satisfy the underlying business process objectives. Coordinator nodes allow us to build control flow structures (fork, choice, loop etc.) to manage the coordination requirements. Since W represents an executed process instance, coordinator nodes types are limited, i.e. $\forall\, n \in C$, CoordType: $n \rightarrow \{fork, synchronize, begin, end\}$.

Consider the following collection of process variants in Fig.2 (V_1, V_2, V_3 and V_4) satisfying same constraints, which are: *T1* must be performed before *T5*; *T2* and *T4* must be done in parallel. PVR can be expected to contain hundreds if not thousands of such variants for a given process.

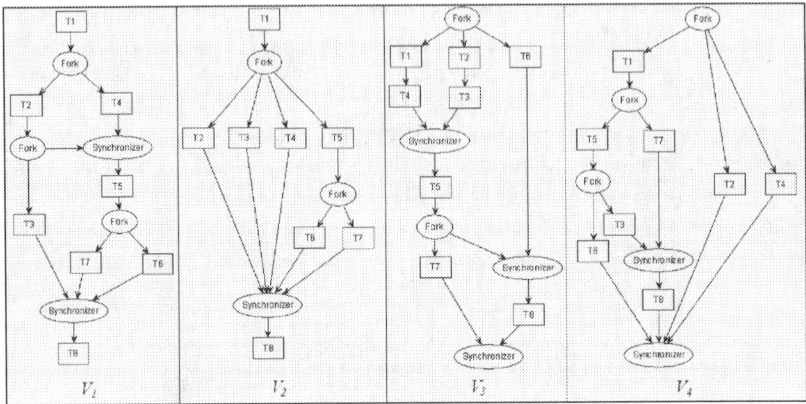

Fig. 2. Example Process Variants V_1, V_2, V_3 and V_4

We propose to define queries on structural aspect as **process fragments**, defined using the graphical language used in *W*. Let *Q* be the process (sub)graph that represents a query, i.e. the criteria for selection of process variants. We define similarity between *Q* and a process variant *V* through two relationships, namely **equivalent** and **subsume** [3]. For example, query graph Q_1 as given in Fig.3, is subsumed by process variants V_1 and V_2.

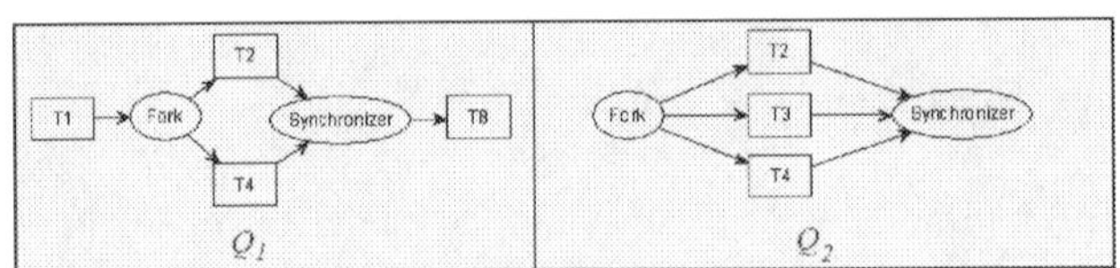

Fig. 3. Example Queries Q_1 and Q_2

In order to determine whether a given variant is in an equivalent or subsume relationship with a specified query, we propose a matching method `SELECTIVE_REDUCE`, which uses graph reduction techniques to determine the match. The method is assumed to be executed on only those variants from PVR where the node set of the variant is a superset of the node set of a specified query. The basic intuition behind `SELECTIVE_REDUCE` is to firstly eliminate from the node set of the variant all task nodes that are not contained in the node set of the query, and secondly to reduce the flow relation using three reduction rules [3], namely *sequential*, *adjacent* and *closed*. Fig.4 illustrates the applications of these reduction rules, where the solid rectangles represent the relevant tasks required by the query and the hollow rectangles the irrelevant tasks. The goal of the original algorithm in [3] is to reduce a process graph into an empty graph in order to verify structural correctness. In our approach, the algorithm is modified to reduce a variant that has an equivalent or subsume relationship with the query, into a structurally identical graph (not empty) as the query. In [4], a detail description of the algorithm can be found.

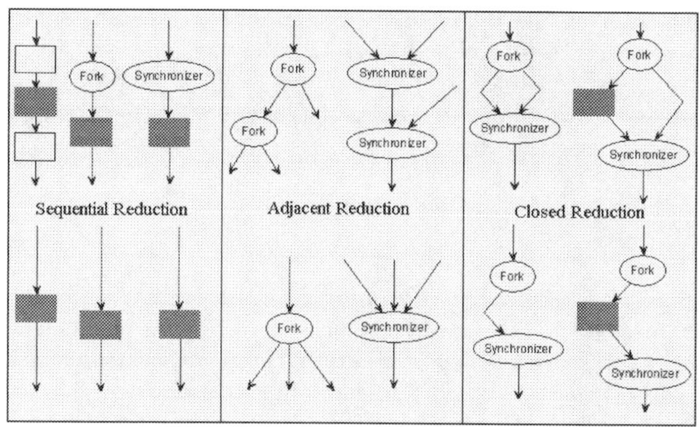

Fig. 4. Sequential, Adjacent and Closed Reduction Rules

Applying SELECTED_REDUCE on all variants given in Fig.2 (V_1, V_2, V_3 and PV_4) for query Q_1 gives reduced structures PV_1, PV_2, PV_3 and PV_4, as illustrated in Fig.5. V_1 and V_2 are said to be **exact matches** with Q_1 since the reduced process graphs of V_1 and V_2 (PV_1, and PV_2) are isomorphic to query graph Q_1. V_3 and V_4 are termed **partial matches** with Q_1 as containing the same set of tasks as the query, but the process graphs are structurally different from Q_1.

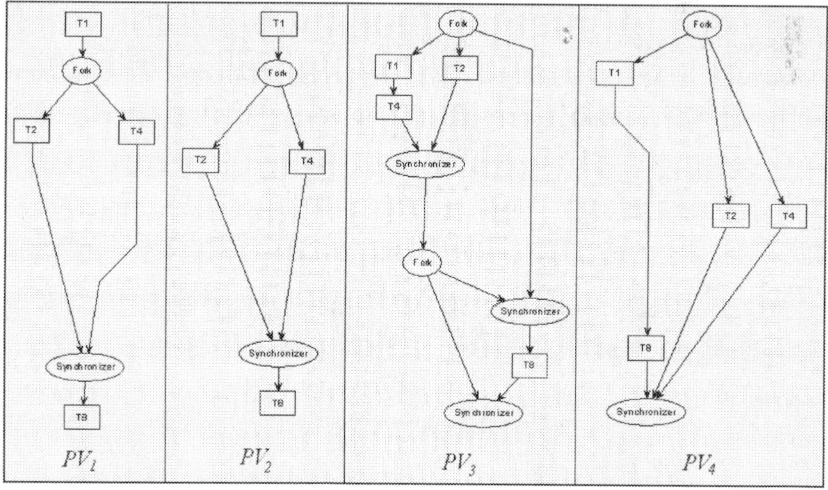

Fig. 5. Reduced process variants PV_1, PV_2, PV_3 and PV_4 against query Q_1

We propose a simple method based on flow (edge) counting to provide further insight into partial matches [4]. The method finds out the similarity between a reduced process graph (of partially matched variant) and a query graph by first comparing the number of matching flows between the two, and the similarity degree is given by the percentage of matching flows among the total number of flows in the reduced process variant. The query facility of PVR can potentially retrieve a very large result, it will be important to provide functionality to further refine query criteria. ***Multi-aspect queries*** will play an important role [5], where structural search is combined with search on operational properties, e.g. find process variants that correspond to the structure of query Q_1 (Fig. 2) and no test was performed by a senior engineer.

4 Related Work

Process models have been regarded as an information resource in many aspects of modern enterprises [6, 7]. The most common way to capture, maintain, manage and diffuse knowledge associated with the best practices can be found in knowledge-based systems [8] and Case-Based Reasoning (CBR) based workflow management [9]. Another predominant technique has been process diagnosis and redesign. The diagnosis activity referred to as Business Process Analysis (BPA), which is assisted by various Workflow Mining techniques [10].

5 Summary

This paper provides methods to benefit from a repository of process variants, namely PVR. The presented methods provide effective means of searching and matching process variants against a given query (example process structure), and generate result sets that can be conveniently ranked. The work reported in this paper focuses on queries on the structural aspect, but can be extended to multi-aspect queries. The results of the proposed query facility in PVR can provide deep insights into ongoing work practices, identify areas of process improvement, and contribute to systematic and well-informed process evolution.

References

1. Lu, R., Sadiq, S., Padmanabhan, V., Governatori, G.: Using a Temporal Constraint Network for Increased Flexibility in Business Process Execution. In: Proc. Seventeenth Australasian Database Conference (ADC2006), Hobart, Australia (2006)
2. Sadiq, S., Sadiq, W., Orlowska, M.: A Framework for Constraint Specification and Validation in Flexible Workflows. Information Systems, Vol.30(5), Elsevier Science (2005) 349 - 378
3. Sadiq, W., Orlowska, M.: Analyzing Process Models using Graph Reduction Techniques. Information Systems, 25(2) (2000) 117 – 134

4. Lu, R., Sadiq, S., On Managing Process Variants as an Information Resource. Technical Report, No.TR-464, School of Information Technology and Electrical Engineering, The University of Queensland (2006)
5. Lu, R., Sadiq, S., Governatori, G.: Utilizing Successful Work Practices as an Information Resource. In: Proc. 9th International Conference on Business Information Systems (BIS2006), Klagenfurt, Austria (2006)
6. Leymann, F., Altenhuber, W.: Managing Business Processes as an Information Resource. IBM Systems Journal, 33(2) (1994)
7. Casati, F.: Industry Trends in Business Process Management: Getting Ready for Prime Time. In: Proc. 16th International Workshop on Database and Expert Systems Applications (DEXA 2005), Copenhagen, Denmark (2005)
8. Dellarocas, C., Klein, M.: Integrating Process Learning and Process Evolution - A Semantics Based Approach. In: Proc. 3rd International Conference on Business Process Management, (BPM 2005), Nancy, France (2005)
9. Madhusudan, T., Zhao, L.: A Case-Based Framework for Workflow Model Management. In: Proc. International Conference on Business Process Management (BPM 2003) Eindhoven, The Netherlands (2003)
10. van der Aalst, W. M. P., van Dongen, B.F., Herbst, J., Maruster, L., Schimm, G., Weijters, A.J.M.M.: Workflow Mining: A Survey of Issues and Approaches. Data & Knowledge Engineering, Vol.47 (2003) 237 – 267

Verification of Business Process Integration Options*

Georg Grossmann, Michael Schrefl, and Markus Stumptner

University of South Australia, Advanced Computing Research Centre, Mawson Lakes, SA 5095, Adelaide, Australia
{cisgg, cismis, mst}@cs.unisa.edu.au.

Abstract. We propose a meta framework architecture for supporting the behaviour based integration of two business processes. The meta level provides basic integration operators to the domain engineer to create integration options for specific domains. Based on semantic relationships between nodes of two business processes these integration options are executed and transform parts of the business processes. The outcome of the model transformation is an integrated business process. Because of the arbitrary combination of basic integration operators, a potentially infinite set of integration options may be applicable, and some of these may lead to an incorrect business process. We analyse our framework according to a set of consistency criteria and propose verification and validation mechanisms to keep the integrated model consistent.

1 Introduction

Research initiatives such as a special issue of *Advanced Engineering Informatics* on Enterprise Modelling and System Support [5] have pointed out the potential of enterprise systems to support integration of various functions in an organisation as well as in value chains and business networks. The implementation, however, is not without problems and failures can be costly. A variety of models, tools and techniques have been developed to address this problem by supporting the analysis of business process structure and performance. Our contribution to this topic is a model driven framework for behaviour based integration of business processes with an underlying metaclass architecture [12]. It represents a generic approach where high-level integration operators can adapt and produce individualized integration options for the integration of processes from a particular domain.

The framework uses instantiation relationships in a metaclass architecture to implement context-dependent integration patterns. In [3,2] we present integration options for business processes which share a common domain or a composite-component relationship. In this paper we go one step further and support the individual development of integration options for various integration purposes, e.g., creating new virtual enterprises.

However the development of customized integration options is error-prone and should not be left without sytem support. The arbitrary definition of integration options and their application may lead to an incorrect business process. Incorrect can mean

* This research was partially supported by the Australian Research Council under Discovery Grant DP0210654.

S. Dustdar, J.L. Fiadeiro, and A. Sheth (Eds.): BPM 2006, LNCS 4102, pp. 432–438, 2006.

that the integrated business process is (1) not **syntactically correct**, (2) not **deadlock-free**, or (3) not **consistent with its input models**. Syntactical correctness of workflows, rules out invalid constructs such as an edge leading back to the source node [10]. Syntax checking can be handled by using a meta modeling tool which can be used, e.g., for specifying Activity State Diagrams. These tools such as DoME or MetaEdit+ [6,7] support an automated verification of the syntax on the meta level and hence syntax verification is not discussed further.

In this paper we are going to check the application of integration options against causing deadlocks. In the Petri net community a deadlock free Petri net is also called a sound and therefore we refer to this issue as the *soundness property* [13]. Furthermore we check the consistency of the integration to its input business processes. This plays an important role in proofing that the activity execution sequence of the input models is not changed through the integration. We refer to this aspect as *sequence constraint* [11,19].

The architecture of the integration framework consists of the meta model level and the model level. The meta model provides a set of basic integration tools which are instantiated on the model level. On the meta level, three steps are undertaken to provide the necessary context for model level integration. On the model level, further four steps must be performed to lead from two separated models given as input to an integrated business process:

1. **Definition of semantic relationships:** On the meta level, the domain engineer defines a set of semantic relationships between element types of a business process.
2. **Definition of integration options:** The second task of the domain engineer is the definition of a set of integration options. Several predefined basic integration operators are available for the development of integration options.
3. **Definition of integration choices:** The last step on the meta level covers the mapping of semantic relationships on integration options in a set of integration choices.
4. **Modeling of business processes:** On the model level, the software developer creates or imports two business processes which are to be integrated into one model.
5. **Set semantic relationships:** The developer subsequently inserts semantic relationship instances between nodes of the two business processes.
6. **Choose integration option:** According to the integration choices defined on the meta level each relationship is mapped to an instance of an integration option. If there exist only one mapping rule then the mapping is done automatically. If there is more than one rule then the software developer has to choose one.
7. **Model transformation:** In the last step, the developer executes all integration options that are related to semantic relationships identified in the second step on the model level.

Our diagram notation is derived from the UML 2.0 Activity Diagrams (UML-AD) [9,8], one of the standard representations for software system behaviour. However, we have adapted activity diagrams to our needs as a result of the experience with our earlier work in this area and call this diagram type ***Activity State Diagrams (ASD)***. First, of the nodes defined as part of the UML 2.0 AD standard, we use a simplified subset that is sufficient to express business process semantics and preserves or even enhances the underlying Petri-net-resembling semantics of Activity Diagrams. Instances of an object type which reside in states or activities are represented by their object identifiers as tokens of a Petri net. On the other hand, we have made three significant extensions. First, we found that both "state-biased" or "activity-biased" diagrams impose limitations on the integration process, and explicitly dealing with states significantly facilitates the clear separation between the different integration options in a number of cases. States represent the situation when an object exists between two activities, a state can hold a token which is waiting for an event that triggers an activity, and states offer the possibility of interrupting a business process before an activity can start. Therefore we introduce an explicit representation of states and include the additional node type *state*. In the diagram a state is represented by a rectangle and labelled with a name similar to the *object* notation of UML-AD standard. Second, on the meta level semantic relationships can be defined which will be instantiated on the model level. They are represented in ASDs by a directed arc with a dotted line between two nodes of two different business processes and are labelled with their type. Third, as described in [2], activity edges are not sufficient for modelling composition and association relationships between business processes, because they always imply passing of tokens, but situations exist where only checking for token existence should occur. Petri nets do not support this constructs either and therefore we have introduced a new edge type, *links*, to handle this situation: We use the *link* elements defined for class diagrams and add them to ASDs to express the sending of messages from one node to another. A link in our notation cannot accept tokens but can hold them in a state or activity or prevent them from entering a node. We use 4 different link types which are sufficient for modeling composite business processes [2]:

invoke: The *invoke link* is defined as $invoke(A, B)$ where A and B are activities. The link is directed, i.e., A is the source and B is the destination node which can hold the instances a and b respectively. The instance a can only leave A if message M was received by b in B and b can only enter B if a resides in A. This link is used for triggering activities, e.g., composite activity A invokes subactivity B.
block: The source and destination node of a *blocking link* can be either an activity or a state. It is defined as $block(A, B)$ and has the following behaviour: b cannot leave B if a has occupied A while b was in B, e.g., in a library system a state "book on loan"(B) is blocked by activity "borrow book" (A).
finished: A *finished link* is defined as $finished(A, B)$ and denotes the opposite of a *blocking link*. If a resides in A and b was blocked through a $block()$ before b can leave B after receiving M from a, e.g., in the library system the activity "return book" (A) releases b in state "book on loan" (B).
enable: The source and destination node of an *enable link* can be either a state or an activity. It is defined as $enable(A, B)$ and means that b can only enter B if a entered A before. In contrast to $invoke()$ a can leave A even if b never occupied B, e.g., in a library system the state "book is available" (A) enables the activity "borrow book" (B).

2 Related Work

In [15], the authors demonstrate a Petri net based approach for modelling interorganisational workflows. Like in our approach they are facing the problem of integrating vis-à-vis workflows but it is not possible to model situations in Petri nets where only checking for token existence should occur, especially in composition and association relationships.

The requirements for interorganisational workflows are discussed in [1]. The authors propose the development of public processes out of cooperative ones which are set between internal processes and so support flexibility, privacy, and the preservation of established workflows. Internal and public processes are connected via producing and consuming cooperative activities where each producing activity is related to a consuming activity. The problem of incompatibilities of cooperative workflows, e.g., the order of producing and consuming activities do not match as shown in Figure 1(a), is not discussed further.

An interesting approach of integrating services at the level of Petri nets is shown in [18]. It discusses the analysis of service interfaces and the detection of service compatibility. Therefore service specifications such as BPEL are mapped to Petri net models. The same approach could be used by our framework as well to integrate services. However compared to [18] our integration process is not automatic but semi-automatic with the advantage that integration options may integrate services even if their public workflows are not compatible.

3 Verification and Validation of the Integration Options

During validation we check if the behaviour of the integrated model is consistent to the input model in regards of sequence constraints. An early detection of these errors is highly desired because it helps reducing development costs [16]. The earliest stage is step 2 on the meta level when the integration option is created by the domain engineer.

Verification on meta level: There exist several publications that discuss the verification of sound workflows and its implementation in tools [13,14,17]. Most of them are based on Petri nets and we are going to use them for the verification and validation on the meta and model level as well. Both issues, the soundness property and sequence constraints of a workflow, can be checked by analyzing the *coverability graph* (CG) which includes all possible transition firings starting from an initial *state* of a Petri net. A *state* is determined by all places that hold a token. To create CG from a ASD diagram we have to translate ASD diagrams to Petri nets first. The mapping of the elements is supported by a meta modeling tool, e.g., AToM^3 [4]. We do not map *links* from ASD diagrams because they cannot accept tokens and there is no equivalent element defined in Petri nets but consider them later.

The verification consists of mapping the integration options to Petri nets, generating a coverability graph CG, and analyzing the CG afterwards. Figure 1(b) shows an integration option for the incompatibility problem of two business processes shown in Figure 1(a). In this example the views of a travel agency on the public processes of two airline booking services do not match. *Airline 1* demands the destination first and then the travel date whereas *airline 2* demands the data in the opposite order. The submissions of data at both airlines are identical activities defined by the semantic relationship *identity* which is represented as a dotted line in Figure 1(a). Identical activities should be executed only once in the integrated business process as shown in the integration option in Figure 1(b). The option consist of four parameters, activities A, B, C, and D

where B and C are merged into one activity and D is automated because it reads the data from datastore which saves the data previously submitted by A. The option can be applied on the business processes by mapping the activity "submit destination" of *airline 1* to A, "submit date" of *airline 1* to B, "submit date" of *airline 2* to C, and "submit destination" of *airline 2* to D. We analyse CG of the integration option by checking if all paths lead to the final node.

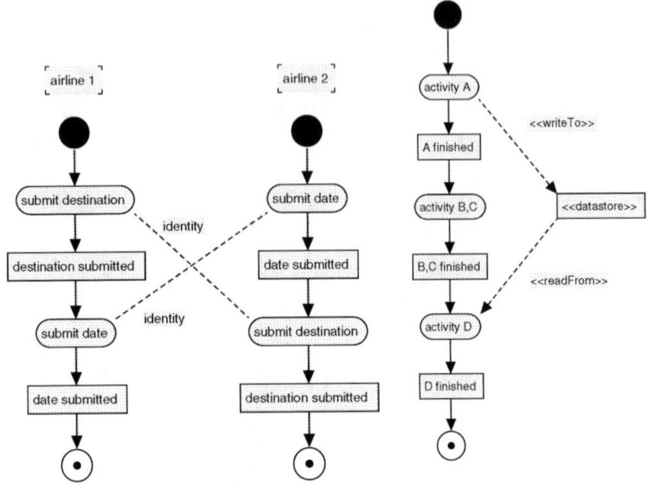

(a) Example of incompatible business processes.

(b) Example for an integration option.

Fig. 1. Example of two airline booking services modelled as business processes

Verification and validation on model level: The soundness and sequence constraint aspect must be verified on the model level. Similar to the verification on the meta level we are going to use coverability graphs CG to check soundness but in this case we will also consider *links*. For validating the sequence constraints we are going to compare the coverability graphs of the input model with coverability graphs of the integrated model.

First, we describe the verification of soundness. We have to investigate all possible initial states of the integrated model O. We start from the set of all possible initial states I of the input models *airline 1* and *airline 2* and map I to the corresponding set of states I' in O. For each state T in I' a coverability graph CG will be created and if CG shows a deadlock, then T will cause a deadlock in the O. However so far, CG contains all possible paths of tokens without considering *links*. Section 1 has explained the semantics of links and how they restrict the behaviour of tokens. We have to investigate paths where *links* have an influence on the behaviour. In the following we explain for each link necessary changes to CG where S is the source and D is the destination place of the link and places correlates with nodes:

invoke: The *invoke link* can hold a token either in S or in the preceding places in D according to the definition in Section 1. We have to check both constraints: (1) If there

is a state $T \in CG$ where $S \in T$ and $D \notin T$ then all following states on that path in CG have to be recalculated: In every following state of T, S must be included till a token enters D. This represents the semantics that a token is hold in S till a token enters D. (2) If the function U = precPlaces(D) returns the set of preceding places U of D and there exists a state $T \in CG$ where $U \subseteq T$ and $S \notin T$ then the states in that path has to be recalculated as well: For each new following state after T, U must be included till S is entered by a token. This ensures that the token in U cannot enter D before a token has arrived in S.
block: If state $V = (S + D)$ and there is a state $T \in CG$ where $V \subseteq T$ then we have to rebuild the remaining path in CG as follows: The token in D is held as long as there is no new calculated state T where $S_F \in T$, $D_F \in T$, S_F and D_F are source and destination places of a *finished link*, and $D = D_F$. This ensures that a token can only leave D if it is released by a *finished link* as explained in Section 1.
finished: This link influences the behaviour of tokens only in conjunction with a *block link* and need not be investigated further.
enable: If U =prePlaces(D) and there is a state $T \in CG$ where $U \subseteq T$, $S \notin T$ then we have to rebuild the remaining path because the tokens are held in U till a state T is reached which includes S. The calculation of new states is similar to previous explained situations.

If there is a path in CG which does not lead to the final places then the initial state T for which CG was created will lead to a deadlock. We can identify the integration option which was applied on the affected places because of the mapping rules defined by the integration options and track it back to a semantic relationship because of the integration choices. The software developer can decide if T is a realistic initial state, choose an alternative integration option or alternative semantic relationships. Depending on the decision the steps 5 and/or 6 must be repeated.

The last aspect is the validation of the sequence constraints. We have to check if the order of activities of the input models have changed during the integration. The order of activities of the integrated model is represented by CG. For comparing the order we have to create two views of CG. The first view CG_a represents the view of object a by omitting all states which cannot accept a. The second view CG_b is in perspective of b. By comparing CG_a and CG_b with the coverability graphs of the input business processes we can find out if the order has changed. The integration option and semantic relationship which cause a violation can be identified by the places which are in a different order. The software developer has two options to solve this violation, (1) choose an alternative integration option or (2) set a different semantic relationship between the affected nodes.

4 Conclusion

This paper has described verification and validation of the integration of two business processes on the different levels of our process integration framework [2]. As correctness criteria we use the soundness of the integrated business process, especially the prevention of deadlock creation through insertion of links, and the maintenance of the sequencing constraints imposed by the two business processes used as input. We are currently developing a meta-modeling tool in DoME [6] supporting our approach and the verification mechanisms. Acknowledge: Part of the DoME framework modifications are due to Rajesh Thiagarajan and Wolfgang Mayer.

References

1. Issam Chebbi, Schahram Dustdar, and Samir Tata. The view-based approach to dynamic inter-organizational workflow cooperation. *Data and Knowledge Engineering*, 56(2):139–173, February 2006.
2. Georg Grossmann, Yikai Ren, Michael Schrefl, and Markus Stumptner. Behavior Based Integration of Composite Business Processes. In *Proc. BPM 2005*, volume 3649 of *LNCS*, pages 186–204, September 2005.
3. Georg Grossmann, Michael Schrefl, and Markus Stumptner. Classification of business process correspondences and associated integration operators. In *Proc. of eCOMO 2004*, volume 3289/2004 of *LNCS*, pages 653–666, November 2004.
4. Esther Guerra and Juan de Lara. A Framework for the Verification of UML Models. Examples Using Petri Nets. In *VIII Jornadas Ingeniería del Software y Bases de Datos (JISBD 2003)*, pages 325–334, November 2003.
5. Elsevier North Holland. Special Issue on Enterprise Modelling and System Support. *Advanced Engineering Informatics*, 18(4):191–253, October 2004.
6. Honeywell Inc. Domain Modeling Environment (DoME). http://www.htc.honeywell.com/dome2.
7. MetaCase. MetaEdit+. URL: http://www.metacase.com/mep/ (last access 07/03/2006).
8. Object Management Group (OMG). UML Superstructure Version 2.0, August 2005. http://www.omg.org/uml, 2005-07-04.
9. James Rumbaugh, Ivar Jacobson, and Grady Booch. *The Unified Modeling Language Reference Manual, 2nd edition.* Object Technology Series. Addison-Wesley, 2004.
10. Wasim Sadiq and Maria E. Orlowska. On Correctness Issues in Conceptual Modeling of Workflows. In *Proc. of ECIS '97*, June 1997.
11. Monique Snoeck. Sequence constraints in business modelling and business process modelling. *Enterprise Information Systems*, 4:194–201, 2003.
12. Markus Stumptner, Michael Schrefl, and Georg Grossmann. On the road to behavior-based integration. In *Proc. of APCCM 2004*, pages 15–22. Australian Computer Society, 2004.
13. W. M. P. van der Aalst. Verification of workflow nets. In *Proc. of ICATPN 1997*, volume 1248 of *LNCS*, pages 407–426, London, UK, June 1997. Springer.
14. W. M. P. van der Aalst. The Application of Petri Nets to Workflow Management. *Journal of Circuits, Systems, and Computers*, 8(1):21–66, 1998.
15. W. M. P. van der Aalst. Loosely coupled interorganizational workflows: modeling and analyzing workflows crossing organizational boundaries. *Information Management*, 37(2):67–75, 2000.
16. Kees van Hee, Lou Somers Natalia Sidorova, and Marc Voorhoeve. Consistency in model integration. *Data and Knowledge Engineering*, 56(1):4–22, January 2006.
17. H. M. W. Verbeek, T. Basten, and W. M. P. van der Aalst. Diagnosing Workflow Processes using Woflan. *The Computer Journal*, 44(4):246–279, 2001.
18. Andreas Wombacher, Bendick Mahleko, and Erich Neuhold. Ipsi-pf: A business process matchmaking engine. In *Int'l IEEE Conference on E-Commerce Technology(CEC'04)*, pages 137–145. IEEE Computer Society Press, 2004.
19. S. J. Woodman, D. J. Palmer, S. K. Shrivastava, and S. M. Wheater. Notations for the Specification and Verification of Composite Web Services. In *Proc. of EDOC 2004*. IEEE Computer Society Press, 2004.

Verifying BPEL Workflows Under Authorisation Constraints

Zhao Xiangpeng[1,2], Antonio Cerone[2], and Padmanabhan Krishnan[3]

[1] LMAM and Department of Informatics, School of Mathematics
Peking University, Beijing 100871, China
[2] UNU-IIST, Macau SAR, China
[3] Centre for Software Assurance, Bond University, Australia
zxp@math.pku.edu.cn, antonio@iist.unu.edu, pkrishna@staff.bond.edu.au

Abstract. Business Process Execution Language (BPEL), or Web Services BPEL (WS-BPEL), is the standard for specifying workflow process definition using web services. Research on formal modelling and verification of BPEL has largely concentrated on control flow and data flow, while security related properties have received little attention. In this work, we present a formal framework that integrates Role Based Access Control (RBAC) into BPEL and allows us to express authorisation constraints using temporal logic. Using this framework, we show how model-checking can be applied to verify that a given BPEL process satisfies the security constraints.

Keywords: Workflow, BPEL, RBAC, model-checking.

1 Introduction

The use of workflows based on web services is a current trend in industry. In this context a workflow can be viewed as a composition of web services which is therefore distributed, decentralized and dynamic. BPEL (Business Process Execution Language) [2] has become the standard for specifying and executing workflow specifications for web service composition. It has been developed to model business processes by describing workflows and interfaces, as well as specifying the technical infrastructure for carrying out business transactions. However, BPEL lacks security and so-called "human workflow" support.

As workflow process modelling is a complicated and error-prone procedure, it is important to ensure that there are no errors when a process definition becomes operational. Thus, effective process verification in the early modelling phase is essential. Fu *et al.* [4] suggest a way to verify BPEL taking into account both control and data flow. Hinz *et al.* [5] describe how to transform BPEL into Petri Nets. However, in their work several details of BPEL, including security, are not considered. We believe that a new model combining both the web service related features and security issues is needed. Our goal is the description, outside the business process, of authorisation constraints that a workflow must satisfy and their automatic verification.

S. Dustdar, J.L. Fiadeiro, and A. Sheth (Eds.): BPM 2006, LNCS 4102, pp. 439–444, 2006.

There are also works that describe injecting authorisation models into workflows [9,1], but without any attempts to give formal verification frameworks. Ribeiro and Guedes [6] use a logic-based method to verify workflows against security policies. Tan, Crampton and Gunter [8] study the consistency of various kinds of authorisation constraints and give an algorithm to determine whether the workflow can be completed under given constraints. However, the authors assume that the workflow has a very simple structure, i.e. a partial order. We believe that verification based on such a simple model is not suitable for real-world workflows. In fact, we want to integrate an authorisation model into BPEL with the ability to verify that a given BPEL business process can actually be completed under the restrictions imposed by the model.

In this paper we introduce security restrictions specified using role based access control to a workflow and show how to verify whether the workflow can still be completed under the security constraints.

2 BPEL and RBAC

BPEL is an XML-based language for the composition of executable business processes based on web services. Since in the business process terminology web services are usually called tasks, we will always use the term "task" in the following. The behaviour of a business process consists of BPEL activities. We distinguish between *basic activities* and *structural activities*.

There are four basic activities: `assign`, to assign value to variables; `receive` and `reply`, to describe data communication with the environment of the business process; `invoke` to describe calls to tasks offered by the environment. The last three activities are called *invocation activities*; they all relate to calling of tasks.

As an example we will describe the process used by a library to acquire a book (Figure 1). The key activities are as follows. Any individual who is a "fellow" of the library can apply for ordering a book. An ordering request consists of the applicant's id, the book name and the book price, described by the `bookData` variable. This request is modelled as a `receive` activity with the name `orderEntry`. The book will be eventually ordered only after the request passes three checks performed by a secretary, an accountant and a manager called `inventoryCheck`, `creditCheck` and `evaluation`, respectively. The manager has a choice (indicated by the `switch` construct) of either purchasing the book (called `purchaseBook`) or sending a reject letter to the fellow (called `sendRejectLetter`).

In invocation activities the name of the web service is described as a tuple (`partnerLink`, `portType`, `operation`). For example, the `inventoryCheck` activity is a synchronous invocation to the operation `check`, which belongs to the secretary partner. It first sends `bookData` as input to `check`, and then waits for the returned result, which will be assigned to variable `inventoryCheckResult`.

Role Based Access Control (RBAC) provides a flexible approach to model access control policies. Permissions are assigned to roles, and roles are assigned to subjects. RBAC is considered as a natural choice in business processes, where

```
<process name="bookRequisition">
  <sequence>
    <receive name="orderEntry" partnerLink="fellowService"
      portType="as:fellowPT" operation="provide" variable="bookData"
      ... ></receive>
    <flow>
      <invoke name="inventoryCheck" partnerLink="secretaryService"
        portType="as:secretaryPT" operation="check"
        inputVariable="bookData"
        outputVariable="inventoryCheckResult"></invoke>
      <invoke name="creditCheck" ... operation="check" ... ></invoke>
    </flow>
    ...
    <invoke name="evaluation" ... operation="evaluate" ... ></invoke>
    <switch>
      <case condition=
        "bpws:getVariableProperty ('evaluationResult','Approved')">
        <invoke name="purchaseBook" ... operation="purchase" ... >
        </invoke>
      </case> <otherwise>
        <invoke name="sendRejectLetter" ...
          operation="sendRejectLetter" ... ></invoke>
      </otherwise>
    </switch>
  </sequence>
</process>
```

Fig. 1. BPEL Source Code for the Library Example

the permissions of performing tasks are usually assigned to roles [8]. Role hierarchy defines inheritance relations between roles, which are usually partial orders. A senior-role is a role that inherits permissions from one or more junior roles.

We model a BPEL specification using a process algebra. The various activities are thus modelled as communication over channels [10]. From the BPEL perspective, partner links can be viewed as roles, and operations as permissions in RBAC. In our framework the assignment of roles to individuals is done explicitly. An agent, which can be any entity performing a certain operation, synchronises with the BPEL process (say by examining the role associated with the `partnerLink`) and executes the particular task. That is, the agent assumes a particular role to complete a task. As an agent can have an iterative behaviour, it can assume various roles within a particular behaviour. Informally, the semantics of an agent only specifies what the agent is willing to do — not what the agent is allowed to do. To ensure that the behaviour of an agent is suitably restricted, we also need to model a controller which checks the basic RBAC constraints. The entire system is viewed as the composition of the agents (along with the individual and role assignments) and the controller [10].

3 Authorisation Constraints and Verification

We now describe the specification of authorisation constraints based on RBAC models. The execution of a task can be associated with a particular individual assuming specific roles. Formally we define the sets $Inds$ (for individuals), $Roles$ (for roles), $Tasks$ (for tasks). The set of all possible states of computation is captured by the set of triples, $Inds \times Roles \times Tasks$. We let the triple (i, r, t) be a typical state and call it an *allocation* for task t. We also support the use of a role hierarchy, which means that if a given role is authorised to play a task, then the roles dominating this role will inherit its execution authorisation. The role hierarchy is a partial order on $Roles$. In general, we can support a variety of structures on $Roles$ (e.g., as proposed in W-RBAC [9]). The focus here is not on properties of the structures associated with such sets; rather it is on how to verify an assignment of individuals to tasks via their roles in a workflow. Using this model we can specify some high-level constraints such as separation of duties.

The trace is defined as a possible "run" of the business process, based on the process definition and the allocation of agents. It captures a specific execution order of the tasks by particular individuals assuming specific roles. A constraint is viewed as a predicate on the "trace". Thus we can use Linear Time Temporal Logic (LTL) to specify the desired properties. We use the standard modalities of LTL ($\Diamond$ for eventually, $\Box$ for henceforth and $\bigcirc$ for next).

We introduce two basic predicates: $canAssume : Inds \times Roles \rightarrow Bool$ and $canPerform : Roles \times Tasks \rightarrow Bool$. These predicates are motivated by our semantics which represents the possible options declared by the agents and the options actually permitted by the controller. We note that these constraints are static and they do not depend on the execution order of the tasks. The execution order cannot be decided until the actual execution of the business process. In order to simplify the verification procedure, we avoid expressing these basic constraints directly as LTL formulae in the implementation. Instead, we express them as a predicate *allow*, which is incorporated within the controller, $allow(i, r, t) = canAssume(i, r) \wedge canPerform(r, t)$. Every valid trace containing (i, r, t) must at least satisfy $\Box allow(i, r, t)$. In general, we use the variables i, r and t as place holders to denote the individual, role and task respectively. For instance, the formula $\Diamond(i = i')$ denotes that eventually the individual i' performs some task. More precisely a trace that satisfies the formula must have the triple (i', r', t') appearing in it for some r' and t'. In this paper we focus only on the verification of security related properties, in particular on "whether the business process can be completed under a set of authorisation constraints". A constrained business process is *completable* under a constraint c if there exists a trace $Tr = \langle (i_1, r_1, t_1), \cdots, (i_n, r_n, t_n) \cdots \rangle$ of the business process such that Tr satisfies c. We are effectively verifying if the workflow description, along with the behaviour of the agents and the controller, actually satisfies the authorisation constraints. While the above infrastructure allows us to define a wide class of authorisation constraints, only a few specific examples are developed below.

Separation of duty (SoD) is an authorisation principle used to prevent fraud and error by requiring that at least two individuals are involved in performing the business process. SoD is also useful when two agents have to co-operate to complete a task but neither agent should know all the details.

The basic form of SoD states that two given distinct tasks t_1 and t_2 must be performed by different individuals. This can be defined as

$$\forall i_0 \in \mathit{Inds} \bullet \neg\Big((\Diamond(t = t_1 \wedge i = i_0)) \wedge (\Diamond(t = t_2 \wedge i = i_0)) \Big)$$

That is, the same individual i_0 cannot perform both t_1 and t_2. We can also define other variations based on the above structure. For example, we can define that task t_1 and task t_2 must be performed by different roles as

$$\forall r_0 \in \mathit{Roles} \bullet \neg\Big((\Diamond(t = t_1 \wedge r = r_0)) \wedge (\Diamond(t = t_2 \wedge r = r_0)) \Big)$$

In this case the tasks may be performed by the same individual; but they must be allowed to assume different roles. We can also define an SoD constraint for a specific agent, e.g., A, which cannot invoke both task t_1 and t_2 as

$$\neg\Big((\Diamond(t = t_1 \wedge i = i_A)) \wedge (\Diamond(t = t_2 \wedge i = i_A)) \Big)$$

As we allow LTL formulae with quantifiers, we can also define constraints that only hold under certain conditions. For instance, we specify below the requirement that if task t_0 is performed by the individual i_s, tasks t_1 and t_2 cannot be performed by the same individual.

$$(\Diamond(t = t_0 \wedge i = i_s)) \Rightarrow \forall i_0 \in \mathit{Inds} \bullet \neg\Big((\Diamond(t = t_1 \wedge i = i_0)) \wedge (\Diamond(t = t_2 \wedge i = i_0)) \Big)$$

That is, the separation of duty only applies if i_s performs t_0 at some time. Such forms of SoD are dynamic, in the sense that they rely on a particular execution of the business process.

We now apply the above discussion to the example shown in Section 2. We have four roles: fellow, secretary, accountant, and manager. We consider a role hierarchy where the fellow is the least element of the partial order, the secretary and accountant are higher than the fellow but incomparable with each other, and the manager is the top element. We have five agents: Alice, Bob, Cathy, David and Elsa. We allow Alice to assume the role of a manager, (formally written as "$canAssume$(Alice,manager)"), Bob to be a secretary, Cathy to be an accountant, David to be a fellow and Elsa to be either a secretary or accountant. For our BPEL specification, we specify that only the manager can execute evaluation, (formally written as "$canPerform$(manager,`evaluation`)"), the secretary to execute `inventoryCheck`, `sendRejectLetter` or `purchaseBook` while the accountant can only execute `creditCheck` and the fellow can only invoke `orderEntry`.

We introduce the following separation of duty constraints:

$$\forall i_0 \in \mathit{Inds} \bullet \neg\Big((\Diamond(t = \mathit{orderEntry} \wedge i = i_0)) \wedge (\Diamond(t = \mathit{creditCheck} \wedge i = i_0)) \Big)$$
$$\forall i_0 \in \mathit{Inds} \bullet \neg\Big((\Diamond(t = \mathit{inventoryCheck} \wedge i = i_0)) \wedge (\Diamond(t = \mathit{creditCheck} \wedge i = i_0)) \Big)$$

which requires `orderEntry` and `creditCheck` be performed by different individuals as well as `inventoryCheck` and `creditCheck`.

The specifics of the verification and synthesis process have been performed using SAL (Symbolic Analysis Laboratory), a model-checker designed by SRI [7]. SAL supports special features such as quantifiers, user-defined data types, functions and infinite data types. We translate the BPEL specification into SAL. The translation is almost straightforward and we only outline the main steps. Channel communications are converted into state transitions with shared variables.

Modules in SAL are distinct transition systems that can be combined together. Each business process or agent is defined as a module. This allows us to build different configurations of the system. We can choose particular configurations to construct the actual system to be verified. Two possible configurations related to our example are are $conf_1$: {bp, Alice, Bob, Cathy, David} and $conf_2$: {bp, David, Elsa}. SAL verifies that configuration $conf_1$ is completable whereas configuration $conf_2$ is not. This is because there is no manager in $conf_2$ to perform the evaluation task. Another configuration $conf_3$: {bp, Alice, David} will also fail, since the separation of duty cannot be satisfied.

4 Conclusion and Future Work

In this paper, we have presented a verifiable framework for BPEL processes that addresses authorisation requirements. We provided a systematic method of integrating RBAC information with the BPEL processes. Based on the trace of the business process, we defined authorisation constraints in temporal logic. Finally, we presented how the business process can be automatically verified for completability under given authorisation constraints using the SAL model-checker. The model-checking procedure is based on the definition of a completable business process using RBAC mechanisms and constraints.

Future work includes adding trust and delegation support to the model, analysing the working draft of BPEL 2.0 [3], and developing efficient translation mechanisms to reduce the state space for the verification process.

References

1. G. Ahn, R. Sandhu, M. Kang, and J. Park. Injecting RBAC to secure a web-based workflow system. In *Proc. of RBAC '00*. ACM Press, 2000.
2. BPEL. Business process execution language for web services version 1.1. `http://www-128.ibm.com/developerworks/library/ws-bpel/`.
3. BPEL 2.0 Working Draft. Web services business process execution language version 2.0. `http://www.oasis-open.org/apps/org/workgroup/wsbpel/`. 2004.
4. X. Fu, T. Bultan, and J. Su. Analysis of interacting BPEL web services. In *Proc. of WWW '04*. ACM Press, 2004.
5. S. Hinz, K. Schmidt, and C. Stahl. Transforming BPEL to Petri nets. In *Proc. of BPM'05, LNCS 3649*, 2005.
6. C. Ribeiro and P. Guedes. Verifying workflow processes against organization security policies. In *WETICE99'*. IEEE Computer Society, 1999.
7. SAL. Symbolic analysis laboratory. `http://sal.csl.sri.com/`.
8. K. Tan, J. Crampton, and C. Gunter. The consistency of task-based authorization constraints in workflow systems. In *Proc. of CSFW'04*, 2004.
9. J. Wainer, P. Barthelmess, and A. Kumar. W-RBAC – a workflow security model incorporating controlled overriding of constraints. *International Journal of Cooperative Information Systems*, 12(4), 2003.
10. X. Zhao, A. Cerone, and P. Krishnan. Modelling and resource allocation planning of BPEL workflows under security constraints. Technical Report 336, UNU-IIST, 2006. `http://www.iist.unu.edu/`.

Selecting Necessary and Sufficient Checkpoints for Dynamic Verification of Fixed-Time Constraints in Grid Workflow Systems

Jinjun Chen and Yun Yang

CITR – Centre for Information Technology Research
Faculty of Information and Communication Technologies
Swinburne University of Technology
PO Box 218, Hawthorn, Melbourne, Australia 3122
{jchen, yyang}@ict.swin.edu.au

Abstract. In grid workflow systems, existing representative checkpoint selection strategies, which are used to select checkpoints for verifying fixed-time constraints at run-time execution stage, often select some unnecessary checkpoints and ignore some necessary ones. Consequently, overall temporal verification efficiency and effectiveness can be severely impacted. In this paper, we propose a new strategy that selects only necessary and sufficient checkpoints dynamically along grid workflow execution. Specifically, we introduce a new concept of minimum time redundancy as a key reference value for checkpoint selection. We also investigate its relationships with fixed-time constraint consistency. Based on these relationships, we present our strategy which can improve overall temporal verification efficiency and effectiveness significantly.

1 Introduction

In the grid architecture, a grid workflow system is facilitated to support modelling, redesign and execution of large-scale sophisticated scientific and business processes [2, 14]. These processes are modelled as grid workflow specifications at build-time stage which normally contain a large number of computation, transaction or data intensive activities [11], then instantiated at run-time instantiation stage by an instantiation grid service [5], and finally executed at run-time execution stage by grid services [5]. In reality, complex scientific or business processes are often time constrained. Consequently, fixed-time constraints are often set in corresponding grid workflow specifications where a fixed-time constraint at an activity is an absolute time value by which the activity must be completed [2, 4, 9].

Temporal verification is conducted to check the consistency of fixed-time constraints. At build-time and run-time instantiation stages, without any specific execution times, we need not consider where we should conduct temporal verification as each fixed-time constraint needs only be verified once statically. At run-time execution stage however, activity completion durations vary and consequently, we may need to verify each fixed-time constraint many times at different activities. However,

S. Dustdar, J.L. Fiadeiro, and A. Sheth (Eds.): BPM 2006, LNCS 4102, pp. 445 – 450, 2006.

conducting the verification at every activity is not efficient as we may not have to do so at some activities. So where should we conduct the temporal verification? The activities at which we conduct the verification are called *checkpoints* [6, 13, 15].

Existing representative Checkpoint Selection Strategies (*CSS*) often suffer from the limitations of selecting unnecessary checkpoints and ignoring necessary ones. Unnecessary checkpoints would result in some unnecessary temporal verification, which eventually impacts the overall verification efficiency. Ignored checkpoints mean some necessary verification would be omitted, which eventually impacts the overall verification effectiveness. Clearly, neither is desirable. In this paper, we develop a new strategy that guarantees checkpoints selected are not only necessary but also sufficient.

2 Related Work and Problem Analysis for Checkpoint Selection

[12] takes every activity as a checkpoint, denoted as CSS_1. [15] sets checkpoints at the start time and end time of each activity, denoted as CSS_2. [13] takes the start activity and each decision activity as checkpoints, denoted as CSS_3. [13] also mentions another strategy: user-defined static checkpoints, denoted as CSS_4. All of CSS_1, CSS_2, CSS_3 and CSS_4 predefine checkpoints before grid workflow execution. However, we may not have to conduct temporal verification at some of them such as those that can be completed within allowed time intervals. Therefore, CSS_1, CSS_2, CSS_3 and CSS_4 may select some unnecessary checkpoints. Meanwhile, CSS_3 and CSS_4 may ignore some checkpoints as we may need to conduct temporal verification at some other activities.

Our earlier works [6, 7, 10] have attempted to improve this situation, but they still have some deficiencies. Specifically, [6] selects an activity as a checkpoint when its completion duration exceeds its maximum duration, denoted as CSS_5. [7] selects an activity as a checkpoint when its completion duration exceeds its mean duration, denoted as CSS_6. [10] introduces a minimum proportional time redundancy for each activity and selects an activity as a checkpoint when its completion duration is greater than its mean duration plus its minimum proportional time redundancy, denoted as CSS_7. However, in Section 6, we will see that CSS_5 may ignore some necessary checkpoints while CSS_6 and CSS_7 may select some unnecessary ones.

Regarding the above limitations of the representative strategies, we may ask: "Can we develop a strategy that only selects necessary yet sufficient checkpoints?". In this paper, we answer the question positively by presenting such a strategy.

3 Timed Grid Workflow Representation

A grid workflow can be represented by a grid workflow graph, where nodes correspond to activities and edges correspond to dependencies between them [3, 12]. Here, we assume that the grid workflow is well structured [1]. We denote the ith activity of a grid workflow as a_i. For each a_i, we denote its maximum duration, mean duration, minimum duration, run-time start time, run-time end time and run-time completion duration as $D(a_i)$, $M(a_i)$, $d(a_i)$, $S(a_i)$, $E(a_i)$ and $Rcd(a_i)$ respectively. If there is a fixed-time constrain at a_i, we denote it as $FTC(a_i)$ and its value as $ftv(a_i)$. If there is a path from a_i to a_j ($i \leq j$), we denote the maximum duration, mean duration, minimum duration, run-time completion duration between them as $D(a_i, a_j)$, $M(a_i, a_j)$, $d(a_i, a_j)$ and $Rcd(a_i, a_j)$ respectively [12, 13]. For convenience, we consider only one execution path in a grid workflow without losing generality. As for a selective or parallel structure, each branch is an execution path. For an iterative structure, from start to end, it is also an execution path. So, we can apply the results achieved in this paper to them.

In addition, four temporal consistency states have been defined in [9]. They are SC (Strong Consistency), WC (Weak Consistency), WI (Weak Inconsistency) and SI (Strong Inconsistency). We summarise their definitions for run-time instantiation and execution stages as our strategy is based on them and is related to those two stages.

Definition 1. At run-time instantiation stage, $FTC(a_i)$ is said to be of SC if $D(a_1, a_i) \leq ftv(a_i) - S(a_1)$, WC if $M(a_1, a_i) \leq ftv(a_i) - S(a_1) < D(a_1, a_i)$, WI if $d(a_1, a_i) \leq ftv(a_i) - S(a_1) < M(a_1, a_i)$, and SI if $ftv(a_i) - S(a_1) < d(a_1, a_i)$.

Definition 2. At run-time execution stage, at checkpoint a_p ($p \leq i$), $FTC(a_i)$ is said to be of SC if $Rcd(a_1, a_p) + D(a_{p+1}, a_i) \leq ftv(a_i) - S(a_1)$, WC if $Rcd(a_1, a_p) + M(a_{p+1}, a_i) \leq ftv(a_i) - S(a_1) < Rcd(a_1, a_p) + D(a_{p+1}, a_i)$, WI if $Rcd(a_1, a_p) + d(a_{p+1}, a_i) \leq ftv(a_i) - S(a_1) < Rcd(a_1, a_p) + M(a_{p+1}, a_i)$, and SI if $ftv(a_i) - S(a_1) < Rcd(a_1, a_p) + d(a_{p+1}, a_i)$.

4 Minimum Time Redundancy

According to [9], for WI and SI, the corresponding exception handling is triggered to adjust them to SC or WC. Hence, checkpoint selection is actually focused on selecting checkpoints for verifying previous SC and WC fixed-time constraints. Correspondingly, minimum time redundancy consists of minimum SC and WC time redundancy.

First, we introduce SC and WC time redundancy from one fixed-time constraint. At run-time execution stage, considering SC $FTC(a_i)$ at a_p ($p<i$), we have $Rcd(a_1, a_p)+ D(a_{p+1}, a_i) \leq ftv(a_i)-S(a_1)$. We have a time difference: $[ftv(a_i)-S(a_1)]-[Rcd(a_1, a_p)+ D(a_{p+1}, a_i)]$. If the succeeding activity execution can be controlled within this difference, $FTC(a_i)$ can still be kept as SC even if the execution consumes more time than scheduled. We define this time difference as SC time redundancy of $FTC(a_i)$ at a_p, and denote it as $TR_{SC}(FTC(a_i), a_p)$ (TR_{SC}: SC Time Redundancy). So, we have Definition 3.

Definition 3 (*SC Time Redundancy*). At a_p ($p<i$), let $FTC(a_i)$ be of SC. Then, SC time redundancy of $FTC(a_i)$ at a_p, i.e. $TR_{SC}(FTC(a_i), a_p)$, is defined as $[ftv(a_i) - S(a_1)] - [Rcd(a_1, a_p) + D(a_{p+1}, a_i)]$.

For a WC fixed-time constraint, say $FTC(a_j)$, we have Definition 4.

Definition 4 (*WC Time Redundancy*). At a_p ($p<j$), let $FTC(a_j)$ be of WC. Then, the WC time redundancy of $FTC(a_j)$ at a_p, i.e. $TR_{WC}(FTC(a_j), a_p)$, is defined as $[ftv(a_j) - S(a_1)] - [Rcd(a_1, a_p) + M(a_{p+1}, a_j)]$.

We now consider multiple SC or WC fixed-time constraints and we have:

Definition 5 (*Minimum SC Time Redundancy*). Let $F_1, F_2, \ldots, F_n$ be n SC fixed-time constraints and cover a_p. Then, at a_p, minimum SC time redundancy is defined as the minimum of all SC time redundancies and is denoted as $MTR_{SC}(a_p)$ (*MTR*: Minimum Time Redundancy).

$$MTR_{SC}(a_p) = Min\{\ TR_{SC}(F_s, a_p) \mid s = 1,2, \ldots, n\ \}$$

Definition 6 (*Minimum WC Time Redundancy*). Let F_1, F_2, ... , F_n be n WC fixed-time constraints and cover a_p. Then, at a_p, minimum WC time redundancy is defined as the minimum of all WC time redundancies and is denoted as $MTR_{WC}(a_p)$.

$$MTR_{WC}(a_p) = Min\{ TR_{WC}(F_s, a_p) | s = 1,2, ..., n \}$$

According to Definitions 5 and 6, we normally have $M(a_p) + MTR_{WC}(a_{p-1}) < D(a_p) + MTR_{SC}(a_{p-1})$. We can develop a method that can dynamically obtain $MTR_{SC}(a_p)$ and $MTR_{WC}(a_p)$, denoted as DOMTR (Dynamic Obtaining of Minimum Time Redundancy). DOMTR can utilise temporal verification computation results without incurring much extra computation. Its working steps are omitted here due to the page limit[1].

5 Checkpoint Selection Based on Minimum SC and WC Time Redundancy

We now first investigate the relationships between minimum SC & WC time redundancy and SC, WC, WI & SI. Then, we present our new strategy. The relationships are shown in Fig. 1. We can further prove why the relationships are as shown in Fig. 1. Again, due to the page limit, we simply omit the proof.

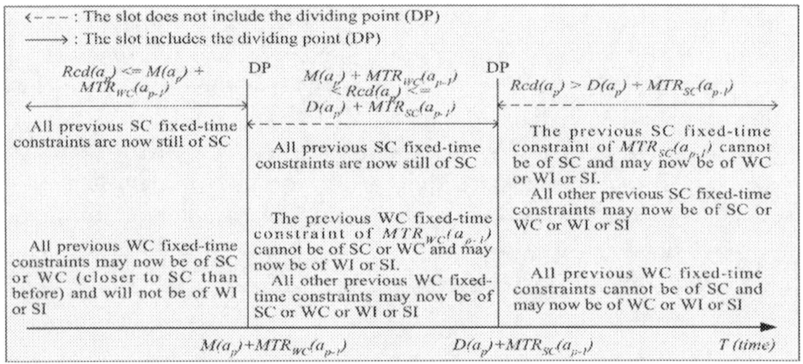

Fig. 1. Relationships between minimum SC & WC time redundancy and SC, WC, WI & SI

According to Fig. 1, we can decide whether to take a_p as a checkpoint. The approach is: *At a_p, if $Rcd(a_p)>D(a_p)+MTR_{SC}(a_{p-1})$, take it as a checkpoint for verifying SC, WC, WI & SI of all previous SC fixed-time constraints, and for verifying WC, WI & SI of all previous WC ones. If $M(a_p)+MTR_{WC}(a_{p-1})<Rcd(a_p)\leq D(a_p)+ MTR_{SC}(a_{p-1})$, take a_p as a checkpoint for verifying SC, WC, WI & SI of all previous WC only fixed-time constraints. If $Rcd(a_p)\leq M(a_p)+MTR_{WC}(a_{p-1})$, do not take a_p as a checkpoint.*

We denote the above approach as $CDA(a_p)$ (Checkpoint Decision-making Approach at a_p). Combining $CDA(a_p)$ with DOMTR mentioned in Section 4, we can derive a new checkpoint selection strategy that selects only necessary and sufficient checkpoints, denoted as CSS_{MTR} (CSS_{MTR}: Minimum Time Redundancy based

[1] In this paper, wherever 'due to the page limit...' appears, please refer to [8] for details.

Checkpoint Selection Strategy). Simply speaking, at a_p, CSS_{MTR} selects checkpoints based on $CDA(a_p)$ while along grid workflow execution, CSS_{MTR} computes minimum SC and WC time redundancy based on DOMTR. We can further derive an algorithm to depict the working process of CSS_{MTR}, but we omit it due to the page limit.

We can rigorously prove that checkpoints selected by CSS_{MTR} are not only necessary but also sufficient. Again, due to the page limit, we omit the proof. Since a large number of fixed-time constraints are often needed in grid workflows, the improvement on temporal verification efficiency and effectiveness by our strategy is significant [8].

6 Comparison and Discussion

According to Section 5, all checkpoints selected by CSS_{MTR} are necessary and sufficient. So, by CSS_{MTR}, there is no unnecessary and omitted temporal verification.

According to Section 2, CSS_1, CSS_2, CSS_3 and CSS_4 may select some unnecessary checkpoints and also CSS_3 and CSS_4 may ignore some necessary ones. Therefore, CSS_{MTR} is more efficient than CSS_1, CSS_2, CSS_3 and CSS_4, and also more effective than CSS_3 and CSS_4 for temporal verification.

According to [6], CSS_5 takes a_p as a checkpoint if $D(a_p) < Rcd(a_p)$. Compared to CSS_{MTR}, CSS_5 omits the situation where $M(a_p)+MTR_{WC}(a_{p-1})<Rcd(a_p)\leq D(a_p)$, i.e. CSS_5 may ignore some necessary checkpoints. CSS_6, according to [7], takes a_p as a checkpoint if $M(a_p) < Rcd(a_p)$. Compared to CSS_{MTR}, the situation is unnecessary where $M(a_p) < Rcd(a_p) \leq M(a_p) + MTR_{WC}(a_{p-1})$, i.e. CSS_6 may select some unnecessary checkpoints. CSS_7, according to [10], introduces minimum proportional WC time redundancy to a_{p-1}, denoted as $MPTR_{WC}(a_{p-1})$. Then, at a_p, CSS_7 takes it as a checkpoint if $M(a_p) + MPTR_{WC}(a_{p-1})<Rcd(a_p)$. However, according to [10], $MPTR_{WC}(a_{p-1})$ is actually part of $MTR_{WC}(a_{p-1})$. Therefore, by CSS_7, the situation is unnecessary where $M(a_p) + MPTR_{WC}(a_{p-1}) < Rcd(a_p) \leq M(a_p) + MTR_{WC}(a_{p-1})$, i.e. CSS_7 may also select some unnecessary checkpoints. In summary, we can say that CSS_{MTR} is also more effective than CSS_5, and more efficient than CSS_6 and CSS_7 for temporal verification.

We can conduct a quantitative evaluation. Again, due to the page limit, we omit it.

7 Conclusions and Future Work

Existing representative checkpoint selection strategies often select some unnecessary checkpoints and ignore some necessary ones, which consequently cause unnecessary temporal verification and omit necessary temporal verification. To overcome such shortcomings, we have proposed a new checkpoint selection strategy, named CSS_{MTR} (Minimum Time Redundancy based Checkpoint Selection Strategy). The checkpoints selected by CSS_{MTR} dynamically along grid workflow execution are not only necessary but also sufficient. Hence, the unnecessary and omitted temporal verification can be avoided, which eventually can improve the overall temporal verification efficiency and effectiveness significantly. With these contributions, we are further working on how to facilitate timed Petri-Net to reason about checkpoint selection.

Acknowledgements

We are grateful for the fruitful discussion with Professor W.M.P. van der Aalst when he visited Swinburne University in Dec. 2005. The work reported in this paper is partly supported by ARC Projects under grant No. LP0562500 and No. DP0663841.

References

1. W.M.P. van der Aalst. Workflow Verification: Finding Control-Flow Errors using Petri-net based Techniques. LNCS 1806, 161-183, 2000.
2. D.Abramson, J.Kommineni, J.L.McGregor and J.Katzfey. An Atmospheric Sciences Workflow and its Implementation with Web Services. LNCS 3036, 164-173, 2004.
3. C.Bussler. Workflow Instance Scheduling with Project Management Tools. In Proc. of the 9th Workshop on Database and Expert Systems Applications (DEXA'98), IEEE CS Press, 753-758, Vienna, Austria, Aug. 1998.
4. R.Buyya, D.Abramson and S.Venugopal. The Grid Economy. The Proceedings of The IEEE, 93(3), 698-714, 2005.
5. D.Cybok. A Grid Workflow Infrastructure. Concurrency and Computation: Practice and Experience, 2005, to appear.
6. J.Chen, Y.Yang and T.Y.Chen. Dynamic Verification of Temporal Constraints on-the-fly for Workflow Systems. In Proc. of the 11th Asia-Pacific Software Engineering Conference (APSEC2004), IEEE CS Press, 30-37, Busan, Korea, Nov./Dec. 2004.
7. J.Chen and Y.Yang. An Activity Completion Duration based Checkpoint Selection Strategy for Dynamic Verification of Fixed-time Constraints in Grid Workflow Systems. LNI, P-69, 296-310, 2005.
8. J.Chen and Y.Yang. Necessary and Sufficient Checkpoint Selection in Grid Workflow Systems. Technical Report, Faculty of ICT, Swinburne University of Technology, May, 2006, http://www.it.swin.edu.au/personal/yyang/papers/2006TR-JChen-1.pdf
9. J.Chen and Y.Yang. Multiple States based Temporal Consistency for Dynamic Verification of Fixed-time Constraints in Grid Workflow Systems. Concurrency and Computation: Practice and Experience, 2006, to appear.
10. J.Chen and Y.Yang. A Minimum Proportional Time Redundancy based Checkpoint Selection Strategy for Dynamic Verification of Fixed-time Constraints in Grid Workflow Systems. In Proc. of the 12th Asia Pacific Software Engineering Conference. (APSEC2005), IEEE CS Press, 299-306, Taiwan, Dec. 2005.
11. E.Deelman, J.Blythe, Y.Gil, C.Kesselman, G.Mehta and K.Vahi. Mapping Abstract Complex Workflows onto Grid Environments. Journal of Grid Computing, 1(1), 9-23, 2003.
12. J.Eder, E.Panagos and M.Rabinovich. Time Constraints in Workflow Systems. LNCS 1626, 286-300, 1999.
13. O.Marjanovic and M.E.Orlowska. On Modeling and Verification of Temporal Constraints in Production Workflows. Knowledge and Information Systems, 1(2), 157-192, 1999.
14. D.R.Simpson, N.Kelly, P.V.Jithesh, P.Donachy, T.J.Harmer, R.H.Perrott, J.Johnston, P.Kerr, M.McCurley and S.McKee. GeneGrid: A Practical Workflow Implementation for a Grid Based Virtual Bioinformatics Laboratory. In Proc. of the UK e-Science All Hands Meeting 2004 (AHM04), 547-554, Sept. 2004.
15. H.Zhuge, T.Cheung and H.Pung. A Timed Workflow Process Model. The Journal of Systems and Software, 55(3), 231-243, 2001.

Faulty EPCs in the SAP Reference Model

J. Mendling[1], M. Moser[1], G. Neumann[1], H.M.W. Verbeek[2], B.F. van Dongen[2], and W.M.P. van der Aalst[2]

[1] Vienna University of Economics and Business Administration
Augasse 2-6, 1090 Vienna, Austria
{jan.mendling, h9950347, neumann}@wu-wien.ac.at
[2] Eindhoven University of Technology
P.O. Box 513, 5600 MB Eindhoven, The Netherlands
{h.m.w.verbeek, b.f.v.dongen, w.m.p.v.d.aalst}@tm.tue.nl

Abstract. Little is known about error probability in enterprise models as they are usually kept private. The *SAP reference model* is a publically available model that contains more than 600 non-trivial process models expressed in terms of *Event-driven Process Chains* (EPCs). We have automatically translated these EPCs into YAWL models and analyzed these models using WofYAWL, a verification tool based on Petri nets, in order to acquire knowledge about errors in large enterprise models. We discovered that *at least 34 of these EPCs contain errors* (i.e., at least 5.6% is flawed) and analyzed which parts of the SAP reference model contain most errors. This systematic analysis of the SAP reference model illustrates the need for verification tools such as WofYAWL.

1 Introduction

There has been extensive work on formal foundations of conceptual modeling and respective languages. However, little quantitative research has been reported on the actual use of conceptual modeling [3]. Moreover, literature typically discusses and analyses languages rather than evaluating enterprise models at a larger scale (i.e., beyond "toy examples"). A fundamental problem in this context is that large enterprise models are in general not accessible for research as they represent valuable company knowledge that enterprises do not want to reveal. One case of a model that is, at least partially, publicly available is the SAP reference model. It has been described in [2,8] and is referred to in many research papers. The extensive database of this reference model contains almost 10,000 sub-models, most of them EPC business process models [7]. Fig. 1 shows the EPC model for "Certificate Creation" as an example of one of these models. The SAP reference model was meant to be used as a documentation for SAP's ERP system. It reflects Version 4.6 of SAP R/3 which was marketed in 2000. Building on recently developed techniques to verify the formal correctness of EPC models [12], we aim to acquire knowledge about how many formal modeling errors can be expected in a large repository of process models in practice, assuming that the SAP reference model can be regarded as a representative example. We will map all non-trivial EPCs in the SAP reference model onto YAWL

S. Dustdar, J.L. Fiadeiro, and A. Sheth (Eds.): BPM 2006, LNCS 4102, pp. 451–457, 2006.

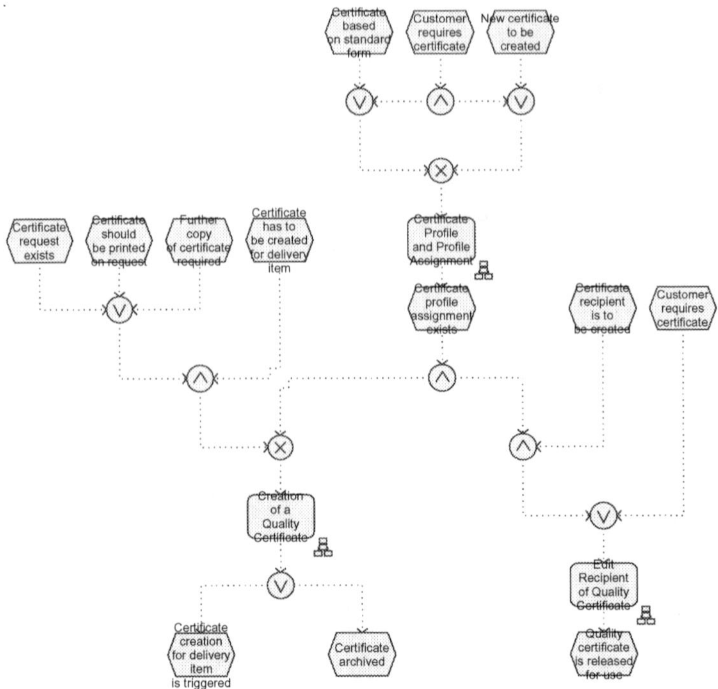

Fig. 1. One of the EPCs in the SAP reference model: the "Certificate Creation" process

models [1] and use the WofYAWL tool [12] for the verification (based on the relaxed-soundness criterion [4]). We have to stress that this analysis yields a lower bound for errors since some errors may not be discovered by this tool. Therefore, it has to be expected that there are more errors than those that we actually identify.

The remainder of this paper is organized as follows. Section 2 describes the research design. In particular, we discuss the mapping of EPCs from the SAP reference model to YAWL models, the analysis techniques employed by WofYAWL, and descriptive statistics that provide a comprehensive inventory of errors in the SAP reference model. Finally, Section 3 presents related work before Section 4 concludes with a summary of our contribution and its limitations.

2 Research Design and Results

In this section, we present the way we evaluated the SAP reference model. We use the ARIS XML export of the reference model as input to several transformation and analysis steps. In a first step, the EPC to YAWL transformation program generates a YAWL XML file for each EPC in the reference model (see Sect. 2.1). These YAWL models are then analyzed with WofYAWL that produces an XML error report of design flaws (see Sect. 2.2). Furthermore, we extract

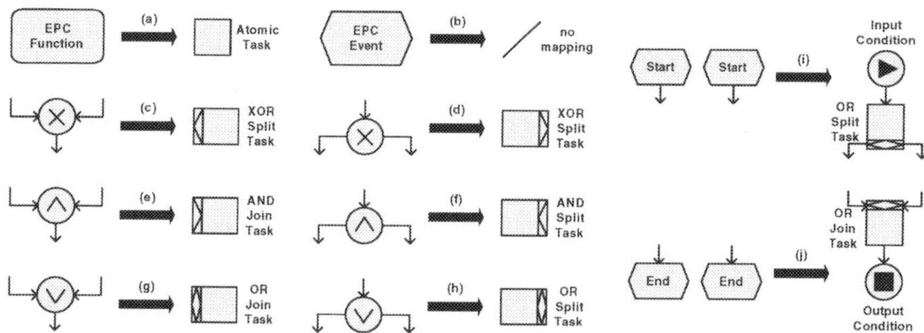

Fig. 2. Overview of the EPC to YAWL Mapping

descriptive information such as the number of elements of a certain element type and whether there are cycles for each EPC model (see Sect. 2.3).

2.1 Transformations of EPCs to YAWL

Several mappings from EPCs to Petri Nets have been proposed in order to verify formal properties, see e.g. [9] for an overview. In this paper, we use a transformation from EPCs to YAWL as defined in [10]. The advantage is that each EPC element can be directly mapped to a respective YAWL element (see Fig. 2). Even though EPCs and YAWL are very similar in this sense, there are three differences that have to be considered in the transformation: state representation, connector chains, and multiple start and end events.

EPC functions can be mapped to YAWL tasks following mapping rule (a) of Fig. 2. The first difference between EPCs and YAWL is related to *state representation*. EPC events define pre- and post-conditions of functions. They do not capture state directly. Therefore, rule (b) defines that events are not mapped to YAWL taking advantage of the fact that arcs in YAWL represent implicit conditions if they connect two tasks. In EPCs connectors are independent elements. Therefore, it is allowed to build so-called *connector chains*, i.e. paths of two or more consecutive connectors (cf. Fig. 1). In YAWL there are no connector chains since splits and joins are part of tasks. The mapping rules (c) to (h) map every connector to a dummy task with the matching join or split condition (see Fig. 2). The third difference stems from *multiple start and end events*. An EPC is allowed to have more than one start event and more than one end event. In YAWL there must be exactly one start condition and one end condition. Therefore, the mapping rules (i) and (j) generate an OR split for multiple starts and an OR join for multiple ends. Fig. 3 gives the result of applying the transformation to the "Certificate Creation" EPC of Section 1. Note that connectors are mapped onto dummy tasks. To identify these tasks they are given a unique label extracted from the internal representation of the EPC, e.g., task "and (c8z0)" corresponds to the AND-split connector following event "Customer requires certificate."

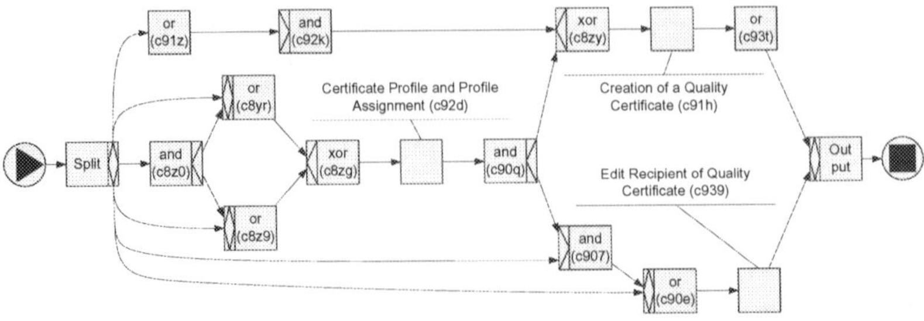

Fig. 3. YAWL model obtained by applying the mapping shown in Fig. 2 to the example

2.2 WofYAWL Analysis

After mapping the EPC onto YAWL, we can use our verification tool WofYAWL [13]. WofYAWL first maps a YAWL model onto a Petri net [11]. Fig. 4 sketches a small fragment of the Petri net that results from mapping the YAWL model of Fig. 3. The fragment only considers the dummy tasks resulting from the mapping of the top four connectors in Fig. 1. Moreover, from the initial OR-split task "Split" we only consider the arcs connected to these four dummy tasks.

The "happy smileys" in Fig. 4 are used to identify net elements that are involved in so-called "good execution paths", that is, the execution paths in the Petri net that lead from the initial state to the *desired* final state. In Fig. 4, there exist two such paths, which join at the XOR-join named "xor (c8z9)". The "sad smileys" visualize relevant parts in the Petri net that are not covered by some good execution path. WofYAWL issues respective warnings. These indicate a problem involving the top four connectors in Fig. 1. Note that the AND-split connector splits the flow into two paths that join with an XOR-join. Hence these two paths cannot be involved in a good execution. Moreover, if the AND-split connector is not allowed to occur, the two OR-joins could as well be XOR-joins. In our analysis we use *transition invariants* to avoid constructing large or even infinite state spaces [12]. Moreover, we have used existing Petri-net-based reduction rules [11] to further reduce the complexity of the models without loosing any information. For further details on this approach we refer to [12].

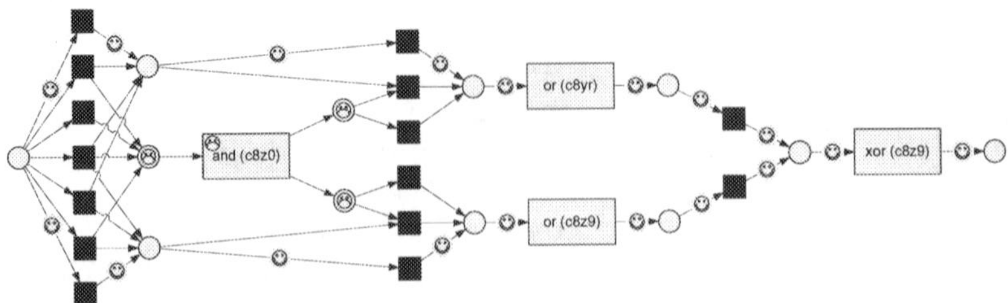

Fig. 4. Petri net fragment of the converted YAWL model

Table 1. Branches of the SAP Reference Model. The columns $E_{av.}$, $F_{av.}$, $C_{av.}$, $A_{av.}$ refer to the mean number of events, functions, connectors, and arcs.

Branch	Model	%	EPC	%	$E_{av.}$	$F_{av.}$	$C_{av.}$	$A_{av.}$	Cycle	Error	%
Asset Accounting	461	4.7%	43	7.1%	13.9	4.0	5.2	23.3	0	7	16.3%
Benefits Administration	50	0.5%	6	1.0%	9.5	3.3	5.8	19.7	3	0	0.0%
Compensation Management	122	1.2%	18	3.0%	7.6	3.4	3.3	13.7	3	1	5.6%
Customer Service	402	4.1%	41	6.8%	16.5	3.6	9.0	29.5	3	1	2.4%
Enterprise Controlling	599	6.1%	22	3.6%	14.3	10.1	6.1	32.1	0	3	13.6%
Environment, Health, Safety	102	1.0%	19	3.1%	3.5	2.7	1.2	7.0	0	0	0.0%
Financial Accounting	614	6.2%	54	8.9%	13.0	4.0	5.1	21.8	0	3	5.6%
Position Management	4	0.0%	0	0.0%	0.0	0.0	0.0	0.0	0	0	n.a.
Inventory Management	184	1.9%	3	0.5%	15.0	7.0	6.0	28.0	2	0	0.0%
Organizational Management	37	0.4%	5	0.8%	12.0	3.0	6.6	24.0	3	0	0.0%
Payroll	541	5.5%	7	1.2%	5.7	3.1	2.1	11.4	0	1	14.3%
Personnel Administration	15	0.2%	4	0.7%	7.3	1.5	4.0	12.3	0	0	0.0%
Personnel Development	60	0.6%	10	1.7%	8.7	2.5	4.4	15.6	3	1	10.0%
Personnel Time Management	87	0.9%	12	2.0%	10.8	3.0	5.3	19.5	1	2	16.7%
Plant Maintenance	399	4.1%	35	5.8%	20.5	4.2	11.4	37.8	9	1	2.9%
Procurement	444	4.5%	37	6.1%	6.7	3.5	2.7	12.4	0	2	5.4%
Product Data Management	366	3.7%	26	4.3%	4.5	5.4	2.2	13.7	0	0	0.0%
Production	296	3.0%	17	2.8%	8.8	3.0	2.9	13.7	0	1	5.9%
Production Planning	194	2.0%	17	2.8%	5.7	2.9	3.0	11.5	0	0	0.0%
Project Management	347	3.5%	36	6.0%	8.5	3.8	2.2	14.0	0	0	0.0%
Quality Management	209	2.1%	20	3.3%	20.5	3.8	11.7	37.8	1	1	5.0%
Real Estate Management	169	1.7%	6	1.0%	12.7	6.5	7.3	27.0	1	1	16.7%
Recruitment	56	0.6%	9	1.5%	7.4	2.6	4.1	13.8	3	0	0.0%
Retail	842	8.6%	1	0.2%	7.0	5.0	2.0	11.0	0	0	0.0%
Revenue & Cost Controlling	568	5.8%	19	3.1%	16.5	10.2	7.9	36.0	1	1	5.3%
Sales & Distribution	703	7.1%	76	12.6%	10.6	3.1	4.3	16.6	0	1	1.3%
Training & Event Management	95	1.0%	12	2.0%	13.0	2.7	6.2	22.2	0	1	8.3%
Travel Management	116	1.2%	1	0.2%	24.0	7.0	16.0	48.0	0	0	0.0%
Treasury	1761	17.9%	48	7.9%	10.5	3.5	4.5	18.1	0	6	12.5%
All 29 Branches	9844	100%	604	100%	11.5	4.0	5.2	20.8	33	34	5.6%

2.3 Descriptive Statistics

The sample of the SAP reference model that was available for this research contains 9844 models, but only a fraction of them represent proper EPCs with at least one start event and one function. There are 604 of such process models as listed in the column *EPC*. Using the transformations and the WofYAWL tool described in Sect. 2, we discovered that at least 34 models have errors (5.6% of 604 analyzed EPCs). Table 1 summarizes the SAP reference model subdivided into its 29 branches. It can be seen that the number of EPC models varies substantially (from none in Position Management to 76 in Sales & Distribution). Furthermore, the EPCs are of different size indicated by the mean number of events, functions, connectors, and arcs in columns $E_{av.}$, $F_{av.}$, $C_{av.}$, $A_{av.}$ respectively. The column *Cycle* states how many EPCs contain cycles, and *Error* for how many models WofYAWL reports an error.

3 Related Research

Work on the verification of process models can roughly be put into three categories: *verification of formal models*, i.e. the model with formal executable semantics is correct or not; *verification of informal models*, i.e. defining subclasses of informal models that are mapped onto formal models, the model is correct or not; and *verification by design*, i.e. the modeling language does not allow for syntactical errors. Examples are block structured models. For related work for each category we refer to [5]. Besides these categories, there are some verification approaches that are a combination of others. For example [6] involves the process designer in the verification process. Therefore, this approach is not applicable for the automatic verification of the entire SAP reference model. The approach we use based on WofYAWL has been introduced in [13]. Yet, it is not complete as there may be errors left undetected. Still, this paper uniquely combines formal error detection with a large set of real-world process models. This way, we have identified a lower bound of 5.6% for errors in the SAP reference model.

4 Contributions and Limitations

This paper provides a lower bound of 5.6% for the number of faulty EPCs in the SAP reference model. Our automatic verification approach is based on a mapping from EPCs to YAWL and on the utilization of the WofYAWL tool. As far as we know, this is the first systematic analysis of the EPCs in the SAP reference model. Yet, our approach still has some limitations: WofYAWL does not find all errors and the SAP reference model is only one specific case of an enterprise model. Therefore, we aim to improve the automatic detection of errors. Moreover, a analysis of further large enterprise models is needed to better understand why and when modelers introduce errors.

References

1. W.M.P. van der Aalst and A.H.M. ter Hofstede. YAWL: Yet Another Workflow Language. *Information Systems*, 30(4):245–275, 2005.
2. T. Curran and G. Keller A. Ladd. *SAP R/3 Business Blueprint: Understanding the Business Process Reference Model.* Enterprise Resource Planning Series. Prentice Hall PTR, Upper Saddle River, 1997.
3. Islay Davies, Peter Green, Michael Rosemann, Marta Indulska, and Stan Gallo. How do practitioners use conceptual modeling in practice? *Data & Knowledge Engineering*, In Press, 2006.
4. J. Dehnert and P. Rittgen. Relaxed Soundness of Business Processes. In K.R. Dittrich, A. Geppert, and M.C. Norrie, editors, *Proceedings of CAiSE 2001*, volume 2068 of *LNCS*, pages 157–170. Springer-Verlag, Berlin, 2001.
5. B.F. van Dongen and M.H. Jansen-Vullers. EPC Verification in the ARIS for MySAP reference model database. BETA Working Paper WP 142, Eindhoven University of Technology, 2005.
6. B.F. van Dongen, H.M.W. Verbeek, and W.M.P. van der Aalst. Verification of EPCs: Using reduction rules and Petri nets. In *Conference on Advanced Information Systems Engineering (CAiSE 2005)*, volume 3520 of *LNCS*, pages 372–386. Springer-Verlag, Berlin, 2005.
7. G. Keller, M. Nüttgens, and A.W. Scheer. Semantische Processmodellierung auf der Grundlage Ereignisgesteuerter Processketten (EPK). Veröffentlichungen des Instituts für Wirtschaftsinformatik, Heft 89 (in German), Saarbrücken, 1992.

8. G. Keller and T. Teufel. *SAP(R) R/3 Process Oriented Implementation: Iterative Process Prototyping.* Addison-Wesley, 1998.
9. E. Kindler. On the Semantics of EPCs: Resolving the Vicious Circle. *Data and Knowledge Engineering*, 56(1):23–40, 2006.
10. J. Mendling, J. Recker, M. Rosemann, and W.M.P. van der Aalst. Generating Correct EPCs from Configured C-EPCs. In *Proceedings of the 21th Annual ACM Symposium on Applied Computing (SAC 2006).* ACM Press, 2006.
11. T. Murata. Petri nets: Properties, analysis and applications. *Proceedings of the IEEE*, 77(4):541–580, April 1989.
12. H.M.W. Verbeek and W.M.P. van der Aalst. On the verification of EPCs using T-invariants. BPM Center Report BPM-06-05, BPMcenter.org, 2006.
13. H.M.W. Verbeek, W.M.P. van der Aalst, and A.H.M. ter Hofstede. Verifying workflows with cancellation regions and OR-joins: An approach based on invariants. BETA Working Paper WP 156, Eindhoven University of Technology, 2006.

A Hybrid Approach for Generating Compatible WS-BPEL Partner Processes

Simon Moser[1], Axel Martens[2], Marc Häbich[1,3], and Jutta Mülle[3]

[1] IBM Böblingen Lab, Business Process Solutions,
Böblingen, Germany
smoser@de.ibm.com
[2] IBM TJ Watson Center, Component Systems Group,
Hawthorne (NY), USA
amarten@us.ibm.com
[3] University of Karlsruhe, Information Systems Group,
Karlsruhe, Germany
muelle@ipd.uka.de

Abstract. The *Business Process Execution Language for Web Services* provides an technology to aggregate encapsulated functionalities for defining high-value Web services. For a distributed application in a B2B interaction, the partners simply need to expose their behavior as BPEL processes and compose them. Still, modeling and composing BPEL processes can be complex and error-prone. With formal methods like Petri nets, it is possible to analyze crucial properties (e.g. compatibility) effectively. In this paper, we present a method that automatically generates compatible partner BPEL processes for a given BPEL processes. Our hybrid approach makes use of formal methods, but also incorporates the structure of the original BPEL process model, such that the generated partner process is easier to understand and manage.

Keywords: Business Process Modeling, Web Service, WS-BPEL, Behavioral Compatibility, Tool based Verification, Petri nets.

1 Introduction

The *Business Process Execution Language for Web Services* BPEL4WS [7] is becoming the standard for modeling Web Service based business processes. A BPEL process implements one Web Service by specifying its interactions with other Web Services (which might be BPEL processes, too). BPEL processes consist of two kinds of activities: *Basic activities* to communicate to the outside, to manipulate data or to interfere with the control flow and *structured activities* to aggregate other activities, i. e. to build the control structures of the process.

For two BPEL processes to interact, interfaces with operations and message types have to be defined separately in WSDL [2] and included into a *partner link* which specifies the interfaces of any given set of interacting BPEL processes. In the online shop example (Figure 1), the client process provides two interfaces: the StartUp Interface towards the initiating component and the Order Client Interface

S. Dustdar, J.L. Fiadeiro, and A. Sheth (Eds.): BPM 2006, LNCS 4102, pp. 458–464, 2006.

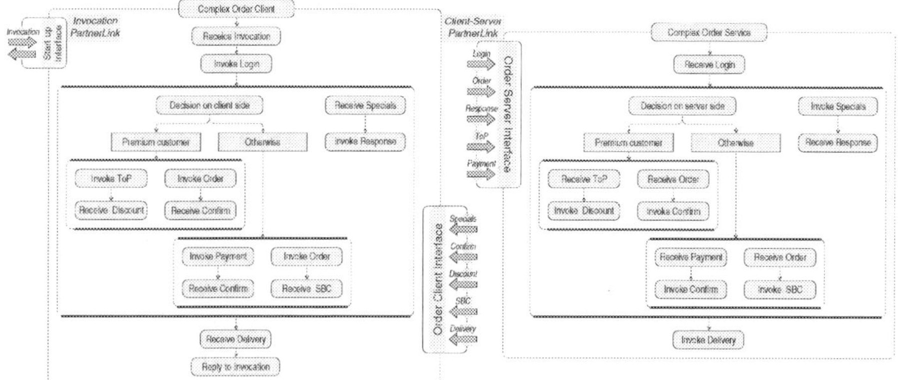

Fig. 1. Online shop example – incompatible BPEL processes of client and server

towards the shop's service. Moreover, the client requires the online shop's Web service to provide the Order Server Interface. Obviously, two BPEL processes can only be composed iff the provided interface of each process equals the required interface of the other. But this *syntactic compatibility* between the interfaces is not sufficient for the successful interaction of two BPEL processes.

An additional requirement – called *behavioral compatibility* [6] – is needed to ensure successful composition. In our example, the client process transmits the login data and makes a decision whether to act as a premium customer or as a regular customer, but its decision is not synchronized with that of the server process, although it is crucial to the further interaction. In case the client acts as a premium customer, it sends its order along with its terms of payment (ToP), and awaits discount information and confirmation. However, the server process might treat him like a regular customer because his last order was too long ago. In that case, the server process will acknowledge the order with the standard business conditions (SBC) and await payment. The concurrent conversation (Invoke Specials) happens regardless of either party's decision. In the end, both processes are waiting and neither can continue on its own - a classic *deadlock* situation. Obviously, the behavior of these two BPEL processes is not compatible.

Handing out an abstract process model to the partner so he can model his process accordingly is one solution to ensure behavioral compatibility, cf. [6]. However, modeling is time consuming and error-prone, and the partner might need many attempts to build a process that is actually compatible. A more elegant solution is to create a template of the partner's process (PP for short) out of the original process (OP) and to hand out this template instead . Thus, the partner only needs to refine the template according to his needs while behavioral compatibility is guaranteed. Similar ideas have been proposed for example in [4]. In this article, we will present a new approach to automatically generating guaranteed compatible BPEL PP in a hybrid approach, which combines the structural and behavioral approaches described in the following.

2 Structural Approach

This approach uses the interaction patterns and control structures defined in BPEL processes. It parses the structure of the OP and reflects it using the *duality* between two BPEL activities (Table 1). The partner generation aims to deliver a process template that interacts correctly with the OP, and that has to be further refined by the partner. Hence, the generation focusses on communicating and structuring activities only, while internal activities of the OP (wait, assign, empty, ...) are ignored/mapped to empty. Communication between BPEL processes is either *asynchronous* or *synchronous*, in which case the activity that calls is blocked until a response has been sent. Structured activities define the *control flow* of a BPEL process. Generally, sequential activities in one process can be mapped to sequential execution within the other. Sometimes the blocking in synchronous communication requires multiple parallel threads in the generated PP (cf. [3]). So the most general approach is to map each sequence into a flow and to express the precedence constraints with flow links. Parallel execution in one process can always be mapped to parallel execution within the other.

Mapping *choices* is more complicated. An *externally* determined choice within the OP (pick) can be mapped into an *internal* choice of the PP (switch), where each case branch exchanges messages w. r. t. the communication style – although the mapping of onAlarm branches is not clear. The mapping of a switch activity into pick activity, however, is not possible in general, because there might be no distinguished messages sent in the case branches at all. Mapping instead a switch into a switch might lead to unsynchronized decisions of both BPEL processes, cf. Figure 1. A switch without communicating activities is just an internal activity. If we see a while activity as a kind of switch that loops in one case and does nothing in the otherwise case, the same problems apply to while (cf. [3]).

The client process shown in Figure 1 was generated using this approach. Since the approach is based on static mapping rules, it is very fast, and the generated

Table 1. Conceptual dualities between BPEL activities

Basic process activity	*partner activity*
receive with/without reply	synchronous/asynchronous invoke
synchronous/asynchronous invoke	receive with/without reply
wait, assign, empty, ...	empty or ignored
Structured process activity	*partner activity*
sequence	sequence (flow)
flow	flow (sequence)
pick	switch
onMessage with/without reply	case branch with sync/async invoke
onAlarm	N/A
switch	pick, switch or empty
while	while
scope	scope
handler	N/A

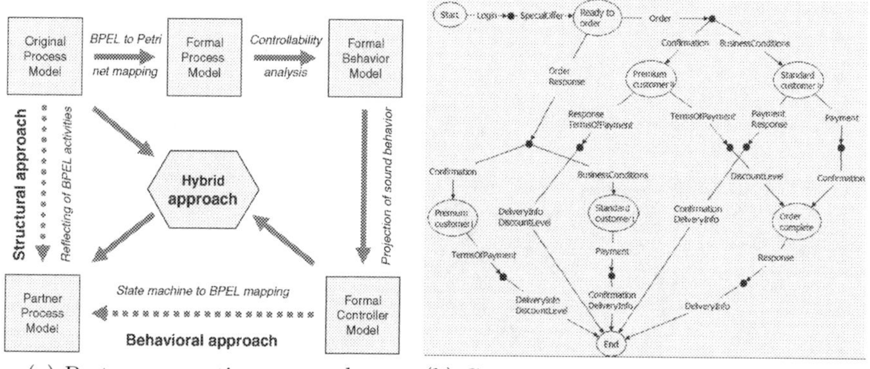

(a) Partner generation approaches (b) Communication graph of server process

Fig. 2. WOMBAT4WS's formal background

PP's structure is as simple (or complex) as the OP. In general, this makes the PP easily manageable/understandable to humans. These are two major advantages. But a major drawback is that compatibility is not guaranteed if internal decisions within the OP influence the communication between the parties. Moreover, the approach does not cover timers, handlers and complex flow link structures.

3 Behavioral Approach

The behavioral approach uses a formal mathematical analysis of the OP model. It consists of four steps, as shown in Figure 2(a). In the first step, the BPEL OP is transformed into a formal Petri Net representation, see also [5,1,8]. To keep the relation to the BPEL process, all Petri net elements are grouped into *block structures*, each representing exactly one element of the process. The resulting formal process model is called *BPEL-annotated Petri net* (BPN) [6].

However, the BPN is intermediary: In the second step, the communication behavior of the BPN is analyzed. Martens [1] presents an algorithm for analyzing the controllability of a BPEL process that generates a *communication graph* of the BPN model. This graph is the external, i. e. the partners', view on the process. Figure 2(b) shows a subset of the communication graph of the server process from the initial example. Formally, it is a state machine with two different kinds of states. A *visible* state (drawn as a white ellipse) refers to reachable states of the BPN in which input messages are expected. Each outgoing edge of such a state is labeled with a message which the BPN is able to receive in this state. A *hidden* state (drawn as a filled circle) is of intermediary nature. Each outgoing edge is labeled with a message the BPN can send in response to the consumed input.

With all possible sequences of input/output messages of the OP, the third step eliminates those sequences that may produce unwanted situations like deadlocks. The described behavior of the initial client process, for example, is one such communication sequence. The projection yields a sub-graph that contains only sound communication sequences and that represents the controller model for

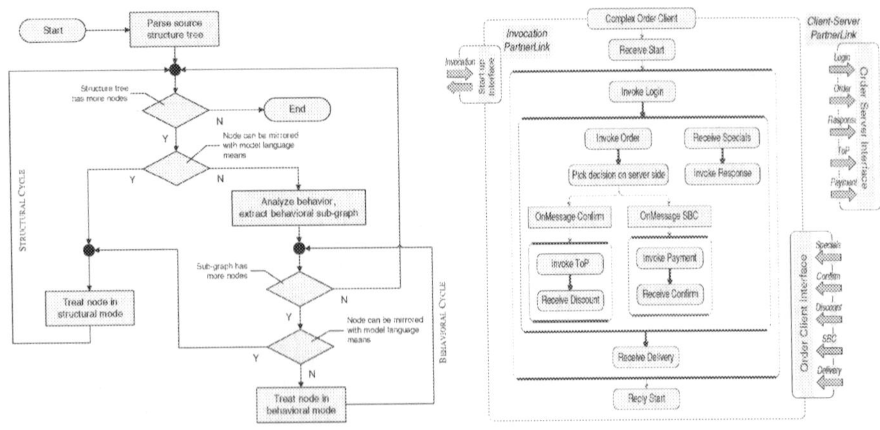

(a) The Hybrid Algorithm (b) Generated compatible client processes

Fig. 3. Hybrid approach for generating behaviorally compatible partner processes

the BPEL OP. Figure 2(b) shows that sub-graph for the server process of the online shop example. The controller model is transformed into the BPEL PP model, by mapping each edge to a communicating BPEL activity while the control flow is built around them w. r. t. the causal order [3]. In contrast to the structural approach, the behavioral method has been proven to produce a behaviorally compatible PP, if there is one possible at all. Still, the main drawback of this method is that it is computationally expensive and will actually consider all possible sequences of communication activities, e. g. for 12 concurrent communication activities in the OP, there are $12! = 47,900,1600$ possibilities to order them. Hence, the method will often yield a PP that is too complex and rather hard for the partner to refine, as Figure 2(b) shows. The generation of the communication graph alone is exponential w. r. t. the size of the OP (cf. [1]).

4 Hybrid Approach

In isolation, both approach have strengths but also drawbacks. The *hybrid approach* combines their advantages without inheriting their deficits: it uses the structural approach *whenever possible*, to make the transformation fast and the result less complex, and the behavioral approach *whenever necessary*, to guarantee behavioral compatibility. The approach combines the hierarchical, tree-like structure gained by parsing the OP into a *structure tree* (so structured activities form intermediate nodes and basic activities form leaf nodes) with the formal controller model of the OP gained with the behavioral approach.

The hybrid algorithm shown in Figure 3(a) always starts in the structural mode (Structural Cycle): It parses the structure tree as defined by the OP. Then, it enters a loop visiting all nodes of that tree. In the so-called *mirror decision*, it decides for each node in the structure tree whether it can be mirrored with BPEL means. If this is true, then on the basis of the conceptual dualities, a corresponding BPEL activity for the current node is generated, named and inserted into the result structure tree. If it is false, i. e. if the activity cannot be reflected by structural means, then the node has to be decomposed into sub-structures, i. e. the behavior of the current activity is analyzed by zooming into it and dissecting it into a sub-tree of connected sub-activities. Now, in the BEHAVIORAL CYCLE, each node of that sub-graph is classified in a decision: If the activity can be reflected with structural means, is handed over to the structural cycle. Else, it is treated in turn according to the formal controller model. Once the sub-graph has been processed completely, the algorithm loops back to the initial *mirror decision* to continue with the next ordinary node. The client process shown in Figure 3(b) was generated using the hybrid approach.

In short, whenever a pattern occurs that cannot be transformed by simply reflecting it, e. g. the internal Decision on Server side (cf. Figure 1), the algorithm switches into behavioral mode to extract information about the pattern's behavior from the communication graph and generates *receive* or *pick*, and *reply* or *invoke* activities for all messages in that sub-graph. Finally, it connects these generated activities by control flow links and/or embeds them into structured activities. Since the structure tree may impose different operation modes, the algorithm will switch back and forth between the two modes depending on the patterns it encounters. For more details see [3].

5 Conclusion

In this paper, a method to automatically generate compatible BPEL partner processes was presented. This method had to satisfy three major requirements: (i) the generated PP had to be a valid BPEL process, (ii) it had to be behaviorally compatible to the OP, and (iii) it had to be sufficiently compact and simple enough to be understood and refined by a human process modeler. Neither a pure structural approach, nor a pure behavioral approach meet those requirements completely. On detailed examination of the two approaches, a third, *hybrid approach*, was developed, which coupled the advantages while overcoming their drawbacks. The hybrid approach connects the structural process elements, as defined by BPEL, with the formal mathematical analysis result (represented by the communication graph). As demonstrated in this paper, the hybrid approach couples behavioral compatibility with human readability and manipulability. A different solution to overcome behavioral incompatibility between two BPEL process models is trying to generate a third one which acts as an *adapter* between those two. This is the topic of a currently conducted research project.

References

1. A.Martens. Analyzing Web Service based Business Processes. In Maura Cerioli, editor, *Proc. of FASE'05*, LNCS 3442, Edinburgh, Scotland, April 2005. Springer.
2. E. Christensen, F. Curbera, G. Meredith, and S. Weerawarana. *WSDL – Web Services Description Language.* W3C, Standard, Version 1.1, March 2001.

3. M. Häbich. Reverse Transformation of Petri Net-Based Communication Graphs to BPEL4WS in Distributed Web Service Environments. Master's thesis, 2005.
4. S. Haddad, T. Melliti, P. Moreaux, and S. Rampacek. Modelling Web Services Interoperability. In *Proc. of ICEIS04*, 2004.
5. R. Hamadi and B. Benatallah. A Petri Net based Model for Web Service Composition. In *Proc. of ADC 2003*. Australian Computer Society, Inc., 2003.
6. A. Martens, S. Moser, A. Gerhardt, and K. Funk. Analyzing Compatibility of BPEL Processes. February 2006.
7. T.Andrews, F.Curbera, H.Dholakia, Y.Goland, J.Klein, F.Leymann, K.Liu, D.Roller, D.Smith, S.Thatte, I.Trickovic, and S.Weerawarana. *BPEL4WS – Business Process Execution Language for Web Services*. Version 1.1, July 2002.
8. W.M.P. van der Aalst. Modeling and Analyzing Interorganizational Workflows. In *Proc. of CSD'98*. IEEE Computer Society Press, 1998.

Towards a Task-Oriented, Policy-Driven Business Requirements Specification for Web Services

Stephen Gorton and Stephan Reiff-Marganiec

Department of Computer Science, University of Leicester
University Road, Leicester LE1 7RH, UK
{smg24, srm13}@le.ac.uk

Abstract. Dynamic assembly of complex software is possible through automated composition of web services. Coordination scripts identify and orchestrate a number of services to fulfil a user or business goal. There exists a need for expressing high level business requirements in such a way that is accessible by businesses. Current solutions fail to include specifications at the appropriate level of abstraction. Our approach defines a graphical notation to depict a business goal in terms of objectives, which are refined by tasks. The specifics of each task as well as overarching business constraints are expressed by policies.

1 Motivation

The advent of Service-oriented Architecture (SoA) makes software "on demand" a distinct possibility. The relatively recent introduction of web services means that automated composition of services can be achieved. Solutions already exist for service discovery and description, though these may be far from complete. Composition solutions also exist, with the Business Process Execution Language (BPEL[1]) the de facto standard.

Attempts to bridge the gap between the business domain and the service domain are often made by expressing business logic through composition or other technologies, but there is a distinct lack of tools which can express precise requirements specifications at the business level. While existing solutions tackle aspects such as functionality and sequencing of business activities, none are complete to encompass all information required at the business level.

The problem that we address in this paper regards business process modelling and analysis, and our goal is to develop a modelling language to accurately express a complete set of business requirements, through the use of policies, in terms of web service usage. One particular aspect is that the notation should be suitable for use by business users (not IT experts) and that it should be simple to use to encourage changes when demand arises.

[1] http://www-106.ibm.com/developerworks/webservices/library/ws-bpel/

S. Dustdar, J.L. Fiadeiro, and A. Sheth (Eds.): BPM 2006, LNCS 4102, pp. 465–470, 2006.

2 Background

Service-oriented Architecture, and its implementation as Web Services, make the vision of just-in-time assembly of applications a distinct possibility. SoA refers to a system architecture where a number of independent services can be composed at runtime into larger applications in order to respond to immediate business needs or goals. For details about SoA we refer to Alonso et al. [1]. The automatic composition (i.e. identifying plans for composing services such that they fulfil some desirable goal) and ways for end-users to express these goals (requirements) are two aspects that still must be addressed. In this paper we concentrate on the latter.

We consider the flow of the business process and the description of the business policies as parts of the requirements specification. Task flow is usually captured in a way that describes the operative nature of the business by using task maps or work flow languages. Task flow is obtained through business modelling as this requires a certain understanding of the business processes involved. Existing composition technologies such as BPEL can express sequence logic in service usage, but they are aimed at the IT level. The Business Process Modeling Notation (BPMN) [2] addresses the problem of expressing business requirements. However, the BPMN specification [2] states that it was "constrained to support only the concepts of modelling that are applicable to business processes", thus not supporting organisational structures and resources, functional breakdowns, data and informational models, strategy and business rules. We believe that BPMN has too many shortcomings to be considered as a complete business solution for expressing business requirements for a web service-based application. In particular, we note that BPMN does not support the expression of non-functional business requirements.

Business policies on the other hand express rules that are of a more generic nature; often they do not apply to a specific business process but rather to specific tasks or the way that the business operates overall. Policies are descriptive in their nature. Policy description languages [3] have been used to express quality of service constraints or access control, that is to describe very low level properties of systems. The APPEL policy language [4] has been defined to express end-user rules in telecommunications systems and we are extending this in our ongoing work to interact with the task maps discussed in this paper.

Our approach builds on the conceptual ideas of BPMN by using a simpler graphical notation, but adding policies to express precise business requirements.

3 Overview of Approach

Our graphical notation is intended to act as a modelling agent for businesses who choose to use web services. The process of requirements elicitation begins with the specification of the business goal. This goal is broken down into objectives that are fulfilled by tasks, which represent atomic business activities. The goal is then expressed in terms of a task map and policies. Now there exists an accurate model for the business requirements.

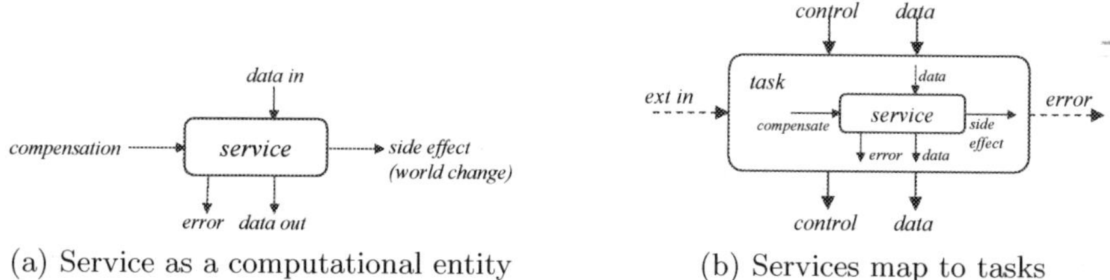

(a) Service as a computational entity

(b) Services map to tasks

Fig. 1. Services

The task map (and policies) are read by a parsing engine, which searches Internet directories for web services that satisfy the requirements. Once all services have been located, their descriptions are returned. A coordination engine generates a coordination script according to the descriptions and flows in the task map.

To define the goal, the business must define the objectives that would satisfy it and the tasks required to satisfy each objective, along with the execution sequences of the tasks. A business goal is likely to be defined at a very high level and thus cannot be easily formalised. Functionality is the core requirement for each task. Functionality can usually be more accurately expressed at the atomic task level, whereas non-functional requirements may be expressed at the composite task level, such that they can propagate through to any subtask. Our approach uses policies to encode rules describing the operation of the business as well as the constraints that apply to certain tasks.

A service is a computational entity that maps input data to output data, respects certain non-functional properties, might change a world condition and has a compensation action (e.g. undo as in [5]). In Fig. 1(a), we see how a service is graphically represented, and in Fig. 1(b) how a service maps to a task (or composite task). Note that the service may be of a composite nature (i.e. composed of other services).

4 Graphical Modelling Constructs

A task is a business activity that contributes to an objective and thus the wider business goal. Each task fulfils a functional requirement. Each task must have a control input and a control output. It has external inputs representing a policy that affects this particular task. Once control has reached a task's input, the task's triggers are activated. On completion of the task, the control leaves through its output channel. Composite tasks are task sub-maps, enabling the designers to separate concerns over aspects of the business goal.

A flow is a sequence of entities (tasks or operators) in the task map and can either be a control flow or a data flow. All tasks inside a task map are subject to policies that are centrally specified by the consuming business or governing law that either restrict the service selection or change the shape of the task map. An example of the former is that a corporate policy may state that the use of

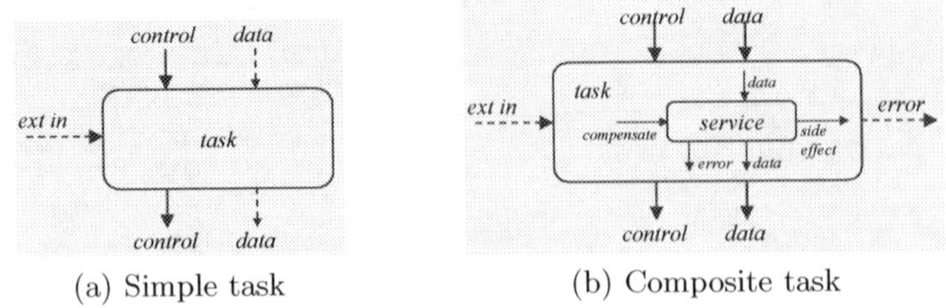

(a) Simple task (b) Composite task

Fig. 2. Tasks

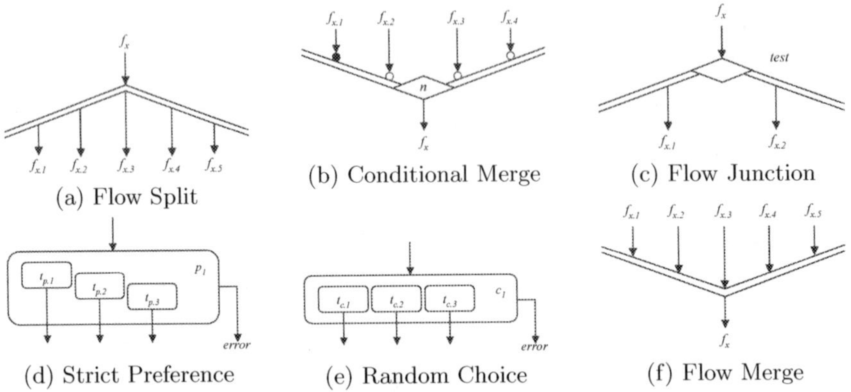

(a) Flow Split (b) Conditional Merge (c) Flow Junction (d) Strict Preference (e) Random Choice (f) Flow Merge

Fig. 3. Operators

a direct competitor's services is forbidden. An example of the latter is a policy that requires the obtaining of at least 3 quotes before a purchase can be made. Note that data and control flow can be independent and we can have partial data flows.

In addition to tasks and flows, which can express simple sequencing, we define operators that are functions on control flows. These further enable a business to accurately model their business goal.

Flow Split. The flow split operator takes a control flow input and produces a set of control flow outputs. In Fig. 3, the operator is pictured with one input and five output flows. When the active control flow reaches the operator, control is distributed amongst the outgoing flows such that each flow progresses simultaneously. For example, in a typical customer-supplier-warehouse example, a product dispatch may involve simultaneously notifying the customer of the dispatch whilst ordering a stock replacement.

Conditional Merge. The conditional merge operator takes a set of active input control flows and, subject to business-defined constraints, merges them with synchronisation to a single output flow. We allow to specify mandatory and optional flows (the filled or empty circles in the graphical notation). Also, the notation allows to specify the number of flows that must reach the operator before proceeding. For example, when looking for airline ticket quotes, one might request quotes from three suppliers, including the preferred supplier. Before booking, we might say that we must have a quote from the preferred supplier, plus one more.

Flow Junction. A flow junction operator diverts the control flow down one of two possible output routes according to a binary test.

Strict Preference. A strict preference operator attempts to execute a series of tasks in a defined order, progressing when one of the tasks is completed. The task with highest priority is attempted first. Each task in the operator specifies its own output flow which is followed when its parent task is completed.

Random Choice. Choice is similar to preference, but without priorities attached to included tasks. When control reaches this operator, all tasks may be attempted simultaneously. When a first task reaches a commit stage all others are cancelled.

Flow Merge. Flow merge is an operator that takes a set of control flow inputs and maps to a single output flow. In order to preserve synchronisation, we say that only one flow of the incoming set must be active, with all others inactive. This may be the result of a prior junction, preference or choice operator.

5 Evaluation

Our approach has been to simplify the requirements specification process for non-IT experts working in the business domain. Despite the existence of other methods, we believe that our method has the following advantages when applied at the business level:

- *Expressiveness:* Our language is able to express as many or as few requirements as is deemed necessary by the business. Task maps are an easy method to understand and, with the aid of a wizard, policies are easy to construct. Despite being at a higher level of abstraction, the task map can be automatically mapped into service coordination scripts. We also include operators in our notation that are non-existent in current notations, e.g. preference, thus increasing the expressiveness for end users.
- *No Binding:* All tasks are expressed without the knowledge of services that are available. The job of matching services to tasks is performed automatically by a search engine, based on ontologies and richer semantic descriptions of web services, which is out of the scope of this paper (there is active research in this area which has led to some preliminary results; most ideas are centred around planning algorithms).
- *Change:* If some aspect of the business goal needs changing to cater for a new or changed business requirement, it can be done with relative ease by altering the task map or underlying policies. The service coordination script is generated automatically, which is subject to any changes made to the specification.
- *Technology Compatibility:* Though not an immediate aspect of business versatility, our solution is able to take advantage of current solutions that exist, e.g. BPEL as the coordination script. In this respect, a business always has the option of altering their executable coordination script before proceeding.

- *Composition Views:* We add that our solution can generate different views that are customized to different stakeholders. In particular, a project manager may be more interested in (composite) task requirements whereas the IT director may be more interested in the global or business-wide constraints. Further low level views include control flow views and data flow views.
- *Workflows:* Our notation is able to support many of the workflow patterns as described in [6].

The conciseness of this paper does not allow to present details on the issues of cancellation, negotiation and how standard workflow patterns are supported.

6 Conclusions and Further Work

We have presented a notation for describing business requirements at an abstract level. A business goal is defined in terms of objectives which are further refined by tasks. Tasks are organised into a task map. Policies define complete requirements and specifications for tasks, and are more generic in that they can be used throughout the task map, providing information to many parts of a business goal, and even across multiple goals. We firmly believe that this solution is able to fill the gap between service levels and business levels.

Our further work includes refinement of the ideas presented on policies, based on the APPEL policy language [4]. We also propose that a workbench be designed to enable designing of task maps and policies through the use of a graphical user interface.

Acknowledgements

This work is funded by the IST-FET IST-2005-16004 project SENSORIA (Software Engineering for Service-Oriented Overlay Computers). Further thanks to Marie-Claude Gaudel for her advice on cancellation and undoing.

References

1. Alonso, G., Casati, F., Kuno, H., Machiraiu, V.: Web Services: Concepts, Architectures and Applications. Springer (2004)
2. Object Management Group (OMG): Business Process Modeling Notation (BPMN) Specification. (2006)
3. Lupu, E., Sloman, M.: Conflicts in policy-based distributed systems management. IEEE Trans. Software Eng. **25**(6) (1999) 852–869
4. Turner, K.J., Reiff-Marganiec, S., Blair, L., Pang, J., Gray, T., Perry, P., Ireland, J.: Policy support for call control. Computer Standards and Interfaces (2005)
5. Gaudel, M.C.: Toward undoing in composite web services. LRI, Paris-Sud University and CNRS, Orsay, France (2004)
6. van der Aalst, W.M.P., ter Hofstede, A.H.M., Kiepuszewski, B., Barros, A.P.: Workflow patterns. Technical Report FIT-TR-2002-03, Queensland University of Technology, Brisbane (2002)

Parameterized BPEL Processes: Concepts and Implementation

Dimka Karastoyanova, Frank Leymann, Jörg Nitzsche,
Branimir Wetzstein, and Daniel Wutke

IAAS, University of Stuttgart, Germany
{karastoyanova, leymann, nitzsche, wetzstein, wutke}@iaas.uni-stuttgart.de

Abstract. This paper presents the concept of parameterized WS-flows and two extensions to the BPEL language for enabling it. Another major contribution is a prototypical infrastructure enacting the execution, monitoring and adaptation of parameterized BPEL processes. The advantages of parameterized BPEL processes are the improved flexibility and reusability.

1 Introduction to Parameterized BPEL Processes

A BPEL [CGK+03] process is a collection of activities and control flow and data dependencies between them. BPEL processes define a business process in an abstract form, with all participants being WSs. Therefore they inherit the independence of platforms, programming languages, data formats and transport protocols. Interaction with partners is defined using partner links where the port types of potential partners are *fixed*. In addition the port type and operation names are a part of the interaction activities' definitions (e.g. <invoke>) that specify a port type and operation of the service to interact with, and the data to be exchanged. BPEL is considered a very flexible model for orchestrating services: process models can be reused with different configuration settings specified during their deployment. However port types (or partner links, respectively) and operation names are hard-coded in process definitions, which limits the loose-coupling and reusability features of processes. Referencing port types is a major drawback because industries can agree upon and standardize the types of messages to be exchanged, but it is nearly impossible to standardize the port types and operations. Thus, process models must be changed to reflect changes of port types across organizations and domains although the messages exchanged remain the same. To tackle this drawback in our previous work we have proposed the concept of parameterized processes ([KHC+05], [KaLB05]). Parameterizing processes eliminates the dependency of processes on partner idiosyncrasies (operation names and port types).

Specifying or modifying endpoint selection criteria during process run time is not yet supported by the existing binding strategies, which limits the process instance repair possibilities and again process flexibility. The drawbacks resulting from fixed portTypes and inability to control selection criteria on ports are eliminated by the concept of *parameterized processes*.

S. Dustdar, J.L. Fiadeiro, and A. Sheth (Eds.): BPM 2006, LNCS 4102, pp. 471–476, 2006.

The goal of this paper is to present prototypical infrastructure implementing this concept.

Parameterized processes contain parameters substituting the port types and operations; hence introduce an additional degree of freedom to process models [KaLB05]. Processes are executable if at run time all partner endpoints are known or can be calculated. Since partner services and their endpoints in our approach are unknown prior to process instance execution, we add a metamodel extension element to supply means of calculating them at run time. The BPEL representation of this element, the <evaluate> element, is shown in the following listing.

```
<invoke name=" " partnerLink="partnerLink" inputVariable="…"
portType="portType" operation="operation" outputVariable="…">
   <evaluate activated="yes|no" changeType =
    "static|prompt|query|fromVariable" substitute="value"/> </invoke>
```

Listing 1. A BPEL representation of the <evaluate> element

We define four mechanisms for parameter evaluation [KaLB05]: "static", "prompt", "query" and "from variable", expressed by the *changeType* attribute of the element. The element can be activated or deactivated by toggling its *activated* attribute (on a per-instance-basis) using external tools (e.g. the monitor in Fig. 1). The input for the parameter evaluation strategy is a proper value of the *substitute* attribute: (1) it contains port type and operation names for the "static" strategy; (2) is empty for the "prompt" strategy because the strategy requires input from a monitoring tool and an authorized user; (3) is a query string or a query identifier for the "query" strategy; (4) a getVariableData() function and a variable name as an argument for the "from Variable" strategy. The query string format we use in this work is presented in Listing 2. The query strategy is indeed a way to specify functional and non-functional requirements on partner services in a declarative manner. In addition, a query may incorporate transition conditions [Wetz06], and so eliminate alternative paths and reduce complexity of process models [KaLB05]. Note that it is designed to be independent of any semantic WS technology. Together with the "from Variable" strategy, the query strategy is executed automatically.

The <evaluate> extension element improves process flexibility because it supports the two basic approaches to flexibility: (i) "avoid change" because port types remain unfixed till activity execution and (ii) process instance adaptation because the extension can be used to modify operations/port types at run time.

For port types selected at run time compliant endpoints have to be discovered. This is done using dynamic discovery of and binding to WS ports – "find and bind" mechanism. This mechanism can be used in reaction to a service bus failure and thus avoid process instance termination. In [KHC+05] we introduce the <find_bind> element to support this mechanism on per-process-instance-basis.

2 Enabling Infrastructure

The prototypical infrastructure supporting parameterized processes contains a process execution engine, an instance monitoring tool, and a message broker (Fig. 1). The

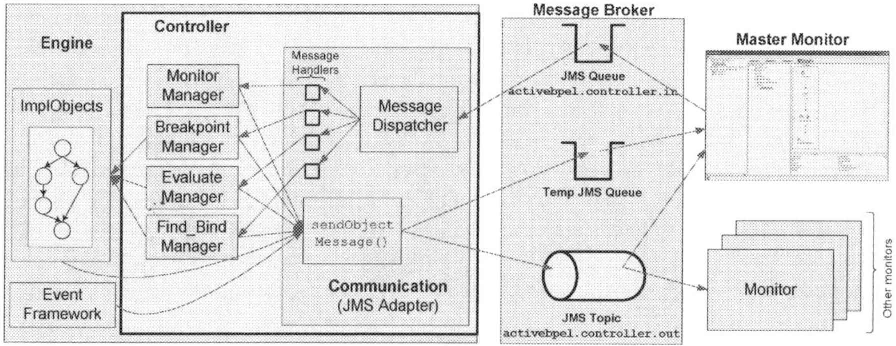

Fig. 1. The Infrastructure Architecture

BPEL engine is an extension to the ActiveBPEL 1.2 engine ([Wetz06], [Wutk06]). Process instances executed on the extended engine are monitored and adapted using a monitoring tool [Nitz06]. A JMS implementation serves as a message broker between engine and monitor.

The *process engine* handles the creation, execution and management of process instances, and alarm events. It is responsible for correlating incoming messages to running instances and their activities or creating new process instances. It schedules service invocations. A work manager assigns work units to separate threads to ensure parallel execution of actions. Time and alarm managers deal with timing issues of process instances (onAlarm events and time-outs). In addition the engine provides an administration module. The engine has an *event framework* for signaling and handling events. Three types of events are signaled by the extended engine: process instance level events, process activity level events and Model Events. Model events are fired whenever a modification in the values of port type and operation is made, as well as upon changes in the attributes of the <evaluate> and <find_bind> extension elements. The events are detected per process instance and are disseminated by the Controller module of the engine to external infrastructure components like monitoring tools. The *Controller* module (Fig. 1) contains the major extensions to the ActiveBPEL engine code. It tackles the communication with the message broker (JMS adapter) and implements managers handling commands from the monitoring tool with respect to changing extension elements attributes and propagating them to the process instances, managing monitoring tools registration and setting breakpoints (EvaluateManager, FindBindManager, MonitorManager, BreakpointManager) (see Fig. 1) [Wutk06].

During process *deployment* the BPEL processes are transformed into the engine internal format – the so called definition objects. These objects have been extended to support the two extension constructs. Definition objects are created once per process model and are *instantiated* as many times as many instances of the process model are created. The engine-internal representation of process instances is in terms of implementation objects containing instance specific data and reference to the process model. They have also been extended to support the semantics of the extension elements.

Whenever <evaluate> and/or <find_bind> elements are present in an activity, their definition objects are transformed into an instance specific object of the type Evaluate and FindBind respectively, and are stored into the corresponding implementation object of the activity. This way all <invoke> activities across all process instances have their own representation of these extension elements. Hence the extension element attributes are kept modifiable at run time on a per-instance-basis. Note that no implementation objects for the two extension elements are created yet.

Process instance execution boils down to executing its implementation objects one after another according to the process model and in compliance with the operational semantics of the WS-flows meta-model. Interaction activities utilize an invoke handler to interact with partner WSs. In this work, alternative invocation handler implementations have been developed to support the <evaluate> and <find_bind> elements.

The invocation handler used by an activity containing an <evaluate> element uses the attributes of the Evaluate object created upon process instantiation to generate an implementation object for the construct, which in turn references an evaluation strategy implementation. The result of the evaluation mechanism is an object (EvaluateResponse) containing the result of the evaluation, namely port type and operation name [Wutk06], [Wetz06]. The implementation objects for the different strategies differ not only in their implementation, but also in the parameters they require (see section 2).

The implementation of the strategy "static" uses the *substitute* attribute value in the Evaluate object to determine the return result. The strategy "prompt" requires the support of a monitoring tool for determining the EvaluateResponse (i.e. the portType and/or operation name); thus administrators are expected to provide parameter values. The result of the *fromVariable* strategy is extracted from the variable specified in the *substitute* field of the Evaluate object. The input for the execution of the "query" strategy is a query string. It enables automatic discovery of candidate service types and uses semantic web service technologies. The design of the BPEL extension, the query string format and the engine design and implementation are independent of any particular semantic WS technology; so far our prototype supports the OWL-S technology. The query string format is presented in the following listing.

```
<query><serviceSemantics><semanticsURI uri=""/>* </serviceSemantics>
    <serviceCategories> <serviceCategory name="" value="" code=""/>*
    </serviceCategories>
    <serviceProperties> <serviceProperty name="" value=""
            comparator="" type=""/>* </serviceProperties>
    <servicePolicies> <wsp:Policy>...</wsp:Policy>
    </servicePolicies></query>
```

Listing 2. The format of the search query in the strategy "query" [Wetz06]

The serviceCategories, serviceProperties and servicePolicies sections are used to specify non-functional requirements to the services, whereas the serviceSemantics section describes the functional requirements in terms of semantic WS description. All these sections may contain conditions similar to transition conditions on connectors in a process model. Based on the data in process variables different service properties may be used as selection criteria across the different instances of a process.

The actual search for and invocation of compliant services in the "query" strategy implementation is delegated to a *service broker* component [Wetz06], which is

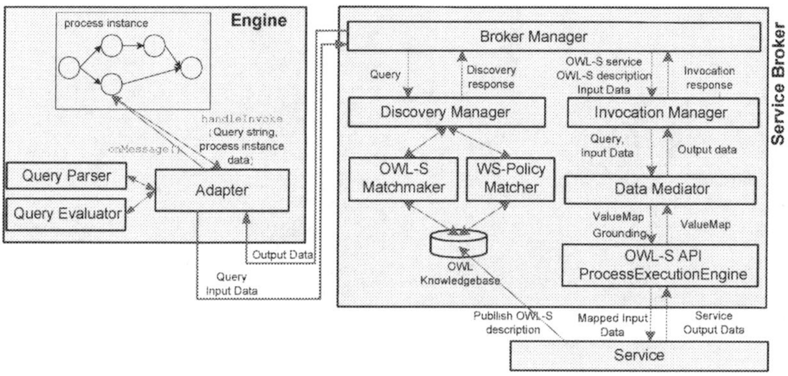

Fig. 2. Extended infrastructure implementing the "query" evaluation strategy

integrated with the engine via an adapter (Fig. 2). The adapter is invoked by the implementation object of an activity containing an <evaluate> construct with changeType="query". The service broker obtains as an input the query string pre-processed for the particular process instance and the input data (input variable) for the service invocation (Fig. 2).

The service broker discovers services based on semantic descriptions, selects the most appropriate endpoint (Discovery Manager) and invokes it (Invocation Manager). For the discovery of semantically compliant services functional semantics match suffices. Additional filtering is applied based on non-functional properties. The invocation manager invokes the service and hands over the resulting output data to the broker manager. For the actual invocation to take place data transformations may be necessary if the input and output data types as required by the process model and the ones used by the invoked service do not match. OWL-S technology supports data transformations using XSL-transformations in the OWL-S grounding.

The result of the "query" evaluation strategy is either the values for the portType and operation parameters or the result of invoking a particular WS operation compliant with the semantic description specified in the query. The former case requires additionally the execution of a "find and bind" mechanism to discover an endpoint and invoke the service. The same mechanism is also performed whenever a <find_bind> element is contained in an interaction activity. It can either be performed by the broker itself, or by another infrastructure component. More details are published in [KHC+05] and [Wutk06].

The *monitoring tool* visualizes process models and the execution status of process instances. It is also used to modify the attributes of the extension elements and to provide parameter values for the prompt evaluation strategy on a per-process-instance-basis. The communication with the engine is handled by the *communication module* (Fig. 3), which consumes engine event notifications published by the message broker and sends messages to the engine's input queue to induce process instance modifications [Nitz06]. The *process manager* is responsible for the monitor-internal representation and management of process models and instances. All changes in the data managed by the process manager are reflected by the *GUI*. All changes in the

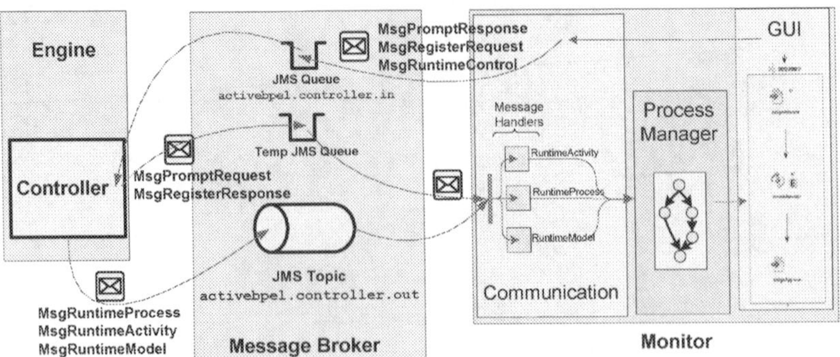

Fig. 3. Components of the monitoring tool, and its interaction with the process engine

activity or process states are published by the engine via the message broker. These events are processed by the monitor's communication module and propagated to the process manager, which updates the states of the corresponding instances and activities affected by these changes. This way the representation of processes and instances in the monitor is synchronized with their state in the engine.

Any modifications (enabled by the GUI) in the extension elements' attributes and breakpoint insertion/deletion are propagated to the engine by the monitor communication module (MsgRuntimeControl). The changes commanded by the monitor are made visible by the monitor only after the engine has confirmed them.

3 Conclusions and Future Work

The concept of parameterized processes improves the flexibility of WS-flows. To enable it the BPEL language has been extended. In this paper report on a prototypical infrastructure implementation supporting flexible BPEL processes. The infrastructure comprises an advanced features BPEL engine and a monitoring and management tool. Parameterized processes aim at improving reusability of process models. Our current and future research work focuses on defining templates for BPEL processes and building a template modeling tool.

References

[CGK+03] Curbera, F. et al.: BPEL4WS 1.1. 2003

[KHC+05] Karastoyanova, D. et al: Extending BPEL for Run Time Adaptability. EDOC 2005.

[KaLB05] Karastoyanova, D. et al: An Approach to Parameterizing WS-flows. ICSoC 2005.

[Leym05] Leymann, F.: The (Service) Bus: Services Penetrate Everyday Life. ICSoC 2005.

[Nitz06] Nitzsche, J.: Entwicklung eines Monitoring-Tools zur Unterstützung von parametrisierten Web Service Flows. Diploma Thesis 2388, Universität Stuttgart, 2006.

[Wetz06] Wetzstein, B.: Dynamische semantikbasierte Suche nach Web Services in parametrisierten BPEL-Prozessen. Diploma Thesis 2372, Universität Stuttgart, 2006.

[Wutk06] Wutke, D.: Erweiterung einer Workflow-Engine zur Unterstützung von parametrisierten Web Service Flows. Diploma Thesis 2401, Universität Stuttgart, 2006.

Behavioral Technique for Workflow Abstraction and Matching

Kais Klai[1], Nomane Ould Ahmed M'bareck[2], and Samir Tata[2]

[1] Technical University Eindhoven
k.klai@tue.nl
[2] GET/INT France
{Nomane.Ould_ahmed_mbarek, Samir.Tata}@int-evry.fr

Abstract. This work is in line with the *CoopFlow* approach dedicated for workflow advertisement, interconnection, and cooperation in virtual organizations. In order to advertise workflows into a registry, we present in this paper a novel method to abstract behaviors of workflows into symbolic observation graphs (SOG). We present in addition an efficient algorithm for SOG matching, which is used for interconnecting workflows[1].

1 Introduction

Research on workflow management has focused on inter-organizational issues and much has been achieved so far [5,1]. Problems to be encountered on this research include mainly autonomy of workflow processing, flexibility, and lack of arbitrary workflow support. To deal with these issues, we have developed the *CoopFlow* approach [3] that consists of three steps: workflow advertisement, interconnection, and cooperation. In fact, for building an inter-organizational workflow, each organization has to advertise, within a common registry, a description of its offered and required activities within their workflows. For workflow interconnection, each organization identifies its partners using a matching mechanism. For matching workflows, we propose in this paper a new algorithm using symbolic observation graphs (*SOG* for short) [2]. The rest of this paper is organized as follows. Section 2 describes our novel method of workflow abstraction based on SOG. Section 3 presents an algorithm for checking whether two workflows could cooperate. Using workflow matching, Section 4 shows how inter-organizational workflow is formed. Finally, the section 5 concludes the paper.

2 Workflow Abstraction

An inter-organizational workflow can be considered as the cooperation of several local workflows. Each one has two types of activities (transitions): cooperative activities that interact with other workflows and local activities that perform local actions. In order to set up cooperation, workflows have to be abstracted to preserve privacy, and advertised into a registry to be found and interconnected to partners' workflows. Workflows are reprenseted by Wf-nets [6]: A WF-net is a Petri net that has one *source* place and one *sink*

[1] This research has been partially funded by the Netherlands Organisation for Scientific Research (NWO) under FOCUS/BRICKS grant number 642.000.504.

S. Dustdar, J.L. Fiadeiro, and A. Sheth (Eds.): BPM 2006, LNCS 4102, pp. 477–483, 2006.

place and all its nodes (places or transitions) should be on some path from *source* to *sink*. To define workflow abstraction and matching, we need to introduce some definitions.

Let σ be a sequence of transitions ($\sigma \in T^*$). The projection of σ on a set of transitions $X \subseteq T$ (denoted by $\sigma_{\lfloor X}$) is the sequence obtained by removing from σ all transitions that do not belong to X. A sequence $\sigma = t_1 t_2 \ldots t_n$ over transitions is said to be accepted if i (resp. o) is in set of input (resp. output) places of t_1 (resp t_n) and σ can be executed by the workflow. The language $L(W)$ of a workflow W is the set of all accepted sequences and the projection function is extended to L as follows: $L_{\lfloor X} = \{\sigma_{\lfloor X}, \sigma \in L\}$.

2.1 Workflow Abstraction Using Symbolic Observation Graphs

In this paper, we originally propose to abstract workflows using the *SOG* structure introduced in [2] as an abstraction of the *reachability marking graph* of a given Petri net within a model checking approach. The building of the *SOG* is guided by the set of the cooperative transitions. Such activities are called *observed*, since they interact with other workflows, while the other transitions are *unobserved*. Then, the *SOG* is defined as a deterministic graph where each node is a set of markings linked by unobserved sequences of transitions and each arc is labeled with an observed transition. Nodes of the *SOG* are called *meta-states* and may be represented and managed efficiently by using Ordered Binary Decision Diagram (OBDD) [7]. The *SOG* technique is suitable for abstracting workflows for many reasons: First, the *SOG* allows one to represent the language of the workflow projected on the cooperative transitions i.e. the local behaviors are hidden. The second reason is that such an abstraction is suitable for checking whether two workflows represented by their *SOG* can be interconnected (see section 3). Finally, the reduced size of the *SOG* (in general) could be an advantage when one plans to store and manage a big number of workflows abstractions in a same registry.

2.2 *SOG* Building Algorithm

We adapt here the SOG technique to our workflow context by representing a workflows by a finite Wf-net associated to an initial marking m_0. A marking description is represented by a fixed vector of boolean variables. Using the enabling predicate for each transition of the system and the transformation, the dynamics of the workflow can be symbolically evaluated by the operation *Img(S,t)* which returns the set of immediate successors of the states of the set S by the occurrence of the transition t. The operation *Img* is naturally extended to a set of transitions T as follows: *Img(S,T)*=$\cup_{t \in T} Img(S,t)$. Algorithm 1 builds the SOG related to an initial state m_0 and to a partition of the set of transitions T into two (disjoint) subsets $Coop$ and $Local$ representing sets of observed (cooperative) and unobserved (local) transitions respectively. The data structures manipulated by the algorithm are the following ones:

- shared OBDD which contains symbolic representations of subsets of reachable sets,
- a standard graph representation with a set of vertices (V) and a set of edges (E). To each node v is associated a set of states $v.set$ that are abstracted by v,
- a stack whose items are tuples composed by a node of the graph and a symbolic subset of states (the interpretation of this set is given below).

Algorithm 1. Building of the observation graph

```
BuildOG (state m0, Transitions Coop);
set S'; vertex v, v';
Vertices V; Edges E; stack st;
Transitions Local = T \ Coop;
S' = Saturate({m0}, Local);
v.set = Reduce(S', Local, 1);
V = {v}; E = ∅; st.Push(⟨v, S'⟩);
repeat
    st.Pop(⟨v, S⟩);
    for t ∈ Coop do
        S' = Img(S, t);
        if (S' ≠ ∅) then
            S' = Saturate(S', Local);
            v'.set = Reduce(S', Local, 1);
            if (∃w ∈ V s.t. w == v') then
                E = E ∪ {v -t-> w};
            else
                V = V ∪ {v'};
                E = E ∪ {v -t-> v'};
                st.Push(⟨v', S'⟩);
            end if
        end if
    end for
until st == ∅;

Transitions Saturate(set S, transitions Local);
set From, Reach, To;
From = S; Reach = S;
repeat
    To = Img(From, Local);
    From = To \ Reach;
    Reach = Reach ∪ To;
until From == ∅;
return Reach;
```

The initialization step of the algorithm 1 allows to compute the first (initial) node of the SOG and to initialize the graph structure. The initial node of the graph is computed in two steps: first, starting from the initial marking m_0, we compute the set of all states that are reachable from m_0 by execution of local sequences of transitions (*Saturate()*). Then, function *Reduce()*, allows to reduce the obtained set by taking only a subset of representative states. Briefly, this function allows to keep one representative of each source strongly connected component in the subgraph abstracted by a node of the SOG (see [2] for a detailed description of this function).

An iteration of the main loop consists in picking and processing an item $\langle v, S\rangle$ of the stack until the stack is empty. The goal of the iteration is to generate the successors of the current node in the SOG. The set of states S corresponds to the states reached by any sequence of cooperative transitions leading from the initial node of the SOG to v. Thus one successively computes the image S' of S by each cooperative transition. If S' is not empty, it generates a new edge of the SOG labeled by the transition. Now one must check whether the node reached by this edge is a new one. So we compute the set attribute of this node. This is done by computing the closure of S' under the action of the local transitions (via *Saturate*) and then compute the representative subset (via *Reduce*). Finally, we look for an identical node in the graph. If such a node is not present we add a new node in the graph and push it on the stack with S'. In fact, we could avoid to push S and retrieve the significant information from $v.set$ but this would complicate the presentation.

3 Workflow Matching

Given a Wf-net W_1 and a registry of potential partners for W_1, we discuss in this section the selection criteria allowing to choose a Wf-net W_2 in the registry as a partner of W_1. Such criteria are based on the observed behavior of W_1, i.e. its behavior on the cooperative transitions, which must match with the observed behavior of W_2. Before presenting the matching conditions, let us introduce some definitions. Each cooperative transition t of Wf-net W is represented by a tuple $t = \langle name, type, msg \rangle$ where $t.name$ is the label associated to t, $t.type$ is a boolean variable saying whether t is supposed to receive a message ($t.type = 1$), or to send a message ($t.type = 0$), and $t.msg$ represents the semantic description of the message (using a common ontology) t has to send or to receive. In order to check whether there exists a correspondence between two cooperative transitions t_1 and t_2 belonging to two different Wf-nets, we need to compare these transitions with respect to their attributes. Two attributes are taken in account: $type$ and msg. For instance, if t_1 is a reception transition then t_2 must be a sending transition and both transitions have to match on the semantic of the exchanged message. We denote by $t_1.msg \equiv t_2.msg$ the fact that messages of t_1 and t_2 deal with the same data type and semantics. Now, if $t_1.type = \neg(t_2.type)$ and $t_1.msg \equiv t_2.msg$, then we say that t_1 matches with t_2 (and vice versa) and denote this relation by $t_1 \sim t_2$. The following hypothesis is important for the remaining part of the paper. It says that, within the same Wf-net W_1, if a cooperative transition occur in a Wf-net more than once then these occurrences are executed in an exclusive way. In this case we denote by $\{t\}$ the set of occurrences of a cooperative transition t in a Wf-net. Let $\langle W_1, m_1 \rangle$ be a marked Wf-net and let *Coop* be its set of cooperative transitions. Then:

$$\forall t_1 \in Coop, \forall \sigma = \alpha t_1 \alpha' t_1,\ where\ \alpha\ and\ \alpha' \in Coop^*,\ then\ \sigma \notin L(W_1, m_1).(H)$$

3.1 The Cooperation Candidate Property

In this section, we define the *cooperation candidate property* that will help us to define formally the fact that a Wf-net W_1 can cooperate with a given Wf-net W_2. For this issue, we need to introduce a renaming procedure $\mathcal{L}_{W_1}$. Let W_1 and W_2 be two Wf-nets and let $Coop_1$ and $Coop_2$ be their sets of cooperative transitions. The renaming procedure $\mathcal{L}_{W_1}$ associated to W_1 is defined as follows:

$$\mathcal{L}_{W_1}(W_2) = \forall t_2 \in Coop_2 \text{ if } \exists t_1 \in Coop_1 \text{ s.t. } t_1 \sim t_2 \text{ then } t_2.name := t_1.name.$$

Now, $\langle W_2, m_2 \rangle$, a marked workflow, is said to be a cooperation candidate for $\langle W_1, m_1 \rangle$ if for any firing sequence enabled from $\langle W_1, m_1 \rangle$, there exists a firing sequence enabled from $\langle \mathcal{L}_{W_1}(W_2), m_2 \rangle$, which both have the same projection on the cooperative transitions (of W_1). In the following, we define such a property. Let $\langle W_1, m_1 \rangle$

and $\langle W_2, m_2\rangle$ be two marked Wf-nets: $\langle W_2, m_2\rangle$ is said to be a candidate for cooperation with $\langle W_1, m_1\rangle$ iff $L_{\lfloor Coop_1}(\langle W_1, m_1\rangle) \subseteq L_{\lfloor Coop_2}(\langle \mathcal{L}_{W_1}(W_2), m_2\rangle)$.

3.2 An Algorithm for Checking the Cooperation Candidate Property

The Wf-net W_2 would be an effective candidate to cooperate with W_1 if the language induced by the *SOG* of W_1 is included in that induced by *SOG* of $\mathcal{L}_{W_1}(W_2)$. To check such an inclusion, the *SOG* of (W_1, m_1) is synchronized against the *SOG* of $(\mathcal{L}_{W_1}(W_2), m_2)$. The inclusion test Algorithm 2 works on the fly i.e. the building of the synchronized product can be stopped at any moment as soon as the inclusion is proved unsatisfied. When the synchronized product is entirely built, one deduces that the inclusion holds. The parameters of this algorithm are the *SOG*s $SoG_1 = \langle s_0, S_1, E_1\rangle$ and $SoG_2 = \langle s'_0, S'_1, E'_1\rangle$ of (W_1, m_1) and $(\mathcal{L}_{W_1}(W_2), m_2)$ respectively. s_0 (resp. s'_0) is the initial meta-state of SoG_1 (resp. SoG_2), S_1 (resp. S_2) its set of meta-states and E_1 (resp. E_2) its set of arcs. The data structures used by Algorithm 2 are a table *Synch*

Algorithm 2. $(L(SoG_1 = \langle s_0, S_1, E_1\rangle) \subseteq L(SoG_2 = \langle s'_0, S_2, E_2\rangle))$?

State s_1, s_2, s'_1, s'_2;
Set of transition f_1, f_2;
stack $st(\langle State, State, TransSet\rangle)$;
$s_1 = s_0$;
$s_2 = s'_0$;
$f_1 = Out(s_0)$,
$f_2 = Out(s'_0)$;
if $f_1 \neq \emptyset$ and $f_2 \neq \emptyset$ **then**
  if $(Names(f_1) \not\subseteq Names(f_2))$ **then**
    return false;
  end if
end if
$Synch = \{\langle s_1, s_2\rangle\}$;
$st.$**Push**$(\langle s_1, s_2, f_1\rangle)$;
repeat
  $st.$**Pop**$(\langle s_1, s_2, f_1\rangle)$;
  for $t \in f_1$ **do**
    $s'_1 = Img(s_1, t)$; $s'_2 = Img(s_2, t)$
    if $\langle s'_1, s'_2\rangle \notin Synch$ **then**
      $f_1 = Out(s'_1)$; $f_2 = Out(s'_2)$;
      if $f_1 \neq \emptyset$ and $f_2 \neq \emptyset$ **then**
        if $(Names(f_1) \not\subseteq Names(f_2))$ **then**
          return false;
        end if
      end if
      $Synch = Synch \cup \{\langle s'_1, s'_2\rangle\}$;
      $st.$**Push**$(\langle s'_1, s'_2, f_1\rangle)$;
    end if
  end for
until $st == \emptyset$;
return true;

and a stack *st*. *Synch* is used to store the states of the synchronized product non completely treated. An item of *st* is a tuple $\langle s_1, s_2, f_1\rangle$ composed of a reachable meta-state of (W_1, m_1), a reachable meta-state of $(\mathcal{L}_{W_1}(W_2), m_2)$ and a set of cooperative transitions enabled in both nodes. Moreover, three functions are used in this algorithm. The two first ones, *Out()* and *Img()*, collect information associated to the *SOG* structure. The first one is applied to a node of the *SOG* and return the set transitions labeling its output edges. The second function is applied to a state s_1 and a transition t (enabled in this node) and returns the reached node. The third function is *Names()* whose parameters are a set of transitions f returns the set of their names.

4 Workflow Interconnection

In this section, we describe how to interconnect two workflows W_1 and W_2 such that W_2 satisfies the cooperation candidate property by connecting the cooperative transitions of W_1 to those of W_2 via a set of buffer places.

Let $W_1 = \langle P_1, T_1, Pre_1, Post_1 \rangle$ and $W_2 = \langle P_2, T_2, Pre_2, Post_2 \rangle$ be two Wf-nets. Let $Coop_k$, for $k = 1, 2$ be the cooperative transitions of W_k, let i_k and o_k be the source and sink places of W_k, and let us assume that W_2 satisfies the cooperation candidate property. Then the interconnection of W_1 and W_2 leads to the Petri net $\Sigma_{12} = \langle P, T, Pre, Post \rangle$ defined, for $k = 1, 2$, as follows:

- $P = P_1 \cup P_2 \cup B \cup \{i, o\}$, where B is a set of buffer places such that: $\exists t_1 \in Coop_1, t_2 \in Coop_2$ and $t_1 \sim t_2$ iff $b_{t_1,t_2} \in B$.
- $T = T_1 \cup T_2 \cup \{in, out\}$
- $\forall p \in P \setminus \{i, o\} \setminus B, \forall t \in T \setminus \{in, out\}$
  Pre(p,t)(resp. Post(t,p)) = $Pre_k(p, t)$ (resp. $Post_k(t, p)$) if $(p, t) \in P_k \times T_k$
- $\forall b_{t_1,t_2} \in B \; Pre(b, t_k) = t_k.type$ and $Post(t_k, b) = \overline{t_k.type}$.
- $Pre(i, in) = 1$, $Post(out, o) = 1$, $Post(in, i_k) = 1$ and $Pre(o_k, out) = 1$.

The following theorem states an interesting feature of the Petri net obtained by interconnecting two Wf-nets: such an interconnection leads to a Wf-net. The proof of the theorem is trivial since the Wf-net properties are ensured by construction.

Theorem 1. *Let W_1 and W_2 be two Wf-nets and let Σ_{12} be the Petri net obtained by the interconnection of W_1 and W_2. Then Σ_{12} is a Wf-net.*

5 Conclusion

In this paper, we have presented an original approach for abstraction and interconnection of workflows. To be advertised in a common registry, workflows' behaviors are abstracted into SOG using the ordered binary decision diagram technique. The abstraction concept provides a high degree of flexibility for participating organizations, since internal structures of cooperative workflows may be adapted without changes in the inter-organizational workflows [4]. To interconnect workflows into an inter-organizational workflow, we have presented an algorithm for matching their SOGs. If the matching result is positive, then the workflows are then interconnected. Results of this work guarantee that the interconnection of workflows nets leads to a workflow net. Algorithms we have presented in this paper are implemented within the *CoopFlow* framework.

References

1. A. Van Dijk. Contracting workflows and protocol patterns. In *Proceedings BPM*, Eindhoven, The Netherlands, June 2003.
2. S. Haddad, J-M. Ilié, and K. Klai. Design and evaluation of a symbolic and abstraction-based model checker. In Farn Wang, editor, *ATVA*, volume 3299 of *LNCS*. Springer, 2004.

3. S. Dustdar I. Chebbi and S. Tata. The view-based approach to dynamic inter-organizational workflow cooperation. *Data and Knowledge Engineering Journal*, 56:2, 2006.
4. W. van der Aalst and K. Anyanwu. Inheritance of interorganizational workflows to enable business-to-business e-commerce. In *The Second International Conference on Telecommunications and Electronic Commerce (ICTEC'99)*, pages 141–157, Nashville, Tennessee, 1999.
5. W.-M.-P. van der Aalst and M. Weske. The p2p approach to interorganizational workflows. In *Proceedings of the 13th International Conference on Advanced Information Systems Engineering*, pages 140–156. Springer-Verlag, 2001.
6. Wil M. P. van der Aalst. The application of petri nets to workflow management. *Journal of Circuits, Systems, and Computers*, 8(1):21–66, 1998.
7. I. Wegener. *Branching programs and binary decision diagrams: theory and applications.* Society for Industrial and Applied Mathematics, Philadelphia, PA, USA, 2000.

Author Index

Lecture Notes in Computer Science

For information about Vols. 1–4064

please contact your bookseller or Springer

Vol. 4185: R. Mizoguchi, Z. Shi, F. Giunchiglia (Eds.), The Semantic Web – ASWC 2006. XX, 778 pages. 2006.

Vol. 4184: M. Bravetti, M. Nuñes, G. Zavattaro (Eds.), Web Services and Formal Methods. X, 289 pages. 2006.

Vol. 4180: M. Kohlhase, OMDoc – An Open Markup Format for Mathematical Documents [version 1.2]. XIX, 428 pages. 2006. (Sublibrary LNAI).

Vol. 4178: A. Corradini, H. Ehrig, U. Montanary, L. Ribeiro, G. Rozenberg (Eds.), Graph Transformations. XII, 473 pages. 2006.

Vol. 4176: S.K. Katsikas, J. Lopez, M. Backes, S. Gritzalis, B. Preneel (Eds.), Information Security. XIV, 548 pages. 2006.

Vol. 4168: Y. Azar, T. Erlebach (Eds.), Algorithms – ESA 2006. XVIII, 843 pages. 2006.

Vol. 4165: W. Jonker, M. Petkovic (Eds.), Secure, Data Management. X, 185 pages. 2006.

Vol. 4163: H. Bersini, J. Carneiro (Eds.), Artificial Immune Systems. XII, 460 pages. 2006.

Vol. 4162: R. Královič, P. Urzyczyn (Eds.), Mathematical Foundations of Computer Science 2006. XV, 814 pages. 2006.

Vol. 4159: J. Ma, H. Jin, L.T. Yang, J.J.-P. Tsai (Eds.), Ubiquitous Intelligence and Computing. XXII, 1190 pages. 2006.

Vol. 4158: L.T. Yang, H. Jin, J. Ma, T. Ungerer (Eds.), Autonomic and Trusted Computing. XIV, 613 pages. 2006.

Vol. 4156: S. Amer-Yahia, Z. Bellahsène, E. Hunt, R. Unland, J.X. Yu (Eds.), Database and XML Technologies. IX, 123 pages. 2006.

Vol. 4155: O. Stock, M. Schaerf (Eds.), Reasoning, Action and Interaction in AI Theories and Systems. XVIII, 343 pages. 2006. (Sublibrary LNAI).

Vol. 4153: N. Zheng, X. Jiang, X. Lan (Eds.), Advances in Machine Vision, Image Processing, and Pattern Analysis. XIII, 506 pages. 2006.

Vol. 4152: Y. Manolopoulos, J. Pokorný, T. Sellis (Eds.), Advances in Databases and Information Systems. XV, 448 pages. 2006.

Vol. 4151: A. Iglesias, N. Takayama (Eds.), Mathematical Software - ICMS 2006. XVII, 452 pages. 2006.

Vol. 4150: M. Dorigo, L.M. Gambardella, M. Birattari, A. Martinoli, R. Poli, T. Stützle (Eds.), Ant Colony Optimization and Swarm Intelligence. XVI, 526 pages. 2006.

Vol. 4149: M. Klusch, M. Rovatsos, T.R. Payne (Eds.), Cooperative Information Agents X. XII, 477 pages. 2006. (Sublibrary LNAI).

Vol. 4146: J.C. Rajapakse, L. Wong, R. Acharya (Eds.), Pattern Recognition in Bioinformatics. XIV, 186 pages. 2006. (Sublibrary LNBI).

Vol. 4144: T. Ball, R.B. Jones (Eds.), Computer Aided Verification. XV, 564 pages. 2006.

Vol. 4139: T. Salakoski, F. Ginter, S. Pyysalo, T. Pahikkala, Advances in Natural Language Processing. XVI, 771 pages. 2006. (Sublibrary LNAI).

Vol. 4138: X. Cheng, W. Li, T. Znati (Eds.), Wireless Algorithms, Systems, and Applications. XVI, 709 pages. 2006.

Vol. 4137: C. Baier, H. Hermanns (Eds.), CONCUR 2006 – Concurrency Theory. XIII, 525 pages. 2006.

Vol. 4136: R.A. Schmidt (Ed.), Relations and Kleene Algebra in Computer Science. XI, 433 pages. 2006.

Vol. 4135: C.S. Calude, M.J. Dinneen, G. Păun, G. Rozenberg, S. Stepney (Eds.), Unconventional Computation. X, 267 pages. 2006.

Vol. 4134: K. Yi (Ed.), Static Analysis. XIII, 443 pages. 2006.

Vol. 4133: J. Gratch, M. Young, R. Aylett, D. Ballin, P. Olivier (Eds.), Intelligent Virtual Agents. XIV, 472 pages. 2006. (Sublibrary LNAI).

Vol. 4130: U. Furbach, N. Shankar (Eds.), Automated Reasoning. XV, 680 pages. 2006. (Sublibrary LNAI).

Vol. 4129: D. McGookin, S. Brewster (Eds.), Haptic and Audio Interaction Design. XII, 167 pages. 2006.

Vol. 4128: W.E. Nagel, W.V. Walter, W. Lehner (Eds.), Euro-Par 2006 Parallel Processing. XXXIII, 1221 pages. 2006.

Vol. 4127: E. Damiani, P. Liu (Eds.), Data and Applications Security XX. X, 319 pages. 2006.

Vol. 4126: P. Barahona, F. Bry, E. Franconi, N. Henze, U. Sattler, Reasoning Web. X, 269 pages. 2006.

Vol. 4124: H. de Meer, J.P. G. Sterbenz (Eds.), Self-Organizing Systems. XIV, 261 pages. 2006.

Vol. 4121: A. Biere, C.P. Gomes (Eds.), Theory and Applications of Satisfiability Testing - SAT 2006. XII, 438 pages. 2006.

Vol. 4119: C. Dony, J.L. Knudsen, A. Romanovsky, A. Tripathi (Eds.), Advanced Topics in Exception Handling Components. X, 302 pages. 2006.

Vol. 4117: C. Dwork (Ed.), Advances in Cryptology - CRYPTO 2006. XIII, 621 pages. 2006.

Vol. 4116: R. De Prisco, M. Yung (Eds.), Security and Cryptography for Networks. XI, 366 pages. 2006.

Vol. 4115: D.-S. Huang, K. Li, G.W. Irwin (Eds.), Computational Intelligence and Bioinformatics, Part III. XXI, 803 pages. 2006. (Sublibrary LNBI).

Vol. 4114: D.-S. Huang, K. Li, G.W. Irwin (Eds.), Computational Intelligence, Part II. XXVII, 1337 pages. 2006. (Sublibrary LNAI).

Vol. 4113: D.-S. Huang, K. Li, G.W. Irwin (Eds.), Intelligent Computing, Part I. XXVII, 1331 pages. 2006.

Vol. 4112: D.Z. Chen, D. T. Lee (Eds.), Computing and Combinatorics. XIV, 528 pages. 2006.

Vol. 4111: F.S. de Boer, M.M. Bonsangue, S. Graf, W.-P. de Roever (Eds.), Formal Methods for Components and Objects. VIII, 447 pages. 2006.

Vol. 4110: J. Díaz, K. Jansen, J.D.P. Rolim, U. Zwick (Eds.), Approximation, Randomization, and Combinatorial Optimization. XII, 522 pages. 2006.

Vol. 4109: D.-Y. Yeung, J.T. Kwok, A. Fred, F. Roli, D. de Ridder (Eds.), Structural, Syntactic, and Statistical Pattern Recognition. XXI, 939 pages. 2006.

Vol. 4108: J.M. Borwein, W.M. Farmer (Eds.), Mathematical Knowledge Management. VIII, 295 pages. 2006. (Sublibrary LNAI).

Vol. 4106: T.R. Roth-Berghofer, M.H. Göker, H. A. Güvenir (Eds.), Advances in Case-Based Reasoning. XIV, 566 pages. 2006. (Sublibrary LNAI).

Vol. 4104: T. Kunz, S.S. Ravi (Eds.), Ad-Hoc, Mobile, and Wireless Networks. XII, 474 pages. 2006.

Vol. 4102: S. Dustdar, J.L. Fiadeiro, A. Sheth (Eds.), Business Process Management. XV, 486 pages. 2006.

Vol. 4099: Q. Yang, G. Webb (Eds.), PRICAI 2006: Trends in Artificial Intelligence. XXVIII, 1263 pages. 2006. (Sublibrary LNAI).

Vol. 4098: F. Pfenning (Ed.), Term Rewriting and Applications. XIII, 415 pages. 2006.

Vol. 4097: X. Zhou, O. Sokolsky, L. Yan, E.-S. Jung, Z. Shao, Y. Mu, D.C. Lee, D. Kim, Y.-S. Jeong, C.-Z. Xu (Eds.), Emerging Directions in Embedded and Ubiquitous Computing. XXVII, 1034 pages. 2006.

Vol. 4096: E. Sha, S.-K. Han, C.-Z. Xu, M.H. Kim, L.T. Yang, B. Xiao (Eds.), Embedded and Ubiquitous Computing. XXIV, 1170 pages. 2006.

Vol. 4095: S. Nolfi, G. Baldassare, R. Calabretta, D. Marocco, D. Parisi, J.C. T. Hallam, O. Miglino, J.-A. Meyer (Eds.), From Animals to Animats 9. XV, 869 pages. 2006. (Sublibrary LNAI).

Vol. 4094: O. H. Ibarra, H.-C. Yen (Eds.), Implementation and Application of Automata. XIII, 291 pages. 2006.

Vol. 4093: X. Li, O.R. Zaïane, Z. Li (Eds.), Advanced Data Mining and Applications. XXI, 1110 pages. 2006. (Sublibrary LNAI).

Vol. 4092: J. Lang, F. Lin, J. Wang (Eds.), Knowledge Science, Engineering and Management. XV, 664 pages. 2006. (Sublibrary LNAI).

Vol. 4091: G.-Z. Yang, T. Jiang, D. Shen, L. Gu, J. Yang (Eds.), Medical Imaging and Augmented Reality. XIII, 399 pages. 2006.

Vol. 4090: S. Spaccapietra, K. Aberer, P. Cudré-Mauroux (Eds.), Journal on Data Semantics VI. XI, 211 pages. 2006.

Vol. 4089: W. Löwe, M. Südholt (Eds.), Software Composition. X, 339 pages. 2006.

Vol. 4088: Z.-Z. Shi, R. Sadananda (Eds.), Agent Computing and Multi-Agent Systems. XVII, 827 pages. 2006. (Sublibrary LNAI).

Vol. 4087: F. Schwenker, S. Marinai (Eds.), Artificial Neural Networks in Pattern Recognition. IX, 299 pages. 2006. (Sublibrary LNAI).

Vol. 4085: J. Misra, T. Nipkow, E. Sekerinski (Eds.), FM 2006: Formal Methods. XV, 620 pages. 2006.

Vol. 4084: M.A. Wimmer, H.J. Scholl, Å. Grönlund, K.V. Andersen (Eds.), Electronic Government. XV, 353 pages. 2006.

Vol. 4083: S. Fischer-Hübner, S. Furnell, C. Lambrinoudakis (Eds.), Trust and Privacy in Digital Business. XIII, 243 pages. 2006.

Vol. 4082: K. Bauknecht, B. Pröll, H. Werthner (Eds.), E-Commerce and Web Technologies. XIII, 243 pages. 2006.

Vol. 4081: A. M. Tjoa, J. Trujillo (Eds.), Data Warehousing and Knowledge Discovery. XVII, 578 pages. 2006.

Vol. 4080: S. Bressan, J. Küng, R. Wagner (Eds.), Database and Expert Systems Applications. XXI, 959 pages. 2006.

Vol. 4079: S. Etalle, M. Truszczyński (Eds.), Logic Programming. XIV, 474 pages. 2006.

Vol. 4077: M.-S. Kim, K. Shimada (Eds.), Geometric Modeling and Processing - GMP 2006. XVI, 696 pages. 2006.

Vol. 4076: F. Hess, S. Pauli, M. Pohst (Eds.), Algorithmic Number Theory. X, 599 pages. 2006.

Vol. 4075: U. Leser, F. Naumann, B. Eckman (Eds.), Data Integration in the Life Sciences. XI, 298 pages. 2006. (Sublibrary LNBI).

Vol. 4074: M. Burmester, A. Yasinsac (Eds.), Secure Mobile Ad-hoc Networks and Sensors. X, 193 pages. 2006.

Vol. 4073: A. Butz, B. Fisher, A. Krüger, P. Olivier (Eds.), Smart Graphics. XI, 263 pages. 2006.

Vol. 4072: M. Harders, G. Székely (Eds.), Biomedical Simulation. XI, 216 pages. 2006.

Vol. 4071: H. Sundaram, M. Naphade, J.R. Smith, Y. Rui (Eds.), Image and Video Retrieval. XII, 547 pages. 2006.

Vol. 4070: C. Priami, X. Hu, Y. Pan, T.Y. Lin (Eds.), Transactions on Computational Systems Biology V. IX, 129 pages. 2006. (Sublibrary LNBI).

Vol. 4069: F.J. Perales, R.B. Fisher (Eds.), Articulated Motion and Deformable Objects. XV, 526 pages. 2006.

Vol. 4068: H. Schärfe, P. Hitzler, P. Øhrstrøm (Eds.), Conceptual Structures: Inspiration and Application. XI, 455 pages. 2006. (Sublibrary LNAI).

Vol. 4067: D. Thomas (Ed.), ECOOP 2006 – Object-Oriented Programming. XIV, 527 pages. 2006.

Vol. 4066: A. Rensink, J. Warmer (Eds.), Model Driven Architecture – Foundations and Applications. XII, 392 pages. 2006.

Vol. 4065: P. Perner (Ed.), Advances in Data Mining. XI, 592 pages. 2006. (Sublibrary LNAI).